The Wars of
GERMAN
UNIFICATION

The Wars of
GERMAN
UNIFICATION

Dennis Showalter
Professor of History, Colorado College, Colorado, USA

HODDER
EDUCATION
PART OF HACHETTE LIVRE UK

First published in Great Britain in 2004 by
Hodder Education, part of Hachette Livre UK,
338 Euston Road, London NW1 3BH

www.hoddereducation.com

© 2004 Denis Showalter

British Library Cataloguing in Publication Data
A catalogue record for this book is available from the British Library

Library of Congress Cataloging-in-Publication Data
A catalog record for this book is available from the Library of Congress

ISBN: 978 0 340 58017 2

Typeset in 10/12pt Apllo MT by Charon Tec Pvt. Ltd, Chennai, India

What do you think about this book? Or any other Hodder Education
title? Please send your comments to educationenquiries@hodder.co.uk

Contents

General Editor's Preface

Historians of the two world wars, searching for nineteenth-century precedents which might have given warning of their scale and destructiveness, are wont to cite the American Civil War. Here, they say, was a portent that was neglected. Dennis Showalter is himself an American. Moreover, his book on the wars of German unification makes some of its points with comparisons derived from those near contemporary events across the Atlantic. It also uses the world wars and even the war in Vietnam in similar fashion. But it is not guilty of the sort of slick hindsight which claims (wrongly) that the American Civil War was ignored in Europe, and that it – not the wars of German unification – was the foundation stone of 'modern war'.

In his concluding remarks, Dennis Showalter stresses that the story of German unification was one of contingency. There was no master plan presided over by Bismarck; instead he was a politician who 'lived on the edge', a man who took his opportunities, and whose achievements and their apparent shape only became evident when all was done. By the same token, there is no straight line from the creation of Germany to Hitler. But the first was, at least, the precondition of the second. In political terms, for anyone living in Europe in the first half of the twentieth century, the wars of German unification were of far greater importance than the American Civil War.

The case for seeing the latter as the first 'modern' war, however, is as much military as political: it was a long war, resolved by industrial might and economic supremacy. The wars of German unification were individually short. If the belief that World War I would be quick had any basis, it lay here. Economic factors, therefore, did not have the opportunity to determine their outcome. Prussia, Austria and France were sufficiently equal to make production indices an unreliable guide as to what would happen if they fought each other. France's superiority at sea became a factor in the winter of 1870–1 but it did not overturn the verdict of events on land. Dennis Showalter concludes that Prussia funded the wars of 1864–71 without really breaking sweat. That with France required it to have recourse to loans and public subscriptions, but France then contributed to the cost of its own defeat with an indemnity, which it in turn managed to pay off in two years. The Napoleonic notion that the ends of war can be greater than the costs incurred – that war can even pay for itself – was partly validated.

The Prussian army was the instrument that warranted the gamble that turned contingencies into outcomes. As Dennis Showalter makes clear, its performance and its subsequent reputation were no more predictable than the consequences of Bismarck's manoeuvring. He rebuts the notion that Prussia was militarist; its evolution up until 1871 lacked that 'peculiarity' detected by historians examining it from the perspective of 1945. In 1864 the Austrian army was built on lines similar to those of other European armies; the Prussian army — with its use of short-service conscripts — was not. It was the product of internal analysis. Its lack of recent battlefield experience was compounded, it seemed, by lower levels of training. Its general staff did give it a command structure that was more coherent than those of the Austrians and the French, but here, too, system followed success more than it preceded it. Much was down to tactics. Outcomes were the products of events on the battlefield, and Dennis Showalter puts the case for restoring the Dreyse rifle, the first universal issue breech-loader, to the pedestal that it occupied in the eyes of many critics in the immediate aftermath of the battle of Koeniggraetz in 1866.

The wars of German unification were 'cabinet' wars, fought — just — within the framework of the Concert of Europe. In this sense they were backward-looking. Dennis Showalter observes that some draw a distinction between the Franco-Prussian War, fought against a France led by an unpopular emperor and concluding with his fall, and the Franco-German War which followed it. The Third Republic represented the people of France and called for national mobilization. Its use of *francs-tireurs* elevated the idea of guerrilla war, and the German reaction both to them and to the resistance of Paris resulted in civilian deaths. But again, Dennis Showalter resists the lure of hindsight. He argues that, in 1871, the Germans were only developing a response to circumstances as they evolved. The *francs-tireurs* were of limited effectiveness, the Germans' reactions were restrained, and in the siege of Paris more damage was done to property than to people. The American Civil War, fought by 'liberal' governments, was far more devastating in its effects, not least because its commanders deliberately targeted the civilian population.

This sense of context is what makes *The Wars of German Unification* the work of a historian at the height of his powers. In 1976, Dennis Showalter launched his career with *Railroads and Rifles*, a study of the tactics and technology which underpinned the Prussian army in the Wars of Unification. It remains unsurpassed. Almost thirty years later, a major scholar, whose output in the interim has embraced almost the entire gamut of military history, has returned to where he began. He has brought to his material a breadth and perspective which inform his discussion not only of military and operational matters, but also of the political and diplomatic. His feel for the circumstances and frustrations of the soldier's lot, and his use of metaphor and simile, enliven a narrative that remains one of the most important in the shaping of modern Europe.

Hew Strachan
Chichele Professor of the History of War,
All Souls College,
Oxford University

Introduction

German unification was, for a century, presented as a natural process. However catastrophic the immediate consequences of events from 1864 to 1871 might have been, they were generally understood as reflecting a set of necessities that caught up Germany with the rest of Europe and placed it in the context of global developments. The industrialized, centralized nation state seemed the defining institution of the modern era, and the stepping stone to the future. Helmut Kohl (as quintessential a conventional German as ever made international headlines) spoke for generations of conventional wisdom inside and outside Germany when he said, 'what belongs together will grow together'.

Beginning in the 1970s, however, a number of alternative perspectives began to emerge. One set, reflecting wider developments in the study of history, concentrated on social and cultural developments, insisting that they need not and must not be understood merely in the context of an emerging German nation state.[1] A second approach emphasized the federal, universalist, 'greater German' (*Grossdeutsch*) aspects of the nineteenth-century experience.[2] Long presented as foils in a nationalist/Borussian context, considered in their own right these factors suggested a spectrum of viable specific alternatives to Bismarck's Second Reich.[3] One was a federal system, based on the German Confederation established in 1815. Another, based on the experiences of 1848–9, involved a centralized nation state based on popular sovereignty and human rights – that alleged European norm to which modern Germany opposed its supposed 'special path' (*Sonderweg*).[4] Somewhat more esoteric, but no less appealing, particularly to Habsburg scholars, was the alternative of shared power – in a Greater Germany, in a hegemony shared by Prussia and Austria, and in a triad, with the third element made up from some combination of the so-called 'lesser' or 'middle' states (which were, in fact, more German than either Prussia or Austria, with their extensive territories alien by history and ethnic identity). The concept of a Third Germany was far from moribund in the nineteenth century's first half, and its appeal extended far beyond special-interest groups.[5]

---

[1]James Sheehan, *German History, 1770–1866* (Oxford, 1989).
[2]Thomas Nipperdey, *Deutsche Geschichte 1800–1866. Buergerwelt und starker Staat* (Munich, 1883). The English version is *Germany from Napoleon to Bismarck, 1800–1866*, tr. D. Nolan (Princeton, 1996).
[3]Hagen Schulze, *Germany. A New History*, tr. D. Schneider (Cambridge, MA, 1998), pp. 147 ff.
[4]Cf. David Blackbourn and Geoff Eley, *The Peculiarities of German History: Bourgeois Society and Politics in Nineteenth-Century Germany* (Oxford, 1984).
[5]Heinrich Lutz, *Zwischen Habsburg und Preussen. Deutschland 1815–1866* (Berlin, 1985).

Supporting this revitalized approach to German unification was an unexpected revival among historians of interest in contingent behaviour. The emergence of Marxism as the dominant intellectual and cultural influence among academics worldwide during the twentieth century further enhanced the appeal of historical determinism. In its fully developed form, the principle that history was shaped not by individual decisions and specific policies, but by abstract, impersonal forces, which might be understood but could not be manipulated, became a kind of gnosis, a secret, higher knowledge open only to the adepts in the faculties of major universities and to their graduate-student apprentices. Had not Bismarck himself said the most he sought to do was listen for the rustle of history passing by and then catch hold of her cloak? Even science fiction, the home of speculative imagination about human futures, was dominated for a quarter-century after World War II by Isaac Asimov's *Foundation Trilogy*, its spin-offs and epigoni, with their common vision of the universe unfolding according to an invariant Grand Design.

The collapse of the Soviet Union, which took intellectual Marxism down with it, left an open field for postmodernist constructivism, with its emphasis on the constructed nature of patterns and connections in history. Even for those scholars who continued to argue that history's truths were discovered and not invented, it became increasingly feasible to question a broad spectrum of received wisdoms about historical causation.[6] It became increasingly respectable to speculate upon alternative outcomes[7] – including, among other things, the Germany that might have been.

That, in turn, exposed another historiographical problem. Military force played a central role in German unification, even in works presenting it as ratifying the inevitable.[8] Moving towards a contingent model only enhanced the importance of armies. The study of operational military history, and of armed forces as military instruments, had fallen into abeyance since 1945. A 'new military history' had emerged, concentrating on social, cultural and political factors – exactly the non-contingent elements reinforcing a determinist perspective on unification. The Prussian army, in particular, was best and most widely understood in the political contexts developed by Gordon Craig and Gerhard Ritter. As a final irony, two of the century's finest war studies, synthesizing traditional and contemporary approaches, were written about the Wars of Unification: Craig's *Koeniggraetz* and Michael Howard's *The Franco-Prussian War*. While they did not exactly sterilize the ground around them, their quality nevertheless required any significant revision, even of narrative detail, to be undertaken with care and respect.

Conceptualizing the present volume, in short, involved a broader spectrum than initially anticipated. Preparing it required integrating four perspectives. One involved general social, cultural and economic developments, considered from a date with significant political implications. The year 1815 symbolized the restoration of European and German order, the recreation of stability, yet it was also the watershed separating the Germany of the Holy Roman Empire from the Germany of the Confederation: the benchmark dividing Germany's past from its future. Resolving that tension required over half a century.

---

[6]Richard J. Evans, *In Defence of History* (London, 1997).

[7]As in *Virtual History: Alternatives and Counterfactuals*, ed. N. Ferguson (London, 1998).

[8]As in Helmut Boehme, *Deutschlands Weg zur Grossmacht. Studien zum Verhaeltnis von Wirtschaft und Staat waehrend der Reichgruendungszeit, 1848–1881* (Cologne, 1966).

The second perspective was political/diplomatic. In an emerging age of parliaments, diplomatic considerations interfaced systematically with domestic politics for the first time in modern western history. The difficulties posed by that new, comprehensive paradigm were exacerbated by a simple lack of precedent and practice in making the new systems work on an everyday basis. In turn, the relationships among changing patterns of government in the German states, the relationships of the states to the Confederation and each other, and Germany's relationship to Europe's power structure, as both participant and playing field, created a network of protean complexities that still challenges analysis.

Unification's third perspective was military. Far from being a period of stagnation and reaction in military matters, the period between 1815 and 1871 was characterized by broad-spectrum concern with change – but in a particular matrix. European states in this period were less impelled by external arms races than by internal considerations, developing their respective military systems according to particular definitions of vital interests and domestic capacities for mobilization. What emerged, in contrast to the years prior to 1756 and 1914, was an asymmetrical search for modernization, in which lesser powers, as well as great ones, sought to maximize their military effectiveness in different ways. Far from the Wars of Unification involving Prussian steel crushing Austrian sawdust and French tinsel, these conflicts engaged alternative concepts of modern war.

That engagement took place, moreover, in a new, untested paradigm of statesmanship. From the Middle Ages to the eighteenth century, war had been 'the ultimate argument of kings', an ace in the hole, to be played when the diplomatic hand failed to produce the desired results. The concept of early modern Europe as an age of limited war may have been a fiction, but it was a fiction on which states agreed. The vision of a state or coalition might encompass an adversary's permanent crippling or its complete disappearance from the map.[9] The achievements were almost inevitably a good deal more modest – not least because of the difficulty of deciding war through battle under early modern conditions.[10]

The revolutionary/Napoleonic era introduced a pattern of higher stakes to war making. Napoleon's essential unappeasability offered two choices: clients or enemies – and accepting either could mean the loss of identity.[11] The reconstructed Europe that emerged from the Congress of Vienna did not seek the utopian solution of ending war altogether. If the mentality epitomized in the Concert of Europe did not emphasize the removal of armed force from the deck used to play Europe's game, then it treated it as a wild card, to be introduced only in extremity and recognized as essentially changing the rules. The military reforms introduced after 1848–9, however, encouraged the post-revolution government's consideration of using armed force as a policy instrument. Diplomacy in the 1850s developed along lines of a constant interfacing of negotiation with force – or its credible threat. Arden Bucholz perceptively compares Napoleonic war to whist, emphasizing both chance and the ability to improvise during play. He goes on to link Moltkean war with

---

[9]C. W. Ingrao, 'Habsburg Strategy and Geopolitics during the Eighteenth Century' in *East Central European Society and War in the Pre-Revolutionary Eighteenth Century*, ed. F. Rothenberg et al. (New York, 1982), pp. 49–66.
[10]Russell Weigley, *The Age of Battles. The Quest for Decisive Warfare from Breitenfeld to Waterloo* (Bloomington, IN, 1991).
[11]Paul W. Schroeder, 'Napoleon's Foreign Policy: A Criminal Enterprise', *The Journal of Military History* 54 (1990), pp. 147–61.

bridge: long-range strategies based on rational calculations of strengths.[12] The multiple synergies of war and diplomacy in mid-nineteenth-century Europe, however, resembled nothing so much as poker – a high-stakes, invitation-only version of a variant like 'Texas Hold 'em', where the values of the cards change with almost every round of play; where cards and money alike become instruments in a mutual exercise of bluff, counter-bluff, and double bluff; where the greatest risk often turns out to be the safest move; and where a sense of the table is as important as rational calculation. Bismarck might have been the most successful practitioner of this new variant, but he had competitors in Vienna and the smaller German capitals, in Paris, Copenhagen and Turin.

The result of all this was a story whose outcomes remained hidden to even the most perceptive contemporaries; whose perspective shifts almost randomly from the antechambers of the diplomats to parliaments, drill grounds and battlefields. It features high politics and low cunning, plenty of violence and a bit of sex. Above all, its telling has been fun. May it bring pleasure also to the readers.

A work this long in gestation accumulates intellectual and emotional debts beyond counting. But since I came to Colorado College in 1969, Bob McJimsey has been friend, colleague and mentor. His learning, his judgment and his good humour make him an exemplar of what a liberal arts professor can be. The book is dedicated to him, in an attempt to say, 'Thanks'.

---

[12] Arden Bucholz, *Moltke and the German Wars, 1864–1871* (New York, 1991), pp. 3–4.

1

Confederation and Revolution

ermany after 1815 was, more than at any time in its convoluted history, a mosaic of
contradictions. On the one hand, the German *Aufklaerung* and the Revolutionary-
Napoleonic Wars had fostered the development of a common culture. The *Aufklaerung*, in
particular, had affirmed the development of a public sphere asserting unity in diversity – a
piety best expressed in Lessing's *Nathan the Wise*, with its fable of the three rings.[1] Goethe
and Schiller were common property, not least for their heavy reliance on the 'Matter of
Germany' for themes and settings. Philosophy addressed questions of identity in contexts of
community. Immanuel Kant's critiques of pure and practical reason, his emphasis on individual consciousness as the fulcrum for universal principles, were developed by Hegel into
a process that synthesized the individual and the collective, the particular and the general.[2]

Behaviours, too, were steadily homogenizing. A new generation of academics was integrating folk ways and folk tales into general analytical structures.[3] A developing print
culture, which offered greatest profit to works with widest circulations, fostered a common
German market in books, magazines and newspapers – especially among a middle class
increasingly able both to pay for its tastes and to establish wider standards.[4] Geographical
mobility was increasingly common among soldiers, officials and clergymen. Degrees from
Halle, Goettingen and, increasingly, Berlin were universal currency between the Rhine and
the Vistula. Gerhard von Scharnhorst's transfer from Hanoverian to Prussian military service
had its counterpart in Johann Gottfried Herder's movements from Riga to Strasbourg to
Weimar as pastor and tutor.[5] Biedermeyer's emphasis on comfortable domesticity even permeated the courts, whose initial post-1815 efforts to sustain the ceremonial grandeur of an
earlier era only looked provincial when compared to the garish extravaganzas of Napoleon.

---

[1]Cf. Horst Moeller, *Vernunft und Kritik. Deutsche Aufklaerung im 17. und 18. Jahrhundert* (Frankfurt, 1986);
Thomas Saine, *The Problem of Being Modern, or, The German Pursuit of Enlightenment from Leibniz to the French
Revolution* (Detroit, 1997); Hans Erich Boedeker, 'Aufklaerung und Kommunikationsprozess', *Aufklaerung* 2,
(1987), pp. 89–112; and T. Yasukata, *Lessing's Philosophy of Religion and the German Enlightenment* (New York,
2002).
[2]Steven Lestition, 'Kant and the End of the Enlightenment in Prussia', *Journal of Modern History* 65 (1993),
pp. 57–112.
[3]Felix Karlingen, *Geschichte des Maerchen im deutschen Sprachraum* (2nd rev. ed., Darmstadt, 1988).
[4]Albert Ward, *Book Production, Fiction, and the German Reading Public, 1740–1800* (Oxford, 1974). Cf. Rolf
Engelsing, *Analphabeten und Lektuere: zur Sozialgeschichte des Lesens in Deutschland zwischen feudalen und
industriellen Gesellschaft* (Stuttgart, 1973).
[5]S. L. Hochstadt, 'Migration in Pre-Industrial Germany', *Central European History* 16 (1983), pp. 195–224,
makes a case as well for a significant degree of regional mobility at lower socio-economic levels.

Yet, at the same time, this developing sense of common identity was a long way away even from the later concept of a 'cultural nation' as expressed by Friedrich Meinecke.[6] Prior to the French Revolution, the 'national idea', in so far as it existed, tended towards a commonwealth or confederation of strongly similar but essentially independent states.[7] German nationalism's modern roots were negative: the *Aufklaerung*'s rejection of what it considered the limited, artificial values of a French Enlightenment copied without comprehension in the courts and salons of the Holy Roman Empire.[8] The Revolution's wars enhanced this negative identity-forming as French attitudes and behaviours in the Rhineland gave the lie to claims of universal fraternity.[9] South-east Germany's dwarf states might no longer serve as foci of identity, but becoming 'French' was an even less desirable option. After Austerlitz and Jena, the German great powers, Prussia and Austria, also stressed a 'non-Frenchness', intended to balance regional and provincial loyalties with commitment to a larger political entity whose welfare was worth fighting for. During the Wars of Liberation, the Prussian army's order of battle depended heavily on the Landwehr, a civilian militia created on mobilization, which learned the craft of war by experience in the field. Prussia's armed forces also included a significant number of units and individuals who had chosen to fight under Prussian colours for a new Germany.[10] Prussia's reform movement, systematically published by the authorities, with its relatively broad and concrete efforts to develop a positive Prussian patriotism with a mass base, seemed, to enthusiasts all over Germany, to offer a springboard for a new era that would both reject the legacies of the old order and avoid the errors of the French.[11]

I

The German Confederation was created at the Congress of Vienna to sustain a central buffer zone that, as both glacis and highway, had been a key to Europe's diplomatic order since the Thirty Years War. As a consequence, direct national integration, to say nothing of national unification, had no practical prospects in post-Napoleonic Germany. At the same time, the French Revolution and the French imperium had demonstrated the risks of excessive local weakness east of the Rhine. The apparent willingness of Prussia to support the wide-reaching aspirations of Russia's Tsar Alexander I also suggested the desirability of

---

[6]Friedrich Meinecke, *Weltbuergertum und Nationalstaat: Studien zur Genesis des deutschen Nationalstaates* (5th ed., Munich, 1919).

[7]Helga Schultz, 'Mythos und Aufklaerung: Fruehformen des Nationalismus in Deutschland', *Historische Zeitschrift* 263 (1996), pp. 31–67. Cf. Hagen Schulze, *Der Weg zum Nationalstaat: Die deutsche Nationalbewegung vom 18. Jahrhundert bis zur Reichsgruendung* (Munich, 1985).

[8]Cf. H. B. Nisbet, ' "Was ist Aufklaerung?" The Concept of Enlightenment in Eighteenth-Century Germany', *Journal of European Studies* 12 (1982), pp. 77–95 and Richard van Duelmen, *The Society of the Enlightenment: The Rise of the Middle Class and Enlightenment Culture in Germany* (Cambridge, 1992).

[9]T. C. W. Blanning, *Germany and the French Revolution* (Oxford, 1983).

[10]Cf. P. Nolte, *Staatsbildung als Gesellschaftsreform. Politische Reformen in Preussen und den sueddeutschen Staaten 1800–1820* (Frankfurt, 1990); Marion Gray, *Prussia in Transition: Society and Politics under the Stein Reform Ministry of 1808* (Philadelphia, 1986); and Karen Hagemann, *'Mannlicher Muth und Teutsche Ehre'. Nation, Militaer und Geschlecht zur Zeit der Antinapoleonischen Krieges Preussens* (Paderborn, 2002).

[11]Andrea Hofmeister-Hunger, *Pressepolitik und Staatsreform: Die Institutionalisierung staatlicher Oeffentlichkeit bei Karl August von Hardenberg, 1792–1822* (Goettingen, 1994) and Robert Berdahl, 'New Thoughts on German Nationalism', *American Historical Review* 77 (1972), pp. 65–80.

establishing a German structure that would be both a counterweight and a magnet for a Prussia too strong to be relegated to regional status in the New European Order. Austria's Clemens Metternich, in particular, urged Habsburg abandonment of any vestigial claims to German hegemony in favour of sustaining harmony among the Confederation's major participants.[12]

The reorganization of Europe after 1815 recognized the developing German sense of common identity and common purpose. The Confederation's boundaries were drawn to exclude the Magyar and Slavic provinces of Austria, and also Prussian Poland. Its censorships did not prevent the diffusion of ideas, however, to say nothing of *belles-lettres*, music and fashion, well beyond their points of origin.[13] If its structure was a federation of independent systems, the number of those systems was drastically reduced from pre-Napoleonic levels. Only thirty-three states and cities were represented in the Confederation's Diet, and over half of these were recognized as being sovereign by courtesy and mutual agreement. The Confederation's focus on France as the 'designated enemy' also sustained the German self-definitions that had been developing since the eighteenth century. The viruses of revolution were no respecters of small-state boundaries, and, by providing a forum for cooperation against liberal movements and impulses, the Confederation facilitated communication and commonality precisely among those elements of the German political order that were most committed to a particularist vision.[14]

Synthesis was only half of the new German dialectic expressed in the Confederation. Economic and legal integration never developed beyond embryonic levels. Its military system, the Confederation's strongest common feature, depended essentially on the armies of Prussia and Austria. Attempts to establish even limited cohesion of armament and tactical doctrines, the military factors most susceptible of homogenization, repeatedly foundered on the middle-sized states' fear of absorption by their neighbours. Even in the early stages of the Congress of Vienna, before the German Confederation ever existed, the middle states strongly protested the projected annexation of Saxony by Prussia, as a matter of both general principle and particular interest. In that context, the single army corps Bavaria provided to the Confederation's theoretical order of battle, the divisions furnished by Saxony, Wuerttemberg and Baden, had more than symbolic value. In the final analysis, they could serve as speed bumps and trip wires, deterrents to any attempts by Prussia or Austria to repeat Frederick the Great's overrunning of Saxony in 1756.

---

[12]See, particularly, Robert D. Billinger, Jr., *Metternich and the German Question: State Rights and Federal Duties, 1820–1834* (London, 1991) and Lawrence J. Flockerzie, 'Saxony, Austria, and the German Question after the Congress of Vienna, 1815–1816', *International History Review* 12 (1990), pp. 661–87. Wolf D. Gruner, *Die Rolle und Funktion von 'Kleinstaaten' im internationalen System 1815–1914: Die Bedeutung des Endes der deutschen Klein-und Mittelstaaten fuer die europaeische Ordnung* (Hamburg, 1985), provides the general framework.
[13]An interesting case study is Manfred Bruemmer, *Staat contra Universitaet. Die Universitaet Halle-Wittenberg und die karlsbader Beschluesse 1819–1848* (Weimar, 1991). Cf. more generally, Frederik Ohles, *Germany's Rude Awakening: Censorship in the Land of the Brothers Grimm* (Kent, OH, 1992).
[14]Cf. Eberhardt Buessem, *Die Karlsbader Beschluesse von 1819: Die endgueltige Stabilisierung der restaurative Politik im Deutschen Bund nach dem Wiener Kongress von 1814/15* (Hildesheim, 1974); M. Jeismann, *Das Vaterland der Feinde. Studien zum nationalen Feindbegriff und Selbstverstaendnis in Deutschland und Frankreich, 1792–1918* (Stuttgart, 1992); and Wolfram Siemann, 'Wandel der Politik – Wandel der Staatsgewalt. Der Deutsche Bund in der Spannung zwischen "Gesammt-macht" und "voelkerrechtlichem Verein" ', in *Deutscher Bund und deutsche Frage, 1815–1866*, ed. H. Ruempler (Munich, 1990), pp. 59–73.

The revolutionary/Napoleonic experience eroded the final legacies of mutual reciprocity that had characterized the Holy Roman Empire even in its final decades. The House of Austria had learned exactly what its historic connections with Germany were worth in a crisis, and correspondingly concentrated on developing its resources, its policies and its identity in a 'black and yellow' context. For Metternich, in particular, the German Confederation was an instrument, a means to the end of internal and international stability throughout Europe. If that end could best be served by Austria playing a facilitator's role, fine-tuning rather than taking strong positions, then so much the better. Nothing in Metternich's philosophy or behaviour, however, indicates any commitment to interests other than those of Austria and Europe – which he perceived as essentially congruent.[15]

State identity was even stronger among the German states with experience as French clients. Napoleon's aims in Germany were concrete and limited. He wanted men and money. He wanted Austria kept out and discontent kept down. Experience of direct rule in such creations as Jerome Bonaparte's Kingdom of Westphalia showed that these goals were best met by cooperating with local systems as far as possible. Experience in the Confederation of the Rhine showed that small political entities required too much material and political overhead for results delivered.[16] As a result, the emperor turned increasingly to an early version of what modern theories of imperialism call mediatizing élites – in this case, the rulers and the administrations of states like Wuerttemberg, Baden and Bavaria. Their territories were increased in proportion to imperial expectations, and they were given an essentially free domestic hand, so long as they delivered money and men for Napoleon's wars.

Such circumstances encouraged the development of strong central administrations and broad-gauged state consciousness. Traditional patterns of loyalty could not be stretched to include the new acquisitions. Nor could they be marginalized or treated as 'provinces reputed foreign', as had been some regions of pre-revolutionary France. Instead, the newly enlarged principalities began consciously fostering patterns Friedrich Meinecke would later associate with a 'state-nation'.[17] Such entities, Meinecke asserts, stress common political identity based on a synthesis of individual affirmation and public performance. For the citizen, and even for the subject, membership in the political body is affirmative, an act of conscious will. In turn, the state seeks to encourage that affirmation by providing services considered – or marketed as – desirable.[18]

Germany's medium states had a history of cameralist proactivism that well antedated any French influence. Princes and their councillors made it a point of Enlightened pride to promote the welfare of their people by direct intervention. A fair number of the ministers and bureaucrats who rose to power during the Napoleonic period – men like Bavaria's

---

[15]Cf. Bertrand Michael Buchmann, *Militaer-Diplomatie-Politik. Oesterreich und Europa 1815–1835* (Bern, 1991) and, more generally, M. Dermdarsky, 'Oesterreich und der Deutsche Bund 1815–1866. Anerkennung zur deutschen Frage zwischen dem Wiener Kongress und Koeniggraetz' in *Oesterreich und die deutsche Frage im 19. und 20. Jahrhundert*, eds. H. Lutz and H. Rumpler (Vienna, 1982), pp. 92–116.

[16]H. Berding, *Napoleonische Herrschafts-und Gesellschaftspolitik im Koenigreich Westfalen 1807–1813* (Goettingen, 1973) and Andreas Schulz, *Herrschaft durch Verwaltung. Die Rheinbundreformen in Hessen-Darmstadt unter Napoleon (1803–1815)* (Stuttgart, 1991).

[17]Cf. as case studies, *inter alia*, L. E. Lee, 'Baden between Revolutions: State-Building and Citizenship, 1800–1848', *Central European History* 24 (1991), pp. 248–67, and Lawrence J. Flockherzie, 'State-Building and Nation-Building in the "Third Germany": Saxony after the Congress of Vienna', ibid., pp. 268–92.

[18]Friedrich Meinicke, *Cosmopolitanism and the National State*, tr. R. Kimber (Princeton, 1970).

Maximilian Montgelas – were committed reformers in their own right, whose ascent was facilitated because they were willing to undertake the comprehensive, large-scale changes that seemed the best response to the maps redrawn and the governments reshaped after 1806. The result was a state consciousness that survived even the losses symbolized by the Munich obelisk commemorating the 30,000 Bavarians who marched into Russia with Napoleon in 1812. Few ever saw home again, whether 'home' had a history of centuries of Wittelsbach rule or had become Bavarian only a few years before its men were conscripted for a war about which few of them cared. Over 16,000 simply disappeared, listed as 'missing in action' into the 1830s. These losses were nevertheless processed in a context of whether any other system and any other approach might have achieved better results. The governments, the state élites and, to a significant degree, those still excluded from their respective political communities, tended to agree, after 1815, that the preservation of autonomy based on patriotism was the best achievable basis for future security. At worst, it provided some freedom in allocating burdens externally imposed and some *sécurité à tous azimuts* – west, north and south.[19]

Prussia, too, had experienced an upsurge of civic awareness between 1806 and 1815. Since the days of Frederick the Great, patriotism had been strong among the native peasants who filled the army's ranks and who perceived Prussia as something more than the faceless authority behind tax collectors and conscription officials. The post-Jena reform movement strengthened public consciousness from two perspectives. Conservatives built on previous grievances to develop systematic depictions and defences of 'old Prussian' virtues, presumably threatened by the would-be Napoleons who believed the best way to beat the French was to become so like them that no one could tell the difference.[20] Reformers, for their parts, argued for nurturing a sense of commitment that would actualize the loyalty they believed Prussians felt for state and crown – the king's subjects would be transformed into Prussian citizens by a network of top-down reforms based on universal military service (most reformers made no secret of their conviction that this revitalized Prussia would become a lodestone for the rest of Germany).[21] This was, however, no new role. The legends that grew up around Frederick the Great had already generated a sense – at least among Protestants – that Prussia was special, different from both the universalist Austrian Empire and the parish-pump principalities of the west and south. After Napoleon's destruction, Prussia would still be Prussia – in a new, improved version.

Prussia's reformers and conservatives found common ground in a sense of unique victimization. Between 1806 and 1815, an increasing body of emotion insisted Prussia was suffering tribulations that merited special recognition. This attitude was reinforced by a

---

[19]Cf. Walter Demel, *Der bayerischen Staatsabsolutismus, 1806/08–1817* (Munich, 1983) and Eberhard Weis, *Montgelas 1759–1799* (Munich, 1971), in the context of Wolfgang Quint, *Souveraenitaetsbegriff und Douveraenitaetspolitik in Bayern* (Berlin, 1971). On the POW issue, see Wolfgang Schmit, 'Das Schicksal der Bayerischen Kriegsgefangenen in Russland 1812 bis 1814', *Militaergeschichtliche Mitteilungen* 47 (1987), pp. 9–26. For a quarter-century afterwards, the Bavarian government attempted to discover the fate of these lost men – a useful case study in the process of transforming subjects into citizens.

[20]See, particularly, Robert Berdahl, *The Politics of the Prussian Nobility: The Development of a Conservative Ideology 1770–1848* (Princeton, 1988).

[21]The government established an embryonic public relations programme to go with its vision. See Andrea Hofmeister-Hunger, *Pressepolitik und Staatsreform: Die Institutionalisierung staatlicher Oeffentlichkeitsarbeit bei Karl August von Hardenberg (1792–1822)* (Goettingen, 1994).

German intelligentsia that, after 1800, increasingly discovered the appeals of political community and as yet possessed little immunity to its negatives. Fichte's *Reden an die Deutsche Nation* were delivered in Berlin. Friedrich Schleiermacher issued his call for a Germany combining cultural identity and political patriotism from Prussia's capital. Professors and clergymen extolled the German fatherland from Prussian lecture halls and pulpits. It was scarcely remarkable that by 1813 even hardened pragmatists in the army and the administration were drinking from the nationalist cup – if only to provide extra courage in the face of what, even after his Russian débâcle, seemed insurmountable obstacles to defying Napoleon successfully.[22]

This did not mean Prussia sought hegemony, or even primacy, in Germany during and after its Wars of Liberation. Baron Karl von Stein's support of a *de facto* dualism, with Austria controlling the south and Prussia the north, and with the autonomy of the lesser states significantly curtailed, was developed to strengthen Germany against France. The aggrandizement of Prussia was a secondary effect, one Stein expected to increase that state's responsibilities more than its power. Karl von Hardenberg, Stein's successor as chief minister in 1810, favoured more than his predecessor the direct expansion of Prussian rule and Prussian control in north-west Germany. He also understood that expansion in a general context of cooperation, first with the small and middle-sized states, and later with Austria, for the sake of strengthening the 'German centre' against both France and a Russia whose messianic Emperor Alexander I seemed to have no more sense of boundaries and limitations than that possessed by Napoleon.[23]

Prussian advocates of both positions perceived Prussia as the dynamic force of the new German order. Such a position was best won by force of arms. The Prussian army of 1813–15 matched its Frederician predecessor neither in relative size nor operational effectiveness. It was, however, unmatched in fighting spirit. Its tone was set in allied councils by Marshal Gebhardt von Bluecher, a fierce old soldier whose character and behaviour harked back to the Thirty Years War and prefigured the Erwin Rommels and Walther Models of a later century. No one ever accused Bluecher of having any more social polish or strategic insight than he actually needed, but he led from the front. 'Marshal Forward' had a rough tongue, unfailing courage and a straightforward sense of honour which inspired the inexperienced conscripts who filled the ranks of both the army's line regiments and the Landwehr, the citizen militia that was the line's stablemate.[24] Bluecher knew only one way of making war: fight without let-up. This mindset informed Prussian diplomacy as well. It was Prussia that took a consistent lead in demanding action as well as negotiation in the months after Leipzig, successfully reminding the Fourth Coalition that peace was contingent on victory, and victory meant Napoleon's removal. During the

---

[22]Cf. Matthew Levinger, *Enlightened Nationalism. The Transformation of Prussia's Political Culture, 1806–1848* (New York, 2000); Thomas Stamm-Kuhlmann, ' "Man vertraue doch der Administration!" Staatsverstaendnis und Regierungshandeln des preussischen Staatskanzlers Karl von Hardenberg', *Historische Zeitschrift* 264 (1997), pp. 613–54; and Joerg Echterkamp, *Der Aufstieg der deutschen Nationalismus* (Frankfurt, 1997).

[23]Philip Dwyer, 'The Two Faces of Prussian Foreign Policy: Karl August von Hardenberg as Minister for Foreign Affairs, 1804–1815' in *'Freier Gebrauch der Kraefte'. Eine Bestandsaufnahme der Hardenberg-Forschung*, ed. T. Stamm-Kuhlmann (Munich, 2001), pp. 75–91.

[24]Meyer Kestnbaum, 'Partisans and Patriots: National Conscription and the Reconstruction of the Modern State in France, Germany, and the United States' (dissertation, Harvard, 1997), contextualizes the Prussian experience with conscription.

Hundred Days it was Prussia, personified once more by Bluecher, that pulled the Duke of Wellington's chestnuts from the fire of Waterloo, transforming 'a damned near-run thing' into a decisive victory.[25]

In these contexts, the smooth and rapid integration of Prussia into the new German Confederation stands among the least logical consequences of the Vienna settlement. The common thread of policy recommendations across the political and ideological spectrum during the Wars of Liberation had involved Prussia developing as a European power in a German context – in other words, recovering the status won by Frederick the Great, only with a new foundation. After 1815, however, Prussia depended on an army of short-service conscripts brought to war strength by mobilized reservists. This was not a force well suited to policies of limited intimidation. Its similarity to the French *levée en masse*, combined initially with Prussia's image elsewhere in Germany as a focal point for 'progressive' forces, including nationalism, generated risk of Prussia being Europe's designated successor to Napoleon's France: an objective military threat combined with a destabilizing and unpredictable ideology.

Prussia was neither able nor willing to sustain such a position. For a decade after Waterloo, the state correspondingly and consciously assumed a facilitator's role in the Concert of Europe, the Holy Alliance of the three eastern empires, and the German Confederation.[26] That same period was characterized by the increasing consolidation of bureaucracy and the accompanying bureaucratization of German political life. Even constitutionalism was increasingly understood as enhancing the special status of the officials responsible for the constitutions' administration. In states like Baden and Bavaria, officials began developing a status much like that of lawyers in the late twentieth-century United States: somehow benefiting no matter what happened because they were the system's fulcrum.[27]

Bureaucratization was also facilitated by industrialization. A cameralist heritage, and Britain's vigorous return to continental markets long denied, encouraged state intervention against traditional but restrictive institutions and practices ranging from guild privileges to tariff barriers. Railway promoters sought public funding in a context of limited private capital markets, and solicited support from army officers who perceived railroads' potential value, even in their early stages, as strategic force multipliers. The Prussian customs union of 1833 was significant less for its direct economic impact than for its reassertion of state control over general economic interests even at the possible expense of traditional and local institutions.[28]

The Europe-wide upheavals of 1830 had a significant impact on this developing structure of centralizing states in a confederation matrix. Unrest in Germany remained strongly localized and highly verbal. Even in the volatile Rhineland, whose Francophilia was

---

[25]Peter Hofschroer, *1815, The Waterloo Campaign* (2 vols., London, 1998–9), overstates the case – but not by much.

[26]See, particularly, Lawrence J. Baack, *Christian Bernstoff and Prussia: Diplomacy and Reform Conservatism, 1818–1832* (New Brunswick, NJ, 1980).

[27]Recent, massive case studies include Bernd Wunder, *Die badische Beamtenschaft zwischen Rheinbund und Reichsgruendung (1806–1871)* (Stuttgart, 1998) and Echhardt Treichel, *Der Primat der Buerokratie: Buerokratischer Staat und buerokratische Elite im Herzogtom Nassau, 1806–1866* (Stuttgart, 1991).

[28]Eric Dorn Brose, *The Politics of Technological Change in Prussia: Out of the Shadow of Antiquity, 1809–1848* (Princeton, 1993) and David T. Murphy, 'Prussian Aims for the Zollverein, 1828–1833', *The Historian* 53 (1991), pp. 258–302.

largely a statement of anti-Prussianism, order was maintained by relatively small forces. These tensions only highlighted the increased legitimacy and power of a 'middle Germany' whose rulers, in general, followed up crowd control through armed force by offering or accepting compromises. Saxony, Hanover and Hesse-Cassel emerged with new constitutions. The number of liberals in the parliaments of Baden and Bavaria increased and their voices grew louder.[29] But as the Hambach Festival of 1832 clearly showed, the opposition still believed it possible to convince governments as opposed to destroying them. That opposition also expected to do its best work in individual states, relating to princes and bureaucrats who had been at least somewhat flexible under pressure. As yet liberalism had not made common cause with nationalism, except in the instrumental context of depicting particular reforms as generally beneficial to the 'German nation', however amorphous that entity might be.[30]

The international context was substantially different. The overthrow of the Bourbon monarchy in France, Belgium's declaration of independence from the Netherlands and the Polish uprising against Russia represented a comprehensive challenge to the Vienna settlement. Russia favoured intervention and mobilized troops to back the policy. For Prussia, Austria and the German Confederation the remedy seemed not much more threatening than the disease. Prussia, in particular, favoured Confederation action to demonstrate the capacity to defend itself against a challenge from either the Rhine or the Vistula.[31]

The Confederation's military organization was based on a force of ten corps. Austria and Prussia were each to provide three, Bavaria one and the lesser states of south, central and north Germany combined their respective contingents into three more. Supreme command would be exercised by an Austrian general. The comparison with the Cold War force structure of NATO is striking — and more than a surface manifestation. Well enough adapted to a clear and present external threat, its applicability to lesser crises and internal tensions was dubious.[32] Prussia, in particular, with its successful history of using armed force as a deterrent, feared that, in the developing context of events, the Confederation would be so slow to move that it might wind up sparking a war instead of preventing one. Both the general staff and the foreign ministry instead favoured bilateral negotiations

[29]James J. Sheehan, *German Liberalism in the Nineteenth Century* (Chicago, 1978) and Dieter Langewiesche, *Liberalism in Germany*, tr. C. Banerji (Princeton, 2000) are the best overviews. Michael Hammer's massive case study *Volksbewegung und Obrigkeiten: Revolution in Sachsen, 1830/31* (Weimar, 1997), makes a case for greater belligerency — at least until the shooting started. Cf. also, Heinrich Volkmann, 'Protesttraeger und Protestformen in den Unruhen 1830–1832' in *Sozialer Protest: Studien zu traditioneller Resistenz und kollektiver Gewalt in Deutschland vom Vormaerz bis zur Reichsgruendung*, eds. H. Volckmann and J. Bergmann (Opladen, 1984), pp. 56–75.

[30]Dieter Dueding, *Organisierter Gesellschaftlicher Nationalismus in Deutschland (1808–1848)* (Munich, 1984).

[31]Cf. P. Burg, 'Die franzoesische Politik gegenueber Foederationen und Foederationsplaenen deutscher Klein-und Mittelstaaten, 1830–1833' in *Aspects des relations franco-allemandes 1830–1848*, eds. R. Poidevin and H. O. Sieburg (Metz, 1979), pp. 17–45; Wolfgang Heuser, *Kein Krieg in Europa: Die Rolle Preussens im Kreis der Europaeischen Maechte bei der Entstehung des belgischen Staates (1830–1839)* (Pfaffenweiler, 1992); and the anthology, *Der Polnische Freiheitskampf 1830–1831 und die liberale deutsche Polenfreundschaft*, ed. P. Ehlen (Munich, 1982).

[32]Lothar Hoebelt, 'Zur Militaerpolitik des Deutschen Bundes: Corpseinteilung und Aufmarschplaene im Vormaerz', *Deutscher Bund und deutsche Frage*, pp. 114–35.

with the principal German courts. This approach was expected to improve collective security and enhance Prussia's credibility in Confederation concerns – the kind of synthesis between doing good and doing well that is a diplomat's delight.[33]

In December 1830, Berlin contacted Vienna with an offer to provide not merely three corps, but 200,000 men, for operations against France should they become necessary. The note also recommended that instead of a single field army, the Confederation employ three. Prussia, supported by the northern and central contingents, would secure the lower Rhine. The Bavarians and the south German corps, probably reinforced by a Prussian corps, would hold the centre, and Austria's contingent would move into the upper Rhine. Such a deployment would require three army commanders, with logic indicating their provision by Prussia, Austria and Bavaria. The Prussian note also suggested that overall command should now be vested in the contingent supplying the largest force and deploying in the area of greatest threat. That, of course, was Prussia.

Considered in purely operational terms, the proposal was not merely a revival of the eighteenth-century cordon strategy Napoleon cuttingly described as best suited to stop smuggling. Prussia's general staff perceived more clearly than the military planners elsewhere in Germany the difficulties of concentrating and supplying eight or more army corps in one place. The Prussians recognized as well that while a Napoleon might be able to command such a force effectively, the German Confederation had no likely future Bonapartes in its armed forces. Finally, Prussia remained committed to its traditional strategy of deterring wars in preference to fighting them. Three corps quickly in place, whatever flags they flew, were more likely to check French opportunism and inspire second thoughts in Paris than was a much larger force concentrated only after hostilities began. That was particularly true given the French army's reconfiguration during the 1820s into a long-service professional force, able to make war from a standing start to a degree impossible in the German armies, which depended heavily on mobilized reservists in order to take the field.[34] The best way to stop the French was before they started.

Metternich temporized. Whatever might be its military virtues, in a political context the Prussian proposal looked suspiciously like a pawn move in a campaign to secure parity with Austria in the Confederation. Creating a separate field army around the south German corps would, moreover, encourage those states to assert themselves in other matters, thereby further destabilizing the Confederation. The south German states, however, were initially interested in Prussia's overtures, not least from concern about being caught in the undertow of Austria's European interests. An independent south German field army had a certain appeal. Prussia's fifteen low-profile years, combined with the relatively low regard in which the state's short-service conscript army was regarded, had diminished anxiety at Prussia's capacity to dominate its near neighbours. And even optimists in the southern war ministries realized that their armies, combined amounting to about two corps, could not by themselves stop a French attack. States needing to be rescued from emergencies by their

---

[33]For the following, Baack, pp. 165 ff., is the best overview in English. Cf. for a briefer analysis, Robert D. Billinger, Jr., 'The War Scare of 1831 and Prussian-South German Plans for the End of Austrian Dominance in Germany', *Central European History* 9 (1976), pp. 203–19 and Juergen Angelow, *Von Wien nach Koeniggraetz: Die Sicherheitspolitik des Deutschen Bundes im europaeschen Gleichgewicht 1815–1866* (Munich, 1996), pp. 87 ff.
[34]For that process, see Gary P. Cox, *The Halt in the Mud: French Strategic Planning from Waterloo to Sedan* (Boulder, CO, 1994).

allies have their claims to autonomy correspondingly diminished. Better to consider arrangements beforehand.[35]

A Prussian military mission making a tour of south-west Germany in the spring of 1831 found widespread support, military and political, for overhauling the Confederation's military system in order to enhance both its defensive capacity and its diplomatic autonomy.[36] Berlin responded by calling for a conference of the south German states, Prussia and Austria. The proposal generated immediate opposition in Vienna, where its consequences were understood as likely to facilitate a coalition of the Confederation's major non-Austrian states. In Prussia, too, critics attacked the initiative as challenging a system that, whether to suppress revolution or deter invasion, needed Austria's positive cooperation. Even Clausewitz, still a sharp critic of what he considered ultra-conservative closeness to Austria, asserted Austria's military importance in any programme of German security. Metternich took advantage of this divided opinion, stressing to Berlin the advantages of a continued 'special relationship' with Austria, while arguing that the lesser states would prove a rope of sand – a prophecy his diplomats in Munich, Karlsruhe and Stuttgart did their best to render self-fulfilling.

The issue grew increasingly moot as a new French monarchy demonstrated its commitment to maintaining the general peace and Russia became enmeshed in reconquering Poland, with the goodwill of Prussian and Austrian governments fearing the spread of nationalist-based disaffection.[37] Metternich succeeded in getting the Confederation to adopt a series of laws, first restricting the states' power to obstruct Confederation legislation directed against revolutionary activity, then strengthening censorship of the press, the universities and political organizations. Lest any doubt remain whether these new laws had teeth, the comic-opera seizure of a police station in the Confederation capital, Frankfurt, by a group of academics expecting to spark a general uprising, led instead to the city's military occupation by troops under Confederation authority. That occupation lasted until 1842 – a sign and a warning to anyone still believing freedom of thought and freedom of action were congruent anywhere east of the Rhine.[38]

Metternich's successful counter-revolutionary campaign made it easier, in the fall of 1832, for Austria to accept a restructuring of Confederation mobilization plans along lines closely resembling the original Prussian proposal. Henceforth 70,000 Prussians, plus the federal northern corps, would deploy on the lower Rhine, with 150,000 Austrians concentrating in the south. It was the central sector that saw the most change. From the weakest force it became the largest; including the two south German corps, the central German IX Confederation Corps, built around the Saxon army, and 90,000 Prussians. By replicating the Confederation in miniature, this field army, though existing only on paper, significantly diminished the southern states' prospects for improving their position in the organization. The command of such a strong force was far more likely to be a subject of controversy than was the case for the original three-corps proposal. In consequence, the south German states never ratified the new system.[39]

---

[35]George Werner, *Bavaria in the German Confederation, 1820–1848* (Rutherford, NJ, 1977).

[36]For Bavaria's position, see Othmar Hackl, *Der Bayerische Generalstab (1792–1919)* (Munich, 1999), pp. 63 ff.

[37]The best work on the military aspect is Frederick W. Kagan, *The Military Reforms of Nicholas I* (New York, 1999), pp. 212 ff.

[38]Billinger, *Metternich*, pp. 144–5.

[39]The draft 'Protokoll' of 3 December 1832 is reprinted in Angelow, pp. 350–65.

This non-cooperation did not mean the end of concern for military reform in the Confederation. A beginning was made in 1830 when the 'dwarf contingents' of the small states of south and central Germany, none stronger than a few battalions, most lacking cavalry and artillery, were withdrawn from the three composite corps and organized into a separate Reserve Division intended for garrison duties. The states still included in those corps subsequently negotiated agreements on the allocation of command appointments, staff posts and similar administrative matters. While these reforms remained largely confined to paper, they nevertheless reflected a collective commitment to being something other than military clients of the great German powers, Prussia and Austria.[40]

The south German states faced a strategic problem as well as an organizational one. Concern for the threat posed by the Orléans monarchy increased as the decade progressed. To a degree, this was the fruit of an internal French issue: agitation for restoration of the 'natural boundaries' of France – especially the left bank of the Rhine – under a government whose legitimacy remained too dubious to challenge its nationalists. Despite continued French assertion of nothing but the most benign intentions in central Europe, newspaper editorials and parliamentary speeches exacerbated fears even among liberal Germans that French goodwill was, at best, ephemeral.

German liberalism at this stage of its history consciously affirmed the role of force in international relations. Those liberals, like Baden's Karl von Rotteck, who focused on security issues, advocated people's armies, various forms of militias, as much on the grounds of their projected operational effectiveness as for their role in giving parliaments a central role in military affairs. The influence of nationalism was also sufficiently strong to foster, if not xenophobia, a healthy suspicion of French intentions. Administrations, for their part, played the security card as a trump in the ongoing game of securing cooperation from this vocal, influential and increasingly economically powerful segment of the political state.

The result was an increasingly harmonious chorus, in an increasing number of south German states, calling for some positive action to assert Confederation commitment to defending German territory against the French threat, without significantly increasing either government power or military budgets, and without repudiating the principle of 'neutrality in all directions' – particularly valued as a counterweight to Prussia's and Austria's respective roles in the great-power system. A decade's experience as clients of Napoleon had provided all the object lessons in that role that south Germany needed.[41]

These objectives, contradictory if not mutually exclusive, were resolved, in practice, by emphasizing fortifications at the expense of field forces. After Waterloo, the victor powers had legitimated the development of a series of strong points in the Rhineland, and supported their construction with 60 million francs allotted from the French indemnity. Over half the cash went directly to Prussia and Bavaria, to improve their respective defence systems. Three locations, Mainz, Landau and Luxembourg, were intended 'Confederation fortresses'. Two more, Ulm and Rastatt, were begun in 1840, in part with money

---

[40]This reform is analysed comprehensively in Wolfgang Keul, *Die Bundesmilitaerkommission (1819–1866) als politisches Gremium* (Frankfurt, 1977), pp. 142 ff.

[41]Cf. Irmline Veit-Brause, *Die deutsch-franzoesische Krise von 1840* (Cologne, 1967); Manfred Mayer, *Freiheit und Macht: Studien zum Nationalismus sueddeutscher insbesondere badischer Liberaler 1830–1848* (Frankfurt, 1994); and Sylvia Krauss, *Die politischen Beziehungen zwischen Bayern und Frankreich, 1814/15–1840* (Munich, 1987).

designated for the purpose that had been accruing interest with the House of Rothschild since 1815.

These were under Confederation authority rather than that of the state in whose territory they lay. The staff and garrisons were mixed. Mainz, for example, was held in peacetime by 8,000 men, half Prussian and half Austrian, supplemented by a battalion from Hesse-Darmstadt. In war, the garrison was increased to 21,000, a third each from Prussia, Austria and the other contingents. Ulm's 5,000-strong garrison was home to 600 Austrian artillerymen; the rest came from Baden and Wuerttemberg. The close association of men from different states did not exactly create a sense of brotherhood. Mainz, in particular, was notorious for brawls between the Prussian and Austrian contingents. Contemporary German critics argued that the sites had been acquired haphazardly and did not form part of a coherent defensive system. The fortresses, however, were important as a minimum common denominator of agreement in the Confederation, and played an increasing role in Confederation strategy. They were expected to absorb enough French attention to make impossible a lightning campaign by the French professional army and offer time for the Confederation's superior numbers to come into action.[42]

Rastatt and Mainz, in particular, were highly regarded among military architects as state of the art. A French study of 1848 described Mainz as a complex system whose approaches could be screened, in part, by flooding, whose garrison had protected access to the Rhine's west bank, and whose magazines could hold around 500 tons of powder. Its garrison had to be neither first-rate nor brilliantly commanded; ordinary competence at all levels would suffice to sustain a long siege.[43]

Such reports, then and now, are often prepared with an eye towards domestic issues such as budgets. Nevertheless, given the consistent French fear during this period of a German invasion, expert professional opinion that Mainz was a stumbling block in the path of even a spoiling attack into Germany may be taken at something like face value. In 1840, French support for Egypt's rebellion against the Ottoman Empire developed into a campaign to secure the Rhine frontier as 'compensation' for modifying its Near East policy. The July Monarchy had deliberately cultivated the Napoleonic mythos as part of its own quest for legitimacy. Foreign Minister Adolphe Thiers insisted France would not compromise, and that any resulting war would be waged on the continent, not in the Near East. To sharpen his point, he festooned his office with maps of the Rhineland.

The south German governments called simultaneously for Confederation neutrality in any European war and for further improvements to the Confederation's military system. Prussia, whose own western provinces were on the French wish list, began in October to bring its Rhine fortresses to war readiness. But if the immediate crisis blew over quickly, it was not least because the French army was not anxious to back Thiers's game to the last card by testing the Confederation and its fortresses in arms.[44]

Thiers's forced resignation in October 1840 restored a surface equilibrium, but left three open sores in Germany. The southern states continued their demand for military reform.

---

[42]Angelow, pp. 57 ff. and Wolfgang Petter, 'Deutscher Bund und deutscher Mittelstaaten' in *Handbuch zur Militaergeschichte*, vol. IV/2, *Militaergeschichte im 19. Jahrhundert*, ed. MGFA (Stuttgart, 1981), pp. 248 ff.
[43]Cox, p. 145.
[44]Cf. Veit-Brause, *passim* and H.-O. Sieburg, 'Napoleon, Napoleon-Legende und politische Gruppenbilding' in W. von Groote, *Napoleon I und die Staatenwelt seiner Zeit* (Freiburg, 1969), pp. 151–67.

Prussia, with a heightened sense of its own vulnerability, began preparing recommendations for systematic changes in the Confederation's approach to a threat from the west. And a burgeoning nationalist movement had an issue, a symbol and a song – 'The Watch on the Rhine' was bad poetry set to worse music. Nevertheless, from its appearance in 1840, it epitomized the 'defence and defiance' (*Schutz und Trutz*) that was the core of the Confederation's military policy, if not always that of its two largest states.

II

Prussia's behaviour was influenced by its new monarch. Frederick William IV assumed the throne in 1840, determined to make the kind of mark in Germany that his predecessor had spent a quarter of a century avoiding. Interested in military matters (along with his brother, Prince William, he played a central role in Prussia's adoption of a breech-loading infantry rifle), Frederick William was nevertheless to disappoint those, especially on the Right, who looked to him for decisively repressive domestic policies.[45] His approach to the Confederation's military system, however, did reflect his primary concern: to create and sustain the monarchical principle in a secular, public, mass age. To that end, Frederick William took the lead in advocating increasing the active components of the German armies. He also urged a policy of 'forward defence', one not accepting the risks of abandoning, however temporarily, German territory to an invader – both for nationalistic reasons and because of his belief that civilians in uniform were not likely to take well the moral and physical strains of an initial retreat that involved fighting on their own territory.

This fundamental challenge to militia advocates in both south Germany and Prussia encouraged the king to pay attention to fortress systems as *couverture* for Prussian and Confederation mobilizations, which, even supported by the railroads coming into service during the decade, demanded time. Prussia used that fact as a starting point to resolve a debate over whether Ulm or Rastatt should be developed into a federal fortress by successfully urging the construction of both. Rastatt's proximity to the major French eastern fortress of Strasbourg made its reinforcement difficult and diminished its prospects for a long-term defence. The first issue was addressed by giving the new fortress a strong peacetime garrison and keeping it fully provisioned. The second, at least in the mind of the Prussian king and his general staff, could best be resolved by a Confederation counter-offensive mounted into France on a broad front along the upper and middle Rhine.[46]

That particular strategic dish was too rich, and too expensive, for the south German states – particularly in the context of Metternich's soothing assertions that 'business as usual' remained viable Confederation policy towards France. Nevertheless, during the 1840s, the

---

[45]Hans-Christof Kraus, 'Das preussische Koenigtum Friedrich Wilhelms IV aus der Sicht Ernst Ludwig von Gerlachs', *Jahrbuch fuer die Geschichte Mittel-und Ostdeutschlands* 36 (1987), pp. 48–93.

[46]Cf. David E. Barclay, *Frederick William IV and the Prussian Monarchy, 1840–1861* (Oxford, 1995), pp. 49 ff.; 'The Soldiers of an Unsoldierly King: The Military Advisors of Frederick William IV, 1840–1858' in *Geschichte als Aufgabe. Festschrift fuer Otto Busch*, ed. W. Treue (Berlin, 1988), pp. 247–66; Robert D. Billinger, Jr., 'They Sing the Best Songs Badly: Metternich, Frederick William IV, and the German Confederation during the War Scare of 1840', *Deutscher Bund und deutsche Frage*, pp. 94–113; and Angelow, pp. 113 ff. For the French perspective, see Cox, pp. 144 ff.

armies of the German middle states in general began to improve.[47] Bavaria, Wuerttemberg and Baden in the south, Hanover in the north, Saxony in the centre – the particularism so often highlighted by outside observers was balanced by certain commonalities as well. These states had constructed their armies along French lines, with some local modifications, during the Napoleonic Wars, and that system had proven itself sufficiently to be retained after 1815. Recruiting was conscription-based, but like its Napoleonic model allowed substitution: the obligation was to provide service, not necessarily to serve oneself.[48] A substitute could be sought privately, furnished by an agency or, increasingly, delivered by the state itself. In each case the pattern was similar. A sum of money, the exact amount depending on the market at the moment, was paid directly to the substitute. Another, larger amount was deposited with the state as a bond. On completion of his term of service the substitute received all or most of the bond – the 'handling charges' could not become too large without disrupting the process.

About a quarter of the men conscripted – or their families – took advantage of the system. It was possible to purchase insurance policies that paid off if the holder's number came up for the draft, and parents who could afford one often did so when their son was an infant, much as parents today invest in saving plans that mature at twenty-one. Often excoriated by nineteenth-century nationalists, the system was in fact a practical response to the development of liberalism and capitalism in societies that did not face direct, comprehensive military threats. The substitute was, in principle, a rational actor, deciding for himself that the bonuses and bounties were worth the six or so years of active service required to collect them, and deciding that military service was a preferable alternative to the civilian labour market. By no means were all, or even most, of the substitutes drawn from society's dregs and outcasts. Apart from men seeking careers as non-commissioned officers – a status fairly easy to acquire in middle Germany – substitution was a path to hard cash in significant amounts. Younger sons with limited prospects of inheriting a farm, apprentices and journeymen perceiving that they were unlikely ever to make their *Meisterpruefung*, and even would-be small businessmen enrolled as substitutes to secure a stake they were unlikely to acquire elsewhere. That many of the hopes went unfulfilled had more to do with the kinds of dreams nurtured by perceptions of opportunity than with any conscious stacking of the conscription deck. Similar motives are a staple of contemporary recruiting programmes everywhere in the western world.

From the viewpoint of those engaging the substitutes, the transaction was a business deal like any other. Military budgets were too low to make universal service possible in any case. There was no reason why planning, as opposed to some form of chance, should not determine an individual's behaviour. The stakes, after all, were not mortal. It is worth

---

[47]Max Ritter von Xylander, *Das Heer-Wesen der Staaten des Deutschen Bundes* (Augsburg, 1842, reprinted 1990), is a comprehensive and reliable handbook. Petter, pp. 359 ff., is an excellent overview of the Confederation from an institutional perspective. Wolf D. Gruner, *Das bayerische Heer 1825 bis 1864. Eine kritische Analyse der bewaffneten Macht Bayerns vom Regierungsantritt Ludwigs I bis zum Vorabend des deutschen Krieges* (Boppard, 1972) and Paul Sauer, *Das wuerttembegrische Heer in der Zeit des deutschen und norddeutschen Bundes* (Stuttgart, 1958), are by far the best studies of their respective armies.
[48]Peter Fleck, 'Konskription und Stellvertretung. Die Behandlung der Kriegsdienstpflicht in hessisch-darmstaedtischen Landtag von 1820 bis 1866', *Archiv fuer hessische Geschichte und Altertumskunde*, Neue Folge 43 (1985), pp. 193–228, is an excellent case study of the system and the controversies it engendered.

noting in this context that the Selective Service System as implemented in the US during the early Cold War only broke down with the advent of Vietnam, when those drafted had a real chance of being killed as opposed to inconvenienced. Nor is there an obvious difference between hiring a substitute, directly or through the government, and fathering a child or becoming a teacher, and thereby moving others ahead of you on the draft board's list. Some moral advantage, indeed, seems to lie with substitution, where the terms are unmistakably clear to all the participants.

Seen in their own terms, the recruiting systems of the German middle states in the middle of the nineteenth century were by no means outdated or retrograde. Nor were the armies thus raised forces of 'rootless cosmopolitans'. At bottom, the relatively small size of the individual states worked against the kind of alienation of soldiers from civilians that was a policy norm in France or Austria. Nor did stringent budgets facilitate regular large-scale transferring of German units from garrison to garrison. The middle German officer corps was significantly less class-bound than their Prussian counterpart. Saxony, Wuerttemberg or Bavaria still did not offer a career open to talent – but they did offer a career open to interest. If a young man from the business or professional classes wished, for whatever reason, to become an officer, he found no insurmountable obstacles in his path. And since a commission lacked the status it possessed in either Prussia or Austria, those who sought one were correspondingly likely to be motivated, at least to some degree, by an interest in the craft of war.

A certain degree of tension nevertheless existed between what might be called the 'parties of movement' in middle Germany and the soldiers whose response was crucial for any movement that hoped to succeed by winning public support. While individual substitutes might make a reasonably good thing of their choice, the bulk of the conscripts, those carried along by the system, regarded their counterparts, middle-class and otherwise, who did not have to don a uniform, more as shirkers than as mentors. When revolution swept Germany in 1848, only Baden's soldiers supported it positively in any numbers. In the other states, the armies kept their ranks and obeyed orders, whatever sympathy they might have felt for the uprising and its representatives. Some Wuerttemberg troops sang songs of freedom before marching off to help suppress the revolt in Baden in June 1849. It did not significantly affect their aim.[49]

The middle-sized German armies did not confront prospective challenges from either popular militias or civic guards raised from the urban bourgeoisie in the pattern of Orleanist France. This reflected the limited friction in constitutional states between governments and parliaments over military questions in the decades after Waterloo: where such institutions existed, their functions were purely political, as a voice for reform.[50] Baden, where Karl von Rotteck remained a consistent, coherent advocate of a democratized militia system, was an arguable exception. Even there, however, Grand Duke Leopold, who

---

[49]Sabrina Mueller, *Soldaten in der deutschen Revolution von 1848/49* (Paderborn, 1999), is masterful in sorting out the social history of the German armies; the anecdote is on p. 315.

[50]Cf. Heinrich Volkmann, 'Protesttraeger und Protestformen in den Unruhen von 1830 bis 1832' in *Sozialer Protest. Studien zu traditioneller Resistenz und kollektiver Gewalt in Deutschland vom Vormaerz bis zum Reichsgruendung*, eds. H. Volkmann and J. Bergmann (Opladen, 1984), pp. 56–74 and Ralf Proeve, 'Civic Guards in the European Revolutions of 1848' in *Europe in 1848: Revolution and Reform*, eds. D. Dowe et al., tr. D. Higgins (New York, 2001), pp. 683–93.

assumed the throne in 1830, tended to strike a balance between liberal politicians and increasingly conservative soldiers, when he did not directly take a liberal position by reducing the army's budgets and limiting its representational functions.[51]

The limited conflicts over military matters, in turn, reflected increasing congruence in matters of finance and foreign policy. The governments of middle Germany grew steadily more liberal than cameralist in their commitment to restricting public budgets as a trade-off for relative administrative independence. Increased spending on entirely new projects, like railroads, usually came at the expense of the army. By 1825 at the latest, it was impossible to find any serious advocacy anywhere in middle Germany of independent operational or strategic planning, except as a stopgap until either the Confederation or the Concert should commit its forces. Nor was there significant consideration in the war ministries of Saxony, Bavaria or Hanover of the grand-strategic or strategic offensive as a desirable policy even in narrow military contexts.[52] Middle Germany's armies were understood as defensive forces to be employed in defensive contexts; the most extreme departures from this generalization involved counter-attacks pushed forward into an aggressor's homeland as part of some general Confederation effort.

Threat assessment was also narrowly focused. France was not merely the major, but the only projected enemy. This limitation reflected, on one level, the impossibility of developing, in the Confederation matrix, contingency plans for military action against either Prussia or Austria. Though either was at least as theoretically credible an antagonist as France, security against the threats they posed had to be provided on the diplomatic level. Nor did Russia figure in middle-state military planning — a consequence of experience as well as geography. Such contexts made easier the establishment of consensus on core issues of military policy; other aspects could be marginalized safely.[53]

Considered individually, the armies of Germany's middle states showed common weaknesses as part of their common matrices.[54] Their cavalry and artillery — both relatively expensive arms, and both requiring high levels of technical proficiency — were generally considered weak points. Individual German regiments and batteries were as good as any in Europe, but there were fewer of them relative to the infantry. The artillery was likely to be armed with guns outdated by half a generation, and both arms suffered from a chronic shortage of horses. The infantry's most obvious shortcoming, as determined by foreign and Confederation observers, was its sharp difference between peace and war establishments, and between peace establishments and men with the colours. A Bavarian regiment expected to mobilize with 2,360 men, for example, had a peace strength on paper of 172 men for each

---

[51]See Reinhard Mielitz, 'Das badische Militaerwesen und die Frage der Volksbewaffnung von den Jahren des Rheinbundes bis zum 48er Revolution' (dissertation, Freiburg, 1956).

[52]See, for example, the Bavarian General Staff's approach in Hackl, pp. 119 ff.

[53]The best overview is Wolf Gruner, 'Der Deutsche Bund und die europaeische Friedensordnung' in *Deutscher Bund und deutsche Frage*, pp. 235–63. See also Peter Burg, *Der Wiener Kongress. Der Deutsche Bund im europaeischen Staatensystem* (Munich, 1984) and Ludwig Bentfeldt, *Der Deutsche Bund als nationales Band 1815–1866* (Goettingen, 1985).

[54]The following is based on Edgar Graf von Matuschka and Wolfgang Petter, 'Organisationsgeschichte der Streitkraeften' in *Deutsche Militaergeschichte*, IV/2, pp. 322–43. Joachim Neimeyer, *Hannoversches Militaer 1815–1866* (Beckum, 1992), offers points of comparison in the context of a state that consistently went its own way in military matters. Cf. the overview by Elmar Wienhofer, *Das Militaerwesen des Deutschen Bundes und das Ringen zwischen Oesterreich und Preussen um die Vorherrschaft in Deutschland, 1815–1866* (Osnabrueck, 1973).

of its eight companies. Only thirty-two men per company, however, were required to be actually under arms at any time. The rest were furloughed for most of the year or only nominally enrolled – 'paper soldiers' in the most extreme form. A Wuerttemberg regiment had 560 men in peace, 1,800 in war, but the actual number of men under arms was determined by the requirements of manning the watch posts in particular garrison towns, as opposed to any operational considerations.

Individual training was restricted, in particular, by the limited amounts of ammunition available for practice. This was significant, less in its consequences for marksmanship – a matter of limited consequence in an era of smooth-bore muskets, flintlock or percussion – than in the inability to accustom partially trained recruits to something approximating the sounds, smells and obscurities of black-powder battles, where the fog of war was a literal phenomenon and where the reflex movements involved in loading and firing were a principal factor keeping men in ranks. Even when German units were able to take the field for autumn manoeuvres, the terrain available to them was often so restricted that one newly minted subaltern ordered to establish security for his unit was told by a peasant that the *Herr Leutnant* had stationed an outpost wrongly: 'it belongs here, by the cherry tree, where it has always been'.[55]

In the context of such professional restrictions, the officer corps of middle Germany nevertheless developed between 1815 and 1848 a flourishing intellectual life. A Saxon captain, Karl Eduard Poenitz, became a leading authority on the use of railroads for military purposes. Other middle German officers specialized in small arms technology or infantry tactics. The *Allgemeine Militaer-Zeitung* began publication in Darmstadt in 1826 and rapidly developed into Germany's leading military journal, combining an editorial eye for technical and professional innovation with a readiness to publish unpopular and unconventional opinions. The latter flexibility distinguished it, in particular, from the *Militaer-Wochenblatt*, which in 1816 began its long existence as the voice of Prussia's military establishment, but was widely read throughout the Confederation. Less familiar journals like the *Zeitschrift fuer Kunst, Wissenschaft und Geschichte des Krieges*, also published in Berlin, featured essays and reviews from officers throughout the Confederation and provided forums for the general exchange of ideas.[56]

Theory and practice, however, too often diverged. In the 1840s, the Confederation authorized a muster and inspection system as an aid to standardizing performance and improving communication among the contingents. Reports were often, one might say, less than flattering. Infantry units fell far short of even their skeleton paper strengths. The cavalry did not know how to ride; the artillery did not know how to shoot; and both arms lacked the horses and saddlery that might have enabled them to practise. Private landowners were unwilling to lease their land for manoeuvres. Public land was either too restricted for more than open-air parades or devoted to other more important purposes. In Bavaria, the royal huntmaster complained that manoeuvres would ruin the shooting for years to come. The various contingents could not even agree on a common field sign to distinguish their units and limit the risk of amicide in combat.

---

[55] A. von Keim, *Erlebtes und Erstrebtes. Lebenserinnerungen von Generalleutnant Keim* (Hanover, 1925), pp. 10–11.
[56] Helmuth Schnitter, *Militaerwesen und Militaerpublizistik. Die militaerische Zeitschriftenpublizistik in der Geschichte des buergerlichen Militaerwesens in Deutschland* (Berlin, 1967), remains a useful overview of the subject.

The Confederation inspection system was not entirely a venture into the world of military operetta. It succeeded in developing common standards for some personnel issues, such as the number of non-commissioned officers to be kept on active service. It succeeded in establishing a common system for procuring remounts. It acted as a clearing house for developments in military-related technology. The development of percussion muskets in the 1830s rendered existing stocks of flintlocks obsolete and the Confederation advocated the purchase of a common design. Confederation states and armies also took a significant interest in railroads. Political and financial considerations might not allow for building a true network of fixed defences, but the railroads offered a possible second-best alternative, enhancing prospects for supporting and reinforcing the confederate fortresses in emergencies. In a wider context, the developing German rail network was concentrated heavily in the Rhine valley, and presented corresponding opportunities for the rapid deployment of troops from outside and within the region to meet a sudden French threat. Confederation inspectors projected railway lines extending from major military centres, enabling the rapid, large-scale movement of forces to support any member state challenged from outside German borders. They also conducted tests, moving troops and equipment on existing rail systems and carefully evaluating the results.[57]

III

The more developed the discussion of such issues became, the more obvious it was that meaningful military reform in the German Confederation depended heavily on its two principal armies. Between 1815 and 1844, Austria's military profile was shaped by three factors. The first was the state's commitment to establishing the army as a reliable internal-security force, capable of acting decisively against liberal activists, ethnic dissidents and over-mighty subjects. Operational planning was less important than political reliability: Metternich and the Habsburgs were all too familiar with the concept subsequently described as 'Bonapartism' to risk nurturing a uniformed challenger to the crown. Indeed, the Habsburg state might well have offered 'Wallensteinism' as an alternative verbal shortcut: since its experiences in the Thirty Years War, the dynasty had taken pains to bind its leading military figures with chains of gold and fetter them with chains of paper – the endless administrative and consultative procedures that enmeshed the empire's every decision. The officer corps was dominated at the higher levels by aristocrats. While this did not guarantee incompetence – the myth that a hereditary title is the equivalent to a prefrontal lobotomy is one of nineteenth-century liberalism's most persistent and pernicious legacies – the complex, conciliar command system it encouraged put further high premiums on connections and collegiality: getting ahead by going along.[58]

In that context, the Austrian General Staff was restricted to the most limited forms of planning and preparing possible future campaigns. In the army's order of precedence, the staff officer corps ranked with the engineers, at the bottom of the official hierarchy and the informal pecking order. There was no danger of the direct militarization of Austrian policy in

---

[57]Allan Mitchell, *The Great Train Race. Railways and the Franco-German Rivalry, 1815–1914* (New York, 2000), pp. 43 ff. Cf. Hackl, p. 79 *passim* and Petter, 'Deutscher Bund', pp. 246 ff.
[58]On the 'Wallenstein question' see Gordon A. Craig, 'Command and Staff Problems in the Austrian Army, 1740–1866' in *War, Politics, and Diplomacy: Selected Essays* (New York, 1966), pp. 3–21.

such a system. Metternich's Austria, indeed, can be considered a model for both civilian control and checks and balances. By the time the high council of war, the council of state, the emperor's direct advisors and Metternich himself finished massaging and spin-doctoring an issue, the original question was likely to have become moot – if only from the passage of time.

That observation should not be taken as poorly veiled sarcasm. The nineteenth century's increasing obsession with rapid decision-making owed much to Napoleon's legacy, and not a little to developing communications technology, which essentially changed the culture of time.[59] One result has been an enduring tendency on the part of historians to privilege the general concept of action, as opposed to analysing proactivity's particular contexts. Given the Habsburg Empire's perceived vital interest in international stability, a system that heard every voice, considered every contingency and periodically gridlocked itself was by no means prima facie dysfunctional – not least because it diminished the anxiety Metternich's policies might otherwise have provoked in Germany and Italy, as well as elsewhere in Europe.[60]

Certainly the Austrian army was unlikely to slip its leash in any conceivable contingency, domestic or foreign. For the sake of economy, men were sent on long-term furloughs, recalled only for inadequate refresher training and emergencies that tended to become disasters because of the inexperience of the purported long-service soldiers. Since ammunition was expensive, men fired their muskets only a few times a year. Since horses were expensive, the artillery's guns spent most of their lives en parc, while the cavalry's troopers were allowed to exercise their mounts only under carefully controlled conditions. In the lower ranks of the officer corps, patronage – facilitated by the continuing and often capricious influence of regimental 'proprietors' – contributed to a pattern of stagnant promotions, encouraged by salaries and pensions low enough to make officers dependent for their livelihood on continuing their careers, but sufficiently promising to discourage adventurism of any kind – political or professional. Austrian regimental officers of the Biedermeyer period were unlikely to compensate for the lack of active-service opportunities by professional study. Instead, they focused on the increasingly complex details of a Byzantine administrative system that offered trap after career-destroying trap for the unwary.

The rank and file were recruited by selective conscription. With terms of service fixed at fourteen years in most of the crown lands and, until 1840, for life in Hungary, 'true volunteers' were few and far between. Nevertheless, to prevent soldiers forming excessively close identities with the civilians of a particular region, infantry and cavalry regiments were constantly transferred, with correspondingly adverse effects on anything beyond elementary training. Pay was nominal, living conditions primitive and discipline correspondingly harsh, with draconian punishments imposed by captains and colonels who exercised power largely unchecked even by a court-martial system.[61]

---

[59]Stephen Kern, The Culture of Time and Space, 1880–1918 (Cambridge, MA, 1983).

[60]See Paul W. Schroeder, The Transformation of European Politics, 1763–1848 (Oxford, 1994), pp. 525 ff.

[61]Gunther E. Rothenberg, The Army of Francis Joseph (Lafayette, IN, 1976), pp. 9 ff., is the standard English overview. Cf. Joachim Niemeyer, Das oesterreichische Militaerwesen im Umbruch. Untersuchungen zum Kriegsbild zwischen 1830 und 1866 (Osnabrueck, 1979). The first volume of Geoffrey Wawro, 'The Austro-Prussian War: Politics, Strategy, and War in the Habsburg Monarchy, 1859–1866' (dissertation, 2 vols., Yale, 1992) is more detailed and exponentially more scathing. Unfortunately, most of it was edited when the dissertation was revised for publication.

The end result in a domestic political context was expected to be a force obeying orders literally at all levels, too cowed or too unreflective to do anything else. The revolutions of 1848 would demonstrate instead that the army's concentration on sticks at the expense of carrots had gone too far, as officers and men alike joined insurgents instead of shooting them down, or just went home. In the next decade, the army would make a more conscious, systematic effort to make 'Habsburg loyalty' a positive concept in the army.

The army's second shaping factor was money. Its best-known historians have consistently depicted a force victimized by cheese-paring economies at all levels, starved of funds for everything from rations to rifles.[62] Recently, however, Geoffrey Wawro has highlighted the 'waste, fraud, and corruption' that in fact shaped Habsburg military spending at least as much as limited budgets. High-paying sinecures for senior officers had first claims on the account. The military bureaucracy absorbed a substantial amount of the balance. What remained after the privileged ones were finished was largely expended in constructing fortresses that contributed little to the empire's security, but much to contractors, their relatives and their connections. Cost overruns were a virtual art form in Metternich's time, and the system largely went unchallenged. Too many highly placed personages profited from both the 'clean graft' of insider knowledge and the other kind, with actual cash discreetly changing hands among gentlemen.[63]

The third factor shaping the Austrian army in the Age of Metternich was exhaustion. The state had used, and used up, its moral and physical resources defeating Napoleon — arguably the final act in three centuries of mortal conflict between Habsburg and Valois/Bourbon/Bonaparte. The dynasty did not emerge from the Congress of Vienna with its stature particularly enhanced, either by domestic revitalization or foreign-policy triumphs.[64] The army had performed effectively but not spectacularly in 1813–14. While Napoleon's grand-strategic deployment during the Hundred Days affirmed his respect for Habsburg fighting power, Waterloo ended the campaign before the Austrians became seriously engaged. That was probably a good thing for a treasury and a replacement system both virtually empty.[65] Like those of France after 1918, Austria's European policies after 1815 were characterized by an increasing gap between commitments and resources. Metternich's virtuosity in negotiations and coalition-building was a 'flight forward' on behalf of a system whose viability made demands that stretched to the limit Austria's own vitality.[66] In that, he resembled no one so much as the Soviet Union's Mikhail Gorbachev. Metternich proved more successful in the short and medium runs. In the long run, however, both men found themselves betting with empty pockets.

---

[62]As in, for example, Heinrich Friedjung, *Der Kampf um die Vorherrschaft in Deutschland* (2 vols., 10th ed., Stuttgart, 1917), vol. I, pp. 375–6 and Oskar Regele, *Feldzeugmeister Benedek: Der Weg nach Koeniggraetz* (Vienna, 1960), pp. 355 ff.

[63]Geoffrey Wawro, 'Inside the Whale: The Tangled Finances of the Austrian Army, 1848–1866', *War In History* 3 (1996), pp. 42–65.

[64]Enno Kraehe, *Metternich's German Policy*, vol. II, *The Congress of Vienna* (Princeton, 1983).

[65]Gunther E. Rothenberg, *Napoleon's Great Adversaries: The Archduke Charles and the Austrian Army, 1792–1814* (Bloomington, IN, 1982).

[66]Cf. Egon Radvany, *Metternich's Projects for Reform in Austria* (The Hague, 1971) and D. E. Emerson, *Metternich and the Political Police: Security and Subversion in the Habsburg Monarchy, 1815–1830* (The Hague, 1968), for discussions of Metternich's domestic use of carrots and sticks.

When these three factors were combined in a German context, the result was benign military neglect. Austria kept troops available for counter-insurgency operations in Poland as part of its relationship with Russia. It was engaged regularly in small-scale military actions and 'operations other than war' along its Balkan frontier – including maintaining a literal *cordon sanitaire* along the border with the Ottoman Empire.[67] But its primary focus was Italy. Metternich perceived Italy as both the linchpin of his European system and the empire's most vulnerable sector. The local rebellions of the early 1820s further concentrated his attention across the Alps. Metternich's Italian client states might be more malleable than the German Confederation, but that only reflected their individual weakness. Naples or Tuscany, Modena, even the Papal States – none possessed the domestic legitimacy of a Wuerttemberg or a Bavaria. And while Prussia was at least susceptible of persuasion that its best interests lay with Austria, Piedmont (the strongest of the Italian kingdoms) increasingly understood its relations with the empire as ultimately zero-sum: one could profit only by the other's loss.[68]

The accession of the Orléans monarchy to the throne of France in 1830 also provided an external challenge to Austria's position on the peninsula. The new government of Louis Philippe mobilized 80,000 men to underwrite its protest against Austria's intervention on the side of the governments in Modena and the Papal States. While those brief uprisings were more gesture than crisis, Metternich did not propose to invite a repetition. Over 100,000 Austrians were stationed in Italy in 1831. While that number was reduced by over half in the next fifteen years, the order of battle continued to include most of the army's best regiments. Under Field Marshal Josef Radetzky, who held command from 1831 to 1857, its training became by far the best in Italy, and arguably the best in Europe. The annual manoeuvres were more demanding, and more realistic, than their Prussian counterparts. Radetzky suspended the more extreme physical punishments, improved rationing, medical services and barracks, and kept his officers busy enough to deter the *routiniers* and attract the energetic. To a degree, the army's effectiveness was enhanced also by the relative hostility the troops encountered from many north Italian civilians. Seldom sufficiently intense to be dangerous, it nevertheless encouraged even the rank and file to believe they were on something resembling active service, and led to correspondingly greater interest in matters of drill and appearance.

In addition to the human factor, the Austrian army in Italy benefited from Europe's best fortress network relative to its mission. The Quadrilateral, the four major fortresses of Pesciera, Verona, Mantua and Legnano, was a mutually supporting system, constantly improved, that absorbed most of the empire's disposable budget for fixed defences. The Quadrilateral was a base area so secure as to be considered impregnable, a rallying point for the forces on the ground, should they be defeated, and a staging area for reinforcements from elsewhere in the empire. Its development was also an economy-of-force policy that enabled the reduction of the field army referred to earlier.[69]

---

[67]Gunther Rothenberg, *The Military Border in Croatia, 1780–1881* (Chicago, 1966), pp. 46 ff. and 176 ff.

[68]The best English-language surveys of Restoration Italy are Henry Hearder, *Italy in the Age of the Risorgimento, 1790–1870* (London, 1983) and Stuart Woolf, *A History of Italy: The Social Constraints of Political Change* (London, 1979).

[69]Oskar Regele, *Feldmarschall Radetzky* (Vienna, 1957), incorporates a favourable presentation of the military aspects of Austria's Italian policy. A. J. Reinerman, *Austria and the Papacy in the Age of Metternich* (2 vols.,

IV

It was hardly remarkable that the German Confederation as a military institution played a limited role in Austria's geo-strategic thinking. Compared to Italy, the Confederation seemed well able to look after itself; the main issue was political – seeing that none of the member states got above themselves or wandered outside the system. Prussia's perspective on Confederation matters was significantly different. The Prussian army of the Biedermeyer era was distinguished by two increasingly complementary features. Its rank and file were rank amateurs and its cadres were highly professional. Neo-Bourbon France and Metternich's Austria possessed long-service forces, able to go to war from a standing start and large enough to support great-power status by the fact of their existence. Prussia's economy could no more support an equivalent in 1820 than in 1740. Instead, the Landwehr was not abolished after 1815. It became the foundation for a military system intended to blend training with enthusiasm.[70]

Even before natural increases in population combined with peacetime cuts in the military budget, the Prussian War Ministry recognized the impossibility of financing a full term of active service – set at three years by the modified Defence Law of 1815 – for every ablebodied man of twenty, except at the expense of everything else – weapons, equipment, food and barracks. The result, within a few years of Waterloo was analogous to the Selective Service System as practised in the US between the Korean and Vietnam wars. Not only was the term of active service frequently reduced by releasing men early; more and more conscripts were administratively assigned to the Landwehr, receiving no training at all. This in turn worked against reducing the theoretical term of active service, since, without a high proportion of fully trained men in its ranks, the Landwehr was no more than so many men with muskets.

The Landwehr, as originally conceived and subsequently defended by the military reformers was expected to be so popular that participation in its drills and exercises would be voluntary. In the long peace after Waterloo, however, the Landwehr lost its novelty. Commissions in its officer corps were no longer sought by the best types of socially ambitious young men from the middle classes. Nor did Landwehr units develop community social roles in the fashion of Britain's volunteers and Territorials or the National Guard in the US. Prussia thus found itself with an increasingly ineffective reserve force and an army that could be operationally effective only with the large-scale mobilization of its reserves, at a sufficiently early stage in a crisis to provide at least some time to correct the most glaring deficiencies. Military preparation on such a scale was as likely to provoke war as deter it; nor could Prussia, still the smallest and weakest of the great powers, risk having its diplomatic intentions misunderstood.[71]

Washington, DC, 1979–89), is more comprehensive than its title suggests for the years up to 1833. Cf. generally, Alan Sked, 'Metternich's System' in *Europe's Balance of Power, 1815–1848*, ed. A. Sked (London, 1979), pp. 98–121. For the Italian garrison's internal dynamic, see Niemeyer, pp. 104 ff.

[70]Heinz Stuebig, 'Heer und Nation: Zur Entwicklung der paedagogisch-politischen Ideen Hermann von Boyen', *Militaergeschichtliche Mitteilungen* 58 (1999), pp. 1–22 and Eberhard Kessel, 'Zu Boyens Entlassung', *Historische Zeitschrift* 175 (1953), pp. 41–54.

[71]For the Landwehr's origins and early years, see Dennis Showalter, 'The Prussian Landwehr and its Critics, 1813–1819', *Central European History* 4 (1971), pp. 3–33 and Dorothea Schmidt, *Die preussische Landwehr: Ein Beitrag zur Geschichte der allgemeinen Wehrpflicht in Preussen zwischen 1815 und 1830* (Berlin, 1981). The analysis in Dierk Walter, 'Preussische Heeresreformen 1807–1870. Militaerische Innovation und der Mythos der "Roonschen Reform"' (dissertation, Bern, 2001) pp. 168–282, is excellent.

The men in control of the state's machinery after 1815 were concerned, in principle, with the re-taming of a Bellona unfettered between 1792 and 1815. This was more than a manifestation of political and social reaction. The essence of the Revolutionary/Napoleonic approach to war was improvisation. The French imperium remained in a state of becoming until Napoleon abdicated its throne. Its military institutions were in a state of constant flux, with orders of battle as evanescent as rank and file were expendable. Waste of all kinds at all levels was as characteristic as long marches and inspired manoeuvres. How could Prussia, a state with a past and a future, with few resources to spare and none to squander, part of a stable international system, begin institutionalizing the positive innovations of the past quarter-century?

The first step was planning, best epitomized in the general staff. The institution had its roots in the 1790s, as the army responded to the state's neutrality by beginning to consider systematically potential enemies and possible theatres of action. By the mid-1820s it had developed a permanent internal structure whose three sections concentrated, respectively, on eastern, western and southern Europe, in both historical contexts and contemporary contingencies. The initial significance of the general staff must not be overrated. It was a small body whose original complement of fifty officers was reduced to forty-five in 1824. About half those officers were assigned to troop units, with individuals regularly rotating between Berlin and the provinces. It was only one department of a war ministry that was primarily concerned with administration. Nevertheless, of all the institutions in Germany, the general staff was most focused on war planning in a military context – not because of any principled commitment to total war, but from an intention to compensate for the structural shortcomings of Prussia's armed forces.[72]

Central as well to the enterprise of planning was the development of military cartography. In 1816 there was still no comprehensive map survey of Prussia. The general staff began remedying that throughout the period between Waterloo and the revolutions of 1848. In the process, the Prussians transformed map-making from an art – based heavily on an individual cartographer's perceptions and drawing skills – to a science, in which mathematics were at least as important as an eye for ground, and then into a technology, keeping pace with mechanical and photo-mechanical techniques to make maps a mass-production item, available not only for the army but for sale to civilian markets as well.

The general availability of identical maps facilitated developing common perspectives of terrain within the officer corps. It correspondingly diminished the element of individual insight into terrain, that *coup d'oeil*, historically described as essential to a successful commander. While the Prussian army never believed it possible to make war from maps (that was why the general staff developed the staff rides that took officers on to the ground they studied), these tended to democratize officers' skills by establishing terrain sense as a skill that could be learned rather than an innate quality. By contrast, as late as mid-century, both Robert E. Lee's Army of Northern Virginia and the French army of the Franco-Prussian War suffered from constant, chronic shortages of accurate maps, and found themselves correspondingly dependent on close reconnaissance that might

---

[72]Cf. Arden Bucholz, *Moltke, Schlieffen, and Prussian War Planning* (New York, 1991), pp. 19 ff. and the excellent comparative study by Othmar Hackl, *Die Vorgeschichte, Gruendung und fruehe Entwicklung der Generalstaebe Oesterreichs, Bayerns und Preussens* (Osnabrueck, 1997).

or might not be present, and local information, the accuracy of which was too often dubious.[73]

Related to planning was organization. After 1815, Prussia institutionalized systems of territorial recruitment, accompanied by territorial garrisoning, on a scale unique in Europe. In theory – and often in fact during peacetime – individual regiments of Europe's armies drew their recruits from a common area. In war, however, replacements tended to be assigned on a needs basis, while higher units were formed with no regard for regional identity. After 1815, Austria's pattern of deliberately separating troops from their home regions was followed by the other great powers as well. In contrast, eight of Prussia's nine army corps were assigned specific regions for recruiting. Each regiment had its own district and, as a rule, was garrisoned in that district. The Guard Corps as well, though theoretically recruited from the entire kingdom, drew most of its active soldiers and all of its reservists from Berlin and Brandenburg. This system reflected the fact that not only were the army's active regiments at little more than half strength in peacetime, but that on mobilization they were integrated with their Landwehr counterparts, one for one. That was the reason for the Prussian army's standard binary organization at brigade, division and corps levels, widely copied after the Franco-German War, despite its obvious inflexibility compared to a system built on threes or fours. It was the best way to put large numbers of reservists in uniform relatively quickly without leaving them essentially to their own military devices. Territorialization also provided a systematic framework for developing tactical doctrines and operational plans. It gave Prussia a stable structure for the field armies that, even in the last stages of the Napoleonic era, were beginning to replace the corps as the dominant large-scale formation. But until mid-century, it was regarded outside Prussia and, to a degree, internally as well, as a second-best solution whose rigidity denied the flexibility introduced to warfare by Napoleon.[74]

The third defining characteristic of the Prussian army was education. Again, well before 1806, an increasing number of officers were paying attention both to the theoretical elements in the craft of war and to the broader intellectual currents of the *Aufklaerung* and the nascent Romantic movement.[75] To a degree, this process reflected a certain boredom with the limited parameters of dissipation available in Prussia. Even Berlin's pleasant vices tended sufficiently towards the banal that study was by no means an unattractive alternative. When Scharnhorst founded the Military Society in 1801, he found ready auditors among captains and majors receptive to the idea of 'an aristocracy of cultivation', where understanding and characters would be developed by the open, systematic exchange of ideas. After 1808, promotion was by examination as well as seniority. When the General War School was established in 1810, it drew faculty from the University of Berlin. Its curriculum was general, with over half the courses being outside the sphere of professional instruction.

---

[73]Bucholz, pp. 25–8 and Walter, pp. 374–6. Cf. William J. Miller, *Mapping for Stonewall: The Civil War Service of Jed Hotchkiss* (Washington DC, 1993).

[74]Walter, pp. 352 ff., perceptively integrates the army's organization with the preservation of a conservative order in the provinces.

[75]Cf. Christiane Buechel, 'Der Offizier im Gesellschaftsbild der Fruehaufklaerung: Die Soldatenschriften des Johann Michael von Loden', *Aufklaerung* 11 (1999), no. 2, pp. 5–23 and Michael Sikora, ' "Ueber die Veredlung des Soldaten": Positionsbestimmungen zwischen Militaer und Aufklaerung', ibid., pp. 25–50. F. K. Tharau, *Die geistige Kultur des preussischen Offiziers, 1648–1806* (Mainz, 1968), remains useful.

The new system was controversial. Both reformers and officers of the old school asserted that emphasizing formal education risked favouring intellect over character. Arguably more important to embedding education into the army's infrastructure was the attitude of the senior officers. Scharnhorst's insistence that the 'new men' were intended to assist rather than supplant colonels and generals meant that, even in the early stages of the process, the Military Society's meetings were attended by generals who might not understand everything the young bucks were saying, but regarded the proceedings with avuncular favour. These were good boys, who would be fine officers once a little gunpowder blew some of the theories out of their heads.[76]

Jena and Auerstaedt inculcated a little humility. When, in 1813, Hermann von Boyen joined the corps of Friedrich von Buelow as its chief of staff, he was uncertain what to expect from a superior who was both a critic of the reform movement and a scion of one of Prussia's greatest military families. Buelow shared a parallel set of doubts, but he welcomed Boyen, listened to him, and gave him full credit for developing the plans that checked the French in front of Berlin and made of plain von Buelow, Buelow von Dennewitz.[77] The almost symbiotic relationship between Bluecher and his chief of staff, Neithardt von Gneisenau, is epitomized by the *bon mot* credited to Bluecher on learning that Oxford proposed to award him an honorary degree. Allegedly, the old cavalryman replied that if he was to be a doctor, Gneisenau should be an apothecary, since they always worked together![78] While that attitude did not inevitably prevail after 1815, neither did the generals regard general staff officers assigned to them as interlopers or outsiders – a significant difference from circumstances in France and Austria.

Military education also had a meritocratizing effect within an aristocratic system. The old Prussian army tended, institutionally, to regard the basic qualities of an officer as sociogenetic – based on a combination of heritage and conditioning that no 'outsider' could replicate. The revolutionary/Napoleonic period, in contrast, incorporated part of the Romantic perspective in conflating officership with leadership, and perceiving the latter as a manifestation of 'genius', a particular spark of divine fire that could no more be replicated institutionally than could the child-development patterns of the Prussian nobility. Military education, general and professional, as it developed in Prussia after 1815, denied the roles of neither breeding nor inspiration. But it did stress in a military context the concept of cultivation, of *Bildung*. The qualities of an officer could be nurtured and enhanced by professionally oriented study.[79]

Analysis was the fourth face of the Prussian army's paradigm. Staff rides, manoeuvres and war gaming provided a comprehensive structure of reflection for an army whose practical experience remained significantly limited compared to its great-power counterparts. Manoeuvres increasingly de-emphasized review and display elements in favour of practical exercises in moving large forces from place to place. There is some irony in the fact that this development was facilitated, in part, because the reservists and Landwehr

---

[76]Charles White, *The Enlightened Soldier: Scharnhorst and the Militaerische Gesellschaft in Berlin, 1801–1805* (New York, 1989).

[77]The relationship is developed in Michael Leggiere, *Napoleon and Berlin* (Norman, OK, 2002).

[78]F. K. Varnhagen von Ense, *Bluecher* (Berlin, 1933), p. 270. If the story is not true, it deserves to be!

[79]Cf. the discussion of officer education after 1815 in Manfred Messerschmidt, 'Die Preussische Armee' in *Deutsche Militaergeschichte* (Munich, 1983), vol. IV/2, pp. 72 ff.

recalled temporarily for refresher training were considered to march so badly that it was embarrassing to display their lack of prowess in keeping rank and step by staging the formal parades that had been a defining feature of manoeuvres in the Frederician era.[80]

War games offered other kinds of opportunities to develop professional skills in a context of 'play'. The *Kriegspiel* that developed from the 'military chess' of the 1780s did not by itself revolutionize an officer corps that, after 1815, remained committed to practical soldiering and correspondingly hostile to 'writing-desk heroes'. But war gaming did offer young officers a learning tool and a test bed, not least because of its competitive aspects. In later years, an anecdote familiar in the Prussian army described Austrian officers being introduced to *Kriegspiel* and asking if one could win money at it.[81] Intended to disparage the alleged professional ignorance of Austrian officers, the joke nevertheless had a certain metaphoric accuracy. In a time of profound peace and few risks, gambling was one way to bring excitement into the routines of garrison service. Few Prussian officers, however, had money to lose — and losing it to each other, a common pattern in small towns where social barriers separated officers from civilian blades, was even more devastating to morale. War gaming was not quite the same rush, but it did offer chances to win or lose, to stand out from the rest, even if only by an unusual run of the dice that decided fates in the map room as well as across the green baize. While this aspect of war gaming should not be over-emphasized, it nevertheless played a role in the players' positive commitment — and perhaps for colonels, too, who were pleased enough to see their junior officers kept busy and out of trouble in their off-duty hours. By the 1840s, Prussian garrison towns were supporting war-gaming clubs that played competitively. While the acknowledged stakes involved bragging rights, accompanied, perhaps, by a dinner and some good wine, it challenges human behaviour to assume that some highly unofficial side-betting was not part of the proceedings as well. In 1844, first place went to Magdeburg, headquarters of IV Corps. Its chief of staff was Helmuth von Moltke.[82]

Planning and organization, education and analysis — all were useful force multipliers, but limited ones. The Prussian army also turned its attention to two new possibilities. One was technology. Prussian soldiers were by no means hostile to either industrialism in principle or to state involvement in economic development.[83] Nor should the vitalist heritage of the French Revolution and the Era of Reform be interpreted to mean enthusiasm and will-power were expected to overcome by themselves superior weaponry. If the army's artillery improved only by slow stages, Prussia took the lead in adopting not only a rifle, but a breech-loading rifle, for its entire infantry. The first 60,000 'needle guns' — so-called because

---

[80]That, in turn, reflected the desire of Landwehr supporters like Hermann von Boyen, recalled in 1841 to the war ministry, to keep the citizen-soldiers free of the line army's emphasis on close-order drill. Friedrich Meinecke, *Das Leben des Generalfeldmarschalls Hermann von Boyen* (Stuttgart, 1899), vol. II, pp. 540 ff.
[81]Kraft Karl zu Hohenlohe-Ingelfingen, *Aus Meinem Leben, 1848–71* (4 vols., Berlin, 1897–1907), vol. I, p. 296.
[82]Bucholz, pp. 28–31 and Werner Knoll, 'Die Entwicklung des Kriegsspiels in Deutschland bis 1945', *Militaergeschichte* 20 (1981), pp. 179–89. Cf. Markus Poehlmann and Dierk Walter, 'Guderian fuers Kinderzimmer? Historische Konfliktsimulation im Computerspiel', *Zeitschrift fuer Geschichtswissenschaften* 46 (1998), pp. 1087–108.
[83]On this subject, cf. Dennis Showalter, *Railroads and Rifles: Soldiers, Technology, and the Unification of Germany* (Hamden, CT, 1976) and, more generally for the railroads, James M. Brophy, *Capitalism, Politics, and Railroads in Prussia, 1830–1870* (Columbus, OH, 1998).

of the long firing pins – were ordered in 1840, though their issue was postponed either until there should be enough for the whole army or Prussia faced a general crisis.[84]

The army also took a significant interest in railroads. The limited carrying capacity of the early railways sharply restricted their ability to move anything other than token amounts of troops or material. Horses, in particular, were a challenge to rolling stock. As late as 1836, a pamphlet accurately demonstrated that a war-strength Prussian corps could cover in sixteen days, marching, a distance that would require twenty days by rail.[85] But a reservist-based army that needed all the time it could buy in order to complete its own mobilization was in no position to overlook any possibility for speeding up the pace of its subsequent movements. A general staff that based increasing amounts of its everyday work on mathematical calculation and linear projections found no difficulty accepting the postulate that railway networks were only going to become denser and more extensive with the passage of time.

The army's interest had a political basis as well. The Rhenish industrialists and entrepreneurs who were the leading advocates of railway development were also among the leading citizens in a region whose loyalty to the Prussian kingdom was still strongly instrumental. Responding favourably to their calls for state support and state subsidy of railroads was a correspondingly sensible political move – even though that response usually took the form of encouraging joint-stock companies as opposed to providing direct subsidies.[86] Other military analysts stressed the compatibility of railroads with Prussia's short-service, reservist-dependent military system by emphasizing steam power's potential to concentrate large numbers of men in critical areas over short periods of time. A highlight of this position, its tendency to equate strategic zones with areas of economic development, reflected a pragmatic reality. Railroads in the 1830s and 40s – and for the rest of the century – were constructed primarily for economic reasons, and therefore linked industrial and commercial centres. It has even been argued that the Prussian state, for all its *dirigiste* aspects, intervened less in railroad development in the 1830s and 40s than the federal, *laissez-faire* American government.[87] Prussian military planners, nevertheless, increasingly considered their maps from perspectives that took account of economic as well as operational factors.

The contexts of German and Prussian military behaviour were pragmatic and reactive. The French Revolution dominated theoretical military writing either directly or as a subtext. For Carl von Clausewitz, and for more popular and familiar writers like Prussia's Karl von Willisen and the Archduke Charles of Austria, it was an endless source of evidence and anecdote. For the Prussian general staff it was a focal point of intellectual endeavour and a lightning rod for intellectual enthusiasm. Questions of history as a source of moral

---

[84] *Das Zuendnadelgewehr. Eine militaertechnische Revolution im 19. Jahrhundert*, eds. R. Wirtgen et al. (Herford, 1991), is a technically oriented narrative of the rifle's origins and adoption by Prussia.

[85] *Ueber die militaerische Benutzung der Eisenbahn* (Berlin, 1836).

[86] Cf. Wolfgang Klee, *Preussische Eisenbahngeschichte* (Stuttgart, 1982), pp. 114 ff.; Jeffry M. Diefendorf, *Businessmen and Politics in the Rhineland, 1789–1834* (Princeton, 1980); and Friedrich Zunkel, *Der rheinisch-westfälische Unternehmer, 1834–1879* (Cologne, 1962). Volker Then, *Eisenbahnen und Eisenbahnunternehmer in der Industriellen Revolution. Ein preussisch/deutsch-englischer Vergleich* (Goettingen, 1997), offers an international perspective.

[87] Colleen A. Dunlavy, *Politics and Industrialization: Early Railroads in the United States and Prussia* (Princeton, 1994).

imperatives clashed with the more up-to-date vision of archival research allowed to speak more or less for itself, establishing parameters of controversy that still persist in the study of military history by soldiers and academics.[88]

Nor was discussion limited by either territorial or professional boundaries. Jomini's writings, quickly and regularly translated into German, were common intellectual currency east of the Rhine, in good part because of their reinforcement of the concept that military competence, as opposed to military genius, could in fact be fostered by study and understanding. Jomini's assertion that war was guided by principles was attractive in another way as well. It provided a template, a grammar for recent military events, which, particularly for those who had experienced them, frequently seemed at the time virtually random processes. Willisen's *Theorie des Grossen Krieges*, in four dense volumes, has been long forgotten even by specialists, but in its time it was widely admired for its author's ability to find common patterns in the nature of conflict. The archduke's three-volume *Grundsaetze der Strategie* enjoyed similar status, even if, like its counterpart, it was more often cited than read.

Clausewitz's writings were similarly rooted in events. His initial search for a pure concept of war, an abstract presentation of its essence, reflected his intellectual grounding in German idealism, particularly its Hegelian version. Like Hegel, Clausewitz understood history as teleological: the unfolding of the Absolute through human instruments, and through failure as well as success. Like all complex behaviours, war tended towards its absolute, an ideal form. The experiential world denied that ideal through what Clausewitz aphorized as 'fog and friction' – the clash of wills and the synergy of mistakes. Yet, at the same time, this 'real war' was not merely a blurred copy of what war 'should' be, any more than a physically realized chair was a defective imitation of the 'absolute' chair.

What Clausewitz sought in his approach was to develop and present the essence of war – its 'warness'. The comprehensive revision of *On War*, interrupted by his death in 1831, was less a modification of his views than their completion in a dialectical context. On the one hand stood the absolute. On the other stood entropy, primeval confusion, the conceptualization of which owed much to Clausewitz's direct experiences as a junior officer in 1806. The 'synthesis' of the dialectic involved developing a conscious purpose for the waging of war. The 'Clausewitzian triad' concretizes this concept, with the people representing chaos, the army, war, and the state, purpose. It is, however, a 'triad' by courtesy – and by virtue of generations of instructors – military and civilian – in English-language institutions who have used as an instructional tool a mathematical trope that fundamentally distorts Clausewitz's perspective. For Clausewitz, as for Hegel, the state in its modern form stood above the passions unleashed by the French Revolution. For Clausewitz, as for the other bureaucratic reformers who began restructuring Prussia after 1806, the state also stood above the army, a governor on that institution's natural propensity to extend the scope and the intensity of war making.[89]

---

[88]Cf. Hans Umbreit, 'Von der preussisch-deutschen Militaergeschichtsschreibung zur heutigen Militaergeschichte' in *Geschichte und Militaergeschichte: Wege der Forschung*, ed. U. von Gersdorff (Frankfurt, 1974), pp. 17–54 and Arden Bucholz, *Hans Delbrueck and the German Military Establishment: War Images in Conflict* (Iowa City, IA, 1995).

[89]Cf. the general analyses in Azar Gat, *The Origins of Military Thought from the Enlightenment to Clausewitz* (Oxford, 1989); Ulrich Marwedel, *Carl von Clausewitz: Persoenlickeit und Wirkungsgeschichte seines Werkes bis 1918* (Boppard, 1978); and Peter Paret, *Clausewitz and the State* (New York, 1976).

V

That Clausewitz was not a seminal figure in the intellectual structure of Prussia's and Germany's armed forces arguably owed less to his linguistic opacity or his intellectual rigour than to the relative conventionality of his positions and conclusions. Certainly his case for the importance, indeed the necessity, of the state as the vector and conductor of the new century's dynamic forces reflected both perception and reality in the capital cities of Germany – and in their armed forces as well.

From the perspective of Paris in 1789, or Petrograd in 1917, the events of 1848 in most of Germany may seem a fairly damp squib. To participants they were cataclysmic upheavals, to be remembered for the next century and more. The revolutions of 1848 challenged the Confederation's military system both collectively and in terms of its individual members. Arguably the most significant military factor was a negative. Austria, already suffering from overstretch, was challenged by revolt in the capital, insurrection in the countryside, civil war in Hungary, revolution in Italy and international war with Piedmont. There was neither armed force nor diplomatic finesse to spare for a Germany that for over two decades had, in any case, been expected by Vienna to look in good part to its own internal security.

Germany's armed forces were not taken entirely by surprise. In Prussia, for example, the 1844 'uprising' of Silesian weavers caught in the web of a market downturn escalated beyond both the physical and the moral capacity of local authorities. Able neither to alleviate privation nor maintain order, they cried revolution and called for the army.[90] Instead of dispersing peacefully, the weavers turned to self-defence. Scythes and axes, clubs and stones, were no bargain against lead and steel. Nevertheless, civilian casualties reaching double figures were unwelcome to an army based on short-service conscription and public goodwill. During the next three years, in Berlin, Cologne and a dozen lesser Prussian cities, soldiers faced civilian protestors at gunpoint. While their immediate causes differed, most incidents followed a similar pattern. Police forces able to enforce laws in a consensus atmosphere had neither the capacity nor, in many cases, the will to act against large, unruly crowds. Troops summoned to the scene, even from local barracks, were likely to arrive late, after alcohol and oratory had reinforced an initially inchoate sense of triumph, of getting away with something. Neither men nor officers had any training in internal-security duties. Initial contempt for civilian rabble was likely to be replaced by fear as the crowds pressed closer. Sometimes horse manure or paving stones began to fly. Sometimes a nervous private fired a shot by accident, or a lieutenant ordered his men to clear a space with bayonets and musket butts. The end result was bodies, usually civilian ones. Nor did the soldiers exactly march back celebrating their triumph. While guns remained pointed in the directions ordered, *post facto* discontent in the ranks reached a point where, in the more unruly provinces, commanding generals began moving units to new garrisons in order to disrupt the comprehensive network of local ties even a barracked military established with the wider community.[91]

---

[90]Hermann Beck, 'State and Society in Pre-March Prussia: The Weavers' Uprising, the Bureaucracy, and the Association for the Welfare of the Workers', *Central European History* 25 (1992), pp. 303–31.

[91]Manfred Messerschmidt, 'Die politische Geschichte der preussisch-deutschen Armee' in *Handbuch der Militaergeschichte*, ed. MGFA (Frankfurt, 1975), vol. IV/1, pp. 129 ff. and Jonathan Sperber, *Rhineland Radicals: The Democratic Movement and the Revolution of 1848–1849* (Princeton, 1991), pp. 88 ff.

Alf Luedtke, *Police and State in Prussia, 1815–1850*, tr. P. Burgess (Cambridge, 1989), contextualizes the government's readiness to use troops for internal security. Mueller, pp. 42 ff., offers a German perspective.

Frederick William's summoning in April 1847 of a Prussian Diet to discuss political reform was overtaken by events, first in Paris and then in western and southern Germany. The violence that shook some thrones and toppled others depended heavily for success on the reluctance of peaceful, legalistic and conservative governments to use armed force against their own people. Three decades of negotiation on the one hand and rhetoric on the other had dulled what might be called the survival instincts of a European system whose ostensible *raison d'être* was to prevent revolutions. In more practical terms, the absence or weakness of police and constabulary forces led to the rapid commitment of troops to a mission in which they had no training and no interest.[92]

Fighting in built-up areas was not an element of tactical training anywhere in Germany or Europe. Confronted with anything but the most improvised resistance, even purported élite forces like the Prussian Guard found their strength dissipated by the need to secure inner cities, where snipers apparently flourished on every rooftop, and where barricades, once taken, seemed to spring up again in the same places as soon as uniformed backs were turned. Nor was clearing the barricades themselves always the easy task assumed by officers imbued with the pride of caste and the valour of ignorance. Cavalry horses were favourite targets for such primitive weapons as sharp rocks and boiling water. The close urban terrain made artillery gun crews vulnerable even to smooth-bore muskets fired from alleys and rooftops. Nor were generals and officials initially comfortable with the notion of destroying cities in order to save them. Using cannon against one's own subjects in a way affirmed the triumph of the very spirit of revolution the Metternich system had spent a quarter of a century resisting. Behind untidy piles of carts and furniture, cut-down trees and baulks of timber, determined men and women could take unexpected toll on infantry unable to develop the momentum of a charge in the twisted streets of a German inner city. And when barricades were in fact taken by assault, the immediate consequence was all too often likely to be the bayoneting of any handy civilians – regardless of age or sex – by troops temporarily beyond control and in any case unable, even when willing, to distinguish foe and friend.[93]

In such contexts, negotiation seemed indeed the better part of valour. After three days of high-casualty street fighting, Frederick William withdrew the troops from Berlin on the night of 18 March. Subsequent criticism of that decision, by conservatives who insisted the army could have 'restored order' if given a free hand, has a significant aura of hindsight. Throughout the summer, morale and discipline in the Berlin area worsened, particularly in the ranks of the Prussian Guard, by its own definition the best and most loyal fighting force the kingdom possessed. Mostly Berliners themselves, they were significantly affected by liberal and democratic propaganda. In August, a cholera epidemic spread to Berlin from the Russian border, and a battalion commander was rumoured to have threatened to punish disobedience with extra night guards until the malcontents fell

---

[92]Ruediger Hachtmann, 'The European Capital Cities in the Revolution of 1848' in *Europe in 1848*, pp. 341–68.
[93]Manfred Messerschmidt, 'Die preussische Armee waehrend der Revolution in Berlin 1848' in *Militaergeschichtlicher Aspekte der Entwicklung des deutschen Nationalstaates*, ed. M. Messerschmidt (Duesseldorf, 1988), pp. 47–63. Cf. Ruediger Hachtmann, *Berlin 1848. Eine Politik-und Gesellschaftsgeschichte der Revolution* (Bonn, 1997), a 1,000-page account of events from March to November 1848. Mueller, pp. 54 ff., offers a German perspective that includes military action in such less familiar situations as rural areas and against populist outbreaks of anti-Semitism.

ill from the night air! In September, a hundred or so men defied their superiors and staged an impromptu demonstration in the streets of Potsdam. Fences and sidewalks were demolished and the police commissioner was beaten up and almost thrown into the canal. Not until midnight was order restored.[94]

Such behaviour was not exactly the stuff of revolutionary ballads. It was, nevertheless, deemed sufficiently serious to lead some officers, at least, to question the worth of their men in future counter-insurgency operations. And it was correspondingly small wonder that middle-state governments like Bavaria, Saxony, Wuerttemberg and Hanover were even quicker than Prussia to seek a middle ground by opening discussions with subjects whose disaffection was optimistically regarded as temporary. The apparent wisdom of this course seemed even clearer as the Habsburg Empire spiralled into civil war, as regional and ethnic loyalties rent the fabric barely re-knitted in 1815. The spectacle of one of Austria's chief cities being bombarded into submission, another retaken at bayonet-point, and the third serving as the focal point of a popular insurrection, even after its recapture, did nothing to enhance the appeal of a violent solution to Germany's political crisis.

It was not lost, moreover, on the professional soldiers of the German Confederation that the Habsburg army was making heavy weather of its domestic mission. Neither its tactics, nor its generalship, nor its logistics seemed adequate – without disproportionate effort – to suppress students with muskets or peasants with scythes, to say nothing of the successfully improvised Hungarian *Honved*. Austria's emperor soliciting the direct intervention of Tsar Nicholas of Russia to restore order in the empire was discouraging to a Germany that had regarded Austria's army as an ultimate guarantor of its security. Even in Prussia the concept of making Vienna's difficulty into Berlin's opportunity was to a good degree negative, the product of a sense that Prussia might have to look to its own welfare after all, instead of placing faith in a wider German system.[95]

The gathering of the Frankfurt Parliament in the summer of 1848 added a new factor to Germany's military situation. Support for the elections to that body had been one of the principal conditions of the civil truces patched up in April and May between governments and insurgents. Prussia's king went even further, donning the red, black and gold sash that was the symbol of the German nationalists and declaring himself ready to lead the movement for German unity without any corresponding ambition to be the head of a German state. The exact mix of fustian and policy in that declaration remains debatable. It was, however, sufficient to alarm those delegates to Frankfurt who saw the risks of the new parliament becoming a stalking-horse for either Hohenzollern or Habsburg – and to encourage direct involvement in international relations.[96]

---

[94]Ruediger Hachtmann, 'Die Potsdamer Militaerrevolte vom 12 September 1848', *Militaergeschichtliche Mitteilungen* 57 (1998), pp. 333–69.

[95]Alan Sked, *The Survival of the Habsburg Empire: Radetzky, the Imperial Army, and the Class War, 1848* (London, 1979). Cf. István Déak, *The Lawful Revolution: Louis Kossuth and the Hungarians, 1848–1849* (New York, 1979) and, for the military aspects, *The Hungarian Revolution and the War of Independence: A Military History*, ed. G. Bona, tr. N. Arato (New York, 1999).

[96]Cf. Dieter Langewiesche, 'Republik, konstitutionelle Monarchie, und "Soziale Frage": Grundprobleme der deutschen Revolution von 1848/49', *Historische Zeitschrift* 230 (1980), pp. 529–48; Manfred Botzenhardt, *Deutscher Parlamentarismus in der Revolutionszeit 1848–1850* (Duesseldorf, 1977); and Guenter Wollstein, *Das 'Grossdeutschland' der Paulskirche. Nationale Ziele der buergerlichen Revolution 1848/49* (Duesseldorf, 1977).

As summer waned, the questions of 'little Germany' versus 'large Germany', the issues of central power and civic rights, which initially dominated parliamentary debates, were challenged and overshadowed by something called the Schleswig-Holstein question. Its complexity is best illustrated by the aphorism attributed to Britain's Lord Palmerston, who declared that only three men ever understood Schleswig-Holstein: a Danish politician who was dead, a German professor who went mad and Palmerston himself – who had forgotten it. That very complexity, however, made it a useful test case for an institution desperately seeking to establish domestic and international credibility.

Expressed in simple terms, the provinces were under the personal rule of the Danish crown. When Denmark proposed to integrate Schleswig more comprehensively into the state's political and administrative structure, at the expense of its internationally recognized connection with Holstein, the Frankfurt Parliament responded with force.[97] It first created a German navy *de novo*, by purchasing vessels that could be converted into improvised men of war, and recruiting crews and commanders, primarily from the Hanseatic cities. The result was arguably worse than if no action had been taken; the flotilla of leaking, badly handled ships invited description as a symbol of the parliament itself.[98]

Denmark did not propose to offer a maritime challenge to anyone. The Danes' stated intention was to establish order 'in their own back garden', using troops only if necessary. The Schleswig Germans responded by forming a provisional government and asking for help. Prussia was first in line. By his declaration of commonality with Germany, Frederick William had left himself no manoeuvring room, while his generals were perfectly willing to bring as many of their reservists as possible under arms and under discipline on any workable pretext. A division-strength task force assembled on the frontier, built around Prussian Guards, despatched to restore a reputation badly tarnished in Berlin. Apart from the pressure applied by domestic liberals and German patriots, Prussia was already too powerful for its immediate neighbours' comfort. Even the limited activism of unilateral intervention in Schleswig could not pass ignored. The Prussians were reinforced by a provisional division made up of contingents from the medium states of north Germany: Hanover, Oldenburg and Braunschweig. Its commander was a British officer in Hanoverian service, Waterloo veteran, Hugh Halkett, now in his mid-fifties and well past an undistinguished best.

Under the command of the Prussian general, Friedrich von Wrangel, the expeditionary force entered Schleswig in April 1848, won a skirmish on 23 April and advanced into Jutland. Wrangel was no Frederick II. He was not even a Duke of Brunswick. His laborious manoeuvring left all too much time for external intervention. From the Frankfurt Parliament's perspective, that was not altogether unwelcome. Anything like a quick victory would have given the soldiers – Prussian ones, in particular – too much credibility for the politicians' comfort. But Wrangel's ponderous movements gave France and Britain time to impose an armistice that bypassed the parliament altogether. One of the few things worse than an over-mighty military is an impotent one.[99]

---

[97]William Carr, *Schleswig-Holstein, 1815–1848: A Study in National Conflict* (Manchester, 1963), covers the international aspects. Steen Bo Frandsen, 'Denmark 1848: The Victory of Democracy and the Shattering of the Conglomerate State' in *Europe in 1848*, pp. 289–311, describes the conflict in a Danish context as a Danish civil war.
[98]Laurence Sondhaus, *Preparing for Weltpolitik: German Sea Power before the Tirpitz Era* (Annapolis, 1997), pp. 19 ff.
[99]Adalberg Graf von Baudissin, *Geschichte des schleswig-holsteinischen Krieges* (Hanover, 1862), describes the

The Frankfurt Parliament soon faced another challenge in the military sphere. The city of Mainz was a stronghold of liberal and republican sentiment, as well as being the site of a major Confederation fortress. Relations between the town's activist citizens and the Prussian elements of the garrison were particularly strained – by some accounts, less for political reasons than because when a civic guard formed in March, off-duty Prussians enjoyed mocking its drills and parades. Two days of small-scale bar-room brawls came to a head on 21 May. It was payday for many civilian firms, and that meant heavy drinking. On the other side of the scratch line, off-duty soldiers were crowding the *Gasthaueser* even in the morning, talking themselves into a fighting mood when their purses were empty. The civic guard strengthened its *Hauptwache*, the riot squad. Towards evening, as the beer took full command, around 400 soldiers started breaking dishes, then turned the sabres they carried by regulation (much as many American police officers are required to go armed off duty) against the watch. When 'recall' was sounded to separate the battlers, the soldiers fell back on their barracks. The civic guard and a number of civilians followed. Then shots rippled from the mass of men.

When the bodies were counted, five civic guards and four soldiers were dead – all of the soldiers shot in the back, presumably while hurrying to escape the guardhouse term that was the penalty for tardiness. To their comrades and superiors, however, they were tangible proof of civilian perfidy. With an enraged crowd threatening to storm the barracks, the garrison's commanders, Prussian and Austrian, demanded the civic guard be dissolved, threatened to bombard the city and fired a few warning shots for effect. Mainz capitulated, but one of its delegates to Frankfurt demanded the parliament take action. The eventual recommendation that some changes be made in the garrison stressed the importance of Mainz for German security – and encouraged the parliament to continue asserting control of the Confederation's military affairs.[100]

Meanwhile, in August 1848, a Prussian parliament, elected in the aftermath of the March Days and correspondingly liberal enough to support anything restricting the military's independence, had demanded that any officer unwilling to support a constitutional legal system should resign. The overt challenge to the army's historic pattern of direct subordination to the crown swung Frederick William's pendulum rightwards. The soldiers were there waiting for him. An officer corps priding itself on being apolitical found no difficulty establishing itself as a sophisticated pressure group relative to a liberal/democratic political order (itself poorly defined) that showed little sympathy for what it considered outmoded caste privileges. The political opposition's influence on lieutenants victimized by poor pay and slow promotion was far outweighed by its difficulty in attracting non-commissioned officers concerned with maintaining their privileged position in securing low-level government appointments on retirement. The events in Potsdam had encouraged a steady, unobtrusive tightening of discipline at regimental levels that defied grass-roots challenges. In mid-November, 13,000 men, supported by artillery, entered Berlin without

---

military operations in exhaustive detail. Cf. Harald Mueller, 'Friedrich Heinrich Ernst von Wrangel. General der Konterrevolution' in *Maenner der Revolution von 1848*, eds. K. Obermann et al. (2 vols., Berlin, 1987), vol. II, pp. 513–36 and Angelow, pp. 140 ff. Lawrence Steefel, *The Schleswig-Holstein Question* (Cambridge, MA, 1932), remains an evergreen on the diplomacy.

[100]S. Mueller, pp. 249 ff. and K. G. Bockenheimer, *Mainz in den Jahren 1848 und 1849* (Mainz, 1906), pp. 66 ff.

resistance from a citizenry either overawed by the display of force or welcoming it as a sign that someone 'up there' finally seemed to know what he was doing.[101]

That was more than the Frankfurt Parliament was demonstrating. The armistice with Denmark had been concluded by Prussia 'in the name of the Confederation'. Radicals and nationalists now demanded a resumption of hostilities for the sake of German honour – as well as to force the middle German governments to take the kind of international chances that would weaken their ability to resist continued domestic reforms. Their opponents emphasized the risk that such a policy might result in an open breach with Austria and a general European war.[102] Moderates and *Realpolitiker* correspondingly fell back on a 'little German' alternative: a federal state with a unified central government, universal adult-male suffrage, and no more than temporary veto power for the monarch.[103] That office was intended for Frederick William IV – who, in November 1848, prorogued the Prussian Assembly and, the next month, introduced a far more conservative constitution, one omitting any requirement that the army swear allegiance to the document or its institutions, while providing wide executive and emergency powers. Call it counter-revolution or call it compromise constitutionalism; this was not the most promising environment for projecting him as the head of a new state that was supposed to be parliamentary as well as powerful.[104]

Alternatives, however, were marked by their absence. In particular, Germany's military situation seemed to be deteriorating both absolutely and relatively. Initially, the Frankfurt Parliament had not been especially concerned with military affairs. Its most vocal speakers on that question either favoured a sentimental pacifism based more or less on Herder's concept of the immutability of national identity as an ultimate deterrent to war, or advocated some form of national militia as the matrix for a wartime *levée en masse*. Moderate opinion tended to resist the disruption of the existing Confederation system in favour of what seemed, at best, a dubious experiment.[105] The Swiss militia system, so long highly praised by German radicals, had hardly been shown to advantage in the Confederation War of 1846, except in the context of the restrictions it imposed on the Swiss factions' ability to damage each other.[106] At the same time the moderates were strongly committed to breaking down the barriers between soldiers and citizens, and ending the extra-constitutional position of Germany's armies. With their strong support, a Prussian general, Eduard von Peucker, was appointed Germany's first war minister in July 1848. Peucker was an archetype of the 'educated soldier' in which Prussia took such pride. A regular writer on issues of officer education, he was also on record as favouring restructuring the Confederation's armies along Prussian lines. He was largely responsible for a series of decrees that doubled the size of federal contingents from 1 to 2 per cent of a state's population, abolishing substitution and

---

[101] Eckhard Trox, *Militaerischer Konservtismus, Kriegervereine und 'Militaerpartei' in Preussen zwischen 1815 und 1848/49* (Stuttgart, 1990), is best on the matrix, and Hachtmann, 'Potsdamer Militaerrevolte', for the events.

[102] Frank Eyck, *The Frankfurt Parliament, 1848/49* (New York, 1968), pp. 288 ff. Cf. for background, Brian E. Vick, *Defining Germany: The 1848 Frankfurt Parliamentarians and National Identity* (Cambridge, MA, 2002).

[103] J. D. Kuehne, *Die Reichsverfassung der Paulskirche. Vorbild und Verwirchlichung im spaeteren deutschen Rechtsleben* (Frankfurt, 1985).

[104] Cf. Guenther Gruenthal, 'Bemerkungen zur Kamarilla Friedrich Wilhelms IV im nachmaerzlichen Preussen', *Jahrbuch fuer die Geschichte Mittel-und Ostdeutschlands* 36 (1987), pp. 39–47 and Alan Kahan, 'Liberalism and *Realpolitik* in Prussia, 1830–52: The Case of David Hansemann', *German History* 9 (1991), pp. 280–307.

[105] Angelow, pp. 148 ff.

[106] Joachim Remak, *A Very Civil War: The Swiss Sonderbund War of 1847* (Boulder, CO, 1993).

requiring members of the Confederation to keep their peacetime armies at regulation strength instead of continuing the long-standing practice of generous furloughs.[107]

Considered in principle, these measures were both militarily desirable and politically correct. If the Confederation possessed any legitimizing principle, it involved providing external security. The Frankfurt Parliament was thus claiming authority in an area recognized as particularly appropriate for a body claiming general competence, while the specific measures enacted were responses to long-perceived problems in the Confederation's armed forces. Perhaps in a climate of external danger, Peucker's initiatives might have succeeded. Denmark, however, scarcely posed a threat of Napoleonic proportions. Instead, the parliament's military reforms helped bring domestic disaster to a state whose liberalism had made it an important sovereign supporter of the proposed new German order.

The government of Baden had made the most extensive adaptations of any state to the revolutionaries' military demands – including the introduction of an oath to the new constitution. Now it sought to meet the parliament's new force structure requirements by recalling men on extended furlough to the colours and inducting large numbers of recruits. Many of the latter were previously exempted from service, or had paid substitutes in accordance with the then letter of the law. Others were recent students in the school of street politics. Apart from individual grievances, the Baden army's infrastructure broke down under the press of numbers it had never been designed to accept. Living conditions worsened to a point where even long-service non-commissioned officers began questioning the system. For many privates, doubts turned to certainty when the payment of enlistment bounties held in escrow was suspended. Whatever might be the state's new agenda, it did not seem to include fulfilling contracts with its long-service soldiers.[108]

By the turn of the year, the disintegration of Baden's army was sufficiently obvious to make generals and administrators elsewhere in small-state Germany reluctant to risk implementing Frankfurt's directives. As for the liberals, their principled distrust of standing armies was now reinforced by fear of Baden's armed masses. That men wore the state's uniform did not guarantee the direction in which they might point their guns. And in the volatile political climate of Germany at the year's turn, anything destabilizing the fragile internal balance of forces and powers was an unacceptable risk.

Events came to a head in April 1849, when Frederick William IV rejected a crown 'from the gutter', declaring himself willing to take the throne only with the agreement of his fellow rulers. His confidant and close advisor Josef Maria von Radowitz took the opportunity to offer the German princes an amended version of the final Frankfurt constitution – a voluntary federation with an elected parliament, but with absolute veto rights vested in the monarch, who would be the King of Prussia. This new empire, in turn, would be federated with the Austrian Empire under a four-person directory, two from each partner. The result would be a compromise between 'big' and 'little' German solutions to the

---

[107]Detlev Bald, 'Bildung und Militaer. Das Konzept des Reformers Eduard von Peucker', *Sozialwissenschaftliches Institut der Bundeswehr, Berichte* (Munich, 1977), no. 10, pp. 1–77.
[108]Rainer Wirtz, 'Widersetzlichkeiten, Excesse, Crawalle, Tumulte und Skandale'. *Soziale Bewegungen und gewalthafter sozialer Protest in Baden, 1815–1848* (Frankfurt, 1981), establishes the matrix. Cf. Karlheinz Lutz, *Das badische Offizierkorps 1847–1870/71* (Stuttgart, 1997) and Franz X. Vollmer, 'Der Nachlass des Johann Martin Bader. Ein Einblick in Mentalitaet und Interessenlage eines in den Sog der Revolution von 1849/49 geratenen Berufssoldaten', *Zeitschrift fuer die Geschichte des Oberrheins* 139, Neue Folge 100 (1991), pp. 333–54.

national question that would, at the same time, bring central Europe under control of a power strong enough to resist any challenges from east or west.[109]

A Catholic aristocrat from Westphalia, Radowitz proved a skilled negotiator. Despite Austrian hostility, he managed to secure support from no fewer than twenty-eight states more or less willing to approve a German constitution with a Prussian king. The southern states, however, were reluctant to accept membership in a body that excluded Austria – not only from fear of Prussian hegemony, but also from growing concern at the hostility expressed by the non-German great powers to the course and pace of events between the Rhine and the Oder. France – even the republican France created in 1848 – considered a unified Germany the greatest possible threat it might face. Indeed, the Prussian ambassador was informed that France would refuse to receive any envoy from a purported German government. Louis Eugène Godefroy Cavaignac, freshly installed as the Second Republic's president, declared himself willing to ally with despotic Russia in the face of German nationalism. British public and official opinion, while not as vehement, was not much more sympathetic when the practical political and economic implications of a unified Germany were discussed. As for Russia's Nicholas I, he had gone so far as to threaten the despatch of an expeditionary force to Schleswig to compel the withdrawal of Confederation forces. Since the armistice he had spared no effort in demonstrating that Prussia's continued flirtation with the Frankfurt Parliament would be at the cost of its Russian connections.[110]

The latter message was hardly lost on Berlin – or Copenhagen. In March 1849, the Danish government denounced the armistice, believing German disorder and Russian disapproval were likely to prevent any consequent response. The Danes, however, reckoned without the small army that the Schleswig-Holstein Diet had raised. An ad hoc mixture of local volunteers with adventurers and nationalists from all over Germany, it was officered in good part by 'temporary resignations' from the northern armies of the Confederation, mostly Prussians, and equipped from a developing German arms market able to provide not only percussion muskets but rifles – albeit muzzle-loaders. While not a force to be confused with Napoleon's Old Guard, it was able to function as a tripwire, holding the line until a new Confederation expeditionary force, mostly drawn from Prussia, reached the theatre and pushed the Danes back into Jutland for a second time, only to see Russia, Britain and France impose another armistice.[111]

The Schleswig-Holstein operation was only part of a process that saw Prussia's army taking centre stage in Germany during 1849. The Saxon capital of Dresden was a focus of revolutionary activity and liberal activism. The king had refused to accept the Frankfurt constitution only when reassured from Berlin that Prussia would assist in any

---

[109]David E. Barclay, 'Ein deutscher "Tory Democrat": Joseph Maria von Radowitz (1797–1853)' in *Konservative Politiker in Deutschland. Eine Auswahl biographischer Portraets aus zwei Jahrhunderten*, ed. H.-C. Kraus (Berlin, 1995), pp. 37–67 and Warren B. Morris, *The Road to Olmuetz: The Career of Joseph Maria von Radowitz* (New York, 1976).

[110]Cf. W. E. Mosse, *The Great Powers and the German Question, 1848–1871, with Special Reference to England and Russia* (Cambridge, 1958), pp. 18 ff.; and, more recently, Lawrence C. Jennings, 'French Diplomacy and the First Schleswig-Holstein Crisis', *French Historical Studies* 7 (1971), pp. 204–25 and William J. Orr, 'British Diplomacy and the German Problem, 1848–1849', *Albion* 10 (1978), pp. 209–36.

[111]Gerd Stolz, *Die schleswig-holsteinische Erhebung: Die nationale Auserhebungen in und um Schleswig-Holstein von 1848/51* (Husum, 1996).

counter-insurgency operations. Massive public protest led to the organization of a Committee of Public Safety on 3 May. Prussia promptly despatched a three-battalion task force. If its strength was not particularly impressive, it was nevertheless doubly a harbinger of the changing craft of war. The troops arrived in Saxony virtually overnight – by rail. A major problem of governments for over a year had been how to deploy forces large enough and reliable enough to overawe or suppress revolutionaries without running the risk of having the troops either trigger an outbreak by their presence or be influenced by their potential enemies. Since the risings of 1849 were largely urban, troops could be moved from city to city without risk of ambushes or demolished tracks. They could be unloaded in areas held by government forces rather than go into action directly from the trains. The nature of urban warfare limited the need for cavalry and artillery forces and elaborate logistic arrangements: the host government could supply rations.

The Prussians brought a tactical innovation as well as an operational one. The 'secret' of the needle gun had been exposed beyond question in June, when the storming of the Berlin arsenal during a brief uprising placed a number of the new breech-loaders in the hands of civilian rebels.[112] Two months earlier, Frederick William and the war ministry had taken the step of disrupting their carefully structured peacetime organization by detaching the four active fusilier battalions of each army corps from their parent regiments and brigading them together. The fusiliers, while not an élite in the sense of the eighteenth century's grenadiers, received, in theory, some extra training in marksmanship and skirmishing, and included a higher proportion of men in their final term of service than did the other two battalions of their regiments. Should revolution spread to the point where some kind of mobile fire brigade became necessary, they were the logical choice. To enhance their capacities they were issued needle guns. The process took over a year, but was greeted with enthusiasm by officers and fusiliers alike. Any suggestion that the rifles be withdrawn was met by the reply that this would devastate the battalions' morale at a time when morale was a scarce commodity.[113]

Sent into Dresden, the fusiliers of the Alexander Grenadiers and the 24th Infantry conducted a bloody seminar in counter-insurgency. Breech-loaders could not demolish barricades. Their rapid fire, however, did keep defenders' heads down while other elements flanked or stormed positions. The revolutionaries, about 3,000 of them, whose core was a civic guard with more cohesion and experience than its counterparts elsewhere in Germany, put up a hard fight. Thirty dead and a hundred wounded was the Prussians' price of victory. About 250 insurgents died and at least 400 were wounded. The latter figure was most probably higher – any rebel who could obtain treatment without entering the official statistics was well advised to do so. By later standards the casualty list was small, and its balance between troops and revolutionaries not so great as to suggest widespread policies of no quarter. But the wave of arrests, indictments and trials that followed

---

[112]The captured rifles had no ammunition, which was stored in a different area. It says much about the nature of the revolution in Prussia that pragmatic insurrectionists promptly sold the weapons back to the army for two or three talers each, as officers in civilian clothes scoured working-class neighbourhoods with cash in hand and no awkward questions. Of around 1,000 missing needle guns, all but thirty eventually found their way back to the arsenal. *Das Zuendnadelgewehr* 82.

[113]Chief of Staff to War Minister Strotha, Carl von Reyher, 19 February 1849, in Carl von Ollech, *Carl Friedrich Wilhelm von Reyher* (Berlin, 1879), vol. IV, pp. 150 ff.

the fighting left no doubt that events in Germany were approaching a straight and narrow passage, where choices were either/or.[114]

The detachment that suppressed the Dresden rising was only the tip of an iceberg. On 2 May the Prussian king had ordered the formation of four provisional divisions for purposes of internal security and external employment. This was done ad hoc, with no regard to tables of organization. About half the battalions involved were Landwehr – part of a process that had brought almost three dozen battalions of that force into active service since November. The gradual call-up was a way of responding to a potentially threatening international situation without the accompanying diplomatic risks of announcing a formal mobilization. It was also a precautionary measure, designed to remove from the civil population as many men as possible with military training under arms. Mobilizing Landwehr battalions was also regarded as a means of re-inculcating any loyalties that might have been temporarily affected by revolutionary propaganda.

That last reflected a significant and enduring difference in practice between military and political reactionaries. The soldiers, no matter how extreme their rhetoric of repression, tended to believe that, at bottom, 'the people' were sound in heart and faith. A few weeks of barracks life and close-order drill would be all that was needed to remind them where their true loyalties rested.[115] This was perceived as true for potentially disaffected regions like Posen and the Rhineland, as it was for Prussia's heartlands in Brandenburg and Pomerania, and was part of the reason why Landwehr was included in the counter-revolutionary task forces without much question of which way they might point their weapons once brought back into uniform.

As a consequence of creating the expeditionary forces for Baden and the Palatinate, a second wave of Landwehr battalions had been called up for garrison and internal security duties. These formations, especially the urban ones, greeted the call to arms with considerably less acquiescence than their predecessors. From the Rhineland to Silesia, public protests escalated into collective refusals of orders, the looting and destruction of supply depots and a general indiscipline serious enough that one trainload of Berliners inspired warning telegrams along their route.

Order was usually restored quickly. A few battalions were deprived of their colours. A few companies were forcibly disarmed. A few men were shot to discourage the rest. The motives for the disaffection, however, were subsequently obscured both by liberals seeking to interpret the Landwehr as a focal point of anti-militarism and by conservatives who either blamed the well-known 'outside agitators' or denounced the Landwehr principle as fundamentally flawed. The Rhenish Landwehr formations were influenced by a general anti-Prussian mood that had peaked since March 1848. In Silesia and other artisan/industrial regions, memories of recent hard times did nothing to foster enthusiasm. Orders

---

[114]For the Dresden fighting and its ramifications, cf. A. von Montbé, *Der Mai-Aufstand in Dresden* (Dresden, 1850) and the articles in *Dresden Mai 1849: Tagungsband*, eds. K. Jeschke and G. Ulbricht (Dresden, 2000). Rolf Weber, *Die Revolution in Sachsen 1848/49: Entwicklung und Analyse ihrer Triebkraefte* (Berlin, 1970), is a general history from a GDR perspective.

[115]Josef Smets, 'Von der "Dorfidylle" xur preussischen Nation: Sozialdisziplinierung der linksrheinischen Bevoelkerung durch die Franzosen am Beispiel der allgemeinen Wehrpflicht (1802–1814)', *Historische Zeitschrift* 262 (1996), pp. 695–738, supports this reasoning by demonstrating the success of little over a decade of obligatory French military service in replacing village-centred mentalities with an outlook accepting military service for a state that remained largely an abstraction.

assigning Landwehr battalions far away from their home districts further exacerbated antagonism among men with farms or shops to run, and workers with no guarantee that their jobs would be kept while they were on active service.

Indeed, the Landwehr's demographics suggested exactly the opposite possibility. As mentioned earlier, the military budget did not make possible the conscription of every eligible man, nor was the army anxious to become more of a militia force than it already was. As a result, increasing numbers of perfectly fit, single men in their twenties were in the crowds that gathered to see the thirty-somethings of the Landwehr on their way to glory, promising them that their businesses, their jobs and their wives would be well and truly cared for.

Once in uniform, the Landwehr suffered from an administration already straining to cope with the challenges posed by constant improvisation. Boots did not fit; blankets were not forthcoming; and food was miserable, even by army standards. The first route marches brought blistered feet and thighs chafed raw by the cheap cloth of government-issue trousers worn with nothing underneath – drawers would not become an item of uniform until after the Austro-Prussian War. Men ignored water discipline, draining their canteens in the first hours, then cursing the sergeants and lieutenants who held them in ranks as they passed by village wells. Open-air bivouacs, which had largely replaced billeting in the Prussian service, aggravated rheumatism and arthritis. Poorly cooked food and unboiled drinking water generated epidemic diarrhoea. All these things might have been acceptable in the context of the kind of national emergency thirty years of propaganda had told the Landwehr it was intended to confront. Instead, the near future seemed to hold nothing beyond close-order drill and garrison duty – a point by no means lost on the more articulate of the rank and file, who were often men of relative substance in their villages or neighbourhoods.

Leadership did not compensate for disaffection. The dichotomy between the political beliefs of the Landwehr officers and those of the active army have often been exaggerated. Men seeking Landwehr commissions, usually drawn from Prussia's commercial and official communities, were usually inclined to favour law, order and hierarchy, while more than a few of the regulars had been supporters of the constitutional aims of the *Vormaerz* liberal movement.[116] The problem involved training. Landwehr officers received little systematic instruction, and almost none of it involved preserving discipline in a context of growing disaffection. It does not require accepting nineteenth-century conservative positions about some classes being 'born to lead' to suggest that the normal routines of a businessman or shopkeeper, a senior commercial employee or a civil servant, did not facilitate the development of skill at exercising authority in the face of challenge.

Prussia was still essentially a culture of small towns and peasant villages, where everyone knew his own place and everyone else's. Deference, while not automatic, was routine. Coming from such an environment, the Landwehr officer had few tools to cope with disobedience. Apart from the sympathy many of them felt with the immediate grievances of their men, the disruption of peacetime territorially based organizations meant – as a rule – they were dealing with unfamiliar superiors. The more senior ones, particularly, were also unsympathetic to the problems of uniformed civilians from another corps district, or

---

[116]Herbert Peters, 'Patriotische Offiziere in der anti-feudalen Vormaerzbewegung', *Zeitschrift fuer Militaergeschichte* 9 (1970), pp. 192–202.

proposed solutions depending altogether too heavily on the court martial and the firing squad to be practical in what was supposed to be a citizen army. In practical terms, the result was a tendency – even in the Landwehr's more reliable battalions – to give as few orders as possible and overlook everything that did not involve open mutiny. Officers of the active army developed a corresponding contempt for counterparts who seemed to confirm every stereotype about pen-pushers in uniform promulgated by every liverish major in every regimental mess of the Prussian active army.[117]

For all the army's internal tensions, the Prussian government did not hesitate in committing it to another counter-insurgency operation, this one well outside both traditional and claimed Prussian spheres of influence in north Germany.[118] The garrison of the Confederation fortress of Rastatt was drawn, in part, from the Baden army. The city's civilian population included several thousand workers on the still uncompleted construction of the fortifications. Many had no families to give hostages to fortune; more had been victimized in recent months by irregular wages and rising prices. In April, when radicals in the Baden Parliament proclaimed a republic and called for an armed uprising, a series of unfocused demonstrations escalated in Rastatt into an equally unfocused mutiny that challenged even the insurrectionists' capacity to bring it under control. Other units of the Baden army drove out their officers and, when they simply did not disband, recognized the revolution. Joined by freelances and volunteers from all over Europe, they formed the first truly revolutionary army seen on the continent in its modern history – an army whose implications far outweighed its effectiveness.[119]

At the same time, a similar outbreak occurred in the Bavarian Palatinate. Here, again, civilian insurgents were joined by mutinous soldiers in proclaiming an independent democratic republic. The Frankfurt Parliament possessed no forces of its own with which to respond to Bavaria's crisis, nor was the kingdom itself willing to test the loyalty of the rest of its army by unilateral action.[120] Austria had no troops to spare. That left Prussia, and the Bavarian ministry had no desire to sacrifice prestige, to say nothing of the wider potential consequences, by turning to Berlin.

---

[117]Curt Jany, *Geschichte der preussischen Armee vom 15. Jahrhundert bis 1914* (Osnabrueck, 1967), vol. IV, pp. 178 ff., summarizes the major troop movements. On the Landwehr, cf. Messerschmidt, 'Preussisch-deutsche Armee', p. 79 *passim* and Walter, pp. 262 ff. Robert Sackett, 'Die preussische Landwehr am linken Niederrhein um die Mitte des 19. Jahrhunderts', *Annalen des Historischen Vereins fuer den Niederrhein* 194 (1991), pp. 167–88 and Mueller, pp. 294–300, focus on the western provinces. For background and detail, cf. R. de l'Homme de Courbiere, *Die preussische Landwehr in ihrer Entwicklung von 1815 bis zur Reorganisation von 1859* (Berlin, 1867) and Conrad Canis, 'Der preussische Militarismus in der Revolution von 1848' (dissertation, Rostock, 1965).

[118]Walter, pp. 278 ff., makes the often-overlooked point that, in the aftermath of 1848/49, official Prussia was loud in its public affirmation of the Landwehr's loyalty and performance during the crisis, and argues convincingly that this was more than window-dressing.

[119]Good general accounts are Franz X. Vollmer, *Vormaerz und Revolution 1848 In Baden. Strukturen, Dokumente, Fragestellungen* (Frankfurt, 1973); Willy Real, *Die Revolution in Baden, 1848/49* (Stuttgart, 1983); and Ralph C. Canevali, 'Armies in Revolution: The Badenese Military Mutiny of 1849' in *Proceedings of the Consortium on Revolutionary Europe, 1750–1850* (1985), pp. 632–43. Mueller, pp. 258 ff., is stronger on the uprising's beginnings than its outcome. Wilhelm Voss, *Der Feldzug in der Pfalz und in Baden im Jahre 1849* (Berlin, 1903), is the Prussian official history, useful for its formidable narrative detail of the fighting.

[120]Joerg Calliess, *Die Armee in der Krise: Die bayerische Armee in der Revolution von 1848/49* (Boppard, 1976), is an excellent general history.

The Palatinate, however, was too close to the already unstable Rhineland for the Prussian government to concern itself overmuch with formalities. By early June, two provisional corps under Prince William of Prussia were ready for action. They were joined by small contingents from Hesse, Nassau and Wuerttemberg, summoned by the Frankfurt Parliament but despatched by their governments essentially to serve as a Confederation fig leaf for a unilateral Prussian action.[121]

The Palatinate was unable to offer significant resistance to overwhelming force. Baden proved a more difficult proposition. Ludwyk Mieroslawski was one of the professional revolutionaries Europe developed in the Age of Metternich. With experience leading uprisings from Poland to Sicily, he and his undisciplined army kept the field for two weeks, danced rings around the clumsy Prussian efforts to force a battle, then withdrew into Rastatt to stand a siege.

Some conservatives called forth apocalyptic memories of Muenster and the Anabaptists in the sixteenth century. Mieroslawski, however, was no Jan Bockelszoon, nor were his followers revolutionaries to the knife. Rastatt held out until 23 July because of the attackers' agreement that the expensive fortifications should not be bombarded. It was, moreover, increasingly clear that the defenders had nowhere to go. Neither Mieroslawski nor the revolutionary government had seriously considered waging a people's war. When Rastatt finally surrendered, those defenders who had not already slipped through a siege that was, in practice, no more than a lackadaisical blockade, were screened, tried and punished. Most of the lesser fry able to tell a convincing story of victimization by outside agitators came off lightly. For the leaders and the visible actors who had not already sought exile, or were unlucky or obvious enough to be captured and escaped being shot out of hand, prison was a much more common outcome than the rope or the firing squad.

In Baden, for example, three emergency courts, staffed by Prussian officers and local lawyers, pronounced 115 judgments between 6 August and 27 October 1849. Thirty-one were death sentences, four of which were commuted to ten-year penitentiary terms. Sixty-two other ten-year sentences were pronounced. Twenty-five defendants were referred to civil courts. One was set free.[122] Rather than suggesting a kangaroo court, that last statistic is an indication that those put on trial were carefully pre-selected from a much deeper pool of potential defendants who were prima facie guilty of what, at the time, were capital offences. Since the emergence of modern laws of war in the sixteenth century, rebels taken in arms had no claim to quarter. From Culloden in 1745 to Vinegar Hill and Ballinamuck in 1798, to Goliad and the Alamo forty years later, the period's history is replete with accounts of condign punishment for insurrection. There was some initial support in Britain for treating the rebellious North American colonies as the Highlands had been treated.[123] Times, however, were becoming gentler. Germany's governments were primarily concerned with

---

[121]For internal developments in the Palatinate, see Sperber, pp. 421 ff. Otto Fleischmann, *Geschichte des pfaelzischen Aufsstandes im Jahre 1849* (Kaiserslauten, 1899), is stronger on the military side. Juergen Keddigkeit, 'Das militaerische Scheitern des Pfaelzischen Aufstandes 1849', *Jahrbuch zur Geschichte von Stadt und Landkreis Kaiserslauten* 22–3 (1984–5), pp. 405–24, is also good on the military aspects.

[122]Mueller, p. 310.

[123]Geoffrey Parker, 'Early Modern Europe' in *The Laws of War*, eds. M. Howard et al. (New Haven, 1994), p. 44. W. A. Speck, *The Butcher: The Duke of Cumberland and the Suppression of the '45* (Oxford, 1981), is an excellent case study.

restoring and recreating order. They had enough to do re-knitting disrupted systems without staging mass executions or organizing a lengthy series of show trials ending in legally sanctioned bloodbaths.

VI

The point, in any case, had been well made. Veit Valentin's long-standard history of the revolution estimates that around 5 per cent of Baden's population emigrated. He quotes a 'lullaby', warning that a Prussian lurks outside the door who has killed Father, impoverished Mother and will surely make short process with a refractory child![124] This politically charged ditty may or may not actually have been sung in Baden's nurseries, but its contents highlighted Prussia's position as the hero of counter-revolutionaries, conservatives and reactionaries throughout Germany and central Europe.

The Baden army re-emerged structured along Prussian models. Saxony, with policies long and legitimately shaped by fear of Prussian ambitions, now stood indebted to Berlin. Even Bavaria was glad enough to reoccupy the Palatinate once Prussian troops had completed its scouring. Meanwhile Radowitz negotiated with the kings of Saxony and Hanover to support the creation of a federal diet, with the aim of working out a constitutional settlement with the remaining states.

By year's end, over two dozen governments endorsed a complex programme for unification from above on a 'little German' basis, with strong safeguards for the lesser states and a parliament based on three-class voting. The Frankfurt Parliament, reduced to a rump of true believers, had sought refuge in Stuttgart, from whence they were sent home by a detachment of the Wuerttemberg army – the only time in modern German history when the proverbial 'lieutenant and ten men' actually did dissolve a parliamentary body. About 150 of its former members, meeting in Gotha, also endorsed Radowitz's idea as the best feasible remaining approach to creating some form of German government.

Austria did not remain idle in the face of this challenge. Its new prime minister, Prince Felix Schwarzenberg, considered the empire's revolution-weakened position best met by assertion on all possible fronts. While his overall German policy remains a subject of dispute, in no case did he intend to allow Prussia to achieve, unchallenged, what amounted to parity with Austria. Through the autumn and winter he played a double-barrelled game in Germany: on the one hand, appealing to Frederick William in the name of tradition and monarchic solidarity, while, on the other, warning the lesser states against the risks of being swallowed whole by a Prussia whose very successes in counter-insurgency warfare had made following its diplomatic lead unnecessary. Simultaneously, Schwarzenberg sought to persuade Nicholas I that Prussia's initiative represented a threat to Europe's status quo that was no less dangerous than revolution. And, as a final card, the foreign minister began making overt, large-scale preparations for military intervention.

This last was by no means a bluff. The Habsburg army had increased significantly in strength during the civil war. By October 1849, it counted 650,000 men. Many of them existed only on paper and many of the formations were undeployable outside the empire, but large numbers of the regimental officers and enlisted men had recent combat experience

---

[124]Veit Valentin, *Geschichte der deutschen Revolution von 1848* (2 vols., Berlin, 1930–1), vol. II, pp. 540 ff.

against organized enemies. The earlier mutinies, moreover, had removed potentially disloyal elements; there was no doubt that any troops sent to Germany would fight, and fight well. Prussia sought to apply the brakes, but in the end had gone too far in advocating a 'little German' federation to withdraw its support from the elections for a parliament that opened on 20 March 1850, in Erfurt, and quickly approved the proposed constitution.

Schwarzenberg again took two roads. While continuing to warn Prussia that it was courting war, he invited the princes to send delegates to Frankfurt to consider restoring the Confederation. Ten responded – all the large ones. Bavaria, Wuerttemberg, Hanover, Hesse and Saxony sent representatives, while assuring Berlin that their intentions were in no way hostile. Prussia, seeing its practical support eroded, pretended to agree while seeking to bring in Russia as a makeweight.[125]

Prussia's success against the German Revolution had been achieved at the price of completely disrupting the army's organization above the battalion level. In addition to the two provisional corps in the south, most of a division was deployed in Schleswig-Holstein and Hamburg. Even after the fighting stopped, two dozen battalions remained in Baden until the state's army could be reorganized. Another half-dozen were stationed in Frankfurt. In contrast to Austria before 1848 or the Kingdom of Italy after 1871, the Prussian army was not organized with preserving domestic stability as a primary focus. Nor, on the other hand, did Prussia have the pretensions of Restoration France as a primary power, a European enforcer requiring an army able to undertake come-as-you-are operations across a broad spectrum of missions and environments. The Defence Law of 1814 and its modifications privileged eventual mobilizable strength over immediate striking power as the basis of Prussia's military effectiveness, and created an organization that lacked the flexibility for task-force operations. In those contexts a good case might be made that the Prussian army had performed admirably. That, however, did not seem the case to a war ministry desperately attempting to untangle and restore its orders of battle while confronting a new, potentially far more serious crisis.

In May 1850, the army began recalling reservists and purchasing horses, putting its eastern and southern fortresses on a war footing and concentrating troops in the south. In the event, half a million men were involved, and the war ministry took advantage of the relatively slow pace of events to move as many of them as possible by rail. The result was compounded confusion. Since no plans existed for systematic military use of the railways, responsibility was assumed by the ministry of commerce. This meant troop trains were fitted into regular schedules on an ad hoc basis, moved seemingly at random along single-track lines from point to aimless point, whose only common feature was the absence of food, water and latrine facilities.

Most of the active regiments had still not returned to their corps districts. In a manner prefiguring France in 1870, detachments of reservists could be found at railway stations all over Prussia, sometimes seeking their parent units and sometimes hoping the affair would be settled by the time they reached them. Landwehr morale appeared somewhat improved over the previous year, but in good part, this was a result of the floggings – not

---

[125]Cf. Roy A. Austensen, 'Austria and the Struggle for Supremacy in Germany', *Journal of Modern History* 52 (1980), pp. 195–225 and 'Metternich, Austria, and the German Question, 1848–51', *International History Review* 13 (1991), pp. 21–37 and Lawrence Sondhaus, 'Schwarzenberg, Austria, and the German Question, 1848–1851', ibid., pp. 1–20.

in a literal sense but a metaphoric one: experience showed bucking the system was clearly futile. A decree providing for family allowances removed some of the still festering griev- ances felt by older, married men at being called up a second time while the young bucks tarried safe at home. The same decree, however, upset local authorities, who were made responsible for paying the new allotments but given no additional money. Stocks of cloth- ing and equipment, already depleted by the unexpected demands of the past year, dimin- ished to the point that some of the Landwehr units found themselves boarding trains in worn-out shoes and without arms of any sort.

On paper, 175,000 men and 500 guns were under orders to move to Prussian Saxony and nearby points. It took two months to concentrate the main body, 60,000 men, around Torgau – without much regard to where or whether that force could move next. An army corps was responsible for mobilizing over 1,000 men in its logistics formations. The total peacetime cadre was two officers and one NCO! Depots fleshed out the army's trains by disposing of their cast-offs: the slow-witted, the intractable, the incompetent. Small won- der that supply units gridlocked as wagons broke down and horses died at the hands of men unaccustomed to caring for any animal larger than a house pet.[126]

Meanwhile, Austria was preparing to deploy over a third of a million men, its own troops plus contingents from Bavaria and Wuerttemberg, on an arc from Moravia through Bohemia into Saxony, and westward toward Hesse. In strategic terms, Austria was far to the north in Germany. On balance, however, Austrian supply systems and Austrian troop movements, while anything but flawless, proved superior to their Prussian counterparts. Austrian operational planning also depended heavily on railroads, initially to secure inter- ior lines of operation, then, once the fighting started, to take the Prussians in the rear or 'do anything circumstances allow'.[127]

As armies massed in a manner reminiscent of the 'Potato War' of 1780 between Prussia and Austria, the Elector of Hesse requested Confederation assistance in suppressing internal disorder generated by his own breach of the constitution. His actions had no wider hidden agenda, but nevertheless proved a catalyst for crisis. Three major roads connect- ing the Rhineland with Prussia proper ran across the Electorate's territory. Prussia was unwilling to allow confederate troops, especially with Austrian support, to gain such an obvious strategic advantage. Frederick William, under conservative pressure, focused through Radowitz, to respond with force, above all did not want war with Austria. He wanted it even less when Tsar Nicholas accompanied his refusal to support Prussia with his own threat of war should his counsel be disregarded.[128]

On 2 November, Prussian troops entered Hesse. Despite promises that they would do no more than secure the roads to which Prussia in any case had right of access, Schwarzenberg responded. A minor skirmish on 8 November resulted in six wounded Austrians and a Prussian troop horse dead: the famous 'Olmuetz grey'. Schwarzenberg and Frederick William exchanged threats and insults for three weeks. On 25 November, Schwarzenberg called the hand, giving Prussia two days to accept the presence of Confederation forces in

[126]Cf. Hermann Rahne, *Mobilmachung* (Berlin, 1983), pp. 16 ff. and Jany, vol. IV, pp. 184 ff.

[127]Hess to General von der Mark, 27 November 1850, in *Feldmarschall Hess. Schriften*, ed. M. Rauchensteiner (Osnabrueck, 1975), pp. 229–30.

[128]For Russian policy generally, see J. Hoffmann, 'Russland und die Olmuetzer Punktation vom 27 November 1850', *Forschungen fuer osteuropaeische Geschichte* 7 (1957), pp. 59–71.

Hesse. With Russia hostile and France and Britain indifferent, on 1 December Frederick William agreed to the 'Olmuetz Punctation'. Its terms included Prussia allowing Confederation troops in Hesse and cooperating with Austria in withdrawing support for the Schleswig-Holstein rebels, leaving the locals to go down at the hands of a Danish army as able as Prussia's to defeat civilian levies. The question of Germany's political organization was to be addressed by a conference of the German states at Dresden.

That conference demonstrated the limited appeal of Schwarzenberg's policies. The middle states were sufficiently frightened by his proposal that the entire Austrian Empire should join the German Confederation that he found himself turning to Prussia, achieving a mutual defence pact that at least suggested Prussia remained willing to sustain some kind of dualism in Germany. Prussia, for its part, understood that the issues of Hesse and Schleswig-Holstein, while embarrassing, were the kinds of things easily enough sent down a memory hole for a suitable quid pro quo. Usually described as a disaster for Prussia, Olmuetz instead represented more of a compromise between two states unwilling to regard their differences as best settled by force of arms – as yet.[129]

---

[129]Cf. Julius H. Schoeps, *Von Olmuetz nach Dresden: 1850–51; ein Beitrag zur Geschichte der Reformen am Deutschen Bund* (Cologne, 1972); Roy A. Austensen, 'The Making of Austria's Prussian Policy, 1848–1852', *The Historical Journal* 27 (1984), pp. 861–76; and Anselm Doering-Manteuffel, 'Der Ordnungszwang der Staatsystems: Zu den Mitteleuropa-Konzepten in der oesterreichisch-preussischen Rivalitaet' in *Die Herausforderung des europaeischen Staatensystems. Nationale Ideologie und staatliches Interesse zwischen Reatauration und Imperialismus*, eds. A. Birke and G. Heyeemann (Goettingen, 1984), pp. 119–40.

2

New Eras

Old clothes may be remade. They may also be mended. The post-revolutionary decade witnessed a series of attempts to revitalize the German Confederation's military system. The significant – and initially unexpected – aspect of these reforms was their external focus. The revamped structure continued overtly to be aimed at France, as opposed to providing mutual support for internal security and counter-insurgency. To some degree, this was a consequence of the success of Germany's governments in dealing with the rebellions of 1848. Aside from such direct inhibitors as firing squads and prisons, the major states established an association of political police forces which, after 1851, met regularly and at close intervals to exchange information on dissidents.[1] Irreconcilables took the hint and chose the path of emigration, usually to the United States, where their presence influenced local governments across the Midwest and contributed to the development of the Republican Party.[2]

Those activists who remained in Germany tended increasingly to work within the post-1848 structures. This development was more than a simplistic exchange of political power for economic opportunity – more, too, than the cooperation of traditional and emerging élites against the common folk. The constitutions introduced or reinterpreted as a consequence of the revolutions offered scope for political development through cooperation. In turn, that perspective made armies – particularly those of the middle states – test beds of policies and intentions. On one side, even the most hidebound supporters of the good old ways saw the wisdom of downplaying the soldiers' internal-security functions in the new contexts of domestic cooperation. On the other, deputies and officials from milieus and interest groups hostile (on pragmatic and principled grounds) to military spending and military values could be convinced to support budgets for armies able to support the state against external enemies – particularly in cooperation with like-minded neighbours.

I

Events from the Frankfurt Parliament to the Convention of Olmuetz had demonstrated the immediate potential for both Prussian–Austrian rivalry and Prussian–Austrian cooperation to challenge the interests of the small and middle states. Concern was not confined exclusively to principled particularists. Advocates of federation along the lines proposed

---

[1]Wolfram Siemann, *'Deutschlands Ruhe, Sicherheit und Ordnung'. Die Anfaenge der politischen Polizei 1806–1866* (Tuebingen, 1985), pp. 242 ff.

[2]Carl Wittke, *Refugees of Revolution: The German Forty-Eighters in America* (Philadelphia, 1952) and *The Forty-Eighters: Political Refugees of the German Revolution*, ed. A. Zucker (New York, 1950).

by Constantin Frantz found common ground with the still significant body of *Kleindeutsch* nationalists who, nevertheless, feared a Germany that might be Prussia written large.[3] Both communities could accept, at least in principle, the desirability of what later generations called a 'credible military deterrent' – armies strong enough and effective enough to encourage caution and negotiation as alternatives to challenge by either France or the two German great powers.

In 1854, the military commission was able to secure approval for mobilizing the Confederation contingents every five years. Inspection teams were to evaluate strengths, administrations, drill and tactics in the context of Confederation requirements. To prevent excesses of zeal, the commission was required to announce its intentions beforehand, with the result that their itineraries were frequently prescribed by the state whose army was the object of the visit. Such manoeuvring is hardly unknown to a later century, but seldom encourages frank evaluations. Its consequences were further exacerbated by the fact that the inspectors were themselves officers in contingents that would be evaluated in their turn. The result was a tendency towards reciprocal whitewashes, characterized by favourable reports and large-scale mutual exchange of lesser decorations. Serious criticism frequently focused on the smaller contingents, more likely to possess clearly visible shortcomings and less likely to be able to exchange favour for favour in the next round of evaluations.

A revision of the Confederation's military constitution, completed in 1855, increased the size of the active contingents members were required to maintain and allowed 'encouraging' individual states to go beyond minimum requirements. The new confederate order required two or two and a half years' colour service; men serving in mounted branches added a year. While long-term furloughing was still allowed, recruits were required to receive at least six months' basic training in addition to any specialized instruction. Every contingent had to be assembled for four weeks' annual training in at least half strength. Every formation was required to participate in brigade- or division-level manoeuvres at least every other year.

As early as 1854, the German states had almost 12,000 miles of railroad track, heavily concentrated in the western regions considered most vulnerable to a French threat. Taken in the aggregate, there was enough rolling stock to transport 170,000 men and 56,000 horses. The various railway systems, public and private, were increasingly used to cooperating with each other and thinking on the large scale. The military commission continued to demand regular reports from individual states on the status of their railways. In 1858, the Confederation Assembly also took responsibility for providing such information. The commission, however, was able to do no more than collect data and make recommendations on establishing common regulations for the wartime use of railways, and on militarily desirable routes. It had no greater success in these spheres than did officers of the middle states who made similar recommendations.

As for fixed defences, while the fortresses of Rastatt and Ingoldstadt were eventually completed, none of the Confederation's members were willing to invest heavily in further large-scale works outside their direct control. This reluctance reflected a general de-emphasis on fortress warfare in mid-century German military thinking. The thrust of opinion outside specialized engineering literature increasingly criticized fortresses as drains on already limited budgets, unable to maintain themselves against modern siege guns, and

---

[3]For Frantz's perspective and influence, see Manfred Ehmer, *Die politische Gedankenwelt eines Klassikers des Foederalismus* (Rhefeld, 1988).

distracting artillerymen, in particular, from their primary purpose of contributing to field operations. In a more practical context, the modern federal fortresses, particularly Mainz and Rastatt, were already too large and complex to be manned effectively by garrisons of the size the lesser states were willing and able to support. And depending on either Prussia or Austria for sufficient troops to sustain any role of deterrence that such fortifications might still possess was a prospect few diplomats – and fewer soldiers – in south Germany accepted with the equanimity of their *Vormaerz* predecessors.[4]

Coordination at the Confederation level remained limited after 1850. Renewed Prussian proposals that command be divided between Austria in the south and Prussia in the north met even stronger resistance from states that feared being compelled to choose sides between the German powers, with an eventual consequence of mediatization. If Olmuetz had demonstrated anything, it was that significant alterations in the organization of Germany were unlikely to be implemented without a war between Prussia and Austria. The scale of that war would dwarf anything experienced in the days of Maria Theresa and Frederick the Great. As much to the point, such a conflict was perceived in middle Germany's capitals as opening the proverbial 'door and gate' to France whose new emperor, Napoleon III, made no secret of his country's claim to primacy (when not hegemony) in Europe.

To some degree, this latter concern reflected Confederation traditions of using a French threat as a means to overcome internal tensions. Nevertheless, particularly after the Crimean War circumscribed Russia's position west of the Vistula and south of the Danube, preserving the German balance, military and political, could legitimately be interpreted as 'speaking for Germany' in a way Prussia and Austria were neglecting. A series of meetings between 1859 and 1861 concluded that a reasonable compromise involved creating three generals-in-chief: one Prussian, one Austrian and a third commanding the other contingents. This movement towards a three-way reorganization of German military power met resistance from Bavaria and Saxony, both reluctant to risk their strategic independence even by such a limited change. The resolution exhausted itself in a series of disputes between states and generals over just who merited such a high post, and whether it should be rotated among claimants.[5]

The Confederation made some progress in rearmament. In particular, the development of the Minié rifle, with its cylindrical, hollow round, which, when fired, expanded to fit the barrel's grooves, produced a weapon with universal appeal. In contrast to the Prussian needle gun, the Minié did not violate existing aesthetics of small arms design. It had a ramrod, a visible lock and hammer and a cartridge that had to be broken open. At the same time, its effective range was five times greater than a smooth-bore, its accuracy ten times greater. In a military environment that increasingly emphasized accuracy over volume of infantry fire, the Minié's flat trajectory and high muzzle velocity seemed preferable to a needle gun that required considerable skill in deflection shooting, even at medium ranges. At least as attractive to war ministries was the fact that existing stocks of smooth-bore percussion muskets could be converted to the Minié system at relatively low cost. Between 1854 and 1858, most German states rearmed their infantries by a process of adopting a new design as standard, introducing it gradually in small numbers and completing the process by issuing converted smooth-bores.

---

[4]Angelow, pp. 162 ff., Petter, pp. 144 ff., Keul, pp. 219 ff. and Hackl, p. 162 *passim*, combine for the details of balancing principle and practice in this period.

[5]Angelow, pp. 171 ff. and, generally, Peter Burg, *Die deutsche Trias in Idee und Wirklichkeit* (Stuttgart, 1989).

Resistance to Prussia's breech-loading needle gun involved questions of procurement as well as ballistics. Even Bavaria, largest and most prosperous of the middle states, did not possess the industrial capacity to produce a new rifle in large numbers at low cost. At the same time, cabinets and administrators were reluctant to sacrifice the independence their small-scale defence industries provided by acquiring weapons from larger neighbours. In comparison with earlier eras, such a process increasingly involved the transfer of complete technologies, involving maintenance and resupply as well as production. To rearm with weapons that might prove dependent on external sources, even for their ammunition, appeared a major step on the road to client status. Thus the three states whose contingents comprised VIII *Bundeskorps*, Baden, Wuerttemberg and Electoral Hesse, adopted a common infantry rifle only after long and complex negotiations that were the despair of their respective field commanders. Even then they settled on a local design, in many ways incompatible with its counterparts elsewhere in Germany.

The principles and materials of cannon construction also began changing significantly in the 1850s. The possible choices involved not only the adoption of rifled cannon, but the introduction of a new design of smooth-bore. Named after the emperor of the French, the Napoleon could use the traditional round shot and canister, but specialized in firing explosive rounds against the open-order formations increasingly used by the major European armies. None of the middle-state war ministries were sufficiently comfortable with any of the various innovations proposed by technologists and tacticians to devote corresponding sums from heavily stressed military budgets to any particular cannon design. Whatever might be the theoretical advantages of being on innovation's cutting edge, practical considerations dictated the wisdom of following patterns established in larger states with larger budgets, states able to correct mistakes in procurement – even if the military price was an increasing dependence on infantry at a time when artillery was beginning to assert primacy on the battlefield.[6]

While its neighbours may have questioned Prussian intentions, cooperation among the Confederation's armies was nevertheless facilitated by the general admiration for Prussian methods and models that spread among Germany's educated soldiers after 1848. The revised military constitution made the larger states responsible for accepting officers and officer candidates from their lesser neighbours into their schools and courses. More and more of the small states of Thuringia and north Germany took advantage of this opportunity to expose at least some of their best and brightest to a Prussian system of officer development, which was held in much higher regard than its Austrian or Bavarian counterparts. States like Braunschweig, Oldenburg and the Mecklenburg duchies adopted Prussian organizations and Prussian manuals for their regiment- and battalion-sized contingents. War ministries and field officers came to the conclusion that the most likely chances for their armies to show to any kind of advantage would be under some form of Prussian auspices – a decision enhanced by the Schleswig-Holstein campaigns of 1848 and 1849, in which Prussia's role had been dominant. The closer these contingents approached Prussian norms, the more likely they were to be given operational responsibilities, as opposed to being relegated to security and garrison missions, and the more leverage their governments would have in Prussian and Confederation councils. North German foreign policies, even

---

[6]Showalter, *Railroads and Rifles*, pp. 94 ff. and Heinz Helmert, *Militaersystem und Streitkraefte im Deutschen Bund am Vorabend des Preussisch-Oesterreichischen Krieges von 1866* (Berlin, 1964), pp. 86 ff.

those of the proudly independent Hanseatic cities, followed suit during the 1850s, increasingly favouring bandwagoning over balancing, accepting *de facto* Prussian primacy in a regional *Kleindeutsch* orientation while attempting to maximize freedom of action within the Prussian sphere.[7]

Among the middle states of central and south Germany, Prussian military influences were less comprehensive, but nevertheless significant. Specialist publications like the *Archiv fuer Offiziere der Koenigliche Preussische Artillerie und Ingenieur-Korps*, along with the increasingly professionally oriented *Militaerwochenblatt*, began finding a place alongside the *Allgemeine Militaer-Zeitung* in mess libraries and on reading lists. This process was facilitated by social and political factors as well as technical ones. The officer corps of the lesser states were developing a stronger and more positive corporate identity than their pre-revolutionary predecessors. That involved various combinations of increased professional competence and enhanced professional self-awareness. Prussian models in both areas were not necessarily attractive *in toto*, but provided clearer benchmarks than either Austria or France. A Hanoverian army arguably less affected than any of its counterparts by the events of 1848–50 made room in the succeeding decade for Prussian ways of war.[8] Baden, under the auspices of Grand Duke Frederick I, organized its army comprehensively along Prussian lines, with limited criticism from an opposition based on an uneasy alliance of clericals and liberals, both prone to look uneasily across the Rhine at an increasingly assertive France.[9]

While none of Baden's neighbours were ready to go that far, neither were they indifferent to change. In Wuerttemberg, substitution was reintroduced in 1851 – but on a free market basis that raised the price of exemption high enough that more and more middle-class men accepted what seemed a nominal obligation rather than make the capital outlay necessary to avoid donning uniforms personally. The rational-actor calculation backfired when the war scare of 1859 summoned the establishment's sons and brothers to the colours, albeit briefly. The experience proved a significant incentive to improve the army's equipment, infrastructure and living standards.[10] Saxony built on its experiences during the revolution to overhaul the army's conscription machinery, its administrative structure and its personnel policies. A reconstituted officer corps paid as much attention to cultivating the morale of the rank and file as to studying the implications of new weapons on tactics and operations. Eventually commanded by a crown prince who developed into an outstanding soldier, within a decade the Saxon Corps stood among the best fighting forces of its size in Germany.[11]

Military reform in middle Germany was, in short, a subject more complex than is conceded either by a military-oriented historiography, insisting on a dichotomy between far-sighted soldiers frustrated by the limited perspectives of bureaucrats and politicians, or by a

---

[7]Georg Hoffmann, *Preussen und die norddeutsche Heeresgleichschaltung nach der achtundvierziger Revolution* (Munich, 1935). Cf. as a case study, Friedrich Herrmann, 'Das militaerische Kontingent des Herzogtums Sachsen-Coburg-Gotha ind seine Vorgaenger 1815–1854', *Zeitschrift fuer Heereskunde* 47 (1983), pp. 37–43.

[8]Joachim Neimeyer, *Hannoversches Militaer 1815–1866* (Beckum, 1992) and Udo Vollmer, *Die Armee des Koenigreiches Hannover. Bewaffnung und Geschichte von 1803–1866* (Schwabisch Hall, 1978).

[9]See Lothar Gall, *Der Liberalismus als regierende Partei: Das Grossherzogstum Baden zwischen Revolution und Reichsgruendung* (Duesseldorf, 1974).

[10]Sauer, pp. 145 ff.

[11]For details, see 'Die Organisation des Koeniglich-Saechsischen Armeekorps und ihrere Entwicklung seit dem Jahre 1849', *Allgemeine Militaer-Zeitung* (1857), nos. 47–8 and 51–2.

'civilian' perspective, emphasizing the risks militarism and militarization posed to responsible government, economic development and public spending for social purposes. In Bavaria, issues involving army reform were comprehensively debated among four institutions and a relatively free press. The war ministry admired the French model of an army with a high peace strength and state-of-the-art weaponry, ready to undertake operations from a standing start in any direction. The king's military household favoured Prussian patterns of universal service and an officer corps closely linked to the monarchy. The parliament was reluctant to abandon traditional patterns of recruiting and furloughing. It was even more reluctant to increase military budgets, particularly at the expense of a comprehensive, state-supported railway network offering economic as well as strategic advantages. The foreign ministry believed Bavaria should be able to operate effectively in potential trouble spots – Baden and the Palatinate against a French threat, Schleswig-Holstein as part of any future Confederation action involving Denmark – but without putting the state forward. Liberal and conservative politicians and journalists protested against what they nevertheless interpreted as a high-risk profile. The result was a series of bitter conflicts in which the war minister narrowly escaped being charged by the parliament with violating the constitution – a harbinger of things to come a few years later, and a few hundred kilometres further north.[12]

II

The newly reconfigured Austrian Empire was a particular source of concern for the rest of Germany. Austria's Italian position had been ostensibly restored in 1849–50. Geographically and diplomatically, however, Lombardy and Venetia not only remained vulnerable, but had been established as the kind of vital Habsburg interest that enhanced the possibility of the German Confederation being called upon to co-sign Austria's Italian diplomatic notes.

At the same time, Austria's foreign policy was based on avoiding 'particular friendships' in favour of seeking a mediating central position in Europe, both for its own sake and to forestall France. In a German context, this meant working to secure the support of both Prussia and the lesser states by a combination of specific concessions to Prussian sensitivities and general efforts to strengthen the Confederation's legislative and majoritarian elements – usually in the face of Prussian protests, and often directly at Prussia's expense.

In great-power terms, the empire's new course was first applied during the Crimean War. Austria might not have 'shocked the world with [its] ingratitude' in denying Russia even benevolent neutrality. However, Habsburg policies did frighten such states as Saxony and Bavaria, which had no desire either to be drawn into the war or to support, however marginally, Austria's efforts at mediation. These left Russia nursing a sense of betrayal, without securing for Austria either gratitude or respect from England and France. By 1855 Austria's international position strongly resembled that of Frederick the Great in the aftermath of the Silesian Wars. By pursuing what amounted to a conflation of its particular interests with the interests of the European polity, Austria had earned no more than suspicion at best, enmity at worst.[13]

---

[12]Cf. Detlev Vogel, *Der Stellenwert des Militaerischen in Bayern (1849–1875)* (Boppard, 1981) and Hackl, pp. 159 ff.
[13]Cf. Paul W. Schroeder, *Austria, Great Britain, and the Crimean War. The Destruction of the European Concert* (Ithaca, NY, 1972) and Bernhard Unckel, *Oesterreich und der Krimkrieg. Studien zur Politik der Donaumonarchie in den Jahren 1852–1856* (Luebeck, 1969).

In principle, Austria's commitment to supporting – or revitalizing – a Concert of Europe that had faded to discords was no mean idea. Sustaining it in the diplomatic climate of the 1850s, however, required the support of a military establishment both powerful and intimidating. Apart from international considerations, the young Emperor Franz Josef recognized the central importance of the army to a centralized state that not only depended on armed force to control its Magyar component, but had successfully antagonized such traditional props of Habsburg rule as the Croats. It was hardly remarkable that Franz Josef insisted on controlling the army as he controlled the court and the bureaucracy. His focus was on the army's dynastic aspects. He sought an officer corps whose identity would be 'black-yellow', one that at all levels perceived the state as the focal point of its loyalties and interests.[14] In that context, the new emperor found little fault with the well-paid sinecures, the generous pensions and the promotion policies producing more senior officers than high-command posts. Money, from Franz Josef's perspective, was easier to obtain than generals who could be trusted. Disinterested public service was an unreliable chimera.

At the same time, the emperor sanctioned opening the ranks of the generals to men whose birth, if not exactly humble, was nevertheless more modest than had been usual since 1815. Men like Ludwig Benedek and Anton von Mollinary were part of a rising new breed whose energy attracted attention, and who were perceived as revitalizing the army from within. Intellectual and institutional matrices, however, remained consciously gerontocratic and correspondingly retrograde. Franz Josef's adjutant-general and chief military advisor, *Feldmarschalleutnant* Karl Ludwig Gruenne, was a courtier and an administrator whose concepts of reform emphasized centralizing power in the emperor's hands – which meant his own. His Byzantine confrontations with the war ministry and the general staff absorbed the attention of both organizations at the expense of their stated primary functions. Nor was Gruenne interested in either technological or doctrinal issues. Not until 1857, years behind even some of the German states, did the army adopt the Minié rifle. And while the *Lorenz-Gewehr* was a fine design of its kind, its production lagged to the point that units sent to the Italian theatre of war in 1859 sometimes received their rifles en route. As for railroads, not until 1858 did Austria make their military use a general staff responsibility, and then the section remained undermanned and marginalized.

The Austrian army in the 1850s did not suffer from financial stringencies. A government that had no doubt of just how much its support rested on bayonets was, by Metternichean standards, unprecedentedly generous. Over 2 billion florins were devoted to military spending in the first decade of Franz Josef's reign. How that money was spent was another story. Apart from the pensions, the sinecures and the parallel appointments, procurement and administration remained swamps of peculation, bribery and outright theft. The emperor refused to alter the long-standing system of favouring certain contractors – a decision that limited even the prospects for new players bribing their way on to the scene. Winks were as good as nods for businessmen and officials who had cooperated so long and so closely that it did not even seem like corruption. Indeed, corruption did not always begin as such. Complex and often contradictory orders and regulations governing every aspect of military contracting invited developing informal understandings as an alternative to gridlock. In many parts of the far-flung empire, 'networking' was deeply ingrained in the

---

[14]István Déak, *Beyond Nationalism: A Social and Political History of the Habsburg Officer Corps, 1848–1918* (New York, 1990), p. 43 *passim*.

commercial culture, and the line between favours and kickbacks might well blur – especially to an officer without private means who was not on the fast track in the military's reward system. Once the line was crossed, complex paper chains facilitated such scams as billing for the shipment of goods purchased on site. When the army mobilized, as in 1850 and 1859, the immediate need for large supplies of food, clothing and forage invited further corner-cutting. And, to adapt modern terminology to an earlier century, widespread mutual involvement discouraged whistle-blowing in favour of compliance, if not necessarily cooperation. Not until the 1860s did a series of trials and suicides – including that of the finance minister – expose the tip of the iceberg, and then neither the government nor the army chose to risk the consequences of a systematic investigation. If every senior officer with questionable connections to the contracting system were to be removed, the army might well find itself effectively decapitated.[15]

While the events of 1866 might indicate that this would have been no bad thing, it is worth stressing that the mid-nineteenth century was undergoing a general paradigm shift in terms of both the standards and the capacities of complex public institutions. In its existing form, the Habsburg war ministry differed neither essentially nor exponentially from its counterparts in Paris, St Petersburg or London. Some general parallels might indeed be drawn with late twentieth-century defence establishments, which have so tested the limits of control and comprehensibility that various forms of corner-cutting, up to and including 'waste, fraud and corruption', can at times become functional ways to achieve public ends as well as private profit.

By the 1860s, however, an increasing synergy was developing everywhere in Europe between a system of bureaucratic ethics emphasizing procedural probity and a system of bureaucratic methods facilitating record keeping and record access. One drove the other, and clearing the administrative underbrush that concealed unauthorized initiatives encouraged comprehensive, self-conscious honesty.[16] Standards, however, were easier to change than institutions. An officer corps that increasingly based its honour on institutional identity and relationship to the state did not find it easy to dismiss the army's administrative morass as the natural behaviour of civilianized pen-pushers. The relative insouciance to the changes technology and bureaucracy were making in the nature of armies and the craft of war, so often described as characteristic of the Habsburg officer corps during the era of German unification, reflected all the usual suspects: anti-intellectualism, miseducation, class arrogance. But it is reasonable to consider as well a certain shoulder-shrugging, an attitude of 'it all counts towards a pension', which can develop in officers who see themselves as powerless to remedy the manifestations of what seems to be a permanent structural crisis.

Armies can compensate for institutional malaise with operational focus. The appointment of Field Marshal Lieutenant (Lieutenant-General) Heinrich Baron Hess as quartermaster general in 1849 seemed a step in that direction. He had served as Radetzky's chief of staff in Italy and carried a reputation as an able planner who combined theoretical

---

[15]Antonio Schmidt-Brentano, *Die Armee in Oesterreich: Militaer, Staat und Gesellschaft 1848–1867* (Boppard, 1975), is the most detailed general presentation; cf. Walter Wagner, *Geschichte des K. K. Kriegsministeriums I, 1848–1866* (Graz-Cologne, 1966). The more or less favourable survey in Rothenberg, pp. 38 ff., is balanced by Wawro's developed indictment in 'The Austro-Prussian War', vol. I, pp. 59 ff.

[16]On this subject, see generally, Eugene N. and Pauline R. Anderson, *Political Institutions and Social Change in Continental Europe in the Nineteenth Century* (Berkeley, CA, 1967).

knowledge with field experience. His acceptance of Franz Josef's direct control of the army spoke more for his acceptance of an unalterable situation than a weak character. More serious was his relative lack of skill at the complex infighting at which Gruenne excelled. The quartermaster general's office steadily lost funding, position and prestige. Gruenne's creation of a corps of adjutants to supervise administration at senior headquarters was ostensibly – perhaps even in principle – designed to relieve staff officers of those burdens so they could concentrate on planning. In practice, the new organization's ranks were disproportionately filled by men from well-connected families, who consistently undercut their rumpled general staff counterparts.

Nor were Hess's circumstances enhanced by the dissonance between Austria's diplomatic geography and its geo-strategy. The foreign office sought to establish Austria at the centre of Europe's affairs, projecting outward an influence expected to be enhanced by its own successes in brokering and managing events. Hess, on the other hand, thought in terms of barriers and ramparts. To a degree, his perspective was influenced by the theoretical writings of Archduke Charles, who reacted to the aggressive-manoeuvre warfare of Napoleon I by emphasizing control – control of terrain, operations and formations. A reasonable case might be made that, when first developed, this approach represented an appropriate playing to Austria's institutional strengths instead of a futile effort to replicate French military behaviour without copying French social and political institutions. A case can also be made that this kind of cautious, defensive perspective best fitted an Austria at once surrounded by potential enemies and possessing defensible frontiers. Nor were prospects of a strategic offensive eastward in the case of war with Russia particularly promising. The tsar's empire offered no obvious objectives within the Austrian army's logistical reach. Instead, Hess advocated the construction of a network of fortresses, not merely on the Russian border, but in every frontier province, east, west and south. In addition, Hess wanted a system of internal strong points. Budapest, Vienna, even Linz, would become part of a comprehensive system of fixed defences that would preserve the monarchy from the worst consequences of any diplomatic overstretch.

For Hess, Italy and Germany were strategic glacis whose vulnerability had increased as the scale of warfare expanded. The 70,000 men permanently stationed south of the Alps were all that Austria's peacetime establishment could sustain without stretching itself too thin elsewhere. As long as the garrison provided a reserve force for the peninsula's client states, as long as Piedmont's army remained ineffective, the status quo could be maintained. But as France developed an overt interest in the Italian question during the 1850s, Hess argued that Austria's deterrent needed to be strengthened. Here, at least, he was constrained to incorporate economic as well as military factors in his calculations. The provinces of Lombardy and Venetia had benefited, since the 1840s, from a state-driven industrial revolution designed to integrate their peoples into the empire. But by 1855 Italy was providing a full quarter of Austria's tax revenues, and operational planning for that theatre had to take corresponding account of preserving the infrastructure from the consequences of campaigning.

Hess was predictable in arguing for an expansion of the region's already elaborate fortification system, and insisting that if the Quadrilateral were properly strengthened, Italy's security would be guaranteed. He was not necessarily wrong-headed. Nor did his insistence that, in case of war with France, the army of Italy must remain on the defensive after reaching its full projected strength of 120,000, necessarily prove Hess a strategic poltroon.

Even assuming Piedmont's hostility, a case could be made that Italy offered no possibilities for decisive action and, therefore, the best policy was an economy-of-force defensive.

It was in Germany where Hess's emphasis on fortresses came to light most fully. In that theatre, Hess projected a total Confederation strength of no fewer than thirteen corps, seven of them based on Rastatt and six on Mainz. This force, far superior to anything the French professional army could muster, was nevertheless to do no more than hold its ground, manoeuvring within a fortress network, which Hess regarded as so vital that he even urged improving the defences of the Saxon capital of Dresden – presumably as a kind of last-ditch point d'appui. For the contingency of war with Prussia, Hess again proposed nothing more daring than a slow advance along the Elbe, taking pains to besiege or blockade every small fortification along the way and providing for a prompt retreat into Bohemia in case of a defeat in the field.[17]

Austrian strategy, in short, was not best calculated to generate elsewhere in the Confederation expectations of dynamic leadership once the guns went off. Austrian tactics in the post-Revolutionary years were, by contrast, strongly aggressive. The experiences of the Napoleonic Wars had indicated that neither firing lines nor skirmish lines were particularly well adapted to mass conscript armies. The Austrians, like the other continental powers, focused correspondingly on shock tactics: attacks pushed home at bayonet-point by closed formations. These formations had the further peacetime advantage of providing impressive spectacles at reviews and manoeuvres with a minimum of training and leadership. The introduction of long-range rapid-fire rifles in the early 1850s generated relatively prompt responses. Instead of being massed in solid blocks, battalions were deployed in 'divisions' of two companies each. In principle, these smaller formations, about 300-strong, were to combine fire and movement, spreading out to fire and concentrating to charge as the tactical situation changed.

The concept was sound enough. Once again the problem lay in its implementation. On the one hand, the peace strength of most infantry units was sufficiently low that they depended heavily on reservists in order to take the field. On the other, those reservists had been trained under essentially different systems. The regimental officers, moreover, were themselves attempting to assimilate the new approach to tactics in a subculture that had tended to be indifferent to such unglamorous details. The Austrian army, in short, was less than optimally prepared at its sharp end when called upon to earn its pay against a foreign opponent.[18]

The Austro-French-Piedmontese War of 1859 was not exactly a surprise. For five years an assertive Piedmont under Camillo Cavour had been increasingly overt both in fostering anti-Habsburg sentiments throughout Italy and in soliciting French support for its position. Nevertheless, every artifice, from sending Piedmontese troops to the Crimea to procuring

---

[17]'Strategische Grundsaetze ueber die Vertheidigung der Oesterreichischen Monarchie und des mit ihr politisch verbundeten Deutschalands, sammt einigen Anhaltspunkten ueber offensive Armee-Operationen nach allen Richtungen (1856)' in Hess, pp. 91–158. Rauchensteiner's analysis of Hess's strategic concepts in Hess, pp. 62 ff., is generally favourable. For the Habsburg position in north Italy generally, see Heinrich Benedikt, Kaiseradler ueber dem Appeninen (Vienna, 1964), pp. 111 ff. and Hans Kramer, Oesterreich und das Risorgimento (Vienna, 1963).

[18]Geoffrey Wawro, 'An "Army of Pigs": The Technical, Social, and Political Bases of Austrian Shock Tactics, 1859–1866', The Journal of Military History 59 (1995), pp. 407–34 and Walter Wagner, Von Austerlitz bis Koeniggraetz: oesterreichische Kampf und Taktik im Spiegel der Reglements, 1805–1864 (Osnabrueck, 1978), pp. 138 ff.

the Piedmontese king's fifteen-year-old daughter as a bride for Napoleon's degenerate cousin Jerome, foundered on the French emperor's unwillingness to be the first to break the continent's peace. Franz Josef was no less cautious. Not until Piedmont opened its borders to Lombardians allegedly fleeing the rigours of Habsburg conscription, not until Piedmont replied to Vienna's protests by summoning its own reserves, did Franz Josef order mobilization.[19]

By the principles and expectations governing its existence, the army – particularly that portion in Italy – should have been ready to go to war from a standing start. Despite the defensive-mindedness fostered under Hess, 100,000 men were, in fact, on the Piedmontese frontier by early April, ready to implement Franz Josef's concept of a first-strike punitive expedition designed not to destroy Piedmont, but to crush its pretensions by forcing demo- bilization before France could intervene effectively. The commander on the spot, however, hesitated for three weeks as French reinforcements poured into the theatre by land and sea. Austrian troop movements, in contrast, were handicapped by a railway system that was a paradigm for everything wrong with Habsburg military administration. The single-track line connecting Vienna with Milan was incomplete when war broke out. No structure existed to integrate the rest of the empire's still developing rail network into mobilization, concentration and logistics plans that were themselves largely the product of improvisation. One Austrian corps took sixteen days to cover forty-seven German miles. It could have marched the same distance in less time, noted one post-war critic, and reached its destination ready to fight.

The notion of marching to contact had merit in theory. In practice, however, any poten- tial seasoning effects that resulted from delays in taking the field were lost because too often the reservists and the organized formations that moved into Lombardy in the spring of 1859 were too preoccupied with finding shoes that fitted, securing their next meal and learning how to load their new rifles, to do any on-the-job training. Once committed to operations, the Austrians were chivvied across eastern Piedmont in a fashion that fre- quently contradictory and poorly executed orders rendered nearly aimless. Straggling and desertion in the ranks, and confrontational arguments at command levels, were the first con- sequences. In limited encounters at Montebello and Palestro, the Austrians suffered defeat, not only at the hands of the French, but also the long-despised Piedmontese. At Magenta on 4 June, Gyulai stood on the defensive, to be outmanoeuvred and outfought by a French army that itself reached the field a corps at a time, then attacked in a disorganized, piece- meal fashion. In the aftermath of defeat, Franz Josef himself assumed command, as much to impose control on his squabbling generals as to assert any presumed *Feldherr*'s talents. He brought with him the equivalent of an entire corps of reinforcements. He also brought Hess and Gruenne, who continued their bureaucratic and professional infighting by advo- cating contradictory strategies. Hess favoured a defensive posture, based on falling back into the Quadrilateral. Gruenne advocated resuming the offensive. Orders and counter- orders generated disorder, exacerbated by administrative collapse. When Franz Josef finally decided in Gruenne's favour, the army that lurched forward had been significantly diminished, not only by the now predictable sickness and straggling, but by foraging parties dispersed in the pattern of an earlier century.

---

[19]On the war's politics, cf. Frank Coppa, *The Origins of the Italian Wars of Independence* (London, 1992); C. W. Hallberg, *Franz Joseph and Napoleon III, 1852–1864: A Study in Austro-French Relations* (New York, 1955); and W. A. Jenks, *Franz Joseph and the Italians, 1849–59* (Charlottesville, VA, 1978).

When, on 24 June, the Austrians stood to arms near the village of Solferino, there had been no systematic distribution of bread for three days. Some regiments had eaten nothing for twenty-four hours. As canteens emptied under a hot morning sun, men fell out of ranks to seek water, no matter how polluted, then fell out again as their bowels loosened. As battle medicine, Franz Josef ordered a double ration of 'brandy' – raw distillate, the initial animating effect of which was wasted because the men were not moving, with its longer-term consequences compounded by empty stomachs and taut nerves. By the time the French and Piedmontese finally attacked around noon, a significant number of Austrian infantry-men were sufficiently impaired that their best chance of hitting anything with their new rifles involved guessing which of the blurred multiple images they saw was the real target.

That, of course, assumed they had a chance to shoot at anything. Austrian engineers sought out first-rate defensive positions, but Austrian generals failed to occupy them, instead holding large sector reserves for counter-attacks that never materialized. Faced with a static enemy, French infantry, well-supported by their new shell guns and light rifled cannon boldly handled in battery strength, thrust into the tactical and operational gaps in the Austrian line. To a degree, this was a form of 'forward flight'. For all their defective training, Austrian riflemen inflicted significant damage on French formations, whose own versions of the Minie were inferior to the Lorenz, and whose marksmanship training was not all that much better. But once the French were on the move, too many Austrians forgot to reset their sights. Too many did not even understand how to do it, or why – initially they had only followed orders to put a small piece of metal in a particular place. Thus, as the French closed the range, they tended to pass under the Minié's killing zone as much as through it. Instead of suffering their heaviest casualties as they approached their objective, companies in the first wave seem to have found their losses dropping. For their part, Austrian officers proved unable to coordinate the new 'divisional' formations, even within battalions. Small isolated blocks of men were overrun by the French or – far more frequently – broke and ran, as much from their sense of isolation as from the actual effect of cold French steel. At the end of the day over 20,000 Austrians were dead, wounded or missing. Another 10,000 had been knocked loose from their units to spread panic in already disorganized rear areas. Franz Josef retreated to the Quadrilateral, the unspoken 'I told you so' of Hess ringing in his ears.[20]

III

Considered from the perspective of a century and a half, the Austrian performance had been marginally – as opposed to exponentially – worse than their principal enemy. French admin-istration, command and tactics had demonstrated the same kinds of shortcomings, whose persistence would be highlighted in the next decade. Nevertheless, the Austrian emperor decided to seek peace. Justifying a decision that sacrificed Lombardy and the military and

---

[20]The best modern accounts are, from the French perspective, Raymond Barque's excellent *Magenta et Solferino (1859): Napoleon III et le rêve italien* (Paris, 1993), and from the Habsburg side, Wawro, 'The Austro-Prussian War', vol. I, pp. 42 ff. and István Déak, 'Defeat at Solferino: The Nationality Question and the Habsburg Army in the War of 1859' in *The Crucial Decade: East European Society and National Defence, 1859–1870*, ed. B. Kiralyi (New York, 1984), pp. 496–516. The Piedmontese army comes off in these as spear-carriers; it plays a more central role in two nationalist/revisionist accounts: Ambrogio Viviana, *Magenta; 4/giugno 1869: dale recherché la prima storia vera* (Milan, 1996) and Mariziano Boignol, *Montebello: 20 maggio 1859, la prima vittoria* (Pavia, 2001).

economic investment in that province required a scapegoat. In explaining himself to his government and his people, Franz Josef savaged Prussia. Instead of honouring its responsibilities to the German Confederation, the Habsburg emperor asserted Prussia had pusillanimously delayed mobilizing and concentrating its troops along the Rhine, all the while pleading operational considerations that were no more than thin smokescreens for bad faith.[21]

To a degree, Franz Joseph was talking for domestic consumption. It was true enough that the Prussian government had been anything but enthusiastic at the revivifying of an Italian crisis hopefully laid to rest in 1848. Frederick William IV, increasingly incapacitated by what were most probably a series of minor strokes, was succeeded in November 1858 by his brother William as prince regent. William promptly sought to mend domestic and foreign fences by inaugurating a 'New Era' based on 'moral conquests'.[22] Translated into a German context, this meant modifying an Austrian policy that, as Frederick William's health declined, had become increasingly confrontational, but with no accompanying general agenda to justify the small-scale obstructionism. As a concrete gesture of goodwill, the regent recalled Prussia's ambassador to the Confederation. Otto von Bismarck's confrontational personality had done as much as his unabashed challenging of Austria's position and policies in the *Bund* to make him *persona non grata* to Vienna.[23] He was reassigned to St Petersburg, where the real diplomatic links were from court to court. Safely 'put on ice on the Neva', Bismarck's rhetoric and ambitions were less likely to damage a Prussian policy William and his advisors proposed to develop as (more or less) *fortiter in re*, but definitely *suaviter in modo*.[24]

The New Era was a response to a decade of development on four fronts in the context of a 'reaction' whose impact had been limited at best.[25] Since the days of the Great Elector, politics, economics, military affairs and foreign policy had been closely related in Prussia — more closely than in any of the great powers, and more closely than in any of Europe's middle-ranking states. By mid-century they had become virtually symbiotic. So much has been written about the Prussian/German *Sonderweg* that it seems appropriate to suggest that, in this respect at least, Prussia instead prefigured the twentieth century in general. And as is the case for twentieth-century states, any discussion that compartmentalizes for the sake of clarity imposes a linear order on what was a synergistic process. To begin with, the state's politics is not to establish priorities; to conclude with the army does not diminish the soldiers' place at the centre of Prussian processes.

In the aftermath of 1848, some Prussian conservatives called for the abolition of a constitution they described as granted under duress. Frederick William IV instead chose to

---

[21]See R. Blaas, 'Die italienische Frage und das oesterreichische Parlament, 1859–1866', *Mitteilungen des oesterreichischen Staatsarchivs* 22 (1969), pp. 151–245.

[22]Guenther Gruenthal, 'Das Ende der Aera Manteuffel', *Jahrbuch fuer die Geschichte Mittel-und Ostdeutschlands* 39 (1990), pp. 179–219.

[23]See Andreas Kaernbach, *Bismarcks Konzepte zur Reform des Deutschen Bundes. Zur Kontinuitaet der Politik Bismarcks und Preussens in der Deutschen Frage* (Goettingen, 1991) and Hubert Kiesewetter, 'Theorie und Praxis deutscher Machtstaatspolitik. Hegel und der Hegelianismus im 19. Jahrhundert', *Jahrbuch des Instituts fuer Deutsche Geschichte* 9 (1980), pp. 273–308.

[24]Otto Pflanze, *Bismarck and the Development of Germany*, vol. I: *The Period of Unification, 1815–1871* (Princeton, 1990), pp. 131 ff.

[25]Hans-Christof Kraus, *Ernst Ludwig von Gerlach. Politisches Denken und Handeln eines preussischen Altkonservativen* (2 vols., Goettingen, 1994), vol. II, pp. 627 ff., establishes the growing discontent of the hardliners.

work within a document whose provisions left control of the army, the bureaucracy and the foreign office in the hands of the crown.[26] In its revised version, the Prussian Constitution also replaced equal male suffrage with the famous – or notorious – 'three-class' system. In its definitive form, this divided voters into three classes, based on the total amount of taxes paid by each class. The result was disproportional representation favouring the well-off at the expense of the bulk of the population.[27] Supported by liberals as well as conservatives, businessmen as well as landowners, it is generally presented as reflecting fear of popular movements whose demands for reform in no way disappeared with the Frankfurt Parliament. In modification of conventional wisdom, however, three points may be suggested. Direct connections between voting and taxpaying existed everywhere in the parliamentary West, at all levels of government, until the second half of the twentieth century. Prussia's tax system during this period neither reflected nor favoured grotesque income inequalities. And given the prevailing pattern of open balloting, opportunities for pressure and corruption were sufficient to encourage Prussian predecessors to America's Mugwumps of the 1880s to support this kind of proportional representation as political reform because it discounted most heavily those votes most subject to pressure. In any case, whether by emasculation, co-option or consensus, Prussia's parliament in the 1850s was a stronger force for stability than dissent.[28]

Political behaviour was also shaped by economic growth. The post-revolutionary years have been described as Prussia's 'take-off period', when a bourgeoisie, freed from both fear of and responsibility for the lower orders, collaborated with an interventionist government to make the state an industrial power whose undertow alone was a sufficient cause of eventual unification.[29] Reality was a good deal less simple; nevertheless, the statistics almost speak for themselves. From power looms to railroad mileage to capital investment, Prussia's numbers increased exponentially. Exports multiplied. New industries developed from backstreet workshops. Industrial concentration reduced the number of businesses and increased the number of employees. Towns grew to cities and merchants became millionaires. News announced by telegraph and newspapers delivered by rail challenged Biedermeyer self-sufficiency in every corner of a Prussia traditionally characterized by its internal differences. The self-confidence of a newly fledged possessing class increased correspondingly.[30] So did the potential tax base available to a government that

---

[26]Hans Boldt, 'Die preussische Verfassung vom 31. Januar 1850. Probleme ihrer Interpretation' in *Preussen im Rueckblick*, eds. H.-J. Puhle and H.-U. Wehler (Goettingen, 1980), pp. 224–46.

[27]Guenther Gruenthal, 'Das preussische Dreiklassenwahlrecht. Ein Beitrag zur Genesis und Funktion des Wahlrechtsoktrois vom Mai 1849', *Historische Zeitschrift* 226 (1978), pp. 17–66.

[28]See, generally, Guenther Gruenthal, *Parlamantarismus in Preussen 1848/49–1857/58: Preussischer Konstitutionalismus-Parlament und Regierung in der Reaktionsaera* (Duesseldorf, 1982).

[29]As in Walther Hoffman, 'The Take-Off in Germany' in *The Economics of the Take-Off into Sustained Growth*, ed. W. Rostow (New York, 1963), pp. 95–118. Cf. Richard H. Tilly, 'The Political Economy of Public Finance and the Industrialization of Prussia, 1815–1866', *The Journal of Economic History* 26 (1966), pp. 484–97.

[30]E. Kiesewetter, 'Economic Preconditions for Germany's Nation Building in the Nineteenth Century' in *Nation-Building in Central Europe*, ed. H. Schulze (Leamington Spa, 1987), pp. 81–106 and Rudolf Boch, *Grenzenloses Wachstum? Das Rheinische Wirtschaftsbuergertum und seine Industrialisierungsdebatte, 1814–1857* (Goettingen, 1991). Cf. Hartmut Kaelble, 'Der Mythos von der rapiden Industrialisierung in Deutschland', *Geschichte und Gesellschaft* 9 (1983), pp. 106–18.

had no thought of withering away in the face of private enterprise, and instead success-fully sought constructive cooperation with the business community.[31]

Both of these mindsets impacted on Prussia's conduct of international relations. German nationalism had not vanished with the collapse of the revolutions. Instead it flourished, and nowhere more than among the 'new men' who at once prided themselves on their hard-headed approach to the present and their lofty dreams for the future. The *Kleindeutsch* concept of the 1840s had suffered from the flaw of being too widely interpreted as Prussia written large. In the 1850s it resurfaced in a different paradigm. On one level the Prussian state appeared to be moving in a liberal, if definitely not a democratic, direction. Even the three-class franchise represented recognition of an open society in which money (which can be acquired) had something like a level playing field with birth (which is unalterable). Particularly given the high degree – and correspondingly high stakes – of government involvement in economic growth, it was not necessarily feckless to postulate the eventual development of an amalgamated upper class.[32] As much to the point, increasing numbers of liberal nationalists, Prussians and others, perceived a situation in which Prussia would become the efficient cause of German unification, but would be unable to sustain its bureaucratic/authoritarian aspects on an enlarged scale. The result would be a necessary turning to those elements with the expertise to run a modern nation state – the same class that saw itself rising to power in Prussia.[33]

The Prussian government's approach to the German question was a good deal more cautious. Karl Marx's observation that Prussia after Olmuetz returned to the Confederation 'like a repentant sinner' oversimplifies the three poles among which the state's diplomats moved in the 1850s. One involved supporting Austria's German and European position on the grounds that international stability best served the vital interests of a Prussia still by far the weakest of the great powers, while conciliation offered the best opportunities for aggrandizement north of the Main. A second paradigm favoured emphasizing Prussia's German status, using the customs union as a diplomatic golden bridge, while presenting Prussia as the best defender of German interests which a newly pretentious Austria regarded as secondary. A third interpreted Prussia as best sustaining its great-power status by presenting itself as an autonomous actor in both European and German affairs: in matters of state as in matters of the heart, a certain distance frequently contributes to achieving desired results.

The resulting foreign policy has most frequently been interpreted in terms of an indecision reflecting either the anxieties of Frederick William IV or the conflicts among interest groups at Prussia's court. More useful is a modification of the model of 'high politics' that Brendan Simms applies so effectively to Prussian decision-making between 1797 and 1806.[34] In the aftermath of 1848, as during the run-up to 1806, foreign relations remained the central focus of Prussian politics, a regulating principle whose demands were reflected in domestic affairs and structures. Foreign policy was conditioned, if not entirely determined,

---

[31]See James M. Brophy, '*Salus Publica Suprema Lex*: Prussian Businessmen in the New Era and Constitutional Conflict', *Central European History* 28 (1995), pp. 122–51.

[32]Dolores Augustine-Perex, *Patricians and Parvenus: Wealth and High Society in Wilhelmine Germany* (Oxford, 1991), develops the point. Cf. M. Gugel, *Industrieller Aufsteig und buergerlicher Herrschaft* (Cologne, 1975).

[33]A. Biefang, *Politisches Buergertum in Deutschland* (Duesseldorf, 1994).

[34]Brendan Simms, *The Impact of Napoleon: Prussian High Politics, Foreign Policy, and Executive Reform, 1797–1806* (Cambridge, 1997).

by geography. Neither representative institutions nor pressure groups were sufficiently developed to diminish significantly the roles of personal ambitions and antagonisms. These were further nurtured by the high level of consensus informing the decision-making apparatus, which reduced the need to compromise differences in order to stand against essentially hostile adversaries such as liberals, and simultaneously made it easier to transfer support from one position to another.

The practical effect of the synergy of possibilities and structures became apparent before and during the Crimean War. Austria's requests for Prussian participation in a policy of mediation generated both fears of alienating Russia and concern with being perceived by France and Britain as an Austrian client. Pursuing a policy of 'active neutrality' meant too many Prussian ambassadors in too many anterooms, vainly attempting to gain hearings from governments committed to war. Asserting leadership in a Confederation which feared being dragged to war for the sake of Austria's ambitions risked permanent alienation of a state whose goodwill was seen as vital to Prussia's great-power status.

In contrast to the course of events in 1806, the Crimean crisis did not find its Napoleon. With its hand unforced, Prussia followed a path activists of all stripes condemned as indecisive. Frederick William began by renegotiating the Austro-Prussian defensive agreement, this time with a clause binding Austria to seek Prussia's agreement before acting in the east. When Austria used this agreement as leverage to force Russian evacuation of the Rumanian principalities of Wallachia and Moldavia, Prussia back-channelled its disapproval to St Petersburg sufficiently convincingly that Russia's anger was focused in the direction of Vienna. Six months later, Austria moved to an alliance with France and Britain and sought mobilization of the Confederation army. Both initiatives were described as necessary to lend weight to Austria's efforts to bring the war to an end. However sincere this interpretation might have been, it did not play in Frankfurt. The middle states, with Prussian support, flatly refused to assume even the limited risk of becoming makeweights in a conflict that by no stretch of any responsible imagination could be described as being in their interest.[35]

That decision contributed significantly to Austria's eventual decision not to assume the risks of direct intervention on the allied side. In turn, the weakening of Austria's European position in the war's aftermath facilitated its resumption of primacy in the Confederation by diminishing its capacity to intimidate the middle states. Prussia, at first glance, seemed to have been left high and dry. Liberals and nationalists, at least some of them, began reality-testing the emerging vision of Prussia as Germany's chrysalis. Prince William grumbled at the consequences of becoming too closely linked with Russia in the minds of the western powers, which, with the Treaty of Paris, were in Europe's driver's seat. Otto von Bismarck asked sarcastically how long his government proposed to play Leporello to the Austrian Don Juan.[36]

Nevertheless, in the context of 'high politics', the mutual cancelling out of conflicting positions left Prussia with playable cards in all of the diplomatic games where the state had a wager. Austria was in no position to turn on its German junior partner. Russia had little

---

[35]Winfried Baumgart, 'Zur Aussenpolitik Friedrich Wilhelms I. 1840–1858', *Jahrbuch fuer die Geschichte Mittel- und Ostdeutschlands* 39 (1987), pp. 132–56, is up to date. The standard older accounts, Kurt Borries, *Preussen im Krimkrieg (1853–1856)* (Stuttgart, 1930) and Christian Friese, *Russland und Preussen vom Krimkrieg bis zum polnischen Aufstand* (Berlin, 1931), remain useful for details.

[36]Pflanze, vol. I, p. 90.

interest in sacrificing its last, best opening to the west. As for the German states, the increasing Prussophilia of their respective nationalist movements, small but vocal, was creating an unexpected window of opportunity for Prussian ambassadors to present images of moderation and reason. Even across the Rhine, a France whose emperor perceived himself as achieving primacy by supporting rather than resisting the tides of liberalism and nationalism saw Prussia as a desirable fulcrum – or, depending on one's perspective, a useful idiot that might eventually be gulled into *de facto* client status as a counter to Austria.[37]

Diplomacy, like poker, is a double-barrelled game, played with both cards and money. The currency in the former case is credible armed force. Prussia's army, in the aftermath of Olmuetz, paid increasing attention to technology as a force multiplier: the technology of railroads and rifles. Despite growing military pressure for nationalizing or subsidizing them, or at least requiring private companies to conform to military requirements in particular cases, after 1848, commercial factors remained decisive in determining Prussia's routes and track systems. Even the Eastern Railway, built during the 1850s at government expense and covering 600 kilometres from Berlin to the Russian border, was developed for economic and political reasons. Neither its routing nor its infrastructure took direct account of military factors.[38]

The rapid growth of track mileage, the corresponding increase in rolling stock and the steady improvements in steam technology and boxcar construction nevertheless significantly enhanced the railways' military potential. In the aftermath of Olmuetz, the Prussian general staff began the processes of developing systems for the large-scale transport of men and supplies. It began its work in the context of a still prevalent assumption that railroads were primarily a defensive instrument, best able to respond to hostile concentrations in a particular sector or reinforce a threatened fortress system. Officers like Helmuth von Moltke nevertheless realized that even these missions required detailed planning, of a scope and on a scale unprecedented in Prussian history. Olmuetz had highlighted, in particular, the logistic risks of bringing the largest possible forces to the largest rail junctions nearest a potential threat. No force much larger than 30,000 men – roughly the size of a war-strength Prussian corps – could be supplied by a single major road and its satellites as long as horse transportation connected railway-created supply dumps with the cartridge boxes, haversacks and nosebags of the forward units. A force 100,000-strong, advancing on a common axis, could not really march. Instead, it inched cross-country, using every accessible track and cow path to move the food and forage on which its effectiveness depended. Even paved roads were not intended to stand the kind of day-in, day-out battering delivered by artillery pieces and heavily loaded wagons, and the Prussian order of battle had no category of labour troops. Finally, complex machinery made its own laws. Boyen had been right in believing railroads fundamentally challenged the vitalism that had been so important to the military reform movement. Metal was indifferent to *Bildung*. Appeals to patriotism and threats of punishment were alike useless in the face of hotboxes, broken axles or tracks that led nowhere operationally relevant.

In combination, these factors made calculation and preparation the keys to the successful utilization of railroads for military purposes on any useful scale. Based on its performances

---

[37]Martin Senner, 'Faire marcher mon jeune empereur d'Autriche: Napoléon III, die Krim und die Grosse Neutraelitaet: Ein Marsch "ins Blaue"?' *Militaergeschichtliche Mitteilungen* 56 (1997), pp. 275–311.
[38]Brose, pp. 230 ff. and Showalter, *Railroads and Rifles*, pp. 28 ff.

in 1849 and 1850 and its existing composition, Prussia's army was unlikely to manage its mobilization and concentration successfully by applying a Teutonic equivalent of the 'muddling through' (System D) of which France boasted. Prussia had nothing like France's cadres of experienced men, at all levels, who could improvise, make do or go without. Indeed, part of the implied contract between the Prussian state and its conscript reservists involved providing boots that fitted, uniforms that did not dissolve in the first rainstorm and regular deliveries of reasonably edible food. Studies of the breakdowns of discipline in 1848–50 suggested strongly that specific problems of command and administration were more common catalytic events than any commitment to revolutionary ideals or hatred of the possessing classes. And while the general staff's competences and capacities to overhaul the entire army were limited, it was in a position to improve its use of railroads for concentration, transport and supply.[39]

Breech-loading rifles had proven their worth from Baden to Schleswig during the revolution. Even inexperienced troops issued needle guns were firmly convinced of their superiority – and, by extension, their own – against anything they faced. That point was particularly important for an army depending on reservists mobilized directly from civilian life. In 1851, the government ordered all future requirements for infantry small arms to be met by versions of Dreyse's rifle.

At the same time, the limited operations of 1848–50 highlighted a growing problem: how to manoeuvre on the battlefield in the face of modern weapons. That France was introducing specially trained battalions of light infantry indicated even the 'ordinary' long-service soldiers of the continent's premier army were expected to find increased difficulty coping with the modern battlefield. Any sophisticated manoeuvring might well prove entirely beyond the skills of the reservists and Landwehr men who would fill Prussia's ranks. Nor could they reasonably be expected to stand in ranks and take punishment at long ranges for any length of time. In the Crimea, even British regulars had faltered when put to such a test.[40]

The Prussian infantry drill regulations, as revised in 1847, interpreted courage as a function of mass and regarded the firefight as a preliminary to the decisive attack of closed columns. That was essentially a response to the perceived problem of maintaining control over units once committed to battle. The needle gun's high rate of fire, and the fact that it could easily be loaded from a prone position, were frequently cited as justifications for reducing the numbers of men deployed as skirmishers instead of being held in closed columns of battalion, half-battalion and company strength. As field and company officers became more comfortable with their new regulations and their new rifles, the concept developed of using the needle gun's firepower to prepare and support attacks, despite continued criticism of the risks of creating a decentralized and uncontrollable 'skirmishers' soup' (*Schuetzenbrei*). Avoiding long firefights, and coming to grips with the

---

[39]Cf. Michael Salewski, 'Moltke, Schlieffen, und die Eisenbahn' in *Generalfeldmarschall von Moltke: Bedeutung und Wirkung*, ed. R. G. Foerster (Munich, 1992), pp. 89–102 and Moltke's '1869 Instructions for Large Unit Commanders' in *Moltke on the Art of War*, ed. D. J. Hughes (Novato, CA, 1991), pp. 171–224.

[40]Showalter, *Railroads and Rifles*, pp. 89 ff.; Hew Strachan, *European Armies and the Conduct of War* (London, 1983), pp. 111–24; Paddy Griffith, *Forward Into Battle: Fighting Tactics from Waterloo to the Near Future*, (rev. ed., Novato, CA, 1991), pp. 62 ff.; and Georg von Ortenburg, *Waffen und Waffengebrauch zur Zeit des Einigungskrieges* (Coblenz, 1990), *passim*.

enemy as rapidly as possible, seemed the most promising option for Prussian tactical theorists.[41]

At the same time, the popular lack of enthusiasm for military service that had developed since the Wars of Liberation was an unspoken argument against the practical prospects for such headlong attacks. Prussian regiments committed to those operations were likely to be neither well trained nor well disciplined. Temporarily exalted by rhetoric, adrenalin or the valour of inexperience, they might indeed push home a charge. They might also charge to the rear with equal energy – or be shot down in windrows before even reaching positions defended by Miniés and Napoleons. Nor could skirmishing any longer be regarded as the collective application of individual initiatives. In the smoke-shrouded chaos of a long-range battlefield, men might easily become lost or go to ground out of confusion. In October 1854, the traditional single-rank skirmish line was replaced by a structure of small fighting teams under the direct control of non-commissioned officers responsible both for directing and controlling the fire of their men and for transmitting the orders of the platoon and company commander.[42]

An army confronting its shortcomings can follow two paths. One is introspection: focusing on internal renovations and modifications. This course was followed by the Wehrmacht in the aftermath of the Polish campaign of 1939, and by the US Army in processing its Vietnam experiences. The alternative involves looking outward, to the government or the society, as focal points of responsibility. The first course is the one most likely to be praised by scholars and analysts, on moral as well as pragmatic grounds. It eschews scapegoating and takes everyone else in the system off the hook of addressing wider issues that are certain to be complex and likely to be painful. It is, however, quite possible for a military system to be given missions whose successful execution with available forces and structures is doubtful. It is not always buck-passing or scapegoating when soldiers assert the need for changes outside the armed forces' immediate sphere.[43]

The Prussian army's efforts to respond institutionally to the shortcomings indicated by the operational circumstances of 1848–50, and the tactical conditions imposed by modern weaponry, increasingly focused on a single issue with implications in both directions: the rank and file, on the whole, were not well enough trained either to maintain cohesion under adversity or to take advantage of their new rifles. This was not a simple matter of blaming the Landwehr, despite the growing social and political hostility to that system within the professional officer corps. It was clear enough that the Prussian Landwehr system could, in fact, put far more men into uniform than were likely to be employable in any future conflict, even one on the larger scale that Olmuetz suggested might become the norm. It was correspondingly possible to sort out the less capable, for whatever reason, and assign them to depots to improve their instruction. But those remaining in the ranks

---

[41] *Exerzir-Reglement fuer die Infanterie der Koeniglich Preussische Armee* (Berlin, 1847). Cf. A. von Witzleben, *Heerwesen und Infanteriedienst der Koeniglich Preussischen Armee* (7th ed., Berlin, 1861), pp. 504 ff. and Wilhelm Ruestow, *Allgemeine Taktik, nach dem gegenwaertigen Standpunkt der Kriegskunst bearbeitet* (Zuerich, 1858).

[42] For the process, cf. Prince William of Prussia's letter of 20 October 1853, and his memorandum to the III Corps, and that of 25 August 1855 to Frederick William IV in *Militaerische Schriften weiland Kaiser Wilhelms des Grossen Majestaet*, ed. Kgl. Pr. Kriegsministerium (2 vols., Berlin, 1897), vol. II, p. 199 *passim*.

[43] See Williamson Murray, 'The German Response to Victory in Poland: A Case Study in Professionalism', *Army and Society* 7 (1981), pp. 285–98 and H. R. McMaster, *Dereliction of Duty: Lyndon Johnson, Robert McNamara, The Joint Chiefs of Staff and the Lies That Led to Vietnam* (New York, 1997).

were not likely to offer much improvement. Growing opinion in the active officer corps insisted that a term of active service that had been reduced in the years before 1848 to two years, and sometimes *de facto* to eighteen months, did not develop trained men – only drilled men, who performed by rote under orders but neither understood nor internalized what they were doing. The result was that even the army's active regiments were, at best, throwbacks to a post-Frederician era whose consequences had been made all too plain in 1806.[44]

The argument that three years were required to develop an infantryman was apparently demonstrated as so convincingly false in the next century that it has been understandably dismissed as specious by scholars and soldiers alike – a self-serving stalking-horse advanced by an increasingly militaristic officer corps determined to assert its influence and maintain its position against the forces of change.[45] Looking down roads not taken, it is indeed possible to hypothesize a response to what might be called the 'infantry crisis' that would be based on overhauling principles of training and concepts of command at company and battalion levels. Maximizing time spent in the field and on the firing range as opposed to the parade ground, developing the NCO's role as a junior leader, reviving some of the literal *noblesse oblige* that had characterized officer–man relations in the days of Frederick the Great – these changes would have required no major alterations in either the army's composition or the pretensions of its officer corps.

Their implementation, however, ran against three interfacing grains. First was the fact that, at mid-century, no army anywhere in the world had developed anything like a functioning method of preparing short-service conscripts for long-range battlefields. It would take decades of trial, error and experience to approximate the appropriate requirements and techniques. Even then, the results were questionable, at best. The hecatombs of 1914 owed at least as much to inadequate training as to defective doctrine.[46] Events by 1918 had gone far to establish the mass citizen armies of Europe's Age of Nation States as a temporary anomaly, created by the Industrial Revolution and rendered at least obsolescent by industrial war. In the mid-nineteenth century, moreover, every other army in Europe accepted the axiom that formal training was no more than a preliminary process; that soldiers could be developed only through apprenticeship. This postulate in part reflected the fact that skill transmission of almost any kind in pre-industrial societies was a function of watching and imitating: the concept of teaching as a formal process carried out in a specific time-frame was still in its early stages. Where contemporary liberals and future academic or military critics perceive months and years wasted in garrison routine, without much being done to develop or refresh soldierly skills, a strong body of common-sense opinion replied that the normal way to learn anything well enough to be really good at it was by osmosis. Nor was it necessarily erroneous to assert that war is sufficiently unlike everyday human activities that the best training is that which develops physical fitness

---

[44]The issue of reduced service is a major theme of *Militaerische Schriften Kaiser Wilhelms*, which includes a large amount of relevant correspondence dating back to 1833 in vol. I, p. 142 *passim*. The issue is summarized in Walter, pp. 244 ff., from a perspective sympathetic to the shorter service.

[45]Contemporary commentaries by external observers, like the authors of 'Die Heeresreform in Preussen', *Allgemeine Militaer-Zeitung* 35 (1860) and 'Die Praeszenszeit', ibid. 37 (1862), tended to take two-year service for granted.

[46]This is a significant theme in Dieter Storz, *Kriegsbild und Ruestung vor 1914. Europaeische Landstreitkraefte vor dem Ersten Weltkrieg* (Herford, 1992) and is mentioned in Hew Strachan, *The First World War*, vol. I, *To Arms* (Oxford, 2001), pp. 110 ff.

and conditioned reflexes. The final element of the compound was a generalized belief among professional soldiers that ordinary people, peasants, artisans and workers, were deficient in the natural moral and intellectual qualities that were becoming premiums on the modern battlefield. Those qualities might be cultivated by appropriate blends of instruction, experience and exaltation. They were, however, unlikely to be sufficiently strong or adequately rooted to flourish without a strong institutional framework demanding and rewarding appropriate combat behaviour.

Thus it was not only concern for domestic political reliability that led France, Austria and Russia, after 1815, to create armies whose rank and file were at least semi-professional by virtue of the length of their conscription terms. Nor was it political reaction that led France, in particular, to emphasize an experienced, long-service rank and file as the best response to the exponential growth of firepower.[47]

These developments in armed forces arguably reflected liberalism's fostering of a new form of class identity based on perceived meritocracy. The experiences of 1848 had provided ample concrete justifications for a liberal distrust of the demos that, at times, seemed to top anything coming from conservative circles. Those benefiting from the new order, the bureaucrats and professors, the manufacturers and businessmen, were also increasingly likely to feel themselves not merely more successful, but better than those remaining behind – an attitude with significant implications for liberal thinking on military affairs.[48]

IV

The Prussian army pursued reform by increments. In 1852, the legal term of active service was restored to three years. Corps were reorganized, each line regiment being brigaded with a Landwehr regiment in the hope of improving the latter's training and cohesion by osmosis while giving the active regiment a greater interest in the welfare of its counterpart.[49] The improvised supply services were replaced by train battalions with their own peacetime cadres, completed on mobilization by men trained as infantry or cavalry who were surplus to the requirements of those arms.[50]

At this stage, questions of planning and mobilization were still the province of the war ministry on the one hand and the corps districts on the other. Friction between and among these agencies was endemic, but for different reasons than in Austria, where state official lines of authority were complex to the point of incomprehensibility. In Prussia, the problems were personal. The organization of the army into permanent, territorialized corps after 1815 created a class of 'demigods': the commanding generals of the corps districts. Combining long seniority, powerful connections and distinguished service, they had no real prospects of further advancement – and, as a rule, were unwilling to exchange

---

[47]These arguments are developed in Dennis Showalter, 'Europe and the World, 1815–1864' in *European Warfare, 1815–2000*, ed. J. Black (New York, 2002), pp. 27–50. For alternative perspectives, cf. David Gates, *Warfare in the Nineteenth Century* (New York, 2001), pp. 55 ff. and Geoffrey Wawro, *Warfare and Society in Europe, 1792–1914* (New York, 2000), pp. 23 ff.

[48]Cf. Lothar Gall, *Buergertum in Deutschland* (Berlin, 1989) and Toni Offerman, *Arbeiterbewegung und liberales Buergertum in Deutschland, 1850–1863* (Bonn, 1979).

[49]'Bemerkungen ueber die Mobilmachungsvorschrift vom 30.6.1851' in *Militaerische Schriften Kaiser Wilhelms*, p. 146.

[50]Jany, vol. IV, pp. 210–11.

their positions for any in the army. Responsible in his person for peacetime administration, wartime mobilization and operational command, a corps commander in the provinces was the closest thing to an independent, absolute authority seen in Prussia since the days of Frederick William I. Prudent war ministers approached them with care and challenged their prerogatives with caution. Most, while not decrepit by the standards of a long peace, were of an age sufficiently advanced to make them set in their ways, and proud of any specific modifications they might make to plans and policies emanating from Berlin — whatever might be the consequences for system and coherence.

The corps system also had an unexpected effect on the development of the general staff. The reformers' initial vision had been of a mutually acceptable symbiosis of staff officers and commanders: age and youth, experience and education, planning and execution. The foundations laid for this during the Wars of Liberation, however, had been eroded by thirty-five years of peace. During that span, most senior officers had acquired, if only by osmosis, competence in routine matters, and most matters had become routine. General staff officers assigned to corps and divisions — over half the total number — as a result spent more time implementing policies than developing ideas. Their roles, in other words, approximated those of their counterparts in other European armies — not the best preparation for broad-gauged thinking on general issues of planning and force structure once one was rotated back to Berlin.[51]

As for the two dozen or so general staff officers assigned to the capital, most of their time was spent on military history, topography and participating in staff rides and war games. No shaping principle existed. For example, Carl von Reyher, chief of staff from 1848 to 1857, has been described as believing that each exercise should reflect the personality and character of the directing officer, with the result that they were uncoordinated.[52] It is not necessary to challenge the fact to provide an alternative interpretation. One legacy of the Napoleonic era had been an emphasis on 'genius' as an indispensable quality of generalship. Even in Prussia, where the re-taming of Bellona had been such a high priority, mass-produced competence was not regarded as a complete substitute for great captains.[53] Staff rides and similar exercises were among the few means available to test and develop officers' capacities and potential for autonomous thinking in something resembling operational contexts. A certain randomness was an acceptable price for giving genius a chance to unfold — even when, like the proverbial second marriage, actual results too often indicated the triumph of hope over experience.

Things began to change when Helmuth von Moltke replaced Reyher in 1857. He had spent forty years in the Prussian army, thirty of them on the general staff. He had spent time as an advisor in the Ottoman Empire, served on the staff of Prince Charles of Prussia and as adjutant to the latter's older brother, Prince William. His appointment, nevertheless, owed something to coincidence. William assumed the regency for his brother the day after Reyher's death from natural causes. He was better acquainted with Moltke than with the other prospective candidates for a post that was, after all, a secondary one; and no one

---

[51]Cf. Eberhard Kessel, *Moltke* (Stuttgart, 1857), p. 200 *passim*; Walter, pp. 302 ff.; and Bucholz, pp. 36 ff.

[52]Kessel, *Moltke*, p. 245. This pattern also arguably reflected the relative balance of power between the *Generalkommandos* and the central authorities, which strongly favoured the former.

[53]Dennis Showalter, 'The Retaming of Bellona: Prussia and the Institutionalization of the Napoleonic Legacy', *Military Affairs* 44 (1980), pp. 57–63.

in any of the court factions seriously questioned Moltke's competence. On 29 October 1857, he was appointed provisional chief of the Prussian general staff.

Moltke was particularly interested in railroads. As early as 1841 he had served on the board of directors of a proposed Berlin–Hamburg railway and put most of his assets into company stock – entrepreneurial behaviour setting him apart from many of his junker-ized counterparts. He had continued to evaluate and cultivate their military prospects. In 1850, as chief of staff of the Rhineland-based VIII Corps, Moltke had integrated railroads into the manoeuvres – an experience that concretized his general conclusion that opti-mum utilization of this new means of transportation required long-term, large-scale plan-ning. Apart from these professional considerations, Moltke, like most new men in senior positions, wished to make a quick, sharp impact. Railways were a useful entering wedge – one, moreover, not directly challenging any other military or civilian bureau. In March 1858, the general staff issued its first general policy statement on the use of railroads for large-scale troop movements. The autumn manoeuvres of that year featured the movement of 16,000 men of V and VI Corps from the manoeuvre ground to the base area around Liegnitz in Silesia. Moltke had played a generally prominent role in the exercises, the first chief of staff to do so, acting as an umpire and spending enough quality 'face time' with William that the regent confirmed his appointment as permanent after the manoeuvres.[54]

That last point is significant in the context of a generally accepted presentation of Moltke's career that owes too much to *post facto* constructions and retrospective pieties, developed after 1871 in the Second Empire and indirectly reinforced for another century by the avowedly meritocratic armies of the western world. In the positive version of this model, Moltke emerges as the archetype of the soldier as a professional, embodying the ethos of being more than one appears, depending for his position on ability rather than arti-fice. Its negative side describes a tunnel-visioned military specialist so focused on the craft of war that he grows blind to the arts of statesmanship.[55] In fact, no officer rises to a high post in peacetime, or retains it, without possessing considerable situational awareness. It is not necessary to paint Moltke as a uniformed courtier to acknowledge his political sense – in particular, his recognition of the central role William, as chief executive, must play in any development of the general staff's position in the Prussian military and state systems.

The manoeuvres of 1858 also highlighted, in Moltke's mind, the need for continuous coordination among the ministries of war, the interior and commerce if railroads were to exercise their growing capacity to move men and material. That concept, however, was at significant variance with a long Prussian history of ministerial autonomy and collegial decision-making.[56] The normal pattern of cooperation involved specific coordination on particular issues. Reyher had followed this practice in dealing with railroad issues during his tenure as chief of staff. Moltke, instead, saw the general staff as the potential (and the logical) vector of permanent administrative cooperation in this area – not least because it had surplus bureaucratic capacity. The general staff's second section was in charge of

---

[54]Kessel, *Moltke*, p. 202 *passim*; Showalter, *Railroads and Rifles*, pp. 29 ff.; and Rahne, pp. 23 ff.

[55]See, particularly, Gerhard Ritter, 'Moltke and Bismarck' in *Sword and Scepter*, tr. H. Nordau (Coral Gables, FL, 1969), vol. I, pp. 187 ff.

[56]Reinhold Dorwart, *The Administrative Reforms of Frederick William I of Prussia* (Cambridge, MA, 1953) and Hans Rosenberg, *Bureaucracy, Aristocracy, and Autocracy: The Prussian Experience, 1660–1815* (Cambridge, MA, 1958), present patterns of a system that endured well into the nineteenth century.

evaluating Prussia's possible military involvement in southern Europe: Switzerland and Italy. Whatever may have been the contingencies forty years earlier, the prospects of direct Prussian commitment to either theatre were sufficiently remote that, in 1859, the section was reconfigured, becoming responsible for mobilization planning and given a special department of railway affairs.

That reorganization followed Prussia's second mobilization of the decade. As its confrontation with Piedmont escalated, Austria sought support from the German Confederation. Prussia had bets down on too many cards to cover them all. The diplomatic prospects of serving as Austria's faithful second while negotiating for an autonomous sphere of influence north of the Main were balanced in Berlin by advocates of an ostensibly Confederation-friendly policy, rejecting or limiting German participation in what seemed to many German soldiers and diplomats a fiasco with its roots in Vienna. At the same time, French involvement in the Austro-Piedmontese dispute engaged nationalist sentiment in Prussia and western Germany. It encouraged realist suspicions of France's intentions towards Prussia, in particular, and Germany, in general. To complicate matters further, Prince Regent William possessed a conscience better able to generate questions than to resolve them. He sympathized with Austria in principle, but was willing neither to deliver that state from its own behaviour nor to exploit its position for Prussia's advantage.

As the crisis deepened, War Minister Edward von Bonin took counsel with Moltke on the practical problems of implementing a mobilization. From the beginning, Moltke emphasized the importance of leverage. Prussia could best contribute to a Franco-Austrian war by moving as many troops as rapidly as possible to the line of the lower Rhine, as a deterrent to French initiatives against Germany and a warning against committing too heavily in the Italian peninsula. At present, he wrote on 14 March, it would require six weeks to concentrate a quarter of a million Prussian troops on the Rhine and Main. At least two weeks could be saved by double-tracking some existing lines and completing another dozen already projected or under construction. Might the ministry of commerce be pressured to expedite the processes?

The war ministry, reluctant to act in the absence of a policy decision, refused even to consider discussing the matter with its fellow cabinet department. The commerce ministry, for its part, replied politely that it was always willing to discuss with the general staff all issues affecting the military use of Prussia's railroads – a piece of bureaucratic boiler plate that left no one ignorant of its real meaning. Meanwhile, as Austrian requests for Prussian support turned into increasingly strident demands, William hung back. Beginning on 22 April, he ordered the army placed on a war footing but held in its garrisons. Only the Austrian defeat at Magenta decided him in favour of mobilizing six corps, on 14 June, and sending them west as a warning to Napoleon of the risks of pressing his success too far.

Moltke and his subordinates had done enough preliminary negotiating with the appropriate ministries of Prussia and the other north German states that the first troop trains were scheduled to depart on 1 July. Then the foreign ministry complicated matters by urging William not to act so strongly without direct Confederation support. Even had there been a consensus among the middle states on the best way to proceed – a counter-factual, particularly in the aftermath of Magenta – this would have taken time the Austrian Foreign Office insisted it did not have. The movement was cancelled, then restored. But on 4 July, when William ordered five corps to the Rhine, the railway rolling stock collected to support the original movement had once again been scattered across

Prussia. It would take, Moltke reported, at least eleven days before any large-scale movements could begin. The subject became moot when, on 11 July, Austria and France concluded an armistice at Villafranca that, for all practical purposes, ended the war. William held his own troops at the ready till 25 July, then ordered demobilization to begin.[57]

The year 1859 was arguably a more significant watershed in European history than 1848. Events in northern Italy had gone far to confirm Napoleon III's vision of a new French imperium, brought to primacy in Europe by its management of the forces of nationalism and liberalism. If Piedmont, in the aftermath of Villafranca, hardly behaved like a grateful client in the traditional sense, that state's self-assertion, its aggrandizement at the expense of the Austrian protectorates elsewhere in the peninsula, could nevertheless be processed in Paris as clearing the board for the future order of nation states.[58] Austria, moreover, while never abandoning its self-defined role as 'the gendarme of Italy', came to terms with its defeat sufficiently to seek French goodwill and French support for its policies in central and eastern Europe, offering, in return, an archduke whose assumption of Mexico's 'cactus throne' did much to legitimate France's drive for overseas aggrandizement, and more to encourage France's 'forward policy' in Germany.[59]

That policy owed more to Gottfried Herder than to Louis XIV. It perhaps reflected also the philosophy of the gaming establishments Napoleon frequented as a younger man. The emperor perceived German integration, if not necessarily German unity, as an idea whose time had come. Considerations of prudence and profit alike suggested France was best advised to act as midwife and broker to this 'new European order'. The practical course of action might involve working with centralizing forces in the Confederation or – far more likely – facilitating Prussia in doing what, from a French perspective, it wanted to do anyway. The latter course of action would involve walking a fine line between Prussia and Austria – but the foreign office was confident of its ability to keep both German players satisfied. The outcome would leave France at the fulcrum of central European politics. And, like the proprietor of any decent gambling house, France would charge the game a reasonable percentage for overhead and protection. In 1859, France's price had been the Piedmontese provinces of Nice and Savoy. A fair return on the more delicate and complicated German question must, of course, be more substantial, but would still remain limited enough to be negotiable.[60]

What France saw as high politics appeared in Germany as low threat. At its beginning, the crisis of 1859 inspired a surge of journalism and rhetoric in support of Austria. Ludwig Bauer's 'O Deutschland hoch in Ehren', later a signature tune of the Second Reich, began as a musical call to arms against the hereditary enemy across the Rhine. Boiler-plate anti-French

---

[57]Kessel, *Moltke*, pp. 265 ff. Hans Kentmann, 'Preussen und die Bundeshilfe an Oesterreich im Jahre 1859', *Mitteilungen des Oesterreichischen Instituts fuer Geschichtsfoerschung, Ergaenzungsband* 12 (1933), pp. 297–415, remains a useful overview.

[58]Michael McDonald, 'Napoleon III and His Ideas of Italian Confederation, 1856–60' (dissertation, University of Pennsylvania, 1968).

[59]Cf. Geoffrey Wawro, 'Austria versus the *Risorgimento*: A New Look at Austria's Italian Strategy in the 1860s', *European History Quarterly* 26 (1996), pp. 7–29; R. B. Elrod, 'Austria and the Venetian Question, 1860–66', *Central European History* 4 (1971), pp. 149–71; Michele Cunningham, *Mexico and the Foreign Policy of Napoleon III* (New York, 2001); and, generally, Hallberg, pp. 314 ff.

[60]William E. Eckard, *Napoleon III and the Concert of Europe* (Baton Rouge, LA, 1983) and E. Ann Pottinger, *Napoleon III and the German Crisis, 1865–1866* (Cambridge, MA, 1962), are solid analyses.

sentiments from 1840 and 1848 were recycled in newspapers and on lecture platforms throughout the Confederation. Magenta and Solferino, however, diminished significantly the enthusiasm of a still embryonic public opinion for a great crusade. Instead, 'realists' across the political spectrum began reinterpreting Austria's difficulty as Germany's opportunity. The rapidity with which Napoleon and Franz Josef concluded peace, combined with increasing rumours of a Franco-Russian alliance, further encouraged demands for a German system strong enough to defend Germany against attack from any quarter.

This new surge of nationalism ran deeper than its more belligerent immediate predecessor. The hundredth anniversary of Friedrich Schiller's birth, in November 1859, was a particular focal point for festivals, parades and speeches celebrating Schiller as the laureate of German identity. Lest the point be missed, allegorical representations of 'Germania' vied with portraits and statues of the poet for pride of place in the public space.[61] The question that remained too embarrassing to answer was how many divisions Schiller had. Increasingly, the political side of the resurgent nationalist movement focused on Prussia. In September 1859, the *Nationalverein* was formed as an umbrella organization. This was an élite body, not a mass movement. It included only a few thousand members, drawn largely and deliberately from the intellectual and commercial middle classes. Its make-up was overwhelmingly liberal, reflecting the growing conviction of businessmen and intellectuals alike that neither the political nor the economic nor – and by no means of minor importance – the cultural goals of the liberal movement could be met within the existing structure of the German Confederation.

However, 1848 had taught wisdom – or, at least, caution. The *Nationalverein's* avowed goal was to move not peoples, but governments, Prussia's government in particular. The *Nationalverein* in no way regarded itself as a stalking-horse for Prussia's unilateral aggrandizement or Austria's expulsion from Germany. Its aims must be evaluated in the context of a constitution kept deliberately vague with the intention of alienating as few potential allies as possible. Reduced, however, to a schema, the *Nationalverein's* approach emphasized the primacy of establishing a central German authority strong enough to defy France in any foreseeable context. Next would come some form of national political assembly. Domestic reforms took third place – not least on the grounds that their issues were the most parochial and divisive.[62]

Prussia's central role in this process was facilitated by its central place in German public consciousness. Frederick the Great had become part of Germany's mythic structure even before his death. His perceived synthesis of intellectualism, asceticism and activism was particularly congenial to a middle class seeing no contradiction between education and property (*Bildung und Besitz*).[63] Frederick's – and, by extension, Prussia's – image of incorporating a tolerant, urbane Protestantism was, for many liberals (particularly north of the Main), a welcome contrast to a Catholicism that under Pope Pius IX was, to its critics, increasingly asserting a politicized universal mission at the expense of every form of

---

[61]R. Notelius, 'Schiller als Fuehrer und Heiland' in *Oeffentlicher Festkultur*, eds. P. Duding et al. (Reinbek, 1988), pp. 237–58.
[62]For the *Nationalverein*, cf. S. Na'aman, *Der deutsche Nationalverein* (Duesseldorf, 1997) and the overlooked contribution by Luis Torres, 'The German Nationalverein, 1859–1867' (dissertation, Minnesota, 1971).
[63]Eda Sagarra, 'The Image of Frederick II of Prussia in Germany in the Century before Unification', *European Studies Review* 4 (1974), pp. 23–32.

human freedom.[64] For academics, the experience of the Prussian state was a convenient framework for structuring the mass of archival material that was reshaping such fields as history and jurisprudence. Prussia's rise also offered an exciting story for an emerging generation of teachers and professors concerned with reaching and inspiring increasing numbers of students. Particularly in universities, speakers and auditors alike no longer viewed the large lecture as something to be endured on the way to the seminars. The 'matter of Prussia' was, for men like Treitschke, Sybel and Droysen, the stuff that could hold an audience, as well as the expression of intellectual conviction.[65]

In more pragmatic terms, the *Nationalverein's* members and supporters accepted the argument that any credible central authority must command credible military force. The mid-nineteenth century is not generally considered a great age of the military amateur, the civilian generally knowledgeable about war. Nevertheless, the growing proliferation of writings on warfare's theory and practice made it possible to develop something other than superficial awareness of military matters – usually accompanied, in this emerging age of professionalism, by a corresponding sense of their complexity. Friedrich Engels is the best known of the first generation of 'defence analysts' – men outside official frameworks who nevertheless manifested interest in and understanding of security issues. Most of them, like Engels and the cashiered Prussian lieutenant Friedrich Ruestow, stood to the left of the political spectrum, and most rejected what might be called the 'classical' German liberal paradigm of a citizen militia. Citizen soldiers, yes, but overwhelmingly, these authors rejected the model of 'domestic mercenaries', soldiers alienated from their societies. But the noun was as important as the adjective. Enthusiasm was a response, not a solution. It was useful only when combined with training and discipline. The exact proportions were open to debate,[66] but by 1859 no one with influence in the liberal/nationalist camp seriously argued that an effective German army could be improvised. Nor was there any faith that the Confederation, or any smaller umbrella organization based on the middle states, whatever might be its other virtues, could develop armed forces to match those of France or Austria. At best, military reform in a Confederation context resembled constructing a model from toothpicks: it offered only a simulacrum of stability.

That left Prussia centre stage, by default. But what if Prussia proved reluctant to play its assigned role? More to the point, what if Prussia performed that role too well? The course of events in Germany between 1859 and 1871, combined with the subsequent history of the Second Empire, has left the liberal nationalists looking more foolish than they deserve. Men like the Hanoverian Rudolf von Bennigsen or Rudolf Haym, founder and editor of the *Preussische Jahrbuecher*, were under no illusions of an overnight transformation of the court of Berlin from goats to gardeners. They, and their colleagues, followers and supporters, reasoned instead that Prussia, particularly given its political history since 1848, possessed neither the administrative capacity nor the internal coherence to run

---

[64]Owen Chadwick, *The Secularization of the European Mind in the Nineteenth Century* (Cambridge, 1975).
[65]Cf. generally, Georg Iggers, *The German Conception of History: The National Tradition of Historical Thought from Herder to the Present* (Middletown, CT, 1983) and A. Lees, *Revolution and Reflection: Intellectual Change in Germany during the 1850s* (The Hague, 1974).
[66]Cf. the essays and articles in *Engels as Military Critic*, eds. W. Chaloner and W. O. Henderson (Manchester, 1959) and Peter Wiede, 'Wilhelm Ruestow (1821–1878): Ein Militaerschriftsteller der deutschen Linken' (dissertation, Munich, 1958).

effectively a Germany unified by brute force. Yet its ambitions, particularly if appropriately encouraged, would not allow for backing down. In 1862, Karl Twesten commented that, should Prussia produce someone able to unite Germany at the expense of treaties and laws, monuments would be erected in his honour.[67] Even in that extreme case, however, the eventual result would be a steady turn towards those supporters of unification who knew how to mobilize and govern a modern system: the liberals and the nationalists. In a kind of lost-wax process, Prussia would be the chrysalis from which Germany would emerge. Or, in the Hegelian language familiar to every educated German, Prussia would fall victim to 'the cunning of reason'.

The rational calculations shaping this position depended strongly on an affirmation of faith: faith in the power of the national idea to generate tectonic changes in political society. In a sense, the rise of nationalism came at liberalism's expense as well, in that it involved a transfer of commitment in the hope of bridging or bypassing some of the tensions and disappointments that had accompanied the liberal movement's ambiguous history since the Wars of Liberation. The most immediate consequence of the approach, however, was its contribution to a paradox. For Prussia to fulfil the destiny assigned by the liberal nationalists, its army's effectiveness, arguably, must be not only sustained but also improved. Fear of Prussia's military power had characterized German liberalism from its beginnings. Now liberalism's nationalist wing would take a different stand.[68]

The Prussian army, for its part, had emerged from the mobilization of 1859 in what might best be described as a state of creative tension. The most obvious lesson from an operational perspective involved not merely the discussable desirability, but the absolute necessity of regulating the administration of railways used for military purposes. In the aftermath of Villafranca, Moltke proposed the creation of permanent committees, including general staff officers and civil officials. The relevant ministries cooperated with goodwill – particularly since a three-week time limit was established for the completion of rail transport from mobilization areas to zones of concentration. This removed the uncertainty that had so plagued ministry of commerce officials in the spring of 1859 – and the problem of sustaining an increasingly rail-based economy without knowing what track lines and how much rolling stock would be available when, or for how long.

The foreshortened transport time was accompanied by a series of administrative reorganizations. A unit-train system was introduced, with war-strength infantry battalions, cavalry regiments and artillery batteries each moved by a single train. Since military traffic had priority during mobilization, neither long halts nor repeated loading and unloading would be necessary. This, in turn, was expected to facilitate maintaining discipline – an issue whose significance was increased by the reduction of notification time for call-ups from five days to one, and the decision to load units at as many sites as possible, rather than foot-march them to rail centres. Since 1815, supporters of Prussia's reserve system had been able to cite the lapse of time between mobilization and deployment as a kind of safety valve, giving units an opportunity to shake down under operational conditions before going into action. Now that lead time was being reduced to the vanishing point, and war was projected as 'come as you are' – warts and all.

---

[67]Cited in T. S. Hamerow, *Social Foundations of German Unification, 1858–1871* (Princeton, 1971), p. 17.
[68]Cf. Dieter Langewiesche, 'Reich, Nation und Staat', *Historische Zeitschrift* 254 (1992), pp. 341–81 and L. Haupts, 'Die liberale Regierung in Preussen in der Zeit der "Neuen Aera" ', ibid. 227 (1978), pp. 45–85.

Nor were these innovations mere paper-framed recommendations whose theoretical promise was nullified by their practical difficulties. In July 1859, V Corps executed a practice mobilization along the new lines. The exercise was successfully completed in twenty-nine days. And while V Corps benefited from being one of the formations earlier brought to war strength in support of Prussia's projected show of force on the Rhine, its garrisons in the rural east and its high proportion of Polish recruits hardly made it a likely showcase for high-technology operations. Put bluntly, if V Corps could do it, the rest of the army had no excuses.[69]

Improving Prussia's military reaction time was by no means regarded as an unmixed blessing. Since the end of the Seven Years War a century earlier, the Prussian army had been regarded by the Prussian government as a deterrent force, whose presence in the right numbers in the right place at the right time was, in principle, part of a carefully calibrated response to a particular situation. If all went optimally, that response would fulfil the state's policy aims without firing a shot. The mobilizations of 1850 and 1859 had been ordered — and must be understood — in that context. The general staff's new mobilization proposals, once implemented, at best, were certain to diminish diplomatic flexibility. At worst, they risked escalating crisis into war by provoking or frightening the adversary into a military response.

Moltke's response was that of a historian rather than a theorist. Since the end of the fighting in Italy he had been sending officers into France to evaluate the nature and condition of that country's railway system. He had assigned other officers to evaluate the large numbers of narratives and the official and semi-official studies published by all the combatants. The picture that emerged was anything but reassuring. France, Moltke asserted, was the main threat to Prussia and the German Confederation — not from any moral or ideological grounds, but because of the nature of its military system. Strategically and tactically, French doctrine emphasized the offensive. The French army, with its large cadres of professional soldiers, requiring no lengthy and complex mobilization to reach war footing, was well matched to the doctrine. The French rail network possessed the capacity to move large forces east, and to sustain them once they reached the theatre. While the administration of the railroads currently left much to be desired, it was in the highest degree imprudent to assume improvements would not be forthcoming.

Moltke believed the most probable French initiative would involve an offensive into south Germany to destroy its armies and secure the advantage of inner lines *vis-à-vis* Prussia and Austria. Only two Prussian corps were based near the threatened area. These could not be reinforced in peacetime by units from other regions without risking a repetition of the confusion of 1850, when it became necessary to call up reserves. Prussian strategy, therefore, must be based on an initial defence, holding the Rhine while concentrating along the Main for a counter-attack — preferably in cooperation with other Confederation forces.[70]

The chief of staff's position was clear. Flexibility as traditionally defined was a snare and a delusion against an army able to make war from a standing start and a state able to send its strike forces into battle behind locomotives. His arguments might well have

---

[69]Rahne, pp. 25 ff. and Kessel, *Moltke*, pp. 272 ff.
[70]Moltke's memorandum of spring 1860 is in Helmuth von Moltke, *Militaerische Werke*, part 1, *Militaerische Korrespondenz*, ed. Grossen Generalstab, *Kriegsgeschichtliche Abteilung* (4 vols., Berlin, 1892–1902), vol. III, pp. 16 ff.

become the focus of a major policy debate — had they not been almost immediately over-shadowed by military decisions with far greater political visibility.

V

The concept of improving the effectiveness of the army's reserves by closer association with the active regiments had generated responses in structural as well as training contexts. A series of limited proposals led to a general statement that initially focused on the growth of Prussia's population from 10 million in 1820 to its current number of 18 million. The annual conscription intake, however, had remained the same, around 40,000. One major result of this was to discredit the principle of universal service by making the draft an increasingly random process that exempted some men entirely while making others liable for decades of active, reserve and Landwehr service. Another consequence was the army's enforced dependence on large numbers of men in their late twenties and thirties. In a long-service army, older soldiers were often the most valuable soldiers. In Prussia, however, the reserve system placed in the front ranks those men whose civil responsibilities were likely to weigh heavily on their minds, and whose diminished vitality was not compensated by increased know-how. Physical fitness had civil responsibilities.

To revitalize the field army, the proposal recommended only men between the ages of twenty and twenty-six should be assigned to the active formations and their reserves. To keep costs within acceptable parameters, the term of active service would be set at two years. Men from twenty-six to thirty-two would serve in the Landwehr and end their military commitment at thirty-two. This rejuvenation could be accomplished by lowering somewhat the existing physical qualifications and conscripting all that met them. The Landwehr, on this model, would become the army's second line, employed primarily as garrisons and on lines of communications.[71]

In February 1858, the war ministry presented its general conclusions to William for consideration. The prince regent had long been a vocal and informed critic of the army's personnel system. The exact mix of social, political and professional elements in his dislike of the Landwehr as it existed in the 1840s and 50s is impossible to determine. William, like most of his professional contemporaries, considered long-service soldiers to be more suited to the new demands of warfare than short-term conscripts. His aesthetic distaste for the Landwehr men, who never seemed to master the intricacies of close-order drill and parade marching, whose uniforms always seemed shabby and whose muskets perpetually wanted cleaning, was well known and frequently expressed. Neither his time as military governor of Rhineland-Westphalia in the 1830s and 40s, nor his experiences in the revolution of 1848 and the mobilization of 1850, had done anything to improve his opinion of citizen soldiers' political reliability.

At bottom, however, the Landwehr was, to William, only one part of a generally defective military system, the reform of which he considered central to the New Era he proclaimed on assuming the regency. As a reformer, he had four problems. One was his age

---

[71]'Motive und Vorschlaege zu einer Reorganisation fuer die Preussische Armee (Konzept des Oberstleutnant von Clausewitz), Juli 1857' in *Militaerische Schriften Kaiser Wilhelms*, vol. II, pp. 326 ff. Cf. the discussion in Walter, pp. 288 ff. and Wolfram Witte, *Die Reorganisation des preussischen Heeres durch Wilhelm I* (Halle, 1910), pp. 37 ff.

relative to his station: a man on the far side of sixty who has spent his life being deferred to is unlikely to change his positions readily on any matter. A second obstacle was sensitivity: William reacted to slights actual and perceived with responses ranging from outbursts of tears and withdrawal of dinner invitations to accusations of treachery. Third came a paternalism that reflected both his years as a senior army officer and his acceptance of the romantic conservatism typical of his class and generation. Believing he knew best because of who and what he was, William found it correspondingly difficult to brook fundamental challenge from those he continued to regard as his subjects. Fourth stood confidence in his own professional judgment: belief that he knew what the army needed better than any politicians, whatever their place in the spectrum. It was not impossible to convince William of something not already a firmly held belief of his own. Neither was it a task lightly assumed.[72]

In July, William received another memorandum on the state of the Prussian army, this one from a source he trusted more than a war ministry that seemed a bit too willing to place military affairs in civilian contexts. Albrecht von Roon is most frequently interpreted in the context established by Friedrich Meinecke, as a blinkered, technocratic opposite to the generous and humane perspectives of the Era of Reform embodied in Hermann von Boyen.[73] Roon was certainly a professional soldier, in the positive and negative contexts of that term. He was also a man informed by the 'realistic' principles that had become increasingly overt in the conduct of international relations since 1848. Roon had served under William while the latter was commanding at Koblenz in 1854, and the prince found both his personality and his ideas congenial. By 1858 Roon was commanding a brigade in Posen, but William had by no means forgotten him. When the war ministry submitted its position paper, William asked Roon for his opinion.

The result was a long and densely written document that gives the lie to Roon's image as a *nur-Soldat*. He began by stressing Prussia's perilous international situation and calling for a build-up in the state's military strength by increasing the conscription ratio. His focus, however, was on a Landwehr that he savaged as a military and political aberration. Universal suffrage, even in its denatured three-class form, had made the Landwehr a political institution by making Landwehr men into voters. That meant, instead of being a work tool of state policy in the monarch's firm hand, in future, the army could be employed only after public debate, and with the consent of its individual members.

Nor were these fetters compensated by operational effectiveness. In presenting familiar evidence of poor training, lax discipline and unqualified officers, Roon highlighted the latter issue a bit more brightly than some of his contemporaries. Amateurs at any level, he argued, could not wage modern war. Men whose primary interests lay elsewhere were no more likely to lead companies effectively than a soldier was to plead a case in court or remove a tumour. The development of specialized knowledge had not rendered *Bildung* irrelevant. It had, however, made necessary a stronger dialectic between cultivation and expertise than Prussia's Landwehr system recognized.

---

[72]There is still no good biography of William I. Karl Heinz Boerner, *Kaiser Wilhelm I, 1797 bis 1888, Deutscher Kaiser und Koenig von Preussen: Eine Biographie* (Cologne, 1987), acknowledges his abilities and affirms his influence, but sees both as being used to sustain an anachronistic social and political system. Erich Marcks, *Kaiser Wilhelm I* (Leipzig, 1897), is both more perceptive and more critical than might be expected from a work that takes such firm stands on political questions. The evaluation of William's character is based on Walter, pp. 287–8.
[73]Friedrich Meinecke, 'Boyen und Roon', *Historische Zeitschrift* 77 (1896), pp. 207–33.

Roon took a similar approach with regard to enlisted personnel. His insistence that three years of active service was the minimum time necessary for inculcating a 'true soldierly spirit' is generally interpreted as demanding the 'militarization' of Prussia's young men in barracks and on parade grounds. His issue was rather the improvement of individual skills and group cohesion. Like Moltke, he agreed that it was fully possible to produce an adequately drilled soldier in less than a year, perhaps no more than six months. Drill and training, however, were not the same. One was the necessary basis for the other, which continued to require a substantial apprenticeship under arms. To facilitate the integration of serving soldiers and reservists, Roon recommended that each battalion of the active army be organized in eight companies, each with a peace strength of one hundred. On mobilization that number would be doubled; each battalion would form two battalions and each regiment a brigade, all essentially homogeneous. To provide cadres, the number of professional officers and NCOs would be increased by expanding the schools that took in sons of career-enlisted men, and by creating NCO academies for conscripts interested in making a permanent career of the army.

When it came to wider questions of politics, at least at this stage, Roon seems to have entertained no delusions about the possibilities of changing a young adult male's fundamental convictions by an extra twelve months in uniform.[74] His reasoning was more subtle. If the revolutions of 1848 had suggested that loyalty could no longer be taken for granted, they also suggested that the masses followed lines of least resistance. Put ordinary human beings into a coherent structure with an avowed purpose, provide effective leadership, consistent discipline and fair treatment, and their convictions would not matter – they would behave as the organization wished.[75]

For Roon, Prussia's real problem was the literal identification, under the Landwehr system, of the soldier with the citizen. The Landwehr man was also a voter, and as long as the Landwehr maintained its corporate identity, the army would be a political institution. The presumption in that context was that the Landwehr as an interest group would support the liberal parties that were its strongest advocates. While Roon did not make it an overt point in this memorandum, like a good many of his counterparts in the mid-upper levels of the officer corps, he was also concerned with the active army's politicization at the other end of the spectrum. Generals, like Edwin von Manteuffel, chief of the military cabinet, and the other military members of the 'camarilla' that had surrounded Frederick William IV, posed a problem not for their principles, which were generally congruent with those of their comrades on staff or troop duty, but because of their visibility and the perceived degree of their influence. When Roon suggested that the standing army should have no right at all to vote, as was the case in Britain, he was also defending the concept of the army as a work tool in the hands of a specialized, professionalized leadership – whose influence over crown, government and its own 'politicized' counterparts would increase correspondingly.[76]

---

[74]The belief that even a few weeks' boot camp are enough to militarize ordinary young adults remains widespread. Thomas Ricks, *Making the Corps* (New York, 1997), discusses this subject perceptively in a contemporary context.

[75]'Bemerkungen und Entwuerfe zur vaterlaendischen Heeresverfassung' in *Militaergeschichtliche Schriften Kaiser Wilhelms*, vol. II, pp. 344 ff. and in Albrecht von Roon, *Denkwuerdigkeiten aus dem Leben des Generalfeldmarschalls Kriegsministers Grafen von Roon* (2nd edn., 3 vols., Trewendt, 1892), vol. III, pp. 521 ff.

[76]Roon, *Denkwuerdigkeiten*, vol. II, pp. 352 ff., shows its author as intelligent and ambitious, by no means merely the work tool of a 'camarilla' whose overall influence, even in its salad days, has been arguably overstated. See David E. Barclay, 'The Court Camarilla and the Politics of Monarchical Restoration in Prussia,

Roon understood, certainly more clearly than he later asserted, that the Landwehr question had ramifications beyond simple questions of conscription legislation. Like William, however, he regarded the direct imperatives for military reform as strong enough to override what seemed little more than semantic objections. The prince regent returned both Roon's and the ministry's drafts, with the comment that he favoured the former as being more comprehensive. The war ministry was correspondingly irritated. Not only was Roon an outsider, but his plans – at least according to Bonin – took too little account of cost. The ministry's officials also criticized Roon's concept of doubling each active company on mobilization as too complicated in the context of the general staff's growing emphasis on speed and simplicity. In February it offered a modified proposal. The term of active service would be set at three years, with the three youngest classes of the Landwehr becoming the reserve of the active army. The number of battalions would be doubled in peacetime, in order to give their officers experience in handling the units they would take into the field. And instead of the 1,000 men currently projected for a war-strength battalion, the new formations would be only 800-strong – half active soldiers and half reservists. These smaller battalions would be easier to command, more flexible operationally and composed of the youngest and fittest men in Prussia – a fair exchange for the overall reduction in the mobilized active army's size that the reorganization would entail.[77]

William began transforming theory to reality on his own initiative in 1859, in the aftermath of the summer mobilization. With no war in sight and large numbers of men under the colours, he ordered the Landwehr and the older classes of reservists in the active regiments to return home – a gesture widely approved. The youngest class of reservists, the new annual intake of conscripts called up on 1 August, and the enlisted cadres of the first-line Landwehr battalions, however, were formed into new 'Landwehr Cadre Battalions' on a one-for-one basis with their active counterparts. In September, the reservists were discharged and replaced by the third-year men of the line battalions, whose place, in turn, was taken by previously unconscripted men between the ages of twenty and twenty-five. These men were legally liable for service even though they had not yet been conscripted. Their position resembled that of American males between twenty-two and twenty-six as Vietnam-era draft calls increased after 1965: previously *de facto* exempt, but nevertheless near the top of local boards' lists for induction, and unlikely to gain much public sympathy – particularly in the context of the hurrah-patriotism sweeping Prussia at the time. Any nascent protests were stifled when, in November and December, the men conscripted in 1856 and kept with the colours a few extra weeks were discharged in their turns. To replace them, each line battalion gave its 'Landwehr Cadre' counterpart 150 more men, bringing the latter up to 418 and reducing the former to 538. That strength was a good deal lower than some professionals, including the king, liked even for a peace establishment. But the systematic introduction of comprehensive three-year service would fill the ranks with men to spare.

This chopping and changing has been presented in detail because it highlights the importance of accomplished fact and 'prompt gradualism' to the Roon reforms. The basic institutional structure of the new system was put in place within three months. Personnel matters

---

1848–58' in *Between Reform, Reaction, and Resistance: Studies in the History of German Conservatism from 1789 to 1945*, eds. L. E. Jones and J. Retellack (Providence, RI, 1993), pp. 123–56.
[77]Cf. the paraphrase in *Militaerische Schriften Kaiser Wilhelm*, vol. II, pp. 301 ff. and the analysis in Walter, pp. 301 ff., which incorporates earlier discussions.

were handled so smoothly that discontent never escalated into protest. Indeed, the government's behaviour was not infrequently applauded in nationalist circles as an appropriate safeguard against a renewal of Franco-Austrian hostilities or some more arcane form of French treachery. In a real sense, the country was not quite sure of what was happening. Semantics, at least, seemed unchanged. No units had been created from scratch; 'Landwehr' was prominent in the title of the 'cadre battalions'. Roon, for one, was well aware of the Landwehr's symbolic position. Keep the name for considerations of tradition and politics, he argued. Indeed, give it to the entire army should that prove a desirable public-relations move.[78]

William was more interested in stabilizing a still provisional framework. In August, he assigned Roon to the war ministry with orders to integrate his proposal with the ministry's into a definitive reorganization plan. Bonin asked to be placed on leave – a gesture of dissent not lost on the regent. Roon, obviously the coming man in the system, found little significant opposition among Bonin's subordinates. Indeed, he was sufficiently impressed by the ministry's financial calculations to approve the 800-man battalions and at least consider some furloughing of active-service troops for the sake of economy. William wanted a full three years of service and insisted on war strengths of 1,000 men for each infantry battalion, to allow for casualties and erosion in the field. The war ministry replied that the larger number would require ten classes of conscripts – three active and seven reserve – to complete. This meant both diluting the number of serving soldiers in the mobilized army and increasing the number of older men in the field force: the precise weaknesses that had led to the proposed reorganization in the first place![79]

Bonin was, by this time, ready to make a stand against what he regarded as unnecessary roughness. He too, it must be remembered, was a man of the 'New Era'. He had served briefly as war minister earlier in the decade, lost his job during the Crimean crisis and been reappointed in 1858, in good part because of a reputation for being able to manage the 'parliamentary' aspects of the position without overtly antagonizing the civilian politicians. The 'liberalism' with which he is sometimes credited consisted primarily of francophobia on one hand and admiration for Boyen on the other. He was no less committed to reforming the army than was Roon, or indeed William himself. During the crisis of 1859 he gave Moltke what amounted to a free hand in operational planning – to the point of allowing him immediate access to the regent. Legally and politically, however, Bonin's was the pivotal position. He had no sense of abandoning it and was confident in his ability to assert decisive influence over a regent whose character Bonin respected more than his intellect or his political sense.

What Bonin recognized, far more clearly than anyone else directly involved, was that whatever the military motives behind the proposed reorganization, its consequences for the Landwehr invited interpretation in the context of the continued attacks on that institution from both the extreme right in parliament and the uniformed reactionaries who had been all too prominent in the entourage and household of Frederick William IV. Again, more than most of his counterparts, Bonin was aware that significant numbers of parliamentary deputies recognized the necessity of overhauling the existing military system. Even men who believed in the Landwehr system, who held commissions as Landwehr officers, understood the institution's shortcomings. But at the same time, they were unwilling

---

[78]Walter, pp. 304 ff. and Jany, vol. IV, pp. 219 ff., combine for the details.
[79]See the correspondence in *Militaerische Schriften Kaiser Wilhelms*, vol. II, pp. 402 ff.

to turn over the central institution of state power to the men who had fought every attempt to introduce constitutional government, however limited, to Prussia.[80]

During the Landtag session of 1859, Bonin fielded questions on the Landwehr by reiterating that the principles of the modified Defence Law of 1815 would be sustained in any reorganization. It was the kind of general answer that aroused no one, but also satisfied no one in parliament and few outside it. Manteuffel, who had never been one of William's favourite personalities, took advantage of the situation to attack the war minister in and out of season, insisting that Bonin's excessive sensitivity to the feelings of ignoramuses on military matters – who were potentially disloyal to boot – would cripple army reform and destroy the 'special relationship' between crown and army.

The exact degree of Manteuffel's influence on the regent during this period is open to debate. Bonin and his liberal friends blamed Manteuffel for encouraging William to make changes to the reform bill that both increased its costs and sharpened its tone to points unacceptable in parliament.[81] Certainly William needed no encouragement to perceive Bonin as something other than a 'team player'. What Bonin saw as lining up support for measures certain to be controversial, William understood as undercutting his authority. 'The warlord commands the army, and not the War Minister', he punningly commented on one of Bonin's letters.[82] Certainly he insisted that Prussia could not afford to subordinate military issues to financial and economic considerations. And whatever may have been Manteuffel's encouragement in this regard, William increasingly believed Bonin lacked the energy needed to implement the army's reorganization. The war minister, increasingly isolated even among his direct subordinates, resigned on 27 November.

Some indication that William was as yet unwilling to risk an open clash with parliament was the length of time he took to announce Bonin's replacement, hoping it would look like a genuine resignation as opposed to a veiled dismissal. Roon's selection for the post came as no particular surprise. He was widely known as the regent's man – a key factor for an office so closely involved with the executive. His appointment placated the reactionaries because of his frequently asserted commitment to the prompt obedience of royal orders. It pleased the technocrats because of his long-standing involvement with the details of army reform. It correspondingly alarmed a parliament already disturbed at the fall of Bonin. In that environment, any proposal for army reform was likely to cause controversy apart from any specific contents.

VI

The government's final recommendations were by this time familiar. The 'Landwehr cadre' units were to be renumbered as active formations, retaining their Landwehr history and honours, but otherwise severing all ties with that institution. The Landwehr's second line was to be disbanded and its four youngest classes assigned to the reserve of the active

---

[80]There is no biography of Bonin. Kessel, *Moltke*, pp. 338 ff. and Craig, *Politics of the Prussian Army*, pp. 141 ff., incorporate the best treatments of his term as war minister.
[81]Gordon Craig, 'Portrait of a Political General: Edwin von Manteuffel and the Constitutional Conflict in Prussia', *Political Science Quarterly* 66 (1951), pp. 1–36, remains a model of analysis. Cf. Ludwig Dehio, 'Edwin von Manteuffels politischen Ideen', *Historische Zeitschrift* 131 (1925), pp. 41–71.
[82]Craig, *Politics of the Prussian Army*, pp. 142–3.

army. The formations that remained – 116 infantry battalions and a dozen regiments of cavalry – would receive new cadres and be used for second-line duties in case of mobilization. The annual conscription intake increased from 40,000 to 63,000, and terms of service were established as three years in the line, five in the reserve and eleven in the Landwehr.

From the war ministry's and the regent's perspectives, these proposals were a long step in the direction of a new model Prussian army, combining traditional Prussian virtues: low cost and high fighting power. The military budget, it was true, would have to be increased by at least 9.5 million talers. Much of this 25 per cent boost, however, could be understood as a one-time investment in infrastructure: barracks, drill grounds and schools of instruction for the extra officers and NCOs that the new system required. Voices in parliament were not so sanguine.[83] The first issue to emerge was financial. The economic 'take-off' referred to earlier in this chapter is more obvious in retrospect than it appeared to delegates who, not infrequently, had direct and uncomfortable experience of the business cycle's vagaries. Nor, at this stage of Prussia's history, were there enough other large categories in the public budget to facilitate reallocating funds among departments. To vote the budget meant either raising taxes or accepting a deficit. Both prospects were uncongenial to the liberals of various types and stripes who dominated parliament's lower house – particularly in a centuries-old German context of Estates whose primary function was to act as guardians of the purse against the ill-considered demands of ill-advised princes.[84]

Given the generally recognized shortcomings of the Prussian army, however, many deputies were also uncomfortable with an overt stand based on accountants' calculations. The proposed reorganizing and repositioning of the Landwehr, by contrast, offered ample opportunity to point with pride to the heroic era of the Wars of Liberation, while viewing with alarm the potential severing of this vital link between army and people. The three-year term of active service was another convenient target. For twenty years in the 1830s and 40s, two-year service – sometimes less in practice – had been the norm, and Prussia had survived without disaster. Moltke himself said that a few weeks sufficed to inculcate the basics of drill.[85]

The accompanying argument that the rest of a conscript's time in service was needed to develop and internalize a set of particular skills and an underlying attitude further opened a door to semantics and linguistics. 'Soldierly spirit', *Soldatengeist*, was a phrase that could be interpreted both in a situational context of 'battlefield awareness', as discussed earlier in the chapter, and as an expression of commitment to the state, the monarch and the army. For William and for Roon the construction was a monad; one concept implied and depended

---

[83]Rolf Helfert, *Der preussische Liberalismus und die Heeresreform von 1860* (Bonn, 1989) and 'Die Taktik preussischer Liberaler von 1858 bis 1862', *Militaergeschichtliche Mitteilungen* 53 (1994), pp. 33–48, are the most detailed overviews of the events described below. Walter, pp. 315 ff. and Messerschmidt, pp. 184 ff., are excellent summaries. Craig, *Politics of the Prussian Army*, pp. 145 ff., remains the best account in English.
[84]Klaus Erich Pollmann, 'Heeresverfassung und Militaerkosten im preussisch-deutschen Verfassungsstaat 1860–1868' in *Parliamentaerische und oeffentliche Kontrolle von Ruestung in Deutschland, 1700–1970*, ed. J. Duellfer (Duesseldorf, 1992), pp. 45–61.
[85]The operational effectiveness of briefly or poorly trained men, even under mid-nineteenth-century conditions was another matter. The Confederate States of America's Army of Tennessee, to a significant degree, embodied the Landwehr ideal of patriotic citizens commanded by local notables. Poor training, however, placed it at a consistent disadvantage relative to its Union opponents. See Andrew Haughton, *Training, Tactics, and Leadership in the Confederate Army of Tennessee* (Portland, 2000).

upon the other. In parliament, however, the phrase invited interpretation as shorthand for an attempt to destroy the constitution by undermining its public support.

Initial criticism of the army bill was also a parliamentary pawn move. Drawing a line on the issue of military reform was both a way of establishing boundaries and a presentation of an initial negotiating position. The generalized necessity for some form of army reorganization was widely accepted in the lower house. Expansion of the active-service force, while more controversial, had a significant number of supporters as well, particularly on the military affairs committee that was responsible for detailed consideration of the measure. That support, however, was significantly eroded by the confrontational approach taken by the officers and officials who testified before the committee. Roon, in particular, challenged the committee's jurisdiction and competence in language unprecedented since the constitution's introduction. At the same time, the proposed reforms attracted increasing interest among Prussia's intelligentsia, the journalists and publicists whose opinions were extremely important to politicians in the days before opinion polls and voter profiling. By the time the military committee completed its report — a complex document accepting the army's expansion but reducing its budget and retaining the Landwehr's traditional role — positions in both the government and the lower house had hardened to the point where the recommendations had no chance of passing.

The administration's response was a neat piece of parliamentary manoeuvring. The original bill was withdrawn. In its place, the government requested a special grant of 9 million talers to cover the next fourteen months. Instead of Roon, Finance Minister Erasmus von Patow, a far less confrontational and controversial figure, made the case before the lower house. The grant, he argued, would only be used to strengthen units authorized under existing legislation. Nor would this grant be considered as prejudicing any further decisions on army organization.[86]

On 15 May the Chamber of Deputies approved the request. Gordon Craig calls the decision 'a tactical mistake of the highest order', and this interpretation has dominated interpretations for half a century.[87] Seen from contemporary perspectives, however, the events of May acquire a different meaning. On a fundamental level, a significant majority of delegates were unwilling to alienate the regent over a measure generally considered necessary, in an area moderate liberals everywhere in Europe considered to be primarily a province of the executive: security. The goal of the parliamentary parties in Prussia before and after 1848 had been to demonstrate that they were competent to participate in governance — not that they possessed the ability to gridlock the state. The Chamber, moreover, stood alone before the vote; an upper house dominated by conservative aristocrats had overwhelmingly supported the government's original military bill. Fourteen months was a long time — time for negotiations to develop, tempers to cool and facts to become accomplished; time as well for deputies ill-informed on the details to learn how the army really functioned.

Time was precisely what extremists on both sides seized by the proverbial forelock. The political officers in William's entourage, Manteuffel their loudest spokesman, insisted that the Chamber's refusal to accept the army bill as presented was a gauntlet thrown down, at

---

[86]Cf. *Stenographische Berichte ueber die Verhandlungen des preussischen Abgeordnetenhauses* (Berlin, 1860), vol. II, pp. 1113 ff. and Fritz Loewenthal, *Der preussische Verfassungsstreit, 1862–1866* (Altenburg, 1914), pp. 39 ff.

[87]Craig, *Politics of the Prussian Army*, p. 148.

best, and a probable harbinger of revolution. In the closed, hothouse atmosphere of the royal court, these views circulated unchecked and virtually unchallenged. They did nothing to discourage the regent's decision, by cabinet orders of 5 May and 4 July, to finalize the new organization. That included renumbering the Landwehr cadre formations. Did this, in fact, breach Patow's guarantee? From Manteuffel's perspective at least, it did not matter. Allowing them to remain as provisional formations rather than confirming them as permanent was to concede parliamentary control over the army. From the perspective of the corps commanders and the general staff, the formations already existed. To disband them, or even to imply that they might be disbanded, was to risk a state of confusion and disorder that would be an open invitation to Prussia's enemies – and devastate as well the morale of the regimental officers already involved in the reorganization.

There was a certain tongue-in-cheek quality to this internal dialogue on reorganization. Formations transformed from Landwehr to line by the lost-wax process initiated in 1859 would be extremely difficult to reconvert without a top-to-bottom revitalization and reconfiguration. Roon saw no necessary contradiction between authorizing what was already an accomplished organizational fact and accepting the commitment to further discussion of wider matters like the term of service and the permanent budget. While the army can probably be cleared in narrow, legalistic terms of violating the guarantees offered by Patow, there can be no doubt that, in a political context, the soldiers' behaviour seemed a clear statement of hostile intent, even to an increasing number of moderates and defence-minded liberals.

Suspicions were fed by the strong journalistic response to the creation of what, in many editorial minds, seemed thirty-six entirely new regiments – four of them, moreover, in a Prussian Guard that since 1848 had been to liberals a major symbol of reactionary militarism. Public opinion played a major role on both sides of the increasingly polarizing issue of army reform. It correspondingly merits mention that public opinion, even in the sense that such a term was understood in the nineteenth century's last quarter, did not exist. Newspapers, magazines, speeches and, not least, gossip, were the means of communicating and transmitting information and ideas. Newspapers were becoming increasingly important to the process, but these were not the mass-circulation dailies that Bismarck would regularly suborn from his 'reptile fund'. Instead they resembled more closely such contemporary publications as *Weekly Standard* or *New Republic* – appealing to target audiences rather than general readers, and built around clear, specific perspectives in their news features and on their editorial pages alike.[88] As for gossip, Berlin during the 1860s prefigured Washington a century and a half later in that politics was still its principal industry. Rumours and inferences flourished in the drawing rooms, salons and restaurants of a city still small enough that it was virtually impossible for people to avoid each other without significant, conscious effort.[89]

What this amounted to was a climate in which increasing numbers of deputies became persuaded that army reform, particularly those aspects involving the Landwehr and the three-year active service, was becoming a 'wedge issue' in a still amorphous, poorly defined polity whose virtual representation by interlocking networks of notables was a

---

[88]Kurt Koszyk, *Deutsche Presse im 19. Jahrhundert* (Berlin, 1966), is a good overview.

[89]There is no better source for that phenomenon than the diaries of Theodor von Bernhardi, who knew everyone worth knowing, and knew enough about enough things to maintain his credibility everywhere he went. The eight volumes of *Aus dem Leben Theodor von Bernhardis* were published in Leipzig between 1893 and 1906 (vols. III–VI cover this period).

vital element of the *Honorationenpolitik* that largely defined Prussian and German liberalism at this stage of its history.[90] William's dedication of the colours of the new regiments at the tomb of Frederick the Great in January 1861 alarmed even his civilian ministers, who perceived the gesture as an unnecessary provocation. Certainly it became a talking point and a rallying point for a coalescing opposition in parliament. The session of 1861 combined heated anti-militaristic rhetoric with sober talk of cutting the military budget. The moderate and the cautious were able to combine in another compromise: the Chamber authorized a second provisional grant, but insisted that the following year the government present a comprehensive military service law for debate and action.

By this time, William had formed an opinion of his own. While susceptible to Manteuffel's influence, he was by no means a man to be moulded by others' wills – as Bismarck, among many others, would eventually discover. The death of his brother on 2 January 1861 was more significant for William than for almost anyone else in Prussia. Regent or king: it was a distinction without difference to those who knew that Frederick William IV's condition had long been irreversible. William, however, for family reasons and from his own convictions on the nature of monarchy, understood an essential change in his status, and his responsibilities, once his brother died. This did not necessarily involve an open break with parliament. Rather, it meant initially that William now felt comfortable asserting what he regarded as legitimate royal prerogatives that also gave him pleasure – like dedicating the flags of the army's new regiments at the tomb of Frederick the Great or staging his coronation not in Berlin the capital but in Koenigsberg, in East Prussia, where he felt more at home.[91]

Whether undertaken for feel-good reasons or as deliberate provocations, these behaviours had political consequences. The dedication of the flags disturbed William's civilian ministers and gave Manteuffel a chance to express once again his acid-tipped contempt for the '... people sitting in a house in the Doenhoffplatz who call themselves a parliament'.[92] The coronation site invited interpretation as a deliberate snub to the new Prussia of railroads, factories and universities to recognize a Junker heritage already too powerful for society's good. To William, however, the public enthusiasm he experienced affirmed his belief that the Landtag represented little more than its own membership.[93]

In the spring of 1861, a liberal politician and intellectual, Karl von Twesten, published a pamphlet warning against policies that might divide army and society in ways reminiscent of 1806. Manteuffel responded by provoking a duel, wounding his opponent and insisting loudly upon serving out the brief spell of arrest that was the usual outcome of 'affairs of honour' in the army. These baroque gestures impressed William, who saw the affair as a 'triumph of democracy', disregarding both Manteuffel's instigation of the affair and the exponential imbalance between even a political soldier and a bookish civilian when it came to pistols for two.[94]

---

[90]Andreas Biefang, *Politisches Buergertum in Deutschland, 1857–68: Nationale Organisationen und Eliten* (Duesseldorf, 1994). Dan S. White, *The Splintered Party: National Liberalism in Hessen and the Reich, 1867–1918* (Cambridge, 1989), establishes the framework of *Honorationenpolitik* in a model case study.
[91]Walter Bussmann, 'Die Kroenung Wilhelms I. – Eine Demonstration des Gottesgnaedigtums im preussischen Verfassungsstaat' in *Politik und Konfession. Festschrift fuer Konrad Repgen*, eds. D. Albrecht et al. (Berlin, 1983), pp. 189–212.
[92]Hohenloe, vol. II, pp. 255–6.
[93]Kessel, *Moltke*, p. 345.
[94]Roon, *Denkwuerdigkeiten*, vol. II, p. 2.

They impressed others as well, but for different reasons. On 6 June 1861, the German Progressive Party came into formal existence. The Progressives were an umbrella party with a platform of two-year military service, the establishment of Prussia as a parliamentary state and the unification of Germany under Prussian auspices. In the elections of December 1861, the new party gained a resounding victory, sending 109 delegates to the new parliament. Other, more moderate, liberal factions totalled 141 votes. The fifty-four Catholic delegates focused on confessional interests. There remained only fourteen conservatives in the lower house. The election results, shocking to the Right, nevertheless did not alter the fundamental conviction that the reform's liberal critics were not representative of the 'real' Prussia. In a certain sense, the three-class voting system and the principle of not paying parliamentary delegates strengthened that perspective. The assembly's membership reflected independent or unearned income only marginally less than the landed establishment of the upper house.[95] More pragmatically, the king could argue that the reorganized army was functioning. Conscripts were reporting on time and doing their duty. Guardhouses and courts martial were no busier under the new order than the old. In William's mind, at least, these facts said more about the views of the Prussian people than any mere election results.

For Manteuffel and his fellows, whether or not a specific number of peasants reported for service was unimportant. Constitutionalism in any form was the enemy, and any steps taken towards its destruction were *ipso facto* justified. In the summer of 1861, the camarilla prepared a comprehensive plan for suppressing insurrection in Berlin — a plan prefiguring the suppression of the Paris Commune in its projected use of artillery, bayonets and firing squads to make an example no one would ever forget. Roon talked and wrote of abolishing the Chamber. Prince Frederick Charles, who would command a field army in 1866 and again in 1870, advocated purging the cabinet of all liberal members and putting Roon at its head.[96]

By the turn of the year, William was sufficiently convinced the state was in danger that he approved a slightly modified version of Manteuffel's internal security plan. From parliament's side, the Progressives secured a lower house majority, supporting an itemized budget and two-year service and rejecting the government's request for funding. William responded by dissolving parliament in March and calling for new elections. In the weeks before they were held, Prussia wavered on the edge of a military coup. Certainly Manteuffel expected some kind of outbreak in the manner of 1848, and openly looked forward to the opportunity to establish himself as the king's strong right arm. The liberal cabinet ministers, for their part, believed the best way to avoid another electoral catastrophe was to offer compromises. William responded by replacing the dissidents, including Patow, with conservative yes-men. When the votes were counted, the opposition had risen to 223 deputies, including 135 Progressives. There were twenty-eight Catholics. The government could count only ten conservatives.[97]

---

[95]W. Gugel, *Die Wahlrecht in der Geschichte der deutschen liberalen Parteien 1848–1918* (Duesseldorf, 1958), pp. 8 ff., establishes a spectrum of connections between *Honoratienliberalismus* and limitations on political participation.

[96]Roon, *Denkwuerdigkeiten*, vol. II, pp. 58 ff.; *Prinz Friedrich Karl von Preussen. Denkwuerdigkeiten aus seinem Leben*, ed. W. Foerster, (2 vols., Stuttgart, 1910), vol. I, p. 268 (hereafter cited as *Friedrich Karl*); and Ludwig Dehio, 'Die Plaene der Militaerpartei und der Konflikt', *Deutsche Rundschau* 213 (1927), pp. 91–100.

[97]The narrative of events at this stage, with the military conflict escalating to a constitutional one, can best be picked up in Eugene N. Anderson, *The Social and Political Conflict in Prussia, 1858–1864* (Lincoln, NE, 1954).

With lines that clearly drawn, all but the most fire-eating reactionaries began entertaining second thoughts. William alarmed his entourage and his administrators with periodic talk of a necessary choice between compromise and abdication. While in principle committed to preserving the crown's prerogatives, he had no desire either to begin his reign with a bloodbath or go down in history as the monarch who presided over a Prussian civil war. Roon also spoke of seeking compromise, even at the expense of three-year service. This was, in his mind, not an optimal decision. However, it could be more or less compensated by increasing the number of long-service soldiers in the rank and file — to as many as one-third of the active battalions. The men who would escape direct conscription under this system would be required to pay a special tax, which, in turn, could support enlistment bonuses for the new career men.

These revisions were hardly innovative. France, Austria and Russia based their armies entirely on long-service soldiers. Boyen himself had advocated substantial cadres of *Kapitulanten* for the active regiments. Whether Roon perceived the modifications as a serious attempt at compromise or an attempt to buy time remains uncertain. He did, however, make periodic references during this period to the career and eventual fate of the Earl of Strafford, the first minister of Charles I of Britain, who, in the seventeenth century, temporarily broke the parliamentary opposition but ended up in the hands of the royal executioner.[98]

Outside the king's immediate circle, most senior commanders and staff officers seem to have agreed in their dislike of politicians in general and liberal politicians in particular. They were committed to the principle of royal command of the army — including the length of active service. They were reluctant to risk the traditional privileges of the officer class. Those beliefs, however, did not make them fertilizer for a military dictatorship. Prussia could sustain a great-power army only by some approximation of general conscript service. Direct experience, and Prussian traditions extending back to Frederick the Great, indicated that popular acceptance of such service was crucial to its success. Effective training of conscripts required their positive participation.[99] Roon might propose, in theory, to increase the number of long-serving 'professional privates' in the army's ranks, but particularly in an expanding economy, the pool of potential volunteers for that kind of career was a shallow one. As much to the point, since the Napoleonic Era, 'mercenary' had become a far more pejorative term in Prussia's officer corps than elsewhere in Europe. For all the rhetorical opposition to 'militias' and 'civilians in uniform', ordinary captains, colonels and generals had made their careers in the environment of a conscript people's army, and correspondingly tended to perceive this as the norm. The purpose of the military reforms was to strengthen the army by making it younger, fitter and better trained — not to emasculate it by filling the ranks with disaffected time-servers kept in order by threats of the guardhouse and military prison.

From the Chamber's perspective as well the time seemed right to seek a middle ground. The Progressives' rapid rise had unsettled those 'old liberals' who feared for their place in the parliamentary pecking order. The businessmen, increasingly influential in the liberal movement, had cooperated very successfully with the administration since William's

---

[98]Cf. Roon's memorandum of 10 October 1863 in *Militaerische Schriften Kaiser Wilhelms*, vol. II, pp. 479 ff. and *Denkwuerdigkeiten*, vol. II, p, 107.

[99]See Dennis Showalter, *The Wars of Frederick the Great* (London, 1996), for an analysis of Old Regime Prussia's conscription and training methods.

accession on issues like property tax reform and the easing of government restrictions on private enterprise. The Prussian bureaucracy was proving itself cooperative when public welfare seemed to clash with private profit.[100] Even the most fire-eating of parliamentary rhetoricians, moreover, did not propose to challenge the government in the streets. That had been tried once.

Did the liberal opposition by now see the issue of military reform as the entering wedge for a parliamentary system? The answer remains unclear.[101] At no time during the constitutional conflict did any party, as opposed to particular individuals, raise that issue. On the other hand, the concept of the state as representing and personifying the community as opposed to particular interests had a long tradition in Prussia – one recently developed in the thought and writing of Hegel, whose work was generally familiar to the university and gymnasium graduates who dominated Prussian politics.[102] In that context, the opposition's working common denominator was to restore a balance that the government was tilting in its favour. The next desirable step was more general cooperation between the government's legislative and executive branches. If German nationalists had been the first to emphasize Prussia's role in the new order, Prussian Progressives were not far behind. The nationalists in their ranks understood a strong army as vital if Prussia were to act as a catalyst of unification.[103] What happened after that might well be left to the stream of time and the cunning of reason.

[100]Cf. Brophy, 'Salus Publica Suprema Lex', pp. 122–51 and Hermann Beck, The Origins of the Authoritarian Welfare State in Prussia: Conservatives, Bureaucracy, and the Social Question, 1815–1871 (Ann Arbor, MI, 1995).
[101]The best discussion of the issue's elaborate historiography is Friedhelm Gruetzner, Liberalismus und Antiliberalismus: Kritische Studien zur Geschichtswissenschaft (Frankfurt, 1986), pp. 15 ff.
[102]Hubert Kiesewetter, 'Theorie und Praxis deutscher Machtstaatspolitik. Hegel und der Hegelianismus im 19. Jahrhundert', Jahrbuch des Instituts fuer Deutsche Geschichte 9 (1980), pp. 273–308.
[103]Andreas Biefang, 'National-Preussisch oder Deutsch-National? Die Deutsche Fortschrittspartei in Preussen 1861–1867', Geschichte und Gesellschaft 23 (1997), pp. 360–83 and the still useful H. A. Winkler, Preussischer Liberalismus und deutscher Nationalstaat (Berlin, 1964).

3

Seeking Resolution

The Prussian constitutional conflict took the course it did, in good part, because it was the first event of its kind in Europe since the era of constitutions began during the 1820s. From Belgium to Bavaria and Berlin to Madrid, these documents had been drawn up so as to finesse whenever possible such 'wedge issues' as those now confronting Prussia. A comparison might be made to the successive French assemblies, which, from the doubling of the Third Estate to the Thermidorean Revolution, proved unable to deal with the concept of a loyal opposition. Another more pointed possibility is to investigate the increasing difficulties of the United States in coming to terms with the appropriate relationship of federal and state authority – difficulties that eventually escalated into the nineteenth century's bloodiest war.

Lack of precedents meant that, from the beginning, no one on either side of Prussia's army-reform issue had any useful models of crisis management. At best, that invited gridlock. With someone like Manteuffel in the picture, it invited polarization. Moving to one extreme or the other was intellectually and emotionally easier than engaging adversaries convinced of their moral rectitude, while simultaneously developing rules and tools of engagement sufficiently sophisticated that the state did not collapse altogether. Participants, moreover, shared a conviction that post-conflict circumstances must be sustainable in the long run, tenable, rather than merely offering a breathing space before the next mortal clash – a mindset not conducive to easy compromise.

I

By 1862, the Chamber did not regard the Landwehr as a non-negotiable issue. In two years the subject had lost much of its headline value. As much to the point, the ongoing discussion of military reform in liberal circles showed, with increasing clarity, that the Landwehr as it existed, as opposed to its mythic image, did not possess a strong interest-based constituency of the kind increasingly important in politics.[1] To explain that, in part, requires stepping backwards in time and sideways in issues, to examine the Landwehr officer corps.[2] In principle, captains and lieutenants were to be chosen by a two-stage

---

[1] Cf. *inter alia*, Ritter, vol. I, pp. 124 ff.; Gugel, pp. 100 ff.; and Walter, pp. 331–2.
[2] The best modern analyses of the Landwehr officer corps are Messerschmidt, *Preussisch-deutsche Armee*, pp. 67 ff. and 87 ff. and Walter, pp. 262 ff. Crouszat is good for details.

method. The Landwehr district was responsible for nominating three candidates for each vacancy; the regiment's officers chose one; and the process was subject to royal review. Battalion and regimental commanders were appointed by the corps district commanders, in cooperation with the king and, increasingly, the military cabinet. The creators and advocates of the Landwehr, Boyen in particular, had expected the pool of candidates to include the 'best and brightest' of the new Prussia – not only men from the developing middle classes, but those of humbler origins interested in and committed to serving Prussia in positions of command. In fact, the overwhelming majority of candidates for Landwehr commissions after 1815 came from the one-year volunteers. These were men of some education – the exact nature and amount could be flexible, but required gymnasium attendance or some equivalent – who were able to pay their own expenses while on active duty. They were eligible for a Landwehr commission if certified as suitable by the regiment in which they performed their active service.

From its inception, the institution of the one-year volunteer never quite found a home in the Prussian army. From the reformers' perspective, it represented a violation of the principle of universal equal military obligation, a temporarily necessary concession to a developing *Klassengesellschaft*, where money and schooling counted as well as birth. The post-reform active army, for its part, remained uncertain whether the volunteers were potential officers or enlisted men with special standing. In either case, they seldom received systematic, specialized instruction, even in the basic duties and responsibilities of a company officer. That did not entirely reflect the caste or professional prejudices of the active officer corps. For young adult 'one-years', the year of military service was frequently understood as a kind of 'latency period' between the burdens of school and the demands of work. Mastering details of drill and administration took correspondingly low priorities in their life plans. A few drinks and a little money in the right places were usually sufficient to minimize pressure from the NCOs who were primarily responsible for the everyday behaviour of these future pastors, professors and businessmen. And then – 'let the good times roll!' was likely to be the watchword.

Once selected and approved as a Landwehr officer, the newly minted lieutenant was unlikely to embark on a rigorous programme of study to make up for the things he had not learned while on active duty. The results were sufficiently plain, at drill, on parade and during field exercises, that increasing numbers of active officers were assigned to junior Landwehr posts. By 1841, almost half the infantry companies were commanded by active officers. Only four of the 108 cavalry squadrons had Landwehr officers at their heads. These figures indicate the mutual interest of Landwehr district committees and professional officers that the Landwehr not become a mere simulacrum of 'the people in arms', a hollow institution where the one-eyed led the blind. And while records on the subject are sparse and suspicious compared to those of a later era, they do indicate that Landwehr soldiers frequently preferred being commanded by active officers. When accounts are made for wishful thinking and special pleading, and with appropriate acknowledgement of the hierarchic, deferential nature of Prussian civil society, a core of evidence nevertheless indicates that Landwehr privates and NCOs respected competent arrogance more than inefficient goodwill.

The impact of these processes on the Landwehr officer corps was substantial. At one end it led to patterns of acculturation. Landwehr subalterns tended to look to the line officers as mentors and role models in military contexts. In turn, that development discouraged industrialists, merchants, commercial farmers – the kind of leading citizens the Landwehr was supposed to attract – from seeking commissions. As liberalism increasingly influenced this section of Prussia's population, the concept of spending large amounts of time in the company, and under the authority, of regular officers became correspondingly unattractive. As a consequence, even before the 1850s, the tone of the Landwehr officer corps was set by bureaucrats from the lower and middle grades, who were still in a position to perceive Landwehr service as useful in their government careers and as a means of social advancement. Far from representing the people as opposed to the aristocracy, far even from representing the rising middle class, the Landwehr officers as a body identified themselves as 'officers of the King, as good as any line officer – and nothing else but.'[3] To the extent the Landwehr maintained an independent identity, it was as a virtual throwback to the eighteenth century: a lesser 'privileged order' that had, at best, a limited voice in the streamlined Prussian Parliament of 1862.

When that situation was factored into the Chamber's general recognition that fundamental army reform was both necessary and, from parliament's perspective, desirable, it became easier to consign the Landwehr to mythic status, a 'thing laid up in heaven' to inspire future generations. That concession, however, did not take place in a vacuum. A new concept began to surface during the summer of 1862 in Berlin's political circles and on the floor of the Chamber. Given the government's own commitment to army reform, and given the fact that the reforms were already well under way, the Chamber's earlier grants of 'temporary' funding might prove to be, *post facto*, the bait on a hook. Since it was impossible to continue meeting the reform's committed expenses without some form of parliamentary consent, all the Chamber needed to do was to stand firm. Rather than either dismantle the reforms itself, or push Prussia over the brink by a coup, the government would come round and negotiate terms that gave parliament an effective voice in the military budget.[4]

This line of reasoning was strengthened when August von der Heydt, Patow's replacement as minister of finance, began discussing possibilities of a compromise. Heydt was ideal for the purpose. His previous tenure as minister of commerce, particularly his interest in railroad matters, had given him extensive contacts and high levels of credibility in both military and civilian circles.[5] In repeated conversations with the war minister, Heydt reinforced Roon's concern over the risks to Prussia's security and integrity posed by the continued deadlock. He knew that concern was exacerbated by Roon's growing conviction that Manteuffel was more than just a rival for the king's ear. The chief of the military cabinet had become a dangerously loose cannon, on the way to losing any sense he once possessed of Prussia's concrete military needs. Since assuming his new post, Roon had insisted on the importance of maintaining the army's position as a safeguard against revolution. But he also believed constitutional methods were best employed to resolve the festering conflict with parliament. On 17 September 1862, he stood before the Chamber and declared himself willing to concede a two-year term of service in return for stabilized

---

[3]Walter, p. 345.
[4]Cf. Wolfram Pyta, 'Liberale Regierungspolitik im Preussen der "Neuen Aera" vor dem Heereskonflikt: Die Preussische Grundsteuerreform von 1861', *Forschungen zur brandenburgischen und preussischen Geschichte* 57 (1992), pp. 179–247.
[5]Alexander Bergengruen, *Staatsminister August Freiherr von der Heydt* (Leipzig, 1908), is a sympathetic narrative biography; pp. 298 ff. focus on his role at this stage of the crisis.

funding. His immediate intention was to use the money to engage more long-service soldiers; his long-term hope was to establish a permanent military budget based on a fixed sum per capita for an army based on a fixed percentage of the population.[6] Old liberals and moderate progressives nevertheless responded positively. A way seemed open for the kind of compromise that would eventually become familiar in plural societies with parliamentary systems and independent executives. Then William entered the discussion.

Almost certainly angered by Roon's failure to consult with him on the proposed settlement, the king declared three-year service essential to the welfare of the army, and therefore to the well-being of the state. Any ministers unable to follow him on this issue were welcome to resign. He was himself ultimately prepared to abdicate rather than go against his judgment and conscience on this matter. Was William bluffing? His own cabinet warned him abdication would be suicide for the monarchy.[7] Certainly he judged Roon shrewdly. His statement independently engaged the war minister's conscience and emotions. Committed in principle to army reform, Roon was even more deeply committed to the principle of the monarch as commander-in-chief. Neither his staff and command service prior to 1858 nor his subsequent activity as war minister had offered much practical experience in developing a more flexible mindset. Roon once described himself as a sergeant in William's company.[8] Confronted with William's resistance, he now reacted like a sergeant instead of a general – a sergeant who feared to lose stripes that depended on his superior's whim. The war minister withdrew his proposal as quickly as he had offered it. Von der Heydt and two other ministers just as promptly resigned. The Chamber cut from the budget the funds already spent on the new army organization, ending the possibility even of further provisional funding pending a settlement. And, on 22 September, William summoned Otto von Bismarck to the royal summer palace.[9]

This turning point in the history of Prussia, Germany and Europe has generally been interpreted as evidence of the Hohenzollern monarchy's authoritarian power, the continued resistance of the officer corps and the bureaucracy to any meaningful parliamentary government, or simply William's intransigence, fuelled by Manteuffel's exhortations. Generally overlooked are the professional bases of William's insistence on the three-year question. Intellectually, William shone nowhere near as brightly as the men who surrounded him – Bismarck, Moltke, even Roon. He was, however, a soldier of long experience. No great theorist of war, his essays and memoranda on practical considerations such as training and armament are nevertheless coherent and intelligent. He took seriously his responsibilities as commander-in-chief. Certainly more than Manteuffel, arguably more than Roon, William paid attention to the progress of army reform at regiment and company levels.

The defence of three-year service and officer professionalization involved more than inculcating 'corpse-like obedience', the infamous *Kadavergehorsamkeit*, and 'purging' the conscript of undesirable 'civilian' characteristics. Its supporters argued, with increasing coherence, that the third year of active service was necessary to polish the conscript's

---

[6]Ritter, vol. I, pp. 147 ff. and Walter, pp. 337–8.

[7]Friedrich III, *Tagebuecher, 1848–1866*, ed. H. O. Meissner (Leipzig, 1929), pp. 494 ff.

[8]Roon, *Denkwuerdigkeiten*, vol. II, p. 151.

[9]Wilhelm Treue, 'Wollte Koenig Wilhelm I wirklich zuruecktreten?', *Forschungen zur brandenburgischen und preussischen Geschichte* 51 (1939), pp. 275–310, is good for the details. Andrea Harbou, *Dienst und Glaube in der Staatanschauung Albrecht von Roons* (Berlin, 1936), pp. 68 ff., empathetically analyses Roon's behaviour.

skills in marksmanship and fire discipline, to develop and inculcate the balance of obedience and initiative necessary to a man carrying a breech-loading rifle and expected to
fight in small formations and dispersed skirmish lines. Certainly two years were more
than long enough to inculcate the basics of drill. But that was only the beginning of making
a modern soldier.

As for the officer corps, reformers insisted that command on a modern battlefield could
no longer be exercised by amateurs. Particularly at company level, where most Landwehr
officers were concentrated, courage and enthusiasm must be complemented by skill in
minor tactics, an eye for terrain, the capacity to act on one's own initiative and the ability
to inspire respect in subordinates, under conditions in which the formal chain of command, with its threats of prisons and firing squads, might seem very remote. With the
best will in the world, these qualities could not be developed on occasional weekends.
They demanded full-time commitment.[10]

By 1860, the presumed tactical lessons of the Italian campaign were lending point and
heft to previously abstract contentions about the value, at regimental levels, of training
and discipline for the men, and professional competence for the officers. Authors throughout Germany praised, in particular, French dash and aggressiveness, determination to
charge home with the bayonet instead of being seduced by the temptations of long-range
rifle fire. Prince Frederick Charles enjoyed a significant reputation as a tactical theorist. In
1861 he published *Ueber die Kampfweise der Franzosen*, a paean to the simplicity and direct-
ness of French regulations and the French soldier's awareness that the best way to avoid
being shot was to get as close to the enemy as possible.

Frederick Charles and his contemporaries had no doubt that the system that worked for
the French was also applicable across the Rhine. The German soldier, bigger, more powerful and less excitable than his French counterpart, had the potential to become an even
more formidable close-quarters combatant. However, since the German states had short-
service armies and no Algerias or Crimeas, soldiers and junior officers alike must be given
peacetime training in developing judgment and initiative. They required training in overcoming the natural reluctance to close with an enemy under fire. They must be helped to
realize that the heavy losses inevitable in that process would be justified by victory. Even
if the first attack were repelled, no enemy could withstand a second or a third charge
delivered with the same intensity. Taking a month's casualties in a day or two was a fair
price for ending a campaign and a war.[11]

As Moltke's observers completed their reports in the aftermath of Villafranca, the chief
of staff also began to accept a modified version of Frederick Charles's reasoning. The general staff's history of the Italian campaign, also published in 1861, suggested that the
increasing range and accuracy of modern rifles, and, in the particular case of the needle

---

[10]Dennis E. Showalter, 'The Prussian-German RMA, 1840–1871' in *The Dynamics of Military Revolution*, eds.
M. Knox and W. Murray (Cambridge, 2002), pp. 92–113. Dierk Walter, 'A Military Revolution? Prussian
Military Reforms before the Wars of German Unification', *Forsvaarstudier* 2 (2001), makes a strong opposing
case, for the limited nature and the fundamental socio-political motivation of the mid-century reforms.
[11][Friedrich Karl], *Eine militaerische Denkschrift (Ueber die Kampfweise der Franzosen)* (Frankfurt, 1860).
Militaerische Betrachtungen ueber einige Erfahrungen des letzten Feldzuges und einige Zustaende deutschen Armeen
(Darmstadt, 1860) and F. G. von Waldersee, *Die Methode zur kriegsgemaessen Ausbildung der Infanterie und ihrer
Fuehrer im Felddienste* (Berlin, 1860), are typical examples.

gun, its high rate of fire, gave the defence an advantage best overcome at the operational and strategic levels. Properly planned concentrations, followed by the hard marching necessary for envelopments and flanking manoeuvres, would create situations when the enemy must attack. Then, Moltke argued, was the moment of the tactical defensive: rifle fire supplemented by artillery to shatter the charges and a counter-attack to turn defeat into rout. A good horseman, Moltke argued in a telling metaphor, does not force his mount against an impassable obstacle. At the same time, no army could afford to base its doctrines entirely on defensive tactics. Sometime, somewhere, it would become necessary to go through an enemy rather than around him. In that case, like it or not, decision rested with closed formations – and the training and discipline to render them effective.[12]

As suggested earlier, the officers who wrote for the military press seem to have entertained few illusions about the army's capacity to change fundamentally the values and attitudes of a conscript's lifetime in either two or three years. What they sought was institutionalization of a fact that they argued the army's liberal critics seemed to misunderstand or ignore. Arguably, since the beginning of the fourteenth century, and certainly since the end of the eighteenth, the demands of war had increasingly diverged from the circumstances of daily life at all social levels. The rise of the modern state had reduced the amount and degree of private, individual violence. The emergence of modern agricultural and industrial economies had reduced the randomness of making a living. Even death was becoming less a matter of haphazard routine and more of a predictable consequence of age or debility.

In short, for the overwhelming majority of Prussian citizens, life was less of a risk and more worth living than at any time in the state's history. What 'technicians' among the army reformers sought was not a return to the good old days of living hard and dying young. They regarded military training as a way of levelling the field, counteracting physically and emotionally what seemed to be dominant cultural assumptions about the nature of the universe with specific enlightenment on the nature of war. More pragmatically, the men who would go into future battles under Prussia's flag deserved a fighting chance to emerge alive – or, at least, for their deaths not to be in vain.

In that context, the broader socio-political consequences of three-year service appear as a kind of synergistic afterthought, broadening the reforms' appeal to conservative circles (inside and outside the army), which were by no means universally pleased either with the new weapons systems and their accompanying tactics, or with the implications that reform would have for an officer corps that would have to be expanded beyond the credible limits of the aristocracy's capacity to provide subalterns.

Officer selection in the active army at the time of the Roon reforms was based on a regulation of 1844, designed to integrate the qualities of practical knowledge, theoretical education and collegiality in the context of a peacetime army. In principle, anyone at least sixteen and a half years old and eligible for the highest level of the classical gymnasium could join the army with the intention of becoming a career officer. After passing a qualifying examination, he served approximately six months as an enlisted man. His company officers, and his battalion and regimental commanders then decided if he was suitable for appointment as an officer cadet.

---

[12]'Bemerkungen vom April 1861 ueber den Einfluss der verbesserten Feuerwaffen auf die Taktik', *Moltkes Militaerische Werke* 2, vol. II, pp. 29 ff.

The candidate's professional capacities increasingly came to be evaluated separately from his 'worthiness' to enter the officer corps. The separation is usually, and accurately, interpreted as a consequence of conservative efforts to reassert the aristocracy's privileged position in the officer corps by making social and economic criteria central to commissioning. Over 40 per cent of the officer corps had been commoners in 1819, in the immediate aftermath of the Reform Movement and the Wars of Liberation. By 1827, the proportion of non-nobles was a quarter, the lowest it was to reach in the half-century. Up to 44 per cent in 1842, the proportion of commoners sank again during the era of liberal activism that followed, years when an army career was not necessarily a social advantage in many bourgeois circles. In the 1850s commoners became eligible to enter the cadet schools, whose graduates were legitimately considered to have a significant advantage over other candidates in meeting criteria of 'worthiness'. By 1861 approximately a third of the active army's officer corps was non-aristocratic in its social origins.

This was a significantly lower proportion than in the armies of Saxony, whose ratio was 50 per cent, and Bavaria, where the proportion of commoners reached two-thirds. It was, nevertheless, unacceptable to Manteuffel, who insisted well before the constitutional conflict that even the limited educational criteria of current policy worked to the disadvantage of noblemen's sons, and who, after 1860, bitterly opposed accepting Landwehr officers into the line to cover the reformed army's increased need for officers. Commoners' prospects for reaching higher rank were limited in any case. In 1855, 13 per cent of the infantry and 11 per cent of the cavalry regiments were commanded by commoners. A decade later the respective percentages were 5 and 6 per cent. A third of the artillery regiments were commanded by colonels of non-noble origins, but the traditional bourgeois presence in that arm was increasingly challenged by aristocrats who perceived the growing importance of artillery to modern war and sought careers by following the guns.[13]

A disproportionate number of commoners in the active officer corps were, moreover, 'bourgeois' by designation rather than from a sense of class-consciousness. Even during the Wars of Liberation, non-noble candidates for commissions in the active army had been heavily drawn from civil servants and civil-service aspirants – a category including clergymen's sons in Protestant Prussia.[14] Given the nature of service in the five decades of peace that followed, its slow promotion and its decades of routine, men were unlikely to seek an army career unless, for whatever reasons, they had accepted the army's norms, well before undertaking the process of commissioning. Whether or not they possessed a 'von' before their family names, Prussian active officers at mid-century were increasingly, though not yet overwhelmingly, aristocrats by ascription.

This by itself was no setback for craft competence. No more than noble birth, commoner status did not automatically confer either aptitude for or commitment to a life in uniform. The exhilaration of expansion and the tradition of 'educated soldiers' kept manoeuvre grounds and officers' messes humming as 'every major, yes, every captain,

---

[13]Karl Demeter, *Das deutsche Offizierkorps in Gesellschaft und Staat, 1650–1945* (rev. ed., Frankfurt, 1962), pp. 11 ff. and 76 ff. and Messerschmidt, 'Preussische Armee', pp. 13 ff. and 60 ff.
[14]This is a central theme of Clinton Grubbs's forthcoming doctoral dissertation at the University of Illinois: 'The Hohenzollerns' Levée: The Mobilization and awakening of Prussian Society during the War of Liberation, 1813–1815'. I wish to thank the author for allowing me to read parts of his manuscript in draft form.

[sought] to invent something new and thereby attract attention to himself.'[15] In June 1861, the army received new manoeuvre regulations. Their preparation had absorbed a good deal more of the army's energy than what seemed to be remote political squabbling in Berlin. Future infantry combat, the document suggested, should seek to engage the enemy in a firefight, manoeuvre him into the open, exhaust his reserves and then destroy him – a process of stages, closer to Moltke's concept than to the prince's advocacy of going in and smashing things. Company columns were recommended as the normal combat formation, with their preferred employment being to manoeuvre rapidly in search of flanks and weak spots, taking maximum advantage of cover in both defence and attack. At the same time, however, battalion columns were encouraged whenever it was desirable to get somewhere in a hurry and in large numbers. The strength of skirmish lines was reduced, on the grounds that the needle gun's firepower allowed for performing the same mission with fewer men. Company commanders were repeatedly warned to keep their men well in hand and not allow them to dissolve into an uncontrollable mass.[16]

In short, the Prussian army was still grappling with the problem of developing functional balances among firepower, shock and moral force. A difficult enough task under any conditions, it was complicated further by the fog and friction inherent in the comprehensive reorganization that accompanied the reforms. Officers and NCOs were promoted and reassigned to units where no one knew anyone else; existing formations saw networks and relationships of decades' standing disappear in a matter of weeks; regiments took the field for manoeuvres when they were still at the company-drill stage. It was scarcely surprising that results were spectacular but unimpressive. In the exercises of 1861, senior officers on both sides deployed their men or held them in battalion columns at suicidally short ranges, attacked strong positions frontally without any preparation and ignored terrain features whenever it suited them. William's son, Crown Prince Frederick, a solid field soldier as well as a royal heir, criticized the performance of the Prussian Guard in tones to which the officers of that élite formation were unaccustomed.[17] French and British observers mocked the Prussian efforts in regimental messes and newspaper columns alike. 'They are compromising the whole profession', the French general, Maximilian Forey, declared loftily.[18] In 1870, French generals would find Forey's words returning to haunt them. But in 1861 they were a barbed reminder to every Prussian policy-maker that the world did not stop for constitutional conflicts, no matter how fundamental the principles at stake.

II

Developments south of the Main only exacerbated Prussian concerns. The débâcle of 1859 had inspired a spectrum of reforms and initiatives in Austria, which, in the minds of many contemporary observers, had the consequence of putting the Habsburg army on a level with any in Europe – the French included. In what it was possible to see as a sharp contrast with Prussian behaviour, Franz Josef extended, if not the hand of fellowship,

---

[15]Hohenloe, vol. I, p. 263.
[16]*Allerhoechsten Verordnungen ueber die groesseren Truppenuebungen* (Berlin, 1861) and the brief commentary in Jany, pp. 231–2.
[17]Friedrich III, pp. 109–10 and 214–15.
[18]Wilhelm Bigge, *Feldmarschall Moltke. Ein militaerisches Lebensbild* (2 vols., Munich, 1901), vol. II, p. 106.

then the fingers of conciliation to the German liberals who were the core of the empire's economic growth and political opposition. The February Patent of 1861 created a bicameral parliament, a Reichsrat whose extensive powers included control over the military budget. The boycotting of the lower house by everyone but the Germans was acceptable for a finance ministry in desperate need of middle-class support for loans and bond issues, and a foreign ministry perceiving the propaganda advantages in the German Confederation of a refurbished Habsburg image as a centralized, liberalized, Germanized state. From the position of the German liberals who dominated the rump assembly, a strong army was a desirable insurance policy against class and ethnic disorder, and influence in the military budget a long step on the way to a true parliamentary system. They were correspondingly cooperative on questions of army financing.[19]

Cooperative did not mean comatose. Spending on the army alone in 1862 was double that of Prussia, almost equal to France, and only a quarter less than in Russia. In that decade, 45 per cent of the state's income went to the armed forces. The budget cuts – from 179 million florins in 1861 to 139 million in 1862 and 118 million in 1863 – reflected, not short-sighted cheese-paring, but parliamentary hostility to the government's transparent attempts to divert army appropriations to non-military functions, particularly the system of pensions and sinecures that continued to flourish. Cuts reflected specific issues raised by specific deputies, ranging from million-florin sweetheart deals with contractors to the number of officers assigned to sinecure posts in archival research.

Budget fights were also, in no small degree, a response to the military establishment's open contempt for civilian politicians – a contempt unbalanced by the reflex deference Prussian soldiers felt, at least for the war ministry. Few armies are ever satisfied with their funding. Indeed, a certain amount of padding in proposed budgets is an understood and accepted part of the game in parliamentary systems. The Austrian army, however, tended by reflex to 'consider the source' of every proposed internal reform connected with the Reichsrat. The war ministry refused to consider modifying the structure of its large – and expensive – cavalry establishment, despite technology-driven changes in war making that suggested the obsolescence of such doctrinal principles as the massed charge, while indicating the enhanced importance of reconnaissance and screening. In another equine controversy, the army was authorized to purchase enough horses to provide teams in peacetime for the entire field artillery. It then sold off 1,300 animals and blamed parliament for refusing to replace the beasts and therefore condemning Austria's gunners to take untrained horses into the next great war. The deputies who responded that the army had used only a fraction of its available cannon in its previous recent campaigns were dismissed as penny-pinching spoilsports. With state security at stake, what were a few horses more or less?[20]

What, indeed? The army had a case to make for the gun-team imbroglio, and for other points of dispute as well. The soldiers and the ministers, however, seldom could be bothered to learn enough of the patterns of parliamentary discourse to engage their critics. Franz

---

[19]*Oesterreichs Weg zur Konstitutionellen Monarche: Aus der Sicht des Staatsministers Anton von Schmerling*, ed. L. Hobelt (Frankfurt, 1994), gives the perspective of a leading participant. Josef Redlich, *Das oesterreichische Staats-und Reichsproblem* (2 vols., Leipzig, 1920–6), remains a useful overview of the reforms and their implications.

[20]Wawro, 'Inside the Whale', *passim* and 'The Austro-Prussian War', vol. I, pp. 191 ff.

Josef had lost none of his determination to maintain control over the army, from issues of policy to questions of regimental proprietorship. He convinced General August Degenfeld, one of the few high-ranking soldiers whose knowledge of finance exceeded putting bills in one pocket and cash in another, to assume the war ministry in October 1860. He sidetracked Gruenne in favour of General Franz Folliot de Crenneville. Hess was retired in 1860 and replaced as chief of staff by Ludwig Benedek. All three were improvements on their predecessors, at least in terms of raw ability. All three immediately ran foul of long-established patterns of entropy in the army and the administration. Crenneville achieved the most success because he was the least interested in changing anything, and the most willing to blow with the winds prevailing around the emperor. As war minister, Degenfeld sought to eliminate the influence that proprietors possessed over 'their' regiments in favour of centralizing control in his office. He attempted to base promotion policies on service and talent as well as birth and favouritism. He tried to establish the general staff as the sole conduit of orders. In each case he was challenged by Crenneville and/or Benedek – who saw these changes as threatening their own prerogatives – and by the even more extreme conservatives whose extra-official connections to the emperor gave weight to their whims. The system of army procurement proved even more resilient; Degenfeld's attacks on corruption and favouritism resembled nothing so much as punching the proverbial sack of wet manure: expended energy and ruined clothes, but no tangible consequences.[21]

As for the general staff, its secondary status was reinforced when Benedek was simultaneously appointed governor-general of Hungary in January 1861 – a full-time job if ever one existed in the Habsburg Empire. Six months later he did give up the post – only to transfer to Italy as commander of a field army in that vital province. More than any senior officer in the mid-century Austrian army, Ludwig Benedek continues to generate controversy. He has been portrayed as a well-intentioned fighting soldier, victimized by the system he served. He has also been characterized as an incompetent blackguard possessing neither ability nor character. Part of his problem was a public persona calculated to endear him neither to the staff officers nor the academics who write most of the books. Benedek belonged to a new breed of generals that emerged as a consequence of the French Revolution and the subsequent development of what might be called public opinion. He was a self-conscious field soldier, a 'general in muddy boots' – at least metaphorically – who constantly called attention to the state of his footwear.

The reality, and image, of the *Haudegen* was nothing new in Europe's armies. The Bourbon Restoration and the long years of peace after 1815, however, had fostered increasingly favourable images of the presumed model of Napoleon's marshals: men who, whatever their birth, earned their rank and status in the front lines. Specifically, Radetzky rather than Archduke Charles was the image to which Austrian officers aspired – those officers, at least, who saw themselves as fighting men rather than sinecurists. 'Vater Radetzky', with his homely proverbs and common touch, his unassuming courage and his driving will – that was an archetype worth emulating. 'In your camp is Austria. The rest is fragments', the poet Grillparzer had written of Radetzky in the darkest days of 1848. Benedek, who had served under Radetzky, may have entertained hopes of inspiring a similar couplet.

---

[21]Ibid., pp. 51 ff. and Schmidt-Brentano, *passim.* Cf. Klaus Koch, *Franz Graf Crenneville: Generaladjudant Kaiser Franz Josephs* (Vienna, 1984), pp. 161 ff.

At the risk of belabouring an obvious point, there is nothing intrinsically dishonest about cultivating a public persona. 'Authenticity' is a virtue more often praised in the abstract than validated in reality – particularly among soldiers who, it may be argued, are required by the fundamental demand of their craft to be ready to behave in ways likely to bring a private citizen to the penitentiary or the madhouse. Nor, in an army where officer–man relationships had become increasingly remote since the Seven Years War, was it necessarily a bad decision for Benedek to seek a bit of the common touch. One thing he recognized more clearly than most of his counterparts was that the development of ethnic identity in the ranks, which had done so much to divide the army in 1848, could not be combated with rhetoric and courts martial. Nationalism was, in Benedek's mind, the principal direct threat to the empire's integrity. Its spread in the army, however, owed less to ideological conviction on the part of the rank and file than to its utility in providing shape and focus for a group identity that was more negative than positive – a consequence of the officer corps' detachment, in practice and in principle, from the men it commanded.

The problem lay in Benedek's choice of methods. He fraternized with enlisted men, drank with them, and took every opportunity to mock idle aristocrats and 'professors in shoulder straps'. He took corresponding pride in his indifference to theories of war, details of administration and any approach to fighting more complex than straightforward head-bashing. It was a style of leadership that distanced Benedek from his ostensible subordinates on the general staff, who found themselves mocked by the man supposed to set an example. Combined with a talent for intrigue, it also alienated him from a significant number of just those senior officers on whom he would have to depend to translate his particular vision of war into operational and tactical realities.[22]

Benedek's approach, however, may be viewed from another perspective. As suggested earlier, it fitted a pattern popular elsewhere on the continent, particularly in the French Second Empire, whose generals and marshals preened their status as warriors, where a senior general allegedly declared that no officer whose name appeared on the cover of a book could expect promotion. At least on the surface, moreover, it was congruent with an area where reform did make significant strides after 1859. Austria's failure in northern Italy was widely – and not inaccurately – viewed by most of the participants as a failure of tactics rather than policy, planning or strategy. Specifically, small Austrian formations, able neither to move nor to shoot, had been isolated, broken or overrun by their larger French counterparts. The response at regimental-officer levels was to improve physical fitness and moral fervour, to increase the size of tactical formations and to emphasize offensive action at every opportunity and under every circumstance. A new generation of company and battalion commanders relearned what their counterparts of 1760 and 1805 had known: few men stood in place long enough actually to be bayoneted. Instead, one side or the other discovered urgent business to the rear. In that context, morale seemed

---

[22]The most scathing indictment of Benedek is Geoffrey Wawro, *The Austro-Prussian War. Austria's War with Prussia and Italy in 1866* (Cambridge, 1996). James G. Huckenpoehler, 'From Cracow to Koeniggraetz: Feldzeugmeister Ludwig Ritter von Benedek and the Shifting Balance of Power in Central Europe: 1849–1866' (dissertation, George Washington University, 1990), is more favourable and less eloquent. Oskar Regele, *Feldzeugmeister Benedek und der Weg nach Koeniggraetz* (Vienna, 1960), speaks with the voice of Austria's military history establishment, offering sympathetic, measured condemnation of Benedek for making Austria look bad while losing.

more important than firepower, and conditioning more significant than marksmanship. In consequence, the standard tactical formation became a battalion column. These columns, however, were not the deep masses usually evoked by the term. They were shallow rectangles of six companies grouped two by two, approximately sixty ranks broad and only twelve deep. They were intended to address head-on a spectrum of problems that seemed more or less intractable under the old order.

Unit cohesion had proven a major problem in 1848 and 1859. When it existed it was paradoxically blamed, however inaccurately, for negative results: collective disaffection in the first case, collective panic in the second. Nationalism, even in the primitive forms that existed in the army's subcultures, was unlikely to disappear. Supplanting it with dynastic identity would take time, if it could be done at all. Moreover, whatever had been the case in the eighteenth century – and even then Austrian infantry had never been remarkable for its cohesion under fire – the current army's morale was ill-adapted to taking a pounding in place. At Magenta and Solferino, battalions dispersed in divisions or massed in reserve had tended to unsteadiness even before the French infantry came forward. But since at least the seventeenth century, armies had understood the value of joint, rhythmic, large-muscle activity for developing common action, in spite of individual wills to the contrary. The Austrian battalion envisaged by the new doctrine was not a dull and lifeless mass. Instead it was an organism, galvanized by systematic group preparation to intimidate an enemy into flight.

The Austrians' ruling concept was that speed did more than mass to create shock. A series of instructions, culminating in the revised drill regulation of 1861, prescribed callisthenics and wind sprints as central to infantry training. Obstacle courses vied for place with drill grounds – at least in principle. Furthermore, cultivating physical fitness was a good thing in itself. In a specifically military sense, the campaign in Italy seemed to have demonstrated that Austria's rank and file found it difficult to endure the rigours of even a limited campaign. Not a little of this, in turn, was due to a combination of early lives of excessive privation with army routines that offered too much idle time and put too much emphasis on bursts of activity – drills, parades, fatigues – as opposed to conditioning men for endurance over long periods. Men who could march with full packs and then charge at full speed were not only the kind of soldiers Austria needed, but the kind of subjects as well.[23]

Close-order assault also played to the presumed strengths of the regimental officers, as opposed to exposing their weaknesses. The ideal of a captain or lieutenant, as developed since Waterloo in most continental armies, was a man of action, uncorrupted by either the pale cast of higher-order military thinking or the shopkeeper's mentality that took time to calculate terrain, weather and enemy positions before ordering a charge. On a more prosaic level, basic communication had proven a major problem under combat conditions in Italy. The image of the Habsburg officer conversant with half a dozen of his multicultural empire's languages is a post-Koeniggraetz construction. Neither at home nor in the cadet academies were junior officers likely to develop fluency in the tongues spoken in their

---

[23]Cf. *inter alia*, Andres, 'Vergleichende Uebersicht des franzoeschen und oesterreichischen Tirailleursystems', *Oesterreichische Militaerische Zeitschrift* (1860), vol. II, pp. 193–9; 'Ansichten ueber ein neues Manoevrierreglement der K. K. oesterreichischen Infanterie', ibid. (1862), vol. II, pp. 46–50; and J. Schweinitz, *Entwurf einer Reorganization der oesterreichischen Armee* (Vienna, 1862).

regiments, save by accident.[24] Even in the 1860s, German was the language of polite discourse everywhere Magyar was not. The other tongues were just beginning to emerge from long-time status as 'kitchen speech', used to communicate on basic levels with low-order servants, and, for upwardly mobile Austrians, not infrequently cousins or grandparents as well. The languages themselves were often still in dialect stages, whose spoken forms could vary sufficiently among themselves to baffle even a willing student. Nor were recruits as likely as in later years to have picked up a 'hearing awareness' of German: a smattering of words and phrases acquired at school or by osmosis. As late as 1854, less than a quarter of them were literate, even by the army's elastic standards.[25]

The army's everyday response to this linguistic chaos was to develop 'regimental dialects' — sometimes fairly elaborate, German-based, with more or fewer loan-words from the languages spoken by the conscripts — which were used to conduct everyday business. Developed as well was a pattern of relying on senior NCOs, men with long service and experience, to function as interpreters, not only in the literal sense, but on broader matters of morale and welfare, much like the Indian officers, the jemadars and subadars, of Britain's Indian army, as they developed after the revolt of 1857.[26] These approaches worked well enough under peacetime conditions in an army that (a leading authority concludes) did not treat its enlisted men badly, on the whole.[27] In the field, however, casualties, fog and friction combined in 1859 to gridlock some formations entirely, and to create significant problems of command and discipline in most others. Claiming inability to understand the *Herr Leutnant* might not be an ideal defence in a court martial. But an officer, trying to hold together, under fire, men who responded to his exhortations with blank stares, might be pardoned if his own bowels began turning to water. Enforcing discipline by direct action was constrained by the fact that even one of the new percussion revolvers held only six shots and took a long time to reload. It seemed more promising to make athletes out of privates than linguists out of subalterns. The new dispensation's emphasis on standing in front of a company, sword in hand, as the bugles blew the charge, was, at worst, a better preliminary to dying well.

A similar mindset informed the army's approach to marksmanship. Shooting in Italy was so bad that, after Magenta, all attacks were required to be made with the bayonet alone. When the issue re-emerged in peacetime, a strong consensus emerged at regimental levels that the ordinary Austrian conscripts lacked the intelligence to comprehend the mysteries involved in setting and adjusting the sights on their new Miniés. Non-commissioned officers, whose grades depended more on length of service and ability to play the system than any particular talent for field soldiering, were unlikely to make up the difference. That perspective involved more than simple class or ethnic prejudice. The Habsburg army

---

[24]'Der Offizier soll die Sprache seiner Mannschaft kennen', *Oesterreichische Militaerische Zeitschrift* (1868), vol. I, pp. 65–6. Déak, *Beyond Nationalism*, pp. 99 ff., establishes the officer corps' collective linguistic limitations, even in the second half of the nineteenth century.

[25]Schmidt-Brentano, p. 70. Klaus Frommert, *Die Sprachenfrage im oesterreichischen Unterrichtswesen, 1848–1859* (Graz, 1963), is a case study of the language issue in another major secondary institution. Cf. V. Zaceck, *Palacky: The Historian as Scholar and Nationalist* (The Hague, 1970).

[26]Cf. D. N., 'Ueber die Truppensprachen unserer Armee', *Oesterreichische Militaerische Zetischrift* (1862), vol. II, pp. 365–7 and David Omissi, *The Sepoy and the Raj: The Indian Army, 1860–1940* (London, 1994).

[27]Schmidt-Brentano, pp. 422 ff.

tended to view marksmanship in terms of what a later generation would call 'athleticism': an inborn — or at least cultural — talent as opposed to a generally transferable, ultimately teachable skill.[28] The mountaineers of the Tyrol and the *Grenzer* of the Ottoman frontier, so the idea went, were born into environments making them hunters and skirmishers from childhood. Until mid-century they had provided the bulk of the Habsburg army's light troops, and set the standards for those formations. The Italian war, however, demonstrated that the *Grenzer*, in particular, had lost to the march of civilization most of whatever cultural heritage as marksmen and skirmishers they had ever possessed. The typical soldier in a *Grenz* regiment by 1860 was a peasant whose everyday life was not essentially distinguishable from his counterparts in Bohemia or Bukovina.[29]

But did the changes in warfare occasioned by developments in weapons technology really require specialized light infantry to prepare the way for the lightning strike of the columns? By 1815, the light infantry regiments of the French army were distinguished from the rest primarily by details of uniform and nomenclature. In 1838, France had formed an experimental battalion of *chasseurs à pied*. It proved so successful that by 1853 there were twenty of them in the order of battle. Armed with rifles, and given a distinctive drill and training emphasizing skirmishing and marksmanship, the *chasseurs* attracted wide attention for their performance in Africa and the Crimea. In the Germanies, professional opinion was initially against what seemed a policy of creating a pool of specialized élite units by skimming the best from the rest.[30] Austria's collective military mind was apparently changed in 1859. In 1848 the army had a dozen jaeger battalions. The number tripled by the 1860s. They remained distinguished, however, more by title than function. Their personnel did not differ significantly from the line units. Their training emphasized close order and bayonet charges. They were enjoined to spend in combat as little time as possible doing skirmish work.[31]

In part, however, the role of preparing attacks was reassigned. The artillery had long been a stepchild of the Austrian army, depending on the train for its drivers until 1850. In 1859 it took the field armed with smooth-bore guns whose basic designs had been unimproved since the Napoleonic era. There was not a dissenting voice from anywhere among the gunners' community when the war ministry put forward a proposal to rearm the artillery completely — and to rearm it, moreover, entirely with rifled cannon. The finance ministry's more desiccated bureaucrats grumbled reflexively about costs, but parliament found this the kind of expense that, in the minds of most deputies, the army should be making. By 1863 the army accepted designs for the new guns; by the end of 1864 the changeover was virtually complete.

There was nothing particularly remarkable about the weapons themselves, four- and eight-pounder bronze muzzle-loaders. Bronze was a well-tested gun metal whose theoretical weaknesses when subjected to the heavier charges of rifle pieces did not outweigh the

---

[28]As in 'Einiges ueber das Feuergefecht der Infanterie', *Oesterreichische Militaerische Zeitschrift* (1863), vol. III, pp. 377–83.

[29]Gunther E. Rothenberg, 'The Struggle over the Dissolution of the Croatian Military Border, 1850–1871', *Slavic Revue* 23 (1964), pp. 63–78.

[30]As in Wilhelm Ruestow, *Geschichte der Infanterie* (2 vols., Nordhausen, 1862), vol. II, pp. 336 ff.

[31]See the critical analysis in 'Ueber Jaegerwesen', *Oesterreichische Miitaerische Zeitschrift* (1863), vol. III, pp. 113–20 and 169–81.

perceived risks of adopting an expensive and untested metal like the cast steel the Prussian artillery was in the process of introducing. Similarly, gunners and technicians alike agreed that the problems of designing and manufacturing a gas-tight breech on a large scale were sufficient to overcome any theoretical advantages. Prussia might favour the breech-loaders offered by Alfred Krupp, but it might also pay an unexpected price when their new cannon began exploding randomly in the field. Nor did the Austrian artillery's rank and file, usually selected for their size and strength, seem promising material for crews of guns whose breeches required systematic maintenance and careful attention. It is, indeed, no exaggeration to say that a good number of men in a good number of Austrian batteries were unfamiliar with how an elevating screw mechanism worked, or how to calculate ranges. But the guns were sturdy and reliable. With shell ranges of around 3,600 metres for the four-pounder and over 4,000 for its heavier stablemate, they would not be outshot by any possible rival.

The revised Austrian artillery doctrine had no place for the recently developed large-calibre smooth-bore shell guns, called 'Napoleons' in America, which continued to form a major element of artillery parks elsewhere on the continent. Paradoxically, this decision, in good part, reflected the demands of the new infantry tactics. The concept of overcoming and overrunning positions by moral shock instead of physical mass was most defensible in a context of infantry against infantry. The principal justification for the shell guns' adoption was their presumed efficacy on the defensive, at short and medium ranges, against skirmish lines and other assault formations. An Austrian tactical doctrine based on the offensive would therefore have little need of them. Rifled cannon, on the other hand, could silence enemy smooth-bores at ranges outside the latter's ability to reply, and keep his outnumbered rifled pieces from interdicting infantry charges whose pace, in any case, would be too fast to allow guns to range on it. Each Austrian brigade was assigned two or three four-pounder batteries as a base of fire, with the rest of the artillery held in corps and army reserve. This decentralization, the norm in Europe, and across the Atlantic as well for much of the Civil War, was considered to maximize the rifle's potential as a precision weapon, able to silence guns and intimidate infantry, not with volume but with accuracy of fire.[32]

In order to implement a general doctrine intended to demoralize and disrupt an enemy by getting inside his decision-making loop, higher structures changed as well. The Austrian army of the Age of Metternich was organized along lines made familiar by Napoleon. Army corps, expected to function as independent tactical entities, were subdivided into divisions, brigades and then regiments. However, 1859 suggested that this structure lacked the flexibility demanded by modern war. The chain of command had too many links – and included too many senior officers who were slow-witted or became confused under stress. A fundamental reorganization abolished the division entirely. An Austrian corps now consisted of three to five brigades (four was the standard), each including two three-battalion regiments of infantry and a battalion of jaeger. With a war strength of around

---

[32]Fritz Wiener, 'Die oesterreichische Artillerie im Feldzug von 1866: Organization, Waffen und Geraet, Kampfweise', *Artillerierundschau* 5 (1966), pp. 101–10, is a good modern overview. Cf. J. F., 'Die oesterreichischen Feldgeschuetzbatterien mit gezogenen Roehren', *Oesterreichische Militaerische Zeitschrift* (1860), vol. I, pp. 47–53; 'Ueber die Beschaffenheit den Gebrauch und die Ausruestung der K. K. Oesterreichischen neuen Feldgeschuetze im Jahre 1863', ibid. (1864), vol. I, pp. 273–83 and 371–84; and 'Ueber Eintheilung und Gebrauch der Artillerie im Felde', ibid. (1865), vol. I, pp. 120–6.

8,000, the brigades had enough mass to do damage, especially if properly coordinated and supported. They were easier than divisions to control under tactical conditions, where noise, smoke and adrenalin created a confused battlefield as well as a dispersed one. They offered independent command opportunities to relatively junior generals, who would now be able to begin taking advantage of fleeting opportunities. They promised flexibility to corps commanders, whose tactical options were now less constrained by conventions like the 'two up, one back' format of modern western armies.

The new-model corps also provided fresh opportunities for a uniquely Austrian institution. The *adlatus* was what amounted to a deputy corps commander. No army has a superfluity of men able to command a corps effectively. On one level, the *adlatus* post was just another Habsburg sinecure: a means of absorbing excess senior officers. On the other hand, a single *adlatus* was less redundant than two or three division commanders, and might readily find useful employment commanding a flank march or a holding attack, without adding a permanent link to the chain of command. He could also step in if his superior became a casualty, without disrupting the chain of command by an emergency promotion or having to find the new corps chief in the middle of a battlefield.[33]

The new tactics and the new organizations involved more than cynicism about the quality of the army's rank and file; more, too, than concern with providing appointments for generals. The craft of war was increasingly being considered, even by its less self-consciously intellectual practitioners, in the context of the rule-of-thumb empiricism fostered by industrialization and *Realpolitik*. Ardant du Picq, a French field officer, went so far as to develop and circulate a questionnaire among his compatriots: a series of inquiries regarding exactly what had happened – and when – to the commands a particular officer had led in battle. Du Picq combined the answers with his own evaluation of classical and early modern experience to conclude that shock was a moral rather than a physical concept, and that fear rather than courage was the starting point for understanding behaviour in battle. Man, asserted du Picq, enters battle not to fight, but for victory. He does everything he can to avoid the first and achieve the second. In practice, no troops could be expected to stand for any length of time under the fire of modern weapons. Nor could unmotivated phalanxes of men massed in close formation be expected to push home an attack. What was required, du Picq concluded, was the mobilization and focus of energy, of *élan vital*.[34]

Austrian officers and tactical theorists reached an essentially similar conclusion in reforming the army's tactics and formations after 1859. The winds of change blew strongly enough in Austria's army to create an impression of successful response to a salutary lesson. Whatever shortcomings might emerge under pressure – and the coming years would parade them in detail – the innovations made at the army's sharp end were remarkably rapid for any complex system, let alone one with Austria's well-merited reputation for gridlock.

---

[33]During the American Civil War, operations were frequently influenced by delays in notifying a new superior that he was now in command, then notifying his successor. An often-cited example is the Confederate attack on the Round Tops at Gettysburg on 2 July, 1863. The wounding of John Bell Hood left his division uncommanded for a critical length of time, and the consequences of the resulting loss of focus remain a subject of intense debate among the battle's micro-historians.

[34]C. J. Ardant du Picq, *Battle Studies*, tr. Col. J. N. Greely and Maj. R. C. Cotton (New York, 1921).

The army's new shock tactics were most likely to succeed in operational and strategic matrices similarly inclined towards the offensive, and as part of a state policy of calibrated assertiveness – picking enemies and opportunities. Instead, in 1861, Hess – whose removal from the general staff had in no way removed him from the emperor's personal counsellors – proposed a complicated plan for increasing the empire's fortress system to the tune of 140 million florins. In its developed version, the scheme called, at one end, for the rebuilding of minor outposts in Transylvania, and, at the other, for the transformation of Vienna itself into a state-of-the-art defensive system. Hess described this in familiar terms, as an economy-of-force measure to serve as bases and sally ports. Critics, both deputies and soldiers, cited the exponential increases in firepower, growth in the size of cities and corresponding increases in the size of garrisons required to make fortresses more than a prize to be seized at will. Meeting even a fraction of the cost of these proposals, moreover, would drain resources from a field army whose mobility and striking power had been the principal selling points for another costly spectrum of innovations. The result was a further exacerbation of strains between war ministry and parliament, with the first considering the second obstructionist, in return suffering accusations of inconsequence, and voices of compromise drowning in mutually hostile rhetoric.[35]

A possible bridge between the factions might have been a mobilization system designed to bring substantial forces to any threatened sector of the monarchy, taking advantage of regional fortifications to support and supply the concentration. That reactive capacity, in turn, would depend on the railroads. The limitations of foot marches had been demonstrated in 1859, especially for an army depending heavily on reservists – and one that continued to station regiments outside their home recruiting districts. In the context of events in 1848, and the continued growth of nationalism in the empire, the common sense of the policy could not be doubted. It created another complicating factor. Because of language differences, no matter how dire the emergency, regiments could not automatically be brought to field strength with reservists from wherever they might be stationed. Bad German spoken by a Slovak was quite unlike bad German spoken by an Italian. Even war's root words, 'water', 'ammunition', 'latrine', often had no common cognates in the empire's varied languages. Disrupting the already delicate language patterns in a unit was an invitation to chaos.

In consequence, an Austrian mobilization required tens of thousands of men, usually in small detachments, to shuttle around the state to find their parent formations. Even in Prussia, where administration was an art form, that was not an invitation to, but a proven recipe for, chaos. It was avoidable only by a long lead time between initiating mobilization and beginning a war – or, perhaps, by a movement to contact that would be rapid enough to compensate for a slow mobilization.

Hess himself recognized the centrality of rail transport for the latter process, arguing that, on the basis of events in Italy in 1859, the empire should emphasize the construction of double-track lines towards Russia and France.[36] In fact, as was the case everywhere in Europe, Austria's railway network had developed along economic rather than strategic lines. Long-standing emphasis on maintaining garrisons and fortifications in traditional

---

[35]Wawro, 'The Austro-Prussian War', vol. I, pp. 156 ff.
[36]Hess, 'Bemerkungen ueber die dringendsten Haupt-Reformen der Armee (1859)', *Schriften*, pp. 352–3.

locations meant that relationships of stations and sidings to centres of troop concentration were haphazard. As late as 1866, formations in such regions as Galicia, Transylvania and Croatia could be over a month's march from the nearest usable railhead.

In contrast to France and Prussia, Austria's staff planners did not begin developing plans for collecting rolling stock and organizing train schedules until 1863. Even then, too many details were left unconsidered. A hot noon meal, for example, was part of the normal marching schedule. Since cooking in wooden boxcars was a high-risk endeavour, formations in rail transit were halted at midday. Since many of Austria's secondary lines were single-tracked, and since a troop train's average speed was twenty miles an hour, concentration took place in slow motion. Nor could the speed of the trains be increased without risking major damage to roadbeds not designed for the pounding of dozens of fully loaded fifty-car trains at short intervals.

Nor could domestic civilian traffic be interrupted as readily as in France or Prussia. This was no simple function of private profit. The principal railroads in northern Bohemia, for example, were not only single-tracked but also served industries providing a good share of the state revenues. The emperor was primarily concerned with the commercial prospects of new construction, even when government funded or subsidized. The war ministry expended what parliamentary capital it possessed on issues of weapons procurement and pension funding. When questioned directly about progress expanding and double-tracking rail routes into Italy that had previously been funded by the Reichsrat, Degenfeld had no answer. The chief of staff of Italy's army expressed indifference as to the particular route a new road would take. In short, whatever might be said for the army's willingness to reform itself at tactical levels, the record indicates that it proposed to win its next war at the sharp end.[37]

III

Austria's dissonances at the higher levels of planning and command seemed to offer promising opportunities for both enhancing middle-German cooperation in a revived Confederation and increasing state autonomy and legitimacy through domestic reform. Saxony's prime minister, Friedrich von Beust, in particular, stood out for his energetic support of a Confederation with an improved army, a strengthened executive and a parliament with real legislative powers, whose delegates would be chosen by the states. Beust even spoke, in occasional unguarded moments, of ministerial responsibility – though that did not diminish post-forty-eighter liberals' rejection of his authoritarian domestic regime. Some policy-makers, like Bavaria's Ludwig von der Pfordten, saw a Confederation revitalized by its middle-sized members as a potential player on a European stage, a balance against Russia to the east and France to the west. This neo-Metternichian concept was, however, a bit lofty for other rulers and politicians, who hoped for no more than the ability to maintain their autonomy by playing off Prussia and Austria against each other.[38]

---

[37]Cf. Burckhard Keester, *Militaer und Eisenbahn in der Habsbuergermonarchie 1825–1859* (Munich, 1998), as a backdrop to Wawro, 'The Austro-Prussian War', vol. I, pp. 119 ff.

[38]Wolfram Siemann, *Gesellschaft im Aufbruch: Deutschland, 1849–1871* (Frankfurt, 1990), provides the model for middle-state activism. Cf. for case studies, Hubert Glaser, 'Zwischen Grossmaechte und Mittelstaaten: Ueber einige Konstanten der deutsche Politik Bayerns in der Aera von der Pfordten' in *Oesterreich und die*

Even the modest visions required underwriting by men under arms. Middle-German critics of 'adventurism' were concerned that their states should not fall hopelessly out of what was emerging as a full-scale *de facto* arms race between Austria and Prussia. Hanover acquired Krupp breech-loaders for its artillery and reorganized its infantry into four brigades on the Austrian model: each with one jaeger and four line battalions. The Saxon corps was similarly restructured, but with Austrian cannon supporting its four independent brigades. In Bavaria, Pfordten and War Minister Ludwig von Lueder, appointed to the office in 1859, agreed on the state's military requirement: an army on the French model, with limited reserve forces but a high peace strength, fully trained, equipped with state-of-the-art weapons and available at short notice to support Bavarian interests in combat. Their vision clashed across the board, however, with a parliament that was economy-minded in principle, and perfectly willing to use the army budget as a lever to force the removal of cabinet ministers whose values they disliked or whose policies they distrusted.

Bavarian constitutional tensions during this period offer an interesting, and overlooked, counterpoint to the similar crisis in Prussia. In neither state were cabinet ministers directly responsible to the parliament. But Bavaria's parliament had forty years of history and a broad base of popular support. A solid majority of its members rejected Pfordten's ambitious policy for a mixture of reasons, ranging from *Urbayrisch* distaste for seeking centre stage, to rational calculation of the state's financial capacities, to dislike of the increasingly erratic personal behaviour of King Ludwig II. The king himself favoured reducing the army's peace strength and cutting expenses rather than risking an open breach with parliament. Lueder asserted the army's requirements with such zeal that the Landtag almost charged him with violating the constitutional limitations of his office. His resignation in 1861 was a clear victory for Bavaria's parliamentary forces. They celebrated by continuing to maintain close control of the army budget. Pfordten responded by using diplomatic finesse as a substitute for guns, pursuing an assertive foreign policy that Bavaria's army was increasingly incapable of supporting with its own resources.[39]

Wuerttemberg's army benefited on two levels from the events of 1859. Its mobilization had been such a disorganized disaster that at least the administrative preparations were thoroughly overhauled. The state's upper classes responded to their involuntary and unwelcome experiences in uniform by increasing military pay and taking a growing interest in the attitudes and effectiveness of an officer corps itself drawn more and more from Wuerttemberg's liberally educated bourgeois. Infantry training was overhauled along French lines, emphasizing assault tactics that combined fire and shock. Light battalions on the French model joined the order of battle. The artillery received new guns: muzzle-loading rifles purchased in Austria. The Wuerttemberg War Ministry expressed increasing interest in Alfred Krupp's cast-steel breech-loaders. By 1866, the state was even ready to sacrifice the decades-spanning effort to adopt a common small arm for the contingents of VIII *Bundeskorps* in favour of introducing breech-loading rifles for its infantry.

The problem lay in choosing the breech-loader. Experimental designs produced by local artisans and officers were unpromising: short-ranged and unreliable. The Prussian needle

---

deutsche Frage im 19. und 20. Jahrhundert, pp. 140–88 and Andreas Neemann, 'Models of Political Participation in the Beust Era: The State, the Saxon Landtag, and the Public Sphere, 1849–1864' in *Saxony in German History: Culture, Society, and Politics, 1830–1933*, ed. J. Retallack (Ann Arbor, 2000), pp. 119–34.

[39]Eduard Wintz, *Eugen Franz Ludwig Freiherr von der Pfordten* (Munich, 1938), is a sympathetic narrative biography.

gun was tested, available – and, by all accounts, obsolescent. The results of Swiss tests made available to the Wuerttemberg army indicated that at least three models of American breech-loaders, proven during the Civil War, were significantly superior to the needle gun. But no one in Wuerttemberg had ever observed Sharps or Spencer rifles actually being used by troops. Purchasing from American sources, moreover, even at favourable post-war prices, meant the rifles would have to be shipped across an ocean, and accompanied by a complete repair and maintenance technology. The final decision was postponed until the Austro-Prussian War made the subject moot.[40]

The debate was a paradigm of the military problem confronting the German Confederation's middle-sized states. By the mid-1860s, Wuerttemberg's army was at a respectable state of effectiveness. Its men were well trained. Its officer corps was solidly professional. Unit for unit, a case can be made that it was at least as good as its Prussian or Austrian counterparts. Its relationship with parliament, and with society at large, was favourable. But it amounted to no more than a single division, at a time when great powers counted their strength in army corps. Baden, Hesse-Darmstadt, Braunschweig, Nassau – everywhere the reality was the same. The military revolution of the mid-nineteenth century had put the middle-sized states of the German Confederation out of the running in the regional-power sweepstakes, at least as independent actors. They were unable to offer numbers. 'Quality armies' had also gone beyond their means in terms of both raw expense and the opportunity costs of diverting resources from other sectors of the private and public economies. A century earlier, similar inability to compete militarily had been translated into cultural activity, with palaces replacing regiments and *belles-lettres* supplanting cannon balls.[41] Arguably a healthy response in the abstract, it had few prospects in an emerging age of blood and iron.

In February 1861, the Confederation did create a special commission to evaluate the German railway system from a military perspective. The body was dominated by its Austrian chair and his Prussian counterpart. Each man reflected his army's institutional and psychological approach to the technical aspects of military reform. Captain Wilhelm Ritter Gruendorf von Zebegeny was a self-christened progressive who had developed an auto-didactic interest in technologies from small arms to steam engines. Primarily a staff officer, a military courtier in what might for Austria be called the good sense of the term, he had positioned himself as one of the token technocrats in the Habsburg army's higher circles, frequently called upon to troubleshoot, or to explain some new tool of war to an old general. Hermann Graf Wartensleben-Carow had begun his career as an officer of cuirassiers, the heavy cavalry with a deserved reputation as the starchiest and most retrograde element of the Prussian army's mounted arm. Assigned to the general staff's second section before it concentrated exclusively on mobilization planning, he caught Moltke's eye during the manoeuvres of 1858 for his reliability, energy and capacity for hard work. He became the first of the 'demigods', the group of junior officers Moltke shaped to the measure of his ideas, and who served as his nervous system in the army at large.

Without dismissing Scharnhorst's original concept of a symbiosis between commanders and staff officers that transcended social origins, Moltke understood that such relationships

---

[40]Sauer, pp. 294 ff.

[41]Peter H. Wilson, *War, State, and Society in Wuerttemberg, 1677–1793* (Cambridge, 1995), is a case study of the phenomenon. Cf. Wilson, *Armies, War, and German Politics, 1648–1806* (London, 1998).

required time to develop and nurture. They were also likely to reflect personal rather than institutional factors. On the other hand, young men like Wartensleben, with aristocratic pedigrees and deep roots in the system, possessed at least the potential for professional development. In 1859, when Moltke needed plans for coordinating railway transport in a hurry, Wartensleben prepared them with a minimum of paperwork. He became the general staff's expert on railway issues – a career move as far as might be imagined from his days as a hard-riding subaltern of cavalry, and one speaking volumes for the success of the post-Jena reformers' concept of 'educated soldiers'. Wartensleben, a War Academy graduate, was no amateur of railroads, as Moltke had been. He acquired his knowledge, and developed the mindset to use it, on the job. In no other continental army was such a process probable, much less successful.[42]

Gruendorf, Wartensleben and their colleagues, one Bavarian and one Hanoverian, spent several months travelling around Germany, discussing the actual and potential capacities of various rail lines with owners and officials. Gruendorf provided the sociability; Wartensleben asked the hard questions; and, on the whole, the committee performed its task well. It may please today's captains and majors, as they confront inquisitorial reimbursement forms, to know that their predecessors took ample advantage of the off-duty hours of their assignment to enjoy themselves at Confederation expense. Their final report, however, was sober enough. It emphasized, above all, the problems of coordinating a railway system whose distinguishing characteristic was entropy. In the south and east, commercial and industrial interests were concentrated in the larger towns and railroads had been heavily subsidized by public funding. The result was a network with a more or less rational structure, but with fewer junctions and fewer miles of track than was the case in the north and west. There, the combination of private investment and the desire of many small states to have their own systems produced a pattern of short lines and many owners. But nowhere in Germany did the railways, public or private, have the capacity or the organization to move masses of men, equipment and supplies without military supervision.

The commission correspondingly recommended creating a central authority to supervise and coordinate the work of the military and civilian agencies operating individual routes. It also prepared detailed plans for the concentration of Confederation forces in the west in case of a war with France. This work, though a theoretical exercise, was nevertheless the first detailed, comprehensive plan for the military use of the entire German railroad network. It embodied as well the basic organizational and technical principles used in Prussian plans for rail concentration against France prior to 1871. It seems almost superfluous to add that Wartensleben did most of the detail work. What, after all, was the purpose of having a Prussian on this kind of commission, if not to make the figures come out properly?[43]

---

[42] *Hermannn Graf von Wartensleben-Carow, koengl. Preuss. General der Kavallerie; ein Lebensbild, 1826–1921*, ed. E. Graefin v. Wartensleben (Berlin, 1923).

[43] For the commission's work, see the engaging, not always entirely accurate, Gruendorf von Zebegeny, *Memoiren eines oesterreichischen Generalstaeblers 1834–1866*, ed. A. Sanger (2nd ed., Stuttgart, 1913), vol. I, pp. 158 ff. Also, Kessel, *Moltke*, pp. 234 and 308–9 and *Bericht ueber die Leistungsfaehigkeit der Deutschen Eisenbahnen zu militaerischen Zwecken erstattet durch die ... Specialcommission* (Frankfurt, 1861). W. Kousz, 'Wilhelm Ritter Gruendorf von Zebegeny' (dissertation, Vienna, 1967), corrects, in pedestrian fashion, its subject's more extreme overstatements.

The Confederation was facing other military challenges in the first half of the new decade. In the aftermath of Villafranca, a new Austrian foreign minister, Count Bernhard von Rechberg, had made mending the Prussian relationship a top priority. Rechberg was a pupil of Metternich and had a reputation as an authority on the German question. William accepted an initial Austrian overture of cooperation in preparing contingency plans for a surprise French attack. But the experts who met in Berlin found little common ground. Moltke, long an advocate of pre-crisis planning, locked horns with a Prussian foreign ministry unwilling to establish binding commitments without concessions on the familiar issues of Prussian command north of the Main and integration of the smaller north German contingents into the Prussian systems of mobilization and command.

As the military conversations faded, a political approach began to emerge. Anton von Schmerling, Austria's minister of the interior since December 1860, had been a delegate to the Frankfurt Parliament ten years earlier as an enthusiastic supporter of 'Great Germany'. Now he urged a policy of making 'moral conquests' north of the Inn by taking the lead in Confederation reform. The initial Austrian proposal was a diplomatic pawn move, recommending the creation of an ad hoc chamber of deputies and an executive committee to address legal issues on a Confederation basis. It promptly encountered Prussian opposition – not least because of its appeal to the nationalist elements in the Confederation, whose support, up till now, had given Prussia what amounted to a free diplomatic ride during its constitutional conflict. Not only was that conflict now generating some second thoughts in those circles, but also Austria suddenly seemed to be following courses congenial to businessmen increasingly inconvenienced by multiple overlapping civil laws, and intellectuals seeking to rationalize and homogenize codes and practices encrusted with generations of procedural cobwebs.

The Diet sent Austria's recommendations to committee in August 1862. Nor did frowns from Berlin retard the endorsement of those proposals by such groups as the Munich-based German Reform Association. Cleverly conducted behind-the-scenes negotiations in the major German capitals even secured for Austria an agreement that, should the Confederation collapse because of Prussian intransigence, a new organization would be formed without Prussia's presence.[44]

This was the kind of diplomatic offensive impossible to ignore, or to challenge by rhetoric alone. Rather than engage directly, however, Prussia turned to economics. What Frank Tipton calls a 'national consensus' shaped for decades an interpretation arguing that the combination of domestic economic development with the customs union of 1833, the *Zollverein*, gave Prussia a *de facto* hegemony in Germany that the Wars of Unification did no more than ratify.[45] In fact, the customs union had, at best, a limited impact on economic development in a Germany that was far more than Prussia writ large, even by the end of the nineteenth century.[46]

---

[44]Richard B. Elrod, 'Bernhard von Rechberg and the Metternichian Tradition: the Dilemma of Conservative Statecraft', *The Journal of Modern History* 56 (1984), pp. 430–55 and the still useful Enno Kraehe, 'Austria and the Problem of Reform in the German Confederation', *American Historical Review* 56 (1951), pp. 274–94, provide the background. William Carr, *The Origins of the Wars of German Unification* (London, 1991), pp. 116 ff., summarizes the events.

[45]Frank Tipton, 'The National Consensus in German Economic History', *Central European History* 7 (1974), pp. 195–224.

[46]The leading proponent of this interpretation is Helmut Boehme. See, particularly, *Deutschlands Weg zur Grossmacht* (Cologne, 1964). Cf. Frank Tipton and H. Berding, 'Die Entstehung des Deutschen Zollvereins als

For a while in the 1830s a south German and a central customs union jostled for places with their Prussian rival. What the three had in common was less economic growth than revenue-raising: rulers interested in escaping from the financial tutelage of Estates and parliaments found the union's profits attractive enough to sacrifice some of their jealously guarded independence.[47] Not until the 1840s did Prussian officials in the foreign ministry and the ministry of commerce begin considering as well the wider political prospects of a *Zollverein* that, by then, had absorbed its competitors. Even then the process began through the back door. As the largest market and the geographic centre of the union, Prussia tended to become the *de facto* mediator of choice in settling disputes among the members. The government was slow to make a systematic effort to translate the influence obtained by primacy in this commercial union into broad-spectrum leverage. Liberal nationalists, however, increasingly interpreted the *Zollverein* as the exemplar of integration through economics – not production and distribution, but economic legislation, regulating the movement of goods.[48] And in the long run, even for states otherwise concerned with maintaining their independence, economic and political cooperation tended to go hand in hand.[49]

Austria was sufficiently concerned at that prospect to initiate, in the aftermath of 1848, discussion of a customs union that would include both the German Confederation and the Habsburg Empire. This classic example of drawing a circle that took in Prussia had its share of appeal, both south of the Main and in Prussian commercial circles interested in the prospects offered by the Danube basin. But Schwarzenberg too quickly interpreted the new organization as a means of returning Prussia to its place as 'faithful second' to Austria's policies. His heavy-handedness, in turn, made the *Zollverein*'s lesser members unusually receptive to Prussian arguments that the German Confederation and the Habsburg Empire had too little in economic common to make possible anything but cooperation on particular issues. The middle states continued to regard some form of Austrian presence in the union as a safeguard against Prussia's expanding influence.[50] But Hanover broke ranks in 1852 by signing a commercial treaty with Prussia, and in 1853 the *Zollverein* treaties were successfully renewed. As a consolation prize, Vienna received a promise from Berlin that Austria's joining the union would become a subject for negotiation before the current agreements expired – in 1865.

Count Karl von Buol, who became Austrian foreign minister on Schwarzenberg's unexpected death in 1852, responded by returning to direct negotiations with Prussia. The result was a comprehensive commercial treaty whose generous terms doubled *Zollverein*

Problem historischer Forschung' in *Vom Ancien Regime zum modernen Parteienstaat. Festschrift fuer Theodor Schieder* (Munich, 1978), pp. 225–37.

[47]Frequently facing opposition from 'middling sorts' seeking to preserve traditional economic orders. See William L. Rapp, 'The Mittelstand and Politics: The Case of Hanover, 1830–1850', *German Studies Review* 4 (1981), pp. 363–81.

[48]Hans-Werner Hahn, *Geschichte des deutschen Zollvereins* (Goettingen, 1984), is the most up-to-date survey of the *Zollverein* and its counterparts. Cf. the case study, Hahn, *Wirtschaftlicher Integration im 19. Jahrhundert: Die Hessischen Staaten und der Deutsche Zollverein* (Goettingen, 1982).

[49]See the case study by Richard J. Bazillion, 'Economic Integration and Political Sovereignty: Saxony and the Zollverein, 1834–1877', *Canadian Journal of History* 25 (1990), pp. 189–213.

[50]Cf. Hans-Werner Hahn, 'Mitteleuropaeische oder Kleindeutsche Wirtschaftsordnung in der Epoche des Deutschen Bundes', *Deutscher Bund und deutsche Frage*, pp. 186–214 and H. Rumpler, *Die deutsche Politik des Freiherrn von Beust 1848 bis 1850* (Vienna, 1972).

imports to Austria in eight years, to over a third of the empire's international commerce. But the flow of commerce in the other direction was far more sluggish. Austria produced few manufactured goods that found ready markets north of the Inn, while the empire's resources in raw materials were as yet undeveloped or untransportable at acceptable costs.

The treaty's terms, moreover, included a most-favoured-nation clause that gave Prussia a pressure point: threatening to cut tariffs to a point at which Austria's 'infant industries' would become vulnerable to French and British competition. Guarantees that Berlin would never practise such low behaviour were appropriately discounted in Vienna, but in the atmosphere of economic optimism flourishing in the 1850s, the risk nevertheless seemed reasonable. Considered in absolute terms, the Habsburg Empire's economy did prosper – particularly the 'German' areas of lower Austria and Bohemia. Trade with Hungary increased and the last economic vestiges of the feudal system were dismantled. Industrialization, however, lagged behind Prussia – not least because it carried the burden of a meddling bureaucracy and dragged the shackles of a public debt that tripled after 1848, and whose servicing required repeated borrowing at rates and on terms that attracted increasing amounts of Austria's liquid capital away from the higher risks and greater uncertainties of investment in industry.[51]

The growing fundamental shift in economic balance between the two German powers was carefully noted in Berlin, where cabinet ministers and lesser officials began considering the possibilities of applying techniques developed in the politics of the *Zollverein* in alternative contexts. The new economic order was remarked elsewhere in Germany as well. When Prussia began seriously considering a recommendation of the newly organized, *laissez-faire* Congress of German Economists to significantly reduce tariffs in the interests of free trade, the *Zollverein*'s south German members blocked the measure – both for the sake of their own special interests and to improve their political standing in Vienna.

Prussia, in turn, looked across the Rhine. More than a tug-of-war with Austria was involved here. The French Empire had celebrated its victory in Italy by negotiating a series of free-trade treaties with Belgium, Switzerland and, above all, Britain, with whom relations had been strained since the Crimean War. Prussia was in no position to be left out of this newly forming commercial loop. Apart from diplomatic issues, a business community, simultaneously dazzled at the thought of expanded markets and frustrated by the *Zollverein*'s reluctance to consider tariff reform, demanded some kind of action. Given parliament's alienation by the issue of army reform, the times were not auspicious to open a second domestic front. Politics has been described as the art of compromise. It is also the craft of compensation. In March 1862, negotiations were completed for a Franco-Prussian commercial treaty that instituted a most favoured nation clause – precisely the thing Austria had insisted it could not accept.

The treaty had strong political subtexts. For Napoleon it was a prospective entering wedge, a step in his long-term policy of establishing Prussia as a combination of ally, client and stalking-horse in central Europe. For Prussia it was a flanking manoeuvre, strengthening the state's position against both the Confederation and the domestic opposition to

---

[51]T. Huerta, *Economic Growth and Economic Policy in a Multi-National Setting: The Habsburg Monarchy, 1841–65* (New York, 1977) and J. Komlos, *The Habsburg Monarchy as a Customs Union* (Princeton, 1973), cover Austria's economic growth. Boehme, pp. 81 ff., presents the German contexts and consequences.

army reform. For Austria it was an opportunity to challenge a Prussia perceived as dragging its feet on Confederation military negotiations, and whose behaviour in the tariff matter had been altogether too high-handed for comfort elsewhere in the *Zollverein*. All of its members had to agree on tariff changes implemented by any member. Berlin had been confident it could make its case – until Rechberg turned his ambassadors loose. Bavaria, Wuerttemberg, Hesse-Darmstadt and Nassau rejected the treaty with no more than minimal arm-twisting from Vienna.

Rechberg followed up this success by offering membership in a new customs union with Austria. Only in Bavaria and Wuerttemberg did significant commercial interests consider the new arrangement even remotely promising. Elsewhere, most businessmen were sufficiently confident of their ability to meet external competition that prospective shares in a large western-oriented market offered a risk worth taking – especially since Rechberg's offer seemed essentially politically motivated, without a convincing cost-benefit element. Rechberg promised to use the new organization he proposed as leverage to negotiate a new commercial treaty with France and Britain – but what was the sense of repeating the steps of the dance? Prussia responded by suggesting that there was no guarantee at all that Austria could cut the kind of deal Berlin had been able to negotiate, and indicated that if the French treaty was rejected, it would have no reason to support renewal of the *Zollverein* treaties when they came up for renewal in 1865.[52]

Prussia also began playing diplomatic hardball, protesting against the Austrian-led decision of the Confederation to restore unilaterally the constitutional order in Electoral Hesse, whose upset had triggered the Olmuetz Crisis. When the elector refused William's near-ultimatum by refusing to read it, the king prepared to send two corps into Hesse. The chances of Austria and the Confederation ignoring such an action were near zero; the prospect of Prussia finding support elsewhere in Europe was even less. It seemed a rerun of Olmuetz was in the making. Moltke was ready to go to war with the Confederation, with Austria and with France, too, should it come to that. He was also willing to pit his improved mobilization system against superior numbers and advantage of position. But even he was not eager for such a desperate struggle. Neither, on reflection, was anyone else, including William. A crown council of 23 June decided to stand down.[53]

Any conciliatory consequences of the gesture were lost when, in July, the Prussian government officially recognized the Kingdom of Italy. That bombshell made the signing of the French trade treaty on 2 August, for which it was an understood quid pro quo, more than something of an anticlimax. Since Villafranca, Austria had been committed to the principle of rejecting the reorganization of the Italian peninsula under Piedmont's auspices. Certainly the other great powers, and most of the other states of Europe, had also recognized the new government. But Prussia's action was a particular cross between a glove in the face and a knee in the groin. More than honour was involved here. The Austrian Empire depended on the dynastic principle for its existence. Making this kind of concession to ethnic nationalism opened the doors to entropy. In concrete terms, Venetia was, if anything, more economically valuable than in the preceding decade; much

---

[52]Carr, *Wars of Unification*, pp. 110 ff., summarizes and demonstrates the synergy of economic and diplomatic factors. Eugen Franz, *Der Entscheidungskampf um die Wirtschaftspolitische Fuehrung Deutschland (1856–1867)* (Munich, 1933), makes a similar case for economics as diplomacy by other means.
[53]The Hessian affair is described in Kessel, *Moltke*, pp. 330 ff.

of the Austrian state's new railway construction was oriented across the Alps – a paying project in peacetime, despite the inordinately high mileage costs. British suggestions that Venetia be transferred to the new state in return for the money Austria so badly needed were correspondingly rejected out of hand.[54]

IV

Then Otto von Bismarck took the helm in Berlin. His course, on assuming the posts of minister-president and foreign minister, has been too often discussed to require elaboration. In his initial discussions with Roon, Bismarck had emphasized the importance of breaking the deadlock between crown and parliament by shifting the focus of Prussia's policy from domestic to foreign affairs. In his first appearance before the budget committee, he announced that the time had come to use the Prussian army to solve the German question 'by blood and iron' – the signature phrase for his entire career. By the time of his official appointment, the internal crisis had reached a point where the statement produced little surprise, and even some relief in liberal circles, where Bismarck's presence had been regarded as the first step in a *coup d'état*. As for his proposed means of solving the German question, force was by no means anathema to certain nationalist elements, who spoke of the need for 'a great genius or mighty tyrant', able to take decisions transcending the complex network of limitations created by lesser political figures.

Outside Prussia, nationalists who had once placed their hopes on that state now hoped for a prompt resolution of a constitutional conflict that, to believers in the grand cause of German unification, seemed increasingly a matter of personal vanities and antagonisms. Inside Prussia, and inside the parliament, perspectives were more nuanced. Not all Prussian liberals were German nationalists. For the sake of a united front, however, opposition to the nationalist position had grown increasingly muted during the constitutional conflict. The nationalists, for their part, were convinced as a body both that unity depended on Prussia and that only a liberal Prussia could make a national revolution. It was an enduring postulate across this spectrum of liberal opinion in the Chamber that the Prussian monarchy could not tap even the vital forces, economic, intellectual and popular, that would be needed to implement an assertive foreign policy, let alone facilitate German unification. Nothing in Bismarck's previous career suggested that he possessed any unusual talent beyond that of antagonizing those with whom he sought to negotiate. To the extent that he had a public reputation, it was that of gadfly and headhunter in the Confederation context. All the opposition needed to do was to stand firm on ground they already held, and the chances were good that Bismarck would do their work for them.

Above all, standing firm meant continuing to refuse funding the new army. Even when Bismarck escalated the conflict by having the entire budget rejected by the conservative upper house and then asserting a 'theory of the gap', by which authority devolved on the crown should parliament fail to vote a budget, the liberals bided their time. This negative policy has been variously described as reflecting some combination of respect for the monarchy, support for its initiatives in the tariff matter, concern that popular support

---

[54]Richard B. Elrod, 'The Venetian Question in Austrian Foreign Relations, 1860–1866' (dissertation, University of Illinois, 1967) and Geoffrey Wawro, 'Austria versus the Risorgimento: A New Look at Austria's Italian Strategy in the 1860s', *European History Quarterly* 26 (1996), pp. 7–29.

for stronger initiatives was lacking, fear of a mass uprising, and inadequate organization of the Chamber majority. Without denying these points, it is also legitimate to suggest a strong subtext of Machiavellian *Realpolitik* in the liberals' behaviour. If, as seemed increasingly likely, Bismarck brought the state into danger by an aggressive, ill-conceived foreign policy, the people would withdraw even their passive support. The king would be in a position where either he would have to turn voluntarily to parliament for help in 'pulling the cart out of the mud', or he could be compelled to listen by cooler heads on both sides of the current divide. The constitution might be ambivalent on budget deadlocks – the *Lueckentheorie* had been asserted by conservatives and rejected by liberals for over a decade – but it clearly allowed for the impeachment of ministers.[55]

It was correspondingly important that the Chamber maintain its position as defender of the law, the constitution and the flag. That last point was particularly crucial. In the context of Prussia's and Germany's subsequent history, a national and international consensus has developed that patriotism in a German context is either the last refuge of a scoundrel or the first recourse of a fool. Prussia's liberals fitted neither category. Apart from any emotional or intellectual considerations, they were beginning to understand the domestic political value of wrapping oneself convincingly in the state's colours. To move towards absolute intransigence was to surrender moral and political ground to the conservatives – ground to which they had no right and which they could not claim unless the liberals allowed it. A comparison might be drawn in this context with the behaviour of the Democratic party in the United States during the 1960s and 70s, when a *de facto* abandoning of patriotism in its conventional senses contributed no little to two decades of Republican control of the White House, interrupted by a single forlorn Democratic interlude.

Bismarck, therefore, had all the rope he needed. It might become a lifeline; it might become a noose. His first months in office were all any liberal deputy might have wished. He began by strong-arming the Confederation Diet to reject Austria's proposals and approve the French customs treaty. Pressure was no new thing in such matters, but Bismarck's blunt assertion that if Prussia lost the vote, it would no longer consider itself bound by the confederate constitution, pushed the envelope of acceptable discourse to tearing point. In November, he repeated William's earlier ultimatum to Hesse – without consulting closely with Moltke, in whom he had no particular confidence as yet. This time it was the elector who blinked as the rest of the Confederation queasily listened to the rattle of Prussian sabres.

On a parallel track, however, as members of the *Zollverein* the small and middle states faced increasing pressure from key domestic sectors to approve the French customs treaty and its free-trade implications. An open break with Prussia might well result in the *Zollverein* dissolving as well. Apart from the internal political conflicts certain to be generated by that event, the economies of Germany had become too interdependent to support

---

[55]The extremely heated atmosphere of Bismarck's first weeks in office is best captured in Pflanze, vol. I, pp. 178 ff., which incorporates a good analysis of the literature on parliament's aims and intentions. Cf. Ludwig Dehio, 'Die Taktik der Opposition waehrend des Konflikts', *Historische Zeitschrift* 140 (1929), pp. 279–347. For the constitutional issues, see Erich Hahn, 'Ministerial Responsibility and Impeachment in Prussia, 1848–63', *Central European History* 10 (1977), pp. 3–27; Winfried Becker, 'Die angebliche Luecke der Gesetzgebung im preussischen Verfassungskonflikt', *Historisches Jahrbuch* 100 (1980), pp. 257–83; and Hans-Christof Kraus, 'Ursprung und Genese der 'Lueckentheorie' im preussischen Verfassungskonflikt', *Staat* 29 (1990), pp. 209–34.

the diplomatic pleasure of telling Bismarck what he could do with his threats. The Austrian proposals lost by a vote of nine to seven on 22 January 1863. But it was a victory purchased at the price of most of Prussia's remaining moral influence in Germany.

As he alienated the Confederation, Bismarck made an equally serious miscalculation on the European stage. In January, long-standing unrest in Russian Poland flared into open rebellion. Bismarck, seeking to solidify relations with Russia, offered support, including military cooperation, should any rebels cross the Prussian frontier. Britain, France and Austria promptly protested against Prussia's initiative from a mixture of feel-good Polonophilia and concern for a resurgent Russian influence in central Europe and the Balkans. And the Russian foreign office was not best pleased at Bismarck's intervention in what it regarded as an internal matter – not least because Bismarck's gesture provided a fig leaf of legitimacy for the censures of the other powers.[56]

Bismarck's relationship with the Habsburg Empire began with a dazzling series of mutually contradictory initiatives. In December 1862 he met with the Habsburg ambassador to Berlin, Count Alois Karolyi. A Magyar magnate with a reputation for quick wits, Karolyi nevertheless was struck by his Prussian colleague's ability to present several mutually contradictory positions before breakfast. Bismarck called for a military alliance, then suggested Austria and Prussia cooperate in Europe while agreeing to disagree in German matters. He urged Austria to allow Prussian dominance of north Germany in return for Prussian support of Habsburg claims in Italy and the Balkans, and talked of war if Austria continued its present policies regarding the Confederation.[57]

Bemused but not befooled by what they regarded as smoke and mirrors, Schmerling and Rechberg proposed to take a leaf from Bismarck's book and redefine the debate's parameters. Franz Josef, after some preliminary grumbling, announced his intention to celebrate his 18 August birthday in Frankfurt, before an assembly of all the German princes – under the red-gold-black flag of the Frankfurt Parliament. The festive surprise was to be a comprehensive proposal for developing the Confederation's administration. A 300-delegate parliament selected by the member states would determine budgets. A five-member directorate, Austria, Prussia, Bavaria and two seats rotating among the other members, would function as the executive. A federal court would have as its first priority rationalizing business and commercial legislation. And a congress of princes, who would retain their respective sovereignties, would supervise the processes.

Accepting the proposal meant some loss of autonomy. But the Austrian incentive put the princes where they most wanted to be – at centre stage, actors instead of ratifiers. The setting facilitated mobilizing support for the reorganization. Instead of men in suits making endless speeches, princes in glittering uniforms surrounded by deferential aides talked themselves towards affirming the new order. And in the midst of it all was Franz Josef, playing, for the last time, the historic role of the Habsburg emperor as the embodiment of the idea of Germany. Only one link in the chain was missing. William of Prussia refused to attend.[58]

---

[56]Hans-Werner Rautenberg, *Der polnische Aufstand von 1863 und die europaeische Politik: im Spiegel der deutschen Diplomatie und der oeffentliche Meinung* (Wiesbaden, 1979).

[57]Pflanze, vol. I, p. 193 and Lothar Gall, *Bismarck. The White Revolutionary*, vol. I, *1815–1871*, tr. J. A. Underwood (London, 1986), pp. 214 ff.

[58]Cf. Hans Scheller, *Der Frankfurter Fuerstentag 1863* (Leipzig, 1929).

His absence was as surprising as it was disconcerting. The entire ceremonial had been developed with an eye toward appealing to William's frequently expressed sense of solidarity with his fellow monarchs. For Prussia's king to refuse to attend a birthday celebration, even one with strong political overtones, was the kind of discourtesy unnatural to someone of William's character and breeding. And once on the ground, it was expected that he could be softened up, if not immediately persuaded.

Schmerling and Rechberg read William correctly. They reckoned, however, without Bismarck. Even the personal suasion of King John of Saxony, sent to restore William's presence to the great chain of German princes, proved futile against Bismarck's adamant opposition. In the first of many emotional arguments that would punctuate the relationship of king and chancellor, William was reduced to tears of frustration as Bismarck smashed a china wash basin.[59] While the vulgar Freudian interpretation of the William–Bismarck relationship has never been developed, the interaction of the two men resembles that depicted in Neil Simon's popular play, *The Odd Couple*, and in dozens of the situation comedies produced for American television during the 1950s and 60s. In that model Bismarck played the 'feminine' role. When 'rational' arguments failed, he trotted out a gamut of emotions that William, the 'masculine' figure of the duo, was unable to match except by conceding the issue. The subtext of the drama – one both parties seem to have understood increasingly well – was that William never called Bismarck's hand by offering to accept his threat to resign, while Bismarck never challenged William's patriarchal authority on its own terms. The king, as a result, was able to give way on particular issues in the simulacrum of a domestic context, which did not threaten his self-images as soldier and monarch.

Bismarck followed his triumph in the royal chambers with a statement that Prussia would accept the proposed reforms only if granted full parity with Austria – and if the assembly of delegates was replaced by an elected parliament. Bismarck had launched the latter balloon before, to see it promptly shot down as a negotiating ploy. Now the context was different. Bismarck's public description of a body elected by 'the entire nation', albeit accompanied by private suggestions that property qualifications might modify what seemed a call for universal male suffrage, was a shot across the bow of Prussia's Chamber as well as Germany's thrones. But Bismarck paid a price for demonstrating that Prussia could say 'no'. A few years earlier he had cuttingly rejected the notion that Prussia should play Leporello to Austria's Don Juan. Now Bismarck seemed well on the way to defining a role for himself as Mephistopheles: 'the spirit that always denies'.

Rechberg was wise enough to fold his cards, abandoning Austria's public effort at Confederation reform in a great-German context but reaping the benefit of a generalized hostility toward Bismarck's high-handedness. It required no great skill to present William's absence from the Frankfurt gathering as both an overt insult to a Habsburg emperor who was still recognized as the first prince of Germany, and a harbinger of Prussia's intentions towards its neighbours. Vienna's boiler-plate rhetoric criticizing Russia's Polish policies won more favour among journalists and publicists than did Prussia's hardline support of

---

[59] *Anhang zu den Gedanken und Erinnerungen von Otto Fuerst von Bismarck* (Stuttgart, 1901), vol. I, p. 74 and Max Lenz, 'Koenig Wilhelm und Bismarck in Gastein, 1863' in *Kleine historische Schriften* (Munich, 1910), pp. 429–74.

firing squads and deportations. Liberals outside Prussia were beginning to question whether the military reforms would only strengthen a reactionary state. Nationalists wondered whether a Germany united under Prussian auspices might in fact become no more than a Prussia writ large. The newly founded (1862) *Reformverein*, originally little more than a Munich-based debating society, attracted attention for its insistence on the diversity of German political life as a source of strength rather than weakness, while the *Nationalverein*'s image as Prussia's stalking-horse cost it members and supporters.[60]

In the event, Austria was undone by its activism. After Frankfurt, the Habsburg Empire was in no bad position to await developments – to give the rulers and governments of Germany time to consider the fundamental decision of how best to safeguard their ultimate interests of economic growth and political sovereignty, and to give Bismarck a chance to eat his fill of the diplomatic soup he had cooked. Instead, Rechberg proceeded from an assumption that, in the final analysis, Prussia would not abandon the principle of monarchic solidarity. 'Honest but stupid', Franz Josef would subsequently characterize a policy that, in the autumn of 1863, opened a door for a Bismarck who might otherwise have tried to kick in a window.

The compromise settlement of the Schleswig-Holstein question negotiated in 1852 had been quietly and steadily eroding for over a decade, under pressure from liberal Danish intellectuals and conservative Danish nationalists.[61] The resulting diplomatic imbroglios were more or less resolved by a series of compromises, internal and international, that increasingly antagonized public and political opinion in the Danish majority. The Danish government, nevertheless, successfully tacked among its own parliament, the German Confederation, the German great powers and the five Great Powers, whose conclusion of the Treaty of London with Denmark in 1852 underwrote both Schleswig-Holstein's special status under the Danish crown and the indivisibility of the duchies – until 1863.

In January of that year, parliament petitioned Frederick to introduce a new unitary constitution for the Danish kingdom and Schleswig. Holstein, the southernmost of the duchies and the one with the highest level of German intransigence, was to receive its own constitution – a more liberal document, in passing, than many of its German counterparts. What began as an initiative to placate opposition flared into an international crisis as Holstein particularists and German nationalists accused Denmark of plotting the annexation of Schleswig in defiance of international law. Their position gained credibility when a mass gathering in Copenhagen rejected any but dynastic connections with Holstein.

While the Danish government had no desire to provoke a crisis, it had reasonable hopes of securing great-power support for its initiative. The French foreign office and the British public seemed to favour Denmark's position. The marriage of the Prince of Wales to a Danish princess in March was unrelated to the issue of the duchies, but nevertheless reinforced the British connection. Germany, on the other hand, seemed too enmeshed in its own controversies to mount a serious challenge to the new constitutional arrangements. It was July before the Confederation acted to condemn the Danish initiative, and it was at this point that Denmark overbid its hand. Not only did it reject the Confederation's

---

[60]Langeweische, *Liberalism in Germany*, pp. 82 ff.
[61]Cf. Hans Kuhn, 'Romantic Myths, Student Agitation and International Politics: The Danish Intellectuals and Slesvig-Holstein', *Scandinavica* 27 (1988), pp. 5–19.

démarche, but it declared that further threats of military response by the Confederation might be regarded as a *casus belli*.

Danish premier Count Christian Hall was by no means an adventurer, a Scandinavian counterpart of Napoleon III or Bismarck. His approach to the issue reflected a generalized conviction that the Schleswig-Holstein situation was an anachronistic anomaly that no modern state could be expected to accept. In that context, he expected the German Confederation to follow a rational-actor model. Having made its *beau geste*, the Diet would take account of Anglo-French attitudes and Austro-Prussian tensions and abandon the field.[62]

Hall reckoned without the galvanic effect of Bismarck's challenge – and, arguably, the Habsburg proposals – on German rulers and Confederation bureaucrats, who resented being treated as pawns. In its four decades of existence the Confederation had, to a degree, prefigured the modern United Nations by forming what amounted to a cadre of administrators, almost all from the lesser states, who identified strongly with the Confederation as an institution. Able to recognize the futility of crossing swords with one of the great powers, they were unwilling to accept a glove in the face from Denmark, and urged action with a unity absent from Confederation councils for years. The German princes took the point. If their sovereignty was in future to be anything more than a kind of watch charm, a hollow charade tolerated by the great powers, they had to prove they could agree to stand against someone, even a minor diplomatic player like Denmark.[63] In October 1863, the Confederation voted with ruffles and flourishes to proceed with armed sanctions. The northern middle powers, Saxony and Hanover, were assigned primary responsibility, with Austria and Prussia to provide further support should that prove necessary.

The guns were still a long way from going off when, on 15 November, Frederick of Denmark died suddenly – and without a direct heir. The Treaty of London had addressed this issue by recognizing the Danish Prince Christian of Gluecksburg as heir to both Denmark and the duchies. Christian, however, assumed the throne under heavy pressure from his cabinet and his parliament to approve the new constitution. Demonstrations outside the royal palace grew so unruly that Copenhagen's chief of police refused to answer for law and order. Christian signed – and opened another door. Duke Christian of Augustenburg headed a cadet branch of the Danish royal house, with some claims of succession in the duchies. As part of the settlement of 1852 he had agreed not to assert those claims. Now he formally renounced them in favour of his son Frederick, who promptly asserted that the dynastic claims of his house superseded any international agreements.

The exact degree of legality embodied in the Augustenburg declaration remains open to dispute. While arcane, it was less spurious than, for example, the dynastic principles cited by Frederick the Great in claiming Silesia a century earlier. They were certainly enough for the German members of the duchies' estates, who requested the Confederation to affirm Frederick as Duke of Schleswig-Holstein. They were also enough for the small-state rulers of north Germany, who quickly followed the lead of Duke Ernst of Saxe-Coburg-Gotha in

---

[62]Carr, *Wars of Unification*, pp. 64 ff. and Mosse, pp. 146 ff., are reliable overviews. Keith A. P. Sandiford, *Great Britain and the Schleswig-Holstein Question* (Toronto, 1975), is broader-gauged than the title suggests. Cf. as well Troels Fink, *Deutschland als Problem Daenemarks: Die geschichtliche Voraussetzungen der daenischen Aussenpolitik* (Flensburg, 1968).

[63]Cf. *inter alia*, as case studies, Liselotte Konrad, *Baden und die schleswig-holsteinische Frage, 1863–1866* (Berlin, 1935) and Lothar Kuehn, *Oldenburg und die schleswig-holsteinische Frage, 1846–1866* (Cologne, 1934).

recognizing Augustenburg as one of themselves. Duke Ernst was no mere transparency. Cousin of the late Albert, Prince Consort of Britain, he was also a leading figure in the *Nationalverein*. His approval of Augustenburg's cause signalled a massive outburst of patriotic advocacy throughout Germany. A Confederation inundated by addresses and petitions refused to recognize Denmark's ambassador. The *Nationalverein* and the *Reformverein* submerged their differences in a rally held in Frankfurt, whose delegates unanimously declared that the cause of Augustenburg was the cause of Germany – and who created a permanent committee to coordinate support for bringing the duchies into the Confederation under Augustenburg's rule.

German public opinion increasingly dismissed international law as no more than a fable on which the powers agreed. Here was a case where popular sentiment – at least of the articulate elements – and historic right went hand in hand. It was time and past time to admit the Treaty of London's provisional nature. It was time and past time as well for the national movement to show its power to the princes – and for the princes to show their strength against Prussia's king and Austria's emperor. Tensions and contradictions among the two impulses were submerged as advocates sought to control the question of the duchies by overtopping each other's calls to action.

Prussian liberals took particular heart from the new situation. Bismarck's assertion that the government would continue to raise taxes and maintain the army reforms without the parliament's consent might be untenable in the long run. But the outburst of national sentiment led to renewed liberal hope that Prussia would take the lead in the question of the duchies – which had been a concern of Prussian policy long before Bismarck – and in the process take the place in creating a new Germany that its liberals had long intended. Bismarck came under corresponding fire in the Chamber. This time his usual critics were joined by an increasing number of conservatives. Some saw Bismarck as a man of neither principles nor conscience: 'slick Otto', too clever by half for everyone else's good. Others were dissatisfied with a foreign policy that seemed simultaneously passive and disconnected. William, in particular, was sympathetic to Augustenburg's cause, and the encouragement he received from his family and associates put heavy strain on his relationship with a Bismarck who, after all, had as yet done nothing obvious to justify the trust he demanded.[64]

Austria, too, sought action, but for different reasons. Another middle-sized state in north Germany, particularly given Augustenburg's current reputation in nationalist circles, might be a useful thorn in Prussia's side. But Austria could not afford to allow Prussia to seize the moral high ground as sole defender of the German cause. At the same time, Rechberg was unwilling to see the empire function as the ratifier and enforcer of a Confederation decision on which it had not been consulted. It seemed time, once again, to turn towards Berlin, and to a Bismarck who might have learned wisdom from his previous failures.[65]

Bismarck recognized the concrete geo-strategic importance of the duchies for Prussia. Their annexation would strengthen the state and give his foreign policy a badly needed public triumph. At the turn of the year, however, he was more concerned with two wider goals. One was making maximum use of the Schleswig-Holstein issue to strengthen

---

[64]Gerhard Ritter, *Die preussischen Konservativen und Bismarcks deutsche Politik, 1858–1875* (Heidelberg, 1913), pp. 84 ff. and Kraus, *Gerlach*, vol. II, pp. 772 ff.

[65]See, most recently, J. V. Clardy, 'Austrian Foreign Policy during the Schleswig-Holstein Crisis of 1864: An Exercise in Reactive Planning and Negative Formulations', *Diplomacy & Statecraft* 2 (1991), pp. 254–69.

Prussia's position *vis-à-vis* Austria. The other was to remove the direct role the great powers continued to play in German affairs.[66] Bismarck remembered the events of 1849, when France, Russia and Britain had combined to check the policies of Frederick William IV. Now he sought to demonstrate the unnecessary and inappropriate risks involved in continuing the effort to fine-tune German affairs from the outside. In the capitals of Europe he repeatedly insisted that Prussia sought only to see fulfilment of the terms of the Treaty of London, had no designs on Denmark's territory or government, and could not be held responsible for the verbal excesses of the Confederation Diet.

To Rechberg this was both a warning and an invitation. On the one hand, Austria could not afford to be pre-empted by Prussia in what remained of the Concert of Europe. On the other, coordinating with Berlin to support the Treaty of London offered an opportunity to re-establish common ground with Prussia, while simultaneously checking any unilateral Prussian initiatives to acquire the duchies either by annexation or as a client. Bismarck's growing reputation for recklessness made the latter enough of a possibility for Austria to decide it was preferable to prevent the consequences of such an act than seek to profit by them. The German and international situations were too intertwined, and too delicately balanced, for Rechberg even to consider presenting Bismarck with that much room for action.

Another factor shaped the thinking of both principals. Napoleon III was using the crisis over the duchies as a springboard to challenge both the Vienna settlement and the German Confederation.[67] His foreign minister was encouraging Prussia's ambassador to consider annexing not only Schleswig-Holstein, but also the other small states of north Germany. Should Bismarck listen – and he made sure Rechberg was kept well informed of the French initiative – Austria would either have to accept a dual solution of the German question under French auspices, or fight a war Rechberg believed the empire could not afford, even if the recent military reforms increased prospects for victory on the battlefield.

Bismarck, for his part, was perfectly willing to pursue a 'policy of diagonals' between France and Austria. He was, however, also willing to consider war as an immediate rather than a general option. He informed his ambassador to Paris that he was 'not frightened of war'. The problem lay in concluding hostilities once begun, and, as early as November 1862, he had requested Moltke, through the war ministry, consider a war with Denmark. The chief of staff, perhaps influenced somewhat by his own Danish heritage, concluded that ending such a conflict in narrow military terms would be difficult in the context of a Danish naval superiority that would allow virtually undisturbed withdrawal of Danish forces from the mainland should that become necessary. Even a perfectly executed strike, implemented with massively superior forces, was unlikely to destroy the Danish army in Schleswig-Holstein, unless the Danes made a series of obliging mistakes.[68]

These considerations made Bismarck more willing than he might otherwise have been to meet Rechberg on the ground of the London Treaties. Rechberg sought a formal guarantee of King Christian's claim to the duchies. Bismarck agreed in principle, while insisting that the strength of Augustenburg's support in Prussia made it impossible to secure William's consent. The exact extent to which Bismarck exaggerated his helplessness is

---

[66]A still useful analysis is Arnold Oskar Mayer, 'Die Zielsetzung in Bismarcks schleswig-holsteinischer Politik von 1855 bis 1864', *Zeitschrift der Gesellschaft fuer Schleswig-Holsteinsche Geschichte* 53 (1923), pp. 103 ff.

[67]Echard, *Napoleon III and the Concert of Europe*, pp. 192 ff.

[68]Kessel, *Moltke*, pp. 359 ff.

impossible to determine. He had already proven his ability to overcome William's resistance. Such success, however, cost influence — especially since, as mentioned earlier, Bismarck had as yet achieved nothing of substance. Certainly Karolyi, nobody's fool, believed Bismarck had done all he could do or would do to secure the guarantee.[69] The next move was Austria's, and, rather than be swept along by events, Rechberg accepted *de facto* cooperation with Prussia and a promise that, in case of war, the status of Schleswig-Holstein would be settled by mutual agreement. For public consumption, the new allies insisted to the Confederation that the London Treaty rather than the Augustenburg candidacy must be the legitimator of any action against Denmark. Should this be voted down, the two German great powers would act in their own interests, independently of the Confederation.

The response of the lesser states mixed shock and outrage. This time Austria bore the brunt of the antagonism. Prussia was behaving about as expected. Austria, on the other hand, in recent years, had made strides towards establishing itself as the advocate not only of traditional legitimacies and sovereignties, but also of forward-looking, broad-gauged projects for taking a revitalized Confederation into the next half-century. Now, put to the test, the Habsburg Empire was demonstrating exactly what it really thought of German cooperation and small-state identity.

The Confederation finally agreed, by a majority of one vote, to accept the treaties as the basis for intervention. That decision owed a good deal to military, as opposed to diplomatic, considerations. Moltke, sent to Frankfurt as a participant in the Confederation commission planning the 'execution', made a general impression as the best mind and the clearest thinker of the soldiers involved. His insistence that military factors demanded prompt action, not only at the risk of losing the initiative to the Danes, but to prevent an outbreak of 'people's war', with volunteer irregulars taking up arms in the duchies' cause, helped cut through the mutually contradictory proposals and accusations permeating the Confederation's atmosphere.

Moltke calculated that at least 60,000 men were necessary to provide the 50 per cent superiority over the Danes that gave at least a minimal chance for an operation to succeed quickly enough to avert action by the great powers. The original plan involved an initial commitment of 12,000 men, half from Saxony and half from Hanover. Hanover, however, was unwilling to act unless Prussian and Austrian troops were also involved. As a compromise, the Saxons were ordered to occupy Holstein while the Hanoverians remained on the frontier in support. As many as 5,000 Prussians and the same number of Austrians were sent north as a rapid reaction force, each with a full army corps available to intervene should the Danes show fight.[70]

The Danish army was not foolish enough to risk destruction by mounting a forward defence in a disaffected province. The Danish government might well not have been all that sorry to see Holstein accede to the German Confederation by *force majeure*, in return for permission to fully integrate Schleswig, with its much stronger Danish sentiments, into the revised constitutional system. Unwilling, however, in the final analysis, to make even a token fight, it resigned. On 23 December, the Confederation task force entered Holstein and advanced without opposition to the line of the Eider River: the boundary between the duchies.

---

[69]Pflanze, vol. I, p. 246.
[70]Kessel, *Moltke*, pp. 370–1.

The initial lack of military opposition encouraged sentiment in the Confederation for continuing the advance into Schleswig and proclaiming the Augustenburg succession. The problem was that 12,000 men were unlikely to make progress against any kind of Danish resistance, except at risks neither their governments nor the Confederation found acceptable. Austria and Prussia responded by insisting that they would invade Schleswig – not, however, as representatives of the Confederation, but in the context of Denmark's continued refusal to implement the London Treaties. A month of multilateral slanging and recrimination culminated on 24 January, when the Confederation simultaneously denounced Austria, Prussia and the London Treaty, insisting in a public appeal to the German people that right was on its side in the struggle for freedom and unity.

It was a document worthy of the 1848 Frankfurt Parliament at its most eloquent, and just about as effective. On 16 January, Austria and Prussia had issued their own ultimatum to Denmark: either suspend the constitution whose provisions violated international law or face military occupation of Schleswig. Like a similar document delivered to another small state fifty years later, this one was meant to be rejected. It was impossible for a constitutional state to act that quickly on a constitutional issue, and Bismarck well knew it.

Then Britain complicated matters. If British public and parliamentary opinion remained strongly pro-Danish, the government, particularly the foreign office, was disturbed by Denmark's persistent violation of both the letter and the spirit of the London Treaty. Even more disturbing was the Danish refusal to yield under increasing British pressure. In that context, Bismarck was unexpectedly emerging as a statesman of stature, establishing his position in London as someone able to ameliorate the demands of the Augustenburg hotheads while insisting on maintaining the existing treaty arrangements Denmark was challenging – with French support.

His new image lent weight to Bismarck's refusal to accept a British-backed proposal from Copenhagen for six weeks' time to hold elections that would amount to a referendum on the constitution. That, Bismarck insisted, was a mere ploy to gain time that no longer existed. If Austria and Prussia did not act promptly to resolve the issue of the duchies, he declared, revolution might break out in Germany! Unstated, but an unmistakable subtext, was the implied question whether the great powers were really prepared to make high politics contingent upon the deliberations of a backwater parliament in a third-rank state.[71]

Meanwhile, Prussian and Austrian troops moved into Holstein. The first team had arrived, and anyone who doubted it had only to see the arrogance with which the Prussians, in particular, made room for themselves. General Heinrich von Hake, commanding the Saxon contingent, protested. Earlier, Bavaria and Saxony had refused to allow the Austrian contingent to cross their territory, compelling their trains to detour through Breslau and Berlin. A meeting of small-state ministers in Wuerzberg resolved to continue supporting an independent Schleswig-Holstein under the Augustenburgs. Bismarck sent troops to the Saxon frontier and secured Austrian support for further armed action if necessary. It was not much – but it was enough. On 22 January the Confederation ordered Hake to stand down and let the big dogs feed.

---

[71]Mosse, pp. 174 ff. Cf. as well Larry Allen McFarlane, 'Anglo-French Relations and the London Conference of 1864' (dissertation, Georgia, 1972).

4

Roads to War

During their first days in the theatre, the Austrian and Prussian contingents spent at least as much time eyeing each other as they did evaluating the Danes they were sup-posed to be fighting.[1] Throughout military Germany, the Schleswig campaign was regarded as a test of systems. Both Prussia and Austria had put time and resources into overhauling their armies, at economic and moral costs high enough to be considered excessive for the results. It was clear as well that the two forces had chosen patterns of reform that were com-prehensively different and, to a significant degree, mutually exclusive. The Austrians were the pragmatists. They had built on continental precedents to develop a 'quality army' of long-service conscripts, intended to secure quick victory through shock applied at all levels. They merited credit also for understanding the capacities and limitations of their personnel, not expecting behaviours outside the capacities of generals, regimental officers and the rank and file.

Prussian approaches were considered to be more theoretical. A mass army of short-service conscripts without operational experience was inherently a high-risk instrument. Its principal weapons, breech-loading rifles and cast-steel cannon, were asymmetrical in a European context, the product of internal analysis rather than the external observation and mutual imitation that were the usual matrices of technological innovation. The Prussians, nevertheless, were regarded as having developed a system that – in principle, at least – compensated for probable shortcomings in execution by comprehensive prepar-ation. Prussia's general staff, in particular, had generated notice over the past decade. The question was whether the Prussians could make war in the field as well as in the library and the laboratory.

I

Both states and both armies were fully conscious they were on display. The Austrian army corps that advanced into Schleswig included some of the army's most highly regarded

---

[1]The campaign produced a surprisingly large body of surprisingly sophisticated writing. In addition to the respective official histories, Wilhelm Ruestow contributed 700 pages on *Der deutsch-daenisch Krieg 1864* (Zurich, 1864), and Theodor Fontane made his appearance in a role now filled in the US by writers like Bruce Catton and Stephen Ambrose, writing solid and literate narrative military history for general audiences, with *Der Schleswig-Holsteinische Krieg in Jahr 1864* (Berlin, 1866). Edward Dicey, *The Schleswig-Holstein* War (2 vols., London, 1864), brings an often shrewd British perspective. Antonio Gallenga, *The Invasion of Denmark in 1864* (London, 1864), covered the war for London's *Times*.

formations, particularly those distinguished for their successful institutionalization of the new shock tactics. There were few reservists in the Austrian ranks; serving soldiers from other active regiments were transferred whenever possible to make up numbers. The general officers were similarly chosen for aggressiveness and panache. The commander, General Ludwig Gablenz, was regarded as one of the army's rising stars, whose experiences in 1859 made him a leading advocate of the new tactics and whose assertiveness made him well able to hold his own in allied councils.

The Prussian contingent similarly reflected the dynamics of its parent force. Moltke initially sought to have a single corps, III Brandenburg, assigned to the operation. It was preferable, he argued, to commit units and officers accustomed to working together than risk forming new relationships in the field. This particular formation was commanded by Frederick Charles, generally regarded as the best of Prussia's peacetime corps chiefs, who had made the most progress of any in the kingdom in adjusting to the new organization and tactics. The recommendation foundered, however, on the rock put in its way by the Defence Law of 1815. To send a corps on a mission not requiring general mobilization disrupted the entire defence plan. Manteuffel spoke for even some general staff officers when he asserted that current political circumstances made it too dangerous to strip a province of its entire active forces. As a result, the Prussian order of battle consisted of one division from III Corps, another from the VII Westphalian Corps (the other formation whose district bordered the theatre of operations), and a composite division from the Prussian Guard.[2]

The transportation of these forces into north Germany was primarily by rail. It went more smoothly than anyone expected – not least because primary responsibility rested with Wartensleben and Gruendorf. Despite their junior ranks, they proved remarkably effective in coordinating government and private rail lines. Gruendorf even convinced the Austrian state railways not to impose a surcharge for the use of their specially constructed stock cars.[3] Even at the beginning of the intervention, the Saxon brigade was moved from Leipzig to the Holstein border in three days. Men, horses and supplies continued to arrive by rail on schedule, and sufficiently unobtrusively that Europe's foreign offices were not subjected to intimidating impressions of a steam-powered juggernaut – the kind of anxiety that had inspired the British volunteer movement a few years previously.[4]

Once on the ground, the Austrians rapidly secured bragging rights. Their men were more accustomed than their Prussian allies to making themselves comfortable in the field, even during a north German winter. The lively bivouacs of the Habsburg regiments, with their blazing fires, their song and music, the shouts and cheers when a general appeared, contrasted sharply with the more drab and sombre Prussian arrangements. Over half the regiments of the Prussian contingent were recent conversions from Landwehr, and still shaking down. Even after calling up their reserves, battalions were at only 80 per cent of full war strength in order to keep the ranks free of older men.[5]

Prussia was also unfortunate in its first military success: naming the overall commander. Bismarck had insisted that an operation in Prussia's backyard, depending on Prussia's

---

[2]Kessel, *Moltke*, p. 371.
[3]Gruendorf, pp. 175 ff.
[4]Ian Beckett, *Riflemen Form: A Study of the Rifle Volunteer Movement, 1859–1908* (Aldershot, 1982).
[5]Cf. Gruendorf, pp. 194 ff., who also mentions that the Austrians' spirit at times needed encouraging, and *Der Deutsch-Daenisch Krieg 1864*, ed. Grossen Generalstab (2 vols., Berlin, 1887), vol. I, p. 46.

infrastructure for much of its logistics, must be under Prussian command. Precedent was on his side as well; since the Confederation's creation, Prussia had been designated the normative commander of operations in the north. Austria, however, imposed two conditions: their troops would serve only under a senior general, and one with combat experience. The Prussian army list was as familiar in Vienna as it was in Berlin; the Austrian government was correspondingly aware that the only man possessing these qualifications who was remotely fit for active service was Field Marshal Friedrich Wrangel. Popular with the Prussian court and Manteuffel's camarilla for his reactionary views, Wrangel was also eighty years old, and old for his years, when he took the field against Denmark. What operational reputation he possessed had been acquired against armed civilians during the revolutions of 1848. It required no particularly Machiavellian turn of mind for the Austrian army and government to see the situation as one in which it was impossible to lose. Either Prussia admitted it had no officer that could meet what were, after all, reasonable criteria, or Wrangel was likely to deliver the kind of lacklustre performance encouraging the German states to think carefully before choosing sides against Austria in any future shooting war.[6]

Things worked out almost too well from the Austrian perspective. Wrangel's erratic and antagonistic behaviour led observers at his headquarters to question his sanity.[7] Frederick Charles, commanding the composite Prussian corps under Wrangel, fell into tooth-grinding frustration as his Austrian counterparts either sympathized with his position or made excuses for Wrangel's latest *faux pas*. In his 'suggestions' to his subordinates, Frederick Charles had recommended the column as the decisive formation, the bayonet as the decisive weapon and close combat as the surest way to victory. He suggested that in a mêlée only the foremost adversaries should be bayoneted. The others 'are to be taken prisoner by shouting a request to them to throw down their arms and surrender. This ... is more practical, since in the time it requires to kill one, five prisoners can be taken'.[8]

In the field, however, the prince showed himself a cautious and methodical commander, unwilling to risk the lives of his men against even improvised Danish field fortifications after 2 February, when a head-down charge against the redoubts of Missunde on the Schlei River cost him over 500 casualties in a few minutes for no results whatever. Frederick Charles responded by going to ground and calling for artillery to blow the Danes out of their position.

This was the kind of obliging behaviour for which the Danish commander Christian de Meza had hoped. The Danish army, though kept on short manpower and financial leashes by the Danish Parliament, was by no means understood as a mere alarm signal for sparking great-power intervention. Like most of its larger counterparts in Europe, it was recruited by a mixture of long-service conscription – the official term of service was four years in the active army and four in the reserves – and substitution. Its active element consisted of two dozen infantry battalions, six regiments of cavalry and an artillery park of ninety-six guns. Its normal authorized strength of 23,000 had, however, been cut almost in half during the past decade, partly to pay the costs of the previous 'incident' with the German Confederation and partly to compensate slave owners in the Danish West Indies, the future Virgin Islands, for the property losses contingent on emancipation of their slaves. That

---

[6]Kessel, *Moltke*, pp. 380–3.
[7]Hohenloe, vol. III, pp. 13 ff., conveys the atmosphere nicely.
[8]'Einige Winke fuer die Offiziere der unter meinen Befehlen ins Feld rueckenden Truppen' in *Friedrich Karl*, vol. I, pp. 279 ff.

meant most of the 35,000–40,000 men called to arms for the crisis were reservists, including married men in their thirties and volunteers with neither training nor experience.[9]

The bulk of this force was deployed forward in Schleswig, manning fieldworks along the Schlei and a line of fortifications begun as the confrontation escalated, called the 'Danish Work', after a medieval fortified line that was also intended to keep the Germans out of Schleswig. In abstract terms, the Danish army was too weak in numbers and too ill-prepared for war to expect to hold improvised forward positions against the forces of two great powers. But abandoning the territory in dispute and withdrawing to the main defences around Copenhagen, without even token resistance, was to concede the question *de facto*. Denmark's poorly trained troops, moreover, were likely to fight better from behind even improvised defences – and the longer the Danes could keep the field, the better the chances of foreign intervention in Denmark's favour.[10]

As Frederick Charles temporized, Habsburg colours went forward to glory. On 2 February, the Austrian Brigade Gondrecourt carried the village of Ober-Selk and the heights beyond it against a Danish force with the advantages of superior numbers and prepared positions. In the best drill-book style, the Austrian troops took their losses, crossed the killing zone of the Danish Miniés and planted their flags on the entrenchments. Wrangel observed the charge and was so impressed that he embraced and kissed Gondrecourt, to the latter's confusion. And it was worth noting that the victors of Ober-Selk were not predominantly the German troops regarded – especially north of the Inn river – as Austria's military backbone. Instead, a regiment each of Magyars and Poles, along with the Sudeten Germans of the 18th Jaeger Battalion, had forced a Danish retreat in a crucial sector and won the nickname of 'Iron Brigade'.[11]

On 6 February, surprised by a new line of field defences at Oeversee, the Austrians turned again to cold steel. At 3.30 on a winter afternoon, there seemed no time for artillery preparation. Instead, Brigade Nostitz charged a fire-spitting maze of stone walls and improvised barricades, broke in and broke through after three desperate attempts. The 9th Jaeger attacked in column formation, along with the 27th Infantry, making more use of their rifles as pikes and clubs than as firearms. Austrian casualties saw 700 killed or wounded, but 600 Danes surrendered when they found their line of retreat severed, and the road into Denmark was wide open. The Prussian Guard division on the Austrians' flank took no part in the fighting – as much by Gablenz's design as by the relative slowness of the Prussian commander, but in any case, definitely to Moltke's embarrassment.[12]

Bismarck was less interested in the military implications of Oeversee than he was disconcerted at the diplomatic implications of the first round of fighting. On the night of 5/6 February, de Meza fell back from his fieldworks to the permanent fortifications at Dueppel

---

[9]Francois de Bas, *L'armée danoise en 1864: le dannewerk et le dybboel: étude historique et militaire basée sur des documents officiels* (Arnhem, 1868), is a good contemporary evaluation.

[10]Hans Delbrueck, 'Dybbol und Alsen', *Preussische Jahrbuecher* 60 (1887), pp. 18–63, is an excellent strategic overview.

[11]Gruendorf, pp. 195 ff. and Hohenloe, vol. III, pp. 27 ff.

[12]Gruendorf, pp. 206 ff. and Hohenloe, vol. III, pp. 45 ff., colourfully describe the fighting – in which a Hungarian hussar regiment repeatedly charged shouting 'to Hell with the Germans' as a battle-cry. Gerd Stolz, 'Oeversee – 6. Februar 1864 und sein oesterreichischen Tradition', *Zeitschrift fuer Heereskunde* 64 (2000), pp. 4–13, is a modern analysis of the action and its consequences.

and up the peninsula into Jutland. From the beginning, Bismarck had insisted to the powers that the joint action mounted by Prussia and Austria was not aimed at the territorial and political integrity of Denmark. As much to the point, Franz Josef and Rechberg were unwilling to risk the possible consequences of invading Denmark proper without a renegotiation – or at least a stabilization – of alliance terms they considered dangerously vague, especially given their minimal trust of Bismarck. The Danish withdrawal, however, had taken Wrangel entirely by surprise, and, once occupied, Dueppel's formidable landward fortifications offered few possibilities for anything but a formal siege. On 11 February, Moltke had been sent to Schleswig temporarily in order to determine Wrangel's intentions. Learning that he was unwilling to waste lives against the Danes' fixed defences by a direct assault, the chief of staff urged instead an immediate advance into Jutland. Stalemate in the field, he argued, was the best guarantee of great-power intervention. He had no difficulty convincing Wrangel. The Prussian Guard and the Austrians pushed towards the frontier, with Frederick Charles left to mask the Dueppel fortifications.

On Moltke's behalf, it must be said that he was in no way informed of the Austrians' position that widening the war would involve renegotiating the alliance. But the immediate reply, a coded despatch from Berlin ordering the Prussian contingent to halt at the Jutland border, was poorly worded, generating some question as to whether Bismarck and William were aware that Wrangel's initial march objectives all lay on the Schleswig side of the frontier. Pending clarification, the field marshal saw no reason to pass on the halt order to his forward elements.

Wrangel – and Moltke, who was aware of the decision – reckoned without the concept of 'mission tactics' and the initiative of Major General von der Muelbe of the Prussian Guard. His men might have missed Oeversee, but they were going to be in the next fight. As the Danes retreated, he kept on their heels. Since maps were few and the Schleswig–Jutland frontier was, for all practical purposes, unmarked, Muelbe's advance guards found themselves occupying the – clearly Danish – town of Kolding on 18 February. His report was predictably late in reaching Wrangel's headquarters: it took some time to compose a credible explanation for the mistake.

Wrangel saw no problem in simply withdrawing the guardsmen to the border. These kinds of mishaps were common enough in war. Since no casualties had been suffered or inflicted, resolving the contretemps offered no insurmountable difficulties. Then another wild card appeared on the table. Prussian Crown Prince Frederick was also present in Wrangel's headquarters. Like Moltke, he was an 'observer' with no official power of command. But he disliked and distrusted Bismarck, and was an unabashed supporter of the Augustenburg candidacy. Frederick correspondingly advised Wrangel to remain in Kolding on the Micawber-like grounds that something would turn up to justify it. Wrangel was an old man. The heir to Prussia's throne was urging him to seize the day. Small wonder he changed his mind, and communicated his decision to remain in Jutland with a melodramatic telegram insisting that if he withdrew his troops from the path of victory, his grandchildren's names would be cursed.[13]

With France and Britain considering intervention, while Austria made no secret of its ruffled diplomatic feathers, it was Wrangel's name that attracted adjectives in Bismarck's office.

---

[13]On the Kolding incident, see especially Kessel, *Moltke*, pp. 388 ff. and Hohenloe, vol. III, pp. 71–2.

Bismarck was unwilling to legitimate any situation he could not alter. The soldiers, on the other hand, were convinced an alliance with Austria was desirable, indeed necessary, in the war most of them expected to grow out of the Danish imbroglio. Moltke, for example, argued that if the western powers wanted war, separately or together, the occupation of Schleswig provided all the excuse they needed. It made political as well as military sense to continue pushing the issue on the ground, thereby encouraging the Danish government to negotiate an end to hostilities before their losses became large enough that only more war could redress them. Even more committed to an Austrian connection was Edwin von Manteuffel, who saw close relations with Vienna as Prussia's best safeguard against revolution, not only from below but laterally, as a consequence of Bismarck's machinations either backfiring or succeeding all too well and sending parliament into the streets.[14] So it was Manteuffel, in a stroke of the genius that comes from recognizing the obvious, whom Bismarck sent to Vienna to obtain Austria's consent for expanded operations in the north.

Manteuffel's performance invites speculation on the course of events in Prussia had he been interested in the career of a uniformed diplomat rather than a military politician. He pursued his mission with a mixture of conviction, tact and charm that won over the Austrians if not completely, then enough for them to approve a plan based on capturing Dueppel and the island – Alsen Island – lying immediately behind it, and also authorizing a full-scale advance into Jutland for the purpose of screening those operations against a Danish counter-offensive.[15]

Rechberg was pleased with what he regarded as a successful assertion of Austria's position. The Prussian army rejoiced at its new position centre stage. For Bismarck, the agreement freed him to respond to increasingly didactic British and Russian demands for an international conference on the question of the duchies. On 7 March, Prussia and Austria declared their joint willingness to participate in such a meeting. That, however, was only one of the cards Bismarck was playing. He began, simultaneously, to prepare public, political and royal opinion for the direct annexation of the duchies to Prussia; and to discuss with France the possibility of supporting Prussian initiatives, at a price to be discussed later. One image that springs to mind is of a chess master playing in a big-city park, moving from board to board with an assurance that can be as intimidating as his actual moves. Another trope is of the pool hustler, carefully setting up both the table and his opponents for the final high-stakes game. But each and all of Bismarck's initiatives increasingly depended on the army. Prussia needed a victory – nothing spectacular and nothing too large, lest it alarm either Austria or the powers, but at the same time, a triumph sufficiently clear to establish Prussia's ability to back its diplomacy with force.

For a man who insisted on conducting the orchestra this was an uncomfortable position. Bismarck began by increasing the pressure on Frederick Charles to finish off Dueppel. The prince responded by stressing the difficulties of the operation. Moltke also saw little point in pursuing a formal siege, but less in attempting to carry the Danish positions by a *coup de main* – itself a flat impossibility without extensive preparation. The Danes had shown no lack of courage in the war's opening rounds – even mobilized civilians armed with Minié rifles were dangerous opponents behind stone walls.

---

[14]Craig, *Politics of the Prussian Army*, pp. 185–6.

[15]Annelise Klein-Wuettig, *Politik und Kriegfuehrung im deutschen Einigungskriegen* (Berlin, 1934), pp. 17–18.

Siege warfare was not a Prussian army strength, and Frederick Charles, an infantryman, was correspondingly dependent on specialist advice whose preparation and presentation took time. Equally important was Frederick Charles's growing conviction that no one in Berlin, including – or especially – Bismarck, seemed to understand that siege operations absorbed men and required resources, in particular, heavy guns, guns whose weight and bulk challenged the capacity of the railways to move them.[16] Even William showed little patience, insisting that the Danes, and by extension the Austrians, needed only a demonstration of Prussian might and Prussian skill to impel their surrender. As men and equipment moved into position to begin the slow-motion ballet of a siege, Moltke hoped for a change of policy that would allow the allies to continue the invasion of Jutland and force the Danes either to negotiate or to risk battle in the open. Instead, he faced – along with Frederick Charles – increasing pressure to fight in front of Dueppel, no matter the cost in lives.

More than militaristic vanity was involved here. Armies differ from all other complex institutions in the limited amounts of time they spend performing their primary avowed function of war making. They have corresponding problems with establishing and maintaining credibility. Navies put to sea; air forces fly; and both thereby provide some sense of their basic competence. By comparison, at best, armies train. At worst, they drill. In any environment involving issues of alliance politics or deterrent policies, the judgment of fellow armies and fellow states can be crucial to decision-making far beyond the operational sphere. During World War II, for example, much of the behaviour of American commanders in North Africa and during the Sicilian campaign was designed to establish the US Army's credibility to both the Germans and the British. A Prussian system that had not fought an external enemy for half a century was on trial more clearly than the Austrians, or even the Danes, who had no pretensions to great-power standing.

As an alternative to siege and storm, Frederick Charles's chief of staff, Karl von Blumenthal, proposed an amphibious operation – a surprise attack in force on Alsen Island to bypass the Danes' defences and force them into the open. Moltke's reservations prefigured those accompanying Operation Sealion in 1940. The proposed landing site could be reached only by crossing up to a mile and a half of open water in the face of a Danish fleet that Prussia had no prospects of neutralizing. It was, Moltke concluded, Dueppel or nothing.[17] For the next six weeks Frederick Charles established gun positions, summoned reinforcements – almost another full corps – and protested against the risks of precipitate action to a point where the Alsen project was revived. Not until 2 April did the bombardment begin – the first real test of Prussia's new rifled field guns in an unexpected milieu. Not until 18 April did Frederick Charles send his infantry forward.

His caution proved justified. The Danish defences were battered, but still essentially intact. The Danish defenders put up a hard fight. The Prussians cleared the redoubts and trenches, but at the cost of over 1,000 casualties – no bagatelle after fifty years of peace. The storm of Dueppel, however, was the kind of operation that lent itself to patriotic enthusiasm. Even the most civilian reporter could not mistake the situation. Here were the Prussians; there were the Danes; and then the Prussians were where the Danes used to be.

---

[16]Graf von Haeseler, *Zehn Jahre im Stabe des Prinzen Friedrich Karl. Erinnerungen* (3 vols., Berlin, 1910–15), vol. I, pp. 204 ff.

[17]Kessel, *Moltke*, pp. 396 ff.

The effects of Prussian artillery fire were as spectacular as they were superficial. The casualties were high enough to lend *gravitas* to the operation, but not so large as to generate shock. Enough humorous and inspiring anecdotes circulated in the storm's aftermath to make imagination superfluous. Newspapers throughout Germany celebrated a victory that simultaneously encouraged agonizing reappraisals among Prussia's liberal opposition, overshadowed the earlier Austrian achievements, and gave Bismarck the operating room he sought to shape the future course of events.[18]

King William was pleased enough to visit the theatre of war in person, review the troops and discuss future operations. Wrangel wanted to replicate Dueppel and take his by now worked-in siege circus to the next large target: the mainland fortress of Frederica. Moltke, not invited to the conference, protested from Berlin that the Danish army was still intact and the Danish government still intransigent. Occupy Jutland, he urged. Deny its resources to the Danes. Leave Frederica to be blockaded by the Austrians, and attack not Alsen but the larger island of Fuenen in force. That combination, Moltke argued, would put an operational halter around Denmark's neck, no matter what happened in London.

The chief of staff's recommendations were greeted with hostility in Denmark, less from Wrangel himself than from his staff officers, who disliked having their shoulders looked over. William was more favourably disposed. When the dust settled and the last telegram had been exchanged, Moltke was on his way to Denmark, for the first time taking the field in a senior position: as chief of staff to the allied army.

He faced a simplifying chessboard. The Danish evacuation of Frederica on 28 April indicated that Denmark had no intention of undertaking any large-scale land operations. That strategic decision was confirmed when two Austrian frigates broke the Danish blockade of Hamburg and forced their squadron to withdraw to the Skagerrak.[19] Moltke organized the virtually bloodless occupation of Jutland. Then he turned to Gablenz and began preparing plans for attacking Fuenen. Moltke believed the assault could be made using pontoons as landing craft, supplemented by locally requisitioned coastal shipping. Naval support was unnecessary for what amounted to an expanded river crossing. Gablenz was by no means so sanguine. His government had not directly authorized an attack on Fuenen. Nor was Gablenz willing to accept casually the feasibility of an amphibious attack on a scale bigger than anything in Austria's history, whose administrative complexities were more obvious than its military advantages. Prussian schoolmasters and writing-desk heroes might be able to work out the details on paper. Their implementation was likely to be a whole other story – particularly for an Austrian army that had a history of rear-echelon problems on dry land, to say nothing of water.[20]

Rechberg, too, was reluctant to pursue a course that seemed to put Prussian generals in charge of events. That was arguably the only risk greater than working too closely with Bismarck. Instead, Rechberg lent Austrian support to the call for an armistice issued by the signers of the London Treaty, who, on 20 April, assembled representatives in the British

---

[18]Cf. the modern analysis, Winfried Vogel, *Entscheidung 1864: das Gefecht bei Dueppel im Deutsch-Daenischen Krieg und seine Bedeutung fuer die Loesung der deutschen Frage* (Koblenz, 1987), with the spirited narrative in Fontane, pp. 194 ff.

[19]Lawrence Sondhaus, *Preparing for Weltpolitik: German Sea Power before the Tirpitz Era* (Annapolis, MD, 1997), pp. 76–7.

[20]Kessel, *Moltke*, pp. 404–5.

capital in an attempt to resolve the Schleswig-Holstein question in an international, as opposed to a regional, context. With the guns temporarily silenced by a ceasefire, Bismarck took full advantage of a continuing Danish intransigence, a refusal to compromise on the Schleswig-Holstein issue that was no less marked because it reflected divided domestic counsels. Since no one could reason with such people, Bismarck declared, the London Treaty's original terms should be replaced by a personal union of the duchies with the Danish monarchy.

The surface plausibility of the proposal was negated by its unacceptability to Danish nationalists – an unacceptability of which Bismarck was better aware than Rechberg, who calculated, without consulting his representatives in London, that the Danes would seize the compromise. Facing flat refusal, left high and dry, the Austrian minister undertook 'flight forward' by proposing an independent Schleswig-Holstein under Frederick of Augustenburg.

This was one of those decisions that seem like a good idea at the time. It mended fences with a Confederation whose support Austria could not afford to lose in either a European or a German context. It responded to the new wave of German nationalism generated by the storming of Dueppel. It removed at least some of the gilt from Prussia's military gingerbread by reasserting the primacy of diplomacy. And it left the London Conference thoroughly off balance. Unwilling to accept the Augustenburg initiative, the Danish government was also unwilling to accept Franco-British initiatives for partitioning the duchies along national lines. The best Britain could manage was consent to the *Dannewerke* as a possible new frontier. Prussia and Austria insisted on a line farther north, from Abenraa to Tonder.

As would be the case on larger scales in 1918, ethnicity, strategy and prestige jostled for place in the discourse. The disputed territory was a true frontier region, where generations and centuries had created a local culture unsusceptible of being honestly separated into Danish and German components. The Danish government wanted to retain the Schlei river line as a forward defensive position, in spite of its army's demonstrated inability to hold it. Prussian and Austrian soldiers and politicians, for all their acceptance in principle that this was a cabinet conflict for limited aims, were reluctant to relinquish at the negotiating table land taken at bayonet-point, without appropriate gestures of subordination from Copenhagen. Britain finally proposed arbitration, with a neutral power determining the frontier. Under Bismarck's urging, Prussia and Austria accepted. Denmark refused.[21]

King Christian and his government hoped, by this gesture, to destroy the conference, expecting that, in turn, to topple the British government. The new elections were expected to favour the Tories, who sympathized more openly with Denmark. As an exercise in contingent reasoning, the syllogisms were impeccable. The real-world consequences were predictable. War resumed on 26 June. The British government survived. On 29 June, Moltke – who had long since given up on securing Gablenz's cooperation – supervised a lesser operation: the crossing of the Alsen Fjord by two Prussian divisions, 25,000 men. The Danish commander had six regiments, plus smaller units: around 10,000 in ranks and under arms. His best chance was to counter-attack at the waterline. Instead, the Prussians encountered no significant resistance, either from an army by now demoralized by three

---

[21]Mosse, pp. 186 ff., is the best detailed overview of the negotiations. Pflanze, vol. I, pp. 249 ff., is the best analysis of Bismarck's role.

months of inactivity, or a navy too committed to the role of a fleet in being to risk its ships in the narrow waters surrounding the island. By 10 a.m. it was all over, with the Danes in retreat across the narrow sound separating Alsen from Fuenen. They left behind 2,500 prisoners, along with 750 dead and wounded. Prussian casualties were around 400 – small price for an operation unique to date in the army's history.[22]

Alsen marked the end of the serious fighting. Moltke busied himself with plans for an attack on Fuenen and an invasion of Zeeland. Allied troops completed the occupation of Jutland. Landing parties picked off a few of the North Frisian Islands against minimal opposition.[23] But ultimately, it was King Christian who decided that further effective resistance was impossible. On 8 July a new government asked for terms. No concessions were forthcoming from anywhere in Germany. Denmark's French and British patrons had no leverage remaining. On 1 August, Christian ceded all rights to the duchies to Prussia and Austria.

II

The year 1864 has usually been presented in political and diplomatic contexts, with its military aspects relegated to footnotes and subsidiary paragraphs. The common perspectives, moreover, are either German or great-power, with the Danes cast as minor players in their own destiny. When a human dimension is included in the story, the most familiar protagonist is Bismarck, with his cold-blooded, unscrupulous virtuosity. The resulting image is of a 'cabinet crisis', highly flexible, depending on nuances for solutions. Seen at a bit of distance, however, three salient points emerge. One is the firm matrix provided to the crisis by Danish policy. Denmark, from beginning to end, followed a pattern of no retreat, no surrender, with which all other participants had to come to terms. Second, and related, is Denmark's autonomy throughout the crisis. No one's client and no one's confidant, this small state acted as an independent player whose calculations may not have been wise or right, but definitely were Danish-centred. The third point is the importance in Danish behaviour of a synergy between policy and force. The initial attempt to hold the *Dannewerk*, the withdrawal to Dueppel and Alsen, the abandonment of the mainland – none of these was a political decision, intended primarily to send some kind of message to Germany or Europe. They reflected, instead, a determination to maintain Denmark's position in arms, to 'negotiate while fighting' as opposed to depending on the London Treaty, the Concert of Europe or any other outside force.

Denmark's behaviour, in turn, enhances the importance of the Austro-Prussian military operations during the first six months of 1864. Had Wrangel and Gablenz, Frederick Charles and Moltke, been less able to determine the campaign's course and pattern, Bismarck's diplomatic performance was correspondingly likely to become more *pas de deux* – or *trois* or *quatre* – than virtuoso solo dance. With the prospect of a next round involving higher stakes and a less obliging adversary, Bismarck took corresponding counsel with himself as he considered how best to maximize Prussia's advantage in the coming end game.

---

[22]For Alsen, cf. *Deutsch-Daenisch Krieg*, vol. II, pp. 634 ff.; Kessel, *Moltke*, pp. 409 ff.; Fontane, pp. 310 ff.; and the excellent summary in Arden Bucholz, *Moltke and the German Wars, 1864–1871* (New York, 2001), pp. 97 ff.

[23]A process depicted in detail in Gerd Stolz, *Die 'Eroberung' der nordfriesischen Inseln im Jahre 1864: eine Affaere aus dem deutsch-daenischen Krieg* (Husum, 1988).

He began, in June, by playing a carom shot, turning to Augustenburg himself to discuss possible territorial concessions in the duchies in return for guarantees of the remainder. The prince, no political naïf, realized that he needed Prussian support for his cause but refused to enter any agreement without consulting the Confederation. His decision was made less from populist principles than from recognition that following in Bismarck's wake would establish him as nothing more than Prussia's client, combined with a shrewd evaluation of just how much Bismarck's word on anything was worth. Bismarck promptly took Augustenburg's intransigence to market, depicting him as ungrateful and inconsequent. The result was a significant discrediting of Augustenburg's cause in the minds of Prussian conservatives who, in any case – from the king downwards – had supported the duke more from adrenalin than from conviction. As for the liberal nationalists, Augustenburg's shield was tarnished by his apparent connection with Bismarck and the Prussian reactionaries.[24]

That left Austria. In Vienna, Schmerling led a faction that argued, both in parliament and the cabinet, for supporting Augustenburg, turning once more to the middle states, and pursuing a forward policy that would compel Bismarck either to fold his hand or expose his cloven hoof. Thus far, the argument went, Prussia had succeeded on Austrian sufferance. The time had come to draw a line. Should Bismarck, William and the whole pack of Junker militarists prove intransigent, then Austria's best course was to pursue alliance with France, even at the expense of an Italian position already so overextended as to be untenable in case of another shooting war. Rechberg, on the other hand, remained committed to a Prussian relationship whose nurturing cost him enough emotional and intellectual effort to be almost self-justifying. 'It increases to a more than ordinary degree', he wrote during this period, 'the difficulties of conducting business when one is dealing with a man who so openly professes cynicism ... '[25] Rechberg also believed that good relations with Prussia were vital if Austria were to maintain its position south of the Alps. No French connection could be fully trusted, particularly if an ill-advised alienation of Prussia created an opportunity to test the Habsburg Empire in Germany and Italy simultaneously. And in considering France and Prussia, Rechberg continued to perceive France as the more dangerous adversary – not least because Prussia's military performance in the duchies fell short of establishing the army's quality as a premier force.

It was in this context that Bismarck, in August 1864, visited Vienna with what seemed to be an offer Rechberg could not refuse: Prussian annexation of the duchies and a solid front against the German middle states in return for a guarantee of Prussian military support against France in Germany and Italy – support not only of the status quo, but for Austrian recovery of Lombardy. Rechberg, in all probability, had no illusions about whether Bismarck would fulfil his side of the bargain willingly under any circumstances. Much of the art of diplomacy, however, involves manoeuvring others into doing what they would otherwise avoid, and Rechberg's dislike for Bismarck was unaccompanied by belief that the Prussian was his superior in that art. When William openly, albeit unwillingly, denied any legal right to the duchies, Rechberg accepted this as sufficient repudiation of Bismarck's more extreme constructions to justify continuing efforts to maintain a 'special relationship' with Prussia.[26]

---

[24]Gall, *White Revolutionary*, vol. I, pp. 251–2 and Pflanze, vol. I, pp. 252–3 and 271 ff.

[25]Quoted in Gall, *White Revolutionary*, vol. I, pp. 261–2.

[26]Walter Lipgens, 'Bismarcks Oesterreich-Politik vor 1866', *Die Welt als Geschichte* 10 (1950), pp. 240–62, incorporates the most detailed analysis of that meeting.

Austria's Prussian policies during this period have so often been interpreted as reflecting either honest stupidity or ill-advised bumbling that it is worthwhile to make overt the point that Vienna, for all its current and future protestations of acting on principle, was not significantly less scrupulous – or less ambitious – than Berlin. To the extent that Austria presented itself as the defender of treaties and precedents, this reflected not only a commitment to principle but also a conviction that it was in the empire's best interests to assert that position. Nor was Austria merely concerned to restrict Prussia's power by underwriting federation as an alternative. Its German policies were increasingly predicated on making common cause with reactionary forces to cripple liberal pressure groups like the *Nationalverein* once their *de facto* Prussian ally and protector should be broken.[27]

Bismarck, nevertheless, was not committed to taking every diplomatic trick in every hand of what he regarded as an ongoing game. He showed his flexibility, in particular, when the customs treaties came up for renewal in the autumn of 1864. Rechberg had temporarily suspended opposition to the Franco-Prussian trade treaty during the Schleswig-Holstein crisis. Now the Austrian requested a Prussian promise to begin – on Austria's initiative – negotiations for a customs union between the German great powers, some time before 1872. Bismarck was willing enough, but could not overcome the opposition of Prussia's various economic ministries, supported by a king not loath to prove he could, in fact, say 'no' to his subordinate.

Facing one frustration too many, Rechberg resigned on 27 October 1864. His successor was a general, a courtier rather than a field soldier, Count Alexander Mensdorff. He assumed office in the context of a significant shift in Habsburg domestic policy.[28] Since 1848, Hungary had been kept at sufficient distance from the empire's levers of power to legitimate already strong feelings of being a conquered people rather than participants in a greater whole. At the same time, the republican- and opposition-minded veterans of 1848 were giving way to a conciliatory faction that stressed legal precedent both for Hungary's rule by the Habsburg dynasty and its identity as a constitutional state. Private negotiations proceeded to the point where, by the spring of 1865, Emperor Franz Josef was promising in public that he would do everything possible to satisfy his Hungarian subjects, and those subjects, in turn, were ready to move into the relative warmth of imperial – or, in this particular case, 'royal Hungarian' – favour. On 30 July Schmerling resigned as minister-president. His successor, Count Richard Belcredi, sympathized with neither Germans nor politicians and was correspondingly willing to further negotiations with Budapest.[29]

Franz Josef had no significant compunctions against a 'brothers' war' with Prussia if the circumstances were favourable. At the same time, he was unwilling either to assume the risks of seeking closer rapprochement with France, or of appearing the aggressor in German affairs. That latter role – should it be cast and acted – he considered better left to Bismarck. It

---

[27] Cf. Elrod, 'Rechberg and the Metternichian Tradition', pp. 454–5 and Wawro, 'The Austro-Prussian War', vol. I, p. 272 *passim*.

[28] F. Engel-Janosi, 'Die Krise des Jahres 1864 in Oesterreich', *Historische Studien. A. F. Pribram zum 70. Geburtstag dargebracht* (Vienna, 1929), pp. 141–95.

[29] Cf. Peter Berger, *Der Oesterreichisch-ungarische Ausgleich von 1867: Vorgeschichte und Wirkung* (Vienna, 1967) and Eva Somogyi, *Vom Zentralismus zum Dualismus: Der Weg der oesterreichischen Liberalen zum Ausgleich vom 1867* (Wiesbaden, 1983). The army's significant role as an instrument of absolutism is presented in Schmidt-Brentano, pp. 335 ff.

was in that context that Mensdorff, in the autumn of 1864, offered Bismarck a choice: either recognition of the duchies under Augustenburg or their annexation to Prussia, with compensation for Austria along the Silesian frontier. Bismarck replied by declaring that his royal master would never consent to surrendering land acquired by the great Frederick, and insisting that the legal succession rights of princes other than Augustenburg must be considered before a new principality was created. In any case, Bismarck asserted, Prussia had special rights in the duchies. Mensdorff pressed for clarification. In February 1865 he received an answer that amounted to making an independent Schleswig-Holstein a Prussian satellite, with its armed forces under Prussian command, a Prussian-controlled canal to be cut through the peninsula and a major Prussian naval base to be established in the port city of Kiel.

Mensdorff struck back hard, challenging Prussian encroachments directly in the duchies and in the Confederation Diet, while simultaneously expressing willingness to negotiate in the context of an Augustenburg succession. By this time, William had become convinced that whatever might be the legal niceties, the blood shed by Prussian soldiers in Schleswig and Holstein legitimated their submission to Prussian rule. Bismarck did not exclude war, especially in discussions with the king. But Prussian money was buying influence with local journalists. Prussian administrators were establishing what amounted to *de facto* governance of both the duchies, despite howls of rage from Austrians on the spot. There was no reason to press forward heedlessly. Tactical concessions on issues such as the amalgamation of the duchies' army with Prussia's, Bismarck argued, would avert the risk of appearing on the German and European stages as a simple land-grabber. Bismarck, however, was unable to convince William to abandon or modify the February declaration.

It is also possible that Bismarck found William's intransigence too useful to turn his full energy to changing the king's mind. William as the 'bad cop' gave extra weight to 'good cop' Bismarck's assumption of the role of spokesman for reason and moderation. In either case, William's inflexibility made war seem a clear possibility in the summer of 1865. That prospect, in turn, discomfited a Habsburg government unwilling to take the risks, unwilling to pay the bills and unwilling to have improving relations with Hungary seem a contingency of conflict with Prussia. Mensdorff was ready to fight because he saw no alternative. Franz Josef, however, took charge. He sent Austria's ambassador to Bavaria, who was also someone he trusted personally, to Bad Gastein, where William had retired for a cure. The official returned with Bismarck's proposal to partition the duchies: Austria receiving Holstein and Prussia Schleswig, with rights of access to and garrisons in Holstein.

Franz Josef saw this as the least worst way out of a high-risk impasse. Mensdorff argued that Austria could not simply agree to partition without an unacceptable loss of position in the Confederation and an unacceptable risk of domestic protest by 'Great German' liberal nationalists, already exercised by the emperor's Hungarian initiatives. Pride of craft demanded, moreover, that the foreign office not merely accept the first offer of someone like Bismarck, whom experience had shown to have hidden agendas at every turn. The Austrian counter-proposal was to retain joint sovereignty over the duchies, while allowing Prussia to administer Schleswig, and Austria Holstein. Schleswig would enter the *Zollverein*; Kiel would become a Confederation port and – eventually – the base for a Confederation navy. Prussia would administer Kiel, but in return, would be responsible for building a canal across the peninsula and a railroad connecting Kiel with Luebeck. Bismarck accepted.

On 20 August, William and Franz Josef formalized this Gastein Convention. Public and political opinion throughout Germany widely considered the agreement no more than a breathing space before a war that increasingly seemed inevitable. The course of events in the next ten months seemed to legitimate that interpretation. The question of why Bismarck negotiated the 'Gastein interlude' in the first place remains a correspondingly intense subject of debate. There seems no doubt that Bismarck was not motivated by any lingering sense of solidarity, dynastic or otherwise, with Austria. He regarded future good relations with the empire as contingent on Austria's abandoning its pretensions to influence in Germany. But how might that policy revolution be brought about to Prussia's greatest advantage? In tactical terms, Gastein was low risk. Austria bore the brunt of middle-state outrage against what seemed simultaneous multiple betrayal of the German nation, the diets of Schleswig-Holstein and the Duke of Augustenburg. Austria, by insisting on retaining the concept of joint sovereignty in the duchies, also gave Bismarck a pretext for creating tension any time he chose, by questioning Austria's behaviour in Holstein. And, at what might be called the operational level, Gastein gave Bismarck opportunities to improve his hand in two crucial areas.[30]

The first was diplomatic. In particular, the government of Napoleon III was concerned at what it considered Bismarck's unwarranted assertion of independence in the aftermath of the Schleswig-Holstein War. In Napoleon's grand design for Europe, Prussia was a supporting player, not a full partner, expected to pursue a German-nationalist policy within parameters ultimately determined in Paris. Bismarck was not much more than another representative of a middle-ranking state whose personal skills, however substantial, were not backed by corresponding material power. That he might occasionally choose to play by himself was acceptable – as long as he did not endanger other and more complicated games.[31]

Bismarck had done nothing to challenge these images overtly. Instead, he reassured France, in language whose deferential, submissive tone was at least as important as the words, that Prussia had no intentions of dismembering Denmark, underwriting Austria's position in Italy or challenging French primacy in Europe. Bismarck's suggestions that Franco-Prussian rapprochement might eventually lead to Prussian cession of the Rhineland was taken less seriously – at least by the French foreign ministry – than is frequently assumed. But that Bismarck might well find himself at a point where cession was the price of French goodwill seemed at least a reasonable contingency. The Prussian's frequent inclusion of Belgium and the Duchy of Luxembourg as other possible areas of French aggrandizement was an even more useful straw in the wind, suggesting Bismarck's interests were German-centred as opposed to incorporating a European perspective. Even his occasional suggestions that French hostility might require a Russian orientation of Prussia's foreign policy were processed in that context: a diplomat placed in the middle by geography, seeking naturally to turn that position to advantage, but unlikely to attach himself permanently to anyone.[32]

---

[30]Chester W. Clark, *Franz Joseph and Bismarck: The Diplomacy of Austria before the War of 1866* (Cambridge, MA, 1934), remains the most reliable guide in English through the details of the negotiations and their background. Cf. Pflanze, vol. I, pp. 258 ff. and Gall, *White Revolutionary*, vol. I, pp. 262 ff., for more recent, analytical treatments.

[31]See, especially, Herbert Guss, *Bismarck und Napoleon III. Ein Beitrag zur Geschichte der Preussisch-franzoesischen Beziehungen* (Cologne, 1959), p. 65 *passim*.

[32]Pottinger, pp. 24 ff., is the best overview of the diplomatic situation from France's perspective. Gerhard Ritter, 'Bismarck und die Rheinpolitik Napoleons III', *Rheinische Vierteljahresblaetter* 15–16 (1950–1), pp. 339–70, remains useful.

For Louis Napoleon, no stranger to strange beds in his personal life, a *maîtresse de convenance* was, in many respects, more congenial than a more committed diplomatic relationship. Gastein nevertheless generated a sharp inquiry from the French foreign office. Bismarck promptly denied any notion of a long-term move towards rapprochement with Austria. Gastein, he declared, was a mere first step in establishing Prussian primacy north of the Main – an unsurprising ambition. Should France approve, Prussia, in turn, would support its aggrandizement 'everywhere in the world French was spoken'.

That phrase covered enough ground that in October Bismarck went to Biarritz to discuss the German situation in more detail with Napoleon and his advisors. It is less likely that he directly sought the price of French neutrality in a shooting war than that he confirmed the instrumentality of Prussia's current relationship with Austria, and suggested that the Rhine was a less congenial site for expansion than the francophone, Gallicized regions of Luxembourg and Belgium. In any case, between two men who had spent their lives and careers as diplomatic salesmen, general impressions were more important than particular issues. Napoleon returned to Paris confident that he had taken Bismarck's measure. Bismarck just as cheerfully reported that France would 'dance the cotillion with us' when and if the ball began.[33]

As for the other prospective dancers, Russia was concentrating on domestic reform rather than foreign initiatives. Its ministries and bureaucrats were concerned with overcoming national tensions, developing a railway network and introducing a mobilization system that would rationalize the state's currently almost random use of its manpower. Russian war plans at this period regarded Austria and Britain as the tsarist empire's most likely great-power enemies, and emphasized repelling invasion rather than power projection.[34] Bismarck found little difficulty reassuring the Russian Foreign Office that the current German crisis was just another in a long series, with no major European implications. Britain, which had long since come to terms with the economic aspects of the *Zollverein*,[35] was absorbed by the imperial issues of Canadian self-government and India's reconstruction in the aftermath of its annexation to the crown. British potential for direct intervention in central Europe was in any case limited by the small size and relative ineffectiveness of its army compared with Prussia's and Austria's.[36] Of the lesser powers, Italy's foreign policy had become a good deal less adventurous since the death of Cavour in 1861. Nationalists and republicans urged direct action against Venetia; the king preferred to negotiate with Austria; the army, which had undergone its own reforms since 1859, looked to Prussia.[37]

---

[33]Friedrich Frahm, 'Biarritz', *Historische Vierteljahrschrift* 15 (1912), pp. 337–61, is the most detailed reconstruction of the meeting and its antecedents. The quotations are from Pflanze, vol. I, p. 265.

[34]Cf. L. G. Zakharovsa, 'Autocracy, Bureaucracy, and the Reforms of the 1860s in Russia', *Soviet Studies in History* 29 (1991), pp. 6–33 and, for specifically military affairs, Bruce Menning, *Bayonets before Bullets. The Imperial Russian Army, 1861–1914* (Bloomington, IN, 1992), pp. 11 ff.

[35]John R. Davis, *Britain and the German Zollverein, 1848–66* (New York, 1997).

[36]On this, see A. R. Skelley, *The Victorian Army at Home: The Recruitment and Terms and Conditions of the British Regular, 1859–99* (London, 1977).

[37]The best overview in English remains Denis Mack Smith, *Vittorio Emanuele, Cavour, and the Risorgimento* (London, 1971).

The resulting gridlock was well suited to Bismarck's methods of management and manipulation. Nothing, however, happened in a hurry in Italy, and, during the last months of 1865, Bismarck was willing to allow that relationship to simmer rather than move towards the kind of relationship that might slam shut the doors to Vienna before he wanted them closed.

The lead time was valuable as well because it enabled recalibration of the relationship between administration and parliament – specifically the financial aspects. In 1864, the Landtag, after bitter debate, had refused Bismarck's request for a one-time grant to pay for the Schleswig-Holstein expedition. By 1865, however, even liberal voices calling for a final settlement of the constitutional conflict were louder and more insistent. Public opinion, it was argued, had grown bored with a gridlock whose details no one understood.[38] The army's victories had shifted the spotlight away from parliament; Rudolf von Benningsen noted that the 'Bismarck course' of honouring military power and diplomatic success was rapidly growing.[39] Might it be time to admit that it was time to cut a deal – even with Bismarck?

In January 1865, the minister of the interior suggested that if parliament was willing to seek another field in which to assert its rights, the government was prepared to listen.[40] William, however, remained intransigent on the issues of three-year service and maintaining the size of the standing army.[41] In the context of events in Denmark this was hardly surprising, particularly since Moltke, whose performance there had made him *persona gratissima* at court, spoke and wrote eloquently for the achievements of the new system under field conditions.[42] Parliament responded by offering proposals for resolving the conflict that were in the same form, tone and language as the previous versions. One is reminded of the definition of insanity as doing something in the same way while expecting different results. It is, in fact, possible to question the wisdom of the lower house's majority in submitting recommendations that prima facie had no real chance of acceptance. The spirit of opposition to the government remained strong, and in some deputies it had hardened into a principled intransigence difficult to distinguish from sheer stubbornness.[43] A more nuanced and accurate interpretation of the Chamber's behaviour, however, focuses on the need to establish a common denominator in a body increasingly divided, not only by the question of how best to proceed on the constitutional question, but on the specific subject of the duchies as well. Annexationists and Augustenburgians fought the issue with a vigour that required careful management in order to avoid another fault line in a parliament that needed to maintain a united front against increasingly sophisticated and comprehensive government pressure. This time, when its army bill was predictably rejected, the administration countered by presenting for consideration new customs union legislation, a series of proposals for state aid in financing railway construction and a bill for financing Kiel's development as a naval base. All three enhanced tensions in the Chamber – but not enough to splinter it before an angry king prorogued the body on 17 June 1865.

Bismarck, whatever his confidence in his own abilities, as yet did not believe in the army's capacity to win an Austrian war quickly and decisively to the extent that he was ready to

---

[38]Martin Philippson, *Max von Forckenbeck: Ein Lebensbild* (Dresden, 1898), pp. 124–5.
[39]Hermann Oncken, *Rudolf von Bennigsen* (2 vols., Stuttgart, 1910), vol. I, p. 647.
[40]*Stenographische Berichte* (1865), p. 62.
[41]William to Roon, 3 June 1865 in *Militaerische Schriften Kaiser Wilhelms*, vol. II, p. 106.
[42]Kessel, *Moltke*, pp. 425 ff.
[43]Gall, *White Revolutionary*, vol. I, pp. 267–8.

proceed without some consideration of financing the struggle. That question had wider ramifications. Bismarck flirted regularly with notions of a *coup d'état*. His methods of dominance were anything but democratic.[44] Governing by force was no more part of his plan than was a continued Austrian presence in Germany. But not only opposition deputies but civil servants, whose loyalties to the crown were, by this time, virtually absolute, were questioning how long the current state of affairs could continue without permanently damaging Prussia's existence as a *Rechtsstaat*. On the other hand, the expenses of a great-power war could be approved *post facto* by the Chamber. But unless that war's progress and outcome gave the state far more leverage than seemed probable at the time, to secure that approval Bismarck would be constrained to approach the deputies, if not cap in hand, then with more respect than he deemed desirable.

That fear was confirmed when the ministry of finance bluntly asked the Landtag to approve the expenses of the Schleswig-Holstein War. It responded by rejecting the proposal and passing a resolution making cabinet members liable for money drawn from the treasury without parliamentary approval. Then a window opened. The Cologne–Minden railroad, one of Prussia's largest and most profitable lines, had been constructed with government assistance whose terms were intended to make the state the line's eventual owner. The principle of public ownership, however, had suffered a setback with the resignation of neo-cameralist commerce minister, August von der Heydt, and the accompanying growth of free-trade ideas among economists. Since 1862, Gerson Bleichroeder, Bismarck's personal banker and confidant, and also the railroad's banker and one of its directors, had been stressing the mutual advantages to be gained should the government abandon its ownership rights in return for a cash settlement. Initially the ministry of commerce rejected the idea, arguing that the state, in the long run, would lose twice as much as the suggested compensation. Bleichroeder, however, was persistent, making his case on the basis of a bird in hand being worth two in the bush. On 18 July 1865, an agreement was reached in which the government renounced its right to purchase company stock in return for 13 million talers in cash and shares.

The ministries of commerce and finance were dubious – not least because these kinds of initiatives risked violating the constitution beyond absolving. Bismarck was overjoyed. The railroad money, he informed Crown Prince Frederick, gave Prussia enough ready cash to pay for full mobilization and a year's campaign. No less significantly, it set Bismarck on the road to Gastein with the confidence that accompanies a gambler who has the funds to back even risky play.[45]

III

Money, however, is not the only tool of war. How far could Bismarck trust the soldiers – not their loyalty, but their effectiveness? At all levels of the Prussian army, the Schleswig-Holstein campaign had initially inspired relief. The reform's wheels had not

---

[44]Otto Pflanze, 'Bismarcks Herrschaftstechnik als Problem der gegenwaaertigen Historiographie', *Historische Zeitschrift* 234 (1982), pp. 561–99.

[45]Cf. Pflanze, vol. I, pp. 278 ff.; Fritz Stern, *Gold and Iron: Bismarck, Bleichroeder, and the Building of the German Empire* (New York, 1977), pp. 62 ff.; and John C. G. Roehl, 'Kriegsgefahr und Gasteiner Konvention. Bismarck, Eulenburg und die Vertagung des preussisch-oesterreichischen Krieges im Sommer 1865' in *Deutschland in der Weltpolitik des 19. und 20. Jahrhunderts*, eds. I. Geiss and B. J. Wendt (Duesseldorf, 1973), pp. 89–103.

fallen off: reservists had reported for duty; officers had shown reasonable competence; and administration had proven more or less efficient. That last competence, indeed, had won the Prussians a significant amount of favourable publicity in European military circles. Not only the effective use of railway transport to move troops into the duchies and bring them home again, but the smooth and rapid movement of siege paraphernalia to Dueppel indicated that, in any future conflict, Prussia's rear echelons would perform notably better than those deployed in the Crimea and Italy. But the Prussians possessed a long-standing reputation for successful paper-shuffling; it was what their general staff was understood to do particularly well. The crucial question was whether, and how well, the restructured army could fight.

Here the verdict was more mixed. In particular, foreign observers noted that Prussian dispersed formations tended to get out of hand. The short-service conscripts were willing enough, but lacked the initiative of men with more time in uniform. Deployed in open order, too many young soldiers got lost or went to ground and stayed there. Only men in the third year of service, argued most company officers, could really be trusted on a skirmish line. The rest, as a rule, wasted ammunition to no purpose. At the storming of Dueppel and, later, Alsen Island, even company columns fell into confusion, failed to press forward attacks or stalled because the captain was uncertain of how best to proceed. Colonel Emil Rothpletz, a Swiss officer, noted that his Prussian counterparts preferred to use battalions rather than companies whenever the terrain permitted, while the Austrian official history stressed the vulnerability of Prussia's small company columns to either counter-attacks or fire action. In short, the position that a mass army of short-service conscripts was most effective tactically when controlled and manoeuvred *en masse* remained conventional wisdom.[46]

Mass, however, was only half the story. The Prussian army was also processing evidence on technology. In the storming of Dueppel, the needle gun seemed to have demonstrated its significance as a shock weapon. While the reports might speak of works carried with the bayonet, direct observers saw little evidence of hand-to-hand fighting. Much of what there was involved not the relatively elaborate bayonet exercises of the parade ground, but close-quarter brawls featuring gun butts rather than cold steel. Asked why he had chosen to use his rifle as a clumsy club rather than a glorified pike, one private allegedly responded in broad dialect that 'when you get mad enough, the thing just turns around in your hands by itself'.[47] As much to the point for anyone willing to spoil a good story, the Prussian infantry seems to have shot its way forward most of the time, shooting from the hip and reloading on the move, halting more or less without orders in the face of opposition, then blasting the Danes out of their way with rapid rifle fire at close ranges.[48]

Just how effective the needle gun could be on the defensive was indicated on 1 July 1864. A half company of the 50th Prussian Infantry, 124 men strong, was surprised in bivouac around the village of Lundby, on the Jutland peninsula, by a Danish force of around

[46]Emil Rothpletz, *Bericht eines schweizerischen Offiziers ueber seine Mission nach Daenemark (1864)* (Bern, 1924), p. 35 and *Der Krieg in Schleswig und Jutland im Jahre 1865. Nach authentischen Quellen bearbeitet ... durch Friedrich von Fischer* (Vienna, 1870), p. 348.

[47]Prince Krafft zu Hohenlohe-Ingelfingen, *Militaerische Briefe*, vol. II, *Ueber Infanterie* (2nd ed., Berlin, 1886), pp. 22–3.

[48]A detailed contemporary analysis is R. Neumann, *Ueber den Angriff auf die Dueppeler Schanzen in der Zeit vom 15. Maerz zum 18. April 1864* (Berlin, 1865).

200 men. The Danes promptly launched a bayonet charge in column. The Prussian captain deployed his men, allowed the Danes to close the range, then ordered platoon volleys: one at 250 metres, one at 200 and the last at 150. When the Danes closed the range to 80 metres, the Prussians opened rapid fire, each man reloading on his own, four or five shots a minute. The charge collapsed. Twenty-two Danes were dead, sixty-six more were wounded. Some were hit as many as seven or eight times. Three Prussians were treated for light wounds. It was the work of twenty minutes.

The outcome of the action was predictable; even the Austrians recognized the need for better odds attacking an unshaken enemy than three to two. What was significant was the disproportion in the casualty lists – and the fact that the men of the 50th had won their fight without breaking a sweat. Fire discipline, ammunition consumption, responsiveness to orders – all the 'little things' of modern war that so concerned tactical conservatives had gone without a hitch. Perhaps the optimists were right. Perhaps a synergy *was* developing among weapons technology, formal training and patriotic enthusiasm.[49]

The artillery had begun following that path as well, introducing rifled cannon in 1861. These were cast-steel six-pounder breech-loaders, designed by an up-and-coming Essen firm, Friedrich Krupp, which had established its initial reputation manufacturing tableware. A lengthy and acrimonious internal debate over the respective value of rifles and the equally new shell guns led, after 1864, under a new and formidable inspector-general, Gustav von Hindersin, to the triumph of the rifles and – though rearmament would not be complete by 1866 – the adoption of an even newer four-pounder alongside its heavier predecessor.[50]

Significant changes had also occurred in the army's internal dynamic. Manteuffel was gone, assigned to Schleswig as governor, against the wishes of a reluctant king. Bismarck and the rest of the cabinet were correspondingly pleased to be rid of someone whose principled anticonstitutionalism and intransigent behaviour were proving increasing embarrassments to developing an agreement with the Chamber. Roon had particular reasons to celebrate Manteuffel's departure. As chief of the military cabinet he had never been willing to acknowledge the war ministry's official superiority, and took increasing advantage of his close relationship to the king to challenge with impunity Roon's policies and decisions. Manteuffel's successor, Hermann von Tresckow, was no less conservative but an altogether easier colleague.[51]

With Manteuffel gone, Moltke's star burned comparatively bright. He, too, was regarded as an easy colleague, whose professional competence and balanced judgment were welcome in councils where overheated tones often did as much as ill-advised policies to inhibit success. Moltke's good working relations with Roon facilitated acceptance of several particular structural recommendations based on conclusions drawn from the Danish campaign. One involved mobilization. The active army's doubling had the unforeseen consequence of

---

[49]The best reconstruction is Bucholz, *Moltke and the German Wars*, pp. 100 ff.; the most detailed is Albert von Boguslawski, *Geschichte des 3. Niederschlesischen Infanterie-Regiments Nr. 50* (Berlin, 1887), pp. 65 ff. The latter account is significant because Boguslawski enjoyed a deserved reputation as one of the Second Empire's premier tactical analysts.

[50]Until the 1870s, 'pounder' expressed the diameter of a gun's bore, not necessarily the weight of the round. The six-pounder, for example, fired a shell weighing around fifteen pounds. For the artillery's rearmament and reorganization, see Showalter, *Railroads and Rifles*, pp. 175 ff.

[51]Pflanze, vol. I, p. 262 and Heinrich O. Meisner, *Der Kriegsminister, 1815–1914* (Berlin, 1940), pp. 21 ff.

increasing the number of garrisons. Where, under the old system, line regiments and their Landwehr counterparts were completed and sent forward from the same location – usually a fair-sized town with corresponding access to railway facilities – the reorganization left fewer than half of the army's infantry regiments mobilizing from a single place. Cavalry and artillery units were similarly distributed. That meant either foot marches undertaken as fast as men were assembled and equipped, or micro-coordinated rail movements, before the principal mobilization could begin. Either required more staff officers, with more direct authority.

Moltke pressed for an increase in his bureau for other reasons as well. The original concept of the staff officer as a universal expert, he argued, had been modified by circumstances. Some technical responsibilities, particularly cartography, were best filled by specialists exempt from the normal patterns of rotation to troop units. During the Danish campaign, a number of these men had been sent into the field, with less than felicitous results. The kind of use made of Wartensleben as a universal troubleshooter for railway affairs was, at best, a provisional solution. In the same context, the Danish campaign had shown the importance of another point first articulated by Scharnhorst. Generals and their chiefs of staff must know each other well enough to be able to work together dialectically. The general acquaintanceships of a professional army in peacetime were not sufficient to overcome differences of professional opinion – particularly when the commanding general was in the mode of Wrangel, an elderly excellency unable to impose his decisions or his will. The solution, in Moltke's opinion, was to provide enough general staff officers, trained to a common pattern, to permit some stability in staff appointments to field formations. Not until 1867 would the general staff officially expand beyond the sixty-four officers authorized in 1853. That number was, however, increasingly supplemented by temporary assignments. The staff was also split by the creation of a subdivision for scientific affairs to deal specifically with technical issues. Now too big for its housing, the staff eventually benefited from construction of a new building – which was only completed after the founding of the empire.[52]

Give the kingdom's loyal sons a stand-up fight against a real enemy, asserted the third-bottle wisdom of the regimental *Kasinos*, and soon the lawyers and professors of the Landtag would be back in their place – which was no place at all. That did not mean Austria was the opponent of choice – only that the army fancied its chances. In fact, however, most of Moltke's attention in the final months of 1865 was devoted to developing a war plan against the Habsburg Empire – and, common sense dictated, against most of the German Confederation as well. Its precondition was diplomatic: the securing of French and Russian neutrality, thereby obviating the necessity for providing security for Prussia's eastern and western frontiers. Within that context, Moltke recommended concentrating eight of Prussia's nine corps against Austria, leaving its German allies to a single active corps supported by Landwehr – whose new role as a second-line force made it ideal for this kind of subsidiary mission – and Prussia's small-state north German clients.

The proposed allocation of forces should give Prussia rough equality with the forces Austria was able to deploy in Bohemia. That province, thrusting into Prussia's heartland like a knife blade into an exposed armpit, was the only theatre where war between the German

---

[52]Kessel, *Moltke*, p. 420 *passim* and Bucholz, *Prussian War Planning*, p. 45.

powers could reach a quick decision. It offered two major operational possibilities: an attack into Silesia or a drive north towards Torgau, with the eventual objective of Berlin. The Bohemian railway network would support either, but since first considering the situation in 1860, Moltke assumed Austria would choose the Berlin option. That initiative suited the Austrian army's new emphasis on dash and aggressiveness. Since, moreover, the Prussian capital was unfortified, loss of a single battle could throw the Prussians into Pomerania, to say nothing of the impact on the international situation.

Moltke's recommendation involved making maximum use of Prussia's rail network to concentrate three corps around Dresden, three more at Goerlitz and two in Silesia to cover that province. Should Austria mount a direct offensive, the chief of staff expected a major battle and a quick decision. If, instead, the Habsburg army should choose the conservative option and thrust into Silesia, the Prussians could either sidestep into that province as well, or attack Bohemia and follow the direct route to Vienna. In either event, Prussia must maintain the initiative, declaring war as soon as any of its enemies – even a middle state – began arming and then moving as fast as possible into the theatre of operations. It was for that reason that Moltke pushed for recalibration and fine-tuning of the mobilization plan. It was for that reason that he chose the concentration sites. Dresden and Goerlitz were south Prussia's major railway centres, each served by several double-track lines and each with extensive maintenance facilities.[53]

Dresden and Goerlitz offered another industrial-age military advantage as well. The kingdom of Saxony's geographic location and its increasingly Austrian-oriented foreign policy made it as big a threat in 1866 as it had been in 1756. In the former case, Frederick the Great had been unable to overrun Saxony or bring its army to battle before Austrian relief forces complicated the scene. Moltke, while unaware of the details of the Saxon army's mobilization system, knew it still depended on marching to reach its concentration areas. He was correspondingly confident that a steam-powered Prussian attack could reach the frontier and occupy Saxony in the kind of *coup de main* impossible for Frederick. This would have political as well as military consequences, by demonstrating to the rest of Germany just how much Austria's protection was worth once the guns went off. At least it might encourage enough second thoughts among the middle states to impede their testing of the second-line opposition that was all Prussia could spare.[54]

Austria, arguably even more than Prussia, regarded Gastein as an interim compromise. In October 1865, when Bismarck called for a joint protest against the free city of Frankfurt's decision to host meetings hostile to the Gastein agreement, Mensdorff temporized. Bismarck blustered to the new ambassador that Austria faced a choice between an 'honest alliance' with Prussia and 'war to the knife'.[55] Franz Josef was unimpressed – and even less so when, in November, Bismarck offered to buy Holstein from Austria for 60 million florins.

It hardly seemed coincidental when Italy made an offer for Venetia: half a million gold francs. The Austrian national debt was five times its annual income. Merely mobilizing the

---

[53]*Moltkes Militaerische Werke* 1, vol. II, pp. 21–45. Cf. Wolfgang von Groote, 'Moltkes Planungen fuer die Feldzug in Boehmen und ihre Grundlagen' in *Entscheidung 1866*, ed. U. von Gersdorff (Stuttgart, 1966), pp. 78 ff. and Kessel, *Moltke*, pp. 437 ff.

[54]Cf. the 1862 memorandum 'Vorgehen gegen Sachsen' in *Moltkes Militaerische Werke* 1, vol. III, pp. 26 ff. and that of 2 April 1966 in ibid., pp. 74 ff.

[55]Quoted in Pflanze, vol. I, p. 266.

Habsburg forces would cost over a hundred million florins. The British Foreign Office, at least, strongly believed Austria would be wiser to take the cash and let the discredit go. Even Bismarck exclaimed that Italy could take the province by force at little more than half the cost. But to have positive consequences, these kinds of transactions – arguably even more than policies of diplomatic appeasement – must be negotiated from strength, or at least from the mutual convenience of seller and buyer. As Mensdorff explained to the British ambassador, apart from any question of principle, abandoning the empire's positions in Germany and Italy without firing a shot would be less harmful to Austria's position than selling them. A financial solution at this point was a rational calculation only in the narrowest of terms.[56]

The government instead negotiated a loan with France's Credit Foncier, whose terms – 18 per cent for 90 million florins – more resembled those of a modern credit card than those offered to a functioning and solvent great power.[57] It nevertheless gave Mensdorff some working room. Austrian ambassadors in Stuttgart, Munich and the lesser courts of southern Germany by now found little resistance when making the case that the time had come to choose sides once for all. Either Prussia must be deterred by a united German front, even at the cost of war, or the question of state sovereignty would be moot by the end of the decade. That did not mean the princes of Germany trusted Austria in any abstract sense. It meant only that Austria was one degree preferable at one particular time to a Prussia whose policies seemed as random as they were aggressive.

Manteuffel obligingly torched the kindling. His high-handed behaviour in Schleswig revitalized the Augustenburg movement to the point where it was able to sponsor a mass demonstration in Altona on 23 January 1866. Since Altona was in Holstein, the Austrian governor had to give his permission. That individual was none other than Gablenz. His later self-criticism has a certain *post facto* tone. While he disliked Augustenburg as a pretentious parvenu, at the time, Gablenz seems to have considered the rally's nuisance value to Prussia as worth the irritation it caused him as an administrator.

Bismarck, for his part, promptly made the molehill into a mountain, informing Mensdorff that either Vienna cooperate in suppressing revolutionary agitation in the duchies or Prussia would consider the alliance abrogated and act independently in pursuit of its interests. Mensdorff saw the *démarche* as, if not quite an ultimatum, a statement of intent that must be answered in kind. While expressing regrets about the incident itself, he informed Bismarck that Austria would continue to govern Holstein as it saw fit. Austria's cabinet, after some delay, decided on 21 February that it was appropriate to begin military preparations for a war that, as yet, no one in Vienna particularly sought, or regarded as imminent.

That was the kind of measured escalation great powers had practised since the Renaissance. Horses purchased, reservists recalled, regiments despatched to the frontier – all were pawn moves in a wider game, designed, in this case, to stress Prussia's fault lines to the point where even Bismarck would consider discretion the better part of valour. The first

---

[56]Ibid., p. 295; F. R. Bridge, *The Habsburg Monarchy among the Great Powers, 1815–1918* (New York, 1990), pp. 80–1.
[57]Cf. Niall Ferguson, *The House of Rothschild*, vol. II, *The World's Banker, 1849–1999* (New York, 1999), p. 130 *passim*; Fritz Hoenig, *Oesterreichs Finanzpolitik im Kriege von 1866* (Vienna, 1937); and Lawrence D. Steefel, 'The Rothschilds and the Austrian Loan of 1865', *Journal of Modern History* 8 (1935), pp. 27–40.

orders to troop units were only sent a week later, and then to cavalry regiments in the east of the empire, as far away from the likely theatres of operation as possible.[58]

Like its Prussian counterpart, the Austrian army had done a good share of self-evaluation in the aftermath of the Danish campaign. Most of it was on the tactical/technical level. Arguably more deliberately than Prussia, Austria had used Denmark as a test bed for its shock tactics. The initial successes mentioned earlier were somewhat clouded by events at a village named Sankelmarkt on 6 February 1864, when Danish riflemen allowed Austrian columns to come to close range before opening fire, and repelled two frontal attacks before succumbing to a turning movement across a swampy fjord through hip-deep, freezing water.[59] But that was the kind of initiative expected from the new tactics; particularly when compared to the cautious, methodical approach of the Prussians around Dueppel, Austrian methods seemed fundamentally sound. If losses had been uncomfortably high, particularly among officers, that, too, was an expected consequence of the new doctrine. Lieutenants, even colonels, were expendable if the objective was carried; a week's casualties in a day was a fair trade for a quick decision.

Prussian comments that the Austrians had benefited from the low quality of Danish troops and the small amount of Danish artillery were dismissed as sour grapes. As for the needle gun that impressed so many observers, the fundamental Austrian reservation remained as defensible in 1866 as it had been in 1860. If the men 'shot like pigs', as one disgusted senior officer had put it years before, and if their levels of education and intelligence combined with language and command barriers to indicate the improbability of developing effective methods of fire control, then there was no particular reason to finance another expensive innovation on the heels of the new artillery equipment.[60]

This, at least, was the dominant opinion at regimental levels – a fact that in Benedek's army significantly handicapped those more senior officers and officials who argued that the muzzle-loader's days as a first-line weapon were numbered. A few models were tested under war ministry auspices. Some vague efforts were made to finance rearmament by floating special loans. In any case, the efforts were arguably misplaced. Had the breech-loader's superiority been generally acknowledged, had parliament made full funding available, had the war ministry thrown its whole ponderous weight behind the project, it is almost certain that between 1864 and 1866, or even with a longer lead time, it still would have been impossible to adopt a design, produce it in mass, train men to use it and develop a doctrine for its tactics, in time to influence the events of 1866. Such an initiative might indeed have proved counter-productive in the short run, disrupting the army sufficiently to disrupt the competences it possessed.[61]

More serious was the general reluctance to consider refining tactics beyond improving the mass and speed of the charge. Some officers noted the needle gun's short range, and a rate of fire that, under conditions more stressful than those encountered in Denmark, might well empty cartridge boxes to no purpose. They suggested the wisdom of taking advantage of the Austrian Minié's additional 300-yard reach and greater accuracy, combining those

---

[58]Carr, *Wars of Unification*, pp. 126 ff.

[59]Cf. Gruendorf, pp. 232 ff. and the Austrian official account, F. von Fischer, *Der Krieg im Schleswig und Jutland im Jahre 1864* (Vienna, 1870), pp. 94 ff.

[60]Wawro, 'An Army of Pigs', *passim*.

[61]Showalter, *Railroads and Rifles*, pp. 121 ff.

with the Austrian artillery's long-range rifles to force the Prussians to attack, then destroying their disorganized skirmish lines and weak company columns by fire before mounting a final charge to complete the victory. Critics countered by evoking memories of 1859, and insisting that Prussian soldiers were too cerebral to withstand the moral impact of an Austrian charge. They dismissed as well the Danish experience on the ground that the broken terrain had slowed the attacks of poorly trained and badly motivated Danish conscripts.[62]

The latter point requires some development in the context of the frequently noted and often (particularly after 1866) criticized tendency of the Austrians to ignore terrain in their tactical practices. Assaults in close columns at top speed were practised from Italy to Galicia, and the expectation was that they would be implemented over virtually every kind of ground. This did not entirely reflect blind faith in the panacea of cold steel. Nor was it the product of indifference to anything beyond the drill field and the manoeuvre ground. Since Austrian regiments were regularly transferred around the empire, a common tactical doctrine was a matter of absolute necessity as a common denominator – much like the British army after 1918 and again after 1945. Any modifications to suit local conditions had to be recognized as exceptions to a general rule. Since that general rule depended on shock, it only made sense to develop the infantry's maximum potential as a shock force, cultivating the ability to advance in order and at speed, even over unfavourable terrain against defenders armed with rapid-firing weapons.[63] Equally significant was that, like any conscript force, the Austrian army was institutionally limited in how much training could be retained. An Austrian column was not understood as a clumsy, unarticulated mass, the successor of the *Gewalthaufen* of the medieval Swiss; its use required no less careful training than did instruction in marksmanship and skirmishing. As for the possibility that the entire army was on a wrong tactical road, the implications prevented consideration in the same way that an equivalent hypothesis will, as a rule, be rigorously excluded from the high councils of a contemporary great-power army. The task was to make the system work in spite of whatever tricks the Prussians had up their military sleeves.

IV

In that context, Otto von Bismarck was increasingly proving himself Austria's best friend at court – at least in the courts and the administrations of the German Confederation.[64] By this time a rift had developed in that body whose moral significance well exceeded its military import. More and more of the small states of north Germany were overtly aligning themselves with Prussia. Their battalion-scale armed forces had long followed Prussian models. Now Lippe, Saxe-Coburg-Gotha, Waldeck, Saxony-Anhalt and even larger entities,

---

[62]Cf. *inter alia*, Andres, 'Das neue Fuesiliergewehr, Modell 1860, in der koeniglich-preussischen Armee im Vergleich mit dem oesterreichischen Infanteriegewehr', *Oesterreichische Militaerische Zeitschrift* (1863), vol. IV, pp. 265–73; J. M. A., 'Die Feuerwaffen und das Bajonett in ihrem Wesen und ihrem Wirksamkeit', ibid., pp. 363–74; and 'Ueber die Ursachen der Misserfolge bei der oesterreichischen Nordarmee im Kriege Preussens gegen Deutschland im Jahre 1866', ibid. (1866), vol. II, pp. 349 ff.

[63]'Zur taktischen Offensive und Defensive der Infanterie', *Oesterreichische Militaerische Zeitschrift* (1863), vols. I–II, pp. 276–86.

[64]For the following, cf. the overview by Richard Dietrich, 'Das Jahr 1866 und das "Dritte Deutschland"' in *Europa und der Norddeutsche Bund*, ed. R. Dietrich (Berlin, 1968), pp. 85–108.

like Oldenburg and Luebeck, were also tailoring their diplomacies to Prussian patterns. The justification was the same in each case: the Confederation no longer offered a reasonable degree of protection against both direct Prussian aggrandizement and Bismarck's growing willingness to take direct advantage of revolutionary forces, liberalism and nationalism to foment uprisings.[65] It was thought best, therefore, to 'bandwagon' and negotiate terms with the threat next door while some room for negotiation remained. It might be a bit early to speak of a domino effect – if only because the states involved were too small and too isolated from the rest of the Confederation to pull anyone down with them directly. Nevertheless, by the spring of 1866, the middle-sized states of the south were sufficiently concerned with being left high and dry in the face of growing Prussian power that Austria needed to offer nothing more positive than resistance to Berlin and its *de facto* dictator to mobilize perhaps the highest level of support it had enjoyed from middle Germany since the Confederation's formation.[66]

Austria's decision for war was facilitated not only by the rallying of south Germany, but also by the impressions of imminent domestic chaos conveyed by the newspapers and the diplomats of Austria's northern neighbour. The constitutional conflict was in no way a secret. Nor was the continuing hostility to Bismarck in public, political and administrative circles. A quick, hard blow – the kind of blow the Austrian army was focused on delivering – had strong prospects for bringing about a cabinet victory in a cabinet war, turning Prussia's political system against itself without either mobilizing any nascent general patriotism or inspiring a revolution that might either spread across Prussia's frontiers or so cripple that state as to force it entirely from the ranks of the great powers. Austria's 'grand policy' towards Prussia, even at this late stage, was designed – as had been that of Maria Theresa in an earlier century – to put Prussia back in its proper place as secondary guarantor of central European stability. As Metternich had calculated and warned in an earlier era, there was no profit for Austria in creating a vacuum north of the Main into which France, Russia or both might move. Nor did even the most 'black-yellow' optimists in the foreign ministry or the general staff believe Austria could long exercise solo hegemony in a Germany that was so rapidly expanding in so many ways.

Victory would not, however, mean simple restoration of the *status quo ante bellum*. At the least, Austria intended to put its influence – and its army – behind conservative efforts to eliminate or emasculate organizations like the *Nationalverein*, and political liberalism generally. Austrian admission into a reorganized *Zollverein*, on the basis of its control of Holstein, was similarly regarded as a given. In both of these contexts, the everyday locus of power in the German Confederation was expected to shift to the middle states, closely cooperating with Austria through governments reorganized along conservative/reactionary lines. The fiction of sovereign equality would give way to a coalition of 'four kings' – Saxony, Wuerttemberg, Bavaria and Austria. The Prussophilic Grand Duke of Baden could either bandwagon or abdicate, while Hanover, the strongest of the northern states, was expected

---

[65]The most detailed general discussion of that crucial subject remains Harold L. Kirkpatrick, 'Bismarck's Insurrectionist Projects during the Austro-Prussian War, 1866' (dissertation, University of California, Berkeley, 1962).

[66]Bavaria was the key to the middle states' decisions, and its policy is discussed in John Eiklors' still useful narrative, 'Bavaria, the Landtag, and the War of 1866' (dissertation, Northwestern University, 1963). Cf. more generally, Gall, *White Revolutionary*, vol. I, pp. 289 ff.

to accept the new dispensation in lieu of the Prussian dominance that seemed the only alternative.

As for direct territorial adjustments, some hotheads – mostly in uniform – considered the prospects of undoing the Seven Years War, by recovering Upper Silesia, at least. With French support this was theoretically possible, and there was gossip about placing the deposed Tuscan branch of the Habsburg family on the new acquisition's throne. The foreign ministry was more cautious. In its favoured scenario, Saxony, Wuerttemberg and Bavaria would be allowed to absorb some of their dwarf neighbours – with perhaps enough slivers from Prussian borderlands to make difficult any future cooperation with the Hohenzollerns.[67]

Mensdorff, for his part, was almost as reluctant as Bismarck would eventually prove to risk creating a permanent *casus belli* by redrawing maps with too free a hand. He was more inclined to appeal to King William, the anti-Bismarck faction at court, particularly the English-born crown princess, her mother Queen Victoria and the Duke of Coburg, and those public figures like the crown prince who were hostile – from conservatism or *Realpolitik* – to the idea of an Austrian war. At best, Mensdorff reasoned, he might be able to avert the conflict at the last moment. Should this be impossible, he hoped to build a 'golden bridge' for reconciliation in the aftermath of Habsburg victory and a 'golden chute' down which Bismarck could be thrown as a symbol of reconciliation.[68]

These, of course, represented speculation and inference more than concrete plans. They invite dismissal as throwbacks to an earlier and simpler time, the days of Hardenberg and Stein, when 'high politics' could indeed shape policy in a medium-sized state like Prussia. Their presentation is nevertheless useful in that it highlights Austria's expectation of victory in the war towards which Bismarck was impelling Germany. That, of course, did not mean one could simply relax and wait for the bayonet to do its work on the plains of Bohemia – the Austrian army agreed with its rival that the decisive campaign would be fought there, rather than somewhere further west in the territories of the German states. Mensdorff's expectation that Austria would benefit diplomatically by being the sole author of the principal victory helped shape this strategic decision. Military questions, however, were even more important. Apart from the limited railway connections into Bavaria and Wuerttemberg, the general opinion in Vienna was that the south German armies were trained in ways incompatible with Austrian doctrines, and not good enough at their own methods to be worth the trouble certain to be caused by issues of supply and command.

With the theatre chosen, two cold equations and a variable came into effect. Prussia was able to mobilize in six weeks to two months – half the time Austria required. That, it is worth emphasizing, was a function of geography as well as general staffs. Austria was larger and less developed, particularly in the empire's southern and eastern regions. The roads and railroads to move troops and supplies quickly did not exist. The second equation, however, was a consequence of decisions made and described earlier. Austria had one railway line leading into the projected zone of operations. Prussia had half a dozen. That, in turn, brought the variable into play. After 1859, as before, about a third of the Austrian army, including some of its best formations, were stationed in Italy. To pull them out and send

---

[67]Cf. the analyses in, *inter alia*, Carr, *Wars of Unification*, pp. 128–9; Wawro, 'The Austro-Prussian War', vol. I, pp. 274 ff.; and Rolf Bauer, 'Oesterreich, Preussen und Deutschland. Der Weg nach Koeniggraetz und seine Folgen' in *Europa und der Norddeutsche Bund*, pp. 57–64.

[68]Clark, pp. 374 ff., remains a sound narrative.

them north over the Alps would not only risk a Piedmontese invasion – even without great-power backing – but it would also send the Prussian general staff the kind of signal it was risky to ignore, the kind that Bismarck could easily fan into a *casus belli* on his terms. Should these risks be accepted, given the difficulties of large-scale rail transport in mountainous regions, the chances were good that the troops in question would arrive too late to do any good. That meant a large part of the northern army must come from the east and south – the very regions where not only railroad but highway networks were the thinnest.

When all the calculations were done, the general staff reported that Austria would need ten to twelve weeks to bring decisive forces into Bohemia. The challenge was to get as much done as possible without provoking hostilities. The foreign ministry, expecting to conclude a long-term peace with Bismarck's successor, was reluctant to abandon negotiations until the last possible moment. Austria's German allies could not be left to stand unsupported against a Prussian attack they had no chance of stopping. Nor should forward Austrian elements be sent into Bavaria or Wuerttemberg, unless absolutely necessary to avert a diplomatic disaster or a Prussian pre-emptive strike. The best operational approach in these contexts was a lightning campaign from a standing start. Benedek, the army's principal hard charger, was ordered to report from Italy to Vienna by 6 March as commander of the North Army. The next day, Franz Josef ordered the completion of preparations for mobilization. As orders of battle were prepared and formation commanders designated, the general staff began turning to its medium-scale maps.

Alfred von Henikstein, Austria's nominal chief of staff, had been appointed in 1864 as Benedek's personal choice, when he decided that he could not simultaneously wear all the army's principal hats. The two men had worked together effectively in Italy, and Benedek considered Henikstein perfectly capable of executing the limited functions that were a planning staff's prerogatives in the Austrian army. Henikstein, on the other hand, doubted his own competence from the day of his appointment. The more he learned of Austria's diplomatic and strategic situation, the more pessimistic he became. It is open to question whether this mindset reflected reasoned calculation or a sense of being overwhelmed by his job's demands, limited as they were. Apart from his self-doubts, Henikstein did not possess the force of character, the institutional leverage or the support of his general staff subordinates to alter state or army policy. By 1866 it was clear that he was not a man to go to war with. At the same time, it went against tradition simply to relieve him. Instead, it was decided to give the North Army an operations chief.

The definition of this post reflected the fact that, at mid-century, the shape of a modern staff system was still indeterminate. The 'chief' was expected to plan the Prussian campaign and confine himself to that single theatre of operations. At the same time, he was expected to keep an eye on the empire's overall strategic situation as it developed. Finally, and not least, the 'operations chief' was tasked with doing most of Benedek's heavy thinking for him, without arousing the latter's military populism to a point where he simply went his own way. The man chosen for the job was Gideon Krismanic. At forty-nine he had been a senior staff officer at Solferino and a professor at the Vienna War School. His specialty was Germany. He and Benedek knew each other from Italy. And even with that experience, Krismanic retained the kind of confidence, moreover, that seemed to indicate an ability to keep from being submerged by his commander.

Most evaluations of Krismanic describe him as among the major human causes of Austria's Bohemian débâcle. He was brought before a court of inquiry after the war, and, if he escaped sanction the same cannot be said for his plan. Krismanic was enough of a historian to be deeply influenced by the defensive campaigns waged by Maria Theresa's generals against Frederick the Great in this same region. He was constrained as well by a template: a rough existing draft of a defensive disposition designed to counter a pre-emptive Prussian strike. Instead of returning to square one when he reached the theatre, Krismanic proposed to use the fortress of Olmuetz as the base for an entrenched camp providing a central position against an invasion from Silesia. Krismanic regarded that as a far more promising route than those leading from Prussian Saxony and Saxony, with their significant natural and man-made obstacles.

There is an interesting parallel between the thinking of Moltke and Krismanic in the months before the outbreak of war. Where Moltke saw the advantages of a straightforward attack on Dresden by the shortest reasonable route, Krismanic considered the distance between the Silesian frontier and Vienna. He evaluated the probable influence on Prussian planning (well known for emphasizing speed and precision) of the four railway lines connecting Bohemia to Silesia and the well-developed system of paved roads in the region. Silesia, he concluded, was Prussia's most likely staging area, and when they came, the North Army would be awaiting them.

Krismanic recognized that he might be mistaken in his calculation of Prussia's main axis of advance. But no matter how reckless Bismarck's diplomacy might be, Krismanic decided Prussia's generals were unlikely to risk bypassing six Austrian corps at Olmuetz in a headlong drive south from Prussian Saxony for Prague and Vienna. If they came from the north, they must turn and fight – on Austrian ground and on Austrian terms, with the mountains in their rear that had dispersed one Prussian army in 1742 and paralysed another in the 'Potato War' of 1780. A rapid-firing, breech-loading rifle lost much of its effect if the man using it was simultaneously looking over his shoulder for sight of the road home. Uniformed civilians were likely to be a good deal less martial at the end of a long supply line than close to their own frontiers and their own magazines.

Considered in these contexts, Krismanic's proposed dispositions were by no means an unmitigated recipe for disaster. Far from planning a 'war of positions' in eighteenth-century style, Krismanic took into account, albeit indirectly, the nature of the armies and the nature of the diplomacies involved. An invasion of Prussia through Saxony, the initiative Moltke had expected, was in fact suggested in May. The balance of forces, however, worked against its serious consideration. Had Austria been able to concentrate its entire army in the northern sector, it was just possible to provide flank security for a 'single thrust' towards Berlin. With three corps in Italy and even minimum security elements left in the east and south, the proposal was a nineteenth-century version of Montgomery's 1944 Operation Market-Garden on a field army scale. Better by far to let the Prussians come, beat them soundly on ground of Austria's choosing, and then advance either into Silesia or across the Inn river into Germany proper.[69]

---

[69]For background and details on Austrian planning in the spring of 1866, Wawro, 'The Austro-Prussian War', vol. I, pp. 325 ff., is at once the most recent and the most critical account. The more favourable analysis is Schmidt-Brentano, pp. 155 ff. Johann Christoph Allmayer-Beck, 'Der Feldzug der oesterreichischen Nord-Armee nach Koeniggraetz' in *Entscheidung 1866* and Wolfgang von Groote, 'Koeniggraetz im Blick der Militaergeschichte' in *Europa und der Norddeutsche Bund*, pp. 109–34, are excellent for the first century of historiography. H. Bonnal, *Sadowa* (Paris, 1901) stands out among the many nineteenth-century studies.

The unavailability of the three corps in Venetia was confirmed as Bismarck came into the open in his search for an Italian connection. Austria still had breathing room in this context. Italy's premier, General Alfonso La Marmora, was not one of the diplomatic community's brighter lights. He was, however, wise enough to evaluate the worth of Bismarck's words. Rather than initiate hostilities with Austria by itself, La Marmora insisted, Piedmont must have a mutual timetable for war as a condition of an alliance. Bismarck stalled as spring went by and secret feelers passed between Turin and Vienna. Mensdorff, however, refused as a matter of principle to surrender Venetia as the price of peace with Piedmont.

In retrospect, the failure to remove the major point of friction between Austria and Italy, particularly since Victor Emmanuel was perfectly willing to secure the province without spilling blood, was questionable. Mensdorff's argument that a dynastic empire could not make this kind of fundamental concession to ethnic nationalism had some merit. So did his argument that Italy's next claims would involve the allegedly Italian areas of Dalmatia and the south Tyrol — both too deeply embedded in the Habsburg heritage to be considered negotiable. But as well as encouraging the pro-Prussian faction in the Italian government, Mensdorff's intransigent position provided a justification for Britain and France to remain at a safe diplomatic distance from an Austria that seemed determined to plunge Europe into war rather than revise parameters outdated by new facts.

For a Britain with no desire to intervene directly in continental affairs, Austria's behaviour challenged the principle — derived from political economy — of rational and businesslike conduct of international relations in a context of tangible objectives. For France — or, at least, Napoleon III — it represented a last stand of the legitimist arguments informing the Congress of Vienna. It also represented a chance to rebuild an Italian position that had remained shaky since the Armistice of Villafranca. Napoleon encouraged Victor Emmanuel to continue negotiations for the Prussian alliance finally concluded on 8 April 1866. By its terms, Prussia had a three-month window to initiate hostilities.

La Marmora promptly began shifting troops towards the Venetian frontier. The premier believed Italy needed a victory to gild a unification that would be achieved by means less than heroic, and to establish the state's position among the European powers. Austrian intelligence — very efficient in Italy — confirmed reports of the Italian movements in the third week of April. While Italy's mobilization in no way resembled the machine-like efficiency of the Prussians, the state nevertheless had 400 battalions, theoretically available for operations against what remained of Austria in Italy.

With the *Schwerpunkt* of the war projected as Bohemia, Benedek's successor south of the Alps must make do with what he had: 75,000 men and 170 guns, plus about another 50,000 men garrisoning the fortresses. These were odds to encourage the truest of believers in Habsburg military effectiveness to demand immediate mobilization rather than risk being caught half-prepared. That Benedek's successor was a matter-of-fact professional, who also happened to be an archduke and the emperor's uncle, only expedited Vienna's decision, made on 21 April, to bring its forces in Italy to a war footing.[70]

---

[70]Coppa, pp. 119 ff., is a good overview. John W. Bush, *Venetia Redeemed: Franco-Italian Relations, 1864–1866* (Syracuse, NY, 1967), focuses on French ambitions. Pflanze, vol. I, p. 295 *passim*, interprets the Prussian alliance with Piedmont in the context of Bismarck's growing readiness to unleash revolution in order to secure his ends.

Linked to the increasing movement of troops into Bohemia, the Austrian decision generated significant alarm in Prussian military circles. Moltke's reliance on the railways to speed Prussian concentration increased as days passed, to become a virtual article of faith. His final proposal divided the army into two equal forces, four corps in Silesia, four more in Prussian Saxony – all with unusually large deployment areas. Only by thus spreading out, Moltke argued, was it possible simultaneously to cover Berlin and Breslau, concentrate the largest force possible in the shortest time and take maximum advantage of the rail network. What he meant was that units were to be moved as far forward as possible on as many rail lines as possible, then advance. Concentration in the familiar sense of that concept would take place only for battle.

Since before his assignment to the general staff, Moltke had argued that autonomy of movement was the operational essence of the army corps system. Corps had to be able to extend themselves like gymnasts, and Moltke constantly warned against being seduced by railroads into massing too many troops in too small an area, leaving them tied to railheads and strangled by limited road networks. The situation in 1866, however, bent Moltke's original concepts out of shape. Not until mid-March would William authorize even preliminary moves to reinforce the fortresses of Schleswig and Silesia; for the remainder of the month he approved nothing but similar limited measures. Moltke's repeated reminders that Prussia was losing time had more intellectual than emotional impact on a monarch from a different culture of time, one measured as much by the sun as the clock. The king, moreover, was viscerally hostile to the concept of a German civil war that he believed could benefit only democrats and Frenchmen. Time and again, Bismarck was able to stimulate anger at particular Austrian behaviour; time and again did the anger dissipate with Bismarck's departure from the royal presence. A sharp exchange of notes between Vienna and Berlin in early April culminated when Mensdorff offered to withdraw the troops already in Bohemia to their normal garrisons if Prussia would reciprocate. Since almost no Prussian troops had yet been moved anywhere, the proposal was sufficiently one-sided to tempt William to insist on a forthcoming response that supported a mutual stand-down on the frontier. The minister complained that he could no longer stand the tension and fell prey to a spectrum of stress-related illnesses.[71]

Then came the Austrian decision to mobilize in Italy. As demonstrated above, in itself this was a rational and appropriate response to a particular situation. There was only one thing wrong with it. Since 1859, Austrian mobilization plans had been sufficiently integrated that the war ministry and the general staff insisted it was impossible to continue the gradual build-up in Bohemia while simultaneously placing the Italian forces on a full war footing. On 27 April, mobilization was ordered for the North Army as well, and some time around that date, Franz Josef seems to have abandoned any lingering hope of maintaining the peace.[72]

William was more sanguine – or simply denser. He took a week to respond to the Austrian initiative, and then did no more than order the mobilization of five of Prussia's nine corps. He still refused to approve their concentration against Austria. Moltke, whose ability to remain calm under these circumstances impressed everyone in his vicinity, insisted once more that time, not mass, was the critical factor. Enough Austrians were already in forward positions to

---

[71]Cf. *inter alia*, Kessel, *Moltke*, pp. 437 ff.; Bucholz, *Moltke and the German Wars*, pp. 112 ff.; and Pflanze, vol. I, p. 296.
[72]Wawro, 'The Austro-Prussian War', vol. I, pp. 330 ff.

mount strong pre-emptive attacks into Silesia and Prussian Saxony. Move two corps into each area, Moltke argued, and leave the Guard in Berlin as a reserve. It posed no problem – if the orders for the movement were issued simultaneously with the orders for mobilization. William, still reluctant to escalate the crisis to flashpoint, temporized.

At this point, it is appropriate to reintroduce the king as an active participant in the processes of decision-making that led up to the Seven Weeks War. Standard person-centred accounts are overwhelmingly presented from the perspective of Bismarck or Moltke. In either case, William – as usual – emerges as a more or less inert force, needing either the repeated galvanic shocks administered by his minister-president or the clearly presented calculations of his chief of staff to impel him to action. William, in fact, was accustomed to making his own decisions, and regarded both Bismarck and Moltke as what they were under the Prussian constitution: royally appointed officials who served at his pleasure. William might not have grasped the details of either Bismarck's diplomacy or Moltke's strategy, but the concepts underlying both were in no way beyond his comprehension. If less willing, in principle, to fight a war than were both of his subordinates by now, the king was beginning to understand the time relationships Moltke had been at pains to explain as the crisis escalated. On the other hand, William sought to give Austria every opportunity either to back away from the crisis or to take such a plainly false step that European neutrality would not depend entirely on Bismarck's gossamer web of negotiation and innuendo.

William did not understand why railway movement orders could not be drafted after a formation was mobilized and ready to take the field. In his mind, that represented a desirable refinement of the strategy of 'gradual escalation' with which he was more comfortable, morally, militarily and politically, than with Moltke's developing concept of war by time-table. Prussian mobilization plans in 1866 were far from the elaborate interlocking structure of 1914, whose disruption, even in theory, caused the then chief of staff to have a walking nervous breakdown. Only in mid-April was the redoubtable Wartensleben transferred to Berlin as head of the general staff's railway section. Not until 1 May did he present a specific proposal for establishing mixed military-civilian 'line commissions' to control and coordinate movement on the route networks leading into the proposed theatre of operations.

Moltke's response to William was crucial for the development of future relations between war and policy. Final preparations for moving a complete corps by rail, explained the chief of staff, were sufficiently elaborate to require at least ten days, even if the actual orders were drafted earlier. Moltke, at this stage of his career, however, in contrast to Bismarck, did not consider it his place to convince the king of anything. He was still breaking new ground, both for his office and himself, and the air was thin at these high altitudes of state policy. As the king remained reluctant to take the final step into war, the chief of staff responded by concentrating his efforts downward, doing everything possible to adjust train schedules and rolling-stock allocations to William's decisions. It required a total of nine separate orders, issued between 3 and 24 May, to bring the whole army under the colours and set it in motion. This was a far cry from the single-step action which Moltke had advocated and hoped for. Nevertheless, it represented the beginning of the process of identifying mobilization with concentration, and concentration with action, which, over the next half-century, would come to dominate the thinking of every general staff and the schedules affecting their particular formations in Europe, and which would survive in modified forms until after the Cold War.

With his hopes for systematic, simultaneous deployment gone, Moltke concentrated on moving individual corps into the theatre of operations as rapidly as possible. Despite some problems caused by senior officers attempting to modify the schedules of their particular formation, both the railroads themselves and their essentially improvised organization did what was asked of them. In a sense, the serial orders whose operational implications had so concerned Moltke were compensated by unexpected administrative advantages. Nowhere was the rail network overloaded beyond the line commissions' ability to compensate. A stray train or two, insufficient rolling stock at a particular place, locomotive breakdowns and track breaks – all proved well within the capacity of private companies and public lines to remedy. Arrangements for providing food and water for both men and horses were correspondingly effective.[73]

This sharp contrast with the events of 1848, 1850 and 1859 seemed a good omen to the officers, and did much to keep the mobilized reservists from consolidating the discontent that accompanied the initial mobilization. Noteworthy in this context is the limited effect of official assertions that uniforms were being donned because it was the king's will. Since 1806, 1815 and even 1848, Prussia's subjects had moved some distance towards becoming citizens, who sought reasons they could understand for risking their lives and sacrificing their wages.[74] The army's ability to minimize immediate grievances, however, significantly diminished individual willingness to voice challenges or give ear to those who might do so. Stomachs were full. Boots fitted. A system that seemed to know what it was doing in these matters might also receive the benefit of the doubt in wider and deeper issues.[75] Finally, and arguably of most importance, the destination points were able to cope with the limited number of trains that arrived on any given day, and, in the process, learn from experience how to keep men, animals, supplies and equipment from piling up haphazardly at the railheads. Here, again, the sense of order and control as one approached the sharp end did much to instil confidence at all levels of an essentially untested army. Even senior officers who might harbour reservations about general staff whippersnappers with inky fingers and superior attitudes could not deny that, so far, all was going well.

Whether the army's dispositions made enough sense to justify the confidence was another question. As Moltke's transport plan unfolded, it was clear that seven and a half corps, almost the whole of the active army, were to be extended like beads on a string around a 400-kilometre arc from Silesia to Saxony. Civilian and military analysts alike described Moltke as resorting to a cordon deployment in the worst fashion of those superannuated generals who had proven such obliging enemies of the young Napoleon. Moltke kept repeating the same points. To counter Austria's time advantage in mobilization, Prussia must reach the zone of operations as rapidly as possible. That meant not just primary but exclusive dependence on steam power, and the major railway junctions in south-east Prussia were extended at regular intervals along the frontier. That fact could not be changed. What was necessary, therefore, was to see the rail concentration as the beginning,

---

[73]Cf. Kessel, *Moltke*, pp. 444 ff.; Bucholz, *Moltke and the German Wars*, pp. 114 ff.; and Dennis E. Showalter, 'Mass Multiplied by Impulsion: The Influence of Railroads on Prussia's Planning for the Six Weeks War', *Military Affairs* 38 (1974), pp. 62–7.

[74]Stig Foerster, 'Militaer und Staatsbuegerliche Partizipation. Die Allgemeine Wehrpflicht im Deutschen Kaiserreich, 1871–1914' in *Die Wehrpflicht*, ed. R. Foerster (Munich, 1994), pp. 55–70.

[75]Frank Kuehlich, *Die deutschen Soldaten 1870/71* (Frankfurt, 1995), pp. 68 ff., describes the mood in the ranks five years later as 'blind confidence' based on 'lower-class' faith in authority nurtured by the war's early success. While there is no similar in-depth study for 1866, the relatively undisturbed mobilization suggests that the army and the government received the benefit of the doubt.

not the end, of the army's deployment. The second stage would begin when the separate corps began marching concentrically toward the enemy.[76]

V

Meanwhile, Benedek's North Army was taking shape. Prussia's military building blocks were preassembled in their respective corps districts. Austria's were fitted together in the field, under a rubric of 'when wood is chopped, chips fly'. Most of the corps and brigade commanders were 'new men', at worst lightly tainted with the disasters of 1859. Most of the corps commanders were also aristocrats whose professional careers owed at least as much to connections as to merit. It may, however, be suggested that no senior appointments made by any army at the start of any war are uninfluenced by similar considerations. Benedek, moreover, had a major role in selecting or approving his immediate subordinates. If he frequently misinterpreted or exaggerated their capacities, this was not necessarily a simple exercise in flattering the powerful or placating the various ethnic and political factions in the army and the government.

The common thread of Benedek's evaluations reflects a search for what later military vocabularies describe as 'thrusters' or 'hard chargers' – men who could reasonably be expected to attack when and where they were ordered. This was in accord with Austrian tactical doctrine – and with a general perspective that emphasized deciding the next war in one or a series of all-out, head-down battles. The brigadiers, whose larger number makes capsule analysis correspondingly difficult, were competent enough in the context of the doctrine they were expected to implement. Combined-arms tactics, general situational awareness, a sense of strategic purpose – these were not primary concerns of the Habsburg army's junior general officers, any more than in any other western army of the period. The men who commanded Benedek's brigades were brave to a fault. They knew how to organize charges, and lead them when it came to that. Most of them could inspire their men even if they could do no more than swear at them in their own languages. Most of them were sober most of the time. There have been worse matrices for victory.

More problematic for the army's command climate than the relative competence of its senior officers was their collective tendency to regard cooperation as a favour and to resist all forms of instruction or correction. These were men who could be driven in a team only by a chief who combined charisma, force and fortune to degrees unusual in any army at any period. Arguably the closest contemporary analogue to the command system of Benedek's army was that of the Confederate Army of Tennessee under Braxton Bragg. Both featured junior generals who were more warriors than *Feldherren,* and seniors whose competence was not so great that they could afford to dissipate energy on faction fighting.

Benedek moved his headquarters from Vienna to Olmuetz on 27 May, and followed his Italian pattern of establishing a public presence, seeking to put his stamp on an army still pulling itself together. Criticism comparing his exhibitionism with the self-effacing sobriety of Moltke combines hindsight and misunderstanding. The Austrian army of 1866 (and indeed throughout its history) responded well to charismatic leadership. The scene at Olmuetz resembled that of Schiller's *Wallenstein's Camp* at least as much as any comparable

---

[76]Showalter, *Railroads and Rifles*, pp. 62–3.

event of the time. For a time it seemed that the North Army had more generals than regiments. Troop staffs were improvised, drawing on officers from all over the empire with no experience of working together. Reports complained constantly about shortages of everything from rifles to underwear. The long marches and slow train trips imposed by the mobilization system worked against any form of refresher training for the reservists, and any opportunity for officers to become accustomed to leading war-strength formations. New innovations such as glass canteens proved unsuitable often enough to diminish faith in the army's 'culture of competence': the belief at lower levels that the system had a reasonable idea of what it was doing on an everyday basis.

Benedek was sixty-three – but an old sixty-three. Years of long days in the field and longer nights of never leaving a full bottle or an empty glass had taken their toll. He had not wanted the North Army's command in the first place, making the case that his expertise was in Italy and he was best left there. For a general who operated essentially by rule of thumb and past experience, the point was a good one. Benedek had no sense of the spatial relationships of this new theatre. He had no 'fingertip feel' for the plains and the passes of Bohemia as opposed to the built-up, fenced-in terrain of northern Italy. And, in contrast to Moltke, theoretical wisdom was not likely to supplement reflexive insight. Benedek's behaviour in Olmuetz suggests someone under constant, unrelievable stress: bursts of random energy followed by what seemed near torpor – at least to those observers who were anxious to begin a campaign that had been characterized on both sides by fits and starts.

The resulting compounding of confusion influenced significantly Krismanic's continued belief that the army was best placed around Olmuetz, as opposed to undertaking any ventures further afield. The Prussians, after all, were not showing any particular initiative in opening the campaign. The outlines of their deployment were as yet uncertain. Moreover, Krismanic argued, the road networks were exponentially better on Prussia's side of the frontier – a fact facilitating the blocking of any partial offensives.

Two men who did not deplore the delay in resorting to force were Mensdorff and Moltke. The Austrian foreign minister was both anxious to secure French support and confident in his ability to do so by playing Venetia as a trump card. Since April he had been floating trial balloons in Paris, receiving definite 'maybes' in reply. Now Mensdorff offered to surrender Venetia, not to Piedmont but to France directly, in return for French support of territorial revisions far more sweeping than those originally considered in Vienna. France would be given a free hand to annex Belgium, and Prussia's Rhine provinces would become a nominally independent state. Austria, in turn, would acquire Silesia. Venetia, of course, would become part of the new state of Italy – but not at Austria's direct expense.

It seemed an offer Napoleon III could not refuse: to profit by doing nothing, thereby giving Austria the 'fair field and no favour' that should be all its army needed against Prussia. The common criticism that it was too much too late does not fully consider the risks of putting too much on the table for a Napoleon whose real problem in 1866 was the compounded multiplicity of his desires and opportunities. The Union's victory in the American Civil War, and the subsequent collapse of Maximilian's ill-fated Mexican Empire, left vulnerable a France increasingly dependent upon plebiscite approval for its legitimacy.[77]

---

[77]Andre Armengaud, *L'Opinion publique en France et la crise national Allemande en 1866* (Paris, 1962). Jean-Guy Larregola, *Le Gouvernement français face à la Guerre de sécession* (Paris, 1970), shows how much political capital the French government expended pursuing the division of the US into two separate and hostile states.

A foreign-policy triumph achieved at no cost, and with no obligation to any of the Second Empire's proliferating domestic factions, was correspondingly irresistible. Gifting Italy with Venetia would both placate what remained of the emperor's conscience and re-establish French influence south of the Alps. A war enabling Prussia to increase its influence north of the Main was good – but a war that would put Berlin under an obligation to Paris was better. Territorial gains for France, moreover, were less likely to attract notice in the context of a general redrawing of central Europe's maps. Napoleon had always been more cautious than his reputation. Now, despite pressure from his entourage to take maximum advantage of the German situation, he remained reluctant to risk developing an image of France as seeking hegemony as opposed to primacy in Europe. At the same time, Napoleon reasoned, Austria must not emerge from the conflict either excessively strengthened or with delusions about its relative place in the European order. In that context, the exchange of Venetia for Silesia was unpromising – to say nothing of the effect brokering it would have on long-term Franco-Prussian relations.

The key to Napoleon's policy was the almost universal conviction of French military experts that Prussia and Austria were an even match. War between them was not, it should be emphasized, expected to endure for months and years. Rather, the balance of forces and competences were such that neither side could reasonably expect to achieve a favourable decision in a time-frame small enough to satisfy their respective diplomats and political systems. Domestic and international considerations, in other words, would encourage accepting – perhaps inviting – French mediation, and sooner rather than later.

This position was reinforced by the French army's structure and culture. This subject will be addressed in more detail in the next chapter. For present purposes it suffices to say that, since at least the 1830s, France had developed its army as a quick-reaction power-projection force, whose high quality and corresponding ability to cope with contingencies enhanced its capacities in situations like the one France presently faced. While the French did not dismiss their potential opponents, they regarded the Prussians as too rule- and desk-bound to be effective in the chaos endemic to modern war. Austrian efforts at improvement had left them no more than a blurred copy of a French original. From the perspective of Napoleon's war ministry, in short, there seemed no reason why a policy of betting on as many diplomatic cards as possible could not be underwritten by force of arms if necessary.

As a consequence, the emperor had no reservations about treading water in March and April as Prussia sought a closer diplomatic connection. By late April he was making vague comments to the Prussian ambassador about major Austrian initiatives, while simultaneously assuring Bismarck of support should Prussia need to defend its interests in the context of an Austrian threat to the European balance of power. In May, he proposed an international conference to discuss the German question – a proposal whose subtext emphasized France's role as honest broker, a role that would merit territorial compensation. Underlying the fustian was Napoleon's hope that Bismarck would make a specific offer without seeking a binding reciprocal commitment from France. By the first week of June, Bismarck was seriously considering concessions in the Rhineland, despite his awareness of the political price – in both Prussia and Germany – he would have to pay for accepting them.[78]

---

[78]Bruce D. Loynd, 'Bismarck and Napoleon III: The Diplomacy of the German Crisis of 1866' (dissertation, University of California, Santa Barbara, 1974), is a good overview.

It was, however, Napoleon who finally called the hand by flatly rejecting both halves of the Austrian offer. Give up Venetia, he informed the Austrian ambassador, and in return France would remain neutral. Otherwise it reserved the option of supporting Prussia by any means that might prove necessary. Nor would the emperor agree to underwrite Austrian claims in Silesia. The French initiative, resulting in the treaty of 12 June, was variously described by Austrian diplomats as a knife at the throat or a gun to the chest. But if the style was less than forthcoming, the substance might have been a good deal worse. Despite operating under the gun, Mensdorff managed to make the cession of Venetia contingent upon Austrian victory over Prussia. As for Silesia, or other German compensation, Mensdorff expected that issue to be resolved in the context of the victory he expected Austria's army to win.[79]

Bismarck, for his part, encountered a stone wall in his final attempts to secure the support of middle Germany. Neither his threats nor his promises had any effect, whether on courts, parliaments or the press. On 9 May the Confederation Diet voted to require Prussia to explain its mobilization. At the end of the month, Austria handed responsibility for the duchies – by now almost forgotten in the excitement – to the Confederation. Mensdorff's expectation was that Bismarck would refuse, and thereby provide a pretext for joint action against Prussia that would appeal to German and international opinion.

He reckoned, once again, without William. The king still hoped for something to come of Napoleon's conference and, in any case, was determined that Austria definitively and overtly breach the peace first. A *casus belli* seemed to emerge when Gablenz, acting on authorization from Vienna, summoned the estates of Holstein for 11 June. Manteuffel, responsible for defending Prussia's rights in Holstein, sent troops north. Given the respective personalities directly involved, both capitals expected the issue to be resolved with gunfire. Instead, Gablenz, with only a brigade under his command, and in a correspondingly hopeless military position, evacuated Holstein while a Prussian band played the Austrian national anthem.

Moltke's silence while all of this was happening did not conceal his concern. Intelligence from across the border was random, considered unreliable by the Prussian commanders on the ground since most of it came from civilian sources. Spies, informants and rumour talked of an Austrian plan prepared by Benedek himself, so ingenious the field marshal was keeping its contents confidential. Frederick Charles, commanding in Silesia, and his chief of staff, Karl von Blumenthal, were convinced initially that the Austrians were preparing for a drive on Breslau. Moltke continued to assume the Austrians would concentrate in Bohemia because he perceived that as the best strategy – that is, the most dangerous for Prussia. Benedek's unexpected inactivity was in any case unlikely to persist over any length of time, and the Prussian army could not indefinitely remain scattered among its railheads. On 29 May, three divisions from the Rhineland, somewhat grandiloquently dubbed the Elbe Army, assembled around Torgau. The II, III and IV Corps in Prussian Saxony shifted eastwards towards Goerlitz, while I Corps moved from Goerlitz into Silesia.

---

[79]Cf. Michael Dendersky, 'Das Klischee von "Ces messieurs de Vienne ..."' Der oesterreichisch-franzoesische Geheimvertrag vom 12. Juni 1866 – Symptom fuer die Unfaehigkeit der oesterreichischen Aussenpolitik?' *Historische Zeitschrift* 235 (1982), pp. 288–353, is the most up-to-date analysis. The cliché referred to is the famous jest that Austria was 'always an idea, a year, and an army late'.

These lateral movements reduced the deployment arc by a quarter, but it still extended over 300 kilometres. Moltke might have requested clarification of his government's intentions, or even made a case in the high councils to which he now had access for the risks of delay. Instead, he accepted them, on 10 June ordering the Guard Corps into Silesia, but simultaneously warning Blumenthal against making any decisions that might unleash a war as yet undecided upon by the king.[80]

That left Moltke with three widely spaced groupings. The Elbe Army's three divisions were at Torgau; the 1st Army's six divisions were 150 kilometres eastward at Goerlitz; and eight more were in Silesia with the 2nd Army, almost 200 kilometres from the 1st Army. By now any chances for a defensive campaign were long gone. Prussia would have to advance into Bohemia, no matter what Benedek decided to do, in order to have any hope of concentrating its forces. Not to worry, Moltke assured William. No matter which way Benedek turned, towards Silesia or to meet the threat from Prussian Saxony, he would be enmeshed in an operational net, with the unengaged elements of the Prussian army closing on his flanks and rear.

For that to happen, however, no more time could be lost in opening hostilities. William, still unwilling to go that far, nevertheless recognized the need for speed and control. On 2 June he ordered that any future operational movements be transmitted to the field commanders by the chief of staff, with the war ministry informed simultaneously.[81] This would eventually prove a key element in the process of establishing the general staff's permanent independence from its nominal ministerial superior. William, however, was concerned with diminishing the immediate prospects for fog and friction should the decision for war be made. And that decision he reserved to himself – until, as it was to do militarily, Austria proved an obliging enemy diplomatically.

With the French negotiations sufficiently in hand that Mensdorff felt comfortable assuming Napoleon's neutrality, he took the offensive in the Confederation Diet. On 11 June the Austrian ambassador denounced Prussia's occupation of Holstein as both a violation of the terms of Gastein and a denial of the Confederation interest in the duchies, which Austria continued to affirm. He called for mobilization of the non-Prussian states against this threat to peace and order. Three days later the motion passed. The vote of eight to five was geographic: the smaller north German states were negative; the southern middle states sided with Austria.

Prussia's ambassador responded by declaring the Confederation dissolved and presenting a detailed plan for a new one – excluding Austria. He then exited the chamber in the wake of outraged rejections of Prussia's position and its proposal alike. The ambassador, of course, was acting under instructions. The Diet's challenge to Prussia finally convinced William that all doors to a peaceful solution to the crisis were closed, and Bismarck had put in place his own contingency plans. On 15 June, the Prussian ambassadors to Saxony, Hanover and Electoral Hesse delivered identical ultimatums, demanding that the states join Prussia's new confederation. Their unanimous rejection brought Prussian troops across their frontiers at midnight. On 18 June, the Diet asked its members to provide military support to

---

[80]Karl Leonhard Graf Blumenthal, *Journals of Field-Marshal Count von Blumenthal for 1866 and 1870–71*, ed. A. von Blumenthal, tr. A. D. Gillespie-Addison (London, 1903), p. 14 *passim* and Kessel, *Moltke*, p. 456.
[81]Craig, *Politics of the Prussian Army*, p. 195.

states under unprovoked attack from Prussia. When Austria declared itself ready to do so, Bismarck interpreted it as a declaration of war – a legitimate interpretation of Austria's intentions.

The absence of a formal declaration is another indication of the desire of both governments – at least their foreign ministries – to retain as much freedom of action as possible, as opposed to enmeshing themselves in the constraints of making official what they were about to do in any case. It was a mindset that would come to full flower in the next century. Meanwhile, elements of the Prussian 1st Army and the Elbe Army occupied Saxony without a fight. On 19 June, Moltke ordered a general advance towards the frontier. Italy declared war against Austria on 20 June, thereby activating the Prussian alliance. On 22 June, Moltke ordered the invasion of Bohemia. The main event was finally on.

5

Iron Dice

If Germany's atmosphere grew more highly charged with each day that passed in June, Ludwig von Benedek was its nitrogen. Militarily, at least, he remained an inert gas. He kept his subordinates on the one hand and his government on the other completely in the dark about his plans and intentions. He kept his formations in place, despite increasingly accurate intelligence information on Prussian concentrations and movements. Such intelligence, it might be added, was significantly facilitated by a combination of large armies and relatively limited railway networks, making both secrecy and deception impossible for any length of time. By the first week of June it was clear that the final Prussian concentration was taking place in two widely separated areas. Benedek remained passive – like the proverbial donkey unable to choose between equidistant bales of hay.

I

Krismanic's original plan had focused on the army's concentration rather than the campaign itself. Nor was he a Moltke *manqué*, whose ideas commanded deference because of their source. If Krismanic continued to urge a defensive posture, Benedek had no reason to accept his advice uncritically. But he neither discussed the issue with Krismanic nor offered his own proposals for the conduct of operations. To complicate matters further, Henikstein had insisted on taking the field with Benedek. While he had also promised not to interfere in operational matters, his mere presence with the North Army, his pessimistic perspective and his acid tongue, created a situation where no one could be sure who was responsible for either planning or execution at the army's highest levels – if, indeed, any coherent plans existed.

Franz Josef was sufficiently concerned to send one of his aides to Olmuetz to clarify the situation. Lieutenant-Colonel Friedrich Beck was one of a new crop of Austrian general staff officers who copied Prussian patterns of behaviour and professionalism. He was also the army's leading staff expert on the Prussian army. His omission from Benedek's staff was, in itself, a significant indicator of the latter's limited preparation for the command he assumed. Beck's tact, however, did not match his ability. He made plain, from the first of the three separate visits he made to North Army, the emperor's bewilderment at what he considered Benedek's lack of enterprise. By now, moreover, Franz Josef believed the Olmuetz concentration to be an example of 'wrong place, wrong time'. Instead, the emperor wanted the army moved into Bohemia, where it would be in a position to support the south German states and thrust directly for Prussia's political heart.[1]

Beck's urging of that policy led to a closing of the North Army's senior ranks against what they perceived as political interference in the conduct of military operations – particularly since they believed, accurately, that Franz Josef was being urged on by Hess and Gruenne, both anathema to the men around Benedek. It was correspondingly easier to reach a negative common denominator of rejecting any interaction with 'outsiders' than to consider the elements of policy that shaped the emperor's behaviour. Bavaria was unwilling to leave its own borders unguarded and march its troops east for a joint drive on Berlin, but a strong Austrian initiative might change minds in Munich. The Saxon government was overtly insisting Vienna clarify its intentions. No one in Dresden, by this time, expected a spectacular rescue effort, with white-coated cuirassiers thundering across the border at the eleventh hour. But Saxon Crown Prince Albert, who would emerge from the war as the best corps-level commander in Germany, did want confirmation that he would have to move his forces south and evacuate his country, or face the Prussians single-handed. He also wanted some assurance that this would be more than a forlorn hope, that an Austrian reception committee – of sufficient strength to keep the Prussians from overrunning his outnumbered exiles – would be waiting across the border.

Benedek and his subordinates were unconcerned with these issues, which they saw as involving them in the multiple problems of coalition warfare while offering no compensating advantages. Under pressure from Vienna, Benedek did send I Corps into Bohemia as a flank guard, and Beck negotiated directly with its commander a plan to move nearer to the frontier than Benedek intended, in order to provide a base for the Saxons to fall back on. Then, on 16 June, as Prussian troops entered Saxony, Franz Josef informed Benedek that events in Germany had made the beginning of operations imperative. Though in principle the emperor left the exact timing to Benedek, there was no doubt of his intention that the North Army should relieve Austria's allies directly by an initiative in Bohemia. That, however, was not what Benedek intended to do. On 17 June, he informed Vienna that he was marching the army west. He described the move, not as the first step in a general offensive, but as a reaction to information from the war ministry that the main Prussian forces were not in Silesia but around Goerlitz. His orders to I Corps were defensive: to hold the line of the Isar river, in cooperation with the Saxons, and fall back on Koeniggraetz if the Prussians forced a crossing.[2]

This all seemed a far cry from the dashing initiatives everyone on both sides had expected. Nevertheless, neither Benedek nor Krismanic took to the field to lose. Neither did they intend to stand in place and be overrun by the Prussians. Reduced to its essentials, Krismanic's concept was for the North Army to monitor the Prussian advance, and then turn on their divided forces in detail as they came within range. That was not an obvious recipe for catastrophe. The focus of the post-1859 reforms had been tactical, not

---

[1] E. von Glaise-Horstenau, *Franz Josefs Weggefaehrte: Das Leben des Generalstabschefs Grafen Beck* (Vienna, 1930), pp. 94 ff., is the most detailed account of Beck's role, consistently giving its protagonist the best of the arguments.

[2] Cf. Wawro, 'The Austro-Prussian War', vol. I, p. 392 *passim* and *The Austro-Prussian War. Austria's War with Prussia and Italy in 1866* (Cambridge, 1996), pp. 125–6. The latter monograph is essentially vol. II of the author's dissertation.

operational or strategic, and Benedek was a tactical specialist. It required no great insight to argue that the 'Austrian fury' would be even more effective against an enemy advancing into hostile country, and at the wrong end of supply lines that – according to Austrian experience – were likely to be tenuous. In addition to the reviews and parades mentioned earlier, Benedek devoted a good amount of attention to large-scale exercises in close formation – scaling the rust from regiments expected to decide the war with steel. As early as 19 May, he issued a directive reaffirming the importance of shock action and closed columns to skirmish lines and firefights. The best way of countering the needle gun, he declared, was never to offer it a stationary target, but to come to close quarters and turn the Prussians out of their positions at bayonet-point. Even frontal attacks, he declared, would succeed, because the Prussians believed them impossible and would be too slow to react.[3]

What seems almost pathetic in the actual context of events takes on a more consequent aspect if the Austrian army is considered in its own terms, as a coiled spring to be unleashed with sudden, violent force against an off-balance enemy. Benedek proposed to march his force from Olmuetz to another small obsolete fortress, Josefstadt – a thirteen-day effort, but still leaving the Austrians with the advantage of interior lines. The North Army would catch its breath, advance to the Isar and smash the 1st Army and the Elbe Army, and then turn on the 2nd Army coming from Silesia.

Moltke, for his part, vigorously pursued the forward concentration that had become central to his operational plan. His geographic objective was the town of Gitschin – less for its terrain, which was well suited to the kind of fast-paced mass tactics in which the Austrians specialized, than for its status as a regional road centre he believed the three Prussian armies could reach before the Austrians did. Moltke's confidence that Benedek's interior lines could be countered by Prussian finesse, the net against the trident as his armies closed in, was in good part *post facto*. In particular, his correspondence with Blumenthal consistently reiterated the importance of taking care in ordering and executing the marches necessary to bring the 2nd Army on to the scene without exposing it to destruction, should Benedek decide to turn first in that direction.

At the same time, the chief of staff emphasized the need to take advantage of any tactical opportunities, and exploit any tactical victories, that might disrupt Benedek's intentions. The nature of Prussia's entry into the war had impelled making a virtue of necessity, resulting not even in a flexible plan, but one that went with the flow of events. It was time and past time now to impose will on circumstances – and, if possible, simultaneously put a spoke or two in Benedek's operational wheel.

After a week on the march, Benedek's army confronted the literal rather than the metaphoric aspect of that trope. The Austrian was moving half a dozen corps, plus cavalry and artillery, in the same direction at the same time, on only two major road axes. The result was a case study validating Moltke's sharp-pencil calculations that an army of the size capable of being assembled in one spot by rail could do no more than inch its way anywhere else. Supplies were misdelivered. Men threw away equipment and weapons. Horses dropped dead and vehicles broke down. Wagon trains contended with troop columns for the right of way on roads that too often faded into little more than cart tracks.

---

[3]Cited in Friedjung, vol. I, pp. 377 ff.

Dust covered everything and choked everyone. While nothing on the scale of the rear-echelon disintegrations of 1859 occurred, the Austrians nevertheless approached Josefstadt sufficiently tired and disorganized that the consensus at all levels was that a few days' rest would be needed under its walls before anyone would have the energy to run at top speed with fixed bayonet against Prussian rifles.

A few days was more than Benedek and his men received. Moltke had intended, from the beginning, to clear his strategic right flank by making a clean sweep of Austria's German allies. Saxony's fate has been mentioned: its future would depend on the war's final outcome. Hanover, further north and correspondingly more vulnerable geographically, had hopes of holding out only if reinforced by the south German VIII and Bavarian VII Corps of the federal army. None of the southern states, however, was willing to risk forcing Prussia's hand by anything as crass and drastic as mobilization, to say nothing of moving troops outside their own frontiers. Strategic caution was operationally reinforced by the defensive advantages conferred on south Germany by the Main river and the wooded, broken country of the Thuringian states separating Bavaria from Prussia proper. On 10 June, the Bavarian chief of staff had travelled to Vienna, and from there to Olmuetz. Three possibilities emerged from the resulting discussions: Bavaria's field army could join the North Army; the Bavarians and the Austrians could advance independently into Saxony, concentrating in the Dresden-Leipzig area; or VIII Corps could cooperate with the Bavarians in an independent south German offensive against Prussia. The final decision was for the first, most cautious solution. But when Moltke's vanguards crossed Prussia's borders, Bavaria was tasked by the Confederation to come to the aid of the invaded middle states. Pfordten and Ludwig complied – at least in principle.[4]

The Hanoverian army, by chance, had been mobilized for annual manoeuvres when Prussia struck. Like the Saxons, it withdrew south, using the kingdom's rail network to outdistance its pursuers and come close enough to the Bavarian frontier that forced marching by one contingent or a sortie by the other might have added Bavaria's two corps to the mix. Instead, the Hanoverians were left to their own devices. Reluctant to risk mobile operations for which their men were poorly trained, its generals decided to hold the naturally strong ground around the Thuringian town of Langensalza and await developments. On 26 June, the Hanoverian army defeated and embarrassed a numerically inferior Prussian force, whose dilatory commander did not take inspiration from Moltke's frustrated efforts to micro-manage the campaign from Bohemia. The victory was, however, no more than a *baroud d'honneur*. Prussian reinforcements, mostly Landwehr and some small allied contingents, pushed the now outnumbered Hanoverians out of their defences and compelled their surrender on 29 June. The terms were generous: universal parole and rail transportation home. The consequence was a confirmed south German determination to hold their own frontiers until relieved either by the Austrian army or the Austrian Foreign Office. Benedek could expect no help from that quarter.[5]

---

[4]Hackl, pp. 204–5.
[5]The best overview of Hanover's war effort is – as so often for 1866 – Wawro's, this time in 'The Austro-Prussian War', vol. I, pp. 419 ff. and 429 ff. Georg Steinberg, *Kriegs-und Friedenserlebnisse eines hannoverschen Jaegers*, ed. R. Sabelleck (Mannheim, 1991), admirably conveys the confusion and lack of grip that informed Hanover's war effort at all levels.

Events south of the Alps, on the other hand, offered greater prospects for optimism. In Venetia, as in Bohemia, the Austrian army initially took up a central position in the face of a numerically superior enemy, deployed in two parts because of delays in deciding on a policy of campaign. As in Bohemia, too, the Austrians maintained that position until the last moment, then reacted to an Italian initiative. With 120,000 Italians concentrating along the Mincio river, just south of Lake Garda, Archduke Albert and his chief of staff, General Franz John, swung their three corps south by forced marches and took advantage of Italian delays getting to and across the Mincio to bring 75,000 men into action against 65,000 Italians around the village of Custozza on 24 June. In a furious see-saw fight, on a day so sultry that men on both sides died of heatstroke, Austrian bayonets and rifled cannon finally mastered the field. As the day progressed and Austrian corps commanders learned to use brigades sequentially and support them with guns from the reserve, Austrian shock tactics proved increasingly effective. Habsburg columns repeatedly broke or overran opposing formations, albeit at the price of heavy casualties and high levels of disorganization. The Italians' heavy loss in unwounded prisoners at Custozza did indicate deep-seated problems of morale and discipline in the army, and of social and economic patterns in wider society. It was also a consequence of the direct moral and physical impact of the battering charges that never seemed to stop. When retreat seemed impossible, men shocked into incoherence by their experiences surrendered, usually expressing relief at finding someone to take responsibility, even if he wore an enemy's uniform. In the aftermath of battle, the festering sense of having been well and truly thrashed led many a uniformed north Italian peasant to bid his own personal farewell to arms, either by straggling or outright desertion. And whatever the moral effect of Austria's losses on survivors without experience of a stricken field – an experience that was frequently traumatic – 5,000 casualties, most of them infantrymen, were not enough, by themselves, to cripple the South Army or prevent its advance into Italy in the wake of an enemy whose demoralization increased with the passing days.[6]

That last point must not be overlooked in any analysis of the wars of German unification. All the major participants were, by the standards of World War I or the American Civil War, significantly sensitive to casualties. The aphorism long attributed to Moltke, that the Civil War amounted to two armed mobs chasing each other round the country, is now generally recognized as apocryphal,[7] although he was certainly well informed about the transatlantic conflict, having followed its course from the beginning.[8] Nevertheless, among the primary reasons given by European armies for not paying more detailed attention to contemporary transatlantic events was the alleged amateurism of the combatants. Thus the Austrians insisted that their professional troops could push home frontal attacks in circumstances where civilians in uniform, that is to say Prussian reservists, lacked the tactical

---

[6]Modern accounts of Custozza begin with Wawro, *Austro-Prussian War*, pp. 100 ff. Best from the Italian perspective remains Alberto Pollio, *Custoza 1866* (4th ed., Rome, 1925), by the then chief of Italy's general staff, a volume whose conventional narrative framework does not whitewash Italy's defects.

[7]Jay Luvaas, *The Military Legacy of the Civil War* (Chicago, 1959), p. 126; Richard L. Di Nardo, 'Southern by the Grace of God but Prussian by Common Sense: James Longstreet and the Exercise of Command in the U.S. Civil War', *The Journal of Military History* 66 (2002), p. 1112, fn. 3.

[8]Justus Scheibert, *A Prussian Observes the American Civil War: The Military Studies of Justus Scheibert*, tr. and ed. F. Trautman (Columbia, MO, 2001), affirms the high quality of the information Moltke received.

skill and discipline to do so. The events of Custozza suggested that there was more than bombast in the concept that the Austrians could hammer any enemy they could reach. What was overlooked was the moral impact of shock on the winners – an impact that had unexpectedly intimidating effects on an army whose experience of war was more limited than it had believed. A Union or Confederate force, comparable in strength to Albert's army, that won a major battle with such a low percentage of losses, would have considered itself master of the theatre of operations as well as the field of battle. Even a lethargic commander would have had to seek hard for reasons not to follow up such a victory in a war where victory usually involved taking casualties over four times higher than those suffered by the Austrians at Custozza. Union losses at Gettysburg, for example, were almost a quarter of the men engaged. The Confederates at Chickamauga came close to a 30 per cent casualty list.

If Albert counted his dead too carefully in Italy, in Bohemia reaching the enemy was the rub – on both sides. Benedek's cross-country march to Josefstadt might have strained his men to their limits, but the Prussians were not doing all that much better.[9] The general staff's elaborate railway timetables had not included post-mobilization logistics, in part, because in the aftermath of the army's concentration the kingdom's rolling stock had to be made available for civilian commercial traffic temporarily interrupted. Instead, each corps was responsible for keeping itself supplied. In earlier wars that meant living off the countryside, by purchase and requisition. But neither Prussian Saxony nor Silesia produced much in the way of agricultural surplus relative to the high numbers of men and horses the railways delivered. As much to the point, corps quartermasters preferred to deal with contractors they knew, firms from their home districts. From the perspective of the general staff and the war ministry, there seemed no reason why the railroads could not be organized to forward supplies as they had earlier moved men, on a district basis. Railway tracks seemed a kind of magic carpet that, for the first time, would free armies from both the limitations of fixed bases and the exigencies of requisitioning.

Results in practice proved far different. Perhaps a bit of peculation might have been welcome in a context where corps intendants, quartermasters and suppliers, determined to keep the men and animals depending on them well fed, purchased and forwarded such huge quantities of food and forage that the processing systems were swamped. In contrast to mobilization, no central authority was responsible for controlling shipments and establishing priorities. The war ministry neither prepared schedules for supply trains nor designated depot areas. Moltke, believing Wartensleben was too valuable to leave behind in Berlin, took him into the field as his operations officer, leaving the general staff correspondingly rudderless in railway matters.[10] The railroads assumed responsibility only for delivering goods – not unloading or storing them.

The results included freight cars arriving in the theatre from as far away as Cologne, loaded to the limits with completely inedible loaves of bread baked at regimental depots. Other freight cars sat for days awaiting the few labourers available in the context of a campaign that virtually ignored administration along the lines of communication. Local military commanders were often long-retired majors and lieutenant colonels, whose active service

---

[9]The following is based on *Heeresverpflegung*, ed. Grossen Generalstab, *Kriegsgeschichtliche Abteilung, Studien zur Kriegsgeschichte und Taktik* 6 (Berlin, 1906), pp. 100 ff.
[10]Kessel, *Moltke*, pp. 456 ff.

had been spent in the cavalry and whose ranks were too low for them to generate results by intimidation. Even under the new organization, about half the army's supply columns were composed of civilian farm wagons, whose durability and weight-carrying capacities were overextended by the demands of keeping fed the constantly advancing forward units. Nor did horses from civil life, accustomed to regular food and dry stabling, respond well to field service conditions. The relative stateliness of the 1st Army's advance owed as much to logistical problems as to the caution of its commander. Requisitions, like those imposed on the town of Reichenberg by the 1st Army between 24 and 26 June, were merely stopgaps, however welcome they might be at the time. Some Prussians would fight the battle of Koeniggraetz on empty stomachs, comforted only by the announcement of Prince Frederick Charles that 'God who feeds the sparrows will also provide for us'.[11]

II

In such contexts, it is tempting to speculate whether a fighting retreat towards Vienna might not have significantly improved Benedek's prospects for victory by overextending Prussian logistical capacities. The point remained moot as the field marshal began deploying for the showdown battle that everyone expected, and that Custozza indicated his army could win. His chosen target was the Prussian advance from Saxony: the nine divisions of the 1st and the Elbe Armies. The 2nd Army of Crown Prince Frederick was the closer enemy. By 26 June, its vanguards reached the mountain passes leading into Bohemia, but its four corps had to separate widely, extending their lines of march to fifty kilometres and longer to make it through and across the constricted terrain.

Critics ever since have suggested that Benedek may well have missed an opportunity, either to strike the Prussians as they emerged from the mountains or – more daring but with a prospect of more decisive results – allow the crown prince to emerge, advance toward the Elbe, and then attack in force before the 2nd Army was fully concentrated. Whatever the operational wisdom of these hindsights, Benedek and Krismanic were agreed that the open ground of western Bohemia was a preferable stage for the Austrian army's particular tactical qualities than the wooded foothills of the north-east. Benedek ordered his I Corps and the Saxons to hold the Isar line at all costs, detached two corps to screen his flank against the 2nd Army and continued pushing west with the remaining four. While he remained vague when discussing time-frames, he seems to have believed still that his main force would reach the Isar in good time to join Clam-Gallas, deal with the Prussian advance from the north and then swing north-east to finish off the crown prince.

Supporting that contention is Benedek's choice of formations and commanders for the flank guard: X Corps under Gablenz, who had been ordered south as the Prussians occupied Holstein, and Wilhelm Ramming's VI Corps. Gablenz had won his spurs and made his bones in Denmark. Ramming was an old Italian hand, and both men were considered hard fighters and competent tacticians, the best in the North Army for temporary independent missions. Benedek's forward commanders were less sanguine. Albert of Saxony and I Corps commander, Eduard Clam-Gallas, had understood their task as a fighting retreat, buying time for the North Army's forward concentration. In that context, they had benefited from

---

[11] *Friedrich Karl*, vol. II, p. 109.

Frederick Charles's refusal to force his pace despite repeated urgings from Moltke. They had been relatively undisturbed when Prussian vanguards reached the Isar at Turnau. Now, with Benedek apparently intending to fight as far forward as possible, it seemed incumbent on the prince and the general to clear the river line by crossing the river further south, at Podol. No more than token Prussian forces were reported in the area, and the town's two major bridges facilitated moving guns and supplies across the river quickly enough to flank the Prussians out of Turnau and establish the kind of forward position Benedek intended.

Clam-Gallas picked his best brigade to lead, and at 8.30 p.m. on 28 June, the Austrians went forward against two companies of Prussian jaeger who were already engaging the bridge guards. The Austrians cleared the town; the Prussians brought up reinforcements; the Austrians mounted a bayonet charge. Thus far, so good – or, at least, all according to doctrine and regulations. Then the Prussians halted, deployed their leading platoons and opened rapid fire. In just over thirty minutes, a single company expended 5,700 rounds, an average of twenty-two per man.[12] Rifle barrels became too hot to handle. Corroded firing pins broke. Poorly galvanized sealing rings failed, with breeches leaking gas so badly that taking aim grew impossible. Instead, men began firing from the hip. And through it all, Austrians died.

Podol, with its stone houses and twisting streets, was an ideal setting for the kind of hand-to-hand mêlée that, time and again, for two centuries, had left victors as demoralized by casualties as were the vanquished. Now the Prussians shot their way forward, clearing houses with fire instead of steel, keeping touch by their rifle flashes as dusk turned to night. Two understrength companies shattered two Austrian battalions in the darkness, firing into the mass by sound and sense, falling back only when cartridge boxes emptied and needle guns jammed hopelessly. At 2 a.m. the Austrians drew off. Of the 3,000 men committed, almost 500 had been shot. Prussian losses were around 130.

Clam-Gallas, who witnessed the catastrophe at first hand, ordered a retreat to Muenchengraetz, handing the Isar's crossings to the Prussians. His rank and file shared his perspective, complaining that 'the Prussians don't fight like honest men' – which implied there was no shame in being defeated by them. Replicating the events at Custozza, a significant number of the losers' casualties were prisoners – over 600 of them, some shocked into disorientation by the fighting and others making a rational calculation that the risks of surrender were less than those incurred by facing the needle gun at close quarters.[13]

To the east, the Prussian 2nd Army was conducting a similar seminar on firepower. On 27 June the crown prince's V Corps emerged from the mountains on to the plateau of Nachod, only hours ahead of an Austrian VI Corps whose march had been delayed by orders, counter-orders and disorders. The Prussians were not much better off, their artillery and supply columns choking the pass for miles behind the infantry. But Karl von Steimetz was a hard driver, and the commander of his vanguard had the sense to deploy his battalions under cover and in open order to screen the arrival of the rest of the corps, as opposed to seeking glory in an attack.

---

[12]K. von Loebell, 'Der Patronenverbrauch inm Ernstfalle und die Kriegsausruestung der Infanterie mit Munitionen', *Archiv fuer die Offiziere der Koeniglich Preussische Artillerie und Ingenieur-Korps* 63 (1868), p. 88.
[13]Cf. Wawro, *Austro-Prussian War*, pp. 133 ff. and Theodor Fontane, *Der Deutsche Krieg von 1866* (2 vols., Berlin, 1871–2), vol. I, pp. 156 ff.

Ramming's response was doctrinally predictable: he ordered a charge. The decision, however, also made tactical sense. Defeating the Prussians in detail and throwing them back into the mountains was preferable to a stand-up fight at even odds: corps against corps. Ramming, despite his original intentions, was unable to concentrate his command for a hammer blow. The needle guns tore his leading brigade to pieces and the rest of VI Corps went in only a brigade at a time – but against an enemy whose strength increased by battalion-sized increments. By a combination of mass and élan, Ramming's assault columns steadily won ground. It was load, fire and reload as Prussian forward elements were over-run and submerged by the Austrians still able to keep in ranks as the needle guns flogged them. But V Corps's lines held. Majors and captains mounted local counter-attacks on their own initiatives. Company columns, skirmish lines and men just pushed out of the way, closed around Austrian flanks unprotected by skirmishers of their own. Opening rapid fire while their cartridges lasted, sometimes at will and sometimes by volleys, the Prussians slowed and disrupted Austrian formations already disorganized by their own successes. Some of Ramming's men had not eaten for almost a day. Others succumbed to a midday midsummer sun. The advance slowed, then stopped, as fresh Prussian battalions shouldered their way on to the Nachod plateau, Prussian guns blocked in the defile came into position and Steinmetz began preparing a general attack of his own.

Ramming pre-empted him by ordering a retreat under the cover of enough artillery to convince even the hard-hitting Steinmetz that discretion was the better part of valour. Once again, in an encounter battle where experience suggested loss ratios should be similar, the Prussians suffered 1,200 casualties against 5,700 Austrians. That figure represented over 20 per cent of VI Corps's strength – sufficient to stagger even the most hardbitten Union or Confederate corps in a pitched battle, to say nothing of a border skirmish.[14]

Eight miles west, at Trautenau, events had taken a different course – at least on a map. The Prussian I Corps debouched from the mountains on the morning of 27 June, pushed back the Austrian X Corps's vanguard and proposed to rest on its limited laurels for the rest of the day. Gablenz responded by bringing up two fresh brigades and his corps artillery, mounting an hour-long bombardment, which silenced the few guns the Prussians had on the field and convinced I Corps's commander that retreat into the Bohemian mountains was preferable to standing against Austrian bayonets. Thus when the Austrian charge went in, the Prussian tactics resembled those of a boxer, shifting balance to his back foot. It was the kind of position tailor-made to maximize the impact of a charge delivered at the double. Even then, the needle guns of the front-line battalions shot the first attack to pieces, stopping both brigades in their tracks. Not until X Corps's fourth brigade reached the field did the Austrians go in for a final try that drove the defenders back into the pass and onto the march formations of the rest of I Corps.

After making reasonable allowances for fog and friction, X Corps had done most things right. Gablenz had used his artillery effectively and kept his attacks more or less coordinated. If his brigadiers were prone to go forward on their own initiatives, boldness was, after all, a significant element of the Austrian system. The Prussians, for their part, had been an obliging enemy, making on *their* own initiative most of the mistakes the Austrians

---

[14]Fontane, *1866*, vol. I, pp. 290 ff., fleshes out the Prussian narrative. Wawro, *Austro-Prussian War*, pp. 139 ff., covers the Austrian side with predictable flair.

would have ordained had they been drawing up I Corps's orders, and complementing command error by a collapse of rear-echelon traffic discipline that made reinforcing the firing lines impossible. But with Steinmetz at Nachod, in positions to threaten his right flank and rear, Gablenz could not hold his ground, much less pursue I Corps back into Silesia. In personnel terms, moreover, Trautenau was close to a catastrophe. With 1,300 Prussians dead, wounded or prisoners, Gablenz's four brigades had lost 4,800 — almost none of them prisoners, and almost all to rifle fire.

The nature of the casualties enhanced their trauma. In the American Civil War, most attacks were made in line, against fire relatively uncontrolled and opened at relatively long range. The usual result was more or less an even distribution of corpses. Post-battle accounts commonly speak of being able to cross a given piece of ground by stepping from body to body. The Prussian I Corps considered itself an élite force, its regiments heir to many of Frederick the Great's victories, and took particular pride in its fire discipline. At Trautenau, particularly in the early hours of the fighting, Prussian platoons and companies held their fire to near point-blank range, then delivered rapid volleys against mass targets. The usual results were literal piles of dead and wounded marking the line of every Austrian advance, blending into impassable windrows as they approached the final Prussian positions. Such sights, often viewed for the first time, boded no good for the morale of men already overmarched and underfed — particularly given the primitive and limited nature of medical arrangements, in no way prepared for such numbers.[15]

Whatever their impact on the army's lower echelons, Nachod and Trautenau did not affect Benedek's determination to continue his advance westward to Gitschin. This decision, like most of those made by North Army's headquarters during the campaign, has been so often criticized that justifying it seems almost perverse.[16] Benedek, however, was by no means ignorant of the tool with which he worked. Operational flexibility, the ability to shift gears suddenly in pursuit of a promising opportunity at theatre level, was not an Austrian strong point. Benedek believed, as suggested earlier, that the terrain and the balance of forces in the Gitschin sector offered better chances for a decisive result on Austrian terms than turning to engage the Prussians coming from Silesia.

Gablenz and Ramming had been requesting, then demanding, reinforcements all day: more men and more guns to finish off I Corps and overrun V Corps while they remained isolated. It was, however, the responsibility of an army commander to fight his battle rather than allow subordinates to set the terms — assuming the North Army could even reach the new sector over the limited road network in time to do more than salute the Prussians as they retreated through the mountains. Since Clam-Gallas had not bothered to establish communication with North Army headquarters, on the night of 27 June, Benedek still believed that his I Corps and the Saxons were established on the Isar, ready to screen the main army's deployment on to what its commander expected would be a killing ground — a delusion sustained by Clam-Gallas's failure to use his corps telegraph to establish contact with his superior. An enduring problem of real-time communications is their facility in transmitting embarrassing information to higher headquarters. Even had Clam-Gallas

---

[15]Fontane, *1866*, vol. I, pp. 364 ff. and Wawro, *Austro-Prussian War*, pp. 145 ff., again, nicely carry the weight of description and analysis for Trautenau.

[16]Cf. *inter alia*, Gordon Craig, *The Battle of Koeniggraetz* (Philadelphia, 1964), p. 64 and Kessel, *Moltke*, p. 469.

been a technical progressive, he was not the first, and would by no means be the last, officer to turn a temporary blind eye to electronics in the hopes of having better news to report later.[17]

Without that information, Benedek ordered VIII Corps to move to Skalitz and take over Ramming's blocking position against Steinmetz. On 28 June, he ordered Gablenz to fall back towards Josefstadt, covering North Army against I Prussian Corps and the Prussian Guard. In case the Prussians should somehow appear somewhere in greater force than the single corps considered the maximum able to negotiate the passes, II and IV Austrian Corps were made available as support. Benedek's intention, however, still remained to fight around Gitschin, on ground he chose and on his terms.

The Prussians, meanwhile, stepped up their pace. Frederick Charles, whose caution had been a marked feature of the campaign, was now convinced he had the Saxons and I Austrian Corps in position for a killing blow at Muenchengraetz. He intended to use the Elbe Army, whose independence had become only nominal, to fix the allies on the Isar by advancing from the west, while sending three of his own divisions to strike their flank and rear. This represented a digression from Moltke's original plan. It also left the 2nd Army much to its own devices, should Benedek turn in that direction. Frederick Charles, however, believed he could do more, both to assist the crown prince and to fulfil Moltke's strategic design, by taking advantage of an immediate opportunity than by rigid adherence to a plan that no one expected to survive contact with the enemy in any case.[18]

Frederick Charles's reasoning was eminently defensible. His execution was a good deal less so. The prince was so busy with preparing orders that he neglected to send his cavalry forward to see if his adversaries were remaining in place for his projected hammer blow. Albert and Clam-Gallas had, in fact, made a joint decision to fall back on the main army rather than risk fighting it out against an enemy coming from three directions – a decision facilitated by the first-class work of their own light cavalry in discovering and reporting the Prussian movements. Frederick Charles's pincers closed on an emptying sack, picking up only 1,400 prisoners, most of them stragglers.

Supplies – or their absence – were increasingly conditioning Prussian operations. The Prussian army was not a worked-in, case-hardened field force, but a structure of mobilized civilians. Their foraging skills and their marching capacities were equally limited. Both had been strained to capacity by the forced marches that had brought them to the Isar, then to Muenchengraetz. Not only the men, but their officers, from captains to colonels, were ready enough to remove boots from swollen feet, ease saddle-sore fundaments and enjoy the good Bohemian beer for which the town was famous, as a partial substitute for the rations that appeared much later – when they arrived at all. Significant lapses of discipline, in contrast to what might have been expected from British, French or Austrian troops in a similar situation, were limited. Most of the Prussian rank and file just more or less quietly drank themselves to sleep as the NCOs and company officers carefully saw nothing.[19] The next day they would be ready to move on. For the moment, however, pursuit was out of the question and no one from, Frederick Charles downwards, seems to have challenged the situation.

---

[17]Martin van Creveld, *Command in War* (Cambridge, MA, 1985), p. 107 *passim*.

[18]*Friedrich Karl*, vol. II, pp. 38 ff.

[19]Fontane, *1866*, vol. I, pp. 180 ff.

The 2nd Army, for its part, began 28 June expecting cold steel rather than cold beer. With his forward corps divided from each other and still largely strung out in the mountain passes that were their respective axes of advance, the crown prince was in the position of a man putting his spread fingers into a multiple thumbscrew and hoping the vice would remain untightened. He took, moreover, the cautious course: swinging the Guard east to relieve pressure on I Corps, while leaving Steinmetz to cope on his own with what might have been as many as three corps had Benedek chosen to fight in that sector. By noon, however, everyone in the 2nd Army was breathing easier. I Corps found nothing in front of its cautious patrols. Gablenz, a hard charger even in retreat, divided his corps to engage the advancing Prussian Guard and lost another 3,700 men around Soor. Steinmetz, pushing forward towards Skalitz, found only a single corps in his path. Benedek had ridden to that sector earlier in the morning and confirmed his previous decision not to engage the Prussians there, particularly since that involved going back across much of the same ground VI Corps had been unable to carry and hold. Whether the commander of VIII Austrian Corps disobeyed the withdrawal order, or whether he did nothing and allowed his troops to be caught in place by the Prussians, remains uncertain. The consequences, however, were pikestaff plain. The Austrian brigadiers sent their men forward in columns – on one occasion, even the artillery following behind instead of preparing the attack. It might have been rage at the casualties inflicted by the Prussian rifles. It might have been raw courage. It might have been the Dutch courage bestowed by a double ration of liquor. But drunk or sober, the men of VIII Corps, Czechs and Poles, Germans and Ukrainians, a cross-section of a polyglot empire, went forward in a way that would have done proud Longstreet's corps on the second day of Gettysburg. Geoffrey Wawro, no admirer of Austria's military effectiveness, speaks of a 'flight of ecstasy'. The whitecoats might indeed have carried the day against any other corps in Prussia's army. But Steinmetz's men had been to the circus and seen that particular elephant the previous day. V Prussian Corps was widely considered the army's ethnic weak link because of its high proportion of Poles from the province of Posen. But the needle gun's language was universal. Battalion and company commanders by now well understood the technique of advancing quickly, taking cover and opening rapid independent fire from front or flank. By 2 p.m. it was all over, with 5,500 Austrians dead, wounded or prisoners, and the rest in a retreat that turned into panic-stricken flight as the effects of alcohol and adrenalin wore off.[20]

The defeat of VIII Corps was paradigmatic for the preliminary battles that did so much to lay the moral groundwork for Koeniggraetz. It was a failure of command as well as tactics. A consistent pattern in all the early actions was the launching of uncoordinated, unsupported charges a brigade at a time. The four brigades of a typical Austrian corps should not have been too many for a commander and a deputy to control effectively. But the new organization was untested, the deputy commander usually ignored by his superior – who was legitimately likely to regard him more as rival than an assistant. The brigadiers, for their part, did what they were expected to do. Concerned with building reputations and qualifying for the Maria Theresa Order, they attacked at every opportunity, making limited use of their organic artillery and soliciting neither help nor support from corps

---

[20]Ibid., pp. 322 ff.; O. von Lettow-Vorbeck, *Geschichte des Krieges 1866 in Deutschland* (3 vols., Berlin, 1896–1902), vol. II, pp. 282 ff.; and Wawro, *Austro-Prussian War*, pp. 165 ff. The quotation is from ibid., p. 171.

headquarters or neighbouring formations until their situation was desperate. As a conse-quence, patching up local disasters took precedence over exploiting local successes.

From the Prussian side, events in both halves of the theatre suggested the virtues of the managed battle, at least at corps and regiment level. The more elaborate Prussian chain of command made possible the regular presence in forward positions of senior officers with some sense of the general situation. Unlike their counterparts, moreover, Prussian colonels and generals did not feel constrained to demonstrate their courage by playing subalterns' roles at the head of attacks. At regimental levels, captains and majors were able to take advantage of the smoke-shrouded conditions produced by rapid-firing black-powder weapons to shift company columns and half-battalions round the field, with relative secur-ity from Austrian rifles, which seldom fired more than once, and Austrian guns, which spent most of their time engaging in long-range duels with their Prussian counterparts.

Firepower is also a form of shock. The needle gun was not an attritional weapon. Properly handled, in large enough numbers, in a matter of minutes it could transform a bugle-blowing, colours-to-the-front attack into wriggling heaps of screaming men and men all too silent, on the one hand, and masses of fugitives with sudden urgent business in the rear, on the other. The Austrians at Skalitz suffered an average of 800 casualties per hour of combat – 40 per cent of the number actually engaged.[21] The needle gun was not a purely defensive weapon either. Against an enemy that regarded a rifle as an elaborate pike, it was possible to come to close quarters, shoot the Austrians out of any position they occupied, and herd the survivors to the rear with jeering shouts of 'about face, at the double', as some Prussians did at Skalitz.

Morale soared, especially in the ranks of the 2nd Army. But within twenty-four hours the Prussians received a stinging contrapuntal lesson in the limits of technological super-iority on a modern battlefield. Moltke, still in Berlin, had grown increasingly concerned with what he regarded as the slowness and lack of strategic grip demonstrated, in par-ticular, by Frederick Charles. At 7.30 a.m. on 29 June he ordered the 1st Army to move towards Gitschin on the bounce, to relieve Austrian pressure on the crown prince. That night, the chief of staff began moving his entire headquarters to Bohemia, keeping in touch as best he could by telegraph with his armies in the field. Learning of the events at Soor and Skalitz, he ordered the 2nd Army to hold in place and be prepared to establish contact with a 1st Army that was presumably advancing 'without pause' in the crown prince's direction.[22]

At this stage of operations, Moltke expected Benedek to attempt what Moltke would have ordered: assume the initiative by attacking the nearest enemy – the Prussians advan-cing from Silesia. Instead, at 8.30 p.m. on 28 June, Benedek drafted orders informing his corps commanders that North Army would now assume a central position on the Elbe, at Koeniginhof, wait for Gablenz to rejoin and the Prussian 2nd Army to come within range, engage and destroy the latter, then march west and finish off Frederick Charles. The unex-pected abandonment of the advance on Gitschin was the kind of fundamental shift in emphasis that can confuse even a smoothly functioning, worked-in operational team.

---

[21]Bucholz, *Moltke and the German Wars*, p. 131, offers that particular breakdown.

[22]Kesel, *Moltke*, pp. 469 ff. For the role of the telegraph in Prussian operations, see Dennis E. Showalter, 'Soldiers into Postmasters? The Electric Telegraph as an Instrument of Command in the Prussian Army', *Military Affairs* (1973), pp. 48–52.

Benedek's decision to go to bed without despatching the orders, which went out at 8 a.m. on 30 June, exacerbated the confusion as units already under way westward retraced their steps, while staff officers and commanders, nerves already stretched, cursed the field marshal for an indecisive incompetent.[23]

It was, of all unlikely subordinates, Clam-Gallas who bought Benedek yet another chance – with major help from the Saxons Benedek had considered expendable. Since the days of Maria Theresa, Bohemia had been a favourite manoeuvre area for the Austrian army and a training area for the Austrian engineers. The wooded high ground north and west of Gitschin had been extensively evaluated for its defensive prospects. It was virtually a matter of 'standard operating procedure' for Clam to deploy his brigades and the Saxons – who arrived late because of their longer line of retreat from Muenchengraetz – against Prussians who attacked off the line of march in late afternoon, with tired, thirsty troops, against an enemy, for once committed to holding ground instead of capturing it.

This time it was Prussian formations that struggled in boggy meadows and broken terrain. It was Prussian columns that felt the lash of Saxon and Austrian artillery firing at marked ranges. It was Prussian skirmish lines that were overrun or scattered by well-timed bayonet charges. And if the Saxons came late to the party, they proved welcome guests. A tactical doctrine that took advantage of the long-range capabilities of their Lorenz-model Miniés gave Prussian attackers more than one 'bad quarter of an hour', as they struggled to cross a killing zone in which their needle guns could make no reply. But Frederick Charles's men were from the II Pomeranian and the III Brandenburg Corps, each regarding itself as the best in the army and correspondingly unwilling to acknowledge themselves beaten. Six companies of them, 1,200 men, accounted for a full quarter of one Habsburg brigade that charged too fast and too far. Other battalions, half-battalions and companies found weak spots in the Austro-Saxon positions and pressed forward on their own initiative, despite rapidly emptying cartridge boxes. The outcome was by no means settled when, around 7.30 p.m., an order arrived from Benedek: fall back on the main army.

Clam-Gallas and his deputy, Count Leopold Gondrecourt, wanted to fight it out, not least because of the risks involved in disengaging, in the dark, from a battle where the troops of both sides were badly mixed. Albert, who may well by now have had his personal fill of the Austrian practice of treating orders as subjects for debate, overrode their objections as the senior officer present. The tactical result was about what Clam and Gondrecourt predicted. The Saxons retired in good enough order – cynics might say that by now they had ample practice in that particular manoeuvre. But the sorely tried Austrian battalions, many of them unfed that day and for several days previous, lost cohesion and scattered, unassisted in any particular by the corps staff. When they rallied the next day, it was to exchange tales of the needle gun that grew with repetition, spreading corresponding alarm and despondency in the ranks of the as yet unengaged troops that first encountered the fugitives once they reached the main army.[24]

Operationally, the story had a different spin. The Prussian 1st Army had lost over 1,500 men by the time it finally secured Gitschin, some time after midnight on 29 June. This time

---

[23]Wawro, *Austro-Prussian War*, pp. 178 ff. and Kessel, *Moltke*, p. 470.
[24]For Gitschin, in addition to Wawro, *Austro-Prussian War*, pp. 183 ff. and Fontane, *1866*, vol. I, pp. 191 ff., see the Saxon official history, *Der Antheil des Koeniglichen Saechsischen Armeekorps am Feldzuge 1866* (Dresden, 1869), pp. 135 ff., which is mildly and pardonably triumphalist.

there was no beer, and almost no energy to drink it had it been available. For many men there was no food either. The stretcher-bearer companies and field hospitals were either too far to the rear, or overwhelmed by the relatively large numbers of casualties. Commanders were reluctant to detail burying parties. The sights, sounds and smells affected even Frederick Charles. Left to his own devices he might have given his men a day or two to rest, as he had done at Muenchengraetz. But there was Moltke's direct order to advance. And there was the presence of the entire royal headquarters – William, Roon, Moltke, Bismarck, Old Uncle Tom Cobbleigh and all – that arrived in Gitschin by rail on 1 July. Frederick Charles and his staff responded by kicking the 1st Army on to its feet and on to the road after the Austro-Saxons – but again, without sending forward anything resembling a cavalry screen. Had he done so, the Prussians would have discovered they were striking at air.

Napoleon's famous aphorism that in war, the moral is to the physical as three to one, has been balanced, at least in the modern era, by the homelier couplet that 'a cannon ball don't pay no mind if you're gentle or if you're kind'. Defeat, nevertheless, remains a moral as well as a physical concept. Viewed objectively, the Austrians on 30 June still had playable cards. The main Prussian armies remained geographically divided. North Army retained its central position and, with the arrival of the three corps of Albert, Clam-Gallas and Gablenz, was numerically superior to either of its enemies. Morale in the ranks was clearly low. That, however, was at least partially susceptible of remedy by logistics: bringing up edible rations and replacing worn uniforms and lost equipment. The previous failures of the army administration in these respects might be appropriately addressed by judicious applications of field courts martial and firing squads. As for the rest, what the army needed was a fighting chance – literally.

Benedek and most of his subordinates were by now aware that successful shock tactics involved a combined-arms battle, coordinated from above. The role of artillery in preparing and supporting attacks had been affirmed in theory but neglected in practice before the war. Now, on 28 June, Benedek issued an order that, without inhibiting the offensive spirit, infantry should go forward only after the guns had opened the way, as Gablenz's batteries had done so effectively at Trautenau.[25] A recipe for victory? No. A set of behaviours beyond the theoretical capacities of Benedek and his officers? Again, no. The start of a vigorous, downward-focused shake-up that might galvanize a front-loaded army into one more good, big fight? Yes. But throughout 29 June, Benedek did nothing but prepare two drafts of a dispatch to the emperor, blaming the course of events to date on everyone except the Freemasons and the Jews, and declaring his intention to 'consider' trusting God and his own 'soldier's luck' in a decisive blow once the army was 'concentrated'. A better gauge of his mood was a private letter to his wife in which he declared, 'it would be better if a bullet found me'.[26] Not until the news of Gitschin reached him did Benedek make a decision to abandon his current position, whose tactical weaknesses seemed excessive, and retreat toward Olmuetz – with a brief pause at Koeniggraetz.

Meanwhile, Moltke was engaging the Prussian army commanders with more force than the latter were engaging the Austrians. Frederick Charles, in particular, insisted that his men were in no fit state to go anywhere until their supply trains arrived. Moltke, arguably

---

[25] *Benedeks nachgelassene Papiere*, ed. H. Friedjung (2nd ed., rev., Dresden, 1904), pp. 369–70.
[26] Wawro, *Austro-Prussian War*, pp. 195–6 and *Benedeks nachgelassene Papiere*, pp. 371–2.

a bit disconcerted by his first physical contact with the realities of war on a large scale, agreed. The Prussian rear services were proving to be well organized only by comparison to Austria's, and rain had softened the unpaved country roads that carried most of the traffic of the 1st and the Elbe Armies. The failure of the cavalry and the intelligence service to produce data on Benedek's whereabouts was mildly disconcerting. There were no indications, however, that the North Army was in a position to deliver a surprise attack from any direction and, in that context, Moltke approved a day's rest for the western armies.

He was less flexible on a second issue. Both Frederick Charles and the crown prince, supported by their respective chiefs of staff, believed the Prussian armies had taken as much risk as was acceptable in marching divided into the theatre of war. Believing the real battle was ahead, they argued that the time had come to fight united. On 2 July, a conference took place in the king's headquarters. The appellation 'council of war' given to it in most accounts was anathema to Moltke, who insisted his was the sole responsibility for advising the monarch on operational matters under field conditions. But with Frederick Charles on the spot and Blumenthal in Gitschin, after a long carriage ride from the crown prince's headquarters, 150 years of precedents favouring collegial decision-making were too strong to deny. As William listened closely, most of the senior officers present argued for drawing the armies closer together.

Moltke, by this time convinced Benedek had withdrawn across the Elbe intending to use the river as a defence line, insisted on the advantages of keeping them separate and advancing simultaneously against the Austrians' front and flank. By now, he argued, the three armies were in fact within easy tactical supporting distance; it was impossible for Benedek to turn against one without being attacked by the other two. William decided in Moltke's favour, not least because he seemed the most sure of himself and had the clearest sense of what to do next – at least until someone discovered exactly where the North Army had gone.[27]

That someone was a colonel commanding a detachment of Frederick Charles's 7th Division, sent forward with other scouting forces on 1 July to secure the route of advance. That night he saw campfires on the high ground west of the Elbe river. The next day, one of his cavalry patrols brought in a prisoner who confirmed that his corps was indeed in that sector. Frederick Charles responded by sending one of his own staff officers forward with a dozen cavalrymen to investigate. After a series of adventures, sufficiently hair-raising to impress Jeb Stuart himself, the patrol returned to report that not one but four Austrian corps were in position west of the Elbe, along the Bistritz river. For Frederick Charles, at least, it was clear that Benedek intended to stand and fight - with a river at his back, the same kind of position that had cost Napoleon so dearly at the battle of Leipzig in 1813. By 9 p.m. on 2 July, he and his chief of staff had prepared orders for his own three corps and the Elbe Army to advance to contact, with the first units on the road by 2 a.m. Only then did the prince send his chief of staff to Moltke with the news, and an account of the 1st Army's initiative.[28]

William and Moltke were both in bed when the officer, Constantin von Voigtz-Rhetz, arrived. The chief of staff's first reply was 'Thank God!' Dressing in haste, he went to the

---

[27]Kessel, *Moltke*, pp. 472 ff.
[28]Fontane, *1866*, vol. I, pp. 457 ff. and *Friedrich Karl*, vol. II, pp. 71 ff.

king, while Voights-Rhetz and Wartensleben – who seemed to appear at every critical juncture of the campaign – began drafting further orders for what was to be the battle of Koeniggraetz. Ten minutes later, Moltke was back with a royal *carte blanche*. His intentions were clear: pin the North Army against the Elbe, cut it off from the fortified crossings to the south, then seek its destruction. Move out as soon as possible, Moltke enjoined Frederick Charles. But instead of directly reinforcing the 1st Army, as the prince requested, the 2nd Army would direct all four of its corps directly against the Austrian left flank. It would be something of a tight squeeze between the Elbe and the Bistritz, but the rivers would also provide an unmistakable guide for the crown prince's axis of advance. Ironically, for an otherwise high-tech campaign, no direct telegraph line connected the respective headquarters. Even had there been one, Moltke might well have been unwilling to trust coordinating what he expected to be the war's decisive battle to something as unfamiliar as electricity. Instead, he sent one of William's aides-de-camp – an officer among the best riders in the army, and with a personal fortune large enough to ensure that his mounts were the best available – to the 2nd Army's headquarters, in the middle of the night, through country alive with Austrian patrols. With a deal of horseman's skill and a bit of soldier's luck, Lieutenant Colonel Finck von Finckenstein reached Crown Prince Frederick's headquarters at 4 a.m. on 3 July. While the 2nd Army's staff officers were drafting and dispatching orders, royal headquarters left Gitschin around 5 a.m. Three hours later, Moltke and the king joined Frederick Charles on the high ground near the village of Dub, just west of the Bistritz River.[29]

What was the North Army doing in the middle of the rapidly closing Prussian circle? Benedek's earlier mentioned decision to retreat towards Olmuetz had been taken in a vacuum. At brigade and corps levels, and in his own headquarters, Benedek received neither advice nor support from officers increasingly concerned with distancing themselves from disaster rather than averting it. For his part, the field marshal did not communicate with his corps commanders. He even ceased talking to Krismanic – though that last might have been understood as improving any future prospects the North Army might have. Further down the army's structure, heavy losses of officers and NCOs in units previously engaged with the Prussians meant that reorganization – sometimes as fundamental as determining the senior officer still on his feet – took precedence over revitalizing men who were over-marched, underfed and ruinously beaten by their enemies. Those formations still unbloodied observed the proceedings with more trepidation than enthusiasm. The North Army lurched into Koeniggraetz throughout the day on 1 July. Benedek, regarding what seemed a hopeless muddle of guns and wagons, infantry and cavalry, decided that an early crossing of the Elbe was impossible. Instead, he ordered the army to bivouac on the river's west bank and begin sorting itself out.

A glance at a map might suggest that the Austrian position at Koeniggraetz at least improved their logistics, since the fortress town was on a main railway line. Reality, however, was that, as so often during the campaign, numbers perplexed. Assembled in one place, the North Army was too large to be supplied by a railway system whose carrying capacity to a particular location was still small relative to what it would become in the

---

[29]Kessel, *Moltke*, p. 476. Cf. van Creveld, *Command in War*, pp. 135–6. A second copy of the order was transmitted by telegraph – the connection being through Berlin, a courier was quicker and surer.

next half-century. Conditions were exacerbated by the continued disorder at corps and regiment levels. A major part of modern war is traffic control. The Austrian army had nothing like a military police force. Nor did any of the generals consider placing cavalry squadrons in the provost role. Columns of wagons with no orders, contradictory orders or outdated orders blocked crossings and broke down dirt roads already softened by the rain that fell on Austrians and Prussians alike. Men, cold and unfed, left their bivouacs in search of food and fire, something to drink and something to smoke. Survivors of Nachod, Skalitz or Gitschin also suffered from the physical reactions that followed from extreme and unexpected stress. Cold and hunger affected them even more deeply than their fellow soldiers, and too many lacked even the energy to help themselves by private foraging. Instead, they huddled in miserable, demoralized groups whose officers were unable to rouse them, even when they themselves had the energy to make the effort.

The general impression of disorganization and demoralization was so great that the governor of Koeniggraetz threatened to close the fortress to the North Army. The sutlers and hawkers that normally flocked to any camp stayed away. Complaints at all levels of command intensified. What, if anything, did Benedek think he was doing? was the question rhetorically asked by generals of anyone they could buttonhole. Friedrich Beck provided a fresh pair of ears. Sent by Franz Josef to view the situation and report, he arrived in Koeniggraetz on 1 July and described an army on the point of collapse. On the same day, Benedek himself telegraphed the emperor that catastrophe was inevitable and urged peace at any price. Beck concurred. When Benedek summoned his corps commanders to a conference on the afternoon of 2 July, most of them expected to discuss the issue of continuing the retreat, with direction being the only issue.[30]

Benedek correspondingly surprised his auditors when he initially spoke of restoring discipline and improving logistics. Then he announced that the army would stay where it was for the next few days. Did that mean the field marshal had elected to fight it out where he stood, even with the Elbe at his back? His subordinates united in agreeing that Benedek said nothing at the conference or afterwards that led them to believe he anticipated a battle any time soon. It must be remembered, however, that their recollections came in the aftermath of a defeat for which the army and the government were eagerly seeking scapegoats. Given the well-known, slightly bowdlerized principle that in military organizations grief rolls downhill, it was to everyone's interest to establish as much distance as possible from a commander who had, in any case, not made himself popular in the earlier stages of the campaign. Geoffrey Wawro presents Koeniggraetz as less a decision to fight than a consequence of failure to decide to do anything – one more in a series of idiocies demonstrating the incompetence of Benedek and the ineffectiveness of the Habsburg military system.[31] Gordon Craig replicates a century of scholarship by stressing the importance of a telegram sent by Franz Josef on 1 July. Declaring immediate peace a political and diplomatic impossibility, it authorized retreat as an alternative. The last sentence asked, 'Has a battle been fought yet?' The question was not the emperor's. It came, instead, from Crenneville, who added it to the original message in the hope that it would

---

[30]Cf. Wawro, *Austro-Prussian War*, p. 192 *passim*; Glaise-Horstenau, pp. 112 ff.; and the general analysis by Eberhard Kaullbach, 'Koeniggraez nach hundert Jahren – zur militaerischen Fuehrung' in *Entscheidung 1866*, pp. 153 ff.
[31]Wawro, *Austro-Prussian War*, p. 204 *passim*.

galvanize Benedek into some kind of action.[32] The insult, however, was not even implied; it was as plain as a backhanded slap to the face.

Certainly Benedek spent a fair amount of energy on 2 July informing his emperor that the North Army headquarters had not exactly been at its best for a while, but that the situation was now improving. The field marshal also seems to have been influenced by what some of his subordinates – and not a few subsequent critics – interpreted as more or less aimless riding around his army's bivouac areas. Benedek's self-concept was of a simple field soldier, out of his depth in issues of grand strategy and high politics. It was correspondingly likely that he would attempt to clear his mind by moving among his troops. What he saw encouraged him to think favourably of prospects for battle, 'if my old luck does not desert me', as he wrote to his wife early on 3 July.[33] It must be understood, of course, that Benedek's perceptions may well have had only tenuous connection to the North Army's realities. But did not Robert E. Lee say, in the aftermath of Pickett's Charge, that he believed his troops could accomplish anything?

Linked to the human side was the rapid progress the army's engineer and artillery officers had made on a network of redoubts and entrenchments covering the army's western flank. These may well have been intended initially as nothing more than force multipliers for a rear guard,[34] but even improvised fieldworks had proven their worth time and again in the American Civil War. To an infantryman like Benedek, the positions conveyed a welcome sense of strength that he did not have to provide in person.

A final factor shaping Benedek's decision to fight might have been the dismal prospects for a retreat under Prussian guns. Throughout the campaign, the North Army had shown itself better at fighting than marching. Stretched out on the roads east or south, it could be devoured from its tail forward. Entrenched on high ground, even on what conventional opinion considered the wrong side of a river, its chances for at least severely bleeding the hitherto triumphant Prussians seemed better the longer Benedek considered the alternatives.[35]

The word 'considered' is itself somewhat misleading. Ludwig Benedek was no complex, self-searching character from a Henry James novel, able to see the fourth side of every three-sided question. In this he was like many – arguably most – senior generals in all armies. War's pivotal events are more likely to originate from their ductless glands than their frontal lobes; their intellectualizing is a *post facto* process. Again, it is not inappropriate to invoke Lee at Gettysburg, drawn into battle on 1 July as much by a sense that this was ultimately a good idea as by any rational calculation of his army's prospects. Ratiocination is usually a staff function. By 2 July, however, the North Army's staff had ceased to function at any level above routine order-drafting, particularly since Franz Josef had ordered both Henikstein and Krismanic relieved. Benedek was on his own – not a good place for that man at that time.[36]

---

[32]Craig, *Koeniggraetz*, p. 80.

[33]*Benedeks nachgelassene Papiere*, pp. 376–7.

[34]Wawro, *Austro-Prussian War*, p. 207.

[35]Frank Becker, ' "getrennt marschieren, vereint schlagen". Koeniggraetz, 3. Juli 1866' in *Schlachten der Weltgeschichte. Von Salamis bis Sinai*, eds. S. Foerster, M. Poehlmann and D. Walter (Munich, 2002), pp. 223-4.

[36]Di Nardo, 'Southern by the Grace of God', pp. 1011–32, is particularly perceptive on the relationships of staff and command in the mid-nineteenth century. For the relief of Henikstein and Krismanic, see Wawro, *Austro-Prussian War*, pp. 312 ff.

III

The Austrian position – like Benedek's decision to fight – was, to a degree, *faute de mieux*. On the right, two corps, IV and II, with a total of 55,000 men and 176 guns, faced northward from the Elbe to the high ground around the village of Chlum. Their assignment was to stand off the 2nd Army. They had the advantage of prepared – or at least semi-prepared – positions along most of their front, and they occupied the tactical high ground. The army's pivot point was on the heights of Chlum. Here Benedek posted his as yet unengaged III Corps, facing west towards the Bistritz. South of it was Gablenz's X Corps, making a total of 44,000 men backed by 134 guns. Extending the line south-east was the Saxon Corps, supported by what remained of VIII Corps – 40,000 men and 140 guns, expected to secure the North Army against any threat to its left flank. In reserve, Benedek retained I Corps, VI Corps, his heavy cavalry and the army artillery reserve: almost 50,000 infantry, over 11,000 horsemen, and no fewer than 320 guns.

Redoubt or deathtrap? The answer is by no means clear when uninfluenced by hindsight. The Austrian positions were compact: correspondingly vulnerable to Prussian artillery and, in the event, to rifle fire as well. Except at Nachod, however, the Prussian army had made limited enough use of its artillery to give the Austrian gunner officers confidence that they could silence or destroy any enemy batteries that showed themselves. To the north, the terrain rose steadily, sloping towards the mountains and, in an operational sense, dominating Austrian entrenchments and concealing them. That advantage, however, was more apparent than objective. The Prussians would have to advance some time, and the ground immediately to the fronts of II and IV Corps offered ample open spaces for tactical killing grounds. The terrain on the left similarly favoured the kind of flexible, firepower-based defence Gitschin suggested the Saxons, in particular, could execute competently. In the centre, the Prussians had to cross a river and climb a series of hills, all the time exposed to entrenched artillery, at ranges so short that the gunners could look and shoot, almost literally, down Prussian throats. Finally, if anything went seriously wrong, Benedek had the advantages that Union general George Meade had exploited so effectively at Gettysburg: interior lines and a large reserve behind them, available either to plug holes as they appeared or – perhaps – to turn a victory into a rout at the day's end.

The position's compactness had another advantage. It improved the prospects for Benedek, and his corps commanders as well, to fight a managed battle. To date, independence and initiative had been counter-productive at all levels. Now, with troops and guns massed in place, the strengths of Austrian tactics and weaponry would not be dissipated by undisciplined over-aggressiveness. If the day went even reasonably well, the final problem of the Austrian position, the existence of only a single line of retreat and that across a major river, would be irrelevant. The only retreating would be done by the Prussians – if they managed to disengage from the final Austrian counter-attack.

The subtleties of this construction were lost on too many of the North Army's regiments, who assumed their posts with glum resignation tempered by disgust at those outfits that still found something to sing about as they marched onto the line. But as the morning of 3 July passed, Ludwig Benedek began looking more and more like, if not Prince Eugène, then at least that master of eighteenth-century battle, Maximilian von Browne. Frederick Charles was initially daunted by his first view of the Austrian positions – a not unreasonable reaction for someone who had never seen fieldworks on that scale in his career. He proposed, almost by reflex, to delay, to feed his men breakfast before sending them into action. Moltke was nursing a bad cold. He was in the company not only of his king, but also Bismarck, dressed for the occasion in his uniform of a major in the Landwehr – a nice ironic touch on at least two levels. The chief of staff's aplomb was correspondingly remarkable. Go forward at once, he ordered Frederick Charles. Fix the Austrians in place until the 2nd Army takes them in flank.

Since no one knew exactly where the crown prince was, William required a bit of persuading, and Bismarck a bit of reassuring – particularly when the Prussian battalions that advanced into the Bistritz valley, beginning around 8.30, were stopped in their tracks by Austrian fire heavier than anything the headquarters worthies remembered from their days in the field against Napoleon. Most of the damage was done by the guns. Dug in, well supplied with ammunition, the Austrian batteries laid down a near impenetrable curtain of fire on the open ground between the Bistritz valley and the Austrian front line. Attempts to go forward collapsed as soon as they began. Austrian jaeger, used for the first time in the campaign as skirmishers instead of shock troops, compounded the Prussian infantry's misery by working forward in small groups, then picking off anyone exposing himself at ranges outside the needle gun's capacity to reply. Officers and sergeants dropped first and most often; leaderless men began straggling backwards, first in twos and threes, but by noon in what seemed entire battalions.

Artillery support for the hard-pressed infantry was ineffective. Senior officers ordered Prussian guns deployed in batteries, without regard for any higher command structure. Fire control was correspondingly impossible. The twelve-pounder shell guns were so outranged that they were able to do no more than draw some fire away from rifled batteries, themselves so hard pressed that they were kept too busy changing positions and refilling their caissons to do the kind of long-range precision shooting pre-war doctrine expected. When, occasionally, a battery did come on target, it soon became apparent that the flat trajectories of Krupp's rifles made it impossible to search the reverse slopes sheltering Austrian caissons and gun teams. In consequence, Prussian gunners abandoned precision shooting for an almost random area bombardment that exhausted their own ammunition supplies to no purpose, and further demoralized the infantry when, as prescribed in doctrine and practice, batteries with nothing to shoot withdrew to the rear to replenish their ammunition while the riflemen continued to endure a pounding that seemed to grow heavier by the half-hour. By noon, the Prussian positions along the Bistritz were sufficiently shaky that royal headquarters and Frederick Charles were concerned that any small event might trigger a general panic.[37]

Just to the north, however, the stage was being set for an Austrian disaster. The process began around 8 a.m., when the Prussian 7th Division entered the Swiepwald. This was no Teutonically disciplined wood with rides surgically cut and trees standing to attention, but a forest over a mile long and half a mile deep, with few trails and underbrush sufficiently tangled to disrupt even experienced bush fighters. The 7th was fighting on this unpromising ground because its commander, Eduard von Fransecky, saw the need both to relieve pressure on the frontal attack and to establish contact with the advancing 2nd Army.

---

[37]For details, cf. *Friedrich Karl*, vol. II, p. 76 *passim*; Kessel, *Moltke*, pp. 477 ff.; and Showalter, *Railroads and Rifles*, pp. 197 ff.

In pursuit of those objectives, he initially took his division forward on his own initiative, and accepted the risk of an exposed left flank that attracted the attention of two Austrian generals.

Count Tassilo Festetics, commanding IV Corps, had posted one of his brigades in the Swiepwald. Driven back by the 7th Division's initial assault, it promptly counter-attacked. Half its men never reached the woods. The rest were shot down as they entered it. Within thirty minutes, all seven of its battalions had been so dispersed that the brigade was finished as a combat force. A cautious general – or a timid one – might well have considered accepting a local defeat. The Prussians had no more chance of advancing over the open ground east of the woods than did their comrades to the south. But Festetics, another of the Austrian army's hard chargers, sent two more brigades into the Swiepwald, charging in battalion columns, played into action by their buglers.

This counter-attack was coordinated by Festetics's second in command, *Feldmarschalleutnant* Anton von Mollinary. Mollinary had been sufficiently underemployed earlier in the day to discover what he perceived as a weakness in Benedek's dispositions: the failure to occupy the higher ground in front of IV Corps's positions. To secure that ground, however, the Swiepwald had first to be cleared. And to clear the woods was also to turn the dangling Prussian left flank. In Mollinary's mind, if ever a time existed for bayonet charges at the double, it was now. Austrian steel had the chance both to create a more secure front against the 2nd Army, and to roll up the heavily engaged 1st Army like a rug before the crown prince could interfere. Mollinary drove, cajoled and cozened the men of IV Corps forward into Prussian rifle fire that dropped them in hundreds. They pushed to the far edge of the woods by mass and élan as the Prussians fell back, then staggered to a halt as the men in spiked helmets closed like a living net around the Austrian columns, firing into their unprotected flanks and rear, driving attempts to deploy back into the mass target the Austrians provided. And if the Austrians tended to huddle together, Prussian tactics fostered entropy, with companies dissolving into platoons and platoons into sections. The Swiepwald became a smoke-shrouded inferno, with organizations on both sides amounting to no more than groups of stragglers and survivors commanded by anyone who could set an example and make himself understood. When Festetics went down wounded, Mollinary took command of the corps and convinced Count Karl Thun of II Corps to support him with two more brigades. At around 11 a.m., these fresh troops drove into the woods to complete the victory. Only two Prussian battalions held the sector under attack. Exhausted by a two-hour firefight accompanied by a heavy artillery bombardment, they faced two dozen fresh battalions. The needle gun once again scythed through the Austrian columns. One jaeger battalion lost over half its men in a few minutes. It was not enough to stop the rush, and Fransecky finally looked over his shoulder.

The 7th Division had absorbed a dozen attacks without support. When its commander finally requested reinforcements, William was ready to commit the 1st Army's reserves to what looked like the crisis point of the field. Moltke intervened, even though there was no sign of the crown prince and no sound of his artillery. Until relief arrived from the north, the two divisions still at the 1st Army's disposal must be kept in hand against a general Austrian counter-attack. 'I know Fransecky', the chief of staff declared, 'he'll hold out'. But by noon the Austrians were in control of the Swiepwald. Prussian infantrymen – those still in ranks – were rifling the cartridge boxes of the dead and wounded to replenish their own exhausted supplies. 'Hold on, boys', Fransecky encouraged those able to hear him, 'it's stand or die'. Company and battalion commanders rallied what was left of their men to meet what seemed sure to be the final attack.

It did not come because there were no Austrians left to make it. The IV and II Corps between them counted a total of fifty-nine battalions. From first to last, forty-three had been sent into the Swiepwald. Only thirteen remained intact. Eight more had been rallied and reorganized – no guarantee by now that they would fight. The remaining twenty-eight were either still tangled in the woods, or had been broken by the needle guns of Fransecky's division, the disciplined courage of the men who wielded them and the tactical skill of their officers.[38]

The situation on the Austrian side is suggestive of that in the Union lines on the second day of Gettysburg. In both cases, a subordinate – Daniel Sickles in one army, Anton von Mollinary in the other – perceived a local terrain advantage and managed, as a consequence, to commit a good part of the army to a close-gripped fight in a sector that the commanding general did not regard as decisive. The process by which Austrian brigades were fed into the mincing machine of the Swiepwald invites comparison with the way Union divisions were committed to the Wheatfield and the Peach Orchard.[39] And the hole that developed in Benedek's line by 11 a.m. was akin to the gap in Meade's left centre around 4 p.m. – a mute invitation to an enterprising enemy with disposable forces. The survivors of Benedek's II and IV Corps stood at the apex of the Prussian left flank. Could they go in with the bayonet one more time? Was this the opportunity the North Army had been seeking since the opening of the campaign?

Benedek was well aware of the vulnerability of his own right flank, seven kilometres long and held, after the morning's movements, by only nine battalions. As early as 10.30 he had ordered Mollinary and Thun to resume their original positions. The major delivering the orders found Mollinary around 11, and he promptly rode to Benedek's headquarters to plead his case in person. That was arguably the worst decision Mollinary could have made. Prompt obedience and close supervision would have somewhat mitigated the moral and physical consequences of pulling back from hard-won ground. Energetic disobedience and a call over his shoulder for support offered promise of a general offensive, if only on the initiative of other generals unwilling to sacrifice the limelight. Convincing Benedek to change his mind took the only vital command presence in the Swiepwald sector out of action as surely as a needle gun round would have.

Then friction struck the Austrians another blow. As part of his effort to motivate Benedek to action, Franz Josef had ordered the dismissal of both Henikstein and Krismanic. Krismanic's replacement as chief of operations was a colonel, Alois Baumgarten, whom Benedek did not know well, who was junior for the appointment and anxious to distinguish himself. On learning of Thun's move to the Swiepwald, he ordered Ramming to move VI Corps from reserve into Thun's now vacant positions. Ramming responded by sending a

---

[38]For the Swiepwald, cf. Craig, *Koeniggraetz*, pp. 105 ff.; Fontane, *1866*, vol. I, pp. 518 ff.; and Showalter, *Railroads and Rifles*, pp. 131 ff. Wawro, *Austro-Prussian War*, pp. 221 ff., tells the Austrian story eloquently. Lettow-Vorbeck, vol. II, pp. 427 ff., once again, is useful for the clarity of his description of the troop movements senior officers intended.

[39]D. Scott Hartwig, ' "No Troops on the Field Had Done Better". John C. Caldwell's Division in the Wheatfield, July 2, 1863' in *The Second Day at Gettysburg: Essays on Confederate and Union Leadership*, ed. G. Gallagher (Kent, OH, 1993), pp. 136–71.

message to Benedek. A better use of VI Corps, he argued, was as part of an all-out attack on the pinned-down 1st Army. Minutes later, Mollinary himself arrived. Breaking contact in the Swiepwald, he insisted, would be a long and costly process for troops as closely engaged as were the Austrians. Retreat would leave them exposed to precisely the kind of rifle flirtations, small columns and skirmish lines closing in and then retiring, at which the Prussians had shown themselves expert throughout the campaign. It was time to take the final risk: to continue applying pressure on the Prussian flank and simultaneously to commit the reserves to a drive forward against the Bistritz, smashing the Prussian centre. Send Ramming to shore up the right flank, Mollinary urged, and hit the Prussian 1st Army with everything else in the sector: with Gablenz's corps, with what could be rallied from II and IV Corps, and with I Corps from the reserve. At about the same time, Gablenz requested more guns and additional ammunition from the army reserve, and asked Benedek when he proposed to send North Army forward.[40]

Benedek temporized. In part, he was concerned with the whereabouts of the 2nd Army, and correspondingly disturbed at the disruption of the two-corps blocking force he had posted to cover his right against its appearance. In part, he was less than pleased with Mollinary for taking part of the battle out of his hands and now attempting to shape the rest. Mollinary has been blamed for establishing the battlefield conditions for Austria's defeat, and lauded as the only senior Habsburg officer on the field with any feel for the battle as a whole. Neither argument can be evaluated without context. Mollinary's determination to establish the Swiepwald as the battle's decisive point had the practical result of eviscerating two corps – two, moreover, of the only three remaining in the North Army that had not previously been savaged by the Prussians. But once his immediate seniors and the commander-in-chief failed to rein him in, the tactical die was cast. Whether he intended to disengage his army from the Prussians closing in on his flanks, or to destroy its centre and send the wings whirling outward on their own, Benedek needed to send his men forward one more time.

What were the prospects of such an attack? Frederick Charles had two full divisions in reserve. His forward formations were badly disorganized and increasingly demoralized, but except for the 7th Division, those were consequences of being hit without the ability to hit back. The 1st Army's artillery was scattered across the front by batteries. Case-shot over open sights, complementing the rapid fire of the best battle rifle in Europe, nevertheless offered better than fair prospects of at least keeping the Austrians in check until Crown Prince Frederick delivered the *coup de grâce* to an army caught lunging forward, wrong-footed for retreating across the Elbe. On the other side of the ledger, the Austrians on most of the prospective front would be engaging tired, hungry, thirsty men whose initial adrenalin rush had long since dissipated. The tactical flexibility that had characterized the Prussians earlier in the campaign, moreover, was far less likely to be evident in the valley of the Bistritz. Not only were the Prussians too shaken and disorganized to be clever, but also they had nowhere to go. The rolling, open ground behind the Bistritz was ideal country for attack by Austrian heavy cavalry organized and trained for just such an action, with three divisions of it massed in the immediate rear of the Bistritz position.

---

[40]Anton Freiherr von Mollinary, *Sechsundvierzig Jahre im oesterreich-ungarischen Heere, 1833–1879* (2 vols., Zurich, 1905), vol. II, pp. 158 ff. and Wawro, *Austro-Prussian War*, pp. 227 ff.

A breech-loading rifle is of little use to a man running away, a man who has just remembered he was a civilian a month ago.[41]

Equally relevant was that Prussia's king and his first minister were in the field, and likely candidates for death or capture should the 1st Army break. Small wonder then that Moltke allegedly responded to William's tentative question about preparations for a 'temporary change of front' by saying that Prussia's existence was at stake and there would be no retreat.[42] Small wonder, too, that scholars of the counter-factual remain bemused by the possibilities of an all-out Austrian attack some time around noon – nothing held back, everything on the line for a legend or a coffin. Even defeat in such circumstances would be a subject of myth and ballad, remembered whenever soldiers and scholars spoke of heroic efforts.

But for all Benedek's pretence of being a field soldier, dice, with its quick decisions based on single throws, was not his game. Instead he stood in place. Around noon, he finally learned that the Prussian 2nd Army had crossed the Elbe at 9 a.m. and could be expected on the field within the hour. Benedek still had time – either to implement Mollinary's death-or-glory recommendation and throw everything into seeking a decision, or to move Ramming into position on the army's right, rally the troops in the Sweipwald and continue the Prussian army's lesson in the role of artillery on the modern battlefield. What he did was fall prey to stress. Baumgarten, Mollinary and Ramming were all acting as though they commanded the North Army. In comprehensive frustration, Benedek ordered Ramming back into reserve, II and IV Corps out of the Sweipwald, and Baumgarten to remember his place – which, by now, in Benedek's opinion, was somewhere under a rock. Krismanic and Henikstein, deposed but not dismissed, stood by like two of the three Fates, silent as the North Army's commander did a credible imitation of an angry child slamming his toy soldiers back into their boxes.[43]

Meanwhile, the crown prince pushed his men southward in a rain cold enough to dampen the most martial spirits and hard enough to turn most unpaved roads into potholed nightmares. There was no *Schwerpunkt*, that 'point of concentration' so beloved by Prussophilic students of war. Instead, the 2nd Army's four corps advanced in line abreast, each making its own best speed. The Prussian Guard, the right-flank formation and the closest to the 1st Army, was handicapped by the presence of a large number of guns with its forward units – the consequence of the corps artillery commander's conviction that his batteries could make a difference in the kind of close-gripped fight which, by 11 a.m., it was clear awaited the 2nd Army. It required all of Prince Kraft Charles zu Hohenloe-Ingelfingen's personal energy to keep his batteries in formation over the objections of senior infantry officers. Then the crown prince rode up. I have two choices, he announced. Either side-slip the army to the right and support Frederick Charles directly, or keep going forward against the Austrian rear. For now, he ordered Hohenloe, form a

---

[41]Paddy Griffith, *Battle Tactics of the Civil War* (New Haven, CT, 1987), pp. 179 ff., develops the controversial but defensible case that firepower technology at this period still fell just short of being able to defeat massed cavalry 'automatically'.

[42]Moltke is also alleged to have reassured Bismarck by carefully choosing the best of the cigars in a proffered case. Both anecdotes are repeated in Craig, *Koeniggraetz*, pp. 110–11.

[43]Wawro, *Austro-Prussian War*, p. 236 *passim*.

gun line; open fire on the high ground around Horenowes, and at least make enough noise to let 'Fritz Karl' know that help is on its way.[44]

It began with two batteries of six-pounder rifles. Ninety minutes later, by 12.30, a total of fifteen batteries, ninety barrels, were in position against two-thirds the number of Austrian guns, many of which had been bombarding the Swiepwald since morning. The Habsburg batteries nevertheless changed front and ranged their new targets with impressive effect. There was no question by 1 p.m. who was victor in the artillery duel. But in the process of dominating their opposites, the Austrian gunners neglected the Prussian infantry, which worked and shot its way forward steadily against elements of II and IV Corps engaged, as per Benedek's orders, in withdrawing from their positions around the Swiepwald, or looking in that direction as the Prussians closed upon them from the north.

The crown prince, meanwhile, had decided side-slipping would take too much time. Instead he ordered his four corps forward, still in line abreast, towards the high ground extending eastward from Horenowes. Marked along much of its length by a stand of trees, it was a visible objective – one that when reached would position the whole 2nd Army for a killing blow at an Austrian flank, by this time almost wide open. Some of the battalions now posted in this sector had been hammered hard around the Swiepwald, then pulled back to reorganize. Shoving and cursing a mass of men into something resembling a military formation was – and is – a necessary first step in restoring order in the aftermath of disruption. The subsequent steps, sorting out companies, reassigning commanders and bringing up food, water and ammunition, were too often untaken, not least because too many of the officers and NCOs who could – literally – speak each other's languages were dead, wounded or shocked.

By 1 p.m., almost before either side noticed it, the high ground of Horenowes was in Prussian hands. Elements of VI Prussian Corps, as yet unengaged in the campaign, were coming up on the Guards' left, crossing the Trotinka river and driving towards the Maslowed plateau, against resistance most charitably described as episodic. The reorganized Austrian battalions were like a water-saturated sugar cube. A few shots from an unexpected quarter – and as the powder smoke thickened, every quarter of the battlefield was unexpected – was sometimes enough to dissolve them, to say nothing of the shock effect of hundreds of needle guns firing as fast as they could be reloaded into their ranks at point-blank ranges. Austrian batteries, left isolated, unsupported and coming under Prussian rifle fire, fought their guns to the muzzle before limbering up and retiring. Across Benedek's entire right wing, increasing numbers of Austrians were giving way before limited numbers of Prussians – a pattern legitimated when Thun, on his own authority, ordered what remained of his corps to pull out of line and retreat towards the Elbe.[45]

As Benedek's right staggered towards collapse, his left began caving in as well. The Prussian Elbe Army had been grinding its way forward, since 6.30 a.m., against a Saxon corps that, once again, showed its skill in fighting a delaying action. Prince Albert's riflemen and artillery kept well at bay elements of three Prussian divisions whose commanders showed no inclination to come to close quarters in the face of the larger engagement to

---

[44]Hohenloe, vol. III, p. 271.
[45]Craig, *Koeniggraetz*, pp. 136–7. Fontane, *1866*, vol. I, pp. 550 ff., is better at describing the Austrians' erosion in this sector than explaining it.

the north, whose outcome seemed increasingly uncertain. When a Saxon brigade, counter-attacking in close formation, almost broke through in one sector, Albert decided to take the initiative with two more of his own brigades and two borrowed from VIII Austrian Corps.

The Saxons hit the Prussian centre in drill-book style and began chewing their way forward. But the Austrians, pressing forward on the Saxon right, were flanked in turn by a Prussian brigade that, aiming at the Saxons, found a closer and more vulnerable target. Advancing in columns, with its skirmishers only a few paces to the front, Brigade Schulz ran headlong into three Prussian battalions, deployed in line and firing as rapidly as the men could reload. A second brigade sent forward to relieve the Prussian pressure was, in its turn, shot apart by the needle guns. Both of the Austrian formations had been engaged at Skalitz, and it did not take long for a sense of *déjà vu* to permeate the rapidly shrinking battalion columns. Some men surrendered on the spot; some ran back along their original line of advance; and others took the line of least resistance and fled south, into the Saxons, turning that attack in moments into a milling mass of targets for every rifle the Prussians could bring to bear.

Thus far in the campaign, the Elbe Army had been the classic attendant lord, swelling progresses and fleshing out scenes. Its commanding general, Karl Herwarth von Bittenfeld, was one of the Prussian army's elderly excellencies, better at awaiting orders than initiating action. Frederick Charles had treated him as a kind of deputy since crossing the border. Now, without waiting for orders, captains and majors of the 15th Division took command of whatever men they could find in the dust and smoke, and pushed towards the gap that had suddenly opened between the Saxon Corps and the Austrian centre along the Bistritz.

Gablenz, alerted by the changing locations of the firing, informed his commander that either reserves must be committed on his left, or he would have to shift part of III Corps to secure the line. But a Saxon brigade opened ranks to let the fugitives through, then reformed and broke the Prussian momentum with a series of well-timed volleys that drove the Elbe Army's leading elements to ground.

It took almost an hour for the officers to get their men moving against fire that broke every rush. Even company columns were too large to be a viable formation against Saxon Miniés and Austrian guns – particularly given the inadequate support they received from their own batteries, which in this sector were all too willing to exchange shots with the enemy gun lines at maximum effective ranges in return for minimum risk to themselves.

The advance regained momentum only around 2.30, when Herwarth received a dispatch from Moltke stating that the 2nd Army was coming in from the north and Prussia had a chance of achieving a double envelopment: a second Cannae. Herwarth responded by sending another full division forward, colours uncased and bands playing. For Prince Albert, it was time to go. By 3.30, the Saxon Corps had disengaged itself, leaving the two Prussian divisions it had engaged so effectively too disorganized to pursue with any alacrity – and leaving Herwarth and his staff sufficiently shaken that they chose not to commit the Elbe Army's third division (which, as yet, had not fired more than a few shots) to keep the attack moving.[46]

---

[46]Fontane, *1866*, vol. I. pp. 480 ff.; Wawro, *Austro-Prussian War*, pp. 229 ff. and 242 ff.; and Craig, *Koeniggraetz*, pp. 98 ff. and 124 ff.

Once again, a subordinate had bought Benedek time he did not use. The tone of some North Army orders, sent as late as 1.30, suggest the field marshal was still considering an attack in the centre, against the 1st Army. But that window of opportunity was rapidly being closed from the other side. Around noon, Frederick Charles had brought up his reserve, the two divisions of III Brandenburg Corps. They made a brave show as they advanced under their regimental colours. They also came in range of Austrian batteries, overjoyed at the new target, and took heavy losses for no immediate tactical results. The Brandenburgers' presence may have had some negative influence on Benedek's in-and-out resolve to go forward. It certainly disturbed Moltke, who, nevertheless, was reluctant to countermand Frederick Charles's orders and withdraw the corps from the fire it could not answer. It was about 1 p.m. when his attention was distracted. In one account, made familiar by its protagonist, Bismarck was scanning the foreground with his telescope when he saw what he had thought to be a line of trees along the Horenowes heights moving forward. He called to Moltke. The chief of staff looked through the telescope and promptly informed William that the battle was won and Vienna lay at his feet.[47]

Had the normally taciturn Moltke burst into music-hall song and executed a few dance steps, the king could not have been more surprised. Nor was William's dusty reply that the chief of staff would do well to keep his mind on events at hand entirely misplaced. Around 1.45, Frederick Charles, seeing victory at hand in his sorely tried sector, ordered the 5th and 6th Divisions forward against the Bistritz heights. Moltke wanted to keep Benedek focused on his centre, not encourage him to retreat. He sent a staff officer – Wartensleben again – to the leading division's commander, telling him to hold his ground. The well-known reply, 'this is all very good, but who is general Moltke?' was an expression of sarcasm, not ignorance. General Albrecht von Manstein was anxious to go forward – or rather, to send his corps forward. In his mind's eye he could see his regimental flags floating above the Austrian positions, and he did not take kindly to what he regarded as a crass violation of the chain of command. It required all of Wartensleben's considerable personal charm and power of persuasion to hold Manstein in place for the fifteen minutes it required to get Frederick Charles to confirm the chief of staff's order – which the prince, *nota bene*, did without protest, despite his subsequent regret at the fame he purportedly sacrificed.[48]

IV

Moltke's intervention was more decisive than he could know. After the capture of Horenowes, the Guard Corps' commanding general, Prince August of Wuerttemberg, proposed to halt until his second division arrived and the VI Corps's advance developed. Major General Hiller von Gaertringen instead took a page from the Austrian book of insubordination and another from the Prussian text on initiative, and sent his 1st Guard Division against what was now clearly the pivot point of the Austrian position in the northern sector: the heights of Chlum.

If the Austrian fieldworks in that sector were a bit skimpy, the same could not be said for their artillery: seven batteries in and around the forward positions, ten on the heights

---

[47]Otto von Bismarck, *Die gesammelten Werke*, eds. H. von Petersdorff et al. (15 vols., Berlin, 1923–33), vol. VII, p. 206.

[48]Kessel, *Moltke*, p. 480 and *Friedrich Karl*, vol. II, pp. 95–6.

themselves, two more immediately available. Against these 152 guns, the guardsmen initially advanced with no artillery support at all. Logically, their attack should have been pinned down within minutes. But the Prussian Guard benefited from a combination of factors. The ground over which it advanced was broken, a network of low ridge lines, dips and hollows. The light cavalry division assigned to the North Army's right flank remained at its far right end, like a drawing pin holding a map in place, eschewing any serious screening and patrolling. The rain that had so hindered Prussian movements since the start of the campaign had been good for the crops: the standing grain in many areas was man-high and better. In the absence of any wind, smoke shrouded the field. Austrian battery officers, accustomed to attacks made in mass, with full ruffles and flourishes, were not particularly impressed by their relatively few glimpses of skirmish lines and company columns working their way forward towards the heights.

Nevertheless, enough guns were in place that their measured, desultory fire was inflicting casualties and disrupting organizations – until the Austrians discovered another target. Hohenloe, acting on his own initiative, took four batteries forward, unlimbered in full view of the Austrians and opened fire, uphill at 1,300 paces – pocket-pistol range for the Austrian rifled cannon. Even when a few more batteries edged forward to join him, Hohenloe was outgunned three to one. But by taking advantage of the ground and moving his pieces freely, Hohenloe attracted and distracted the Austrian gunners long enough for Hiller's infantry to come within killing range.[49]

The Austrians holding in the sector, one brigade from IV Corps and one from III, had not established outposts. One choleric and short-sighted colonel dismissed reports of men in blue coats approaching his position, asserting that they must be Saxons![50] The brigadier from IV Corps, still expecting an order to attack the Swiepwald, had deployed his men facing west, with only a single battalion holding Chlum as a flank guard. It was around 3 p.m. By then, the 'fog of Chlum', so often cited in Austrian sources to explain the next thirty minutes, had lifted from the field, but remained as a metaphor. In a fashion prefiguring the March offensives of 1918, the forward elements of the 1st Guard Division had infiltrated an Austrian position occupied not by coherent, cohesive formations, but isolated brigades, out of touch with each other and lacking awareness of events around them. The battalion in Chlum village was destroyed before it knew what was happening, 400 of its men surrendering almost without a fight to Prussians that seemed to appear from nowhere. Two more battalions attempted a counter-attack and had 600 shot down in a few minutes. Over 1,000 more threw away their rifles and shouted to the Prussians to come and get them. Three companies of the Guard bypassed the fighting in the village, instead advancing downhill, through the tall summer grain and along a sunken road into the neighbouring village of Rosberitz, whose outskirts touched the Austrian army's jugular vein: the high road to Koeniggraetz and the Elbe river. Half a dozen more companies followed the temporary line of least resistance, and began turning Rosberitz into a field fortification, loopholing walls and building barricades against the counter-attack that was sure

---

[49]Lettow-Vorbeck, vol. II, p. 437; Fontane, *1866*, vol. I, pp. 518 ff.; and Hohenloe, vol. III, pp. 282 ff.
[50]Fontane, *1866*, vol. I, pp. 527 ff. At some risk of overkill, it should be noted that had the colonel been correct, given the Saxons' original position, their presence in the Chlum sector could only be a sign of disaster elsewhere, and a signal for immediate and drastic action. The incident epitomizes the lack of information and lack of grip too often characteristic of the Austrian army at regimental levels in 1866.

to come. Other companies and half-battalions of guardsmen moved seemingly at will across the high ground, shooting up battery positions and scattering local, small-scale cavalry charges, able to use neither mass nor surprise against the needle guns. Prussian officers did not even need to form square in order to see off the Austrian horsemen, who, in turn, repeatedly added to a growing general discomfiture by charging in and out of their own infantry.

Some Austrian commanders responded to the Prussian eruption by abandoning their positions. Other brigadiers, colonels and majors took battalions into improvised counterattacks. Austrian doctrine asserted (and subsequent German experience in two world wars demonstrated) that the best way of restoring this kind of desperate situation was by throwing back the enemy before he could reinforce or consolidate his newly gained positions. Around Chlum, however, the needle gun was trump. Bayonet charges melted away in the smoke, their leading files shot down and the rest trailing away to the flanks and rear. What remained of Benedek's II and IV Corps were dissolving, their men seeking any way out of the smoke-shrouded inferno. The Austrian III Corps was also beginning to fade back from its positions along the Bistritz, its brigades fighting individual battles to cut lines of retreat through Prussian Guardsmen who appeared, as if by magic, on all sides of their formations.[51]

The exact timing is impossible to determine, but the best evidence indicates that Field-Marshal Ludwig Benedek had abandoned thoughts of an offensive around 2 p.m. His subsequent attention was initially devoted to keeping an eye on the Bistritz sector, then to shoring up his left flank, where, as previously described, the Elbe Army was driving the Saxons in slow motion. Then, around 2.45, a staff colonel arrived at headquarters with a report that not only had the 2nd Army reached the field, but the Prussians were in Chlum, and he had dodged enough of their bullets to be certain. An incredulous Benedek rode to see for himself, first experienced Prussian rapid fire at 200 yards, then came under friendly fire that dismounted half a dozen staff officers. A Habsburg partisan might be forgiven for wishing that either the Prussians had been lucky, or that the Austrians had, for once, set their sights a little higher. It was donkeys and not horses that had led them to ruin that day.[52]

Reverting briefly to the role of a field officer, Benedek rallied a shaken regiment, the Magyar 52nd, and sent it against Chlum to by now predictable destruction by the needle gun. Then, finally acting like an army commander, he rode back to VI Corps, still in reserve, and ordered Ramming to throw the Prussians out of Rosberitz and Chlum. Ramming had profited from his experience at Nachod – and from the fates of his fellow corps commanders, Festetics, Thun and Mollinary, earlier in the day. He had also been warning Benedek for over an hour that the entire position around Chlum was in peril. Now, whether something of the battle could still be salvaged, or if he could do no more than hold open a line of retreat, Ramming was going to demonstrate how to conduct a counter-attack. Ignoring Benedek's repeated appeals for haste, ignoring as well the arrival of more and more Prussian troops in the Chlum sector, he delayed sending his infantry forward, instead stabilizing their formations while 120 guns bombarded the villages and the heights behind them. The ground was too broken, Austrian staff work too haphazard, for a coordinated, multi-brigade

---

[51]Fontane, *1866*, vol. I, pp. 561 ff. and Wawro, *Austro-Prussian War*, pp. 249 ff., can be combined to reconstruct confusing events whose exact sequence often remains uncertain.
[52]Ibid., pp. 252–3.

attack. Instead, VI Corps was committed sequentially, by brigades, too often by battalions. But the attacks, nevertheless, went in like sledgehammers.

Their first objective was Rosberitz. Brigade Rosenzweig swept into the village, a jaeger battalion in the van. Its men (Ruthenians, as they were called then) were yokels from Carpatho-Ukraine, one of the empire's remotest corners. They had no economic interest and no national stake in the fighting's outcome – just, perhaps, a pride of craft and colours that carried them forward into streets and outbuildings against the sleeting rifle fire of Prussians readier themselves that day to die than to run. Austria had no guard formations, but alongside the jaeger in the first wave was the 4th Infantry Regiment, the *Hoch-und-Deutschmeister*, Vienna's own, and as proud as any northerners wearing guard-braid on their uniform coats. As its corner-boys, factory hands and shopkeepers' assistants measured bayonets and rifle butts with the Prussians, Rosenzweig's second regiment, whose original objective was the high ground beyond the village, was also drawn into what was becoming the closest gripped fighting of the war. With Prussian rifles overheating and Prussian cartridge boxes emptying, one last shrieking Habsburg charge forced the surviving defenders from the village and back up the heights. A sergeant and twenty men, all that remained in ranks of the 2nd Foot Guard's 11th Company, brought out the battalion colours – to a more jaded age, perhaps, a meaningless *beau geste*, but to the men on the spot a sign of defiance, a statement that it was not over yet. Other companies, spotting the withdrawal, came up in support. Two gunner captains pushed their batteries forward from Chlum without orders to take the Austrians under fire at hundred-yard ranges.

The Prussian Guard has gone down in modern military writing as an institution dedicated to aristocratic pretensions and retrograde tactics. At mid-century, its officer corps was filled with 'von und zu' scions of Prussia's nobility. Its regiments cultivated elaborate *couleur* relationships, or barely acknowledged each other's existence, for reasons incomprehensible outside the 'Guard family'. Its training and discipline were proverbially rigorous. But the corps also prided itself on being at the cutting edge of tactical effectiveness – a vanity piqued by a long-standing rivalry with its neighbours of III Brandenburg. Many of its active soldiers and most of its reservists were Berliners, city boys accustomed, in their own eyes at least, to responding to the unexpected. Now they shot Rozenzweig's brigade to pieces as its commander personally led it in a rush that almost reached the outskirts of Chlum, successive waves struggling to make progress across the open ground and up a nameless trail that by day's end bore the grim sobriquet, 'Dead Man's Way'.[53]

As is so often the case in shock warfare, the first charge got the farthest. The rest of VI Corps swung up the Chlum slopes against a thin line of guardsmen from half the companies in the 1st Division, commanded by anyone able to set an example. Ramming took one attack forward in person, using up a career's worth of good fortune in escaping unscathed from Prussian fire that mercilessly sought out the mounted officers. 'Crazy courage and a crazier formation', Hohenloe later described the Austrian mass attacks.[54] But one by one, his batteries ran out of ammunition. One by one, the cartridge boxes of

---

[53]Craig, *Koeniggraetz*, pp. 144 ff. and Wawro, *Austro-Prussian War*, pp. 260 ff. are good on Ramming's attack from an Austrian perspective. For the Prussian side, cf. Fontane, *1866*, vol. I, pp. 594 ff. and the history of the 2nd Foot Guards, which bore the brunt of the defence of Rosberitz, Col. von Pape, *Das zweite Garde Regiment zu Fuss in dem Feldzug des Jahres 1866* (Berlin, 1866), pp. 106 ff.
[54]Hohenloe, vol. III, p. 292.

the infantrymen emptied. There were no reserves in sight, and the Austrian bayonets were closing in.

Ramming later declared his attacks were intended to do no more than hold off pursuit of the beaten North Army.[55] He did not communicate that limited mission statement to senior Prussian officers, who saw the battle slipping away. Chlum had fallen too quickly for the information to percolate to higher headquarters. On Frederick Charles's front, things looked so bleak that around 3 p.m. the commander of II Corps, whose men had spent the day in the woods under Austrian fire, was convinced it was necessary to retreat.[56] The 2nd Army's headquarters had done almost nothing to control or coordinate the actions of its forward corps. 'What's happening?' was the first question addressed to anyone who came near the crown prince with powder smoke clinging to his uniform. Further forward, Hiller von Gaertringen sat his horse, hoping at least to inspire men he could not reinforce. Then he saw something to his rear. Given the disorder on this part of the field it might even have been those wandering Saxons. Instead, it turned out to be elements of the 1st Jaeger Battalion, and behind them the whole of I Prussian Corps, coming fresh to a fight their presence sent into its final rounds. 'Now everything will be all right!' rejoiced Hiller to the jaegers' commander. Moments later he was mortally wounded by a bursting shell – a scene that would seem impossibly contrived if presented in a movie.

Hiller died as the leading elements of I Corps took position among the surviving guardsmen, sharing cartridges, building up a firing line strong enough to see off Ramming's final attack, then slowly moving forward towards the Koeniggraetz high road, across ground so covered with dead and wounded that officers were constrained to dismount and lead their chargers over the bodies.

A little earlier, William – with one eye on his chief of staff – ordered a general advance on the 1st Army's front. Initially it met little opposition. Benedek's III Corps had long since been caught up in the collapse on the right. Gablenz had begun withdrawing X Corps without orders, as the Elbe Army's advance bit deeper and deeper into his exposed left. Even so, the Prussian advance was tentative, particularly since the Austrian guns were still active and accurate. The king himself came under fire sufficiently heavy that Bismarck, whose own tolerance for shelling was not particularly well developed, successfully insisted the monarch restrain his enthusiasm and fall back at least to a longer range.[57]

The North Army had begun the day with two of its corps in reserve – Ramming's VI and I Corps, now commanded by its former *adlatus*, Leopold Gondrecourt. Maintaining a reserve of this strength was sufficiently important to Benedek that he had refused to commit it when it might have brought victory. With disaster upon him, the field marshal appeared initially to have had some intention of committing both corps simultaneously against Chlum in a last attempt to turn the day in Austria's favour, while sending his reserve cavalry to stand off the troops of Frederick Charles. After ordering Ramming's counterattack, however, Benedek again reverted to the behaviour of a colonel, dashing almost at random around the field, to the despair of staff officers unable to deliver questions or

---

[55]Wawro, *Austro-Prussian War*, p. 260.

[56]The frequent description of this behaviour as a harbinger of the officer's post-war mental collapse (itself probably a form of Alzheimer's Disease) is convincingly refuted in Lettow-Vorbeck, vol. II, p. 490. Cf. Craig, *Koeniggraetz*, p. 137.

[57]Fontane, *1866*, vol. I, p. 609.

reports. If he was looking for a bullet, he did not place himself at the head of attacks until one found him. If he was functioning as a commander, he did nothing to coordinate the movements of VI and I Corps with each other or with the cavalry.

His men deserved better. By itself, the Austrian reserve cavalry managed to stop the 1st Army for about an hour. Numerical superiority — forty squadrons against thirty Prussian — was for once accompanied by tactical skill. The Austrian troopers always seemed to have a few squadrons in the right places with a few more in reserve; and the Prussian regiments were roughly handled as long as the contest involved horse against horse. But the field of Koeniggraetz was restricted at best, offering little open ground at the beginning of the day and less as the advancing Prussians squeezed the pocket tighter. One of the paradoxes of the modern battlefield, as it developed between 1848 and 1914, was that it was simultaneously emptier and more crowded. Time and again Austrian troopers trying to shake themselves out or reorganize after an engagement came within range of Prussian rifles or artillery, and paid the price in men and horses. Nor was it easy to find enough room either to deploy in numbers large enough decisively to sweep the Prussian horse from the field, or to develop sufficient momentum to generate real shock effect. The result was a series of mêlées, swirling sabre duels that decided nothing, but did at least enmesh the Prussian cavalry and clog their infantry's lines of advance.[58]

Another of Benedek's improvisations reaped greater results. By 3.30, the Prussian Elbe Army was almost in a position to cut the North Army's line of retreat by default. All Herwarth had to do was advance towards a highway left open by the destruction of VIII Corps's two brigades and the retreat of the Saxons. As the afternoon waned, Prince Albert appears to have considered prudence a greater virtue than 'Nibelungen loyalty' to an ally whose behaviour, since before the war, had been significantly and overtly motivated by self-interest. With his country under Prussian occupation, the crown prince was unwilling to risk the destruction of its army as well. Despite the steady courage that was a consequence of sensible tactics, his battalions were tired and shaken. As they withdrew from around Prim and Problus, they were also withdrawing from the war.[59]

Neither Herwarth nor his senior generals, however, could see beyond the disorganization of their forward units, or beyond the empty stomachs and canteens occasioned by the early hour of the Elbe Army's advance. Benedek ordered a brigade of I Corps into a counter-attack. Once again, the battalion columns were shattered and most of the company officers shot down in minutes. But Prussian aplomb was shattered as well, at least in that sector. Herwarth even considered withdrawing artillery that seemed threatened by the Austrians' desperate valour. His infantry held their positions, but failed to push forward with any enthusiasm.[60]

Three more brigades of I Corps went up the Chlum heights. The corps had been left to its own devices so long that it lacked space and time to form the assault in regulation fashion. Instead, the Austrians went in by columns of march, only a few files across and dozens deep. The guardsmen and their West Prussian reinforcements took what cover they could find and allowed the Austrians to close, sometimes to ranges as short as 300 paces. One

---

[58]For the cavalry fight, see Lettow-Vorbeck, vol. II, pp. 502 ff.; Fontane, *1866*, vol. I, pp. 611 ff.; and 'Das Kavallerie Korps Prinz Adalbert in der Schlacht bei Koeniggraertx', ed. A. Schmidt, *Forschungen zur brandenburgischen und preussischen Geschichte* 39 (1937), pp. 260–74.

[59]Paul Hassell, *Aus dem Leben des Koenigs Albert von Sachsen* (2 vols., Berlin, 1898–1900), vol. II, pp. 296 ff.

[60]Lettow-Vorbeck, vol. II, pp. 488 ff.

Austrian battalion, led by the corps commander, almost managed to reach the crest, at the cost of over 500 casualties. Otherwise, results were predictable. By 5 p.m., I Corps had lost over 10,000 officers and men – above half the strength it took into action. It was the work of thirty minutes of breech-loading rifle fire. And it set the seal on catastrophe.[61]

By now the Prussian VI Corps was well into the Habsburg rear, with V Corps coming up rapidly on the Prussian far right – the conceivable spearhead of a tactical envelopment that might put all of North Army in the bag by day's end. Well before the crushing of I Corps, the Austrian rear had been overrun by masses of men knocked loose or shocked loose from their formations, wandering more or less aimlessly but always heading more or less towards the safety promised by the Elbe and its bridges. Even more than in earlier battles, commanders had been generous with alcohol as a boost to morale and a substitute for undelivered food rations. As the liquor died out, dissociation set in. It escalated to panic as men sought escape from a Prussian pursuit that seemed increasingly personal.

Reality was more pedestrian – and more heroic. Two battalions of the army's artillery reserve, originally posted on the Chlum heights, had fallen back to the lower ground east of the Koeniggraetz road. Benedek visited their commander and received his reassurance that the guns would stand to the last. Unsupported by infantry, but joined by other batteries with a few rounds and some fighting spirit remaining, they shot it out on even terms with thirty-three batteries from three Prussian armies, until the late July night finally fell and enough order had been restored to get a North Army – by now composed of demoralized survivors – across the Elbe.

Not a single one of Benedek's Austrian infantry brigades was combat-effective by the evening of 3 July. Over 40,000 men were dead or wounded (the latter arguably a worse fate in an inefficient and overloaded hospital system that was unable even to keep reasonable records of the numbers of deaths under its dubious care) and 20,000 were prisoners – a number that, in conventional contexts, indicated a complete collapse of morale. The army's ethnic groups were already pointing fingers, with Poles accusing Magyars of shirking, Germans decrying the cowardly Czechs, and everyone despising the Italians. A determined pursuit might well have applied the *coup de grâce* – in hindsight.

Moltke, who had spent most of the day awaiting information and presenting an image of calm confidence, was, in fact, uncertain if his victory was 'a Magenta or a Solferino'. He did not as yet perceive it as a 'crowning mercy'. In later years, the chief of staff became more willing to describe Koeniggraetz as his 'most elegant' battle, a particular masterpiece of concentration on the field in the face of the enemy.[62] Reality, as twilight deepened, was elements of three armies milling around in a killing ground that had become a slaughterhouse. A Prussian front covering over thirty kilometres when the fighting began had been compressed into a pocket less than four kilometres across. Even the few veterans of the Wars of Liberation still occupying senior posts were shocked by the sheer numbers of dead and wounded Austrians strewn across that small area. Prussian battalions and squadrons were almost as disorganized by victory as their opponents were by defeat.

With adrenalin wearing off, hunger set in – not the usual hunger accompanying a day's hard physical work, but a gnawing, painful demand whose origins were as much

---

[61]Wawro, *Austro-Prussian War*, pp. 256 ff. and Fontane, *1866*, vol. I, pp. 601 ff.
[62]Kessel, *Moltke*, p. 481.

psychological as physical. Not to be overlooked was the effect of a long and strenuous day on senior officers normally at least in their fifties, at a time when geriatric medicine and physical fitness were both embryonic concepts. Moltke himself was approaching his sixty-sixth birthday and, after thirteen hours in the saddle, King William was willing to admit that he was no longer a young buck either.[63] Most of the Austrian army was over the Elbe, and a night battle to secure bridgeheads seemed a second, set-piece operation rather than a 'bouncing' of the river line. There seemed, in short, ample reason to regard the day of Koeniggraetz not as a thing in itself, but as the end of the beginning and the beginning of the end.

V

In the historiography of the wars of German unification, the campaign and battle of Koeniggraetz have tended to be overshadowed, on the one hand, by the more arduous, more glamorous and better reported operations against the French Empire and Republic, and, on the other, by the spectacular diplomatic virtuosity of Otto von Bismarck before and after the war. General histories present the war of 1866 in a 'Whig' context: part of a linear process resulting ultimately in the establishment of the Second German Reich. Austria's expulsion from Germany seems correspondingly predictable, almost natural. This approach has been facilitated because specific accounts of the Seven Weeks War strongly reflect an emphasis on specific military factors, especially technology and staff planning, which tends to juxtapose the modern Prussians and the retrograde Austrians.[64]

Another, related, contributing factor is a persisting Habsburg nostalgia that is the central European counterpart to the gunpowder-and-magnolias 'lost cause' school of writing on the American Civil War. For black-and-yellow pietists, the battle of Koeniggraetz is the counterpart of the third day at Gettysburg: a time when it is not yet 1 p.m. on 3 July, the cannonade has not begun and, once it does, life will never be the same. Austria's defeat becomes a kind of mythic tragedy, fated by powers beyond the control of man − 'the stars in their courses' fought against Benedek, as they did against Robert E. Lee.[65]

Geoffrey Wawro has recently sought the jugular of that approach with a scathing, comprehensive indictment of Austria's military ineffectiveness. Nevertheless, his seminal work too often conflates fog and friction with incompetence and ineffectiveness. His descriptions of the Austrian attacks on 3 July, for example, significantly resemble both contemporary and academic accounts of the Confederate side at the battle of Chickamauga in September 1863. That, too, was a dogfight, where command and control collapsed and no one was sure where anyone else was. But it broke the Union line in one of the hardest-fought tactical victories of the Civil War, and opened strategic prospects whose non-exploitation had nothing of substance to do with the battle itself.[66]

---

[63]Craig, *Koeniggraetz*, p. 163.

[64]See, for example, Jeremy Black, 'European Warfare 1864–1913' in *European Warfare 1815–2000*, ed. J. Black (New York, 2002), pp. 53 ff.

[65]As in Emil Franzel, *1866. Il Mondo Casca* (2 vols., Vienna, 1968).

[66]Peter Cozzens, *This Terrible Sound: The Battle of Chickamauga* (Chicago, 1992), deals best with the effects of 'fog and friction' on the fighting.

Was Koeniggraetz, then, an effort doomed from the start by genius on one side, fate or fecklessness on the other? An evaluation of the evidence suggests the contrary: that both the campaign and the battle were near-run things. On the Prussian side of the line, Moltke's reliance on the railroads to deploy his armies was a calculated risk that paid dividends at the policy level, but committed Prussia to an operational approach offering a reasonably enterprising enemy significant opportunities to decide the issue by defeating the two major armies in detail. Once the campaign began, neither Frederick Charles nor the crown prince was extraordinarily successful in overcoming the problems inherent in moving large forces of inexperienced men into enemy territory. Nor is there any evidence that they understood the implications and possibilities of a forward concentration, whose nature was clearer in retrospect than prospect even to its author, Helmuth von Moltke.

This did not mean the Prussian advance was a disaster waiting to happen at the operational level. In the context of 1866, however, Austria did not need an Austerlitz or a Jena. A partial victory, an Antietam, a Gettysburg, or a reasonable facsimile, was almost certain to reshape the political factors that were closely and inextricably bound at all levels on both sides of what was understood as a policy war. Napoleon III, Bismarck's domestic opponents, even King William, would have been likely to reconsider their options fundamentally had the 1st Army been fought to a standstill at Gitschin and the 2nd been thrown back into Silesia. If even the day of Koeniggraetz had ended with a hard-hammered North Army still holding high ground west of the Elbe and ready for another day's fight, might the Prussian high command – which was also the Prussian government – have reconsidered its military and diplomatic options?

That shifts the focus of analysis to the North Army. To what extent was Benedek in a position to structure victory at the war's operational, theatre level? His initial decision to concentrate at Olmuetz was defensible – not obviously worse than the major alternatives. His initial refusal to lunge into south Germany to pick up their armies was also sensible. Apart from the problems of transportation and logistics that had accompanied Austria's mobilization, the Austrian army perceived its strength as being tactical, not operational. Clever manoeuvres in the Napoleonic style were less its forte than a decisive battle on a chosen killing ground. Allowing the Prussians to thrust their necks into a noose was preferable to improvising an operation that would, in Benedek's mind, do no more than encumber him with another 50,000 or so second-rate troops, to be fed from an already stressed supply system.

As discussed earlier, once Benedek left Olmuetz and started west, he had two proactive options as the Prussians advanced. He could do what most of his later critics recommend: turn on the 2nd Army in force and kick it back through the mountains. He could also leave two or three corps to block the passes and push on with the rest of North Army to join I Corps and the Saxons at Gitschin, then take on Frederick Charles in the kind of battle, and on the kind of terrain, that suited his army's doctrine and training. In the event, Benedek made a series of small decisions but no big one – nothing that suggested anything like either a grip on the course of events or a will to shape those events. The result was a set of local defeats whose material and moral consequences, at all levels, had seriously weakened the North Army's fighting power by the time Benedek determined – again, to a certain degree, *faute de mieux* – to make some kind of fight at Koeniggraetz.

Benedek's handling of that battle, from the inattention to the entrenchments covering his northern flank to his failure to take charge of his subordinates in the Swiepwald, reflects the indecision characterizing his earlier conduct of the campaign. Punching home an attack in the Swiepwald, mounting a counter-attack across the Bistritz and allowing the Prussians to attack his field defences all offered risks, and each offered prospects. Benedek chose none of them, and, as a result, let the Prussians structure his battle for him.

That brings us to the last level of analysis. Time and again, armies have made good unfavourable strategic and operational circumstances by tactical effectiveness or sheer fighting power. Above the regimental level, there was little to choose in ability between the combatants. The major discrepancy was the Austrians' difficulty coordinating operations. Benedek could not keep control of his corps commanders; neither could they keep control of their brigadiers. This reflected less incompetence than inexperience. An Austrian brigade at field strength, around 6,000 strong, was virtually impossible to command from horseback on a black-powder battlefield, a quarter of an hour after it was committed. As yet, no army had developed even ad hoc means of coordinating large-scale tactical movements; the Prussian attacks of 1870 would fare little better than did the Austrians in 1866.

That leads to the most familiar criticism of Austrian tactics: the commitment to shock. Of itself, this was no bad idea at this date. Shock tactics' relative failure in the American Civil War arguably owed as much to the improvised civilian armies on both sides as to the effects of 'modern' firepower on the battlefield. A case might – and can – be made that Austrian generals willing to accept a campaign's worth of casualties in a few hours, able to lead or drive forward soldiers conditioned to accept those kinds of losses, had reasonable prospects of success – as long as they faced muzzle-loading Miniés instead of breech-loaders like the needle gun.

At no time during the campaign, except perhaps at Trautenau, did Prussian artillery contribute significantly, much less decisively, to the repulse of an Austrian attack. Instead, it was the rifles they carried that gave the Prussian rank and file confidence in their own ability to shatter the most fearsome charge, then herd and harry the survivors like wolves among deer. It was the needle gun that gave point to Prussian tactics emphasizing company columns, by acting as a force multiplier for the relatively small numbers. Arguably, it was also the needle gun that helped make combat leaders out of inexperienced captains and lieutenants, by making it possible for even small numbers to compensate for a tactical error like misreading terrain or failing to see enemy movements. The 'mission tactics' so often held up as an example of the German way of war at its best require a high capacity for self-correction. Ideally, this is a product of skill, but in 1866 the needle gun was a useful facilitator. In short, Austrian tactics made them in 1866 an 'obliging enemy' – an enemy who not only made errors, but of his own volition made the kind of errors that maximized his opponent's advantages.

VI

On 4 July, Gablenz appeared in Prussian headquarters under a flag of truce. He asked for a three-day armistice, ostensibly to tend the wounded and bury the dead. Moltke, Bismarck and William rejected the proposal out of hand as a ploy to gain time for the North Army to make good its escape. That escape, it developed, was in the direction of Olmuetz. Benedek's decision to fall back eastwards toward the fortress rather than south on Vienna, in part, seems to have been a reflex process: he came from there and he would return to there. In more rational terms, his decision was defensible on the grounds that the North Army needed immediate rest and reorganization. Olmuetz was only half as far from Koeniggraetz as was Vienna. Should the Prussians follow him, the capital was at least temporarily safe, and the government in a position both to negotiate foreign intervention and concentrate reinforcements. Should Moltke and William march directly on the Austrian capital, perhaps it might even be possible for a rallied and revitalized North Army to execute the original strategic intention of striking the Prussians' exposed flank.

In the event, Moltke delayed. Apart from the near-traumatic effect of victory on his own army, initially he was unsure exactly where Benedek was going: a month in the field had not improved the Prussian cavalry's skill at operational reconnaissance. On 6 July, Moltke finally ordered the 2nd Army to advance on Olmuetz and fix Benedek there while the 1st Army and the Elbe Army took the high road towards Vienna.[67] The question was whether they could march faster than the diplomats could talk. On 2 July, Mensdorff had contacted Paris, requesting French mediation of a war whose prospects seemed dubious, whatever the outcome of Benedek's as yet unfought battle. The despatch itself was disconcerting to an emperor and a foreign ministry expecting a relatively long campaign of mutual exhaustion – an expectation that arguably encouraged Mensdorff to request mediation in the first place. On 5 July he further sweetened the pot by ceding Venetia directly to France.

That gesture, however, was overshadowed by the news of Koeniggraetz, reported with colour, verve and only moderate exaggeration in the British and French presses. Napoleon had no plans for such a contingency. On 4 July, he contacted William and proposed the extension of the armistice to Prussia. The next day, his government, following the lead of Foreign Minister Drouyn de Lhuys and Empress Eugénie, decided 'armed mediation' would better serve French interests. The sight of 80,000 French regulars on the Rhine frontier would catch the attention even of a Prussian government labouring under an extreme case of victory disease. Napoleon, suffering from a painful and debilitating kidney problem, initially agreed, but continued to prefer 'friendly mediation'. He believed the public opinion on which his plebiscitary empire increasingly depended would not support serious military action against Prussia. He also listened to the pessimists among his advisors, who stressed the current economic and military weaknesses of an empire already suffering overstretch in Mexico. The result was vacillation – and a hotter frying pan for Bismarck.[68]

The Prussian minister-president blew familiar smoke in the direction of Paris, simultaneously threatening Napoleon with a German national revolution that would set Europe ablaze and extending hope of compensation on France's eastern frontier. But Bismarck's main concern was to bring the Austrian war to a quick and acceptable end. In that he received support from Benedek. The field marshal had been surprisingly successful in reorganizing his shattered army in the days after Koeniggraetz. The price he paid – a predictable one – was staying so long at Olmuetz that the Prussians were able to cut the Olmuetz-Vienna rail line. When Benedek began to march south before his supplies ran out, the Prussians stung his flank guards badly in several minor encounter battles. Rather than risk a running fight, Benedek took his army across the Carpathians and into Hungary, eventually reaching Vienna by way of Pressburg – more of a tourist itinerary than a military manoeuvre.

---

[67]Kessel, *Moltke*, p. 482.

[68]Cf. Pottinger and Armengaud, *passim*. The most detailed account from the diplomatic trenches is Willard Allen Fletcher, *The Mission of Vincent Benedetti to Berlin, 1864–71* (The Hague, 1965), pp. 80 ff.

It was fortunate that elements of Archduke Albert's army had reached the capital earlier. It was even more fortunate that the Prussian advance had been slowed to a crawl by logistics problems that did not approach solution until mid-July, when Wartensleben – again – and his junior associates began integrating the railway lines of occupied Bohemia into the army's forward delivery systems, at the same time clearing bottlenecks further back along the lines of communications, often by simply destroying spoiled food and ruined clothing.[69] Forced marches in hot weather contributed to the delay as well, less from a collective outbreak of sunstroke than because of thousands of small breakdowns in water discipline. Officers whose entire training and conditioning had been oriented to fighting battles were too often indifferent when their hot, thirsty men drank from dubious sources of water. Even when the streams and wells were not polluted, their bacteria were different from those to which the north Germans' systems were accustomed. Diarrhoea became endemic, in degrees far greater than official reports acknowledged. Deceiving one's superiors as to the condition of one's troops is not a twentieth-century invention. But it was harder to conceal the cholera that began spreading in some regiments as the Prussians approached Vienna. Anything like a siege or a blockade, and disease bade fair to do to Prussia's still unseasoned campaigners what the Austrian army had failed to do: break its operational effectiveness. From Austria's perspective, the rapid spread of the disease to the civilian population in the zone of operations only highlighted the risks of continuing the war in the north, where Prussian requisitions were already stripping the countryside of its resources.[70]

In the aftermath of Custozza, the Italian army took no further initiatives for a month. Archduke Albert's corresponding failure to follow up his victory had the unexpected consequence of making troops immediately available to reinforce Vienna. Irregular forces under revolutionary hero Giuseppe Garibaldi achieved some successes in the Trentino, but did not generate a popular uprising. When, at the urging of its government, a numerically and technically superior Italian navy finally brought the Austrians to battle, Admiral Wilhelm Tegetthof inflicted a defeat as stunning as it was humiliating, off the Adriatic island of Lissa on 20 July. Austria, in short, was now in a position to approach a conference table as something other than a suppliant.[71]

Bismarck, by his own subsequent accounts at least, was willing to invoke not only German nationalism but Magyar separatism, rather than back down before French intervention and Habsburg intransigence. Mensdorff, at least, was not prepared to put him to the test. On 22 July, the two diplomats agreed to an armistice. William had no similar compunctions. The king, his entourage and his generals wished Austria to pass under the yoke. A victory parade through Vienna and a peace whose final terms were dictated from royal headquarters was the least they would accept. William entertained visions of revising frontiers everywhere in Germany, reclaiming such territories as Ansbach-Bayreuth, which had been Prussian more by courtesy than right or power. Austria, too, was expected to pay in land – less for diplomatic or strategic reasons than as a public, permanent symbol of

[69]Wartensleben, pp. 52–3 and *Heeresverpflegung*, pp. 124 ff.

[70]Heinrich Mast, 'Die Erignisse im Ruecken der preussischen Armee inm Juli 1866', *Oesterreichische Militaerische Zeitschrift* (1966), vol. I, pp. 21–6.

[71]For Lissa and its consequences, see, particularly, Lawrence Sondhaus, *The Habsburg Empire and the Sea: Austrian Naval Policy, 1797–1866* (Lafayette, IN, 1990), pp. 252 ff.

defeat. Bismarck had no use for such gestures. At this stage he had no real vision of a grand design that would eventually produce a dual alliance between the 'Germanic' powers of central Europe. But he remembered the consequences of Frederick the Great's misbegotten relationship with Maria Theresa. Koeniggraetz had been a decisive victory – but on the face of it, so had Chotusitz, Hohenfriedberg and Leuthen. What was important was to resolve the issue of Austria's expulsion from Germany without creating the kind of long-running antagonism that in future might force Prussia to make policy in a context of compensating for Habsburg hostility.[72]

When Bismarck made his case, William exploded. To some degree, the king's intransigence reflected a desire to reassert authority that he had not exercised on the field of Koeniggraetz. William was enough of a professional soldier to be well aware who had been the architect of that triumph. But he did not take kindly to accepting the role of a figurehead. At one point in the high-decibel dialogue, Bismarck ran from the room and fantasized jumping through an upper-storey window. In a slightly calmer mood, he considered resignation, but the crown prince talked him out of any precipitate action and took it upon himself to bring around his father. William eventually agreed to 'bite the sour apple' of a moderate peace.[73] He would almost certainly have done so even without his son's intervention. William could be stubborn, but he was no man's fool for long. The king could see as well, if not as clearly, as did Bismarck the disadvantages of a permanently irreconcilable Austria. And the preliminary terms, concluded at Mensdorff's Nikolsburg hunting lodge on 26 July, were mouth-watering. Prussia received an indemnity of 40 million florins – a budget restorative that cut the heart out of parliament's refusal to fund the war. Austria accepted the abolition of the Confederation and recognized the legitimacy of a new association of the states north of the Main river. Prussia was given a free hand to negotiate terms with the south German states, at as near to gunpoint as made no difference. Prussia was also allowed to annex directly Hanover, Electoral Hesse, Hesse-Nassau and several smaller north German territories, including Schleswig-Holstein, the original ostensible apple of discord. In 1598, Henry of Navarre justified his conversion to Catholicism with the quip that 'Paris is worth a mass'. William of Prussia, not a man given to aphorisms, might nevertheless well have reflected that all this was worth sacrificing a parade.

---

[72]Cf. *inter alia*, Gall, *White Revolutionary*, vol. I, pp. 299 ff.; Pflanze, vol. I, pp. 314 ff.; and Craig, *Politics of the Prussian Army*, pp. 199 ff.

[73]*Friedrich Karl*, vol. III, pp. 470 ff.

6

When to Hold and When to Fold

The German Confederation was ended with steel, not ink. Its inglorious disappearance highlights the importance of choice in public policy. While not designed to cope with either cold or hot war between Prussia and Austria, the Confederation had the potential to adapt to that situation – particularly since it developed over at least a decade.[1] Middle Germany, however, was unwilling to accept the social, financial and political demands of supporting armed forces sufficiently effective to act as a magnet and a deterrent for Prussia and Austria alike. Added together and including Hanover, the lesser states had a minimum Confederation responsibility for maintaining about four corps, and were at liberty to increase their contingents as they saw fit. Four corps were certainly not negligible when compared with the deployable forces of Prussia – nine corps – and Austria's seven or eight. Four *good* corps had every possibility of holding the diplomatic and military balance in German affairs. The individual and collective decision to de-emphasize the military aspects of security, and instead put faith in negotiations and pieces of paper, meant Confederation policy in 1866 was the stuff of words, blown away this time not by a whiff of grapeshot, but by the fire of the needle gun. Thus ends the lesson – which remains as pertinent for the twenty-first century as it was for the nineteenth.

I

Prussia's Chamber of Deputies faced a situation similar to the south German governments: a lost wager for high stakes. The war had generated an outburst of hurrah-patriotism that, even before Koeniggraetz, had reshaped the Landtag. Elections held on 3 July gave the conservatives a majority in the lower house and encouraged an agonizing reappraisal among the liberals. Well before the war, Bismarck had been extending olive branches, talking of golden bridges and mutual cooperation in pursuit of mutually desirable goals – national ones in particular.[2] After 3 July, it was apparent – by any measure – that public opinion was on the minister-president's side, especially when the day's casualty lists were not repeated. That was important in a state where, since the Roon reforms, virtually every family from every social class had one or more males in uniform. And after Nikolsburg, it was clear that, far from becoming fatally enmeshed in his own shortcomings, as liberals had expected, Bismarck was now the arbiter of central Europe.

---

[1]Karl Bosl, 'Die deutsche Mittelstaaten in den Entscheidung von 1866', *Zeitschrift fuer bayerischen Landesgeschichte* 29 (1966), pp. 665–79, stresses the limitations of Confederation options at the finish.
[2]For the effect, see H. A. Winkler, *Preussischer Liberalismus und deutscher Nationalstaat* (Tuebingen, 1964).

What next? The immediate debate focused on the issue of an indemnity bill: essentially accepting Bismarck's apology for his behaviour in exchange for absolution from past constitutional sins. The document finally approved on 3 September 1866 was hard even for some of its supporters to accept, especially when its government version omitted any promise not to rule without a budget in future. But the risk of making a devil's bargain was overcome by the fact that Prussian liberalism had evolved from a movement to a party. It was a player and a participant in political life.[3] And, to quote a long-time nineteenth-century master of the American urban machine, 'politics ain't beanbag'. Liberals saw that the Prussian government had effectively pre-empted the nationalist and foreign-policy aspects of their programmes. As for legitimacy, Bismarck and the king could claim to speak for a good many more of Prussia's citizens than did the newly minoritized liberal fraction of the parliament. Despite the expansion of industrialization, Prussia's – and north Germany's – social structures were still largely agricultural, artisanal and commercial-bureaucratic. In 1816, three-quarters of Prussia's people lived on the land. By 1867, that figure had been reduced to two-thirds, but the decrease was hardly a demographic paradigm shift. Nor, given liberalism's internal divisions and the rhetorical successes of social-ist leader Ferdinand Lassalle, was it exactly certain that liberalism could count on being the wave of Germany's political future.[4]

In a movement as strongly individualized and personalized as German liberalism, personal changes of opinion played a role as well. Some were influenced by the trappings of success. One-time radical, Gustav Mevissen, experienced his epiphany while watching a victory parade.[5] After Koeniggraetz, a professor at Goettingen – whose pride in its prin-cipled liberalism was as great as any politically correct British or American university of the 1990s – described himself as bowing before Bismarck's genius and repenting having once considered this great man's behaviour criminal.[6] But not all changes of position reflected adrenalin rushes. Even before the war, intransigence over the budget had seemed a dead end to an increasing number of liberal deputies. What now were the hopes of maintaining any political credibility by denying funding to the government that had won Koeniggraetz and united north Germany? Liberal leaders, like Eduard Lasker and Rudolf von Bennigsen, were convinced that refusing to participate in shaping the new North German Confedera-tion would set liberal aspirations back for half a generation and more.

Bismarck, moreover, was not exactly the template of a tyrant. His image in recent years is equal parts statesman of genius and Bonapartist authoritarian. In either case, he emerges as someone sure of his intentions and behaviour. The minister-president's reality in 1866–7 was more complex. He proposed to extend Prussian power in Germany and Europe. He recognized that liberalism was too important and too powerful to be perman-ently marginalized. And he understood the commitment of Prussia's traditional élites to maintaining an authoritarian political system in the face of undeniable and irreversible social and economic change. In the long term, he was in the position of the man in the

---

[3]The process is discussed in Langeweische, *Liberalism in Germany*, pp. 102 ff.
[4]The classic self-analysis is Hermann Baumgarten, 'Deutscher Liberalismus: Eine Selbstkritik', *Preussische Jahrbuecher* 18 (1866), pp. 455–515 and 575–628. Cf. K.-G. Faber, 'Realpolitik als Ideologie. Die Bedeutung des Jahres 1866 fuer das politische Denken in Deutschland', *Historische Zeitschrift* 203 (1966), pp. 1–45.
[5]Pflanze, vol. I, p. 331.
[6]Quoted in Faber, pp. 15–16.

riddle, seeking to get a goat, a wolf and a cabbage safely across a river in a boat that was too small. At the same time, however, Bismarck's recent experiences highlighted the virtues of operating in short-range contexts, allowing seemingly intractable facts a chance to modify themselves. Delay, as well as activity, could solve problems.

Specifically, on his return from Bohemia, Bismarck emphatically rejected any notion of using Koeniggraetz as a springboard for a *coup*. He reiterated his intention to establish a parliament for what would become the North German Confederation. From a liberal perspective, these were straws in the wind, suggesting Bismarck might be amenable to other modifications of policy and behaviour. In that context, the Indemnity Bill was only one measure in a continuing dance.[7]

Anyone doubting possible alternatives need only look at the map of north Germany that emerged in the aftermath of Nikolsburg. States vanished like soap bubbles, absorbed into a 'great Prussia' that now included such long-time sovereign bodies as Hanover. Most of the acquisitions were smaller: the Mecklenburgs and the dwarf states of Thuringia. Many were compromises, negotiated positively rather than under the gun.[8] The deposition of a king, an elector, two dukes and other assorted legitimate governments nevertheless left Prussian conservatives reeling. Liberals, by contrast, saw an opportunity to establish themselves once more at the forefront of a surge of patriotism that re-energized an already solid commitment to a *Kleindeutsch* approach to the national question north of the Main. Ludwig von Gerlach, one of the intellectual and political luminaries of Prussia's conservative movement, might declare his state had 'violated the ten commandments of God' through a 'depraved pseudo-patriotism',[9] but in 1866–7, liberalism did not perceive itself in a position to indulge such niceties of feeling. It should be remembered as well that Prussian and German liberalism, especially in their post-1848 versions, were more about doing than being. The concept of standing permanently in opposition, of pointing with pride, viewing with alarm and retiring to the *Stammtisch* to praise each other's purity, was uncongenial to these men of affairs. Better by far to consolidate ground gained during the constitutional struggle and continue holding Bismarck's feet to the fire to make the state a more liberal one.[10]

As the constitution of the North German Confederation developed, military issues emerged as focal points of discussion. And it was here that liberals, in particular, were most willing to make concessions. In the aftermath of Koeniggraetz, there seemed few defensible arguments against making *de jure* a Prussian military hegemony that was already established *de facto*. But otherwise, especially as written, the Confederation constitution was a strongly federal document. To placate conservatives, reassure rulers and, not least, attract those German states still outside its provisions, central institutions were

---

[7]Rainer Wahl, 'Der preussische Verfassungskonflikt und das konstitutionelle System des Kaiserreichs' in *Moderne deutsche Verfassungsgeschichte (1815–1914)*, eds. E.-W. Boeckenfoede and R. Wahl (2nd ed., Koenigstein, 1981), pp. 208–31. Some of the sharpest criticism of the indemnity came from conservatives critical of the war with Austria and dubious about Bismarck's willingness to violate the constitution. Kraus, *Gerlach*, pp. 821 ff., is a good overview.

[8]Hans A. Schmitt, 'From Sovereign States to Prussian Provinces: Hanover and Hesse-Nassau, 1866–1871', *Journal of Modern History* 57 (1985), pp. 24–56.

[9]Quoted in Carr, *Wars of Unification*, p. 139.

[10]See Alan Kahan, 'The Victory of German Liberalism? Rudolf Haym, Liberalism, and Bismarck', *Central European History* 22 (1989), pp. 57–99.

kept to a minimum. The armed forces were not only the most visible symbol of the new Confederation, but they were also virtually the only one, absorbing no less than 99.5 per cent of the Confederation's revenues in 1868. In those contexts, liberals could – and did – calculate that emphasizing the centralizing, syncretic aspects of the army was the best possible step away from particularism, in both its small-state and old Prussian versions.

In specific terms, each member of the Confederation was to provide a contingent, whose chief was the ruling prince. Local administration, internal security and appointment of most officers were left in state hands. When it came to operational matters, however, the army of the North German Confederation was not a combination of contingents, but a unitary force with a single commander-in-chief and a single general staff. Its senior officers were appointed by the King of Prussia and swore allegiance to him. Its soldiers also swore oaths of obedience. Prussian military law and Prussian drill regulations were adopted for the whole army. Formations might bear local titles or honorific designations, but were numbered sequentially – with the 'old Prussian' regiments taking pride of place. The commander-in-chief was given *carte blanche* to secure uniformity in all aspects of armament, training and administration that affected preparation for war. The army's peacetime strength was fixed at 1 per cent of the population of each state, with every male obliged in principle to serve three years in the active army, four years in the reserves and five in the Landwehr. Finally, lest any doubts remain who had emerged victor in this aspect of the Prussian constitutional conflict, an 'iron budget' fixed annual military appropriations for an indefinite period on a per capita basis – 225 talers per soldier. Only amounts in excess of that sum were susceptible of discussion in the new North German parliament.[11]

Among the Confederation's lesser members, only Saxony protested seriously against the limiting of its military independence, and here Bismarck and William were ready to compromise. The Saxon contingent would be organized and equipped on Prussian lines, but was to remain a separate army corps, with its own war minister and its own officer training system. At the same time, Saxony was guaranteed access to all the common institutions of the new army, including technical schools and the general staff. On the whole, this seemed a reasonable recognition of Saxon pride and Saxon performance in the late war, especially since Prince Albert became the first commanding general of what was now XII Corps of the army of the North German Confederation.[12]

The Saxon Corps and the contingent of the Grand Duchy of Hesse, organized as an independent division, initially retained a few minor institutional characteristics: Hessian regiments were not renumbered and had only two battalions; and the Saxon Corps included an extra rifle regiment and an extra jaeger battalion. Essentially, however, both forces were homogenized, restructured according to Prussian tables of organization. Other states and territories of the new Confederation were even less privileged – and that included Old

---

[11]The best general discussions of the North German Confederation's constitution are Pflanze, vol. I, pp. 341 ff. and Otto Becker, *Bismarcks Ringen um Deutschlands Gestaltung* (Heidelberg, 1958), p. 211 *passim*. For the everyday conduct of affairs, see Klaus Erich Pollman's massive *Parlamentarismus im Norddeutsche Bund 1867–1870* (Duesseldorf, 1985).

[12]Cf. Richard Dietrich, 'Der preussisch-saechsische Friedensschluss vom 21. Oktober 1866', *Jahrbuch fuer die Geschichte Mittel-und Ostdeutschland* 4 (1955), pp. 109–56 and James Retallack, ' "Why Can't a Saxon Be More Like a Prussian?" Regional Identities and the Birth of Modern Political Culture in Germany, 1866–67', *Canadian Journal of History* 32 (1997), pp. 26–55.

Prussia as well as its new acquisitions. The aftermath of the Austro-German War posed a major challenge to a Prussian army which had just spent five years remaking itself under difficult circumstances, and now was constrained not only to reorganize once more, but also to incorporate and accommodate former enemies, whose military self-identification was often based as much on hostility to Prussia and things Prussian as on positive loyalty to the Duchy of Gerolstein or the Palatinate of Ruritania.[13] How could the *muss-Preussen* of Hanover, Nassau and the Hanseatic cities best be socialized into the new military order? How could conscription on Prussian lines be introduced with minimal friction? Could territorial recruitment be sustained without risking internal stability? Where were the officers of the new formations to come from? Even more to the point, what about NCOs? Could sergeants from Posen or Pomerania, where hard words and heavy hands were the order of the day — in civil society as well as in barracks — be transferred without further ado to companies where they might well not even understand the dialects of the men they were supposed to instruct and command?

The answers began with organization. The Prussian army was directly increased by three corps: IX organized in Schleswig-Holstein and the Hanseatic states, X in Hanover and XI representing the lesser Thuringian states. The formations of Prussia's allies during the war — Oldenburg, Braunschweig, the Mecklenburgs — were assigned to these corps with new numbers and a minimum of internal restructuring. Most of their units, however, came from Prussia proper. When the army was demobilized in 1866, every infantry battalion formed a fifth company. These were then organized by divisions into new regiments and assigned to garrisons in the new provinces. Twelve companies of the West Prussian 1st Division, for example, became the 73rd Infantry Regiment. Those from the 6th Brandenburg Division formed the 77th, and both regiments were stationed in Hanover. The 81st and 82nd Regiments were formed from companies from the 9th and 10th Divisions of Posen's V Corps.

Most of the defeated states had sent their reservists and conscripts home after the war, retaining only the professional cadres of their active units. These, in turn, were integrated with the new regiments assigned to these new provinces: the four Electoral Hessian regiments into the new 80th, 81st, 82nd and 83rd regiments, the two Nassau regiments into the 87th and 88th, and so on. The Hanoverian army was the exception in that it had been completely disbanded after Langensalza. But in November 1866, the men enlisted in that year, whether as conscripts or substitutes, were ordered to complete their military service by reporting to a new regiment responsible for absorbing men from a particular formation of the old army. Men from the old 7th Hanoverian Regiment, for example, went to the 73rd, and men from the 5th to the 77th.

Some regiments were temporarily exchanged. As late as 1870, four of the eight infantry regiments of X Corps, where Hanoverian loyalties persisted, were from the 'old Prussian' army — the neighbouring province of Westphalia. The IX and XI Corps had two 'old' regiments apiece, with the former having a third attached as an extra formation. These anomalies were by and large corrected after 1871, but they indicated the high command's refusal to take either political or operational chances with the new formations by concentrating

---

[13]Richard Dietrich, 'Preussen als Besatzungsmacht im Koenigreich Sachsen, 1866–1868', *Jahrbuch fuer die Geschichte Mittel-und Osteuropas* 5 (1956), pp. 273–93 and Fritz Dickmann, *Militaerpolitische Beziehungen zwischen Preussen und Sachsen, 1866–1870* (Munich, 1929).

too many under one command. Similar procedures were followed with the cavalry and the artillery. The result was that, by the time of the spring call-ups in 1867, recruits in the new corps districts were joining functioning formations whose administrations, at least at the company and battalion levels most important to trainees, were both efficient and effective.

About a third of the privates in most companies were men in their second or third years of service who, if not always happy at being further from home than expected, found compensation in accelerated promotions to the grade of lance-corporal – usually difficult to reach for any conscript not intending to seek a military career. They also benefited from the perquisites of old soldiers: light duty and soft jobs at the expense of the recruits, and drinks and tips for showing the new men how to survive in a Prussian uniform. Enough NCOs from the former state armies transferred to Prussian service to provide protection against the kinds of abuse based on regional differences and length of service that so eroded the Soviet army in its later years. And their colleagues from the 'old nine' of the Prussian army seem to have been a generally well-selected group.

After 1860, the expansion of the army made an NCO's career increasingly attractive by providing accelerated opportunities for promotion – a factor also encouraging young and ambitious corporals and junior sergeants to transfer to the new companies when they were first formed. The establishment of training schools further contributed to the growing self-identification of Prussian NCOs as belonging to a specialized profession, distinct from the officers but no less worthy, and specializing in training men, not breaking them. Civil service appointments for retired NCOs, originally a poor state's substitute for disability pensions, now became available at the end of only twelve years. A man could start a well-paid second career at thirty-five, a fringe benefit that – when extended to the new Prussian provinces in 1868 – was a powerful incentive for experienced NCOs from then disbanded armies to complete their terms of service in the new system, giving it legitimacy in the eyes of the conscripts that it might not have possessed had all the orders been given in the accents of Brandenburg or Pomerania.[14]

Officers were a slightly different matter, and here the Prussian army found itself in an ironic double bind. Institutionally, the Prussian army was short of officers, and certainly did not have enough to provide cadres for three full army corps. Politically, as French experience had shown during the Bourbon Restoration, little could be worse for the new North German Confederation than to have large numbers of disgruntled ex-officers on small and premature pensions acting as a potential source of unrest. Individuals, particularly in a Hanoverian officer corps, where loyalty to a dynasty in exile still persisted, were urged to consider carefully their moral obligations and personal prospects in the new German order before going into retirement.[15] 'Co-ordinated' rulers, even deposed ones,

---

[14]*Die Schlagfertigkeit unsrer neuen Armee-Corps im April 1867, von einem preussischen Offizier* (Cassel, 1867), focuses on the organization of XI Corps. Cf. Jochen Klenner, 'Die Geschichte des Bundeskriegswesens des Norddeutschen Bundes', *Wehrwissenschaftliche Rundschau* 19 (1969), pp. 388–410 and Klaus-Dieter Kaiser, 'Die Eingliederung der ehemals selbstaendigen norddeutschen Truppenkoerper in die preussischen Armee in den Jahren nach 1866' (Ph.D. dissertation, Berlin, 1973). Jany, vol. IV, pp. 244 ff., offers a brief schematic overview. For the NCOs, cf. also Messerschmitt, *Preussische Armee*, pp. 193 ff.

[15]Julius Hartmann, *Meine Erlebnisse zu hannoverscher Zeit, 1839–1866* (Wiesbaden, 1912), discusses the situation from the perspective of a Hanoverian major.

were correspondingly encouraged at least to free officers from previous obligations. Thus a total of 336 others from Hesse, Nassau, Hesse-Homburg and Frankfurt entered the Prussian army. Fifty-eight others from the states, and all but five of the Frankfurt contingent, were pensioned. Only forty-one refused to take the oath to Prussia.[16]

Young men from the new provinces after 1866 were favoured candidates for places in the army's cadet schools. A disproportionate number of these officers and officer candidates were bourgeois. Apart from the social structures of the new territories, in which the aristocracy was much less significant than east of the Elbe, sons of the academic, official and business classes were more likely than the noblemen to have been influenced by their fathers' sympathy for nationalism in its *Kleindeutsch*, Prussian context, and more willing to serve as officers. The proportion of noblemen in the army, already declining in the aftermath of the Roon reforms, dropped further as the Prussian officer corps adjusted to the kingdom's new demographics. The inner dynamic of old Prussian regiments changed as freshly commissioned subalterns from the new provinces were assigned to them to facilitate their acculturation.

Particularism was also challenged by professionalism. For the officers of the new regiments, there was the challenge of creating something new from whole cloth, while at the same time – at least for the veterans of the small-state armies – learning how to play in the senior league. Prior to 1866 it was difficult, to a degree, for a captain from Hesse or a major from Hanover to take his profession seriously in anything but a limited sense. But in the North German Confederation there was every reason to refresh and enhance skills uncultivated through inanition.

All of this is hardly to suggest that the Prussian army became more liberal, more humanitarian, kinder or gentler during the era of the North German Confederation. It did, however, function admirably as an instrument of national integration, a sign that the new order in the process of development could work, and work out positively, without making massive demands on the individual conscience.[17]

Nor was that merely an abstract exercise. If Austria's place in Germany had finally been decided, France remained a diplomatic threat. Even more to the point for the workaday warriors whose place was the drill ground or the company office rather than the map rooms of the general staff, the Seven Weeks War had demonstrated that Prussia and/or the North German Confederation had a long way to go in overcoming shortcomings in doctrine, equipment and performance. As the first state to introduce paper-cartridge breech-loaders, Prussia was also the first to suffer in a modern context the problem of technological obsolescence. The needle gun might have been devastating on the battlefields of Bohemia, but its basic design was a quarter of a century old. France was in the process of introducing the chassepot, a similar design with a longer range and higher reliability than its Prussian rival. Magazine rifles and metallic cartridges had been widely used by the Union during the American Civil War. German designers were developing their own versions of next-generation small arms. In the aftermath of the Franco-Prussian War, the German army would again take the lead in small arms by adopting the Infantry Rifle M1871, the first in

---

[16] *Unsrer neuen Armee-Corps*, pp. 14 ff.

[17] Manfred Messerschmitt, 'The Prussian Army from Reform to War' in *On the Road to Total War. The American Civil War and the German Wars of Unification, 1861–1871*, eds. S. Foerster and G. Nagler (New York, 1997), pp. 263–82, is an excellent overview.

a long line of bolt-action breech-loaders from the firm of Mauser Brothers. The weapons, moreover, would be produced by state-of-the-art machine tools imported from the US. The firm of Pratt & Whitney provided tools, jigs and gauges enabling the production of weapons with truly interchangeable parts, at a rate that enabled the almost immediate rearmament of the entire infantry with a weapon as good as any in Europe.[18]

Infantry tactics as well as infantry armament were being called into question by veterans of the Bohemian fighting. On the one hand, no future opponents were as likely as the Austrians had been to present mass targets for rapid rifle fire; on the other, the campaign had demonstrated more strongly than expected the problems of maintaining control of men once dispersed under fire. Even against the tactically unenterprising Austrians on 3 July, entire Prussian battalions had straggled, shirked or become honestly lost in the smoky confusion. What would be the results against an enemy like the French, who had a history of open-order tactics and regarded the rifle as something more than an appendage to a bayonet?

The senior officer corps, King William and Moltke himself shared a commitment not to skirmish lines regarded as too prone to disorder and producing too little striking power for their numbers; but company columns and their doubled version, the half-battalion, Moltke argued, were an acceptable combination of control, flexibility and survivability. Repeatedly, in 1866, they had manoeuvred under Austrian fire without losing too many men.[19] After the war, terrain exercises in small closed units absorbed training time, even at the expense of parade drill in some regiments. Men were drilled in holding fire and closing distances, as opposed to engaging chassepot-armed Frenchmen at ranges beyond the needle gun's capacity. In the process, a certain synergy developed between the army's role in fostering patriotic identity and military morale, and the tactical requirements imposed by a current, though presumably correctable, technological imbalance. North German spirit and Prussian training would compensate for the French infantry's superior firepower.[20]

Relevant as well in this context was the army's increasing commitment to homogenized effectiveness. This sharp contrast to other continental armies, with their large forces of élite light infantry and guards, reflected, in part, the need to integrate the new formations from the new provinces as seamlessly as possible, minimizing the kind of regional pecking order that had existed under Frederick the Great. Homogenization reflected the expansion of Prussia's military perspective from the battle to the campaign. The experiences of 1866, and their post-war influences on operational doctrine, meant that any corps of the army might find itself in the position of striking the decisive blow in a particular action. The Guard Corps prided itself not only on its socially élite officer corps, but also on being the best trained, the bravest and the toughest soldiers in the army; but its recruits were by no means as carefully selected as their Russian counterparts or the Guards of the French Second Empire, created initially by levying picked men from the line regiments. Nor were the soldiers of III Brandenburg, II Pomeranian or any other corps of the North German army prepared to concede bragging rights to the men who wore the

---

[18]Ulrich Wengenroth, 'Industry and Warfare in Prussia' in *On the Road to Total War*, pp. 249–62, especially pp. 256 ff.

[19]'Memorien ... ueber die bei der Bearbeitung des Feldzuges 1866 hervorgetretene Erfahrungen', *Moltkes Militaerische Werke* 2, vol. II, pp. 93 ff.

[20]Showalter, *Railroads and Rifles*, p. 216.

Garde-Litzen, the distinctive braid on their collars. The closest the army came to an élite in the commonly understood sense of the word was its dozen jaeger battalions, and these specialized riflemen existed as much to meet the demand for gamekeepers and forest rangers in civil society as from any perceived military value.[21]

Between 1866 and 1870, the North German army began compensating for the short-comings of its infantry rifle by developing another source of firepower. The Prussian artillery's performance in 1866 had been disappointing but predictable, in a sense – at least to senior generals whose memories of the Wars of Liberation did not include the hurricane bombardments of Napoleon at his tactical best, and had been overlaid by five decades of regarding the gunners as something less than proper soldiers. Initial contro-versies after the war involved technical issues: the final replacement of smooth-bore shell guns by rifles and the possibility of replacing steel with bronze in gun construction. The latter question arose because half a dozen steel barrels had burst without warning in the course of the campaign, calling into question the reliability of Krupp's cast steel among artillery officers still caught up in an engineering mentality.[22]

The result was a final struggle for power within the artillery between the technicians and the tacticians. It was also a struggle between old and new, bourgeoisie and aristocracy – but here the familiar parameters were reversed. It was the older officers from middle-class backgrounds, men who guarded the artillery's technical mysteries as a source of power in a hostile environment, who were being challenged by a new generation of gunners. These were disproportionately noblemen, less concerned with details of metallurgy than with making artillery a socially respectable and militarily useful arm of service. They also per-ceived that the two goals were synergistic: the more necessary the artillery became, the less possible it would be to marginalize its officers.

Hindersin remained the guru and mentor of the young Turks, but by this time was him-self becoming a bit too old to lead charges, even on doctrinal fields. That responsibility was increasingly assumed by Hohenloe, and by a rising generation of battery command-ers in the Guard Artillery and III Brandenburg, the two gunner regiments near Berlin. For these officers it was no longer enough merely to find and engage a target. Future officers, and their crews, must be able to observe fire, correct errors and understand the full poten-tial of the rifled cannon with which they were equipped. Lecture series at regimental levels, creation of an artillery school and training in long-range firing, contributed to an operational climate where, by 1869, battery officers regularly, within minutes, could bring all six of their rifled guns on to targets at ranges of up to a mile.[23]

This, by itself, was enough to impress powerfully foreign military observers, including the French military attaché.[24] But improving the quality of individual batteries was only a first step. Hohenloe, in particular, argued that the future role of artillery lay in preparing

---

[21]Dennis E. Showalter, 'German Army Elites in World Wars I and II' in *Elite Military Formations in War and Peace*, eds. A. Ion and K. Neilson (Westport, CT, 1996), pp. 135–66, especially pp. 138–43.

[22]Baron Stoffel, *Rapports militaires écrits de Berlin, 1866–1870* (3rd ed., Paris, 1871), pp. 87 ff.

[23]Cf. Kraft Karl zu Hohenloe-Ingelfingen, *Militaerische Briefe*, vol. III, *Ueber Artillerie* (2nd ed., Berlin, 1887), pp. 43 ff.; *Aus meinem Leben*, vol. III, pp. 375 ff.; and 'Die Ausbildung der preussischen Fussbatterie', *Archiv fuer die Offiziere der koeniglich preussische Artillerie-und Ingenieur Korps* 67 (1870), pp. 64–79, 95–130 and 236–74, and 68 (1871), pp. 97–154.

[24]See the report of 25 October 1869, in Stoffel, pp. 338 ff.

infantry attacks. The traditional artillery duel was obsolete because it was irrelevant. The dominant pre-war concept of guns bombarding enemy batteries at extreme ranges to force them out of action, while the infantry provided its own fire support, had been outdated by the general adoption of the breech-loading rifle. At 1,000 metres, combat range for the new rifled cannon, a battery of artillery was thirty times as effective as a war-strength rifle company. But softening a determined enemy required time, particularly if that enemy occupied even improvised field entrenchments. It also required accepting a status as the primary target of the enemy artillery while sacrificing retaliation on any scale. That meant no more withdrawals of batteries whose ammunition was exhausted. If they could not shoot back, at least they could draw fire until their caissons arrived from the rear echelon. The historic practice of holding significant numbers of guns in corps and army reserve meant those pieces were seldom where they were most needed. Instead, enough guns must be brought into position and kept in position to sustain bombardment in spite of losses. Instead of moving from position to position, rifled cannon must take advantage of their long range to reach out and touch new targets from the same location. It meant deploying the largest possible number of guns at the earliest possible moment as well, and keeping those guns under central control. Decentralizing command, allocating batteries permanently to divisions or brigades, meant dispersing fire – which, in turn, meant delaying the infantry attack and virtually guaranteeing heavier casualties when the company columns finally went forward.

The Prussian artillery's organization was essentially unaltered on paper after 1866. Each corps assigned one battalion of its organic artillery regiment to each of its divisions and kept the remaining guns – usually a battalion and one or two batteries of horse artillery – under corps control. But instead of being a support and feeder for the divisional batteries, the corps artillery became the core of the firefight, its gun lines absorbing and moving divisional guns as needed. Artillery's normal position became close to the head of a march column instead of to the rear. An artillery regiment's primary loyalties focused not on the branch of service, but on the army corps to which the regiment belonged.[25]

Artillery officers were still regarded as specialists, unqualified to command higher formations. Not until 1913 would a gunner general take over an army corps. But the new, younger generation of generals who took over the divisions and corps after 1866 were far more prone than their predecessors to regard their senior artillery officers as colleagues as well as subordinates. The infantry-artillery combat team, whose foundations were established between 1866 and 1870, would prove itself in the Franco-Prussian War and set a tactical and operational example that survived into World War II.

Planning structures kept pace with institutional changes. The size of the general staff was increased to 101 officers, with approximately half in Berlin and half in the field at any one time. Fresh blood was secured by Moltke's policy of recruiting a dozen or so of the best officers from each War Academy class and assigning them provisionally to the general staff. Those selected for permanent appointments – if they accepted, and a fair number did not – did their next tour as staff officers with operational formations, then

[25]Cf. in particular, Hohenlohe, *Ueber Artillerie*, pp. 73 ff. and Helmuth von Moltke, '1869 Instructions for Large Unit Commanders' in *Moltke on the Art of War*, ed. D. Hughes, tr. H. Bell and D. Hughes (Lincoln, NE, 1993), pp. 311 ff. By this time an artillery battalion had two batteries each of four- and six-pounders. The horse artillery battalion had three four-pounder batteries, with one or two usually detached to the independent cavalry divisions organized on mobilization.

returned to Berlin, and so on in a cycle that, by 1870, gave every corps and army commander a chief of staff experienced in the system, yet young enough to be both energetic and flexible. Making maps and developing railroad schedules grew more important than ever. Military attachés were assigned particular intelligence missions as well as their traditional, more general responsibility of keeping Berlin informed of the mentalities of Europe's armies. Particularly after the Luxembourg Crisis of 1867, the western frontier area became a focus of staff rides and theoretical exercises.[26]

Evaluating and synthesizing recent experience also engaged the army's intellectual energies. In 1867, the general staff's military history section published *The Campaign of 1866 in Germany* – among the first modern official histories and a model for successors ever since. Critics frequently and legitimately condemned its tendency to present Prussian plans, procedures and behaviour in the best possible light, sometimes virtually in spite of contrary evidence.[27] But the volume is also a mine of easily accessible information on tactics and operations – the sort of data regimental officers previously found almost impossible to obtain. Worth noting also is that the book's primary intended consumers were able to read between its lines. Most of the whitewashed incidents were already the stuff of discussion, gossip and speculation, a good deal of which found its way into print and still remains available to any student seeking to contextualize the official story.

The Campaign of 1866 was, in any case, only a counterpoint to Moltke's 'Instructions for Large Unit Commanders'. Prepared from the same body of data as the official history, available in preliminary form in 1868 and published the next year, this work remained the theoretical basis for conducting large-scale war for three-quarters of a century.[28] It is still a classic compendium of the techniques of war making in the mid-nineteenth century, and equally important as a guide to the thinking of a great captain who distrusted systems of all kinds. Instead, Moltke stressed the importance at all levels of responding to circumstances. Strategy, operations and tactics alike, depended on the capacity to understand what was, as opposed to what should be.

The experience of 1866 left Moltke convinced that the army corps remained superior to the division as the basic operational formation. Its field strength, 25,000 infantry and seventy-two guns, gave it striking power and sustainability. Its numbers were a challenge to control, but since corps were permanent organizations, their subordinate formations – and officers – were accustomed to working together. That, combined with the development of troop staff, gave a North German corps enough of a nervous system that it could respond with reasonable speed and sophistication to the changing circumstances of a campaign or battle.

At one time, Moltke had hoped to dispense with corps commands as unnecessary links. In 1866, Frederick Charles had handled four of the 1st Army's divisions directly – those of III Corps, which was his peacetime command, and IV Corps, whose commanding general was seventy-five and in such fragile health he could not take the field.[29] The experience had not been particularly successful. Another reason for retaining the corps, rather than

---

[26]Rahne, pp. 52 ff.; Bucholz, *Prussian War Planning*, pp. 48–9; and Kessel, *Moltke*, pp. 501 ff.

[27]See Arden Bucholz, *Hans Delbrueck and the German Military Establishment: War Images in Conflict* (Iowa City, IA, 1985).

[28]Hughes, *Moltke on the Art of War*, p. 171.

[29]Kessel, *Moltke*, p. 452.

establishing the smaller, more flexible division as the basic large unit, was that it was easier to find a dozen generals than two dozen who were able to act independently and willing to cooperate closely with their chiefs of staff. Prussian corps commanders in 1866 had been the products of seniority.[30] The Seven Weeks War had provided at least some alternative reasons for promoting and reassigning generals. By the time war broke out in 1870, Eduard von Fransecky, hero of the Swiepwald, commanded II Corps, the Pomeranians. The Alvensleben brothers, Konstantin and Gustav, had been promoted respectively to III and IV Corps, with the former a 'below the zone' reward for his energy as a troop trainer. Von Manstein's rhetorical questioning of Moltke's place in the chain of command at Koeniggraetz did not hinder his assignment to VIII Corps two years later. Noteworthy as well was the appointment of Constantin von Voigts-Rhetz to command the new X Corps. In 1866 he had been the 2nd Army's chief of staff; his new assignment was tangible proof of the link between line and staff appointments in the Prussian system.

II

Crucial to Bismarck's goal of transforming Prussia into Germany was his policy of building 'golden bridges' across the Main. To south German states, embarrassed by the ease of their defeat at Prussian hands, and left diplomatically isolated by Austria's withdrawal from the German stage, military reform was a *sine qua non*, no matter what their monarchs and parliaments decided about their future status. Not until the beginning of July had the formations of VII and VIII *Bundeskorps* done any fighting. Instead of the collection of reservists and battalion-sized north German contingents that made such heavy weather of the Hanoverian campaign, they faced a *Mainarmee* built around first-line troops: the 13th Division, the only active division not sent to Bohemia, and a provisional division composed of a brigade drawn from Schleswig and four independent regiments of the active army that had been garrisoning the Rhine fortresses before the war.

The south German armies had the flaws to be expected of small contingents, and none of the qualities required to implement the Austrian regulations or the French spirit that were supposed to be their central advantages against the formulism of the Prussians. Smooth-bores and rifled cannon purchased from the arsenals of their neighbouring great powers jostled each other in south German gun lines. South German infantry, in peace, tended to consider a casual approach to drill regulations a sign of panache. South German planning and administrative staff spent more time debating spheres of authority than addressing operational issues. South German generals proved consistently ineffective at strategic and operational levels. The Bavarian commanding general and his chief of staff initially could not agree on an operational plan, so the whole corps remained in place as the Prussians advanced.

The south Germans achieved occasional tactical successes, as at Hammelburg on 10 July, when two Bavarian battalions stopped the advance of a Prussian division for several hours by using their Podewils-model Miniés to keep their needle-gunned adversaries at respectful ranges. More often they died well, as on 13 July at the Bavarian village of Frohnhofen,

---

[30]See Nikolaus von Preradovich, 'Die Fuehrer der deutschen Heere 1866 in sozialer Sicht', *Vierteljahrschrift fuer Sozial-und Wirtschaftegeschichte* 53 (1966), pp. 370–6.

when elements of two Prussian battalions stood off the bayonet charges of six Hessian battalions for four hours, inflicting almost 800 casualties for a loss of sixty-eight of their own. No army is likely to keep the field if such exchange rates are the norm.[31]

After Koeniggraetz, it was plain no help was forthcoming from Austria. Honour, such as it might be, was satisfied. It was time to negotiate, and Bismarck initially took no prisoners. He demanded treaties of alliance that would place the armies and the railway networks of Baden, Wuerttemberg and Bavaria under Prussian control in wartime. The price of refusal would be high indemnities and accompanying territorial losses. All three states acquiesced with little overt protest – particularly when Napoleon III made plain the folly of expecting support from across the Rhine.[32]

On paper, the treaties created the strongest connection between north and south Germany since the Thirty Years War. Bavaria's new minister-president, Count Chlodwig zu Hohenloe, sought to sustain south German autonomy by coordinating the foreign and military policies of the southern states among themselves, rather than have each deal separately with Prussia.[33] Instead, Baden, Wuerttemberg and Bavaria were unable to agree on such core matters as length of service, training and armament. Even in Baden, where the administration was Prussophile and *Kleindeutsch* liberalism strong, protests arose against the human and financial costs of implementing three-year service – and against the 'militarization' of society by introducing Prussian methods of drill and discipline. The Bavarian parliament and the Wuerttemberg war ministry favoured the alternative of a system modelled on the Swiss militia. In any case, south German planning staff and officer corps were determined that their contingents would be more than rear-echelon and garrison forces in any future conflict.

Baden moved fastest and furthest. Parliament was brought to support reform by the promise – eventually fulfilled – of liberal domestic reforms whose consequences did much to foster Baden's reputation as the *Musterlaendle* of the Second Reich. The grand duke then negotiated a series of conventions allowing his cadets and officers to be trained in Prussian institutions. He appointed Prussian officers to senior military posts in the Baden army.

---

[31]Fritz Hoenig, *Die Entscheidungskaempfe des Mainfeldzuges an der Fraenkischen Saale* (Berlin, 1898), is the best tactical/operational narrative from the Prussian perspective. Eugen Frauenholz, *Die Heerfuehrung des Feldmarschalls Prinzen Carl von Bayern im Feldzug 1866, Darstellungen aus der Bayerischen Kriegs-und Heeresgeschichte*, ed. Bayerischen Kriegsarchiv (Munich, 1925), vol. 25, is its Bavarian counterpart. Theodor Fontane, *Von der Elbe bis zur Tauber: Der Feldzug der preussischen Mainarmee im Sommer 1866* (Bielefeld, 1867), takes his familiar unit and individual perspective. Sauer, p. 330 *passim*, is a modern analysis of south German military shortcomings from Wuerttemberg's perspective. Hackl, pp. 206 ff., performs that function for the Bavarians. Hugo Arnold, *Unter General von der Tann* (Munich, 1896) gives a Bavarian company officer's perspective. *Feldzugs-Journal des Oberbefehlshabers des 8ten deutschen Bundes-Armee-Korps im Feldzuge des Jahres 1866 in Westdeutschland* (Darmstadt, 1867), expresses Alexander's frustration on every page.
[32]Lothar Gall, 'Bismarcks Sueddeutschlandpolitik 1866–1870' in *Europa vor dem Krieg von 1870. Maechtekonstellation-Konfliktfelder-Kriegsausbruch*, ed. E. Kolb (Oldenbourg, 1987), pp. 23–32, argues that Bismarck's policies were not so unsuccessful as to drive him to seek war with France. The most detailed treatments of the negotiations remain Gustav Roloff, 'Bismarcks Friedensschluesse mit den Sueddeutschen im Jahre 1866', *Historische Zeitschrift* 146 (1932), pp. 1–70 and Johannes Petrich, 'Die Friedensvershandlungen mit den Sueddeutschen 1866', *Forschungen zur Brandenburgischen und preussischen Geschichte* 46 (1934), pp. 321–51.
[33]Ernst Salzer, 'Fuerst Chlodwig zu Hohenloe-Schillinfuerst und die deutsche Frage', *Historische Vierteljahrschrift* 11 (1908), pp. 40–74.

Baden's new war minister was a Prussian major general. The army was reorganized on the lines of a Prussian division, its armament and regulations adjusted to Prussian patterns.[34]

In Wuerttemberg, Foreign Minister Friedrich von Varnbueler remained determined to preserve the state's actual as well as theoretical independence by extending no more than minimal cooperation to Prussia.[35] He benefited from the government's prudent securing of parliamentary support before declaring war in 1866. As a consequence, public enthusiasm was sufficiently strong that, even after Koeniggraetz, some newspapers called for popular resistance on the model of Spain against Napoleon. That mindset continued after the peace treaty in the high degree of public support for a militia system as an alternative to Prussian-style conscription. Critics, including the overwhelming majority of the officer corps, argued for the inapplicability of Swiss methods in the kind of wars Wuerttemberg could expect to wage. In 1867, an equally dubious king replaced his war minister with a figurehead whose adjutant, Albert von Suckow, was the driving force for army reform, eventually becoming Wuerttemberg's chief of staff.

A Mecklenburger by birth and an admirer of Prussian methods by conviction, Suckow nevertheless made haste slowly, beginning with the adoption of the needle gun. It was difficult for anyone to defend the Minié in the aftermath of Koeniggraetz, and it seemed only a logical consequence when, shortly afterward, Suckow adopted Prussian drill regulations as well. Since the Wuerttemberg army would be fighting in a Prussian context, reorganizing it as a Prussian-style division was hardly a resignation of independence. Sending officers as students or observers to Berlin was hardly controversial if the two armies were expected to fight side by side. Or so, at least, Suckow defended his innovations. Rather than risk the charge of Prussianizing Swabia's sons, he even imported drill instructors from Baden.

Wuerttemberg's parliament was not willing to be led by the nose – or any other organ – indefinitely. As in Prussia a decade earlier, the term of active service was the crucial sticking point. Suckow had learned from the experience of his northern counterpart: he compromised, over the fierce opposition of conservative court circles and in the face of sharp criticism from Berlin. Not only was the term of active service in the Wuerttemberg army set at two years, but also candidates who qualified for the status of one-year volunteer could apply for government support if their family was unable to pay their expenses – a significant departure from a Prussian practice that was making the *Einjaehrig-Freiwillig* status increasingly popular among segments of the upper middle classes (upwardly mobile professional families and merchants seeking to distinguish themselves from mere shopkeepers).

Even these concessions were insufficient to avert a storm of public protest, spearheaded by a People's Party perceiving this as the kind of wedge issue that Wuerttemberg's liberals had been unable to develop for twenty years. Opponents of the new conscription laws collected over 150,000 signatures on a petition criticizing the innovations. This was about

---

[34]Willy Riese, 'Die badische Wehrmacht 1866–1870/71' (dissertation, Heidelberg, 1934), incorporates a narrative overview of the military reforms. Gall, *Regierende Partei*, J. Becker, *Liberaler Staat und Kirche in der Aera von Reichsgruendung und Kukturkampf. Geschichte und Strukturen ihres Verhaeltnisses in Baden, 1860–1876* (Mainz, 1973) and Stefan P. Wolf, *Konservatismus im liberalen Baden: Studien zur badischen Innen-, Kirchen-, und Agrarpolitik, sowie zur sueddeutschen Parteigeschichte, 1860–1893* (Karlsruhe, 1990), cover the wider politics and their social aspects.

[35]Folkert Nanninga, 'Zur "deutschen" Politik des Wuerttembergischen Aussenministers von Varnbueler in den Jahren 1864 bis 1879', *Zeitschrift fuer Wuerttembergischen Landesgeschichte* 32 (1973), pp. 113–49.

three-quarters of the usual number of voters in state elections, and a clear indicator that even Bismarck's military treaties with south Germany stood in danger, to say nothing of his wider concept of bridges over the Main.[36]

Initially, the Bavarian army seemed willing enough to copy Prussian methods, if not always Prussian values. King Ludwig, whose madness, like that of Hamlet, often seemed to depend on the direction of the wind, reached deep into the army for a war minister. Colonel Sigmund von Pranckh was primarily a staff officer who, nevertheless, had performed effectively in field assignments. He introduced conscription on the Prussian model, with neither exemptions nor substitutions. He overhauled the army's drill regulations. He introduced regular field manoeuvres. But as in Wuerttemberg, there were straws in the wind. One was sartorial. The Bavarian army continued to wear its distinctive light-blue uniforms and crested infantry helmets – the kind of gesture that was significant because it was so obvious. A second anomaly was technical. Instead of adopting the needle guns available in large numbers and at low cost, Bavaria converted its Miniés to breech-loaders. The ballistic shortcomings of the reworked rifles were compensated, at least for the government and the war ministry, by the fact that the conversion system was the work of a Bavarian designer. Bavaria went a step further in 1869 by adopting another domestically designed rifle, the Werder, whose metal cartridge and improved breech made it at least the equal of any military rifle in the world, and clearly superior to the needle guns still carried north of the Main – even if there was only enough time and money to issue them to four of the army's battalions by the outbreak of war in 1870.[37]

Even at that late date, the direction in which Bavaria's rifles would be pointing was not as clear as Bismarck or Moltke hoped. Conflict between the liberal-nationalist majority in the lower house of parliament and an electorate rapidly turning particularistic and clerical in its political expressions, led, in 1869, to a significant conservative victory. The progressives responded by challenging the results, only to be even more soundly defeated in a new election in November. When the new parliament met, the military alliance with Prussia was a focal point of the conservatives' attack on a government they denounced as near traitors, seeking, through underhand means, to transform Bavaria into a spike-helmeted province of a German Union that was only Prussia written large.[38]

Hohenloe's resignation did little to alleviate the tension. His successor insisted that the Prussian alliance was defensive, not offensive. That only increased the credibility of a demand, supported by the left wings of both liberal and conservative parties, for the introduction of a militia based on only eight months of active service. As in Wuerttemberg, a government, itself not exactly committed in principle to the Prussian-style reform of its army, looked to Berlin for support against an opposition centred in parliament. But this was

---

[36]Cf. *Rueckschau von Albert von Suckow*, ed. W. Busch (Tuebingen, 1909), p. 111 *passim*; Sauer, pp. 196 ff.; and, more generally, Dieter Langewiesche, *Liberalismus und Demokratie in Wuerttemberg zwischen Revolution und Reichsgruendung* (Duesseldorf, 1974).

[37]Hackl, pp. 219 ff., offers an excellent overview of the reforms and their wider implications. Max Leyh, 'Die bayerische Heeresreform unter Ludwig II 1866–1870' in *Darstellungen aus der bayerischen Kriegs-und Heeresgeschichte*, ed. *Bayerischen Kriegsarchiv* (Munich, 1923), vol. 22, pp. 9–96, remains a useful source of details.

[38]See, for background, Frank D. Wright, Jr., 'The Bavarian Patriotic Party, 1868–1871' (dissertation, University of Illinois, Urbana-Champaign, 1975).

too close to the pattern of events in 1849–50 to be congenial to Bismarck, whose plans involved winning hearts and minds rather than commanding bodies. Nor was it welcomed by the general staff, who, while still unconvinced that even at their best the south German contingents would be of much use in a great-power war, nevertheless had no desire to direct the next campaign against Munich rather than Paris.[39]

That contingency had seemed unlikely in the first months after Koeniggraetz and Nikolsburg. Relative to pretensions, the real loser in 1866 was Napoleon III. Instead of territorial compensations or diplomatic concessions, he received assurances that the German reorganization would remain geographically and politically limited. Bismarck's initial suggestions to the French ambassador that the frontiers of 1814, or even some Belgian land, were distinct possibilities proved to be as ephemeral as all the other ploys he had dangled in front of all the other French statesmen over the preceding eighteen months. But particularly given the impact of Koeniggraetz on the French army's institutional confidence, Napoleon was in no position to do more than swallow hard and cope.[40]

That the emperor had delayed rather than risk a war for which France was ill-prepared, did not blind him to the dynastic, diplomatic and plebiscitary risks of Prussia's emergence as the primary power of central Europe. If France could not play the self-defined role of mediator central to its pre-war policy, some tangible recognition of its primacy was even more necessary. Based on Bismarck's previous statements, there seemed to be no insurmountable difficulties when, beginning in August, France initiated serious discussions for the annexation of Belgium and Luxembourg. In return, Napoleon proposed acceptance of a federal union between the south German states and the North German Confederation, and offered the new Germany an offensive and defensive alliance – the latter to be kept a secret.

For Bismarck, this was entirely too comprehensive, too binding and too politically risky. He was well aware of Luxembourg's status as a member of the former German Confederation, and of its potential propaganda role as a glacis in a developing culture war between Teuton and Gaul. He declared himself willing to back French initiatives within Luxembourg, as opposed to supporting French annexation directly and openly. For Paris this was not enough – especially since no tangible support for a French connection existed in Luxembourg, or could be created for a reasonable price. As Bismarck delayed, pleading ill health and domestic commitments, Napoleon and his new prime minister, Eugène Rouher, were caught in a cleft stick. In addition to growing newspaper criticism of seeming weakness in confronting the compensation question, the legislature was due to meet in February, and even deputies friendly to the government were unlikely to ignore an issue offering such inviting prospects for leverage.

The imperial response was a package of procedural reforms improving dialogue between deputies and ministers, and a blunt statement by the emperor that he accepted

---

[39]Cf. inter alia, C. Stache, *Buergerlicher Liberalismus und katholischer Konservatismus in Bayern 1867–1871* (Frankfurt, 1981); Theodor Schieder, *Die Kleindeutsche Partei in Bayern* (Munich, 1936); and Wolf D. Gruner, 'Bayern, Preussen, und die Sueddeutschen Staaten, 1866–1870', *Zeitschrift fuer Bayerische Landesgeschichte* 37 (1974), pp. 799–827. The latter, particularly, stresses Bavaria as an independent actor.

[40]Wilfried Radewahn, 'Europaeische Fragen und Konfliktzonen im Kalkuel der franzoesischen Aussenpolitik vor dem Krieg von 1870', *Europa vor dem Krieg von 1870*, pp. 33–64, is an excellent overview. For military aspects, see E. R. Defrasne, 'L'Armée française au lendemain de Sadowa', *Revue Historique de l'Armée* 24 (1968), no. 2, pp. 121–36; and for more detail, Paul Bernstein, 'The Rhine Problem during the Second Republic and Second Empire' (dissertation, University of Pennsylvania, 1955).

the principle of nationalism as recently implemented in Germany. It met a counter-attack by parliamentary spokesmen for the balance of power, and for the right of a great power to compensation when that balance shifted significantly. In losing sight of those facts, asserted opposition leader Adolphe Thiers, the government had committed every mistake possible. No errors remained to perpetrate on the people of France.

Thiers was an optimist. On 19 March 1867, Bismarck revealed Prussia's military treaties with the south German states. The decision had more to do with domestic than foreign policy: Bismarck sought to forestall criticism in the Prussian parliament that the post-war organization of Germany left room for alliances between the south German states and 'external powers' – a polite euphemism for France. But the announcement caused an explosion in the Parisian press. It made Thiers look like too much of a statesman for Napoleon's comfort. He had already initiated negotiations with the King of the Netherlands to buy Luxembourg for 5 million gulden and a French security guarantee. From the perspective of The Hague it seemed a fair offer. Bismarck's revelation of the treaties, however, generated enough second thoughts for the king to seek Prussian approval of the arrangement.

For Bismarck, the timing could scarcely have been improved. The constituent parliament assembled to decide the organization of the North German Confederation was approaching critical votes on the issues of the military budget and ministerial responsibility. There was no better solvent of unseemly debates on subjects better left undiscussed than an issue tailor-made to arouse patriotic, nationalist emotions – particularly since French agents in Luxembourg city were organizing large and loud demonstrations supporting annexation to France. The enthusiasm might last no longer than the free beer that fuelled it, but the German newspapers, particularly in cities along the Rhine, had found a new subject for scare headlines.

The actual results were mixed. Bavaria and Wuerttemberg, in particular, accused Bismarck of using a trumped-up national issue to win on the street what he could not achieve by negotiation: south German accession to his new order. Bismarck promptly changed venues, calling for an international conference on the Luxembourg question. Meeting in May, the powers called for neutralization of the duchy and withdrawal of the Prussian garrison that had occupied the old fortress of Luxembourg for half a century. For Bismarck this was a setback. For Napoleon, however, it was a glove across the face – especially compared to his original intentions and in the context of the setbacks the Second Empire had suffered in Mexico and after Koeniggraetz. The Second Empire did not commit itself in principle to teaching Prussia a lesson – but was unlikely to let a similar incident pass a second time.[41]

Bismarck continued floating trial balloons southward. In February 1867, he had proposed a reorganized Customs Union – this one with a parliament as its decision-making

---

[41] By far the most comprehensive analysis of the crisis is Christian Calmes, *1867: l'Affaire du Luxembourg* (2nd ed., Luxembourg, 1967); not least of its values is its Luxemburgian perspective, which somewhat resembles that of a football in the World Cup. Pflanze, vol. I, pp. 371 ff.; Gall, *White Revolutionary*, vol. I, pp. 334 ff.; and Carr, *Wars of Unification*, pp. 154 ff., are general analyses from the more usual great-power position. The most recent treatment, Herbert Maks, 'Zur Interdependenz Innen-und Aussenpolitischer Faktoren in Bismarcks Politik in der Luxemburgischen Frage 1866/67', *Francia* 24 (1967), pp. 91–115, stresses Bismarck's unwillingness to go to war for the sake of his domestic political ends. Fletcher, pp. 141 ff., particularly develops the shortcomings of French diplomacy.

body, rather than the old council made up of state representatives. Again, Wuerttemberg and Bavaria protested against what they considered the 'Prussianization' of a key German institution, giving way only under heavy pressure from their business communities. Bismarck hoped that the Customs Parliament, whose elections were held on the principle of universal male suffrage, might become a precursor of a political body, accustoming south Germans to the idea. Instead, particularists, state patriots, anti-Prussians and Catholics south of the Main staged campaigns with different words but a common idea: send Berlin a message. Out of eighty-five south German delegates, only thirty-six were avowed supporters of political unification through the Customs Parliament. The initial meeting of that body showed, moreover, none of the general support for unification that Bismarck had expected. While no state was willing even to consider seriously withdrawing from the organization and abandoning the benefits of economic integration, the delegates took pains to address only economic affairs.[42]

In practical terms, that may have been no bad idea. Given the continued growth of anti-Prussian sentiment south of the Main, the less said about political integration the better in any public venue. The slow progress of unification also led increasing numbers of Prussian liberals to question the bargain they had made in the aftermath of Koeniggraetz. In February 1870, Eduard Lasker, no admirer of Bismarck's, proposed a motion in the finally functioning north German parliament, the Reichstag, that Baden be immediately admitted to the North German Confederation. He spoke for a National Liberal Party seeking simultaneously to force Bismarck's hand and test the will of France. If Napoleon did nothing, then the holdouts below the Inn might join rather than risk being last on board. If France responded by declaring war, the south German states would either participate voluntarily in the national conflict or join under Prussian pressure. Neutrality was not considered an option by the liberals; nor was south Germany's closer association with France. For them, this was an issue to be settled by blood and iron.[43]

Bismarck responded by denouncing both coercion and warmongering. Instead, he made public an initiative that would make King William 'Emperor of Germany' – a symbolic title that might help alleviate enduring southern suspicions of 'Prussianization'. The initiative, shaky, at best, because of William's opposition, collapsed when the Reichstag's liberal majority suggested ministerial responsibility as an appropriate quid pro quo, and expired when the other German princes manifested no support for William's elevation.[44]

Bismarck was, by now, apparently playing a hand without face cards. His repeated insistence that the south would come round in time was being challenged fiercely in the newspapers and the parliaments of the three states in question. Some scholars go so far as to describe a burgeoning domestic crisis in Bavaria, and perhaps Wuerttemberg as well, with an 'establishment' of throne, bureaucracy and army confronting a mass popular

---

[42]Walter Schuebelin, *Das Zollparlament und die Politik von Baden, Bayern und Wuerttemberg 1866–1870* (Berlin, 1935), remains the most comprehensive treatment of the subject. For background, cf. Wolfgang Zorn, 'Die Wirtschaftlicher Integration Kleindeutschlands in den 1860er Jahren und die Reichsgruendung', *Historische Zeitschrift* 218 (1973), pp. 304–34.
[43]J. Becker, 'Bismarck und die Frage der Aufnahme Badens in den Norddeutschen Bund im Fruehjahr 1870. Dokumente zur Interpellation Laskers vom 24. Februaer 1870', *Zeitschrift fuer die Geschichte des Oberrheins* 119 (1971), pp. 427 ff.
[44]Pflanze, vol. I, pp. 430 ff.

opposition with a strong religious element.[45] The central issue, as it had been in Prussia a decade earlier, was the cost and the nature of the army. Protestors demanded a return to a traditional militia-oriented system. Conservatives relied, paradoxically, on a newly reorganized mass army to keep them in power. The domestic tension south of the Main, however, must not be exaggerated. The real issue at stake was not the size of south Germany's armies, but the policies of south Germany's governments, perceived by their critics as sailing too closely in Prussia's wake for comfort, and far more closely than was necessary. At the same time, the opposition coalitions represented a loosely linked aggregation of naysayers, offering no comprehensive positive alternatives to an ever closer association of the southern states with the North German Confederation – an association likely to be encouraged by French reaction to Prussia's growing military power and diplomatic influence.[46]

From his earliest days as president of a Second Republic he intended to destroy, Louis Napoleon Bonaparte was committed to continuing and fulfilling France's self-defined post-Waterloo role as the fulcrum of Europe. Recognizing his uncle's mistake of insatiability and his own shortcomings as a war leader, the new Napoleon correspondingly fancied himself a statesman. Between 1791 and 1815, twenty-five years of general war waged by armed masses, inspired by a revolution and an emperor, had exhausted France's material and emotional resources. Instead, Napoleon III sought aggrandizement by persuasion and example.[47] Force, at least in European contexts, was a choice of last resort. Its application must be surgical: the kind of deep, clean, painful cut inspiring the recipient to sober second thoughts as an alternative to pursuing the disputed issue in arms, encouraging observers to choose their next actions prudently, and, not least, demonstrating to the French people that their ruler knew how to use power competently and effectively.[48]

For over a decade, the combination had been at least reasonably successful. In the aftermath of what he considered the Luxembourg fiasco, Napoleon took it to market once more. His ambassadors described the threat to European order generated by Prussia's pretensions and Bismarck's shamelessness. They stressed the value of a common diplomatic front against the newcomer – a front underwritten by a French army that, during the Bourbon/Orléans/republican era, had been structured for a primary mission of deterring challenges to the French state's self-defined primacy. Britain remained sceptical, especially after a clumsy French initiative to acquire shares in Belgian railroad lines during 1868–9. The possibility of French invasion might be more remote than it had seemed a decade earlier. The possibility of a French army with easy access to the port of Antwerp,

---

[45]See, especially, George Windell, *The Catholics and German Unity, 1866–1871* (Minneapolis, 1954).

[46]Rolf Wilhelm, *Das Verhaeltnis der sueddeutschen Staaten zum Norddeutschen Bund (1867–1870)* (Husum, 1978), develops this line of argument convincingly.

[47]Cf. Echard, *Napoleon III and the Concert of Europe*, and two useful dissertations, J. R. Bloomfield, 'Count Walewski's Foreign Ministry, 1855–1860' (dissertation, University of Pennsylvania, 1972) and Warren F. Spencer, 'Edouard Drouyn de Lhuys and the Foreign Policy of the Second Empire' (dissertation, University of Pennsylvania, 1955).

[48]On that last vital point, see Lynn M. Case, *Public Opinion on War and Diplomacy during the Second Empire* (Philadelphia, 1954).

however, altered that situation enough to keep Britain at a distance from situations which its armed forces – the army, in particular – were in no shape to modify directly.[49]

In Vienna, matters initially seemed more promising. Austria's generals, those still retaining credibility in the aftermath of the débâcle in Bohemia, were loud in advocating a second round with the Prussian usurper. Had words been shells, Berlin would have lain in ruins six weeks after Koeniggraetz. In October 1866, moreover, Franz Josef had appointed Count Frederick von Beust to the foreign ministry. Beust had been minister-president of Saxony until that state's accession to the North German Confederation. His new appointment, part of a long tradition in which men moved from smaller German states to larger ones, also seemed to signal Franz Josef's belief that the rivalry between Prussia and Austria was far from settled. 'From oxen', Bismarck grumbled, 'one can expect nothing but beef; from Beust nothing but an ambitious, intriguing Saxon *Hauspolitik*'.[50]

The observation seemed supported when, in April 1867, Beust rejected Bismarck's proposal, made through Bavaria, for a central European alliance aimed at France. That did not, however, make Beust an unslaked revanchist. During the Luxembourg crisis the French ambassador also floated a huge trial balloon in his direction. Duke Antoine de Gramont suggested an offensive-defensive alliance that, in the aftermath of a short, victorious war with Prussia, would give France the Rhine frontier, restore Silesia to Austria and divide south Germany into spheres of influence: Baden for France, Wuerttemberg and Bavaria for Austria. Beust rejected the concept as too high-risk and too crude. His intention was not to challenge Prussia in arms directly, but rather to cultivate Austrian influence in south Germany, reinforcing anti-Prussian, Catholic, particularist elements whenever and however might be possible, and acting as south Germany's patron in great-power discussions. As a second step, Beust hoped to isolate Prussia by using recent developments in the Balkans as a 'wedge issue'. In 1866, the island of Crete had embarked on one of its periodic rebellions against Ottoman rule. Beust proposed to use this as a catalyst to organize the western powers in a common diplomatic front against Constantinople. This, in Beust's mind, would have the positive effect of re-establishing Austria in the position of Europe's coachman that it had enjoyed until the mistaken policies of the Crimean War. It would trump a similar but less ambitious Russian initiative, and correspondingly encourage Russia to seek support in Berlin. Bismarck could be expected to reply affirmatively. Even if it did not come to a war of West against East, Beust counted on Bismarck's liberal supporters either to break with him or to cause enough trouble in parliament that he would reconsider his policies towards Austria and south Germany.

Seen in hindsight, this elaborate theoretical construction, with its dependence on interlocking contingencies at every stage, seems like a modern board game, where complexity becomes proof of quality. Beust, however, was neither a charlatan nor a fool. He recognized the growing reluctance of France to support either Russia or Austria in a large-scale Balkan initiative. In August 1867, Napoleon and Empress Eugénie paid a visit to Franz Josef at

---

[49]Peter Alter, 'Weltmacht auf Distanz: Britische Aussenpolitik, 1860–1870' in *Europa vor dem Krieg 1870*, pp. 77–90, highlights Britain's *de facto* withdrawal from continental affairs. Cf. Thomas F. Gallagher, 'British Military Thinking and the Coming of the Franco-Prussian War', *Military Affairs* 39 (1975), pp. 19–21 and Kurt Rheindorf, 'Der belgisch-franzoesische Eisenbahnkonflikt und die grossen Maechte, 1868/1869', *Deutsche Rundschau* 195 (1923), pp. 113–36.

[50]Quoted in Pflanze, vol. I, p. 434.

Salzburg, ostensibly to express sympathy at the execution of his brother Maximilian by the victorious Mexican republicans of Benito Juarez. It did nothing for imperial cooperation that Franz Josef believed Maximilian had been betrayed and abandoned by the French government that had put him on the throne. It did much when Beust put forth his Balkan proposition as a talking point, designed to put further negotiations on a basis acceptable to both parties. France wanted support against Prussia. Beust's intention was not to set Europe ablaze to undo Koeniggraetz, but rather to establish a deterrence structure strong enough to convince Bismarck to modify his ambitions without creating a risk either of the proposed principal partners, France and Austria, would find unacceptable. The front against the Ottomans was a lost-wax process, designed to produce an entirely different diplomatic sculpture.[51]

Beust's foreign policy was also rendered one-sided – arguably more so than at any time in Habsburg history – by domestic considerations. The Compromise of 1867 that replaced the Austrian Empire with a dual monarchy gave Austria and Hungary separate parliaments and administrations while providing for a common army and foreign ministry. The Magyar half of the new system promptly asserted its reluctance to support any policy aimed at restoring the monarchy's position in Germany. This position reflected nationalism: a desire to minimize German influence in the monarchy. It also reflected a desire to establish Hungary as an equal partner in foreign policy, by taking a stand on a particular point; and it was rooted in the reasoning of Julius Andrassy, who emerged from the *Ausgleich* negotiations as Hungary's leading political figure. Committed simultaneously to enhancing Magyar influence and maintaining the dual monarchy as a great power, Andrassy argued for conciliation wherever possible – at least until the armed forces were in shape to underwrite an assertive foreign policy.[52]

Beust was no less aware of partition's drastic impact on what, in principle, was supposed to remain a common army. In 1868, military service became universal and short, on the Prussian model of three years with the colours and seven in the reserves. The same body of legislation also established two second-line organizations, the Landwehr in Austria and the Honved in Hungary. Hungarian politicians viewed the Honved as the first step to a Hungarian national army, and did everything they could to improve its quality and enhance its distinctiveness. While German was the 'language of command' in the common army and the Landwehr, for the Honved it was Magyar, and this was only one

---

[51]Hans Schmitt, 'Count Beust and Germany, 1866–1870: Reconquest, Realignment, or Resignation?' *Central European History* I (1966), pp. 20–34, is a good interpretative introduction to the subject. For details, cf. Heinrich Potthoff, *Die deutsche Politik Beusts von seiner Berufung zum oesterreichischen Aussenminister Oktober 1866 bis zum Ausbruch des deutsch-franzoesischen Krieges 1870–71* (Bonn, 1968); K. P. Schoenhals, 'The Russian Policy of Friedrich Ferdinand von Beust, 1866–71' (dissertation, Rochester, 1964); and the magisterial overview of Heinrich Lutz, *Oesterreich-Ungarn und die Gruendung des Deutschen Reiches: Europaeische Entscheidungen, 1867–1871* (Frankfurt, 1979). Still good for the Salzburg meeting is Josef Redlich, 'L'entrevue de l'empereur François-Joseph et de l'empereur Napoléon à Salzbourg 13–18 août 1867', *Le Monde Slave, Nouvelle Serie* 3 (1926), pp. 143–51. A. Lorant, *Le Compromis austro-hongrois et l'opinion publique française en 1867* (Geneva, 1971), contextualizes the French position.

[52]Isztvan Dioszegi, *Hungarians in the Ballhausplatz. Studies on the Austro-Hungarian Common Foreign Policy*, tr. K. Balos and M. Borsos (Budapest, 1983). Andrassy's stock has recently risen among historians: cf. Tibor Simanyi, *Julius Graf Andrassy: Baumeister der Doppelmonarchie, Mitstreiter Bismarcks* (Vienna, 1990) and Rainer Schmidt, *Graf Julius Andrassy: vom Revolutionaer zur Aussenminister* (Goettingen, 1995).

example of a policy that, within a few years, created what was appropriately called a military concordat – an alliance of three armies under a common flag.[53]

Reorganization had a cataclysmic effect on an institution that, at its previous best, had never been noted for adaptability. Successive ministers of war, Generals Franz John and Franz Kuhn, increased pay and improved living conditions at regimental levels. They introduced a new infantry rifle and new guns for the field artillery. They ordered the introduction of a corps system on the Prussian model, with fixed districts and permanent garrisons. This and more was done against the determined opposition of Archduke Albert, hero of Custozza and patron by default of the school of thought that continued to suspect the kind of centralization that the war ministry sought to implement. The general staff also resented the challenge to its privileged position that seemed implied in the war ministry's efforts to bring general staff officers into closer, more systematic contact with field formations and their commanders.

Always in the background loomed the problem of finance. The dual monarchy required the assent of two parliaments to the military budget – one dominated at this period by German liberals, the other by Hungarian nationalists, and each, for its own reasons, inclined to cast a jaundiced eye on any figures submitted by the war ministry. The issue was less the amounts voted – at this stage, at least, usually more or less in line with what the ministry expected to get, if not necessarily the amount originally submitted – than the energy expended in discussion, debate, manoeuvring and string-pulling. Winning the budget battle became the psychological equivalent of winning a campaign in the field.

Added to that problem was the administrative energy required to bring the Landwehr and the Honved into existence, to transfer officers to them until they could provide their own, to reorganize the dual monarchy into the new corps districts and to assign regiments and battalions to their new homes.[54] When all was said and done, or rather, ordained and ordered, the Austro-Hungarian army was in a state of flux that precluded its commitment except in the direst of national emergencies. That was demonstrated painfully in 1869, when eighteen battalions, supported by cavalry, artillery and warships, were unable, after six months, to force the surrender of 1,000 or so Dalmatians protesting in arms the introduction of universal military service.[55]

Franz Josef understood the problems of the new common army better than those fire-eating generals of the old guard who periodically encouraged their French counterparts as to the prospects of an Austro-French connection. In 1870, just before the outbreak of the Franco-Prussian War, one of Napoleon's close military advisors, General Barthélemy Lebrun, visited Vienna to discuss with Archduke Albert the outline of a joint campaign against Prussia. Franz Josef approved the operational details, but added that he would have to be forced into such a war. That did not mean he had become a convert to pacifism. He understood, rather, that the Austro-Hungarian army as it then stood was in no condition to take

---

[53]Gunther E. Rothenberg, 'Toward a National Hungarian Army: The Military Compromise of 1868 and its Consequences', *Slavonic Review* 31 (1972), pp. 807–11.

[54]Cf. Scott Lackey, *The Rebirth of the Habsburg Army: Friedrich Beck and the Rise of the General Staff* (Westport, CT, 1995) and Walter Wagner, 'Die K. (u.) K. Armee – Gliederung und Aufgabenstellung ... 1866 bis 1914', *Die bewaffnete Macht*, p. 551 passim.

[55]Josef Rausch, 'Der Aufstand im Raum Kotor im Jahre 1869', *Oesterreichische Osthefte* 25 (1983), pp. 95–126 and 223–49.

the field against a first-line opponent – unless, of course, someone else did the heavy lifting.[56]

Napoleon quickly grasped the Austro-Hungarian subtext. In the summer of 1868 he raised the possibility of 'passive alliance' should Vienna take diplomatic or military action in the case of either Bismarck or the south German governments seeking to cross the line of the Main. In such a contingency, France, the emperor asserted, would support Austria to the limit, but could not take the lead itself. German national identity was, by now, a point too sore to be addressed from Paris. Beust responded by reminding Napoleon that Austria could not afford to alienate German nationalists – including those within its own frontiers – by allying with France. Beust suggested, instead, that Napoleon call for general European disarmament. Should Prussia approve, it would lose the support of the nationalists who believed only war could fulfil their aims. Refusal, on the other hand, would cost Prussia and Bismarck the 'moral high ground' in the next rounds of diplomatic confrontations.[57]

That exchange is best understood as a final round of fencing. Napoleon and his advisors found it as difficult to take Beust's proposition seriously in a literal sense as they did to accept the risks of a general European war that seemed to them so clear in Beust's Balkan scheme. The latter came to an unmourned end in February 1869, when a conference of the powers, brokered by Bismarck, met at Paris and demanded Greece cease supporting the Cretan insurgency. That unlikely juxtaposition of person and place, the defusing of a crisis by allowing someone else to walk point in the minefield, was an example of the emperor's ability to side-slip difficult situations of his own making.[58]

Paradoxically, the mutual demonstration that neither France nor Austria was willing to assume the initiative in an alliance facilitated their agreement in May 1869 on a more limited proposal. The agreement guaranteed each other's territories, provided for common action in European affairs and accepted 'in principle' offensive-defensive military cooperation should 'symptoms' of war appear. Compensation in the aftermath of the latter contingency would be arranged by mutual agreement. By conventional standards that was not much to show, particularly since the agreement itself remained unsigned and Beust continued to insist on Austria-Hungary's right to remain neutral if its interests so dictated.[59]

Napoleon, however, had made a career of making success out of unpromising matrices. He next sought to bring Italy into the arrangement, offering a tempting spectrum of financial and territorial concessions in return for aiding France against Prussia and assuming the same obligations as France to support Austria in a future war. King Victor Emmanuel was ready to fight just about anyone to prove Italy's virtu and complete Italy's unification. Unofficially, he informed Napoleon he would join him against Prussia, sounded Bismarck on a possible war with France and suggested to Austria that he might

---

[56]Scott Lackey, 'The Habsburg Army and the Franco-Prussian War: The Failure to Intervene and its Consequences', War in History 2 (1995), pp. 151–79.

[57]Cf. Die Rheinpolitik Kaiser Napoleons III. von 1863 bis 1870 und die Ursprung des Krieges von 1870/71, ed. H. Oncken (Berlin, 1936), vol. III, p. 12 passim; and the narratives by Potthoff, pp. 200 ff. and Lutz, p. 126 passim.

[58]Wolfgang Elz, Die europaeischen Grossmaechte und der Kretische Aufstand, 1866–1867 (Stuttgart, 1988), is a detailed analysis of the uprising in the context of continental diplomacy.

[59]The text is in Rheinpolitik, pp. 185 ff. Cf. Potthoff, pp. 267 ff.

be ready to take on both France and Prussia if the circumstances were right! Beust was unimpressed, although he was interested in establishing an Italian alliance to strengthen Austria's position *vis-à-vis* both France and Prussia.[60]

Apart from the continued presence of a French garrison guaranteeing Rome and the Papal States against Italian invasion – not exactly a facilitator of Napoleon's proposed alliance – the new Kingdom of Italy had a spectacular spectrum of domestic problems, ranging up to an undeclared civil war in its southern provinces. Victor Emmanuel's belligerence, correspondingly, found little resonance. Even conservative elements in parliament were reluctant to give a monarch remarkable for slow-wittedness a free hand in international affairs. The Italian high command had no interest in committing its fragile army even to a theoretical prospect of hostilities with Prussia, much less fight such a war under Austrian auspices. The foreign office stressed the liabilities of allying with France as long as Napoleon kept a garrison in Italy to secure the Pope's temporal power. Victor Emmanuel, for his part, was unwilling to take any risks to depose 'the poor devil in St Peter', who, after all, had conveyed a papal blessing when the king thought himself on the point of death in 1869.

The result was a compromise note, delivered in September, in which Victor Emmanuel agreed to an alliance in principle, contingent upon French military withdrawal from Rome. The document was intended more to paper over differences of opinion within Italian policy-making circles than to convey any definite diplomatic intentions. Neither the king, the army, nor the foreign office expected France to do anything of the kind for the foreseeable future.[61]

Napoleon, for his part, seems to have considered the Italian alliance a done deal, whose implementation depended only on removing a garrison that, in any case, was a hollow deterrent in the diplomatic climate of the late 1860s. France's Austrian connection also appeared to him morally ratified, if not completely set on paper. Most analyses of Napoleon's behaviour at this stage describe some form of diplomatic death wish, a loss of grip and focus that eventually proved fatal against Bismarck's virtuosity. Certainly Napoleon's declining physical health impacted on his judgment. Also the emperor was significantly distracted in these months by the final stages of what amounted to a long-term 'velvet revolution' in France and the installation of a parliamentary government under Emile Ollivier.[62] Since his rise to power, however, Napoleon had been reluctant to commit France to any firm, overt alliances. This reflected his concept, discussed earlier, of France as Europe's primary power, at once the continent's more or less honest broker, source of political ideas and court of last resort. All of those positions were likely to be endangered, or at least diminished, should France appear to *need* help – even when it did. For Napoleon III, successful diplomacy involved doing exactly what he believed he had done with Austria and Italy: create an 'agreement in principle', then take initiatives that encouraged the other parties to follow France's lead – and preserve France's standing among the powers.

---

[60]Lawrence Sondhaus, 'Austria-Hungary's Italian Policy under Count Beust, 1866–1871', *The Historian* 56 (1993), pp. 41–54.

[61]Cf. Rudolf Lill's overview, 'Italiens Aussenpolitik 1866–1871' in *Europa vor dem Krieg 1870*, pp. 93–101; Mack Smith, *Victor Emanuel, Cavour, and the Risorgimento*, p. 343 *passim*; and F. Engel-Janosi, 'The Roman Question in the Diplomatic Negotiations in 1869–70', *Review of Politics* 3 (1941), pp. 319–49.

[62]For the history and implementation of this process, see especially Roger Price, *The French Second Empire: An Anatomy of Political Power* (New York, 2002).

III

This high-risk diplomatic technique depended, above all, on an army – and an army of a specific type. Imperial France kept relatively few men in uniform – no more than 380,000, even in the crisis year of 1870. Limiting the army's size was by no means a second-best solution to the army's commanders. French generals after 1815, accepted the necessity of fighting outnumbered in any general war. They also believed it possible to fight outnumbered and win. The wars of the revolutionary/Napoleonic era had shown an increasing tendency for armies to outgrow their nervous systems. Even under the emperor's hand, the conscript masses of Borodino and Leipzig had proved significantly less effective than the lean strike forces of Lodi, Marengo and Austerlitz. In the post-Waterloo years, not a few of Napoleon's marshals advocated a return to smaller forces susceptible to precise operational control on military, as opposed to social and economic grounds.[63]

A small army was conceived as a quality army. The Second Empire, in particular, placed great emphasis on what a later generation of soldiers would call 'combat multipliers'. The army was quick to introduce rifled small arms for its infantry – muzzle-loaders first, then, in 1866, the famous chassepot, the ultimate development of the paper-cartridge breech-loader, exponentially superior in range, accuracy and reliability to the better-known Prussian needle gun. The French artillery adopted rifled cannon in the 1850s. If, by 1870, they had fallen behind the Prussians, this was due to the inevitable disadvantages of being first off the mark. The *mitrailleuse*, too, was a promising supplement to French fire-power, handicapped more by an excessive secrecy, which prevented effective training in its use, than by significant conceptual flaws.[64]

Post-Napoleonic consensus in France regarded the fully developed French soldier as essentially different from the mercenary cannon fodder of the *ancien régime*. A professional warrior and a master craftsman, able to outmarch, outshoot, out-think and outfight his enemies, he could act on his own initiative in camp and battle, then effortlessly become part of a team. French tactics stressed the offensive, even in the face of modern firepower. But 'offensive', especially under the Second Empire, meant neither the headlong charges of Jemappes nor the massive columns of Borodino. Instead, the high morale and the operational efficiency of the French rank and file was considered to facilitate a more sophisticated approach: controlled, limited counter-punches directed against an enemy previously brought to point of wavering by French firepower. The French army of the mid-nineteenth century did not expect to match European enemies man for man and gun for gun. Victory in battle depended on timing and manoeuvre, on encouraging the foe to beat himself by exposing and exhausting his forces, then coming together to overrun him.[65]

Men, rather than machines, thus remained the central factor in French definitions of military effectiveness. Even in an age of rapidly expanding railroad networks, operational

---

[63]Cf. *inter alia*, Cox, *Halt in the Mud*; P. G. Griffith, *Military Thought in the French Army* (Manchester, 1989); and E. Carrias, *La Pensée militaire française* (Paris, 1960), pp. 226–62.

[64]The backbone of the French artillery in 1870 was the four-pounder muzzle-loading bronze rifle adopted in 1859 – about ninety batteries of them, supplemented by two dozen more of twelve-pounder shell guns that had been rifled to increase their range. Richard Holmes, *The Road to Sedan: The French Army, 1866–1870* (London, 1984), p. 199 *passim*, surveys the army's weaponry.

[65]Cf. P. Contamine, 'Puissance de feu et manoeuvre en 1870–71', *Revue de défense nationale* (August–September 1970), pp. 1310–18.

mobility depended on soldiers' legs. Especially in an age of rapidly improving weapons, combat effectiveness depended on soldiers' skills. Work patterns in a still industrializing society depended less on brute strength expended in spurts than on know-how steadily applied. At the end of a long day in the field or shop, a father, even a grandfather, would be on his feet when the young bucks were panting from exhaustion.[66] Older men were considered more resistant than youngsters to both familiar diseases and the exotic ones that accompanied overseas expeditions. They were less prone as well to *nostalgie, mal du pays* – the emotional shock at being severed from everything familiar that left young men susceptible to even minor physical illnesses. Endurance and expertise alike were perceived in France as consequences of experience, long service in uniform, preferably in the same formation and among the same comrades. They involved, one might say, permanently institutionalizing the positive qualities of Napoleon's *grognards*, the 'grumblers' who had carried the tricolour from Madrid to Moscow.[67]

How were such paladins to be mass produced in peacetime? Since the Bourbon Restoration, successive French governments had rejected the concept of a nation in arms and the principle that all fit males owe the state a term of military service. The alleged political unreliability of such a force was only one factor in its perceived incompatibility with French interests. 'The empire is peace', Napoleon III had promised his people. One way of keeping his word was to keep the responsibilities of military service as unobtrusive as possible. France possessed neither the surplus manpower nor the discretionary wealth to recruit a professional army of true volunteers who proactively chose military service. Instead, the army was sustained by a form of selective service based on a lottery. A 'bad number' could mean seven years of active service – and seven years of bad luck. A man in his mid-twenties was too old for an apprenticeship and out of the social networks that determined marriage into a farm. Casual labour was his best prospect; the worst did not bear consideration.[68]

Unlike its twentieth-century successors, however, French conscription legislation required *furnishing* military service as opposed to *performing* it. In other words, it allowed substitution. For the middle classes, the draft became something against which one could take out an insurance policy. For the state, the funds thus raised provided a source of bounties for enlistees and bonuses for veterans. The army of 1870 included over 200,000 substitutes. To its critics, republicans and otherwise, substitution appeared an obscene trafficking in human bodies. To a society increasingly permeated with bourgeois values at all levels, substitution seemed to be no more than a logical application of an economic system in which men took their skins to market and accepted substantial physical risks in the process, whether in mill, mine, field or barracks. If not democratic, the principle of substitution was liberal in its openness to anyone able or willing to make the financial sacrifices. On the other side of the equation, substitution's bounties and bonuses enabled choice on rational-actor models. Prudently managed, they might even provide for an

---

[66]See, generally, Peter Stearns, *Work in a Maturing Industrial Society* (New York, 1975).
[67]See, particularly, the discussion of the 1832 military service law in Douglas Porch, *Army and Revolution: France, 1815–1848* (London, 1974), pp. 62 ff.
[68]On civil-military alienation, see David M. Hopkin, '*La Ramée*, the Archetypical Soldier as an Indicator of Popular Attitudes to the Army in Nineteenth-Century France', *French History* 14 (2000), pp. 115–49.

adequate retirement. If high personnel costs meant fewer soldiers, those soldiers would be good ones, motivated by two quintessentially bourgeois virtues: self-interest and pride of craft.[69]

Along with this went the self-cultivation among the rank and file of a cult of the 'old soldier'. A fighting man was expected to drink hard, drink constantly and, above all, drink in company – 'acting Swiss', playing the tightwad, was a good recipe for ostracism or worse. One French general described a routine that began with a little wine in the morning, proceeded to hard liquor in the course of the day and ended with an aperitif before going to sleep. The officer in question was a reformer, and correspondingly concerned with painting as dark a picture of the status quo as possible. His image of an army that spent much of its waking time either hung-over or in an altered state of consciousness, nevertheless underwrites other frequently observed patterns of behaviour. Particularly in French garrisons, enlisted men refused to take seriously the forms of discipline soldiers of a later generation lump together under the appellation 'chickenshit'. Insolence – the 'dumb' or mute kind of 'body English' so long a staple of British Army orderly-room charges, or the more verbal variety – characterized the French soldiers' relationships with their superiors. They talked among themselves in ranks and on exercises. They reported late for parades and roll-calls. They walked away from details they did not feel like performing. They left everything unbuttoned but their flies.[70]

These manifestations, in turn, were widely tolerated as signs of the 'warrior spirit' the French military system sought to inculcate. Men who were hard to handle in garrison were exactly the sort of men wanted in the field. In any case, punishment had little or no deterrent effect. Part of being a real soldier was the ability to take anything the system handed out in terms of extra duties and 'cells'. A sentence to the disciplinary companies in Algeria was reserved for the extreme hard cases, men whose behaviour was unacceptable even to their fellow soldiers.

The imperial army, in short, might well be described as *faute de mieux*, having 'defined deviancy downwards', accepting what it could not prevent. On the other hand, the operational consequences of that kind of behaviour should not be exaggerated. Parallels might be drawn with twentieth-century paratroopers and similar élite forces that have taken pride in ignoring regulations and routines, policing themselves internally, confident that everything will be 'all right on the night'. The question – one impossible to answer until the actual test of battle – is when internal discipline has been crippled by arrogance.

In the French army, the issue was complicated by the shortcomings of a non-commissioned officer corps that, on the whole, commanded neither the respect nor the obedience of junior enlisted men. That, in part, reflected the French Army's growing pattern of promoting its officers from the ranks. Unlike his British or Prussian counterpart, a French NCO with some ambition and some education was very likely to seek a commission – or have one handed to him. In consequence, instead of developing an institutional identity as a corps of junior

---

[69]The standard work on the issue of recruitment is Bernard Schnapper, *Le Remplacement militaire en France. Quelques aspects politiques, économiques et sociaux du recrutement au XIX siècle* (Paris, 1968). Cf. the more general and accessible essay by François Choiseul, 'Du Tirage au sort au service universel', *Revue Historique des Armées* 37 (1981), no. 2, pp. 43–60.

[70]General Louis Jules Trochu, *L'Armée en 1867* (Paris, 1868), is virtually constructed around these kinds of anecdotes.

leaders, the imperial army's NCOs tended to be polarized between those on the way up and those left behind. The latter included a high proportion of the senior sergeants, a crucial group whose influence over the rank and file was correspondingly limited.[71]

The officer corps of Napoleon III had been handed what its advocates — including the army's political masters — reckoned to be a well-tempered épée, rather than a hastily forged broadsword. How well could it be expected to wield such a weapon? In terms of military culture, the match was a good one. A French officer of any rank was supposed to be a warrior, not a clerk; a man of the camp, not of the study. As in all armies, selection for the highest posts depended on attracting attention; and the Second Empire's water-walkers were expected to make their mark against the Second Empire's enemies, rather than in staff or administrative appointments. The ethic of combat performance was fostered by the fact that about two-thirds of the army's officers began their service in the ranks. These men, whose early formal educations, as a rule, had been significantly limited, were hardly likely to be attracted by a system of higher military education that depended on abstractions at the expense of practical, operational problems. They were unlikely to be attracted by any educational system at all. A lieutenant's average age in 1870 was thirty-seven, a captain's forty-five — well past the prime years of intellectual flexibility. An officer's ability to hold his liquor and lead his men outweighed by far any attendance at fancy schools.[72] This mindset is best epitomized by the cavalry general who, in 1870, allegedly dismissed geography and topography as 'a pile of shit', and described tactical intelligence as telling a peasant, 'Son, you're going to take us where we want to go, and then we'll give you a little drink and a pretty coin. If you steer us wrong, we'll blow your head off'.[73]

The anti-intellectual image of the Second Empire's officer corps must not be exaggerated. Strategic and administrative considerations were by no means ignored. Both, however, tended to remain secondary elements of war making in the context of a national strategy that focused specific military requirements at tactical and operational levels. The army's task in a great-power context was to win battles quickly and decisively enough to convince the enemy to sue for peace. It was scarcely remarkable that the French general staff developed as an isolated, self-proclaimed *corps d'élite*, distinguished only by its intellectual pretensions.[74] Officers with career ambitions shunned staff work — and with good reason. Unlike their Prussian rivals, who had nothing to do but study, French soldiers had ample experience in what arguably still remains the best school of military instruction: war itself.

Since 1815, the French army had been almost constantly engaged in what Paddy Griffith calls 'small wars and big riots'. From Paris and Lyons to Spain, Greece and Algeria, Bourbon white and imperial tricolour had been carried in every possible military environment. Every theatre and every enemy provided a specific challenge that could not be prepared

[71]See Holmes, pp. 119 ff. and, from a slightly different perspective, Terry R. Streiter, 'The Sous-Officiers of the French Army, 1848–1895: A Quantitative Study' (dissertation, University of California, Santa Barbara, 1977).
[72]Cf. William Serman, 'Les Généraux français de 1870', *Revue de défense nationale* 26 (August–September, 1970), pp. 1319–30 and *Les Origines des officiers français, 1848–1870* (Paris, 1979).
[73]Paraphrased from Raoul Girardet, *La Société militaire de la France contemporaine, 1815–1939* (Paris, 1953), p. 110.
[74]Still useful on the subject is Dallas Irvine, 'The French and Prussian Staff Systems Before 1870', *Journal of the American Military History Foundation* 2 (1838), pp. 192–203.

for through staff work and theorizing. Recent experience, in the Crimea, northern Italy and Mexico, only heightened the perceived importance of context in making war. Well before the Second Empire, the army had developed a cult of field experience that insisted war could not be micro-managed from capital cities or remote headquarters. The army's famous – or infamous – System D (*se débrouiller*), or 'muddling through', was by no means a manifestation of insouciance. It reflected, rather, a firm belief that victory depended on adaptability: throwing away the book and relying on one's own response to circumstances. Too many abstractions dulled a soldier's cutting edge, making him more sensitive to concepts than realities.

The French imperial army was particularly conscious of the importance of confusion at all levels of war. Emphasizing flexible responses, based on instinct cultivated by experience, seemed the best practical way of avoiding the risk of what the first Napoleon had described as 'making pictures'. And nothing in the past half-century suggested otherwise. Even in 1859, the closest thing to a major war France had fought since 1815, the French remained well inside the Austrians' loop of initiative. Magenta and Solferino had intimidated a great power into seeking terms, not because it had been overthrown, but because it had first been baffled, then outfought.

The army's organization and administration were shaped by its tactical orientation. No permanent operational command structure existed above the regimental level, and the regiments themselves were regularly transferred to new garrisons. This policy reflected fear that political reliability would decline if soldiers were allowed to grow too close to the population.[75] It also incorporated the army's belief in flexibility. It was important for the French way of war that its fighting men not become too settled, too well adjusted. Similarly, the absence of permanent higher formations allowed for a task force system, tailoring troop lists and command structures precisely to specific situations. For soldiers as professional as the French felt themselves to be, the inevitable friction accompanying this policy was an acceptable difficulty.

Administrative circumstances were less reassuring. The war ministry was disorganized, its bureaux operating virtually independently of each other. The army's emphasis on war's operational aspects meant military administrators tended to be failures in their own eyes as well as their fellows': *routiniers* waiting for orders and hiding behind regulations. In Mexico and Algeria, living off the countryside became almost *de rigueur* in an environment of inadequate supply systems. Closer to home, poorly loaded ships and poorly organized railroads had plagued the army in 1854 and again in 1859. These shortcomings were likely to prove even more significant should large numbers be concentrated in a relatively small area – as would be the case in 1870.[76]

In the four years prior to the outbreak of the Franco-Prussian War, the French military was significantly overhauled. Even before the Prussian victories of 1866, reformers argued that the army had become too front-loaded, with too many of its assets in the store windows. Particularly given France's expanding imperial responsibilities, critics argued, the empire needed a larger army and a more comprehensive reserve system. Napoleon and his war minister, Marshal Adolphe Niel, proposed reducing active service to a term of six years

---

[75]That concern was by no means imagined. Cf. Douglas Porch, *Army and Revolution. France 1815–1848* (London, 1974).
[76]Cf. Holmes, pp. 73 ff. and the contemporary critique, *L'administration de l'Armée* (Paris, 1867).

and requiring all fit men to receive training in a reserve force. The government failed to mobilize either popular or legislative support for what one critic called the process of turning France into a barracks. Instead parliament approved cutting the term of active service to five years and authorized a 'mobile national guard', theoretically including all men not conscripted for the active army. Since this force was allowed to train on only four-teen days a year, it was accurately dismissed by the regulars as virtually useless.[77]

These purported reforms were, and could be, no more than cosmetic. Their advocates sought to change the French army's military culture, to make the army into something dif-ferent, in essence, from what it was. But in the half-century after Waterloo, France had developed an army generally and accurately regarded as the kind of army its government wanted and its people would support and pay for.[78] It saw itself as effective, innovative and flexible, able to take on all comers in the context of the national strategy it was designed to implement. The imperial government did not alter that strategy in the years before 1870. Instead it implemented changes that overlooked or denigrated possibilities for improvement within contexts that were no less modern than those of a mass conscript force.

Reformers obsessed with numbers paid little attention to enhancing effectiveness by, for example, improving coordination between the military planners and the civilian direct-orates of France's railways, or by overhauling the army's logistical and administrative sys-tems.[79] A soldier – even a paid substitute – can be illiterate, inarticulate and, simultaneously, a proud and formidable fighting man. The abolition of re-enlistment bonuses in 1867 was undertaken as a budget-cutting measure and a means of rejuvenating an army its critics saw not as mature, but overripe, with too many fifty-somethings in the rifle companies. It sig-nificantly reduced the number of long-service men in the ranks. It also made many of those who remained feel marginalized and unwanted, increasing already high levels of bloody-mindedness.[80] Consequently, the new intakes of conscripts and the reservists who filled the ranks in 1870 too often entered an environment where neither patriotism nor professionalism was strong enough to compensate for the shortcomings that exist in any military system – to say nothing of overcoming the fog and friction inevitable in modern war.[81]

IV

When, in early 1870, Napoleon took stock of France's military/diplomatic position, in his mind, the Second Empire had recovered its footing after the lapses and setbacks of 1866–7.

---

[77]Cf. Jean Casevitz, *Une loi manqué; la loi Niel, 1866–1868; l'armée française à la veille de la guerre de 1870* (Paris, 1960) and L. Thiriaux, *La Garde nationale mobile de 1870* (Brussels, 1909).

[78]Gordon Wright, 'Public Opinion and Conscription in France, 1866–1870', *Journal of Modern History* 14 (1942), pp. 26–45.

[79]Thomas J. Adriance, *To the Last Gaiter Button. A Study of the Mobilization and Concentration of the French Army in the War of 1870* (Westport, CT, 1987), pp. 33 ff. and François Jacquemin, *Les chemins de fer français pendant la guerre de 1870–71* (Paris, 1872), pp. 32 ff.

[80]Making civil service posts available to retired NCOs began in 1868, but had only a limited impact before the war. C. A. Thoumas, *Les transformations de l'armée française. Essais d'histoire et de la critique sur l'état militaire de la France* (2 vols., Paris, 1887) vol. I, p. 391 and Holmes, pp. 122 ff.

[81]David M. Hopkin, 'Sons and Lovers: Popular Images of the Conscript, 1798–1870', *Modern and Contemporary France* 9 (2001), pp. 19–36, surveys the state's efforts to make conscription popular by establishing it as a male rite of passage.

That did not mean France could afford more mistakes and defeats. It did, however, put the ball back in Bismarck's court. What the Prussian chancellor did with it has been central to the study of European history for a century and a quarter. Contemporary opinion laid primary responsibility for the events of 1870 at the door of France – specifically, of Napoleon III, who was described as forcing a conflict to shore up his unstable regime. Beginning in the 1890s, primary responsibility was increasingly shifted to a Bismarck who allegedly set out deliberately to provoke a war with France and was not above forging diplomatic documents (the Ems Despatch) to achieve his ends. Germany's subsequent behaviour, from 1900 to 1945, lent further credibility to the thesis that the War of 1870 was just another manifestation of 'blood and iron'.

Both approaches incorporated a deal of hindsight. Napoleon III had been the focal point of Europe's diplomacy – and, to his critics, the disturber of Europe's peace – for so long that it was almost natural to assign him responsibility for the war, despite its disastrous outcome for the empire and the dynasty. Similarly, Bismarck, by the turn of the century, was so well established as the cicerone of great-power diplomacy that it was difficult to imagine him not orchestrating a sequence of events so vital to the future of his own state.[82]

A third perspective developed with the growing sophistication of both Bismarck biography and diplomatic history. Otto Pflanze and Lothar Gall interpret the events of 1870 in the context of Bismarck's insistence on keeping as many options as possible open for as long as possible.[83] For these scholars, and for those diplomatic historians who integrated domestic factors into their analyses, Bismarck's primary objective was the resolution of a German question that seemed to be growing beyond the matrices established in 1866.[84] He had not given up hope of gradual unification along the lines later described by Helmut Kohl: 'what belongs together grows together'. At the same time, he saw the new developments in France as offering two possibilities. On the one hand, the empire's new domestic order might absorb so much energy that France would have no interest in obstructing German unification. On the other, it might open the doors of revolution and adventurism in the style of the 1790s. A dynamic France would create immediate opportunities for Prussia – and, from Bismarck's perspective, therefore evoke immediate action. Bismarck was, moreover, not quite an independent actor. He was well aware both that the force of German nationalism had been easier to unleash than to harness, and that it was increasingly generating dynamic internal and

---

[82]Carr, *Wars of Unification*, pp. 178–9. The historiography of the war could easily be the subject of a separate monograph. Lawrence Steefel, *Bismarck, the Hohenzollern Candidacy, and the Origins of the German War of 1870* (Cambridge, MA, 1962), incorporates an excellent analysis of earlier material. S. William Halperin, 'The Origins of the Franco-Prussian War Revisited: Bismarck and the Hohenzollern Candidacy for the Spanish Throne', *Journal of Modern History* 45 (1973), pp. 83–91, extends it by a decade. David Wetzel, *A Duel of Giants. Bismarck, Napoleon III, and the Origins of the Franco-Prussian War* (Madison, WI, 2001), incorporates a comprehensive survey of the literature and is a model of learning lightly worn. The first volume of Josef Becker's magisterial source collection, *Bismarcks spanische 'Diversion' 1870 und der preussisch-deutsche Reichsgruendungskrieg* (Paderborn, 2002), unfortunately appeared too late to be incorporated into the present work's research base.

[83]That is also the conclusion of Patricia Kollander, 'Crown Prince Frederick William and the Hohenzollern Candidacy Revisited', *European Review of History* 3 (1996), pp. 171–85.

[84]Cf. particularly, Josef Becker, 'Zum Problem der Bismarkischen Politik in der spanischen Thronfrage', *Historische Zeitschrift* 212 (1971), pp. 529–607 and 'Der Krieg mit Frankreich als Problem der kleindeutschen Einigungspolitik Bismarcks, 1866–1871' in *Das kaiserliche Deutschland, 1870–1918*, ed. M. Stuermer (Duesseldorf, 1970), pp. 75–88.

external opposition. In his own mind, Bismarck was riding a tiger in the final months of 1869. He had every intention of avoiding the fate of the 'young lady of Niger', and keeping the smile on *his* face when the next hand was played out.

If Bismarck prided himself on a particular skill at this stage of his career, it was to step into a situation and stir things up, confident that he could respond to confusion exponentially better than his associates and opponents. Yet Europe in 1870 seemed more settled than at any time in the past five years. The international uncertainties that existed were to the benefit of France: Austria and Italy might not be Napoleon's allies, but they were something more than his neighbours. Russia, to be sure, was anxious to improve relations with Prussia in light of Beust's assertive Balkan policies. Tsar Alexander had even offered, in case of a Franco-Prussian conflict, to mobilize 100,000 men on Austria's frontier as a guarantor of the latter's neutrality. Bismarck responded that Prussia could handle France by itself if the situation arose. From his perspective, the risks of a general war reached unacceptable limits whenever Russia became involved – a mindset congenial to a Russia seeking to remain disengaged from the conflicts and crises of central Europe for the sake of its ambitions further east.[85]

Then Spain played a wild card. In 1868, revolution had forced the queen into exile. No one in the Iberian peninsula who was acceptable to the major interest groups could be persuaded to assume the throne. The ruling junta looked elsewhere, including across the Pyrenees. One of their prospects was Prince Leopold of Hohenzollern-Sigmaringen. He was the scion of the Catholic branch of the House of Hohenzollern, which had remained in south Germany when the cadets of the family relocated to Brandenburg in the Middle Ages. His father was currently military governor of the Rhineland and Westphalia; Leopold himself was a Prussian officer who had served in 1866. He was the husband of a Portuguese princess, offering the possibility, attractive in Spain at that time, of eventually reuniting the Iberian thrones. He had several healthy sons to carry on the line. He was related to the Bonapartes as well as the Hohenzollerns; not closely, but enough for dynastic purposes, with a bit of goodwill on all sides.[86]

Despite Leopold's Bonaparte connections, the impact on France of a Hohenzollern accession was impossible to overlook, and the other great powers were correspondingly likely to have a say in the issue. From the time of the first Spanish initiatives in September 1869, Leopold and his father insisted, in particular, that acceptance was impossible without the full support of William, both as head of the House of Hohenzollern and as King of Prussia. William opposed the idea, believing that no foreigner could rule Spain, even nominally, for any length of time. Bismarck, for all his subsequent insistence that the whole thing came as

---

[85]Pflanze, vol. I, pp. 436–7 and Lutz, p. 158. For Russia's policies, see Dietrich Beyrau, 'Russische Interessenzonen und Europaeisches Gleichgewicht 1860–1870' in *Europa vor dem Krieg 1870*, pp. 65–76 and the more focused *Russische Orientpolitik und die Entstehung des deutschen Kaiserreiches, 1866–1870* (Munich, 1974).

[86]Steefel, *German War*, pp. 22 ff. and Hans-Otto Kleinmann's excellent 'Die spanische Thronfrage in der internationalen Politik vor Ausbruch des deutsch-franzoesischen Krieges' in *Europa vor dem Krieg von 1870*, pp. 125–49. It is easily forgotten that the candidacy was, from the start, a Spanish issue and determined by Spanish considerations. Javier Rubio, *España et la guerra de 1870* (3 vols., Madrid, 1989), does an excellent job of establishing Spanish agency throughout the process. His arguments are summarized in 'La vacance du trone d'Espagne (1869–79) et l'équilibre européen. Une révision du problème des candidatures', *La guerre de 1870/71 et ses conséquences*, eds. P. Levillain and R. Riemenschneider (Bonn, 1990), pp. 33–85.

a surprise to him, had kept abreast of the issue from its beginnings. He responded by urging William to allow the candidacy to proceed, for a mixture of dynastic and geopolitical reasons that left Prussia's monarch even less convinced than before of the wisdom of the idea.[87]

By this time, the Hohenzollern candidacy had developed a life of its own in Spain, where the spectacle of the crown of Charles V and Philip II being hawked unsuccessfully around the minor courts of Europe was draining the junta's limited credibility. Leopold declined again – then, with encouragement from Bismarck's agents, as well as the Spanish delegation, he changed his mind. William finally, grudgingly, agreed, and the agent of the Cortes telegraphed Madrid to prepare for Leopold's immediate election. A clerk decoded the message incorrectly – one of those historical ball-bearings on which great events so often turn.[88] Instead of confronting Europe with a *fait accompli*, the Cortes dissolved and went home to escape the hot Madrid summer. It was scheduled to meet again in November. But on 2 July the Paris press broke the story with ruffles and flourishes, and France erupted.

Had that been Bismarck's intention from the first? To take seriously his repeated assertions that the Hohenzollern candidacy was defensive and dynastic, in the words of Otto Pflanze, 'make[s] the lion of European diplomacy look like a house cat'[89] – one that has had a recent close encounter with a veterinarian. Even had Leopold's accession been implemented as planned, Bismarck had to expect serious diplomatic consequences. Apart from the long-running two-handed game between Bismarck and Napoleon III, since the sixteenth century, France's geo-strategic nightmare had involved being sandwiched between dynastically connected powers. Europe had fought almost two centuries' worth of wars to bring closure to a Habsburg challenge that the Hohenzollerns had now resurrected. Rhetorical questions as to whether Bismarck intended to provoke a war, or merely force the collapse of Napoleon's regime, tend to overstate Bismarck's belligerence while underrating his self-confidence. The Hohenzollern candidacy was designed to provoke a crisis with France. But it was so managed that at each stage, the final initiative, the final choice, remained with Paris. Bismarck recognized that war was an extremely likely outcome of the situation. At the same time, however, he was testing the intentions of the emperor, his new 'liberal empire', and France itself.

Bismarck's repeated insistence that William's approval of the candidacy was a dynastic issue, having nothing official or essential to do with Prussia, is usually dismissed, either as a fig leaf to conceal his own role, or a tacked-on insult to France, unable to credit such a transparent fabrication without critical loss of face.[90] Diplomacy, however (especially the cabinet diplomacy that still prevailed at mid-nineteenth century), is, in good part, composed of exactly those kinds of ploys and the gavottes that surround them. An international incident is what one of the parties involved wishes to define as an international incident.

---

[87]The most complete analysis is Jochen Dittrich, *Bismarck, Frankreich, und die Hohenzollernkandidatur: Die 'Kriegsschuldfrage' von 1870* (Munich, 1962). Eberhard Kolb, *Der Kriegsausbruch 1870. Politische Entscheidungsprozesse und Verantwortlichkeiten in der Julikrise 1870* (Goettingen, 1970), is persuasive within its limits.

[88]See the discussion in Wetzel, pp. 88 ff.

[89]Pflanze, vol. I, p. 459.

[90]As in ibid., p. 457 and Gall, *White Revolutionary*, vol. I, pp. 354–5.

Without that desire, sunken ships and shot-down airliners have been known to disappear as completely as any alleged victim of the Bermuda triangle. Negotiating room remained in the first days of July 1870. The question for Bismarck was what uses would be made of it. The Hohenzollern candidacy might well become the focal point for serious negotiation of France's position *vis-à-vis* south Germany, and its relationships with Austria and Italy — relationships developed largely to intimidate Prussia, in general, and Bismarck, in particular. That, however, was a game two could play, as Bismarck had just demonstrated. Now the time had come for posturing to end and statesmanship to begin — should Napoleon pick up that subtext.

Or perhaps not. If France broke in the other direction, developing the candidacy into a *casus belli*, then the card of German nationalism could be played as a counter. Bismarck's problem was that he could not know whether it would prove a trump or a joker. Would Prussia emerge as the standard-bearer for a long frustrated 'German spirit'? Or would the nationalists, always volatile, turn from a state whose dynastic posturing had put the German dream at unconscionable risk? It was something to ponder, over dinner and a drink — or several drinks, presumably of something stronger than the mineral water to which the chancellor was purportedly confined since he began a 'cure' on 8 May at his country estate.

From a French perspective, the Hohenzollern candidacy was a 'short crisis'.[91] It burst so unexpectedly that even the editors who ran the story were initially willing to give the government time to define the parameters of the issue before writing new headlines in order to sell more papers. Viewed militarily, the projected dynastic connection was more a nuisance than a threat — 1870 was not 1570. The days when a monarch could send armies to the frontier on a whim were long past, especially in a Spain that had enjoyed good relations with France for half a century. In any case, Spain's armed forces were in a sufficient state of decay that French second-line troops should be well able to hold the line of the Pyrenees until the regulars settled accounts with Prussia.

In his better days, Napoleon might have taken advantage of the coding error and encouraged the junta to rethink the circumstances of its offer. After all, nothing had yet happened that could not be undone, then spun to French advantage in the ways Napoleon knew so well. Another promising approach involved opening negotiations with Berlin, encouraging William to withdraw his support for the candidacy and sounding out Bismarck on his price for brokering Leopold's withdrawal. That pattern, too, was familiar to Napoleon and his foreign office, but the domestic matrix of the Second Empire had changed drastically since the last time the emperor played a game of smoke and mirrors. In May 1870, a new constitution had been introduced and overwhelmingly approved by plebiscite. Its principal author, Emile Ollivier, was no disguised republican. He favoured a combination of a strong central government with a strong parliament, both functioning in an atmosphere of civil liberty — including freedom of speech. While not intending to reduce the emperor to a figurehead, Ollivier clearly saw himself standing at the power centre of this new order. And long before the Hohenzollern candidacy became an issue, Ollivier believed that the best way to that position was to defend French honour and French interests in the public forum. Only then might revolution and socialism, on the

---

[91]Stephane Audoin-Rouzeau, *1870. La France dans la Guerre* (Paris, 1989), p. 19.

one hand, and militarism and autocracy, on the other, cease to threaten a France in the process of rebirth.[92]

It was an unpromising matrix for caution – and Napoleon had exacerbated his problems further in that respect by promoting Gramont from the Vienna embassy to the foreign ministry in May. Gramont, volatile in temperament and virulently anti-Prussian, was strong medicine even for Ollivier. But the new minister's extreme clerical sympathies served to quiet those conservative circles grumbling that the 'liberal empire' was taking the adjective in its title too seriously. 'I will be the French Bismarck', he declared on leaving Vienna. He had assumed his office with the general expectation that he would test Prussia's mettle at the first opportunity. Now one had, almost literally, fallen on his desk.[93]

Gramont began by asking Berlin for the full extent of Prussia's involvement. Bismarck called the question insolent. Gramont dismissed the reply, that officially Prussia knew nothing about the matter, as insulting. This was provocative but not decisive. Bismarck was away from Berlin, which Gramont knew when he drafted his message. It was answered by an under-secretary – acting for Bismarck and speaking in Bismarck's words, but nevertheless a flunky.[94] The Council of Ministers, however, backed Gramont when, on 6 July, he read a prepared declaration to the *corps législatif*, denouncing the candidacy as a threat to Europe's balance of power and to the honour and the vital interests of France. 'Peace if that is possible; war if that is inevitable', was the policy of a government that, Ollivier asserted, could now count on the support of all its citizens in a time of crisis.[95] Gramont followed up his rhetorical effusions by sending France's ambassador to Prussia, Count Vincent Benedetti, to Ems, where William was taking a cure. Benedetti's mission was to confront the king and convince him to end Leopold's candidacy once for all. If not – 'c'est la guerre', noted the suddenly laconic minister.[96]

Any doubt of how seriously Gramont regarded the issue was dispelled by his instruction to seek out William at Ems. Interrupting any public figure, much less a ruling monarch, under those circumstances, was the rough equivalent of what barging into his bathroom might be in this less reticent era. Reading Gramont's text on 8 July, Bismarck described it as a statement of intent to go to war. But did he believe it? He did not respond by contacting the war ministry and the general staff; instead, he ordered the newspapers turned loose to inflame public opinion and waited for news from Ems.[97]

William was initially conciliatory – not least because he was once again nursing a serious case of 'I told you so' in regard to his chief minister. The candidacy, he informed

[92]Theodore Zeldin, *Emile Ollivier and the Liberal Empire of Napoleon III* (Oxford, 1963), remains a good introduction. Cf. Douglas W. Houston, 'Emile Ollivier and the Hohenzollern Candidacy', *French Historical Studies* 4 (1965), pp. 125–49. Ollivier speaks for himself on the subject, eloquently and interminably, in *L'Empire libéral; études, récits, souvenirs* (18 vols., Paris, 1895–1918).
[93]There is no scholarly study of Gramont. The critical capsule sketch in Pierre de la Gorce, *Histoire du Second Empire* (7 vols., Paris, 1899–1905), vol. VI, pp. 216–17, is a reasonable beginning, which Gramont's own memoir, *La France et la Prusse avant la guerre* (Paris, 1872), does nothing to modify. The quotation is from Wetzel, p. 34.
[94]R. H. Lord, *The Origins of the War of 1870: New Documents from the German Archives* (Cambridge, MA, 1924), pp. 30–1.
[95]Ollivier, vol. XIV, pp. 92 ff.
[96]Gramont to Benedetti, 7 July 1870, in Vincent Benedetti, *Ma mission en prusse* (Paris, 1871), pp. 319–21.
[97]Pflanze, vol. I, pp. 464–5.

Benedetti, was not exactly a mistake, but certainly of itself not intended as a *casus belli*. Benedetti came away reasonably convinced that William could be counted upon to use his good offices to squelch a project he considered ill-advised, and reported to Gramont accordingly. But he added to his despatch a generalized warning that the king might be buying time for Prussia to prepare for war. Whether this was common-sense boiler plate or involved a desire to cover himself against his superior's predictable rage, it had a greater impact in Paris than the rest of the despatch put together – not least because the initial telegraphic transmission was garbled, and much of the more conciliatory material was lost. First impressions were what counted. Gramont ordered Benedetti to confront William and obtain a definitive answer.[98]

William stalled – particularly when requested to end the candidacy because the French government requested it and French public opinion demanded it. He was, however, no more responsive to the increasingly desperate telegrams from Bismarck urging him to stand firm. Instead, William contacted directly the Prussian ambassador in Paris, ordering him to inform Gramont personally of Prussia's desire for peace. On 12 July it suddenly appeared the situation had become moot. William had contacted Leopold's father on 10 July. On 12 July, the prince, alarmed at the war talk spreading throughout Europe, declared his son was no longer interested in the throne of Spain.[99]

Crisis management demands, above all else, a firm, consistent grasp of affairs by the managers – or at least one of them. It was in that spirit that Bismarck left Varzin, early on 12 July, for Ems, to oversee directly William's contacts with Benedetti. His route lay through Berlin, and at the railroad station a number of newly arrived telegrams were thrust into his hands. These included a report on Karl Albert's decision to terminate the candidacy, messages from Paris describing the provocative stories in the French press and, not least, a number of reports on William's courteous and conciliatory attitude towards the French ambassador. Bismarck riffled through them and considered resigning. Prussia, he thought to himself, had just suffered its worst diplomatic humiliation since Olmuetz.[100]

Otto Pflanze describes Bismarck as reacting from frustration at seeing the war he by now wanted slipping through his fingers.[101] Frustration played a role in Bismarck's immediate reaction, to be sure. But if any one thought ran white-hot through his mind, it was most probably some variant of 'His Majesty has done it to me again!' William's common-sense approach to defusing the immediate crisis had instead put Prussia in a position where every chancery in Europe would process the event as a French victory – a victory, moreover, won by 'standing tall' and confronting Prussia directly. What state would be next to apply the same method of direct confrontation in its dealings with Prussia? It was a question better left unconsidered for the moment.

Bismarck telegraphed William *please* to refrain from announcing Leopold's renunciation. He reassured the crown prince, the Russian foreign minister (who happened to be

---

[98]Benedetti, pp. 325 ff., describes the exchange in detail. Cf. Lord, pp. 50–1.

[99]William I to Karl Anton, 10 July 1870, in *Briefe, Aktenstuecke und Regesten zur Geschichte der Hohenzollernschen Thronkandidatur in Spanien*, ed. R. Fester (2 vols., Leipzig, 1913), vol. II, pp. 64–5 and Karl Anton to William I, 12 July 1870, in *Bismarck and the Hohenzollern Candidature for the Spanish Throne*, ed. G. Bonnin (London, 1957), pp. 251–2.

[100]Otto von Bismarck, *Die gesammelten Werke*, vol. XV, pp. 305 ff.

[101]Pflanze, vol. I, p. 466.

passing through Berlin) and the Italian ambassador that the crisis was over. He informed the Berlin press and the Prussian diplomatic corps that the Hohenzollern candidacy was officially ended – an early form of 'spin control' by taking charge of breaking news. At the same time, Bismarck sent another message to the ambassador to France, declaring that he wanted an official explanation of recent French conduct. He also floated to the press a trial balloon that involved recalling parliament to discuss further action should the French response be unsatisfactory.[102]

Taken together, these improvisations combine less to indicate a coherent desire for war than a familiar pattern of keeping options open. Noteworthy, too, was Bismarck's increasing use of the telegraph to fine-tune and micro-manage a diplomatic situation whose denouement now seemed more a matter of hours than days. But his moves became moot with the beginning of another sequence of events during the afternoon of 13 July in Paris.[103] Gramont presented Leopold's renunciation to the *corps législatif* only to face a barrage of questions and challenges whose burden was 'too little and too late'. The session did nothing to calm a man already half convinced that this was a time to push the issue by getting William himself to announce Leopold's withdrawal. He took the argument to Napoleon.

Like most of the Paris diplomatic corps, the emperor had been prone to regard the outcome as a victory – the first unmistakable triumph France had scored over Bismarck. But Gramont was a powerful advocate in one-on-one situations. He had help, moreover, from Empress Eugénie. Conservative, Catholic, authoritarian to her fingertips, she had been outraged by political reforms she believed would leave her son Louis merely the simulacrum of power when he should ascend the throne. She made no secret of her conviction that war with Prussia was just what the empire needed to restore its vitality and credibility.[104] Napoleon, by this time in increasing pain as stress worked on his kidneys, approved new instructions for Benedetti. The foreign minister promptly drafted a telegram to Benedetti, instructing him to obtain a guarantee that the King of Prussia would not again authorize a Hohenzollern candidacy for the Spanish crown, and to respond as quickly as possible.[105]

Gramont, Ollivier, Napoleon and just about every other key figure in that decision at some time cited public opinion as a major factor in their thinking.[106] In fact, the run-up to the war of 1870 was a 'cabinet crisis' as well as a short crisis. No one in authority took any consequent pains to mobilize French opinion in any direction, despite years of practice in that craft. Prefects remained unbriefed and journalists unbribed. Even the Paris press did not speak with one voice during the crisis. Whether that reflected a progress too fast for 'pack journalism' to develop is debatable; the major Paris liberal-democratic papers had a history of equating Prussian enlargement with the advance of liberalism and the

---

[102]Steefel, *Hohenzollern Candidacy*, pp. 165 ff. and Wetzel, pp. 140 ff. and 151 ff., combine for Bismarck's deeds, attitudes and dissimulations on 12 and 13 July.

[103]Cf. Steefel, *Hohenzollern Candidacy*, pp. 195 ff.; Wetzel, pp. 142 ff.; and Ollivier, vol. XIV, pp. 337 ff. – the latter modified and supplemented by Pierre Muret, 'Emile Ollivier et le Duc de Gramont les 12 et 13 juillet 1870', *Revue d'histoire moderne et contemporaine* (1909–10), vols. XIII, pp. 305–28 and XIV, pp. 178–213.

[104]Eugénie's role is analysed in detail in Nancy Barker, *Distaff Diplomacy: The Empress Eugénie and the Foreign Policy of the Second Empire* (Austin, TX, 1967), pp. 186 ff. Eugénie was a formidable woman – Napoleon's kidneys were not the only vital imperial organs at risk during the crisis.

[105]Gramont to Benedetti, 7 p.m., 12 July 1870, in Benedetti, p. 369.

[106]Case, pp. 225 ff., particularly stresses the impact of a public 'will to war' on policy formation.

prospects of compensation on the Rhine.[107] The Paris police reported significant loci of opposition to the government's belligerence. Opinion in the provinces, so far as it can be determined, was even more lethargic. Public behaviour certainly became more volatile during the last half of the month – especially in Paris, where crowds of 600 to 1,200 assembled to shout war cries, dispersed, then reformed again a few blocks away. By and large, however, enthusiasm developed after the fact, as a consequence of the government's behaviour – not as a cause of it. Even before the first shots were fired, the groundwork for a national war was in place.[108] Like the Prussian monarchy, however, the French Empire proposed to wage a cabinet war, a dynastic war, a war for limited aims.

If, that is, war should be necessary. Gramont was pushing his hand to the limit. But given William's previous behaviour, and his apparent good rapport with Benedetti, it was a fair probability that he could be convinced to give the guarantee France was demanding. Undocumented, but a probable factor in that calculation, was the opinion – common in French government circles as it was elsewhere in Europe – that William lacked the intelligence quite to know when he was being manipulated, whether by his own minister-president or by the French ambassador. The facts are familiar: Benedetti's repeated requests for an audience; William's refusal, accompanied by a recommendation that further discussion of the question be conducted through Bismarck; the final encounter between the monarch and the ambassador in the Ems *Kurgarten*; William's tip of the hat and polite withdrawal as a public scene seemed in the making.[109]

William's anger at Gramont for challenging his word did not spill over into his refusal to renounce the candidacy permanently. Such commitments are not made hastily or informally. The uses Bismarck made of the telegram reporting the incident generated an entire academic subculture, based primarily on Bismarck's own editing of the message so that the encounter read like an insult to Prussia and Prussia's king. The shortened version Bismarck gave to the press is essentially congruent with the full telegram. Both, it must be reiterated, made the confrontation between Benedetti and William more confrontational than it had been – certainly more confrontational than Benedetti reported. Certainly, as well, publication of the 'Ems Despatch' in the major German papers brought crowds to demonstrate in front of the French embassy in Berlin, and provoked similar responses when translated and published in Paris.[110]

The despatch was also enough for Gramont and Ollivier. Gramont called it an intolerable affront to national honour. Ollivier considered it sufficiently provocative to call a council meeting for the afternoon of 14 July. Gramont opened the session with a dramatic demand for war. War Minister Leboeuf demanded immediate mobilization of the reserves. Despite some dissenting voices, at 4 p.m. mobilization was approved and Leboeuf departed to issue the necessary orders. Then Benedetti's despatch, with full details of the last meeting, arrived. It became apparent that Prussia had publicly refused

---

[107]Wilfried Radewahn, *Die pariser Presse und die deutsche Frage unter Beruecksichtigung der franzoesischen Pressepolitik im Zeitalter der Bismarkischen Reichsgruendung 1866–1870/71* (Frankfurt, 1977).

[108]Antoine-Rouzeau, pp. 37 ff.

[109]Lord, pp. 83 ff., is the most detailed reconstruction.

[110]W. L. Langer, 'Bismarck as a Dramatist' in *Studies in Diplomatic History and Historiography in Honour of G. P. Gooch*, ed. A. O. Sarkissian (London, 1961), pp. 199–216, remains the definitive account of the editing of that document.

the guarantee France demanded, but William had insulted neither France nor its representative.

Were the grounds for war sufficient? What if, suggested one council member, this incident became the springboard for an international council discussing the problem of princes accepting vacant thrones without great-power consent – a conference, of course, to be held in Paris. Napoleon and Ollivier, each for his own reasons, seized upon the idea. Leboeuf suggested that the government make up its mind. By the time the council reconvened at 10 p.m. that evening, Empress Eugénie and Ollivier's family had had time to work on their wavering significant others. With the end of the work day, the crowds had grown larger and noisier. As much to the point, Ollivier at least believed that anything but a recommendation for war would have no chance in the legislative assembly. That left two choices: show the liberal empire was a sham by ignoring parliament and possibly encouraging revolution as well, or roll the iron dice. Now the ball lay in the army's court. When – or whether – Leboeuf actually proclaimed the military ready 'to the last gaiter button' was less important than the air of confidence he had been projecting since the crisis began escalating. 'Give us a chance', his manner projected. 'The soldiers will bring France through'. At a time of increasing uncertainty in all other quarters, it was not surprising that the council meeting ended by approving continued mobilization. It was even less surprising when, on 15 July, the council formally approved war and the assembly overwhelmingly voted the necessary credits.[111]

William, as reluctant a belligerent now as he had been in 1866, had resisted Bismarck, Moltke, Roon and his son, the crown prince, for most of two days as they demanded mobilization. The news from Paris convinced the king that no alternative remained. On the evening of 15 July, the North German Confederation issued its mobilization orders.

---

[111]Steefel, *Hohenzollern Candidacy*, pp. 198 ff.; Pierre Lehautcourt, *Les Origines de la guerre de 1870: la candidature Hohenzollern 1868–1870* (Paris, 1912), pp. 493 ff.; and Ollivier, vol. XIV, p. 354 *passim*, combine for a reconstruction of the events of 14 and 15 July.

7

War Against the Empire

The Franco-Prussian War began almost on duellists' terms. Neither party had a significant advantage in mobilization; neither had undertaken preliminary preparations. It was a classic 'come-as-you-are' war, and its initial advantages rested with the French. That was the kind of conflict around which their military system had been developed and refined. The Prussians depended on playing catch-up, compensating for instant readiness with speed and system, showing what they could do in 1866, albeit against what, in hindsight, seemed a second team. To participants and observers alike, *retiarius* now faced *secutor* in an asymmetric contest whose outcome was anybody's guess.

I

'Come-as-you-are' is not a euphemism for 'haphazard'. Since 1866, French planning for war with Prussia/Germany had been based on forming three field armies. One, three corps strong, would concentrate around Strasbourg, and another of equal strength at Metz; the third, of two corps, would remain at Châlons in theatre reserve. In so far as a single war plan ever held sway in imperial councils that can best be described as flexible or ramshackle, France's strategy was projected as defensive: drawing the Prussians into the natural killing ground on the French side of the frontier.[1]

The diplomatic situation in 1870, however, seemed to demand the quality the French army was most supposed to embody: quick reaction. Napoleon III had never intended to take on the North German Confederation single-handed. On 9 July, before the candidacy crisis broke, Beust promised no more than diplomatic support. On 18 July, responding to Russia's threat to occupy Galicia should Austria enter the war, Franz Josef proclaimed neutrality. Beust was at some pains to inform Gramont that neutrality was merely a ploy. The Austrians, he murmured, would be all right on the night. Napoleon, however, took that sentiment for what it was worth. Across the Alps, Italy's parliament and cabinet refused to honour Victor Emanuel's informal commitments to Napoleon.[2]

---

[1] Cf. the summaries in Adriance, pp. 55–6 and Holmes, pp. 169–70. 'La Guerre de 1870' in *La Guerre de 1870–71. Preparation à la guerre*, ed. Section Historique de l'État-Major de l'Armée (35 vols., Paris, 1901–13), vol. I, pp. 79 ff., reprints part of the most comprehensive pre-war strategic proposal.

[2] Cf. Isztvan Dioszegi, *Oesterreich-Ungarn und der franzoesisch-preussische Krieg, 1870–71*, tr. J. Till (Budapest, 1974) and S. William Halperin, *Diplomat under Stress: Visconti-Venosta and the Crisis of July, 1870* (Chicago, 1963). The presumed allied war plan, as it was understood in Paris, is presented in Barthelemy L. Lebrun, *Souvenirs militaires 1866–1870* (Paris, 1895), p. 71 *passim*.

Both decisions were disappointments; both policies were subject to change – at least in the minds of an emperor and a government accustomed to flexible, ephemeral agreements. A quick, impressive victory or two – the kind of victories the French reasonably expected to win – and the winds from Turin and Vienna were likely to blow more favourably. By July 1870, Napoleon intended to combine the armies of Metz and Strasbourg, cross the Rhine south of Rastatt, then swing north-west and hit the Prussians while they were still unloading their troop trains. The two corps from Châlons would advance to Metz and cover the Lorraine frontier against any Prussian threat from the Rhineland. The plan had political as well as military elements. Apart from its expected positive effect on Austria and Italy, a French invasion was expected to cause the south German states to think twice about involving themselves in Bismarck's war.[3]

The latter was not mere wishful thinking. In the days following the candidacy crisis, strong political and journalistic warnings were raised everywhere south of the Main against blindly joining in a second great-power conflict in less than five years. What, the opposition argued, did Bavaria have to do with the question of whether a Hohenzollern prince wore the crown of Spain. Even in Baden, where Prussophilia ran deepest, hawks were reminded that the state was on the geographic front line of any war with France that it might join. Not until the aftermath of the Ems Despatch did the neutrality movement collapse – and then, in good part, because of Austria's half-hearted support.[4] Nor could the still untempered North German Confederation reckon automatically on internal stability.[5] Apart from potential political dissent, the Berlin stock market reacted to the war's outbreak by panic selling, major stocks dropping as much as 30 per cent from their price on 1 July. An initial government attempt to raise a 100 million taler loan by public subscription also failed. A second, far more modest attempt was launched successfully, but only after the victories of August.[6]

Napoleon initially sought to strengthen his diplomatic hand by a second military initiative. On 11 July, he informed the war minister that he had decided to concentrate France's active forces in a single Army of the Rhine, eight corps strong, under his personal command.[7] A force that size, with a paper strength of between 300,000 and 350,000 men, would have strained the capacities of his uncle. Such a mass of manoeuvre nevertheless offered the promise, if used boldly, of an immediate thrust into Prussian territory – and damn the risks. Insouciance had been part of the French way of war since before Napoleon the Great. Now, from his nephew's perspective, it was a necessity. The French war minister, at least, believed Napoleon planned to hammer his way across south Germany and link up with the Austrian

---

[3]The plan is summarized in Napoleon III, *Des Causes qui ont amenés la capitulation de Sedan* (Brussels, 1871), pp. 4–5. Cf. Adriance, p. 56 and Holmes, p. 170.

[4]Cf. *inter alia*, Becker, pp. 691 ff. and Lutz, pp. 222 ff. E. Weis, 'Vom Kriegsausbruch zur Reichsgruendung. Zur Politik des bayerischen Aussenministers Graf Bray-Steinburg im Jahr 1870', *Zeitschrift fuer bayerische Landesgeschichte* 33 (1970), pp. 787 ff. and Potthoff, pp. 344 ff., cover the diplomacy. Erich Schneider offers a case study in public opinion with 'Die Reaktion der deutschen Oeffentlichkeit auf den Kriegsbeginn. Das Beispiel des Bayerischen Rheinpfalz' in *La Guerre de 1870*, pp. 110–57.

[5]Alf Luedtke discusses 'The Permanence of Internal War: The Prussian State and its Opponents, 1870–71' in *Road to Total War*, pp. 377–92. Cf. Stewart A. Stehlin, 'Guelph plans for the Franco-Prussian War', *Historical Journal* 13 (1970), pp. 789–98.

[6]Cf. Stern, *Gold and Iron*, pp. 130–1 and Theodore S. Hamerow, *The Social Foundations of German Unification: 1858–1871: Struggles and Accomplishments* (Princeton, 1972), pp. 400 ff.

[7]Ollivier, vol. XV, pp. 105–6.

army, which he expected to respond to his initiative.[8] One might call it the right idea for the wrong reason. Above all, the empire needed to shape the campaign's conduct while Prussia was still at the stage of concentrating its numerically superior forces. Attacking across the Rhine from a standing start to open the campaign offered the same kind of prospect as beginning a fight with a kick to the groin.

In the event, neither speed nor shock was forthcoming. The problem was not material. France's railway network was arguably the best in Europe from a military perspective. As a pre-war German study noted, almost two-thirds of its lines were double-tracked. France had a third more rolling stock per track mile than Prussia. Stations in the French eastern provinces were larger, and marshalling yards better equipped, than their German counterparts.[9] While private enterprise and private capital were central to railway construction in France, almost from the beginning a strong public element was involved as well. Strategic and operational factors influenced route choices far more than anywhere else in Europe, though the army by no means always got its way on such issues as laying track on the side of a river furthest from the German frontier. In contrast to the Prussian pattern, commercial and military interests were generally considered compatible. If the primary reason for constructing track or facilities was military, the state assumed an appropriately higher liability. In 1856, for example, the war ministry subsidized the fortification of part of a line from Paris to Muhlhouse in Alsace. In 1863, the government agreed to compensate the Eastern Railway Company 62,800 francs for building what was essentially a complex of unloading facilities for military trains. The result was a regional network of lines along the eastern frontier, connecting the major fortresses and facilitating the lateral movement of troops, combined with a web of lines extending outward from the hub of Paris. If anything, the synergy between soldiers and railroads was too close. Maintaining rolling stock, operating engines, even loading trains, were the responsibilities of civilian railwaymen; not until mid-July in 1870 was the army authorized to organize its own maintenance units.[10]

Deployment to the zone of operations from peacetime stations was less of a problem than is generally assumed. The Imperial Guard was already organized as a corps, and concentrated in Paris. The line regiments in or near the capital became III Corps; those training at Châlons formed II Corps. A significant number of the other regiments assigned to the Army of the Rhine were already stationed on the frontier. Nor were regiments from the interior assigned haphazardly. Following the network layout described above, units from the north, as a rule, were shipped to Metz, those from central France to Châlons and Nancy, and regiments from the south and Algeria to Belfort or Strasbourg. The devil lay rather in the details – those details overlooked in the pre-war concern with numbers. As it concentrated in the relatively remote countryside of Alsace-Lorraine, the army depended on regular supplies. Instead, provisions, uniforms, even ammunition, piled up haphazardly as an overstrained administrative system suffered one short circuit after another. The army's policy of sending reservists first to their regimental depot and then to the front generated such spectacular odysseys as the discharged zouave recalled to service, sent

---

[8]That, at least, was his testimony in the post-war *Procès Bazaine* (*capitulation de Metz*, etc.) (Paris, 1873), p. 208.

[9]H. L. W., *Die Kriegfuehrung unter Benuetzung der Eisenbahnen* (Leipzig, 1868), pp. 74 ff.

[10]See, especially, Mitchell, pp. 31 ff. and F. Jacqumin, *Les Chemins de Fer pendant la Guerre de 1870–71* (Paris, 1874), pp. 111 ff.

from his home in Alsace to his depot in North Africa, then returned to his regiment in eastern France.[11]

Small numbers of such peregrinations could be tolerated. But the French army of 1870 was no longer structured top to bottom for making war from a standing start. The recent reforms had made it dependent (almost as much as its Prussian rival) on call-ups to bring its regiments to war strength. Reservists chivvied all over France as individuals and small groups had far too many opportunities to ask themselves if the trip was really necessary. Armies depend for cohesion and effectiveness as much on a 'culture of competence', a sense that 'the system' knows approximately what it is doing in matters like rations, marches and mail, as on inspired combat leadership. There were no institutional or cultural reasons making inevitable the national railway system's poor performance in moving masses of men and equipment efficiently. Instead, competence had been assumed. And as a result, instead of coiling for a deadly strike, the Army of the Rhine thrashed haphazardly in the war's first decisive weeks, a victim of reforms misdirected and changes not undertaken.

Administrative shortcomings were not compensated by command expertise. The French army's operational effectiveness depended heavily on focused direction. It received, instead, the dubious presence of a Napoleon increasingly uncertain about the conflict's wisdom, suffering ever worse pain from his kidney stones, and, at his best, no more than a dilettante of war. France's senior generals were as jealous as so many chorus girls. Peacetime emphasis on will-power and self-assertion produced no patterns of deference, nor did France have anything like the Prussian structure of corps and divisions to restrain competing personalities. Marshals Achille Bazaine and Patrice MacMahon were Napoleon's senior subordinates in the theatre. Both were ambitious. Both had well-deserved reputations as battle captains. Both were honourable and courageous men, well regarded by their colleagues. While Bazaine had been caught in the political currents following his questionable handling of the Mexican expedition, in a military context, even that fiasco suggested, at worst, that Bazaine was unsuited for independent high-level command.[12] A third marshal of France was also with the army. Jean-Baptiste Canrobert may have been the best of the lot: an old Algerian hand who had commanded with distinction in the Crimean and Italian campaigns. But Canrobert also had a sense of his ceiling, and perhaps the situation; and refused to consider any appointment above that of the VI Corps he commanded. Among the rest, Ladmirault of IV Corps and Felix Douay of VII were relative unknowns, who proved competent but limited when field-tested. Froissard of II Corps was an engineer with a high reputation as a planner and no experience in field command. The Imperial Guard's Charles Bourbaki was another senior officer with a well-earned reputation for leading from the front, but a corresponding image as less than the sharpest mind in the army.

Nevertheless, taken as a whole, the French corps commanders were no worse than their Prussian counterparts.[13] Had they been able to concentrate on getting to know their officers and imprinting their personalities on their men, the improvised French corps might

---

[11]There are many accounts of the French mobilization, and many of those are more colourful than accurate. The official *La Guerre de 1870–71. Mesures d'organisation depuis la commencement de la guerre*, pulls few punches. Cf. as well, A. Martinien, *La Guerre de 1870–71. La Mobilisation de l'Armée* (Paris, 1911).

[12]Maurice Baumont, *Bazaine; des secrets d'un maréchal (1811–1888)* (Paris, 1978), especially pp. 95 ff. and 376 ff., convincingly establishes the marshal's qualities and limitations.

[13]An opinion shared by Michael Howard, *The Franco-Prussian War* (London, 1961), p. 66.

have developed into effective units. Instead, they were constrained during the war's initial stage to do what they did most poorly: administration, and with only small, improvised personal staffs to help. The result was that their subordinates of all ranks tended to see 'the old man' at his worst rather than his best – not a promising preparation for combat.

A French corps in the summer of 1870 was typically built around three or four divisions, each with two brigades of two three-battalion regiments, a battalion of light infantry, and three artillery batteries: two of light rifled cannon and one of the new mitrailleuses. The corps commander also had at his disposal a cavalry division of four or six regiments and an artillery reserve of half a dozen or so batteries. This structure was neither significantly better nor worse than its Prussian counterpart. What it lacked in system it compensated for in flexibility. French infantry regiments at their usual maximum strength of around 2,000 men were only a little over two-thirds the size of their Prussian counterparts; French infantry companies (six in a battalion instead of four) were over a hundred men smaller – a size considered easier to control on battlefields dominated by firepower.

In the event, the speed Napoleon demanded impelled dispersion after all. Terrain for bivouacs was simply not available in one place. Railheads could not handle the train schedules required by the originally planned deployment area and the originally projected offensive timetable. By the time the trains had completed their work, five French corps were based around Metz, but the other three had concentrated a good way further south, around Belfort and Strasbourg.[14] Not until 5 August did Napoleon give each wing its own commander: Bazaine and MacMahon, respectively. Even then, the emperor limited their authority to military operations only. With the Vosges Mountains between them, the Army of the Rhine's halves had correspondingly limited possibilities of cooperating flexibly against a reasonably competent enemy.

The French, however, were showing their weak points in expected areas: in the rear and at the top. An army that regarded administration as of secondary importance could hardly expect to be perfectly supplied and reinforced from day one. An army projected as the work tool of a flexible foreign policy could hardly count on possessing specific plans for every possible strategic and operational contingency. The French army defined itself as a battle instrument, able to make good its deficiencies when the shooting started. All it needed to make things right was an enemy its men could see.

The conflict would prove to be a land war, despite France's overwhelming maritime superiority. Its navy had been constructed to measure itself with England, and was designed for global operations. In 1870, it included over 400 warships. Its fighting core was a dozen or so broadside ironclads, built in the 1860s. While inferior to the best British designs, they were exponentially better than their three unreliable counterparts that were the core of the North German Confederation's otherwise mixed bag of unarmoured wooden cruising ships, gunboats and civilian conversions.

French naval plans had been made accordingly: an aggressive campaign against merchant shipping, a close blockade of the major north German ports of Kiel and Wilhelmshaven and, ultimately, a landing of 30,000 men in Schleswig – on the relatively sheltered Baltic side. Since no navy had the material or the doctrine to mount an amphibious operation on such a scale from an open ocean against opposition, Danish participation was a necessity,

---

[14]Adriance, pp. 110 ff.

and French plans assumed 30,000 Danes, cooperating with their own landing force against local objectives like Kiel and Hamburg, then perhaps penetrating even deeper inland. The rapid and successful invasion of France, however, left Denmark unwilling to assume the risks of another war, which, in turn, left French maritime strategy in the northern theatre high and dry.

Once the transportation of French forces from North Africa was completed, both the Atlantic and the Mediterranean squadrons of the French fleet did eventually take position off the German coast, maintaining a month's worth of relatively successful blockades against German shipping. About 200 merchantmen altogether were captured, with a correspondingly crippling effect on the Confederation's overseas trade. The Hamburg–America Line went so far as to suspend transatlantic sailings altogether. British ships, by contrast, entered and left German ports and waters almost at will: the French had no desire to risk British reaction.

The combination of defeat on land and the onset of autumn weather brought the blockade's abandonment. The navy's major contribution to the rest of the war was on land, though its smaller ships did sporadically patrol the Channel and keep a weather eye open for a German fleet that, with a few exceptions, prudently and appropriately confined itself to harbour.[15]

On the Prussian side of the battle line, Moltke and Roon were living up to their army's definition of modernity. The issue of Moltke's contribution to the development of what has been called 'operational art' – the shadowy level between strategy and tactics – is best understood in two contexts.[16] One is the pragmatism that became increasingly central to Moltke's view of war during the 1860s. The other is Moltke's understanding of the relationship between war and policy. As chief of staff he accepted a sharp distinction between the two spheres. In peacetime, the army's job was to plan and prepare for the next war. It was the government's task to establish that conflict's paradigm and define its parameters.[17] When, in 1867, Bismarck peacefully concluded the Luxembourg crisis, Moltke offered only the dry comment that the minister-president's decision 'will cost us a lot of blood later'.[18] Yet, in the same context, he accepted as given Bismarck's later assurances that Austrian intervention in a future war with France need not be feared.

That kind of yin-yang symbiosis with Bismarck gave Moltke, by early 1870, a single-contingency military situation: planning a war against France. Like all of Prussia's wars, it would have to be decided quickly – even more quickly than usual. While Bismarck's diplomatic virtuosity had given Moltke a free hand operationally, his international constructions were as fragile as they were elaborate. For Moltke, the best way of ending the war quickly

---

[15]For north German naval activity, cf. Sondhaus, *Preparing for Weltpolitik*, pp. 85 ff. and Hans Otto Steinmetz, 'Im Schatten der Armee und der Grossen Politik: Eine Betrachtung zum Einsatz der preussisch-deutschen Marine im Krieg, 1870/71', *Marine Rundschau* 70 (1973), pp. 212–29. French policy and strategy are admirably presented in Theodore Ropp, *The Development of a Modern Navy: French Naval Policy. 1871–1914*, ed. S. Roberts (Annapolis, MD, 1987), pp. 22 ff. and Hans-Justus Kreker, 'Die franzoesische Marine im Kriege von 1870–71', *Marine Rundschau* 7 (1973), pp. 276–86.
[16]Michael D. Krause, 'Moltke and the Origins of the Operational Level of War' in *Generalfeldmarschall von Moltke*, pp. 141–64, is a useful introduction.
[17]Rudolf Stadelmann, *Moltke und der Staat* (Krefeld, 1950).
[18]Kessel, *Moltke*, p. 533.

was to advance on Paris, because in that direction was likely to lie the war's true objective: the French army. Paris was the heart of France and of the Second Empire: it could not be sacrificed in a strategic withdrawal that was foreign to the French way of war anyway. Engaging the French army and decisively defeating it would convince other powers, Austria, in particular, to let half-drawn swords return to the scabbards. Moltke did recognize that since the Second Empire depended so heavily on its army, defeat might generate revolution. But since Moltke believed Prussia wanted nothing from France, peace could be readily concluded with the new government. In any case, that was not part of his brief.

The next question was how best to achieve the campaign's political/military goal. Initially, Moltke expected to have about 360,000 men for his offensive, plus whatever the south Germans might provide – superior numbers, but not exactly overwhelming, especially for an attacker. His corresponding decision was to concentrate in the Rhineland/Palatinate area of Prussia. The initial centre of gravity, the *Schwerpunkt*, would be around Homburg, where two armies – in the event, a single, oversized 2nd Army – would advance in two echelons, ready to attack to its front or swing to either flank. On the right, a 1st Army of two corps would cover the 2nd's advance and be ready to act offensively against the French should an opportunity arise. A 3rd Army, concentrating somewhat further south than the other two, would advance north-west into Alsace on the left. Its strength was initially set at two Prussian corps, with a third to follow and the south German contingents adding what amounted to two or three more if they showed up. Like the 1st Army, the 3rd was to serve as a flank guard and itself engage a French flank should opportunity offer. In specific terms, Moltke planned to swing south of the French fortress of Metz, then advance on the Moselle between Lunevillle and Point à Mousson – a line of advance dictated more by logistical than operational conditions. 'There we have two railroads to the rear', he declared. A major battle should take place before reaching the river, and 'thereafter nothing can be predicted in detail'.[19]

This presentation is often cited in general works as illustrating Moltke's aphorism that no plan survives contact with the enemy. It also illustrates the chief of staff's accompanying contention that therefore the initial plan must be a good one! Moltke provided regularly updated timetables for the advance of each corps from the assembly area – detailed to a point of specifying what locations each formation would reach on a particular day. Moltke also insisted that circumstances made it necessary to regulate corps and division marches in the theatre of operations from above.[20] He allocated most of the army's cavalry to reconnaissance and screening missions, designed to keep the French in the dark regarding his movements. Even the cuirassier regiments, wearing steel breastplates and initially armed with nothing more lethal than single-shot pistols, took their turns. The lancers, or uhlans, considered before the war primarily suited to large-scale mounted charges, were sufficiently

---

[19]Moltke's plan of campaign for 1870 has been the subject of near theological exegesis. His 'Erste Aufstellung der Armee', begun in the winter of 1868–9, and most recently reworked in July 1870, is in *Moltkes Militaerische Werke* 1, vol. III, pp. 114 ff. Cf. the memo of 6 May 1870 in ibid., pp. 131 ff. The quotation is on p. 132. Among the many analyses, Bradley J. Meyer, 'The Operational Art: The Elder Moltke's Campaign Plan for the Franco-Prussian War' in *The Operational Art. Developments in the Theories of War*, eds. B. J. C. McKercher and M. Hennessy (Westport, CT, 1996), pp. 29–49; Kessel, *Moltke*, pp. 538 ff.; and Bucholz, *Moltke and the German Wars*, pp. 155 ff., stand out for perception and clarity.
[20]*Moltkes Militaerische Werke* 1, vol. III, p. 133.

ubiquitous that they gave their name to the entire German mounted arm – whose losses on patrol would be significantly heavier than those suffered in pitched battles.[21]

Moltke's schematics recognized the risks of gridlock inherent in deploying forces of the size at his disposal in a relatively small sector on a fairly narrow line of advance: the sixty or so miles between Metz and the Vosges Mountains. He also recognized the possibility that the French, if they did not strike immediately into Germany, might assume the natural defensive positions in which the region abounded, meet the Prussian attack, then counter-attack a weakened, confused enemy. Artillerymen like Hohenloe might be confident in their guns' ability to provide sufficient firepower to compensate for the shortcomings of the infantry's rifle. At the operational level, however, in 1870, Moltke put his faith in tight control of the advance for as long as possible, for the sake of immediate mutual support and cooperation against the French flanks.

Moltke's emphasis on flank operations was, in good part, a response to tactical technologies. His repeated insistence that modern small arms increased defensive capacities exponentially more than offensive ones was complemented by his growing awareness that the increased size of modern armies meant reserves could be echeloned more deeply than in previous wars, and thus shift more effectively to shore up a flank at risk. The increased range of modern weapons meant that rifles and artillery could engage an outflanking move from its inception. For optimal success, flank attacks were best undertaken from outside the zone of frontal engagement, and in significant strength – a corps at least.[22]

Putting together the specific features of the theatre of operations, and Moltke's general concepts of the effect of technology on tactics, it is easy to see why the chief of staff emphasized control of the campaign's initial stages. Control was the best available measure against the development of something like a continuous front, with Prussia's three armies acting on their own initiatives, in response to specific situations, and pushing the French back steadily enough – but too slowly to fulfil the war's policy objectives.

Moltke's operational plan correspondingly depended on the railroads. Where, in 1866, he had improvised existing lines and based his plan on the extrinsic deployment that resulted, his concern from 1867 to 1870 was to funnel as many men and horses as possible into a relatively small area on Prussia's western border as quickly as possible. That was easier said than done – not least because the patterns of railway construction in Germany had, for thirty years, clearly favoured north–south lines as offering commercial advantages obvious enough to overcome enduring southern particularism in railway matters.[23]

At the heart of the restructuring was the railway section of the general staff. It had passed its first test in 1866 on an ad hoc basis. After the war, its establishment was increased and its position enhanced – to a point where officers in the planning sections at times complained that the railway tail was wagging the operational dog. But newly promoted Colonel Baron Hermann Wartensleben-Carow, and his 1868 successor, Major Karl von Brandenstein, understood how to work with a railroad system that included over fifty separate lines, some public, some private and others a mixture of the two. In November 1867, corps headquarters received detailed mobilization instructions, providing for the mobilization and despatch

---

[21]Hermann Kunz, *Die deutsche Reiterei in den Schlachten und Gefechten des Krieges von 1870/1871* (Berlin, 1895), pp. 369 ff., is a good overview of the cavalry's wartime performance.
[22]'Instructions for Large Unit Commanders', pp. 214 ff.
[23]Mitchell, p. 65.

of each unit in the corps. A military transportation plan established rail schedules for the entire army. Three permanent line commands were created, with ten more to be added in wartime: one for each major east–west rail route in the North German Confederation, to coordinate movement, maintenance and administration of specific rail networks during mobilization. Integrating general staff officers with civilian administrators and technicians, they heralded the synergy of bureaucracy and technology that, for the next century, defined the nature of war. The new organization removed the major obstacle to rapid long-distance troop movement: using the tracks of several companies with different ownership structures in the same operation. In case of war, the civilian authorities would work under military command. Another harbinger of total war was the complete suspension of civilian traffic during mobilization. Never before had a government asserted the power to control the movement of its citizens in such detail as a matter of routine.

Tested in a November 1867 war game, the military transport plan required thirty-two days to move the Prussian field army into its designated zone of operations in the west. A year later, that time had been reduced to twenty-four days. By 1870, it was twenty days. As the declining rate of improvement suggests, fine-tuning was becoming increasingly important. Enough slack must remain in the schedule to enable the process to continue without disruption. Prussian troop trains did not move particularly rapidly. In some cases, at least during the mobilization of 1870, it was possible for men to jump out of the train, grab a loaf of bread or a can of coffee from civilian bystanders and catch up with their assigned boxcar – all without attracting serious attention from the NCOs. What was important was that the trains moved systematically, reached their destinations predictably and unloaded in safety.[24]

Increasingly, Moltke accepted the railway section's recommendation that it was preferable to concentrate at the principal railheads – behind the Rhine if necessary – and temporarily sacrifice German territory rather than risk disruption or disorder in unloading and returning the trains.[25] Moltke accepted as well the accompanying argument that the army should move in echelons rather than risk straining a rail network that, even under the diplomatic conditions of the late 1860s, did not add lines or tracks for strategic reasons. No fewer than seven of the North German Confederation's twenty-seven active divisions remained behind when the first trains rolled west in 1870. One of them was assigned the mission of defending the western coast against any French attempts to use their superior navy to support amphibious operations. The other six – I, II and VI Corps – were left in their peacetime districts, not for security reasons vis-à-vis Austria – though Moltke had considered that issue – but because moving them immediately from West Prussia, Pomerania and Silesia risked overstraining the carrying capacities of the railroads further west. Given the actual speed with which they were eventually moved to France, those three corps might be called a second strategic echelon. Moltke, however, would have preferred to have them closer at hand than the specialists' timetables allowed.[26]

---

[24]Cf. Wolfgang Petter, 'Die Logistik des deutschen Heeres im deutsch-franzoesischen Krieg von 1870–71' in *Die Bedeutung der Logistik fuer die militaerische Fuehrung von der Antike bis in die Neuzeit*, ed. *Militaergeschichtliches Forschungsamt* (Bonn, 1986), pp. 109–33; Rahne, pp. 52 ff.; and Bucholz, *War Planning*, pp. 48 ff.
[25]Kessel, *Moltke*, p. 548.
[26]Ibid., pp. 537–8.

The nature of the Prussian mobilization system helped to explain the refusal of the general staff and the war ministry to react to reports that the French were gaining the initiative by transporting reservists from Algeria or moving supplies from one point in eastern France to another. When the order for mobilization was issued, the Prussians had no fewer than six organized rail routes, each able to handle two or three corps in succession: eighteen trains a day over double-track lines, twelve on single-track routes. Beginning on 15 July, over 1,500 trains reached their destinations, discharged their cargoes and, not least, turned round and went back for another load. By 3 August, the nineteenth day of mobilization, the field force was ready to advance. And a mere lieutenant-colonel had directed the whole process: Freiherr Karl von Brandenstein, the first third-generation general staff officer who had made his military career with the railroads. Moltke trusted him implicitly. Roon complained that, as war minister he had too little to do because of the youngsters! Even when allowances are made for hyperbole, the mobilization and concentration of the Prussian army in 1870 marked the beginning of a new era of war making, with administrative preparation and peacetime planning at least as important as operational virtuosity. But when it was all over, sighs of relief went up from a good many desks.[27]

The south Germans had three lines of their own, running from Augsburg, Noerdlingen and Wuerzburg to the southern sector of Moltke's designated zone of concentration. The success of those three states in keeping pace with the Prussian concentration, over rail-roads with a generally lower carrying capacity and without the elaborate Prussian staff organization supporting the operation, should not be dismissed in a footnote. It demonstrates the significant improvement in the operational effectiveness of all three armies – and suggests as well that the military establishments of Baden, Bavaria and Wuerttemberg were anxious to demonstrate that they were more than mere spear-carriers for their larger ally across the Main.[28]

Ironically, just as the south German contingents demonstrated that they could keep pace with Prussia, at least in the early stages of mobilization and concentration, Moltke's operational plans encountered an unexpected snag. The logistical shortcomings of the Koeniggraetz campaign had not gone unnoticed by Moltke and his subordinates. After the war, Brigadier General Albrecht von Stosch, the 2nd Army's chief quartermaster in 1866, was appointed to overhaul the military economy department. Stosch was as close to a Renaissance professional as was possible in the context of the Prussian army's development in the nineteenth century, with a breadth of administrative talent that eventually made him an effective minister of the new German navy. He also believed in militarizing management as far as possible. In contrast to Wartensleben, he sought to remove civilian officials and contractors from the supply system. Too many of his military appointments were officers partially disabled by wounds or illness, with no other obvious qualifications

---

[27]The most detailed account is Gustav Lehmann, *Die Mobilmachung von 1870* (Berlin, 1905). Rahne, pp. 59 ff., is a good modern overview. Cf. Conrad von Hugo, 'Carl von Brandenstein, Chef des Feldeisenbahnwesens und engster Mitarbeiter Moltkes 1870–71', *Wehrwissenschaftliche Rundschau* 14 (1964), pp. 676–84.

[28]L. Sukstorf, *Die Problematik der Logistik im deutschen Heer waehrend des deutsch-franzoesischen Krieges 1870/71* (Frankfurt, 1994), pp. 64 ff., surveys the south German mobilizations and concentrations. Cf. K. Thoma, 'Die Eisenbahntransporte fuer Mobilmachung und Aufmarsch der K. Bayerischen Armee 1870' in *Darstellungen aus der Bayerischen Kriegs-und Heeresgeschichte* 5, ed. K. B. Kriegsarchiv (Munich, 1896), pp. 151–81.

as administrators. Too many of the civilians responded by what one authority calls 'inner emigration', a pattern of working to rule that boded ill in any emergency situation.[29]

Stosch did much to improve the organization of the army's logistics. Instead of moving the bulk of the army's provisions by rail from the interior of Germany, as had been the case in 1866, he established a general principle of obtaining supplies locally, in 'enemy country', by requisition and purchase. Even with a reduced burden of food and forage, however, the problem of transportation remained. Since wagons and draught horses of each corps were in its later rail echelons, supplies delivered to railheads could initially be distributed only on an improvised basis. The more troops that assembled in the zone of concentration, the less possible it was to meet their needs from local resources. Once the advance began, matters grew worse, as supply trains clogged roads and obstructed junctions – problems far beyond the capacity of the relatively few military police to resolve. Empty wagons were arguably more of a problem than the loaded ones that received what priorities there were. Too often, instead of returning promptly to the depots established along the rail lines, supply columns found themselves diverted to the least desirable routes: roads that were little more than local trails, which broke down quickly under the pounding of heavy wheeled traffic. The 3rd Army lagged well behind Moltke's original schedule, in part because of the difficulties posed by the poorly organized supply trains of its two Bavarian corps, but even more because of the relative scarcity of any kinds of secondary roads along its axis of advance.[30]

Since 1859, the Prussian army had possessed specialized 'railroad detachments', responsible for minor repairs and emergency construction. A front-loaded order of battle, however, had no room for equivalent road-maintenance formations. The army's pioneers, at the ratio of a battalion for each corps, could hardly be spared for rear-echelon duty, and, in any case, saw themselves as combat troops. Converting Landwehr battalions to labourers in uniform still carried with it significant political risks. Instead, the rear echelons muddled through.[31]

II

That logistically determined delay would produce immediate operational consequences, exacerbated by command issues at the highest levels. Moltke's three army chiefs were what amounted to 'natural' choices. Crown Prince Frederick and Prince Frederick Charles had led field armies in 1866. Neither had shown particular inspiration; neither had demonstrated the kind of incapacity that made their sidetracking in this war a clear necessity. Both their armies – initially five corps and seven corps respectively – were too large to be commanded effectively by a 'good ordinary general'. But somewhat like the Union's Army of the Potomac when it was reorganized after Gettysburg, the Prussian army had no obvious

---

[29]For Stosch's achievements, see Petter, 'Logistik', pp. 115 ff.

[30]See, particularly, Sukstorf, pp. 114 ff., and, for details, 'Truppenfahrzeuge, Kolonnen und Trains bei den Bewegungen der I. und der II. Deutschen Armee bis zu den Schlachten westlich Metz', Kriegsgeschichtliche Einzelschriften 17, ed. Grosser Generalstab (Berlin, 1895).

[31]H. Kaehne, Geschichte des Koeniglich Preussischen Garde-Train-Battalions (Berlin, 1903), pp. 129 ff., tells one unit-level story. Replacing horses was a particular problem, given the weight of German vehicles and the corresponding preference for two- or four-horse teams, as opposed to the six draught animals favoured by both sides in the American Civil War.

candidates at corps levels for higher command, and Moltke considered it preferable to have fewer armies than more unknown quantities.

For that reason, the remaining army command went, virtually by default, to Karl von Steinmetz. In his seventies, he was long in the tooth for field service. He was showing increasing signs of substituting temper for judgment – including recent marriage to a girl of eighteen, which had set tongues wagging in an officer corps still small enough to mind each other's business.[32] But Steinmetz had been the best of the corps commanders in 1866, showing solid tactical skill at Nachod; and with three corps, VII and VIII in the first wave and I scheduled to arrive later from Pomerania, his army was the smallest. It seemed a reasonable risk.

Moltke and a royal headquarters that, as in 1866, amounted to the effective government of Prussia, marched with Frederick Charles's 2nd Army – not least to keep an immediate eye on him. That was a poor recommendation for a man with such a crucial mission, but Frederick Charles, too, held his particular appointment by default. No one except the crown prince, heir to Prussia's throne, had the standing to exercise unchallenged authority over the south German contingents that made up half of the 3rd Army. Crown Prince Frederick's chief of staff was, moreover, among the better horses in Moltke's stable. Karl von Blumenthal was as competent as he was acerbic. He had been with Frederick in two previous campaigns; the crown prince trusted him and was willing to take his advice almost without question. Again, by default, it was the team best suited to operate away from Moltke's direct supervision.

Moltke's may not have been an optimal senior command system, but the revised French deployment seemed to minimize its disadvantages. Moltke's final modified plan was for the 1st and the 2nd Armies, under his direct command, to hold the French in place on the Saar, while the 3rd Army dealt with MacMahon's three corps to the south in Alsace. The crown prince would then swing north against the now-exposed French left flank. It seemed simple enough. But as Blumenthal evaluated the logistic situation, he insisted that the 3rd Army could not meet Moltke's 30 July deadline for the initial advance. Nor, Blumenthal declared, was he willing to engage three French corps with only two Prussian ones. He insisted on having VI Corps in his order of battle before going forward. While he did not exactly dismiss the Bavarians as a liability, he came sufficiently close that it required a special envoy from Moltke himself to restore allied harmony and get Blumenthal, who was supported up to the hilt by the crown prince, to agree to a compromise: an advance postponed until 4 August to sort out the rear echelons, but made without VI Corps.[33]

If Blumenthal was cautious, Moltke's 1st Army jumped the starting gun because of its commander's dreams of glory. Karl von Steinmetz was a general of the old Prussian school – which is to say, of no school at all. He neither understood nor sympathized with Moltke's strategic concepts. For Steinmetz, anything more complex than a kick to the groin was useless in war. An enemy to the front was an enemy to be attacked. Instead of holding back, as the general plan intended, Steinmetz ordered his VII and VIII Corps south, towards Saarbruecken and the nearest large body of uniformed Frenchmen.

---

[32]Paul Bronsart von Schellendorf, *Geheimes Kriegstagebuch 1870–1871*, ed. P. Rassow (Bonn, 1954), p. 70. Bronsart was chief of Moltke's operations section.

[33]Cf. Julius Verdy du Vernois, *With the Royal Headquarters in 1870–71*, ed. Capt. W. H. James (London, 1897), pp. 45 ff.; Blumenthal, pp. 84 ff.; and the analysis in 'Moltke in der Vorbereitung und Durchfuehrung der Operationen', *Kriegsgeschichtliche Einzelschriften* 36, ed. Grosser Generalstab (Berlin, 1905), pp. 119 ff.

Steinmetz's initiative had its first consequences on 6 August, around the border village of Spicheren. Prussian cavalry patrols mistakenly reported a French retreat. Steinmetz responded by launching a pursuit that ran into a buzz-saw. A single French corps held the high ground of Spicheren against growing odds. But it was II Corps, commanded by Froissard, the engineer who proved the right general for the right place. Well-sited French positions and well-timed French counter-attacks frustrated what amounted to increasingly bull-headed Prussian determination, at all levels, to carry the day by raw courage and force of numbers. Steinmetz's Rhinelanders and Westphalians had played relatively undistinguished roles in 1866. Opinion in the lower-numbered corps from the kingdom's eastern marches counted the westerners as a cut below top quality, and their senior officers, at least, were determined to prove otherwise. One division commander even sent a cavalry regiment charging in column up a sunken road, running uphill at a steep angle! Though at some points it came to bayonets and rifle butts, in general, the chassepot rifle proved itself master of the field, inflicting most of the 4,500 Prussian casualties. But the French high command sent no reinforcements. Nor did nearby French generals, unlike their Prussian German counterparts, march to the sound of the guns. As superior numbers began working around their flanks, at dusk, the baffled, frustrated French drew off, exhausted and angry at a local success that somehow had turned to a defeat.[34]

On the same day, the German 3rd Army encountered another isolated French corps around the Alsatian villages of Froeschweiller and Woerth. Two days earlier, on 4 August, three of the crown prince's corps had crushed an isolated French division around the border town of Wissembourg. The taste of victory – an allied victory won by Prussian and Bavarian troops side by side – had obscured the effect of French rifle fire on attack formations whose commanders, inspired by a desire to advance as quickly as possible, mixed company columns, 250-man oblong masses, with skirmish lines so thick that, in some cases, the men were advancing virtually shoulder to shoulder in eighteenth-century fashion. And the apparent success of the infantry attacks had, in turn, obscured the central role of the German guns in silencing their French counterparts and checkmating the chassepots.[35]

MacMahon did not miss the points, but nevertheless believed the Germans could be stopped. He concentrated the three remaining divisions of his 1st Corps at Froeschweiller and summoned the other two corps under his command, the 5th and the 7th, to move up in support. Both took their time – so much so that, on 6 August, MacMahon was to fight an isolated battle: one corps against four. MacMahon's decision to stand was, nevertheless, a reasonably sound one – especially since his strategic alternative was to abandon both Alsace and the initiative to the Germans. MacMahon was an old combat hand, and 1st Corps included some of the French army's best fighting men. Its six regiments of Zouaves and Turcos (*tirailleurs algeriens*) were famous as shock troops. Most of the line regiments had been transferred from Algeria and were correspondingly field-experienced.

---

[34]For Spicheren, see Howard, pp. 89 ff. and the brief analysis by Ronald Zinz, *La bataille de Spicheren, 6 août 1870* (Annecy-le-Vieux, 2001); for the German perspective, see Georg Cardinal von Widdern, *Kritische Tage*, vol. III, *Die Befehlsfuehrung am Spicheren und am Tage darauf. 6. und 7. August 1870* (Berlin, 1900); and for the French, see Frossard's *Rapport sur les operations du deuxième corps de l'armée du Rhin dans la campagne de 1870* (Paris, 1871), pp. 43 ff.

[35]Howard, pp. 101 ff. Cf. Ernst von Hoffbauer, *Die deutsche Artillerie in den Schlachten und Treffen der deutsch-franzoesischen Krieges*, vol. I, *Das Treffen von Weissenburg* (Berlin, 1876).

A rainstorm on the night of 5/6 August led to unauthorized campfires, which disclosed the French main positions. It produced high levels of straggling, particularly as men from Africa drifted away from their bivouacs to seek shelter from the raw cold to which they were unaccustomed.

That kind of sergeant major's nightmare, however, was characteristic of the imperial army. When the bugles sounded the call to arms at dawn, MacMahon's ranks were reasonably complete. Their ground was good, with a shallow river to the front acting as a moat for a network of woods and broken ground, which, in turn, channelled movement towards the open slopes for the wine grapes that supported the four small villages running along the line of Froeschweiller ridge. In a way, the terrain resembled a greener version of Algeria, and colonels and captains fresh from North Africa knew how to take advantage of every metre.

Froissard's handling of Spicheren and MacMahon's deployment at Froeschweiller/Woerth are frequently used to support one of the major erroneous generalizations about the campaign of 1870: that the French army abandoned its previous and traditional offensive tactics based on skirmishers and assault columns for a relatively static defensive system based on infantry fire and regimental-level counter-attacks. The introduction of the chasse-pot and the experiments conducted at manoeuvre camps during the 1860s did significantly diminish confidence in the all-out mass bayonet charge in the fashion of Magenta and Solferino. But a fundamental principle of the Second Empire's way of war was that there were no fundamental principles. The revised infantry drill regulations issued in 1869 offered no firm doctrinal guides. The absence of permanent higher headquarters left regimental commanders most of the everyday control over training, and the colonels were, by and large, pragmatists. The bayonet charges of 1859 had been a response to a particular circumstance: the French had muskets and the Austrians had rifles. In 1870, the Prussians had rifles and the French had better ones. It made corresponding tactical sense to pick positions with a good field of fire, and then give the Prussians a chance to defeat themselves.[36]

Neither Blumenthal nor the crown prince was planning for a fight that day. The battle began with a series of exchanges between outposts and detachments.[37] A Bavarian corps went forward to support what its commander thought was an attack of the Prussians on his flank. Then the artillery, first of XI, then of V Corps, took a hand. The guns did enough visible damage, especially to their French counterparts, that the infantry COs sent their men forward into French rifle fire and French counter-attacks that, between 10 a.m. and noon, held the Prussians in place with increasingly heavy losses.

Frederick initially attempted to break off the action. Instead, V Corps's commander, Lieutenant-General Hugo von Kirchbach, informed the crown prince that withdrawal was presently impossible. Kirchbach, contrary to the stereotyped image of the machine-like Prussian, would have fitted well in the Army of Northern Virginia. He had won Prussia's highest decoration for valour, the *Pour le Mérite*, in 1866, commanding a division of V Corps from the front. He had been badly wounded in the shoulder at Wissembourg, again doing a colonel's job at short range, and was still unable to mount a horse. Instead,

---

[36]Holmes, pp. 208 ff., covers the development of French infantry tactical practice before 1870.

[37]For Woerth, or Froeschwiller, as the French call it, cf. Howard, pp. 99 ff., for the overview. Hermann Kunz, *Die Schlacht bei Woerth am 6. August 1870* (Berlin, 1908); Guillame A. Bonnal, *Froeschwiller* (Paris, 1899); and, more recently, Victor Moritz, *Froeschwiller, 6 août 1870* (Strasbourg, 1970), provide the details and war stories.

he rode a wagon to the field, then walked forward, briefly considered the situation, and committed his second division.

Confronting a *fait accompli*, Crown Prince Frederick and his chief of staff came forward and took charge. The two Bavarian corps, by then seeking to flank the French position from the right, made heavy going of the broken, wooded ground and the numerous fast-flowing streams in their sector. The crown prince, normally the soul of discretion, finally sent the Bavarian attaché at his headquarters to warn his countrymen against abandoning their allies or disgracing themselves.[38] The principal result was to increase the casualties inflicted by the Zouaves on the Bavarians' front – the best bush fighters in Europe, living up in full to their reputation that day, albeit at the price of heavy casualties, keeping the Bavarians at bay for as long as it mattered by rapid fire mixed with local counter-attacks.

On the other flank, events took a different course, for reasons arguably neither the French nor the Prussians expected. The Prussian corps assigned to the 3rd Army had been determined by railroad layouts. Yet had it been possible to select two corps for a secondary theatre, V and XI were likely to head most of those lists of expendables all armies deny maintaining. At the core of XI Corps, cynics might mutter, were the former armed forces of the Thuringian 'dwarf states' so bitingly satirized in Thackeray's *Vanity Fair*: battalions glued together like toothpicks, with a few 'old Prussian' regiments as 'corset stays', plagued by heavy straggling even at this early stage of the campaign. The V Corps had kept its ranks well, even though many of its men were marching barefoot, their new and ill-fitting army boots sucked off as dirt roads turned to mud. But the corps was recruited in the province of Posen, and its ranks contained a high number of Poles – about 15 per cent. In contrast to the Russian and Austrian armies, who considered their respective Polish soldiers and formations as highly strung, 'nervy' and prone to 'charge like hell – both ways', the Prussian army used 'stupid polack' almost as a single word. Discipline in V Corps was likely to be enforced with a fist, a boot or imaginative verbal abuse; its suicide rate stood consistently high in the army averages.[39] German soldiers described their Polish squad mates as dishonest, dirty, fond of strong drink and prone to brawling.

This was not promising material, on the face of it, for a frontal assault over open ground against the best rifle in Europe, in the hands of experienced men. But the Poles and the central Germans kept moving, answering the bugles while they sounded, following the officers as long as they survived, beating off counter-attacks, rallying, then coming again. Frederick, no mean judge of fighting men, would later call V Corps the core of his army.[40] And, as its infantry bled on the slopes in front of Froeschweiller, the Prussian artillery discovered how to do its share of the day's work. With the last of his infantry committed, the commanding general of V Corps, almost by default, turned to his guns as a tactical reserve. Over a dozen batteries formed the initial Prussian gun line. They were joined by the six-pounders and four-pounders of XI Corps, coming up on the left, taking position

---

[38]Frederick III, *The War Diary of the Emperor Frederick III, 1870–1871*, tr. and ed. A. R. Allinson (reprinted, New York, 1988), p. 36.

[39]In 1895, for example, V Corps was second at 8.87 per 1,000; VI Corps stood sixth of sixteen at 8.17. 'Zur Selbstmordsterblichkeit in der Preussischen Armee', *Militaerwochenblatt* 9 (1896) and Kuehlich, p. 94. Kuehlich also speaks of a 'good, sometimes even warm' relationship between the army's Poles and Germans. One wonders how he would describe a hostile one.

[40]Frederick III, *War Diary*, p. 109.

anywhere they could find a place in a firing line whose ominous power became plain as the morning wore on.

The Prussian advantage was a matter of organization and fuses. French artillery doctrine expected the divisional batteries to do most of the work, with the corps artillery employed only briefly, and at decisive moments.[41] As had been the case in battle after battle during the American Civil War, that decisive moment never came. Instead, MacMahon's reserve artillery was engaged by batteries at best, leaving the Prussians free to concentrate as many as a hundred guns at a time on individual French batteries, which, one after another, were overpowered, silenced or forced to change positions. As more and more French guns went out of action, Prussian gunners turned on French infantry positions.

Whether shrapnel or common shell, black-powder rounds were a weapon of attrition, with limited destructive capacity. Nor, as previously mentioned, did a breech-loading gun on a fixed carriage have a faster rate of fire than a muzzle-loader, particularly as crew fatigue set in. What the Prussian guns did have were reliable percussion fuses. Improved since 1866, these impact rounds could be neutralized if they landed in soft mud. They could not deliver the spectacular airbursts still beloved by directors of movies set on nineteenth-century battlefields. But most of the time, they exploded where they struck. The days when infantrymen would trust the gunners to fire over their heads in direct support were decades in the future. But by sheer weight of metal, the Prussian guns began forcing the French infantry out of one position after another. With the Bavarians closing on their left as the Prussians grappled with their right and centre, by mid-afternoon the French were compressed into a mile-square killing zone, every yard of it under enemy artillery.[42] The corps was able to extricate itself only by a series of suicidally desperate improvisations. A brigade and then a division of heavy cavalry, by brigades, were thrown in over broken ground to cover the withdrawal of part of MacMahon's infantry. Since the introduction of firearms, that mission had never been understood as anything but a gesture of desperation: glory purchased at the price of casualties. What was significant is that the Prussians were barely discomfited; the horsemen were destroyed by infantry that found it unnecessary to form squares, or do much of anything else, even though shaken and disorganized by a day's hard fighting.

The Algerian professional soldiers of the 2nd *Tirailleurs* bought the main body more time in a rearguard fight to the finish, losing over 2,100 men, including more than 700 prisoners – most taken, according to German accounts, with empty cartridge pouches. The regiment would earn a record number of *Légions d'honneur* that day, and the citations combine for a record of heroism seldom matched in any war. The Turcos and the Zouaves, indeed, had proven so effective that German rumour and German propaganda cranked out a seemingly endless supply of atrocity stories, varied with lurid denunciations of the French for employing 'black savages' in a civilized war. The Zouaves, in fact, were European, at this stage, mostly French volunteers, and the Germans were often mistaken in their interpretation of a deep suntan. Nevertheless, the stereotypes – positive and negative – of the African soldier would survive two world wars. French force structures would include increasing numbers of Africans and treat them as élite shock troops. German cultural and military mythologies

---

[41]For details, see Thoumas, vol. II, pp. 125 ff.

[42]For the role of the artillery, see Otto Leo, *Die deutsche Artillerie*, vol. II, *Woerth* (Berlin, 1876), *passim*.

would insist on the 'Black disgrace' (*Schwarze Schande*) of using Africans in European warfare, and periodically emphasize disapproval by shooting captured tirailleurs out of hand.[43]

The war's opening rounds offered little to choose tactically between the performances of the opposing forces. MacMahon's corps lost around 6,000, killed and wounded, but inflicted almost twice as many casualties on a 3rd Army that was so shaken it took five days to advance thirty miles. It was the wider implication of the engagements that mattered. They were not triumphs of military aesthetics. The Germans were 'winning ugly', by a process of getting stuck into their enemy virtually at random, then seizing hold and turning him the proverbial every way but loose. Steinmetz, Kirchbach and a dozen lower-ranking officers were in positions to be relieved for insubordination; it required two sharp letters from the king himself before Steinmetz held his tongue, albeit temporarily, about Moltke's shortcomings.[44]

But the German generals were responding, however clumsily, to Montrose's toast: 'He either fears his fate too much/Or his desserts are small/That dares not put it to the touch/To win or lose it all'. They were also doing what the French had been expected to do. These were the kind of first battles the French army was supposed to win – and win convincingly enough to influence and intimidate neutrals as well as enemies. As late as 20 July, Beust discussed the possibility of a French army, 300,000 strong, standing on Austria's border within a week, and said such a force could bring the dual monarchy into the war whether or not it was pledged to do so.[45] Instead, Spicheren and Froeschweiller/Woerth ended any French hopes of support from an Austria seeking revenge for Koeniggraetz, or from an Italy hoping to profit by mounting a French bandwagon.

Rather than risk launching a counter-attack to recapture the operational initiative, Napoleon, sick and dispirited, ordered a general retreat. An obvious and militarily sensible option would have been to have the five corps around Metz fall back to the south and join the three corps retreating from Alsace. Thus concentrated, the French could threaten with reasonable confidence any German advance into the heart of their country.[46] Moltke gave them three days to do it when he eschewed an immediate pursuit in order to bring royal headquarters forward and give his own shaken and entangled forces time to recover their footing. Such a movement, however, would also throw the country's increasingly volatile capital on to its own resources. In Paris, press and parliament were already calling for a return to 1792 and the arming of the people for a war to the finish. Nor was that an isolated manifestation of confusion and disaffection in the rapidly eroding empire.[47]

Another military alternative involved trading space for time by bringing both wings of the Army of the Rhine back to the fortified camp of Châlons to join the second-line forces assembling there. But choosing that option also meant leaving large amounts of French territory open to the enemy. A strong government could have taken either risk. A weak one, getting weaker by the day as the emperor's health declined, and depending on military

[43]See the impressive analysis by Christian Koller, *'Von Wilden aller Rassen niedergemetzelt.' Die Diskussion um die Verwendung von Kolonialtruppen in Europa zwischen Rassismus, Kolonial-und Militaerpolitik (1914–1930)* (Stuttgart, 2001).

[44]Kessel, *Moltke*, pp. 552–3.

[45]Oncken, vol. III, pp. 464–5 and Potthoff, p. 370.

[46]Adriance, p. 128.

[47]Bertrand Taille, *Citizenship and Wars: France in Turmoil, 1870–71* (London, 2001).

victories for political stability, instead ordered a withdrawal north-westward, to the fortress of Metz.[48]

From the French side of the line, holding Metz was, in principle, a necessary prerequisite for any successful counter-attack. In reality, the city held the promise of becoming more death trap than *point d'appui*. Instead of marching to join Bazaine as initially ordered, MacMahon had on his own responsibility withdrawn to Châlons – the first position in his sector he believed possible to hold without facing disaster, but well out of operational touch with Metz. Both retreats strained the French army at its vulnerable points: staff work and administration. With routes of march haphazardly assigned, corps and divisions became entangled. Supplies arrived with exasperating inconsistency. Constant rain added to the men's misery. Straggling increased. The circumstances were certainly enough to discourage recent conscripts and recalled reservists. But the old soldiers who might silence the newcomers with the French equivalent of 'it all counts for twenty' were themselves silent. 'An inert crowd', observed one officer, '... scarcely moving even if you kicked them, grumbling at being disturbed in their weary sleep'.[49] Pre-war neglect of tempering the army's cutting edge in favour of redefining its nature had given France too many men who were neither patriotic warriors nor professional soldiers, but armed civilians, mortally discouraged by a month's adversity.

Their Prussian opponents did not look much better. Uniforms grew ragged and boots wore out. Beards sprouted on men once clean-shaven. The infantry was restricted in its movements by the few paved roads. Guns bogged in the mud. Supply wagons lagged behind the men and horses they were supposed to feed. The cavalry, untrained in and unaccustomed to that kind of steady outpost work, had constant difficulty maintaining contact with the French. Where, in 1866, the Prussian army had held its cavalry divisions back as a reserve force, in 1870, all six of the divisions organized on mobilization were thrown forward to screen and scout for the main armies. But almost half the regiments assigned to them were heavy cavalry, whose training was almost entirely in battlefield shock. Not until 10 August did Moltke have enough information from various lost patrols of bedraggled troopers to be certain that the French were retiring in two different directions: towards Metz and Châlons.[50]

He reacted to dispersion by concentration, issuing orders designed to bring his three armies abreast of each other along the Moselle: a sledgehammer with a front of no more than forty miles, its striking power further enhanced as the railroads brought up the three Prussian corps of the second wave. Moltke gave his subordinates and their staffs two days to sort out the confusion in their rear echelons, and then repeated his orders for an advance. Beginning on 12 August, the three German armies were to go forward in line, swing first to the south of Metz, then drive north-west against the French around the fortress.[51]

---

[48]Froissard, p. 142, claimed credit for first originating the idea of falling back on Metz. No one else seriously challenged his claim to that dubious honour.

[49]Maurice d'Irisson d'Herisson, *Journal of a Staff Officer during the Siege of Paris* (London, 1885) p. 18. An indication of how low morale had sunk is that this supercilious commentator did not meet with an 'accident' while putting the boot in.

[50]Gerhard von Pelet-Narbonne, *Die Reiterei der ersten und zweiten deutschen Armee in den Tagen vom 7. bis 15. August 1870* (Berlin, 1899).

[51]*MMK* 1, vol. III, pp. 207 ff. Cf. Verdy, pp. 61–2; Bronsart, pp. 37 ff.; and Kessel, *Moltke*, pp. 552 ff.

The 3rd Army took its time pushing forward against no serious opposition, reaching Nancy only on 14 August. On 13 August, however, Moltke learned that the French had not yet crossed the Moselle. He modified his dispositions accordingly, ordering the 2nd and 3rd Armies to swing north while Steinmetz attracted the French attention without so threatening them that they retreated faster than the Germans could follow. It was not an impossible assignment, but it required a good deal more 'fingertip feel' than Steinmetz had possessed even as a much younger man. Now, stung by Moltke's blunt rebuking of his impetuosity at Spicheren, he delayed his advance. Then he lost a day by allowing one of his brigadiers to pick a fight with elements of the French rearguard that drew in all three of his corps, ended in a stalemate and left Moltke wondering whether the French might follow up with a general counter-attack.

The chief of staff was correspondingly relieved when, on the morning of 15 August, his armies faced nothing more formidable than the detritus of an abandoned battlefield and saw nothing more dangerous than heavy dust clouds from the far side of Metz. Moltke responded by ordering an advance that amounted to a general pursuit, sending the 2nd Army towards Verdun with the objective of catching Bazaine on the march. The decision, taken without knowledge of the growing breakdown of command and discipline in Bazaine's ranks, reflected his continuing respect for the French army's reputation for hard marches and quick recoveries. Frederick Charles acted on that same principle – only he sent three of his corps west, instead of north as ordered, in an effort to re-establish contact with an enemy the prince believed so nearly out of fighting range that he established twenty-five miles as the next day's march norm.[52]

In fact, the only Frenchmen beyond Prussia's grasp were those escorting Napoleon, who, on 16 August, departed for Châlons, where a new army was forming around MacMahon's three corps. He left Bazaine with the understanding that the marshal was to continue retreating to Verdun as soon as possible and not compromise the army.[53] Neither the emperor nor his marshal, however, had made any preparations for withdrawing over 170,000 men through a walled fortress city, or for marching them along the tangled network of small roads in the surrounding countryside, or for clearing the main route west of the civilian refugee traffic that, unhindered and unregulated, blocked the road at every turn.

Nor did anyone have any idea where the Prussians were, or where they might be going. The corps cavalry divisions, theoretically responsible for screening and reconnaissance, instead kept close to the infantry bivouacs. The army's three regiments of *chasseurs d'Afrique*, scouts and patrollers without parallel, with years of experience in the Algerian *bled*, had been massed in a single division as part of the cavalry reserve. When two regiments were finally detached from that unnatural assignment, it was to escort the emperor on the first stage of his journey. When Bazaine, who himself had been wounded in the shoulder on 14 August, decided to take another morning to sort out his ranks, feed his men a hot meal and give the situation time to develop, it was little wonder that he remained undisturbed by reports on Prussian movements. With most of his five corps,

---

[52]Cf. Howard, p. 139 *passim* for the narrative; Verdy, pp. 69 ff. and *Friedrich Karl*, vol. II, p. 172, for the immediate decisions; and Fritz Hoenig, *Dokumentarisch-Kritisch Darstellung der Strategie fuer die Schlacht von Vionville-Mars-la-Tour* (Berlin, 1899), for the controversies that grew up around them.

[53]*Procès Bazaine*, pp. 159 ff.

and almost 350 guns and mitrailleuses, more or less in position on the plateau west of Metz, there seemed little to worry about in any case.[54]

This time, 'System D' was not enough. Around 9 a.m. on 16 August, German shells began bursting in the camps of a French cavalry division, caught with its horses on picket lines. They were followed by the infantry of III Prussian Corps, under Konstantin von Alvensleben.[55] Prussia's system of territorial recruiting gave each of its corps an identity; III Corps had an attitude as well. Most of its men were from Brandenburg – not yet the built-up conurbation of 1914, but the Mark, the network of estates, villages and towns immortalized by Theodor Fontane, its sons leavened by factory workers, shopkeepers and corner-boys from a Berlin that already prided itself on *Schnauze*. With most of its units stationed around the capital in peacetime, III Corps was accustomed to working together, and against its historic rival, the Prussian Guard. The Guard might show to advantage on the drill ground; and its elegant uniforms might impress the girls at the weekend. But the men of III Corps prided themselves on their field skills as skirmishers and marksmen – prided themselves, too, on never giving up, whether the weapons were belt buckles and beer mugs in a *Gasthaus* brawl, or something more lethal.

At first, Alvensleben believed he faced only a rearguard, and had no hesitation in committing his corps to cut off as many French stragglers as possible. Instead, almost at once, his two divisions found themselves with their hands in a wasps' nest, engaged with three corps' worth of bloody-minded Frenchmen, determined to show they could fight when their generals gave them a chance. Some Prussian commanders brought their men on to the field in battalion columns, but even skirmish lines melted away under the chassepots. Alvensleben turned to his guns: fifteen batteries' worth deployed by 11 a.m. on high ground around the village of Flavigny, in position to sweep the French positions as their counterparts had done at Froeschweiler/Woerth. By the end of the day they would fire over 20,000 rounds – most of them in direct support of III Corps – and ammunition columns were pushing forward into the gun lines to refill caissons and limbers.[56] Alvensleben's men pushed forward, as much to keep from being shot down by the chassepots as for any tactical reason: advancing was the only way to bring their own shorter-ranged rifles into play. They captured the village of Tronville. Around 11.30 they took Vionville, cutting the Metz–Verdun road, only to have French rifles and French artillery turn the sector into a killing ground. Alvensleben, believing his best chance involved continuing his own attack,

---

[54]Achille Bazaine, *Episodes de la guerre de 1870 et le blocus de Metz* (Madrid, 1883), pp. 80 ff. The wound was more of a serious bruise from a shell fragment. He frequently mentioned that it pained him, and while not disabling, it was the kind of close call that can diminish even a brave man's ability to concentrate by reminding him of his mortality.

[55]Howard, pp. 152 ff., is for once trumped as narrator and analyst by David Ascoli's model, *A Day of Battle: Mars-la-Tour 16 August 1870* (London, 1987), which describes Alvensleben's fight on pp. 131 ff. 'Das Generalkommando des III. Korps bei Spicheren und Vionville', *Kriegsgeschichtliche Einzelschriften* 17, ed. Grossen Generalstab (Berlin, 1895), is detailed and critical. The familiar argument, most recently presented in Sven Lange, *Hans Delbrueck und der 'Strategiestreit': Kriegfuehrung und Kriegsgeschichte in der Kontroverse 1879–1914* (Freiburg, 1995), that Germany's general staff historians were uncritical, or too prone to interpret past history in the context of present doctrine, merits modification, in that specialized monographs primarily for in-house use, like this one, were often quite scathing – as opposed to general histories, the 'flagship books' written for general circulation in the army and among civilians.

[56]See Ernst von Hoffbauer, *Die deutsche Artillerie in den Schlachten bei Metz* (4 vols., Berlin, 1872–5), vol. III, pp. 97 ff.

struck north across the main road and east towards Rezonville, taking the village of Flavigny about noon. As the manoeuvre developed, III Corps found itself moving ever deeper into a potential French noose. But it was one that Bazaine, concerned for the security of his own left flank, refused to tighten. As elements of four French corps remained passive, an unsupported French cavalry charge was shot to pieces in front of the village of Flavigny. By that time, Alvensleben's infantry was so closely engaged that he, too, ordered a cavalry charge to buy time and win breathing space.

The 'Death Ride' of the von Bredow brigade arguably did more than any single event after Waterloo to extend the half-life of Europe's horse cavalry. Six squadrons from the 7th Cuirassiers and the 16th Uhlans, around 800 men, took advantage of broken ground and powder smoke to come within sabre range of a French gun line, cut down the crews, scatter the supporting infantry and give a good account of themselves against most of a French cavalry division before falling back into their own lines. It was magnificent. It was war as well, for the French 6th Corps, victims of the charge, played no further role in the day's fighting.[57] But the troopers' heroism brought no long-term relief to a III Corps whose left flank now stood open to a full corps – the 4th, under Ladmirault – moving on to the French right wing without orders, advancing to the sound of the guns.

Finally, it seemed, things were happening as they should. Ladmirault sent his three divisions forward against Prussian infantry with empty canteens and empty cartridge boxes, their officers down and their organization disrupted by six hours and more of the hardest fighting III Corps had ever experienced, though some of its regiments could trace their history to the days of Frederick the Great. The Brandenburgers fell back, less panic-stricken than disorganized, moving in flocks across the Metz high road as surviving officers sought to restore order in the scattered companies. With his left flank turned, Alvensleben pulled his survivors towards the corps gun line and the high ground around the villages of Flavigny and Tronville. He had been promised reinforcements, but at this stage it did not matter. The III Corps would hold its ground or die standing as long as Alvensleben was in command. If all else failed, he intended to make a fighting retreat west, towards Verdun. 'Bazaine could beat me', he said, 'but he wouldn't be rid of me for a long time yet'.[58]

As the Prussians regrouped for what seemed a last stand, French colonels and brigadiers suffered second thoughts. Like Confederate General Richard Ewell at Gettysburg, they wondered if their men, tired, thirsty and disorganized, could make headway against the Prussian guns facing them, guns that all afternoon had torn French ranks to pieces, and surely would now be fought to the muzzle. And while the French wavered, the balance of time swung against them. The first Prussian reinforcements reached the field: elements of X Corps, coming into action at the end of an eight-hour forced march that brought them twenty-five miles from their bivouacs at a cost of heavy straggling – but in time.

---

[57]Bredow's thoroughly analysed, often misunderstood charge is described in Major Kaehler, 'The German Cavalry in the Battle of Vionville-Mars la Tour' in *Cavalry Studies from Two Great Wars*, tr. C. Reichmann (Kansas City, MO, 1896), pp. 166 ff. This edition of Kaehler's monograph is especially useful because it is printed along with a similar study of the French cavalry in the battles of the frontier and the Union cavalry at Gettysburg. The strong comparative dimension highlights, in particular, the Europeans' disregard for dismounted tactics.

[58]Thilo von Krieg, *Konstantin von Alvensleben, General der Infanterie. Ein militaerisches Lebensbild* (Berlin, 1903), p. 109.

The leading battalions of the 20th Division swung into line beside the Brandenburgers around Tronville. Then came the guns: almost the whole artillery of the corps, going into battery as best it could and ranging against the targets III Corps was engaging. With Alvensleben's position stabilized, Voigts-Rhetz sought to seize what seemed like an opportunity. He sent the 20th Division forward across the Verdun road and into the woods north of Tronville, while swinging the corps's other division, the 19th, westwards against what appeared to be an exposed French right flank. The leading 38th Brigade, advancing in company columns for the sake of speed and shock, without benefit of reconnaissance, found itself looking into the rifle muzzles of a full, fresh French division at 300 yards' range across a ravine whose existence was completely unsuspected. With no time to call for artillery support, the commander ordered a charge. The forward companies deployed as best they could, and went ahead into sleeting rifle fire that stopped the attack and drove the survivors into the bottom of the valley, where they remained clumped for another ten minutes as Ladmirault's infantry emptied their cartridge pouches into the mass, then went in with the bayonet and drove the stunned Prussians back up the hill, over the bodies of their own dead and wounded.

Over 2,500 of the brigade's 4,500 men had been shot. Three-quarters of the ninety-six officers were down, and the Prussian Army's reluctance to expand its officer cadres turned around and bit as no one remained to rally survivors. The 38th's fragments scattered in all directions, carrying rear-echelon elements with them.[59] Had Ladmirault kept his men moving, the chances for enveloping the Prussian line from the left and rolling it up like a rug were as promising as any opportunity either side had seen the entire day. Instead the Frenchman hesitated, refusing to drive his forward elements in the absence of support from the army reserves.[60] The trumpets of the cavalry division backing up his flank remained silent. It was from the other side of the line that half a dozen squadrons of cavalry, attached to X Corps from the Prussian Guard, charged into Ladmirault's infantry, covering what remained of the 38th Brigade. And it was by Voigts-Rhetz's orders, around 6.45, that a full division of Prussian horsemen rode against 3rd Corps's right flank. This time they were intended not to check a defeat but to complete a victory. The movement, in turn, galvanized the French cavalry into action. For thirty minutes, 5,000 troopers charged and counter-charged across terrain that might have been designed for mounted action. The immediate result amounted to two chess players exchanging knights: situation as before. But the Prussians kept the field, and the French made no more attempts to reach the Verdun road in that sector.[61]

---

[59]The brigade's fate and its causes generated almost as much controversy as the more familiar disaster suffered two days later by the Prussian Guard. The definitive 'official' account is 'Der Kampf der 38. Infanterie Brigade und des linken Deutschen Fluegels in der Schlacht bei Vionville-Mars-la-Tour am 16. August 1870', *Kriegsgeschichtliche Einzelschriften* 25 (Berlin, 1898). Cf. Fritz Hoenig's iconoclastic *Die Wahrheit ueber die Schlacht von Vionville-Mars-la-Tour auf dem linken Flugel* (Berlin, 1899).

[60]After the war, Ladmirault bitterly blamed himself for not advancing, saying 'if only I had known'. J. de la Faye (pseud.), *Le général Ladmirault (1808–1898)* (Paris, 1904), pp. 208 ff. The general's birth date suggests part of an explanation – sixty-two can be long in the tooth for high field command, and Ladmirault had a demanding couple of weeks behind him. Alvensleben, on the other hand, was sixty-one and hardly lacked energy. Lifestyles seem to have played a role: while Prussian senior officers were hardly ascetics, as a group they seem to have devoted less attention to the pleasures of the table and the bottle than their French counterparts.

[61]Kaehler, pp. 190 ff.

By 7 p.m. it was all over. Frederick Charles's belated effort to force a breakthrough on his army's left, around Rezonville, with elements of III Corps, did little but swell casualty lists already staggeringly high. Two Prussian corps had cut and held the Metz–Verdun road, at the cost of around 16,000 men, compared with 1,000 fewer for the French. Prussian artillery, deployed in masses, had silenced French guns and inflicted heavy casualties on French infantry. But time and again the chassepots, this time supported by gunners who stood to their pieces while a round remained in the limbers, had stopped both frontal attacks and flank marches in their tracks. At day's end, in most sectors the French were holding their ground, in front of fields carpeted with Prussian bodies. To the rank and file and their regimental officers there seemed no reason why the Army of the Rhine should not go over to the attack the next day, smash the enemy still in its way and reach Verdun in triumph.

Bazaine was less sanguine. Moving from sector to sector in the course of the day, he had amply resolved any questions about the effect of age and good living on his physical courage. But in repeatedly performing the functions of a company officer, Bazaine failed consistently to act as a field marshal. He allowed his corps commanders to conduct what amounted to a series of separate battles, neither coordinating the movement of reserves nor timing his appearances in ways that might have galvanized subordinates caught up in the affairs of their own sectors. The list of missed opportunities was long. It included failure to strike hard at III Corps in mid-afternoon, and to drive Ladmirault forward in the aftermath of his local victory. It included Bazaine's neglecting to push his unengaged corps forward along the Verdun road, and to use some of his cavalry to clear his gridlocked rear areas.

As important as any specifics, Achille Bazaine had spent a day confronting his own shortcomings. He was not stupid. Nor was he the first or the last senior officer to revert under stress to a level of command at which he felt comfortable. Union corps commander Gordon Granger spent part of the Battle of Lookout Mountain acting as a gun captain. Another American major general fought, albeit for better reasons, as a bazookaman while his division disintegrated in the early days of the Korean War. Nor did direct impressions provide reassurance. If, by the end of the day, Bazaine was convinced in his own mind the battle was lost, it was not least because he had seen so many stragglers and wounded. The proportion was probably no greater than in any other battle of the Second Empire. The absolute number, however, was much larger. It gave weight to reports complaining that the men were unfed and low on ammunition. The nearest magazines were at Metz, and the city's walls had drawn Bazaine like a magnet long before Frederick Charles's abortive late-evening attack strengthened his fear that the Prussians' real intention was to cut him off not from Verdun but from Metz. Around 10 p.m. he assembled his staff and told them he intended to retire on the fortress. Any subordinate with a better idea was invited to contribute it.[62] Not surprisingly, the retreat began at first light the next morning – to the accompaniment from the ranks of sulphurous denunciations of Bazaine for abandoning a victorious field without first taking the trouble to provide soup and coffee.[63]

---

[62] Ascoli, pp. 206–7, overstates the impact of Frederick Charles's initiative on Bazaine's decision. Baumont, *Bazaine*, pp. 115 ff., sympathetically presents Bazaine's situation without concealing his essential loss of grip.

[63] As in Leonce Patry, *The Reality of War: A Memoir of the Franco-Prussian War, 1870–1871*, tr. D. Fermer (London, 2002), pp. 94–5. Patry, a regular officer, was, at the time, a company commander in the 6th Infantry, IV Corps.

The comments might have been even stronger if the Frenchmen had been aware of the Prussian reaction. The reports he received from the field of Vionville convinced Moltke that Bazaine was more likely to hold his ground than cut his way through to Verdun – but it was well into the early morning of 17 August by the time he had a clear picture. The corps commanders engaged the day before were of a common opinion that their men badly needed rest. Moltke himself was not unwilling to sort out his forces as his enemy remained conveniently in place. An extra day would be useful for what he had in mind.[64]

III

Today's armchair strategist, following on a map the respective moves of the French and Prussian corps after Vionville, may well be pardoned for seeing one side offer a catastrophe in slow motion while the other refuses the gambit.[65] Moltke began by route marching over 200,000 men across Bazaine's front – a process of stretching out one's throat for the knife that even a lethargic foe would find difficult to misinterpret or ignore. When the move was successfully completed, Moltke had achieved the movement of most of his army in a half-circle. The Prussians now faced towards Germany, and would be attacking backwards towards their own lines of communication! Even a local defeat could have a disastrous effect on a supply system by now sustained as much through will-power as anything else. It says much for the Prussian army's faith in its chief of staff that no one in royal headquarters verbalized the opinion that, if these dispositions reflected genius, then what might illustrate incompetence?

At least part of Moltke's confidence, which never wavered in public, was a product of poor reconnaissance. The Prussian cavalry spent most of 17 August recovering from its exertions of the day before, making no systematic effort to discover precisely where the French were and where they were going. Moltke wound up relying on dust clouds more than patrol reports, and not until the morning of 18 August did he discover that Bazaine had given himself one last chance to turn the tide of the campaign – and the war.

The French cavalry had been no more active than its Prussian counterpart, paying more attention to covering the army's retreat directly – and thereby protecting themselves by remaining under the infantry's rifles – than in taking their skins to market and investigating the Prussian-generated dust clouds to the left. Had French troopers brought back reports of the 2nd Army's high-risk manoeuvre across what had now become Bazaine's rear, the marshal might have been tempted to revert to his days in Africa and try for a lightning slash across the Prussian jugular. Instead, on the evening of 17 August, Bazaine began deploying his army in arguably the strongest tactical positions French troops had occupied in the whole campaign.

The 'Lines of Amanviliers' ran along high ground about a mile outside the fortress of Metz, from the village of St Privat in the north, through Amanviliers and Gravelotte in the centre and centre-left, down to the wooded terrain covering the Mance ravine, which bent the French left into a fishhook. When the two are juxtaposed, the French position strongly resembles that of the Union at Gettysburg, with St Privat as the Round Tops and the

---

[64]Thanks in good part to Bronsart, who completed thirty hours in the saddle by bringing the news to headquarters. Cf. Bronsart, pp. 42–3 and Kessel, *Moltke*, p. 556.

[65]Kessel, *Moltke*, pp. 556–7 and Howard, pp. 164 ff. Still good as a step-by-step guide is Fritz Hoenig, *24 Stunden Moltkeischer Strategie entwickelt und erlaeutert an den Schlachten von Gravelotte und St. Privat* (Berlin, 1891).

Mance ravine as Cemetery Hill/Culp's Hill. If anything, the French were even better off than the Yankees had been: most of the ground on the right and centre was bare and gently sloped, offering perfect fields of fire for the chassepot, while the sides of the Mance ravine, steeper even than the slopes of Culp's Hill, were all but impassable in the face of any significant opposition.

Bazaine brought his corps into position with no more than the now standard amount of quarrelling and friction. Froissard's 2nd Corps held the Mance sector: a natural assignment for an engineer and a defensive specialist with Spicheren on his record. The 3rd and 4th Corps deployed in the centre, digging in along the low Amanviliers–Gravelotte ridge line, marking ranges and improving fields of fire for their guns and rifles. The right of the line fell to 6th Corps. Operationally, like the Union left at Gettysburg, its right flank was open. Bazaine proposed to guard against envelopment by having the corps deploy echelons to the north-east. Canrobert, more concerned with the expected threat to his front, proposed to take his chances on the flank and focus his defence from St Privat south-west towards the 4th Corps sector. Canrobert had a decade's seniority on Bazaine; Bazaine had always served under his orders. It hardly seems necessary to say that Canrobert prevailed and left his flank hanging.[66] Surely the Prussians would not be able to get that far north – not across the front of an entire army!

Bazaine, too, expected the main Prussian effort to come against his left and centre. His principal reserve, the Imperial Guard, was deployed to support that section of the line; he took no pains to compensate for Canrobert's 'modification' of his orders by backing up his right. If things went as Bazaine expected, Moltke's corps would advance by echelon into a killing ground almost ideally structured for French weapons, French tactics and, not least, French circumstances. Bazaine's orders, and his plan if he had one, did not incorporate instructions for a general counter-attack should the Prussians in fact be defeated on the slopes before Metz. Instead, Bazaine most probably expected his subordinates to develop victory by local ripostes, and only then initiate a pursuit. On the other hand, should the day go against him, Bazaine could fall back into Metz and wait for the emperor to bring the strength of France to his relief in a style appropriate to the age of Louis XIV. In either case, the decisions he must make would be few and obvious.

On their side of the front, the Prussians began 18 August by assuming that role of obliging enemy hitherto reserved to the French. Moltke initially planned to launch the 2nd Army in a five-corps 'sickle cut' against the French right. The advance would pivot on IX Corps, the formation nearest the Verdun road. The Guard and the Saxons would come up on the left, with the heavily reduced III and X Corps following in direct support. Steinmetz would provide the holding force against an unexpected French riposte. The 1st Army's VIII and VII Corps would go forward from a standing start against the Mance ravine – but only when the 2nd Army's left hook was in position. In contrast to previous *de facto* improvisations, Moltke intended this time to fight a theatre-level battle, committing the 1st and 2nd Armies simultaneously in a hammer blow that would render Bazaine's intentions irrelevant by leaving nothing of his army except fragments. The objective was to force the French either to fight or to retreat north into Luxembourg, internment and disgrace.[67]

---

[66] *Procès Bazaine*, p. 166.
[67] *MMK* 1, vol. III, pp. 231 ff.

Virtually every standard account of the battle lays the blame for the next sequence of events on Moltke's subordinates. The familiar scenario has Frederick Charles encounter French positions on the Amanviliers ridge at around 10 a.m., mistake the troops occupying them for the flank of an army in retreat and respond by prematurely swinging his army eastward. The decision was probably facilitated by that cautious general's discomfort at discovering he was marching in columns of divisions across an enemy front. For the sake of speed, the prince, in preparing his orders for the advance, had eschewed the normal 'long, thin' columns of march in favour of divisional masses, the kind used at reviews and parades, difficult to deploy quickly and correspondingly vulnerable to surprise. He also took pains, however, to establish that the march in that formation was not a tactical but an administrative movement, extending no further than the Verdun road, to be followed by a midday halt and – presumably – fresh orders.[68]

The prince's decision to swing hard right seemed validated when, at 10.30, Moltke ordered both the 1st and 2nd Armies to attack. That decision was based, in turn, on the chief of staff's assumption that the French were massed further south than he had originally believed, and that the position observed by Frederick Charles represented their right flank instead of, as was the actual case, their centre. He correspondingly ordered the Guard and the Saxons to turn eastward and envelop the French right flank, which he presumed was somewhere around Amanviliers.[69]

The chief of staff and the prince were initially undisturbed by reconnaissance reports from the cavalry at Frederick Charles's disposal which, on this day, without specific orders, stayed close to the main body. Such patrolling as it did had been to the north and west – not the east, where the French in fact were. Prussian infantry was neither oriented towards nor structured for direct reconnaissance. The jaeger battalion assigned to each corps was generally used as a shock element once battle was joined, rather than a force of scouts to expose enemy deployment.[70] Nor did the prince's mass formation exactly facilitate the detaching of infantry platoons to test unknown ground in the way regiments in the American Civil War routinely put out a company or two as skirmishers.

This neglect of reconnaissance might have owed something to another problem that the higher headquarters had created between them. On 17 August, the Saxons had been ahead of the Guard on the Nancy–Metz road when Moltke issued his orders. Instead of following logic and giving XII Corps the bivouac areas further west, Moltke's headquarters organized the lines of march so as to bring the Guard into position for the night on the Saxons' left. Frederick Charles's orders, in turn, reversed that, setting the Saxons' march objective as Jarny on the left and the Guard's as Doncourt on the right. That meant the Saxons had to cross the Guard's line of advance. It also cost the latter corps three hours, and required significant efforts to keep the two corps from becoming entangled. When informed of the problem, the prince confirmed the original orders.

Post-war army gossip alternately described the imbroglio as reflecting the Prussians' desire for the Guard to strike the finishing blow at the French, and their decision to give the Saxons that honour for political reasons. A second dichotomy suggested alternatively that Frederick Charles did not trust the Saxons and so gave them the role of flank guard,

---

[68] *Friedrich Karl*, vol. II, pp. 228–9.
[69] *MMK 1*, vol. III, p. 234.
[70] See Hermann Kunz, *Die Thaetigkeit der deutschen Jaeger-Bataillons im Kriege von 1870–71* (Berlin, 1896).

or credited the prince with wanting the better corps commander, Albert of Saxony, on his open flank. Frederick Charles never discussed the issue afterwards. Less controversial, but probably most correct, is that the situation was a consequence of a lapse in staff work and a corresponding misunderstanding on the prince's part, which he found easier to go along with than to undo.[71]

Arguably more significant than the actual time loss were the consequences of increased stress on commanders, most facing their first action of the war, at the beginning of a day that would call, above all, for cool heads who remembered things like comprehensive patrolling. Frederick Charles received his reality check by a series of reports from small scouting forces that had probed eastwards. They all said the same thing: St Privat was swarming with Frenchmen and seemed to be strongly fortified.[72] To the prince, this indicated that the French were not retreating after all, but instead were present to his new front in strength. He responded by ordering IX Corps, the one by now nearest to the French positions, to hold in place until the Guard and the Saxons could move to its support. Manstein had missed his chance for glory at Koeniggraetz. He had also paid close attention to the nature of the fighting in this war – it had cost him a son, killed at Spicheren. The forward battalions of IX Corps were expecting the order to shift from company columns and half-battalions into the skirmish lines that prefigured a fight. Instead, Manstein sent nine batteries ahead of the foot troops – an hour ahead in some cases – to establish a gun line and 'shoot in' his riflemen before the French responded to what was hitting them.

It was a good idea, but the execution did not match the conceptualization. Not until around noon did the Prussian guns open fire. Even then, by a negative miracle of non-existent French reconnaissance, the surprise was complete. But instead of breaking, Ladmirault's regiments abandoned their tent lines, fell in, deployed and proceeded to give the Prussians opposing them a lesson in infantry fire tactics. Manstein's artillery officers, seeking commanding ground, had deployed well within chassepot range. Their crews suffered heavy losses as French skirmishers got close enough to capture and remove four guns.[73] By the time Manstein's infantry went forward, the French were waiting for them. He had two divisions, his own 18th and the independent 25th, from the Grand Duchy of Hesse, attached to replace a division left on coast watch. The corps suffered heavy losses in initial attempts to advance, then went to earth. The men in the ranks could calculate odds, and even the most fire-eating field officers quickly understood the folly of attacking massed chassepots over billiard-table ground. Manstein, no fool, accepted front-line wisdom and waited for the guns and the Guard to buy his corps some manoeuvring room. The day was still young.

The mitrailleuse, by this time, was coming into its own along the French front, especially in Ladmirault's sector. The weapons consisted of twenty-five rifle barrels built into

---

[71]Cf. *Friedrich Karl*, vol. II, pp. 230–1 and Hohenlohe, vol. IV, pp. 64 ff. Ascoli, p. 263 and Philip Howes, *The Catalytic Wars. A Study of the Development of Warfare 1860–70* (London, 1998), pp. 522–3, are typical of the recent comments. The 'modernization' of the Prussian army in 1870 can easily be exaggerated. Hohenlohe, still commanding the Guard's artillery, makes the point (p. 64) that while the Guard Corps daily synchronized its watches to the chief of staff's, the 2nd Army did not have a common time. The difference on 18 August was twenty minutes – 'and given today's critical importance of firepower, twenty minutes can be decisive'.

[72]From here, Howard, p. 169 *passim*, can be used alongside the excellent *Der 18 August 1870, Studien zur Kriegsgeschichte und Taktik*, ed. Grossen Generalstab (Berlin, 1906), a model of detail that can become confusing.

[73]Hoffbauer, *Die deutsche Artillerie in den Schlachten bei Metz*, vol. IV, *passim*, focuses on the guns.

a cylinder, loaded from the breech by a plate cartridge holder and fired in sequence by turning a crank. They were prone to jamming and breakdowns, the firing pins, especially, corroding with use. They had a limited cone of fire and no traversing ability apart from shifting the entire mount. But a good crew could go through three plates a minute – no mean force multiplier, even for infantry armed with breech-loaders.

The weapon looked like a cannon, was mounted on a wheeled gun carriage and, on mobilization, had been assigned to the artillery as a replacement for one of the four-pounder rifle batteries in most of the divisions. In the war's early stages, that battery was usually deployed in gun lines with the rest, despite the fact that the range of a mitrailleuse was no more than that of a rifle. This initial misuse of the weapon is usually cited to condemn pre-war secrecy, or to illustrate the technical backwardness of the French army of 1870. In fact, the technical aspects of the mitrailleuse did not call for a rocket scientist, and French gunners, in particular, were usually able to count above ten without removing their boots. By 18 August, mitrailleuse battery commanders and their superiors understood that the new weapons were best employed forward, with the infantry. Despite drawing disproportionate amounts of Prussian fire, dug in by ones and twos, mitrailleuses did much to convince any Germans under their sights of the wisdom of keeping their heads well down. Even Hohenloe, listening to their distinctive snarl, found himself wondering whether Prussian experts had been wrong in dismissing this innovation, as he rode forward to see how his gunners were standing up under its fire.[74]

As at Vionville, however, Ladmirault neither took the risk of mounting sector counter-attacks on his own initiative, nor assumed the responsibility of informing Bazaine what was happening on that part of the front. In the meantime, Moltke had been distracted by developments in the sector of the 1st Prussian Army. Steinmetz, listening to the ever-increasing roar of artillery in Manstein's sector, put his own spin on an earlier despatch from Moltke instructing him to hold his position and use artillery to prepare the 1st Army's eventual attack.[75] Beginning around noon, the old man concentrated most of the guns of VII and VIII Corps around Gravelotte – 150 barrels, the largest artillery force employed in the campaign to date. In so doing, he reassumed *de facto* control over VIII Corps, which had been removed from his orders by Moltke after Vionville, in hopes of limiting the damage Steinmetz might cause by limiting the forces at his disposal.[76] At the time, it seemed a preferable alternative to relieving him for cause – not least because Moltke had no one available that he trusted to assume command.

Decisions thus finessed have a way of rebounding. When Steinmetz began issuing orders to VIII Corps, no one on the staff, from the commanding general down, was prepared to dispute the issue, especially at the start of the biggest battle in the corps's history.[77] Moltke himself had moved forward to Rezonville, the better to keep an eye on Frederick Charles's

---

[74]And received a royal rocket from Wuerttemberg for exposing himself unnecessarily. Hohenloe, vol. IV, p. 70. Cf. Holmes, pp. 206–7; A. von F., 'Ueber den Werth der Mitrailleusen mit besonderer Ruecksichtsnahme auf das in Oesterreich-Ungarn eingefuehrte System Montigny-Christophe', *Jahrbuecher fuer die deutsche Armee und Marine* 10 (1874), pp. 303–23. For events in the French centre generally, see *La Guerre de 1870–71. Les operations autour de Metz*, vol. III, pp. 194 ff.
[75]*MMK* 1, vol. III, p. 235.
[76]Bronsart, p. 69.
[77]Gebhard Zernin, *Das Leben des Generals August von Goeben* (Berlin, 1897), vol. II, p. 56.

movements. The relocation left him out of sight and out of touch with his right wing. If the chief of staff heard anything at all, it was Steinmetz's guns, whose roar rose over most other sounds, while they presumably continued to prepare the attack, as Moltke had ordered.

By every appearance, those guns were doing a thorough job. Farms with names like Moscou and St Hubert crumbled into blazing ruins as other Prussian batteries hammered French positions along the high ground on the far side of the ravine:

> Limbs and bodies were blown thirty to fifty paces apart, and the stones and sand ... were covered with pools of blood ... Some French were found burned in their defensive positions, and a large number of wounded showed marks of the flames ...[78]

Small wonder that the brigadiers of VIII Corps, on Steinmetz's left, began trying their luck in local attacks – and no wonder at all that corps commander August von Goeben supported them, despite their lack of success. Not all of the defenders were burned alive. French infantry in well-camouflaged positions scattered Prussian skirmish lines and pinned down Prussian company columns with heavy losses.[79] In a pattern that would be repeated throughout World War I, German officers tended to commit reinforcements in companies, with limited regard for battalion – and, as the situation worsened, regimental – chains of command. The result was a series of small-scale rushes more or less at random, whose effect resembled eroding a rock with handfuls of boiled peas. Casualties mounted by the half-hour, and no one on the spot was senior enough and willing enough to report the true state of affairs to higher authority. Instead, Steinmetz proposed to develop the attack by bringing his guns to closer range – which he defined as the side of the Mance ravine in Prussian hands. That terrain, however, was well within chassepot range, and VIII Corps was ordered to get across the ravine and drive the French from its other side.

Schwerpunkt of the effort was the farm of St Hubert, a forward position blocking the only decent road across the ravine. Its capture would eventually enable guns to cross the obstacle – while casualties came back in the other direction. Three brigades of VIII Corps went up the slope, to stick fast in tangled woods and underbrush scourged by French artillery and rifle fire. A dozen companies from half a dozen regiments managed to work close enough to rush St Hubert around 3 p.m., against a garrison whose survivors accepted a no-quarter fight to the finish that left victors as exhausted as the few prisoners they took. By the end of the day, forty-three companies would be represented at St Hubert. Steinmetz, convinced he had the French on the run, ordered VII Corps into the ravine on VIII Corps's right to complete the victory. Goeben, by now reasonably informed of what was happening to his forward elements, protested that there were already too many men on the ravine's floor and its German side: the shell-shocked, the lightly wounded, the stragglers, the lost. Steinmetz paid no attention; Goeben was unwilling to do more than raise the issue.[80]

The VII Corps was less well commanded at all levels than its stablemate. It was attacking the most formidable terrain of the French line, whose defenders had been on the alert for hours. Prussian drums beat the charge shortly before 4 p.m. Within minutes, the leading elements, advancing in skirmish lines, were fleeing before some of the heaviest rifle

---

[78]Hoenig, *24 Hours*, p. 63.
[79]The French side of the fight is in *Metz*, vol. III, pp. 188 ff. Ascoli, pp. 248 ff., is Prussocentric.
[80]Zernin, vol. II, p. 56.

and mitrailleuse fire of the day. A few minutes more and they crashed into the rest of the corps, coming up in company columns that, in turn, melted like sugar lumps in hot water.

By now the floor of the Mance ravine was a tangled mass of dead and wounded men and horses, destroyed wagons and disabled guns. An oblivious Steinmetz, convinced VII Corps was on top of the ridge in force, sent a full division of cavalry down the western slope, with orders to pursue the French to the gates of Metz! He also sent forward VII Corps's artillery. The horsemen and the guns were to advance along the road through St Hubert – a daunting task even had that forest path not been crowded with dead and wounded. A single cavalry regiment and four batteries got across the causeway at the bottom of the ravine. The troopers were promptly shot to pieces. Two of the batteries were knocked out; another stayed in action for two hours; the fourth kept a single gun firing until nightfall. Everything else stuck fast in a ravine that became a killing ground as French gunners, no longer plagued by VII Corps's counter-battery fire, found the range and took revenge for a long day's pounding.[81]

Had the French in this sector mounted anything like a counter-attack, the German rear lay wide open. But Bazaine took no action. His generals remained in their headquarters. The regimental officers, themselves exhausted, were unwilling to take the risk of advancing into ground choked with the debris of a Prussian defeat as complete as any in that army's history, where blood stood in pools and ran in streams, and fragments of men still made noises. By 7 p.m., moreover, they had other concerns. The Prussian II Corps, under Lieutenant General Edouard von Fransecky, officially part of the 2nd Army, was part of the second wave of formations transported to the theatre of war. It had been marching hard to overtake the advance – the king himself had authorized Fransecky to take the road at 2 a.m., another of his periodic interferences with the chain of command[82]– and it now arrived, in what seemed to Steinmetz like the nick of time. The Pomeranians had a high reputation in the army (in fact, about one man in ten of II Corps was actually Polish, reflecting an army policy to distribute Polish conscripts and reservists among as many units as possible without disrupting mobilization).[83] But they were tired, their canteens and stomachs empty. Steinmetz nevertheless asked not Moltke but William for permission to use them in a last charge. William agreed, over Moltke's eloquent silence.[84]

Behind them, the Mance ravine burst like a boil. Soldiers, horses and wagons poured out of its western end, running in the general direction of Gravelotte, all order lost, with no more thought than to get away. Officers of the general staff, and the king himself, sought vainly to stop the rout, beating panic-stricken men with the flats of their swords as Prussia's monarch demonstrated that he had not entirely forgotten the drill-ground vocabulary of his youth. Not until Rezonville did the routed men stop, and then it was more a pause for breath than a rally.[85]

---

[81]Hoenig, *24 Hours*, pp. 119 ff.; *18 August*, pp. 273 ff.; and Verdy, pp. 84 ff.

[82]'Koenig Wilhelm auf seinen Kriegszug in Frankreich 1870. Von Mainz bis Sedan', *Kriegsgeschichtliche Einzelschriften* 19, ed. Grosser Generalstab (Berlin, 1897), p. 37.

[83]Kuelich, pp. 92–3.

[84]Verdy, pp. 84 ff. Moltke later went on record as saying he would have been better advised to keep II Corps in hand for the next day. Helmuth von Moltke, *The Franco-German War of 1870–71*, tr. and rev. Archibald Forbes (London, 1893), p. 78.

[85]Hoenig, *24 Hours*, pp. 149 ff.; and Wilhelms Kriegszug, pp. 43–4.

Almost simultaneously on that long August day, II Corps began its advance down the western slope of the ravine. There were no skirmish lines. Instead, the Prussians moved in company columns, partly to avoid the dead men and wrecked vehicles, partly to avoid coming apart in the gathering darkness, and partly because Fransecky and his subordinates believed, like Steinmetz, the French could be finished off by one more blow, delivered by the closed fist of closed formations: a few minutes of point-blank rapid fire, then the bayonet and the 'Pomeranian gun butts' (*Pommersche Kolben*), celebrated since the days of Frederick the Great as the province's preferred alternative to steel at close quarters. But by the time the Prussians started to climb the ravine's eastern slope, the French had reformed their lines and replenished their ammunition. The muzzle flashes of hundreds of chassepots reached for the Prussian columns. The leading files returned the fire — mostly into the backs of the survivors of successive assault forces still holding out around St Hubert. Silhouetted by the fires, they made natural targets for the green Pomeranians. Taken by surprise from the rear, these sorely tried men nevertheless faced about and confronted what seemed a new enemy. At least this was one they could see! For perhaps thirty minutes, the two Prussian forces tore each other to pieces at close range. Around 8 p.m., enough proved enough. The garrison of St Hubert broke, running through ranks that only then discovered the nature of their enemy. Fransecky reached the scene in time to order his buglers to sound 'cease fire' and halt his men — those still in ranks — in place in the ravine and on its blood-slippery slopes.[86]

A now exhausted William and his discomfited chief of staff were considering the possibility of at least a tactical withdrawal in this ill-omened sector, when news from the north changed their minds. Moltke had left Manstein's IX Corps at mid-morning, pinned down by rifle, mitrailleuse and artillery fire, awaiting relief from the advance of XII Corps and the Prussian Guard on its left. Shortly after noon, as scouting reports continued to arrive, Frederick Charles and his staff finally agreed that St Privat was the anchor of a French position that extended well to the north of where he and Moltke had initially thought. St Privat was also directly in the path of the Guard's advance. A frontal attack uphill against a built-up strong point was no part of Frederick Charles's personal tactical doctrine. As the Guard reached the lower slopes of St Privat, at around 2 p.m., it received new, blunt orders: wait for the Saxons to come up on the left.[87]

It took another hour for XII Corps to reach the first defended obstacle in its path, the village of Ste Marie les Chenes. West of St Privat, and at the foot of the slope leading up to it, the village formed an outpost of the main defences, held by a regiment of infantry and a battery of four-pounders. Hohenloe built up a dozen-battery gun line and blasted the village into ruin before elements of the Saxon Corps and the Guards stormed and cleared it. In the process, the Germans took heavy losses from a diehard garrison that kept its ground to the last at odds of twenty to one, then fell back on the main position in a model holding action.

---

[86]Hermann Kunze, 'Das Nachtgefecht vom 18. August', *Kriegsgeschichtliche Beispiele* 1 (Berlin, 1897), does an excellent job of clearing the underbrush from what happened during II Corps's disastrous attack. Cf. 'Der 18. August 1870', pp. 317 ff.

[87]*Friedrich Karl*, vol. II, p. 246. To the specific sources on St Privat may profitably be added, Herman Kunz, *Der Kampf um St Privat La Montagne* (Berlin, 1899). *St. Privat. German Sources*, tr. Harry Bell (Ft. Leavenworth, KS, 1914), is a compendium originally produced for internal instructional purposes by the US Army, and correspondingly good for specific episodes.

With their fingers thus well burned, neither corps commander, the Guards' Prince August of Wuerttemberg, nor the Saxons' Crown Prince Albert, was eager to throw his men forward directly against the St Privat heights. Instead, the Saxon infantry pushed north and east, looking for a way round. Their corps artillery deployed on the left of the Guards; the batteries of III Corps came up to reinforce IX Corps's gun line; and for almost three hours, 200 German field pieces tore up a French position never intended to withstand that kind of pounding. When it first moved to the front, VI Corps had left its tools behind and had small chance of improvising field entrenchments.[88] As his casualties mounted, Canrobert repeatedly called for support. He received only a few hundred rounds of artillery ammunition – little help as German guns silenced battery after French battery, while increasing numbers of stragglers drifted away from a fire nothing in their experience had prepared them to endure.

Then the Prussians – or rather, a Prussian officer, the Prince of Wuerttemberg – seized the initiative. Hohenloe, as good an artilleryman as was to be found on that side of the Atlantic, saw his task as attritional: wearing down the French by a steady, disciplined fire as opposed to trying to sweep them away by blasting at random into the middle distance.[89] But the Prussian guns were kept at long range by the chassepots of French skirmishers, who had a relatively free hand because of the reluctance of the Guard's infantry officers to deploy a battalion or two to drive them off. Hohenloe's crews took brutal losses as sharpshooters marked their ranges. Inevitably, their shooting suffered. Nor were the blast or the fragmentation effects of black-powder shells as spectacular as the explosions indicated.

Alvensleben had used his experiences at Spicheren and Vionville to warn his colleague of the danger of committing his infantry in haste. Prince August had initially ordered Hohenloe to save his ammunition and wait for the Saxons to come in on the French right flank. Then he changed his mind. The decision to send the Guard forward against St Privat has been described as made from a desire to keep the Saxons from bearing off the day's glory, a belief in the power of the offensive spirit to overcome any obstacle and a response to Moltke's original order to attack the French wherever they might be found. Another – albeit unlikely – story had Frederick Charles, who was no admirer of the Prussian Guard, baiting Wuerttemberg by making remarks about the corps's sluggishness. Perhaps, too, Wuerttemberg remembered past glories on the heights of Chlum. The French position in front of him seemed no less *Sturmreif* (ripe to be assaulted), the day was waning and the Saxons seemed to be making no progress finding the French flank, to say nothing of driving it in.

Frederick Charles, himself increasingly concerned for the Saxons' whereabouts, agreed.[90] Just before 5 p.m., a brigade of the Guard Corps mounted a diversionary attack to pin down the right division of the French 4th Corps. Its head-down charge over open ground diverted the French well enough – at a cost of 2,500 casualties in three-quarters of an hour, with so many officers down that one battalion was commanded by a cadet. At 5 p.m., the Guard's

---

[88]Constant Bapst, *Le Maréchal Canrobert. Souvenirs d'un siècle* (6 vols., Paris, 1898–1913), vol. VI, pp. 77 ff., describes the limited preparations for defence in VI Corps's sector.
[89]Hohenloe, *Aus meinem Leben*, vol. IV, pp. 74 ff., describes his gunners' work in the early afternoon of 18 August, with frequent recourse to the first person singular. But it's not bragging if you can back it up. Hohenloe could and did, time after time.
[90]His perspective is presented in detail in *Friedrich Karl*, vol. II, pp. 250 ff.

main attack sent in its other three brigades – not simultaneously but one after another, in a manoeuvre similar to Longstreet's initial assault at Gettysburg on 2 July. The Prussians went in by half-battalions, behind their unfurled colours, drums beating. They were carrying full packs and equipment, close to a hundred pounds, and faced 3,000 yards of open slopes. The French had to do no more than set their sights and open their cartridge pouches.

By 6.30, almost 8,000 of the original attacking force of 18,000 were casualties. The main assaults collapsed at a common distance of around 1,000 yards from the French position: approximately the chassepot's effective killing range when used in large numbers against mass targets. Had VI Corps had mitrailleuses in position, the butcher's bill would have been even higher; Canrobert bemoaned their absence at Bazaine's court martial.[91] It says much for the courage of the men, and for the initiative of the junior officers and NCOs who took command of the shattered companies, that the guardsmen continued to inch forward in small groups, in some sectors, working their way to within 600 yards of St Privat. That, however, could hardly be described as a tactical movement, especially since the alternative involved going back – alone – across the same killing zone and risking a bullet in the back. Most who tried it were, in fact, shot down.

To decide the day in France's favour, all that seemed necessary here, as well as in the south, was one substantial counter-attack. Again, it never came. Bazaine, with the French Imperial Guard ready to his hand, remained inactive. When the Guard's commander did despatch one of his divisions to the front, it was to the wrong sector – to support a 3rd Corps that was still well able to hold on. Canrobert's corps, in contrast, was fought out. A few local initiatives to clear the remaining guardsmen from its front were checked by artillery that, caissons refilled during the infantry attack, resumed a bombardment heavy enough to pin even the boldest French regiments in position. Nor were there troops to spare against a Saxon flanking movement, which, by 7 p.m., had hammered its way through Canrobert's brigade-strength flank position around Roncourt and was on the way to St Privat.

It had become a battalion commanders' fight in the Saxon sector. Senior officers had long since lost effective contact with their forward units, and the majors were turning towards 'the sound of the guns' – the heavy fighting in the Guard's sector. The 1st Battalion of the 107th Infantry lost half a dozen colour-bearers, and the 2nd lost four, grinding down a still desperate local resistance.[92] As the Saxons penetrated St Privat from the north, around 7.30, the survivors of the Guard mounted a near spontaneous rush of their own against their tormentors. Batteries from both corps advanced to what seemed point-blank ranges, aiming at flashes as growing darkness made true observation impossible. In a sixty-minute hand-to-hand brawl with quarter seldom asked or given, the Germans cleared St Privat and its environs as Canrobert fell back south-east with what remained of his corps.

The rest of the main French position unwound predictably, falling back from right to left into Metz as much by reflex as by orders, first 4th Corps and then 3rd, 2nd and, finally, the Guard. At a cost of 13,000, they had inflicted over 20,000 casualties on a Prussian army by now lacking both the organization and the energy to do more than thank God things had not gone worse. The officer corps was still small enough to be close-knit, and had never experienced casualties at such levels. Bismarck's son had been wounded at Vionville; few

---

[91] *Procès Bazaine*, p. 224.
[92] Hassel, vol. II, p. 388.

of the army's planners and commanders were not mourning friends or relatives. One staff officer gave up asking; the only answers he received were 'dead' or 'wounded'.[93]

IV

The events of 16–18 August are a case study in operational asymmetry. Moltke sought a decisive battle that would crush the Army of the Rhine in the open field. Bazaine perceived himself as fighting a series of rearguard actions, preliminary to the withdrawal into Metz that was his real intention. Seen in that context, his reluctance to mount general counter-attacks, even under highly favourable tactical conditions, makes sense. As he informed the emperor on 19 August, the army was exhausted. And as Stalingrad was to do to Friedrich Paulus on a larger scale in 1942, Metz acted as an irresistible magnet to a field commander tried beyond his capacities. But Bazaine's army still represented a force in being far too formidable merely to be blockaded.

Another French force was, moreover, by this time ready to take the field. The Army of Châlons counted 130,000 men and over 400 guns – no bagatelle, especially if allowed the initiative, and Moltke was initially uncertain how best to proceed. He spent a day reflecting and refining his plans. The corps he left to finish off the French in Metz were some of the best in the army, despite their recent heavy losses. The Brandenburgers and the Pomeranians, the north Germans of IX Corps, the Rhinelanders and Westphalians so mishandled by Steinmetz, had borne the burden of the campaign to date. Gravelotte-St Privat, fought and won entirely by regiments and officers with their roots in the age of Frederick the Great, the Wars of Liberation and the Roon reforms, was the swansong and the valedictory of the old Prussian army. For the final round against the Second Empire, Moltke found himself leading a different kind of field force: a German one almost 250,000 strong.

Three corps, the Guard, the Saxon XII and IV, were formed into the new Army of the Meuse. Its commander was the Crown Prince of Saxony – a reflection of Albert's seniority, and his more than competent performance at St Privat. With royal headquarters and the 3rd Army's Prussians, Bavarians and Wuerttembergers, it marched west on 23 August. Moltke's initial orders were to advance on a broad front towards the Meuse river, then converge on Châlons with 3rd Army on the left, keeping a day's march ahead of the Army of the Meuse. An attack against either one could thus be met with a flank attack, as had been done to the Austrians at Koeniggraetz. As for Steinmetz, Moltke obtained the small personal satisfaction of removing him entirely from the theatre of war, sending him east as governor of Posen: the closest thing to a backwater the Prussian Army could offer.[94]

In the Army of Châlons the Germans faced a weakened reed. The regulars that were supposed to form its core were tired and dispirited, their officers unable or unwilling to bring them back to the mark. The French army has never been known for gentle discipline. A judicious use of courts martial and firing squads might have 'encouraged the rest'. Instead, the army's tone had been set by eighteen battalions of mobile national guardsmen from Paris, who responded to cries of 'long live the emperor' by chanting 'one, two, three, shit!'[95] This behaviour arguably reflected not so much principled revolutionary republicanism as

---

[93]Verdy, p. 103.
[94]*MMK* 1, vol. III, pp. 235–6 and 239–40, and Bronsart, pp. 71–2.
[95]d'Herisson, p. 21 and Adriance, p. 77.

the kind of collective bloody-mindedness often best addressed by hard marching with a victory at the end of it. To secure that victory, the Army of Châlons had two obvious possibilities. It could retreat on Paris, drawing the Germans after it, and act as a nucleus for a nation in arms. It could also advance on Metz to relieve Bazaine.

There remained a third, grand strategic option, the negative side of the Second Empire's chosen way of war. Logic suggested the wisdom of accepting defeat and opening negotiations. But that choice seemed a guarantee of revolution in a France whose government was disintegrating faster than its army. Ollivier had been forced to resign on 9 August, in what one scholar calls a veritable usurpation of power by the empress.[96] The new cabinet and the council of regency, which Napoleon had left behind in Paris, insisted that the regime could not survive without making an attempt to rescue Bazaine. The council's president and new minister of war, General Charles de Palikao, considered the movement eminently practicable, even in the context of the past two weeks.[97] Instead, Napoleon and his senior generals initially decided to abandon Châlons and withdraw towards Paris.

After three excruciating days, the army staggered into Reims, where the council had despatched Eugène Rouher, president of the senate and staunch Bonapartist, to change the emperor's mind. What this experienced administrator and politician saw convinced him, instead, that prompt withdrawal was the best solution at the empire's disposal. The Army of Châlons had a better chance of restoring the situation in Paris than of beating the Germans. But as soon as Rouher left for Paris, the situation changed again. On 21 August, Bazaine's report of Gravelotte finally reached Napoleon's headquarters. Dated 19 August, it declared that he had fallen back on Metz, planned to rest his troops two or three days, then proposed to break out to the north, advancing on either Châlons or Sedan.[98] Neither Napoleon nor MacMahon saw any alternative to joining him. On 23 August, the Army of Châlons broke camp and headed not west to Paris, but north-east towards Sedan.

To Bazaine's limited credit, let it be said that he did make some efforts on 26 August to break out of what was, at that stage, still more a blockade than a siege in the conventional sense. But the weather was against him. Heavy rains bogged guns and wagons whose teams were already suffering from short rations and sore backs – the latter a consequence of the poor harness discipline that would plague French armies into 1940. Troop movements were under constant observation from Prussians occupying the high ground. The sortie came to nothing. From Bazaine to the rear-rank reservists, the French were rapidly developing a first-rate case of what later military generations would call 'bunker psychosis' – unwillingness to test their chances outside of their defensive systems.[99]

That left it up to MacMahon. The original Army of the Rhine just might have slashed through, at least getting close enough to Metz to galvanize Bazaine into action. The Army of Châlons exhausted itself reaching the zone of operations. One corps moved no more than five miles in a day, over open terrain and a reasonably good road network. For an operation that would require a rapid crossing of the Meuse, MacMahon had forgotten to bring along the army's bridging trains. Supply arrangements made in Reims collapsed, and the advancing

---

[96]Audoin-Rouzeau, pp. 111–12.
[97]Charles C. de Montaubin, Comte de Palikao, *Un ministère de la guerre de vingt-quatre jours, du 10 août au 4 septembre 1870* (Paris, 1871), pp. 96 ff.
[98]Bazaine, pp. 107–8.
[99]A point highlighted by the account in ibid., pp. 158 ff.

units began living off the countryside. Some regiments sent out organized foraging parties, but in most cases, systematic requisitioning degenerated into indiscriminate plunder, with as much wasted as eaten.[100] By 27 August, the Army of Châlons had advanced no more than forty miles. It had also come under the detailed scrutiny of a Prussian cavalry screen, whose patrols found little difficulty brushing aside their French counterparts.

The Army of Châlons was facing an enemy confident in itself and its leaders. The unit cohesion facilitated by territorial recruiting made the heavy losses of 16 and 18 August particularly staggering. On 4 August, the average strength of a battalion in V Prussian Corps was 935; by 1 September, it was 640. The XII Corps had left its depots with an authorized strength of over 1,000 men per battalion; on 21 August, the average was down to 800. But here and there, lightly wounded back from the dressing stations sported bandages on heads or arms with the pride that can come from 'seeing the elephant' at close range. Stragglers who had fallen out at earlier stages of the campaign were rejoining. So, too, were men knocked loose from the ranks in the fighting around Metz, returning now with unverifiable stories of prodigies of valour performed with other regiments, and welcomed, nevertheless, because they were alive. The rank and file of the German regiments knew they were winning. They had seen the backs of their enemies from the border all the way into Metz. Paris was the next stop.[101]

Helmuth von Moltke, on the other hand, was in a temporary quandary. He considered the most logical French course of action to be a retreat on Paris. Instead, his wide-ranging cavalrymen informed him of the French movement from Châlons to Reims. Reports from the telegraph agencies of Reuters in Britain and Wolff in Berlin confirmed the shift. But why? The concept that politics might dictate operations – in this case, compelling MacMahon to march to Bazaine's relief, regardless of the military situation or the army's condition – did not immediately motivate the Prussian chief of staff to turn his forces in pursuit. Instead, he slowed the pace of the advance, shifted its axis slightly in the direction of Reims, waited for information and passed the time in working with his staff, calculating march tables for the various possible contingencies.

Among Moltke's favourite relaxations was whist, and he saw no reason to give up his evening foursome just because Prussia was at war. On the evening of 25 August, however, he was interrupted by a batch of recent Paris newspapers, describing in various degrees of detail the planned advance of the Army of Châlons to the relief of Metz, accompanied by a telegram from London passing on an article from the usually reliable *Temps*. Moltke put down his cards and remarked that 'the dummies will pay for this'.[102] The next day, both of his armies swung north into the Argonne Forest: 150,000 men, 600 guns and their supply trains, with rain turning the few decent roads to quagmires and sending up the sickness rate as wet feet and wet bivouacs bred respiratory problems and stiff joints. But the supply wagons were more or less keeping pace with the rifle companies. The 'kitchen bulls' were usually able to produce hot soup and hot coffee at the end of most marches. It was not much, but the French had less.[103]

---

[100]Barthélemy Lebrun, *Guerre de 1870. Bazeilles-Sedan* (Paris, 1884), pp. 42 ff., is an impressionistic account of the march by one of the corps commanders.

[101]German morale is analysed generally in Kuelich, pp. 175 ff.

[102]Kessel, *Moltke*, pp. 562 ff.

[103]Sukstorf, pp. 239 ff.

A week of stop-and-go mud marching might have put the prospective combatants on a more even footing of exhaustion and confusion. But that same afternoon, German troopers – Saxons from XII Corps, which had a full division of organic cavalry and used it to maximum advantage in the Sedan operation – crossed sabres with patrols from MacMahon's vanguards. The armies were close enough for Moltke to pass the word down the Germans' chains of command: close it up and keep moving.

The French continued their advance east throughout 27 August, every kilometre bringing them nearer to the Germans, moving north through the Argonne towards the Meuse. By day's end it was clear to MacMahon that, to reach Metz, he was going to have to fight his way through at least one layer of Germans. That was the only thing clear about his situation. Lacking any information on the whereabouts of either Bazaine or Moltke, MacMahon hesitated, informing the government that he now proposed to retreat to Paris, after all. The response was a flurry of telegrams warning of revolution, culminating in a direct order to continue to Bazaine's support.[104]

Napoleon could have countermanded the order, but by this time was a broken man, no more than a 'battle bum', following army headquarters. MacMahon, an old field soldier, could have refused to comply on his own responsibility. But 'responsibility' was the operative word. Patrice MacMahon was not the brightest military light in France, but he had seen enough service to know when a situation was disintegrating. In such circumstances, he was not the first, nor in any way the last, senior officer to cling to superior orders as a drowning man clutches a piece of flotsam. At least somebody, the somebodies in the government and on the council of regency, knew what they wanted to do. And maybe – just maybe – MacMahon could bring it off.

On 28 August, the marshal ordered his forward elements to cross the Meuse between Sedan and Stenay. The French marched – or rather, lurched – forward in a hard rain, under the eyes of German horsemen on the high ground to the south. The sense of being constantly observed, with no reaction from their own cavalry, did nothing for French morale.[105] When patrols found the Stenay bridges in the hands of Saxon infantry and the direct route to Montmédy blocked as well, the bad news spread like wildfire through MacMahon's disgruntled ranks. MacMahon shifted his march routes north. By evening, his two left-flank corps were in position to cross the Meuse unopposed. The other two, harassed by German cavalry, had lagged behind – and a Prussian patrol had captured a courier bearing MacMahon's revised orders.[106]

Moltke responded by ordering a general advance for 30 August. The Army of the Meuse was directed towards Beaumont, the Saxons on the right, around Stenay, with IV Corps extending the line to the south, the Prussian Guard in reserve behind them, and a demigod (in this case, Verdy) officer at Prince Albert's headquarters to make sure he did not go chasing after glory on his own. The 3rd Army, coming up on the left, received

[104]*La Guerre de 1870/1: l'Armée de Châlons*, vol. I, doc. annexes, p. 279.

[105]Prince George Bibesco, *Campagne de 1870. Belfort, Reims, Sedan. Le 7e Corps de l'Armée du Rhin* (Paris, 1872), p. 80. Pierre Lehautcourt (pseud. for Gen. B. Palat), *La Cavalerie allemand et l'armée de Châlons* (Paris, 1912), is an acknowledgement of the German troopers' effectiveness from the perspective of a knowledgeable enemy.

[106]Bronsart, p. 53.

orders to swing wide to the west, its two Bavarian corps directed on Buzancy, and the rest of the army towards le Chesne.[107]

To spare the roads and minimize rear-area congestion, Moltke ordered 'light marching order': no more than three days' food and ammunition. By this time, too, Prussian officers were learning something about traffic discipline. The Saxons and IV Corps, in particular, moved so smoothly through the thick forests in front of Beaumont that they caught a French corps – once again – in bivouac, with sentries unposted, horses unsaddled and guns unmanned. For the first hour or so, the course of events was predictable. Prussian artillery shelled the French camp into confusion, with demoralized soldiers and terrified refugees scattering in all directions and small-scale French counter-attacks crumbling under Prussian fire. But by 3.30, the French, Failly's 5th Corps, had set up a gun line a mile to the rear of their lost camp. French infantry rallied to the cannon, their chassepots stinging Prussians and Bavarians advancing over open slopes. Failly's men were ready to take out their frustration on anyone they could shoot at. The Germans, for their part, were by no means as eager as they had been a month earlier to sound the charge and go forward with drums beating. Instead, they brought up their artillery, probed for flanks and kept up a steady, unspectacular pressure that by day's end, pushed the Frenchmen into rout once more.[108]

It almost goes without saying that 5th Corps fought its battle alone. Its nearest neighbours were tangled in the forest and reinforcements arrived too late to do anything but cover the disaster: 5,000 men lost, plus guns, horses, wagons and the treasury of the supply services – 150,000 francs in hard money that could not be replaced easily under current circumstances. Small wonder that MacMahon decided the better part of wisdom was to fall back on the fortress of Sedan and sort out his army – and his thoughts – once more.

Sedan itself was less important than the terrain surrounding it. The marshy ground of the Meuse valley restricted any attacks from the south and west. To the north lay high, open ground, sloping downward to the city and offering a network of promising defensive positions – to an army large enough to hold them. Otherwise, once the line was breached, the sector could easily become a death trap: there was nowhere to go except downhill into Sedan. MacMahon knew that at least as well as his many subsequent critics. He knew that Sedan's magazines contained neither food, forage, nor enough ammunition for a fight to the finish. But MacMahon did not see his withdrawal as prefiguring some kind of last stand. He intended to remain at Sedan no longer than was needed to regroup and resume the march to Metz. If, in the process, he was able to bloody the Germans' noses, or perhaps even stage a second Gravelotte, that would be a bonus. Before moving in any direction, however, he needed to know where the Germans were. On 31 August, he ordered his cavalry to scout the terrain around Sedan in force the next day. For the rest of the army, 1 September would be a day of rest and reorganization.[109]

Given his intentions, MacMahon's deployment on the Sedan heights was logical, with 7th Corps holding the northern sector, 1st the east and 12th the south-east, its right flank

---

[107]*MMK* 1, vol. III, p. 263 and Verdy, pp. 112 ff. Cf. Kessel, *Moltke*, p. 565.

[108]Cf. H. von Hopfgarten-Heidler, *Die Schlacht von Beaumont* (Berlin, 1897) and Pierre Louis de Failly, *Opérations et marches du 5e Corps, jusqu'au 31 août* (Paris, 1871).

[109]Howard, pp. 204 ff., is a solid analysis of intentions MacMahon – at best – expressed obliquely at the time.

anchored on the fortified village of Bazeilles. What was left of 5th Corps constituted a reserve MacMahon did not expect to need. There was no reason to waste energy constructing field entrenchments, as some of his subordinates requested. After all, the army would be on the march again on 2 September. Fresh troops were on the way – a 13th Corps cobbled together in Paris. But instead of more men, another senior general arrived: a replacement for the now disgraced Failly. Emmanuel de Wimpffen, a veteran African fighter with a good reputation, was more than he seemed. He also held a 'dormant commission': if anything happened to MacMahon, he was to assume command of the army. It had been intended by the war ministry as a security blanket to prevent Napoleon, still with the army, from doing something stupid in an emergency.[110] Seen in hindsight, MacMahon was doing that quite well enough on his own.

Moltke, for his part, was driving his subordinates at all levels to overtake and overrun the French. He was sufficiently confident of victory that he even asserted a right of 'hot pursuit' into nearby Belgium. The orders for 31 August were simple enough to seem obvious. The Army of the Meuse would advance west between the Belgian frontier and the Meuse; the 3rd would advance north towards the river, extending its left flank far enough to cut off a French retreat. By nightfall, the Guard and the Saxons were in position, with IV Corps backing them up. In 3rd Army's sector, elements of II Bavarian Corps managed to seize a bridge over the Meuse and fight their way into Bazeilles long enough to cover the laying of two pontoon bridges as well. Further west, XI Corps's vanguards had seized another undamaged bridge at Donchery, and V Corps, behind them, was in position to swing across the French rear and establish contact with the Guard, making the envelopment of the Sedan position complete.[111]

On a map, however, the best that the French could conclude was that it was 'déjà vu all over again' – or, at least, Vionville all over again. The Prussians were closing in on Sedan; XI Corps, with V supporting it, was in position to repeat Alvensleben's manoeuvre should the French seek to retreat. That situation was bad enough, even though MacMahon seems not to have seriously considered the option of withdrawing – not least because, even at this late date, the French commander seemed to have no real idea of the forces against him. With a fecklessness prefiguring Dien Bien Phu, what passed for the intelligence service of the Army of Chalons did not take the trouble to add up the formations identified by patrols, or from casualties, in the various sectors of what was rapidly becoming a 360-degree front. Had they done so, elementary calculation would have shown they were outnumbered nearly two to one, even with maximum allowance for previous German losses and minimum deductions for French stragglers. The Germans, in contrast, kept careful track of the parent units of French stragglers and prisoners, and were correspondingly able to identify both the presence and the positions of all four of MacMahon's corps.[112]

At least MacMahon's army was in fighting position. But most of the comfort that circumstance provided dissipated as the Germans lit their bivouac fires for the night. The semicircle of flame beginning around Donchery and extending to the Belgian frontier was almost unbroken. 'We have them in a mousetrap', rejoiced Moltke. General Auguste

---

[110]Emmanuel Felix de Wimpffen, *Sedan* (3rd ed., Paris, 1871), p. 124 *passim*.
[111]*Moltkes Militaerische Werke* 1, vol. III, pp. 264–5. Cf. Kessel, *Moltke*, p. 565 and Howard, pp. 206–7.
[112]Howes, pp. 542–3 and Bronsart, p. 56.

Ducrot, the hardbitten commander of MacMahon's 1st Corps, found another metaphor: 'we're in a chamber pot, and tomorrow we're going to be shit on'.[113]

It was the Bavarians who opened the ball. Moltke wanted to give his wings, XI and V Corps, the Saxons and the Guard, time to tighten the noose, but General Ludwig von der Tann of I Bavarian Corps had other ideas. He was the senior Bavarian officer in the field and, as such, had a dual military/political responsibility that, in practice, resembled that of British Commonwealth commanders in World War II. Bavaria, the most powerful of the German middle states, could not afford to play a passive or secondary role in the battle that von der Tann believed was likely to decide the war. He had three bridges across the Meuse in his sector; his men had been forced to retreat yesterday; and he was able to convince himself that the French to his front sector might be preparing a withdrawal. Around 4 a.m., von der Tann sent his infantry forward against Bazeilles – and into a hornets' nest.

Bazeilles, the south-eastern anchor of the French line, was held by the best men in MacMahon's army: the *Troupes de la Marine*. These regiments were under the navy ministry – hence their name – but were not marines in the British or US sense. They were, rather, an élite expeditionary force of long-service professionals. From Mexico to China, from Senegal to Tahiti, the *Marsouins* had seen it all and done most of it. Now they fought for Bazeilles with a grim determination learned in campaigns where surrender was seldom a viable option.[114] The Bavarians initially advanced without artillery, and were shot down like rabbits in the streets. They occupied some of the empty buildings, brought up guns and began fighting their way forward, house to house. Bazeilles burst into flame as both sides sought to burn out strong points that defied bayonet charges. In that kind of close-gripped fighting, the rules of war grew remote. Von der Tann himself noted that 'excesses' took place. Frenchmen who threw down their rifles were shot or bayoneted. While most of the civilians had left, a few remained in their homes. Some denied soldiers were in their houses. Others were swept up when strong points were overrun. A few were taken with rifles in their hands.

The Bavarians, like the rest of 3rd Army, had encountered small-scale irregular warfare since entering Alsace. Most of it involved stragglers rather than civilians, and, in any case, standing orders required civilians suspected of partisan activity to be held for trial. In Bazeilles, proceedings were more direct. French mythology initially described a general massacre of the town's 2,000 inhabitants. After the war, however, French authorities verified only thirty-nine civilian deaths. Eight had been burned or asphyxiated – mostly children and the elderly, dying in the ruins of their homes. Thirty-one were listed as having been killed, wounded or missing as a direct result of the fighting.

That was a long way from a massacre. Nor were military prisoners killed either in groups or in cold blood; most of those who died with their hands empty had taken a bit too long to surrender. It is clear, nevertheless, that French civilians in Bazeilles were shot out of hand – and that the Bavarians regarded such punishment as appropriate. War was a matter

---

[113]Blumenthal, p. 110 and C. Sarazin, *Récits sur la dernière guerre franco-allemande* (Paris, 1887), pp. 114–15. Sarazin was senior medical officer of the division in whose ranks Ducrot spent the night.

[114]Bazeilles remains a centrepiece of the French marines' identity and mythology, similar to the places Iwo Jima, Inchon and Hue hold for the US Marine Corps. The battle is featured on the website and in the museum of the *Troupes de la Marine*. The defence of one strong point, 'The Farm of the Last Cartridges', is commemorated annually on the site.

of armies, and an affair of men. While only one woman was an official casualty of the fighting for Bazeilles, Bavarians reported seeing armed women everywhere, brandishing weapons and uttering curses. These *Flintenweiber* may have been largely constructions of imagination, phantoms of a kind of close-quarter street fighting that seemed unnatural to soldiers trained exclusively to fight in the open. They symbolized a comprehensive loss of control – some of it inherent to street fighting, some of it reflecting the later emergence of people's war in Paris and the provinces.[115]

The issue of civilian deaths in Bazeilles has attracted such disproportionate attention that it is worth emphasizing that the Bavarians' chief concern was taking the place, and they were by no means sure of the outcome. As 12th Corps moved promptly to support the garrison, Ducrot extended 1st Corps south to cover his neighbour's flank by occupying the village of Daigny. That was the Saxons' sector of advance, and Prince Albert took pains to deploy most of the artillery of his corps – sixteen batteries – to shoot in his riflemen. Not until 10 a.m. did the Saxons establish firm contact with von der Tann's sorely tried Bavarians and take firm hold of Daigny.

'Firm' was the master adjective on the French side of the line as well. MacMahon had ridden promptly to the sound of the guns around Bazeilles. Around 6 a.m., he took a shell fragment in his leg – a wound just serious enough to impel him to turn over command. His designated successor was Ducrot, easily the hardest fighter among the corps commanders, and a correspondingly logical choice. He received news of his elevation two hours later, just about the time the Saxon attack on Daigny was developing, and just as the advance units of the Prussian Guard began approaching Ducrot's hitherto unengaged left flank.

Then the German gunners got lucky once more. A shell burst killed the general commanding the division at Daigny – the last of Ducrot's pre-war senior subordinates, and the one he most trusted. At this stage of the battle the French still had options. Bazeilles was holding; the Saxons and the Guardsmen were taking their own time to advance. But Ducrot had not seen MacMahon in days and had no idea of his immediate intentions. He knew only vaguely the positions of the other French corps and the German forces. His corps staff was a force of aides and couriers, not a planning body. It was scarcely remarkable that Ducrot acted on the general impression he had pithily expressed the night before. He ordered a general retreat.

He also met a prompt challenge from one of his former colleagues. General Barthélémy Lebrun's 12th Corps was holding its positions nicely, but its projected line of retreat lay through some of the roughest terrain on the field. Given the army's previous problems with moving over broken ground, might it not make more sense to fight it out? Ducrot, who, for practical purposes, continued to command his own corps as well as the army, replied that the Germans were fighting no more than holding actions; the real threat came from the flanks. Surprisingly, given his temperament, he did not issue Lebrun a direct order to retreat until later in the morning, and by that time a wild card had appeared on the field.

Wimpffen initially did not attempt to exercise his dormant commission, but when he learned of Ducrot's withdrawal order he rode to Lebrun's headquarters, announced that he

---

[115]See the excellent analysis by Mark Stoneman, 'The Bavarian Army and French Civilians in the War of 1870–71: A Cultural Interpretation', *War in History* 8 (2001), pp. 271–93.

was in command and declared that the Army of Châlons would stand and fight. 'We need a victory', he informed the enraged Ducrot. Wimpffen, also, was more aware than Ducrot of the speed and scope of the German flank movement to the west. Stretched out in line of march, the Army of Châlons was likely to be overrun in detail. If it stood its ground, the *baraka*, the warrior's luck so prized by the Army of Africa, might still be with it at day's end.[116]

Helmuth von Moltke was not superstitious. March discipline, firepower, speed and shock – this was the stuff of Prussia's way of war. The 3rd Army's XI and V Corps had been on the march since before dawn, first north, then east along the high road from Mezieres to Sedan – Ducrot's projected line of retreat. The road, in some places more of a wide track, could not support the simultaneous advance of both corps, especially since both commanders had learned their lessons and had every gun they could muster as far forward as possible in their respective columns. At a village called Floing, the advance divided, V Corps (under some protest by its commander, who feared missing out on the glory) swinging north and left, XI Corps following the main road to the sound of the guns.

Julius von Bose, the corps's original commander, had taken a wound at Woerth that troubled him for the rest of the war.[117] His successor, the 22nd Division's Major General Konstantin von Gersdorff, on 1 September 1870, was the epitome of the good, ordinary general who often determines the course of battles at their sharp ends. By 10 a.m., most of his corps artillery was in position to take the French 7th Corps under fire. He had only a minimal screening force of infantry, but those half-dozen battalions were more than enough to smash desperate French efforts to overrun the gun line. As V Corps's batteries came into position on his left, 150 guns began a systematic bombardment of 7th Corps's positions. From the other direction, the Prussian Guard, its officers determined not to be overshadowed a second time by the plebeian Saxons, drove forward under cover of its own corps artillery, massed by a Hohenloe determined to avert another St Privat. As patrols of the Guard cavalry linked up with V Corps's infantry to complete the envelopment in the north, the artillery of the two Bavarian corps and IV Prussian Corps, whose infantry was still mostly in reserve, came into line in the south.[118]

The French responded by deploying to meet an attack in the style of Woerth, Vionville and St Privat: expecting heavy skirmish lines, followed by columns of infantry, to be mowed down by the chassepots. Instead, the German guns kept up their relentless hammering. In every sector, men began to straggle out of the line – by ones and twos, then in larger groups, ostensibly supporting wounded comrades. The French artillerymen, outnumbered, outranged and outshot, stood to their guns. Some batteries emptied their caissons in an effort to provide at least moral support to the hard-hammered infantry. Others hunkered down, saving what ammunition they had for the final charge that eventually had to come.

But the rules of combat were changing. As the day began to turn, the German infantry still held their positions, still let the guns do their work. Wimpffen sought to mount a

---

[116]Cf. A. Ducrot, *Journée de Sedan* (Paris, 1871); Sarazin, pp. 120 ff.; Lebrun, pp. 101 ff.; and Wimpffen, p. 162 for direct accounts of interchanges and intentions. Albert du Casse, *Le Général de Wimpffen: Réponse au Général Ducrot par un officier supérieur* (Paris, 1871), makes Wimpffen's case. Howard, pp. 209 ff., is the best reconstruction.

[117]Bronsart, p. 355.

[118]The official *The Franco-German War 1870–71*, ed. Grosser Generalstab, tr. Capt. F. C. H. Clarke (5 vols., London, 1874–84), vol. II, pp. 353 ff., offers a coherent general narrative. Hohenloe, vol. IV, pp. 177 ff., gives a gunner's perspective on what rapidly became an artillery battle.

breakthrough southwards around Bazeilles. He pulled together what he could of 5th Corps, and part of 1st, even borrowing a division from the hard-pressed 7th and asking Napoleon to put himself at the head of the sortie. It was the kind of *beau geste* that, even in failure, might become the stuff of legends, enough to preserve, at least for a while, an empire whose fragility had been apparent to Wimpffen well before he left Paris.[119]

Napoleon did not appear. Instead, German shellfire continued to reduce the French rear areas to chaos, with every path, track and ride under the kind of steady bombardment that precluded organizing a large-scale counter-attack. Facing almost no opposition from the French artillery, Prussian batteries, in particular, maintained almost peacetime procedures. As caissons emptied, they were replaced from the rear echelons, and these, in turn, were refilled from the ammunition trains pre-war conservatives had often dismissed as redundant. The still inexact craft of ranging, the unequal quality of black-powder rounds and the steady shrinking of the battlefield meant that 'friendly' fire inflicted increasingly heavy losses – particularly when batteries were firing in support of other than their own corps. Nevertheless, from the German artillery's perspective, at least, on the afternoon of 1 September, everything was going by the book: the book as rewritten by Prussia's artillerymen after 1866.

An end to horror was preferable to horror without end. It was 7th Corps that broke first. By 1 p.m. its right-flank regiments were pinned in place, their survivors able to do no more than rally on their colours and stand their ground as the skirmish lines and company columns of V Corps flowed into the gaps between them. At the same time, elements of XI Corps were enveloping 7th Corps's other flank, left exposed by the silencing of its artillery support. The key to the sector, the high ground around the *calvaire d'Illy*, was defended by little more than stragglers and fragments of Ducrot's corps when the Prussians closed in on it around 2 p.m. By 3 p.m., French soldiers were leaving the line by companies, some heading for woods like the Bois de la Garenne, others for Sedan itself, with its illusory promise of shelter from the shells that seemed to come from everywhere and never seemed to stop.

On the eastern side of the envelopment, the Saxons had pushed their gun line to the high ground west of Daigny. Further north, Hohenloe brought most of the Guard's batteries into position to hammer the Bois de la Garenne. Here, it was scientific gunnery on a new scale, with each battery sighting one piece on a specific point at the wood's edge, then the other five taking the same aiming point and increasing the range by another hundred paces, bringing the forest under a controlled rain of shellfire to a depth of over 500 paces. Should the French look like mounting an escape attempt in any sector, the guardsmen concentrated on the target of opportunity, then resumed their assigned fire plans. What remained of French unit coordination vanished as regiments, then companies, dissolved into amorphous bands of survivors moving aimlessly from place to place. Prussian shell and shrapnel were contact-fused. As would happen again in the Huertgen Forest and the Ardennes, tree bursts scourged the French to a point where, at times, it seemed at though the men were being herded, rather than driven, by the guns.

As the barrage was getting under way, one of the Guard's division commanders approached Hohenloe and suggested he stop showing off. 'I want to storm the woods over there', General von Pape declared. Hohenloe replied, '... you probably want to lose as many men again as you

[119]Wimpffen, p. 218; Lebrun, pp. 119–20; and Henri de Castlenau, 'Sedan et Wilhelmshoehe: Journal du Général Castlenau, aide-de-camp de Napoleon III', *Revue de Paris* 36 (1 and 15 October and 1 November 1929), p. 853.

did two weeks ago. If you attack those woods before I've worn the people over there all the way down, I'll open up on you!' Pape, who probably meant the whole thing as a joke, called Hohenloe 'a rough cob' (*ein grober Kerl*) and betook himself to his infantrymen – who, in one regiment at least, were taking off their spiked helmets, with the glittering eagles that revealed their position to the French.[120] Even the Prussian Guard could learn from experience.

It was 2.30 when the Duke of Wuerttemberg finally sent the Guard's skirmish lines forward. The Saxons and XI Corps, by now under its third commander in a month – Gersdorff having been mortally wounded by a rifle shot – followed suit. Most of their work was mopping up: accepting surrenders, collecting swords and flags, doing what they could for the wounded until the stretcher-bearers arrived. In some cases, Frenchmen fought Frenchmen, as units still seeking to break out confronted comrades ready to shoot their own countrymen to make an end.[121] By 5 p.m., the 1st and 7th Corps of the Army of Châlons had been removed from the board.

Earlier in the afternoon, as 7th Corps began to unravel, Ducrot arrived in its sector, acting on what amounted to his own unauthorized initiative. Unable to stop by himself the steady erosion of the French position, he returned to his *idée fixe* of a breakout to the west. By this time, the Army of Châlons had exhausted its infantry reserves. There remained, however, a cavalry division: four regiments of *chasseurs d'Afrique*, hard veterans of the empire's wars on four continents, but with no experience of charging *en masse*. Now Ducrot rode up to their commander, General Jean Margueritte, and did not spare the melodrama. 'Take your people', Ducrot ordered, 'and open a road for the rest of us! Cut a way through for what infantry can still be saved!' Margueritte responded promptly. As his regiments fell into line, he made a personal reconnaissance of the ground over which they were to charge. A stray bullet ripped his face open; he had only enough energy to point towards the German positions before collapsing. With shouts and mutterings of 'vengeance', the chasseurs moved from walk to trot to gallop.

Their panache left even the King of Prussia applauding. 'Ah! Les braves gens', William murmured as the chasseurs' attack crested. The Westphalians and Thuringians facing the charge were less impressed – both ways. The skirmishers in the van dropped to the ground, beneath the sweep of the chasseurs' sabres. The formed units to the rear opened fire. Few men could hear the shouts attempting to organize volleys. No officers considered forming square. The chasseurs were shot down *ad hoc*, dead men and dying horses piling up in front of the German rifles. But the speed of the charge and the endurance of the little Arab barbs the men rode, kept their losses lower than might have been expected. Enough survived and rallied that Ducrot was able to send them in twice more over the same ground. 'As often as you like, my general', replied Margueritte's successor, General Gaston de Gallifet, 'as long as there's one of us left'. It was a *beau geste* that made Gallifet's career. But having seen off the chasseurs once, the infantry of XI Corps made short work of the later attempts. A pleasing counterpoint to the legends of murder in cold blood surrounding Bazeilles has Gallifet, at the head of a few survivors, riding past a Prussian regiment whose men held their fire, and whose officers saluted as a tribute to their enemies' courage and honour.[122]

---

[120]Cf. Hohenloe, vol. IV, pp. 196 ff. and Howard, pp. 214 ff.

[121]*La Guerre 1870/1, l'Armée de Châlons*, vol. III, doc. annexes, p. 191.

[122]Ducrot, pp. 410 ff.; Charles Rozat de Mandres, *Les Régiments de la Division Margueritte et les charges à Sedan* (Paris, 1908); and Jean Guirec, 'La Division Margueritte', *Revue Historique de l'armée* 27 (1971), no. 1, pp. 128–34.

As the cavalry died and their corps dissolved, Lebrun, Douay and Ducrot separately followed a common course: find the emperor. Growing mobs of French soldiers surged around the small fortress of Sedan, whose governor had locked the gates. Most of these men were from the rear echelons, detached from their companies as cooks and baggage guards, wagon drivers, the mildly sick excused duty and the lightly wounded. Napoleon had earlier ridden aimlessly around the battlefield, vainly seeking a death that came to so many better men. Now, demoralized and nearly incoherent with pain, he raised a white flag and demanded that a delegate be sent across the lines to discuss surrender terms. His generals protested.[123] But as word of the truce flag spread, any hope of rallying the demoralized masses crowding down the slopes and into the town vanished.

Wimpffen, an eternal optimist, still wanted to fight. He and Lebrun managed to galvanize a couple of thousand men for one last charge. By chance, the sortie hit II Bavarian Corps, driving it back and helping to establish a legend of Bavarian fecklessness that survived well into the Great War. But the Bavarians rallied and the German guns reopened fire. The rush dissolved as rapidly as it began. What remained were isolated rifle shots, a few artillery salvoes, and then silence, as even the most fire-eating battery commanders realized that there were no more targets.[124]

Moltke had noticed the white flag flying from Sedan's walls and sent one of his young staff officers to investigate. Napoleon replied with a message. Unable to die at the head of his troops, he commended his sword to the hands of his brother, William of Prussia.[125] Bismarck sent his answer: Napoleon's surrender was accepted; Moltke would negotiate the details of handing over the Army of Châlons. After a bitter argument, Wimpffen agreed to act for France. He was accompanied by an officer of the imperial suite, General Henri Pierre Castlenau, as Napoleon's spokesman, and entertained hopes of salvaging something from the débâcle. But when Wimpffen threatened to continue the fight, Moltke asked him what he proposed to use for an army. When Wimpffen appealed to generosity as the best basis for a lasting peace, Bismarck responded by attacking France as the historic disturber of Europe's equilibrium. He excoriated the Jacobin democracy that had ignited the current conflict. He insisted on Germany's securing territory and frontiers as safeguards against future aggression.

Then the chancellor cut to the chase. Was Napoleon surrendering himself or France? If France was capitulating, Bismarck broadly hinted, matters might be arranged in an entirely different fashion than his earlier words suggested. Castlenau, apparently stunned by the question and the tirade preceding it, stammered that the surrender was personal. Neither Moltke nor Bismarck pushed the issue – not least because even the lesser victory in their hands exceeded all but the wildest hopes of the most extreme pre-war optimists. The rest was a matter of formalities: Wimpffen consulting his generals and surrendering the Army of Châlons as prisoners of war; Napoleon meeting briefly with William, then disappearing into gilded captivity at the castle of Wilhelmshohe; and Moltke and Bismarck considering their next moves in a conflict that suddenly seemed to stretch before them on an unmapped road.[126]

---

[123]Lebrun, p. 123 and Ducrot, p. 130.
[124]Wimpffen, pp. 173 ff.; Lebrun, pp. 135 ff.; and *Franco-German War*, vol. II, pp. 397 ff.
[125]Bronsart, pp. 58 ff.
[126]Castlenau, pp. 857 ff.; Wimpffen, pp. 329 ff.; the report in *La Guerre 1870–71: l'Armée de Chalons*, vol. III, pp. 248 ff.; and Verdy, pp. 136 ff. combine for the surrender negotiations.

8

The Republic Strikes Back

From the conventional perspectives of cabinet war, it was all over. France's armies were destroyed or neutralized; France's emperor was a prisoner. The catastrophe of Sedan struck a country already conditioned to bad news from the front. But the hostility of both the French masses and the French élite had a focus: the empire had led the country to disaster. They also had something unique in Europe: a template for replacing a government while continuing a war. France had done that before, with an alien enemy at the gates, in 1792. Now in Paris, General Louis Trochu became president of a council of national defence, the striking arm of a new republic. Leon Gambetta, a provincial politician more noted for charisma than judgment, took over as minister of the interior. The empress went into exile, and what remained of the imperial administration was integrated into a re-energized war effort as Right and Left alike rallied to a new iteration of 'the Fatherland in danger'.[1]

I

Across the line, Prussian royal headquarters was increasingly suffering from an artificial, hothouse atmosphere, where too many strong-willed people, deprived of their normal routines, had too little to do. The resulting patterns of backbiting, tale-bearing and grievance-nurturing were a poor matrix for mutual understanding.[2] A quarter of a century later, Bismarck told of overhearing, in the train taking him to the front at the start of the war, a senior staff officer saying that this time Bismarck would be kept from meddling in operational affairs.[3] Nevertheless, in the campaign's early stages Bismarck had no significant difficulty accepting the dichotomy between 'military' and 'political/diplomatic' spheres that Moltke insisted was necessary for effective war making. Certainly, Vionville and Gravelotte offered little room for the exercise of his characteristic skills. At the same time, for Moltke there was no question of challenging the chancellor's central position in the negotiations at Sedan. The chief of staff, on the other hand, was sufficiently casual about his own place and status in those proceedings that, as French resistance collapsed, he took dinner in his quarters and, after a few celebratory glasses of wine, fell fast asleep. Shaken

---

[1] Audoin-Rouzeau, pp. 143 ff., comprehensively surveys the events of 4 September and their immediate consequences.

[2] Bronsart's diary describes the environment admirably. Like many of his counterparts, military and political, Bronsart was not a 'natural' intriguer, but susceptible to its chief temptation, gossip, when not kept busy.

[3] Eberhard Kolb, 'Strategie und Politik in den deutschen Einigungskriegen: Ein unbekanntes Bismarck-Gespraech aus dem Jahr 1895', *Militaergeschichtliche Mitteilungen* 48 (1990), p. 131.

awake and told the French had come to surrender, Moltke cleared his head by thrusting it into a basin of cold water.[4] He would have been well advised to remember that sensible act in subsequent weeks and, perhaps, even repeat it.

Bismarck had never intended to destroy the French Empire – only to conclude peace on terms involving the permanent weakening of France. Squaring that circle depended on negotiating the kind of settlement which left enough on the table to deter the loser from later attempts to reverse the situation through war. And that, in turn, required an opposite number who understood how the game was played. Had Napoleon's surrender 'spoken for France', the possibility existed of concluding a tentative peace agreement with some standing in international law, regardless of what might subsequently transpire in Paris or elsewhere.[5] Instead, the capitulation was personal. The republic was not opposed to negotiating a peace – but its terms must require France to yield 'not an inch of her soil nor a stone of her fortresses'.[6] It was brave talk for an improvised government with an enemy army deep in its territory. What would it take to change minds, if not hearts, in Paris? Could it be done without a still embryonic Germany conquering itself to exhaustion in a total war whose outlines had appeared on the slopes of St Privat and the heights of Sedan?

Bismarck considered giving the French time to understand how desperate their position really was – time for the adrenalin of revolution to exhaust itself, and time for the new government to establish enough domestic and international legitimacy to give its decisions credibility. Moltke saw the problem from a military perspective, and advocated a prompt advance to Paris as the next step in completing the kind of victory of which even Frederick the Great had only dreamed. No one at royal headquarters, least of all Bismarck, was prepared to argue.[7] On 7 September, the victors of Sedan broke camp. By 20 September, the 3rd Army and the Army of the Meuse had completed the encirclement of Paris. The Army of the Meuse took position around the city's northern half with no problems. The 3rd Army swatted away a poorly organized sortie, whose survivors fled with a cry soon to become all too familiar – 'we are betrayed' – and Blumenthal expected no more than token resistance in general. One of his subordinates declared the Bavarians would penetrate the city's defences while on their routine foraging expeditions, which by now were becoming a running joke in the rest of the army.[8]

'The attack on Paris is being eagerly studied', noted Bronsart on 7 September, in that German passive voice construction that removes direct responsibility from anyone in particular.[9] Should resistance prove serious, the Germans had three alternatives: storm the city, starve it out or compel its surrender by bombardment. The first alternative was rejected out of hand even by the most reckless fire-eaters. A city the size of Paris would absorb and digest the 150,000 or so available Germans without a belch, drawing them into exactly the kind of street-by-street fighting that maximized the strengths of the new Republic's

---

[4]Kessel, *Moltke*, p. 568.
[5]See Joachim Kuehn, 'Bismarck und der Bonapartismus im Winter 1870/71', *Preussische Jahrbuecher* 163 (1916), pp. 49–100.
[6]The *défi* of 6 September, in *Dépêches, circulaires, décrets, proclamations et discours Leon Gambetta*, ed. J. Reinach (2 vols., Paris, 1886), vol. I, pp. 6 ff.
[7]Cf. Howard, p. 229 and Kessel, *Moltke*, p. 569.
[8]Bronsart, p. 94.
[9]Ibid., p. 67.

improvised levies. Logistics were the rub of both other prospects. If it remained in one place, the German force was too large to live off the country, especially since the rapid advance from Sedan had left the countryside in question barely occupied and hardly conquered. It must be supplied primarily from Germany. Two major railway lines were available. Both had suffered from the effects of French demolitions. Both were blockaded directly by small fortresses the German advance bypassed, and threatened by other, larger works in their neighbourhoods. Lille, Peronne, Soissons, Thionville, Toul, Strasbourg – the list read like a Baedeker of obsolescent defences that had not been worth the cost of updating, even to the French. The Prussian army deliberately devoted little attention to siege operations, regarding them as costing time and resources best applied to decisive operations in the open field. The small and medium-sized works that dotted the landscape of eastern France had been dismissed before the war as mantraps, whose garrisons of second-line troops would surrender once their field armies were defeated. Instead, the bypassed fortresses were now either stalling or openly defying summonses to surrender made by forces of a few battalions and a couple of field batteries.[10]

Meanwhile, in front of Paris, negotiations between Bismarck and the republic's representatives went nowhere. Jules Favre, the new government's foreign minister, was a long-time moderate republican who had fallen into an intellectual pattern of ascribing primary responsibility for Europe's problems to an aggressive and incompetent Second Empire.[11] His position that Prussia should be grateful for Napoleon's exit and would be well advised to seek the goodwill of a new French order foundered when he spoke of restoring the *status quo ante bellum* in terms more appropriate to victors in a pitched battle than to revolutionaries besieged in a capital they controlled largely by force of arms. Talk of no annexations received an even more dusty answer in the context of Prussian plans that, even in the war's early stages, expected to redraw the eastern frontiers to provide security against the war of revenge believed certain to come.[12] Strasbourg, Bismarck said, Strasbourg and Alsace, part of Lorraine as well – those were the minimum demands of an emerging German Empire. Favre collapsed in tears, accused Bismarck of trying to destroy France and returned to Paris.

Meanwhile, the new government continued to mobilize the internal human and material resources of France for a defence *à outrance*. Most of France was still well outside German reach. Local lines of authority might be unclear, and local popular enthusiasm might be limited, but there was an ample supply of arms, with more available every week to a France whose navy controlled both its coastal waters and the open ocean.

The provinces' war effort was further galvanized on 7 October, when Gambetta escaped from Paris across Prussian lines in a hot-air balloon. His critics suggested that the mode of transportation was particularly appropriate. Nevertheless Gambetta brought his own driving energy – less homicidal, but no less determined that that of Robespierre and Danton a century earlier. He brought ministerial authority to the national mobilization.

---

[10]Cf. Hans-Justus Kreker, 'Die franzoesischen Festungen 1870/71', *Wehrwissenschaftliche Rundschau* 20 (1970), pp. 505–17 and the stupefyingly detailed work of Herman Frobenius, *Kriegsgeschichtliche Beispiele des Festungskrieges aus dem deutsch-franzoesischen Krieges 1870/71* (2 vols., Berlin, 1899–1906).

[11]The account of these negotiations is based on Jules Favre, *Gouvernement de défense nationale du 30 juin 1870* (3 vols., Paris, 1871–5), vol. I, pp. 156 ff.

[12]Eberhard Kolb, 'Der Kriegsrat zu Herny am 14. August 1870: Zur Entstehung des Annexionsentschlusses der preussischen Fuehrungsspitze im Krieg von 1870', *Militaergeschichtliche Mitteilungen* 9 (1971), pp. 5–13.

And he conveyed as well an understanding that Paris was not in a position to defeat the Boche with its own resources. To win the war — and Gambetta accepted nothing else — revolutionary capital and still cautious provinces would have to synergize their efforts.[13]

A few of the old army's regiments had, by one means or another, escaped the débâcle of the frontiers. The *Troupes de la Marine* emptied their depots, providing both steady infantry and experienced gunners. Algeria furnished a small contingent, including the Foreign Legion, previously forbidden by law from serving on French soil. Paramilitary bodies, the gendarmerie and the customs guards also made their contributions. The core of the new armies, however, were the provisional regiments raised by combining or expanding the depot battalions of the imperial regiments and filling them out with reservists and recruits. Manpower was not a problem. In a still agricultural country, with the harvest largely in, and local commerce disrupted by the war, men were willing enough to report to the army and eat government *soupe* for the winter months. The rank and file were mostly youngsters, twenty-one or less, unmarried, last hired and first fired, limited hostages to the tyranny of every day. The bulk of the rest of the new army came from the mobile guards, originally projected as a second-line force, of men not drafted for active service in peacetime. Over 300 battalions of them existed on paper by the time of Sedan; over 250 would eventually serve in the provincial field armies. Despite the despair of regular officers for their lack of formal discipline and of republicans for their refusal to be galvanized by patriotic rhetoric, the mobiles, on the whole, gave what they had and improved with experience. Their artillery, eventually over 150 batteries, did well both in the field and behind walls throughout the republic's war. Finally, there was the national guard. Originally a middle-class volunteer force, it had been reorganized as part of the Niel reforms as a second-line local defence force, a *Garde sedentaire* complementing the *Garde mobile*. It expanded to become the eventual major focus of national mobilization, with over 700 battalions in existence — and half of those in the field — by the end of the war. Lacking both cadres and training, these guardsmen saw relatively little combat — but there were a lot of them, with promise of more to come.

Exact orders of battle for the republic's armies are difficult to construct, but in most cases, commanders sought to send their best units to the front and to equalize experience. At the end of November, for example, the Army of the Loire had six corps. Its assigned infantry strength on paper was approximately thirty-five regiments of mobiles, twenty-five provisional regiments formed from line depots, and ten more of regulars, *Troupes de la Marine* and the Army of Africa. Standard practice was to brigade as far as possible a regular or provisional regiment with one of mobiles, in the pattern of line and Landwehr in Prussia before the Roon reforms, as opposed to concentrating the established formations.

For practical purposes, the new armies had no cavalry — only improvised formations of untrained men on unfit horses, capable of short-ranged scouting, at best. The artillery depots and the factories furnished sufficient guns to field enough batteries to make

---

[13]The most recent and comprehensive study of Gambetta's chequered career is Pierre Antonmattei, *Leon Gambetta: héraut de la République* (Paris, 1999), with pp. 77–136 concentrating on the war years. James R. Lehning, 'Gossiping about Gambetta: Contested Memories in the Early Third Republic', *French Historical Studies* 18 (1993), pp. 237–54, analyses the processes of constructing Gambetta's historical image. Still useful on the specific subject of national mobilization are Colmar von der Goltz, *Gambetta und seine Armeen* (Berlin, 1877) and Henri Dutrait-Crozon, *Gambetta et la défense nationale* (Paris, 1914).

adequate noise to give the infantry hope. After the battles of the frontier, after Sedan, French artillery officers expected to do little more than stiffen the improvised infantry levies that were going to carry the war's burden. There were enough rifles for most of those that could be expected to fight. In particular, the arms manufacturers of a (Re)United States were more than willing to pass on, at knockdown prices, the vast surplus of now unsaleable rifles from the recent Civil War. Many of them were metallic cartridge breech-loaders, arguably superior to the chassepot itself and relatively easy for the new infantry of a new government to learn how to use.

What was missing were regimental cadres and senior leadership. Gambetta's abolition of pre-war restrictions on promotions and assignments at least enabled the opening of opportunities to ambition, if not always the opening of careers to talent. Enlisted men and cadets from the military schools donned the *galons* of junior officers. A crop of majors and colonels, some from the depots, some recent retirees, and some who escaped or evaded the surrenders, became instant generals. Admirals were assigned to command divisions and corps – doing very well on the whole, it might be added. But company and battalion commanders remained scarce – particularly those able to drill men. Paradoxically, the French Imperial Army had not needed to pay attention to the details of training recruits quickly on a large scale. The *bleus* tended to learn by imitating the veterans. The captains and majors – especially those their parent regiments chose to leave behind when the war started – were correspondingly able to say, 'carry on, *chef*', and retire to the casino for a little refreshment.

Apart from the professionals' shortcomings, the right of the national guard to elect its own officers, a right later extended to the mobiles, virtually assured the development in the republic's armies of a pattern of 'command by consensus', with NCOs and regimental officers taking pains to avoid, whenever possible, giving direct orders that might be challenged by their recipients. That pattern was not – indeed is not – uncommon in citizen armies. Nor does it guarantee entropy and ineffectiveness. It does, however, depend for success on experience – and on enough initial successes to generate confidence in the army's institutional competence.[14]

What were the chances of winning such successes against Moltke's armies? In retrospect, German field officers and staff men alike had no doubts their trained and tempered forces could defeat any multiple of newly raised, undisciplined levies. The actual mood in the fall of 1870 was less sanguine.[15] It was not that they lacked troops – they just were not quite the right kind of troops. The front-loaded mobilization system of the North German Confederation had brought all of the active army's organized higher formations into the field and sent them to France. Apart from a division left behind in north Prussia for coast defence, and a few scattered regiments, further reinforcements depended on mobilizing Prussia's Landwehr. In theory, each regiment formed two battalions for active service, and, eventually, no fewer than four divisions built around the Landwehr would see

---

[14]Audoin-Rouzeau, pp. 184 ff., is the best modern overview of the republic's levies. The official volume, *La Guerre de 1870/1: La Défense Nationale en Province*, offers a wealth of supporting detail. Specialized works include Hermann Kunz, *Die Zusammensetzung der franzoesischen Provinzialarmeen im Kriege von 1870/71* (Berlin, 1892) and L. Girard, *La Garde nationale, 1814–1871* (Paris, 1964).

[15]See Stig Foerster, 'Optionen der Kriegfuehrung im Zeitalter des "Volkskrieges" – Zu Helmuth von Moltkes militaerisch-politischen Ueberlegung nach den Erfahrungen der Einigungskriegen' in *Militaerische Verantwortung in Staat und Gesellschaft*, ed. D. Bald (Munich, 1986), pp. 83–107.

action, ranging from local security in quiet regions, to sieges like Belfort and Strasbourg, to taking the field alongside the active army in the war's later stages. The Landwehr's primary mission, however, was rear security in occupied France, and no local commander ever admitted he had enough of them. About 130 of the almost 170 non-divisional Landwehr battalions mobilized during the war would be sent to France.[16]

A major objective of the Roon reforms had been to avoid using the Landwehr in any numbers, and to depend, instead, on trained, young men to fight Prussia's wars. But by mid-September, the Prussian army had suffered 70,000 battle casualties. Another 130,000 men were in hospitals. The depot battalions were just about able to replace the combat losses, providing about 50,000 men in September – but at the price of nearly exhausting the supply of pre-war-trained men. What remained available were wartime conscripts and volunteers, and only about 50,000 of those. 1870's class of conscripts was called up only in September, and would not be ready for service until into the new year.[17]

The longer the war continued, in other words, the more the limitations of the system introduced in 1860 emerged. It correspondingly behoved Moltke and his subordinates to return to the pre-Sedan days of defining the war on their terms – initially by breaking their active corps formations free for field service against the Republic's new armies. The most obvious source of trained and organized manpower was the siege works around Metz, where Bazaine continued to contemplate a breakout and determine his exact relationship to the new government. He tested the first alternative on 31 August, in an attempted sortie to meet MacMahon's presumed advance. Initially well supported by their artillery, the French infantry drove deep into Prussian positions in the valley of Noisseville. But slack command and poor cooperation at corps level were compounded by Bazaine's (by then) predictable failure to exercise even normally decisive command. The Germans rallied, brought up their ubiquitous guns and shelled the French back into Metz the next day.[18]

The high command still regarded itself as the servant of the empire, even after learning of MacMahon's surrender. Thoughts of transferring allegiance to the republic were blurred by practical considerations. If the former Army of the Rhine pledged a new allegiance, should it seek to strike for a Paris itself besieged, and accept the risk of another and worse defeat? The Prussians made their victory at Noisseville look sufficiently easy that very little optimism about reversing the results survived at regimental levels.[19] To stand siege to the limit, the other military alternative, depended on some realistic hope of being relieved. The republic's main armies were forming in the Loire valley: operationally, about as far away from Metz as the dark side of the moon. Indecision led to inconsistent rationing policies, and to conflicts with the civilian population. As forage ran out and the army began slaughtering its horses, a sortie in the grand style became less and less practical because the guns and wagons supporting it could no longer be moved. Bazaine and his senior officers increasingly sought a political solution to their dilemma. On 10 October,

---

[16]*The Franco-German War*, vol. I, app. 5, gives the field strength of the North German and allied armies as 474 battalions on 1 August, backed up by 328 replacement and garrison battalions – about 1,200,000 men, including cavalry, artillery and supporting arms. Replacement battalions were training and holding units that did not take the field. Statistics on the Landwehr are from Jany, vol. IV, pp. 264–5; exact figures vary slightly.
[17]Sukstorf, pp. 282 ff.
[18]Hermann Kunz, *Die Schlacht bei Noisseville am 31. August und 1. September 1870* (Berlin, 1892).
[19]Patry, pp. 119 ff., is typical of the declining mood.

a council of war decided to seek honourable terms. The marshal conceded the war was lost and offered to use the imperial army to guarantee a regency under Empress Eugénie, with vague assurances of a stable government and a long-term peace.

Bismarck saw the position as promising. From Moltke's point of view, however, Bazaine was making promises he could not keep. The safest place for his army, especially given the republic's military resurgence, was in POW camps. The issue became moot when Eugénie, by now in British exile, refused to underwrite Bazaine's offers. Even Bismarck saw no more was to be done in that quarter and ended negotiations. Out of food and out of hope, the French garrison of Metz surrendered on 29 October.

So much type has been set over Bazaine's behaviour at Metz, so much attention given to the question of whether he could have 'saved France' somehow by doing something different, it seems worth noting that, even had Bazaine broken out of Metz earlier in August, strategically he had no further prospects. Frederick Charles may not have been the most enterprising of generals, but it is unlikely Bazaine was going to outmarch him long enough to reach MacMahon. The most probable positive outcome of a successful sortie (as opposed to being overrun in detail, for example) was pursuit by the erstwhile besiegers, an eventual standing at bay on tactically favourable ground, and another pitched battle somewhere between Metz and Paris, about the time Moltke was finishing off the Army of Châlons. The chances of Bazaine's army, or what might remain of it, eventually reaching Paris under those circumstances are best understood, not in the sphere of contingency, but rather as part of the realm of the counterfactual. The discussion of whether Bazaine was a traitor, an incompetent, or simply in over his head, becomes correspondingly theoretical.[20]

The Prussian army's sun was at noon. Bazaine refused the honours of war, so there was no formal surrender, no last parade with its ritual offering of swords and their customary return to gallant enemies. To twenty-first-century minds, orchestrated capitulations seem artificial when not hypocritical. Such exercises, however, have a significant effect in reaffirming the common identity, as soldiers and men, shared by victor and vanquished. Union General Joshua Chamberlain may not have offered a formal salute to the Confederates surrendering at Appomattox; the Confederacy's John Brown Gordon may never have answered it – at least in the ways they later asserted. But the formal ceremony nevertheless provided material for a 'myth of closure', eventually useful and welcome to both sides.[21] The Metz ceremony's aftermath only provided material for arrogance, by confirming the image of the French as an adversary unworthy of respect. Instead, the capitulation resembled a rat-hunt, with the ragged survivors of once-proud regiments being disarmed *en masse*, then enumerated for loading into boxcars and despatch to Germany as so much live freight.[22]

---

[20]The routines of the siege are presented in two recent accounts: Patry's first-person narrative, pp. 128 ff. and Matthias Steinbach, 'Metz 1870: Zum Alltag einer Belagerung im deutsch-franzoesischen Krieges', *Militaergeschichtliche Mitteilungen* 55 (1996), pp. 1–49. Howard, p. 266, outdoes himself on the politics of the siege on both sides. Maurice Baumont, *L'Echiquier de Metz: Empire ou République?* (Paris, 1971), considers the wider implications.

[21]Cf. William Marvel, *A Place Called Appomattox* (Chapel Hills, NC, 2000) and David W. Blight, *Beyond the Battlefield: Race, Memory, and the American Civil War* (Amherst, MA, 2002).

[22]POWs were, however, treated correctly, and often humanely on their arrival. See Manfred Botzenhardt, 'French Prisoners of War in Germany' in *Road to Total War*, pp. 587–93.

'Victory disease' is a subtle infection. A second source emerged at the fortress of Strasbourg. In the days of Vauban it had been one of the major bastions of the French frontier. By 1870, its defences were obsolete and encapsulated by the industrial city that had grown up around them. The 17,000-strong garrison was a mixed bag of stragglers and fugitives from the battles of the frontier, locally raised mobiles and national guardsmen, with a single regiment of the line standing at its core. Crown Prince Frederick detached 3rd Army's Baden contingent, a division's worth of men and guns that he considered eminently dispensable, to capture the city. Reinforced by two freshly raised divisions of Prussian Landwehr, they invested the place and started throwing shells into it more or less at random in mid-August.

Karl von Werder, a Prussian general also considered dispensable by his own army, was under pressure from Moltke, and from the Baden government, to conclude the operation quickly and with low casualties. He decided his best option was to use the limited amount of artillery at his disposal to bombard the town and intimidate the civil population into demanding capitulation. While not exactly *de rigueur*, this had been done before, during the wars of Frederick the Great and Napoleon, and, besides, the French had set a precedent by shelling Strasbourg's neighbour city of Kehl, on Baden's side of the Rhine. Initial results were spectacular. Public buildings went up in flames; weeping women begged the commandant to surrender; the Catholic archbishop himself called for a ceasefire. Then everyone calmed down. The city and the fortress held. Werder, his ammunition running low and his guns wearing out, switched tactics and began a formal siege that ended in an equally formal capitulation on 28 September.

Strasbourg's fall assisted rapid resumption of service on one of the main rail routes to Paris. In both France and an emerging Germany, Strasbourg also had a high symbolic value as the cultural capital of a frontier zone each regarded as the key to its respective house.[23] And the operation offered an example of what might have been – if the frightfulness had been more intense and longer lasting. Strasbourg's Vauban-style fortifications had been vulnerable to even semi-modern heavy artillery. For critics of Werder's deliberate methods, all that were needed were enough guns, sufficient ammunition, and the will to use them ruthlessly.[24] As a counterpoint, Toul, the other main obstacle on the rail line, also surrendered, after another six-week siege, on 23 August – but endured only a single day's bombardment from a siege train of no more than a couple of dozen modern guns.[25]

Victory in siege and battle kept morale high, even as it seemed the war was not going to end tomorrow. But medical services helped. Prussia's conscription system included prospective medical students, who eventually progressed to doctors in the army reserve. Many of these, in passing, were Jewish. While a doctor did not hold an officer's commission, he had the next thing to it and that was a useful safety valve for social aspirations.[26] In sharp contrast to other armies, whose medical services in war, as in peace, depended on whomever

---

[23]The phrase was first used by Jules Favre and adopted by Bismarck. Roth, pp. 227–8 and Howard, pp. 231–2.

[24]Jean Nouzille, 'Le dernier siège de Strasbourg (11 août–28 septembre 1870)', *Revue Historique de l'Armée* 37 (1981), no. 1, pp. 77–95, is a good modern overview. Reinhold Wagner, *Geschichte der Belagerung von Strasburg im Jahre 1870* (3 parts, Berlin, 1874–8), is Teutonically thorough.

[25]See another work only a technician could love, Hermann von Mueller, *Die Thaetigkeit die deutsche Festungsartillerie … im deutsch-franzoesischen Kriege, 1870–71* (4 vols., Berlin, 1898–1904), vol. II, pp. 93 ff.

[26]A. Cohn, *Meine Erlebnisse im Feld, 1870–71. Von einem alten Landwehrarzt* (Berlin, 1907).

they could lure into uniform, the best and brightest of Prussia's young doctors automatically joined the colours on mobilization – one for every 290 men in 1870. Until the 1840s, German medicine had been virtually a branch of philosophy, with limited practical aspects. The young Hegelian movement, by stressing setting the dialectic 'on its feet' once more, encouraged a more practical approach: collecting and evaluating data in the context of the rigorous testing that was already characteristic of the university seminar. Within individual lifetimes, German medicine became an exact science, incorporating a strong experimental aspect and correspondingly ready to consider evidence from a wide variety of sources.

In 1866, a Prussian army with a high proportion of unseasoned reservists suffered heavily from dysentery and typhus, along with the post-Koeniggraetz cholera epidemic that encouraged making peace. Over 10 per cent of the wounded died in hospital – not a high ratio by the standards of the American Civil War, to say nothing of the Crimea and earlier, but, nevertheless, more than the Prussian medical profession anticipated or found acceptable. The large-calibre, soft-lead bullets fired by modern rifles, and the large fragments created by artillery shells of low-grade metal, created such traumatic wounds that, where limbs were involved, amputation was not merely the preferred treatment but the necessary one – often even by today's standards. Before 1870, the best that could be done to improve survival chances was perform the surgery as quickly as possible, thereby minimizing further shock to the victim's system. Even cutting-edge doctors spoke learnedly of 'laudable pus' as patients died of post-operative infection at rates approaching 50 per cent.

English surgeon Joseph Lister first learned of the work of French chemist Louis Pasteur in 1865. Pasteur's germ theory of infection encouraged Lister to experiment with methods of antiseptic surgery, which, by 1870, had reduced the percentage of deaths in amputation cases to below 1.5 per cent – and that in traumatic accident cases whose nature approached a battlefield as closely as was possible in civilian life. His methods and ideas were strongly resisted for years and decades – except in Germany. Doctors took at least rudimentary antiseptic techniques into the field with them in 1870, and linked them to army regulations and practices regarding sanitation.

Soap was not an army issue item. Clean clothing was a hit-and-miss operation. Soldiers could not always be bothered to use latrines. Lice were a plague from the war's early days. Typhus and dysentery remained the most common major illnesses. Yet compulsory vaccination, another Prussian innovation, held smallpox rates to a third those of the French, and only 300 of the 5,000 cases died. Even under unpromising conditions, German officers and NCOs managed to prevent dirt-borne epidemics of the kind that historically debilitated armies. Cleaning latrines and picking up trash were, after all, time-honoured ways of keeping conscripts busy. Cleanliness, no matter how relative, also became a way of distinguishing German from French, 'us' from 'them', that has long endured.

The Prussian army's modern approach to medical treatment in combat began when a man was first hit. Each soldier had a first-aid kit, with bandaging material and sterile lint as an absorbent. While other armies depended on regimental medical services, whose stretcher bearers were often improvised or provided from regimental bands, the train battalion of a Prussian corps, by 1870, also included three medical detachments, totalling twenty-one doctors and about 450 stretcher-bearers, with rudimentary training in things like applying tourniquets. Each corps also had a dozen small field hospitals, whose thirty-man staff included five doctors. Their 200-patient capacity diminished the impersonal butcher-shop ambience associated with the large facilities that were the norm in other armies, and where casualties piled up in anonymous misery hundreds of yards around the tent or building housing the surgeons. The relatively limited casualty loads also facilitated a 'conservative' approach that resorted to amputation only in extreme cases rather than as a matter of routine. To adherents of germ theory, the high risk of post-operative infection in amputation cases legitimated taking lesser, though still high, chances to save the limb. One result was a long list of grateful patients who vastly preferred a stiff leg or deformed arm to a missing one. In the rear zones, the principal distinguishing feature of Prussian/ German military medicine was a policy of evacuating seriously sick and wounded back to Germany as soon as possible. German hospital trains were widely admired for their quality; and soldiers and their families were grateful for the result. A wound that became a *Heimatschuss* was usually easier to bear. Despite occasional serious gridlocks, particularly around Metz after the August battles, the medical system contributed significantly to the army's specific image of institutional competence and the new Reich's aura of progress.[27]

French military medical services, on the other hand, were unique in their degree of bureaucratization. The *Intendance*, the army's administrative services, exercised rigid, comprehensive, pettifogging control over personnel and arrangements. Even treatments were prescribed, with Lister's antiseptic techniques specifically forbidden. The shortage of doctors was chronic. During the war the ratio was one for 740 men, while the veterinary services had one vet for every 250 horses! The republic's attempt to bridge the gap by using civilian volunteer units led to further confusion and tension, with turf battles taking precedence over patient care. It was small wonder that the death rate from amputations was 75 per cent — 10,000 out of 13,000 cases, fingers and toes included. Throughout the war, a wounded Frenchman's best chance involved being left for the Germans — not a major contribution.[28]

II

Morale, in the sense of will-power, was increasingly on Moltke's mind as he redeployed his forces for the war against the republic. At least as well as Bismarck, the chief of staff understood the risks of protracted war for Prussia and its allies — though as yet not in the contexts of mass mobilization and popular insurgency. His concerns were still the historic ones that had shaped Prussia's strategy for over a century: limited resources and outside intervention.[29] The 1st Army, now under the command of I Corps's Edwin von Manteuffel, was ordered north, to deal with the Republic's forces in that region and clean up any fortresses still holding out between Paris and the frontier. Frederick Charles was directed southwards, to a more threatening region.

Geographically, the Loire basin, depending on one's point of view, might become a basis for a secondary interior line of resistance against an overextended enemy, a counter-attack

---

[27]Cf. Richard A. Gabriel and Karen S. Metz, *A History of Military Medicine*, vol. II, *From the Renaissance through Modern Times* (Westport, CT, 1992), pp. 199 ff.; Sukstorf, pp. 222 ff. and 327 ff.; and Kuehnlich, pp. 267 ff. and 402 ff.
[28]William B. McAllister, 'Fighting Reformers: The Debate over the Reorganization of the French Military Medical Service, 1870–1889', *Essays in History* 35 (1993), pp. 1–13.
[29]Dennis E. Showalter, 'German Grand Strategy: A Contradiction in Terms?' *Militaergeschichtliche Mitteilungen* 48 (1990), pp. 65–102.

north and east, or a redoubt for a last national stand. Gambetta saw the republic's primary requirement, strategic, political and diplomatic, as relieving a Paris unable to break the German siege with its own resources. He concentrated his new armies as far north as possible, around the city of Orleans – one organized corps, the 15th, two more in the process of formation, and a penumbra of unattached battalions and squadrons.[30] Well before the surrender of Metz, Moltke took the threat seriously enough to weaken his siege lines. Over the cautious William's objections,[31] he detached I Bavarian Corps, a division of XI Corps, and a couple of divisions of cavalry and sent them south to clear the French away from the German rear, take Orleans and Chartres and, if opportunity offered, push as far as Tours, where the provisional government had established its temporary base.

These were scarcely modest objectives. Von der Tann was neither an enterprising commander nor an insightful one, while the Bavarians who composed the bulk of his force were, by this time, regarded as inferior in training, discipline and effectiveness to the worst of the Prussian active corps.[32] In no way ready for an open-field battle, the French fell back, deciding to abandon Orleans itself. But when the Bavarians and Thuringians caught up with the French rearguard on 10 October, they got all the fighting they could handle from infantry who had neither to manoeuvre nor counter-attack – just hold their ground. Neither frontal attacks nor flanking manoeuvres produced quick results. The Bavarian artillery proved less effective than its Prussian counterpart. At the end of the day, von der Tann nevertheless found himself in possession of Orleans, and around 1,500 prisoners, who seemed barely worth confining in terms of their formal qualities as soldiers. His own casualties were about 1,000 – scarcely crippling, but nevertheless sufficient to encourage him to remain where he was.[33]

The limitations of that idea became apparent as von der Tann's force found itself encapsulated by growing numbers of more or less irregulars. The terrain was as unsuitable for German-style operations as might be imagined. Today only vestiges of its former self, the Orleans forest in 1870 was in a near-natural state, poorly charted, with few roads and sparse networks of trails and tracks known only to the local inhabitants. Efforts to use the cavalry to clear space and obtain information were handicapped because the divisions' light regiments were poorly trained in dismounted tactics, while the heavy regiments, the cuirassiers and uhlans, had no firearm more formidable than a pistol, primarily intended for signalling purposes. Most of those sent in the Loire were distress signals. Even after

---

[30]Howard, pp. 285–6, describes the Loire region's military geography. Antonmatteri, pp. 110 ff., summarizes Gambetta's intentions.

[31]Frederick III, *War Diary*, p. 148.

[32]Arthur Coumbe, 'The Reputation of an Army: Foreign Opinion of the Bavarian Army in the Franco-German War, an Illustrative Case Study' (dissertation, Duke University, 1985), is a mine of valuable data and analytic insight on the Bavarians' achievements and problems.

[33]Cf. Hugo von Helvig, *The Operations of the I Bavarian Army Corps under General von der Tann*, tr. Capt. G. Sali (London, 1874), pp. 141 ff. and Fritz Hoenig, *Der Volkskrieg an der Loire im Herbst 1870* (2nd ed., 5 vols., Berlin, 1893–7), vol. I, pp. 34 ff. Hoenig was one of the most perceptive, and correspondingly the most controversial, of the 'second generation' of campaign analysts. He proposed to write 'critical military history', and succeeded to the point of being challenged to at least one duel. His history of the Loire campaign is advocacy history in its emphasis on the high command's mistake in not recognizing the capacity and potential of the republic's levies. The work, however, also incorporates the most detailed tactical/operational narrative of the campaign. See also Joachim Hoffmann, 'Der Militaerschriftsteller Fritz Hoenig', *Militaergeschichtliche Mitteilungen* 5 (1969), pp. 5–25.

captured chassepot carbines were issued to them, the heavy troopers could neither use the weapons effectively nor fight on foot, except in a hit-and-miss fashion.[34]

Despite urging that amounted to arm-twisting from Moltke and the crown prince, von der Tann refused to push further south than Orleans. His isolated force, further weakened when its Prussian division was detached, drew the French like a magnet – or perhaps a *fata Morgana*. Michael Howard shows how, in October, the republic was assembling significant forces on both strategic flanks of the invasion. In the north, a network of small fortresses provided a base structure for armies able to draw equipment through the channel ports and from the factories around Lille. In the east, the rough terrain of the Vosges was a natural breeding ground for irregulars and a shelter for new formations to gain experience as supplies arrived from the Midi and Marseilles. The Army of the Loire could draw on the south-east for men and the Atlantic ports for weapons. Howard goes on to make the point that overrunning even one of these three zones would absorb most of the German forces not needed around Paris. His accompanying implication is that the republic might have been best served by a cape-and-sword technique, using its regional forces to threaten and wear down the invaders. At the same time, that process would build their own professional competence to a point where a joint relief effort for the capital could be mounted with a fair chance of success.[35]

Any strategic wisdom in that approach was overshadowed by political considerations. The strained relations between the people of Paris and their far more moderate government outside the city allowed no time for finesse. Less tangible, but no less significant, the republic had established its legitimacy in unoccupied France largely by its energy. To switch to a policy of buying time and building force meant a corresponding risk of a fragile domestic consensus collapsing in confusion. Nor could the imperial prisoners of Sedan, and subsequently Metz, be entirely overlooked. Napoleon and Eugénie might be in exile, but London was just an afternoon away from the German headquarters in France. Should Moltke and Bismarck choose to do so, it was within their power to create the nucleus of a counter-revolutionary army with a few telegrams.[36]

Gambetta, his ministers and his associates correctly perceived themselves as being in the position of a person who stumbles while running downhill. The best chance of avoiding a fall or worse involves running faster in order to re-establish one's balance. And for the first time in the war, the Germans seemed to have overreached themselves. Moltke intended the division detached from von der Tann, the 22nd, to return to Paris and reinforce the siege. On its way back, it was ordered to swing west and clean out the detachments and stragglers reported in the area of Châteaudun and Chartres. The Thuringians walked into a wasps' nest of mobile guards and partisans who sometimes scattered, other times fought to the last man, and increased both casualties and anxiety levels in a formation that had been

---

[34]Assigning detachments of infantry and pioneers to the cavalry improved their firepower but crippled their mobility. The added expedient of mounting the foot troops in commandeered wagons, useful in more open country, too often failed in the Loire's sparse road network. Dennis E. Showalter, 'Prussian Cavalry, 1806–1871. The Search for Roles', *Militaergeschichtliche Mitteilungen* 19 (1976), pp. 16–17.
[35]Howard, pp. 289 ff.
[36]The generals in Metz were unsure whether the empire or the republic bore most blame for France's catastrophe. Mirrors seem to have been in short supply. See Robert Tombs, *The War against Paris 1871* (Cambridge, 1981). pp. 13 ff.

in the field from the war's first days. Discipline in some regiments began to loosen, with officers and sergeants looking the other way as chickens disappeared into camp kettles and fence rails stoked bivouac fires, in defiance of orders and regulations.

As the 22nd approached Châteaudun, a centre of partisan activity, sniping incidents and ambushes multiplied. A Prussian detachment was overrun, and captured men and horses brought back to Châteaudun in triumph. On 18 October, the town was summoned to surrender. Its defenders, 2,000 local mobiles and national guards and 1,600 partisans, commanded by a Polish exile with a lieutenant-colonel's commission and some experience in street fighting, refused. They easily threw back the first Prussian companies, which entered the town almost off the line of march and attacked with a tentativeness suggesting reluctance to be among the first casualties of the battle or the last ones of the war.

General Friedrich Wilhelm von Wittich was a solid division commander, and this was the kind of battle he knew how to fight. He responded by bringing up artillery and mounting a full-scale assault that took most of the day to prepare. Part of the preparation was a series of energetic reminders to his subordinates that the war was far from over; reputations and careers were on the line. The French defenders, meanwhile, had been able to distribute ammunition, loophole walls and shed their less enthusiastic elements. Townspeople and peasants from surrounding villages, including some women, joined their ranks armed with everything from army rifles to pitchforks. When the Prussians came again, they found themselves in a street brawl that made Bazeilles pale by comparison.

After the war, the French accused the 22nd of sacking the town, and honoured Châteaudun's heroic stand by adding the Cross of the Legion of Honour to its coat of arms. The Prussian reports and narratives are less forthcoming than those of the Bavarians at Bazeilles, but similar in describing a situation where there was neither time nor opportunity to check opponents' identities and genders. Fighting was house to house; bayonets and rifle butts time and again supplanting bullets. Superior artillery was of no use in a rapidly falling winter night, at ranges so close that casualties were coming back with powder burns on their uniforms. Whether all the dead Frenchmen were males in uniform, whether some were killed out of hand or shot in the aftermath of a strong point's overrunning, was left to rumour and legend.

The Germans took no physical reprisals beyond the individual looting that was and remains a standard and predictable accompaniment of an assault of that kind. Some prisoners were deported to Germany. Wittich fined the community 400,000 francs – no small sum – for its participation in the resistance. He described the destruction of over 200 homes as an unintended consequence of the fighting, fuelled by a brisk wind. Châteaudun, however, increasingly became a touchstone as German officers argued among themselves over the best way to handle irregular resistance in a hostile countryside. Chartres, at least, took the lesson and surrendered without a fight a few days later.[37]

---

[37]Cf. L. von Wittich, *Aus meinem Tagebuche, 1870–71* (Kassel, 1872), p. 93 *passim*. Among many contemporary and near contemporary French accounts, cf. Ernest de Lipowski's *Ablis ... Châteaudun ... Alençon Colonne mobile du général de Lipowski (1870–71)* (Paris, 1897); Paul Montarlot, *Journal de l'invasion. Châteaudun (4 septembre 1870–11 mars 1871)* (Châteaudun, 1871); and Edouard Ledeuil, *Châteaudun – 18 Octobre 1870* (2nd ed., Paris, 1871). As might be expected, the perspectives are virtually irreconcilable. If the Prussians have the best of it in the above narrative, it is because the *Châteaudunois* seem to have had little or no idea of the level of violence in even a small-scale modern battle.

As resistance in the Loire Valley increased, the Bavarians in Orleans invited attack – especially when it became plain that Moltke did not propose to reinforce them. On 7 November, the French advance on the city began. Its core was the new 15th and 16th Corps, under General Claude d'Aurelle de Paladines. His name hardly suggests a good republican, and the old imperial veteran had no illusions about the overall quality of his newly christened Army of the Loire. But when all the small forces in the region were calculated, he had about 100,000 men against fewer than 25,000 Bavarians. He had been able to give the regiments of 15th and 16th Corps at least the rudiments of tactical training. A few spectacular military executions had silenced the worst of the rank-and-file grumblers and those zealots who equated republicanism with indiscipline.[38]

Von der Tann was enough of a general to understand the risk of being trapped in Orleans, poorly fortified and too large to defend with the troops he had. Instead, he took the bulk of his corps a short distance north-west and began digging in around the village of Coulmiers. It was good defensive ground, and it took most of 8 November for the French to force the Bavarians out of their positions and into retreat northwards. Morale in the Army of the Loire soared. The victory owed much to the replacement of the French artillery's ineffective time fuses with percussion ones – a long overdue field modification, introduced by the new government, that came as a considerable shock to the Bavarians. Tactically, this was the first time during the entire war that French attacks had been made for any purposes beyond countering Prussian initiatives. On the whole they had succeeded, despite high losses. Perhaps, after all, there was something to the legends of the *furia francese*. Tomorrow, Orleans; next week, Paris![39]

Aurelle was less sanguine. Instead of following in hot pursuit of the Bavarians, he established Orleans as a base and a training centre for the battalions the provisional government forwarded in seemingly endless numbers. His original two corps expanded to five by the end of November. If three of them were composed of new formations, untrained and poorly commanded, that made little difference to political authorities like Charles de Freycinet, Gambetta's official spokesman in the military matters of whose details he was essentially ignorant. Freycinet, an engineer in his day job, played a major positive role in administrative matters. Without him, indeed, the Army of the Loire may well not have gone beyond the stage of a rabble in arms. His achievements gave him leverage when he insisted that Aurelle move immediately to the relief of Paris.[40]

Freycinet's motives were operational as well as political. Moltke had initially done everything possible to ignore the republic's assembling levies. In part, this reflected his continuing belief that civilians were civilians whether or not they carried rifles and wore something approximating uniforms. Training made soldiers – training and good officers. As late as 7 October, Moltke proclaimed the war over and the French thrashing aimlessly, with no more major fighting to be expected anywhere.[41] Mass, however, has its own qualities. In the

---

[38]Claude M. d'Aurelle de Paladines, *Campagnes de 1870–71. La première Armée de la Loire* (2nd ed., Paris, 1872), p. 9 *passim*.

[39]For Coulmiers, Pierre Lehautcourt (pseud. Gen. B. Palat), *Campagne de la Loire en 1870–1871* (2 vols., Paris, 1893–5), vol. I, pp. 130 ff., is a good overview. Cf. Helvig, pp. 179 ff. and Aurelle, pp. 102 ff., for the commanders' perspectives.

[40]Charles de Freycinet, *La Guerre en Province pendant la siège de Paris 1870–71* (Paris, 1871), is sharper-edged than his account in *Souvenirs, 1848–1893* (2 vols., Paris, 1912), vol. I, pp. 139 ff.

[41]Alfred Graf von Waldersee, *Denkwuerdigkeiten*, ed. H. O. Meissner (3 vols., Stuttgart, 1922–5), vol. I, pp. 101–2.

immediate aftermath of Bazaine's surrender, Moltke had ordered Frederick Charles to move his 2nd Army towards Paris, simultaneously to reinforce the lines against a sortie from the city and to provide close cover for the siege against an attack from the Loire. On 14 November, he sent the prince south with three corps and a new mission: hold the main road from Orleans to Paris. At the same time, Moltke put von der Tann's old task force, now of I Bavarian Corps, the 17th and 22nd Prussian Divisions, and three cavalry divisions under the Grand Duke of Mecklenburg-Schwerin, and sent him west from Chartres towards Le Mans. The latter town was the major French base in the region. Moltke also expected it to be the concentration point for a full-scale attack on Paris from the west. The Army of the Loire by itself, the chief of staff reasoned, had no chance in a frontal, breakthrough battle, especially with Frederick Charles's hard veterans. Let it sidestep to the west and join forces with the French in that sector, and the story might be different.[42]

Moltke's logic was not universally affirmed. Blumenthal, for one, considered the approach an exercise in *Flickwerk*, which invited a series of small defeats, and preferred accepting the risks of concentrating enough force for a decisive operation.[43] Mecklenburg, moreover, was a general of neither great experience nor particular merit. He had also been sent on a fool's errand. There were no sizeable French forces around Le Mans for him to engage. His own army detachment was too large to move quickly, and too small to inhibit a local resistance that improved with experience and, literally, had the Germans in that sector chasing themselves from town to town, as first their boots, then their legs, gave out. When Moltke ordered the duke east to support Frederick Charles, it was as much for logistical as operational reasons: the men and animals were exhausted.[44]

Moltke did hope as well that the presence of another four divisions would galvanize the Red Prince into acting more like the hussar officer whose uniform he affected. Moving faster than his wont, by 24 November, Frederick Charles had the 2nd Army in position along the north edge of the Orleans forest, its cavalry probing for French positions difficult to discover. He was no more comfortable with the terrain he faced than von der Tann had been. Even at maximum discount for exaggeration, the French had the advantage of numbers. The civilians among whom his men marched and on whom they were billeted were increasingly and overtly hostile, to a point where one corps made a policy of keeping its supply trains with its combat units rather than detailing train guards – a definite handicap to the kind of mobility Moltke expected from his major formations.

Frederick Charles had a chance to make his case directly when King William, increasingly frustrated by the confused course of events, on 25 November sent a personal emissary to Frederick Charles's headquarters. Colonel Alfred von Waldersee was one of the best of the middle-ranking general staff officers, on good terms with Moltke and respecting him, but not identified as one of the inner circle of 'demigods'. It was a good choice, and Waldersee was impressed with the prince's frankness. Frederick Charles admitted he did not know where the enemy was, could not find him and called that reason enough for not seeking an encounter battle. The best way of dealing with the Army of the Loire, Frederick Charles and his chief of staff believed, was to take enough time to swing the 2nd Army south-east around the French right flank, have Mecklenburg close from the

---

[42]*MMK* 1, vol. III, pp. 372–3 and 376 ff.
[43]Blumenthal, pp. 179–80.
[44]Helvig, pp. 227 ff. and Hoenig, *Volkskrieg*, vol. I, pp. 120 ff. and 307 ff.

other direction, and force another in the series of 'battles of annihilation' that had swept French armies from the field since the war's beginnings. But, added the prince, no one could be sure. The power of lawyers' politics might even send the French boiling out of the trees, into open country where German troops could move, and on to German artillery and German rifles as MacMahon had done in the Sedan campaign.[45]

'From your mouth to God's ears', is a familiar Yiddish wish. Another, higher-flown aphorism says those whom the gods wish to destroy, they strike mad. Freycinet and Gambetta had been demanding action from Aurelle for days. Aurelle temporized until 22 November, when Freycinet sent him a direct order to prepare his corps commanders for an advance on Paris. When Aurelle protested through appropriate channels, Freycinet replied that a general who did nothing on his own initiative had no right to complain when others took the reins from his hands.[46] It was the kind of backhand slap across the face Aurelle could not ignore. The French advance began on 24 November.

Aurelle, by this time, more or less commanded half a dozen corps, with a theoretical strength of well over 200,000 men. On his far left, a 21st Corps that existed mostly on paper had its headquarters in Le Mans. Next came the 17th Corps, originally deployed around Châteaudun and still confronting Mecklenburg in that region. On Aurelle's far right stood an 18th Corps that was further along than the 21st, but still in the early stages of formation. The heavy lifting would be done by the army's centre. The 16th and 15th Corps, the victors of Coulmiers, stood respectively on the left and right of the Orleans–Paris highway. Beginning on 15 November, they were reinforced by a newly formed 20th Corps, mostly raw levies poorly armed and poorly officered, moved by rail from the Sâone valley.[47]

The French offensive promptly ran into Frederick Charles's forward elements, and the sharp initial fighting mostly went in favour of the French, who, in addition to possessing superior numbers, performed better than expected at regimental and company levels. It was reports of these defeats that finally decided William to send Waldersee on the mission described above, accompanied by the gloomy warning that, if Frederick Charles was defeated, the siege of Paris must be abandoned. Moltke, too, took action, responding to Mecklenburg's apparent lack of grip by putting him directly under Frederick Charles's command, and transferring the redoubtable Stosch from his post of intendant-general to be Mecklenburg's chief of staff.[48]

When all the moves and changes were accomplished, the battle was left in Frederick Charles's hands: his to win or lose. Expecting the French to press their attack in the direction of Paris, the prince intended to use his X and IX Corps as a blocking force, the 'shield', with III Corps, the Brandenburgers, acting as the 'sword' — perhaps 'rapier' would be a more accurate metaphor, given their previous losses — thrusting at the French

---

[45]Waldersee, vol. I, pp. 107 ff.; *Friedrich Karl*, vol. II, pp. 337 ff.; and Hoenig, *Volkskrieg*, vol. I, p. 266 *passim*. Hoenig, vol. I, pp. 246 ff., also makes the point that the 2nd Army had lost part of its marching capacity in the trenches of Metz and required a few days to harden up.

[46]Freycinet, *Guerre*, pp. 114 ff.

[47]Lehautcourt, *Campagne de la Loire*, vol. I, pp. 206 ff.

[48]Albrecht von Stosch, *Denkwuerdigheiten* (Stuttgart, 1904), pp. 206–7; and Hoenig, *Volkskrieg*, vol. I, pp. 334 ff. Petter, 'Logistik', p. 125, suggests that the assignment was also meant to give Stosch the field experience that would confirm his expected post-war replacement of the elderly Roon as war minister.

left flank as opportunity offered. In the event, the French did much of the Germans' work for them at the fortified village of Beaune-la-Rolande on the morning of 28 November.

Beaune-la-Rolande and its satellite hamlets formed the central position of X Prussian Corps, with its mixed bag of Westphalians, Hanoverians and other north Germans. Two brigades held the position, backed by a dozen batteries of the corps artillery. Two full corps, 60,000 French, were under orders to carry the sector. But if the French that day were fire and flame, the men of X Corps prided themselves on a dourness that resisted both enthusiasm and despair. They had fought well at Vionville, attacking in support of III Corps, and had learned that battle's defensive lessons even better. Beaune-la-Rolande still had part of its town wall on the south side – ten feet high in some sections. The Germans had built firing platforms behind it, and measured ranges. The houses were mostly of heavy stone; their walls now loopholed for mutual support and to catch attackers in crossfire.

As was – and is – often the case in such attacks, French efforts were drawn towards Beaune itself, as opposed to clearing the outlying defences that throughout the day choked off manoeuvres and blocked reinforcements. The village witnessed some of the war's hardest fighting, as waves of French stormed repeatedly through its streets, only to fall back again before the rifles of a dozen companies of the Westphalian 16th and 57th Infantry.

This was the 38th Brigade, so badly shot up at Vionville. Most of the men were weavers and factory workers, not the farm boys so prized in the Prussian system. Compared with the Prussian Guard, they were short: stunted by malnutrition, stooped by labour. But their steady volleys and disciplined independent fire once again put paid to the long-standing canard that ordinary soldiers could not be trusted with rapid-firing weapons. The needle gun's range might be shorter than the chassepot's, but at 200 yards it was no less devastating. The Westphalians, indeed, made it look so easy that not until early afternoon did Frederick Charles begin feeding in reinforcements from III Corps's 5th Division – which had marched to the sound of the guns on its commander's initiative.

It was high time. The survivors of Beaune's garrison were counting their cartridges and eyeing their bayonets when the 5th Division's guns opened on the flank and rear of the last French charge and hammered its survivors out of the village. With the burning town for a backdrop, the Brandenburgers' leading companies marched in, cheered to the echo by anyone from the 16th and 57th who had not lost his voice or been silenced forever. Over 800 Germans had been killed and wounded. French casualties amounted to 3,100, including 1,800 prisoners – sufficient witness to the close-gripped nature of fighting that left many of the leading waves unable to obey the bugles when they sounded 'retreat'.[49]

Beaune-la-Rolande left French commanders on the spot less than optimistic. The best efforts of two corps had been blocked, at the crucial point, by little more than a regiment. German artillery had been the dominant element of the war against the empire. Beaune-la-Rolande demonstrated that, as long as its ammunition held out, German infantry was also an extremely dangerous opponent for the republic. French reports and accounts stressed the cold-blooded fire discipline of the Prussians – the officers' ability to keep their men in hand until the last possible moment. Those, French officers declared, are *real* soldiers! Ours are, at best, an untempered tool. From corps commanders downwards, commanders complained of what they lacked: uniforms, blankets, rations. In particular, General

---

[49]Hoenig, *Volkskrieg*, vol. II, pp. 80 ff. and *Friedrich Karl*, vol. II, pp. 356 ff.

Crouzat, whose freshly raised and newly organized 20th Corps had done some of the day's hardest fighting, spent more time bemoaning shortages than encouraging men who were at least susceptible to being told that they were winning.[50]

The Loire Army's shortcomings were real enough. They were also being viewed from the perspective of men who had seen little field service, and that long past. A few regimental officers more accustomed to the friction of war, a few brigadiers who recognized that a fight like Beaune-la-Rolande hurts the enemy too, and perhaps the Army of the Loire might have challenged fortune again the next day. Certainly, Frederick Charles had been sufficiently set back on his heels that in the next few days he expected to be attacked from flank as well as front, and ignored repeated orders from Moltke to go over to the offensive himself.[51] Instead, Aurelle and Freycinet exchanged correspondence, fiery on one hand and frigid on the other. With each despatch Aurelle found more reasons why his situation offered no promise. Freycinet, galvanized into near exaltation by fresh news of a sortie from Paris, again overrode his field commander and ordered the offensive continued. This time a single corps was to cover Orleans; the other four would drive on Paris.

Some indication that Freycinet's initiative was more than a politician's folly was offered on 1 December, when 16th Corps, on Aurelle's left, mounted a local offensive to separate Mecklenburg's detachment from the 2nd Army. It was a good day to attack. The ground was frozen hard enough to move guns and men; and the French hit the Germans' weak link: I Bavarian Corps. By the end of November, the corps had had almost 21,000 men hospitalized for sickness and suffered over 7,000 battle casualties. Bavaria's replacement system had broken down to the point where most of the battalions were at less than half strength, working in pairs to form one tactical unit. On 11 December, for example, the corps's twelve battalions included approximately 1,300 active soldiers, 700 Landwehr men and 2,000 wartime recruits with a maximum of three months' training. That kind of mixed bag put a heavy premium on leading from the front, which, in turn, increased the losses of the cadres. Most companies had only a single officer, and he was likely to be a second lieutenant. First lieutenants were commanding no fewer than five battalions. The sergeants and corporals were increasingly spot promotions, whose authority was correspondingly less than that of their long-service predecessors. In recent weeks, the corps had been overmarched, underfed and regularly embarrassed by an enemy whose presence was more often sensed than seen. The supply system was on the ragged edge of collapse:

> Some had scarcely any boots on their feet, some walked in wooden shoes, and others even in slippers ... Blankets in all colours and sizes ... served against the wet cold and for protection at night ... Our ranks dwindled in an alarming fashion through sickness, and it was no rarity for 15, even 20 men from a company to be left behind because of exhaustion ... then drag themselves along in a wagon or on foot at night.[52]

The middle of France was a long way from Munich and the Isar. The wine was sour and the beer non-existent. What were honest Bavarians doing, taking their skins to market in

---

[50]Freycinet, *Guerre*, pp. 130 ff. and Aurelle, pp. 269 ff.

[51]*Friedrich Karl*, vol. II, pp. 378 ff.

[52]Dietrich Freiherr von Lassberg, *Mein Kriegstagebuch aus dem deutsch-franzoesischen Krieges 1870/1* (Munich, 1906), p. 213.

this *Saupreuss* war? Like their spiritual successors in the US Army in Vietnam during the early 1970s, the Bavarians would fight when they had to, but their skills were eroding and their enthusiasm was long gone.[53]

It was scarcely surprising that, unlike X Corps at Beaune-la-Rolande, the Bavarians had done nothing to improve their position by fortifying the villages they occupied. Their limited ability to manoeuvre under fire meant companies could not support each other, and regiments were driven from one position after another by a French attack that gained momentum as it gained success. The corps owed its survival in good part to its artillery, which, throughout the day, stood its ground under French counter-battery fire and set high prices on French bayonet charges. One battery, two of its guns knocked out, fought the remaining four to the muzzle in two directions at once, supported only by a worn-down infantry company with largely empty rifles, whose commander had ignored an order to retreat and instead stood by the guns. The Bavarians made a final stand around the chateau of Villepion, and bade fair to hold their ground until Admiral Jean Jarigueberry, commanding one of the French divisions as though he were on a quarter-deck, led a boarding party of four battalions in a wild rush that sent the garrison flying and drove the rest of the Bavarians into retreat.[54]

The admiral might be said to have fought Waterloo's last hours in reverse by carrying the counterpart of Hougoumont Farm. The next morning, 16th Corps went forward again. Stosch, by now barely acknowledging Mecklenburg even as a figurehead, had spent the night preparing a counter-attack, and the unexpected French initiative caught his troops off balance. Jarigueberry's division, flushed with victory, drove back the Bavarians in their front, but failed to clear the chateau of Goury, where part of the 4th Bavarian Brigade stuck like a bone in the throat of the French onslaught, taking brutal casualties in the process. During a long, slow afternoon, the 17th and 22nd Divisions worked around the French right flank, as Prussian and Bavarian artillery took steady toll of the mass formations that were the only way the republic's levies could move quickly and coherently in any direction. The 16th Corps gradually fell back on Loigny, with increasing numbers leaving the ranks.

The men who stayed fought all the harder. Repeated German attempts to rush the village melted under the chassepots. Some commanders ordered their bands forward to 'play in' infantry far too played out to respond to musical inspiration, no matter how thumpingly martial. It was neither lead nor steel but fire that decided Loigny's fate. As the village began to burn, set ablaze by German shelling, the French fell back rather than burn in it.

The Germans pressed forward by companies towards the next strong point, the village of Villepion, when suddenly new columns of French appeared to their front. They were from the 17th Corps, whose commander had marched to the sound of the guns and, in the process, lost touch with most of his men. In 1862, at the Battle of Sharpsburg, Confederate General A. P. Hill had turned the tide by a similar action. But General Henri de Sonis, though he had potential in that direction, was no A. P. Hill. His recruits were not Hill's Light Division. The units he faced were commanded by officers who had spent their professional

---

[53]I Bavarian Corps's decline is discussed in Sukstorf, pp. 306 ff. and 389 ff. For the statistics, see Herman Kunz, *Die Schlacht von Loigny-Poupry am 2 Dezember 1870* (Berlin, 1893). Hermann Rumschoettel, *Das bayerischen Offizierkorps 1866–1914* (Berlin, 1973), p. 46 *passim*, discusses the army's problems securing officers before 1870 and the post-war development of procurement policies.

[54]Hoenig, *Volkskrieg*, vol. III, pp. 236 ff. and Helvig, pp. 258 ff., combine to describe the fighting.

lives preparing for such emergencies. Two battalions, the last sector reserve, met the French head-on. Eight more companies, from three different regiments, hit them in the flank. De Sonis went down, badly wounded. Over 1,000 of the men who followed him in that last rush were killed, wounded or captured as well – part of a French total of almost 7,000 lost during the day to a German defence as solid as anything mounted in the war.[55]

Aurelle, meanwhile, had spent the day listening to the sounds of battle and awaiting an opportunity to attack that somehow seemed never to come. When the outcome was clear, he ordered a general retreat on his own responsibility. Mecklenburg and Stosch, each with visions of *Pour le Mérite* dancing in his head, wanted to move south and west to cut off the French retreat, with Frederick Charles reinforcing and supporting their advance. Frederick Charles, who disliked Mecklenburg personally and distrusted – with good reason – his competence, was not inclined to assume the role of second lead. Also, even after the events of the past two days, he remained concerned that should he shift too far west, the French might simply march around his left and on to Paris. Moltke, however, was convinced that the main French strength was concentrated on and west of the high road. On 2 December, he ordered Frederick Charles to advance directly on Orleans with the objective of engaging and destroying the enemy. It was an example of that exercise of command from a distance which Moltke himself warned of when the telegraph had been introduced, and Frederick Charles protested. Overruled, he ordered IX and III Corps to take the lead, with X Corps falling back into reserve, and Mecklenburg's detachment to cooperate directly with the main attack by driving the French into Orleans from the west. When Stosch reasserted his proposal for something fancier, along the lines of a deep envelopment by his four divisions, Frederick Charles told him to obey orders, like everyone else in the Royal Prussian Army.[56]

The prince's prudence was the result of reflection as well as temperament. Both the initial battles along the frontier, and the more recent encounters in the Loire Valley, had demonstrated that French villages and large farms, held even by improvised garrisons of a few hundred, could dominate a sector for a long time. They had too much stone construction to be easily set on fire. Their buildings were too sturdy to be readily dismantled by field guns. The kind of close-quarter grappling necessary to capture them with infantry deprived the Germans of their advantages in training and discipline, and swelled casualty lists already long enough due to sickness and exhaustion. The III Corps's battalions averaged below half their authorized strength, with IX Corps not much better off – neither situation surprising after Vionville and Gravelotte.

The infantry's relative numerical weakness also unbalanced tactical structures. Since the artillery's losses had been low and easily replaceable, the proportion of guns to rifles increased steadily. By December, it was six guns and more to 1,000 infantry in the 2nd

---

[55]For the German side of the fighting, see Kunz, *Loigny-Poupry* and Hoenig, *Volkskrieg*, vol. IV, *passim*. Helwig, pp. 268 ff.; Aurelle, pp. 306 ff.; and Freycinet, *Guerre*, pp. 141 ff. cancel out each other. Henri de Sonis, *Le 17e Corps à Loigny* (Paris, 1909), does a good job reconstructing the impact of combat on inexperienced men and formations. Pierre Bertin, 'La Contre-Attaque de Loigny (2 decembre 1870)', *Revue Historique des Armées* 26 (1970), no. 3, pp. 35–43, is an excellent up-to-date overview.

[56]*Friedrich Karl*, vol. II, pp. 378 ff.; Bronsart, p. 202 *passim*; and Stosch, p. 213. Bronsart notes that Frederick Charles's chief of staff was not best pleased with Moltke's orders – a good indication that the Prussian army was, as yet, a long way from having a two-track system of higher command.

Army. March columns, in turn, grew relatively clumsier and less flexible because of the higher proportion of guns, caissons and battery vehicles. Post-war analysts sourly observed that the new order slowed advances and led to an unhealthy dependence on firepower at the expense of the infantry assaults central to Prussian tactical doctrine: shock. In contrast to Grant and Sherman in 1864, however, neither Frederick Charles nor his corps commanders ever seriously considered rebalancing their force structures by leaving some batteries out of action. Their infantry commanders, particularly below regimental levels, understood too well the value of the guns. Those captains and lieutenants quick to order a charge against fire-spitting stone walls were frequently no longer present in ranks. A growing rifleman's consensus argued for letting the gunners blast out or burn out strong points before taking the bayonet to them. The weather was worsening, wind-driven snow blocking the few roads. Nevertheless, whatever it took on the slippery roads, the guns were kept to the front when the Germans began to move towards Orleans around daylight on 3 December.

Elements of III Corps met their first serious resistance at the village of Chillery. Alvensleben managed to bring up every gun he had, all fourteen batteries. The ground was too broken to form a gun line in the style of Sedan, but by batteries and battalions, the Brandenburg artillerymen shelled the French out of position after position. Alvensleben sent his infantry forward only to complete the local victories, when the French guns were silent and their infantry had begun to withdraw. His corps suffered only around a hundred casualties in the entire day – something of a record for any mid-nineteenth-century army in that kind of fighting, and a tribute to Alvensleben's learning curve. With Mecklenburg's 22nd Division coming up on its flank, IX Corps made similar use of its artillery from the first contact with a division of the 15th Corps just north of Artenay. The terrain in that sector was more open, and the 9th Artillery Regiment's commander deployed no fewer than eighty-eight guns against the final French position in that sector. Frederick Charles himself forbade the infantry to go forward as darkness approached and the French pulled out. The prince saw no reason to multiply losses by night attacks on what he still believed to be prepared defences.

In fact, the Army of the Loire had been too busy preparing its Paris offensive to pay any attention to anything so mundane as entrenchment construction. Nor, and of far more consequence, had its major units practised mutual support. Having fought its battle alone, by day's end, 15th Corps had begun to disintegrate; 16th and 20th Corps, falling back as their flanks were exposed by 15th's unravelling, also began leaking men as they drew nearer to Orleans. The temperature dropped; snow fell harder as the night deepened. The Germans had some winter coats and were able to build fires without interruption. Half-frozen Frenchmen, officers and men swarmed into Orleans looking for warmth wherever it might be found – and in whatever form. Even small amounts of liquor had devastating effects on men who had fought all day on empty stomachs, or stood in ranks as the cold ate into their bodies and spirits. No one at the top was willing to try the effects of a vigorous attempt to restore discipline and morale. Instead, Aurelle asked Freycinet and Gambetta to authorize a general retreat.

Not until late in the afternoon of 4 December did permission arrive. The German advance had been even slower than the day before – consequence of a now general consensus that shells saved blood, combined with the few targets offered by the remnants of the French rearguards. It was 8 p.m. when the 17th Division's commander summoned Orleans to surrender or face bombardment. Major General von Treckow, a former royal adjutant, was also a hard driver, a sound tactician who took pains to limit his casualties whenever possible, and a man with at least a rudimentary sense of humour, since his artillery had been left far behind and the bombardment would have been composed of snowballs. The local French commander nevertheless welcomed the opportunity to secure free passage for his survivors. The Duke of Mecklenburg hurried to the scene to take charge of the negotiations, and, around 12.30, the 17th began its now unopposed advance into Orleans. In the city square, in front of the statue of Joan of Arc, Mecklenburg and Treckow held an improvised review, the men falling into step and the regimental bands playing under the winter moon, as French stragglers gazed on the spectacle or formed up one final time to surrender their rifles. It was a contrast neither army would forget.[57]

The Loire campaign was over. Aurelle was dismissed in disgrace. One wing of the defeated French army marched towards Le Mans, now under the command of Chanzy. The other turned east, and would make its final fight under that most protean of French captains, Marshal Charles Denis Bourbaki, late of the Imperial Guard, late of the Army of the North, and hero of a dozen missed opportunities. He may, in passing, have missed another in not closing to threaten the Germans' flank and rear when Frederick Charles finally marched out of Orleans towards Le Mans on 7 December.[58]

The prince had been in no hurry, despite Moltke's importuning telegrams. His regiments needed replacements; his men needed rest and re-equipment. While he kept his own counsel on the subject, Frederick Charles seems also to have come to three related conclusions: France was a big country; a stern chase is a long chase; and the war was going to last a while longer than Moltke expected. The final opinion was strengthened when Mecklenburg ran into Chanzy's two corps on 7 December. Chanzy was a solid field captain, one of the 'Africans' who had reached France too late to be caught up in the empire's débâcle. His 16th and 17th Corps had paid high tuition costs for the lessons, but the Germans had taught them how to fight and how to soldier. The regiments had shed the worst of their unable and unwilling members. The officers who remained commanded respect by character rather than insignia. At the risk of some stretching, Chanzy's corps resembled the Army of the Potomac in mid-1862: not the best troops in the field, but given a fair chance, they would do well. At Beaugency, on the high road to Le Mans, they proved it, stopping Mecklenburg in his tracks on 7 December, and almost driving him back the next day in a series of back-and-forth fights for the farms and villages that anchored the front lines. The tide turned the next day as German experience finally told. But Mecklenburg's troops had been hammered hard; I Bavarian Corps, in particular, was all but finished as a fighting formation – 'they can positively do no more', said Stosch, who was sufficiently concerned that he telegraphed Moltke for reinforcements.[59]

The chief of staff had none to send. All he could do was order Frederick Charles to support the grand duke. He sent X Corps in that direction, ordering III to take position to

---

[57]For the battle and occupation, see, primarily, Hoenig, *Volkskrieg*, vol. V, *passim* and Herman Kunz, *Die Schlacht von Orleans am 3 und 4 Dezember 1870* (Berlin, 1894).

[58]Stosch, p. 214, at least mentions Frederick Charles's concern at the possibility.

[59]Cf. Antoine de Chanzy, *Campagne de 1870–71. La deuxième Armée de la Loire* (4th ed., Paris, 1872); Helvig, pp. 299 ff.; and Stosch, p. 215. Philippe Le Moing-Kerrand, *Les Bretons dans la Guerre de 1870: le camp de Conlie et la bataille du Mans* (Plougoumelen, 1999), is a regionally focused account of the fate of the Breton levies, thrown into the final weeks of a lost war.

block any movement by Bourbaki. That captain found it easier to complain about the quality of his troops than to attempt to restore their morale. Left correspondingly isolated, Chanzy fell back – to the detriment of his army's cohesion, as hundreds of men fell out of ranks, headed for home or to the partisans. The survivors reached the Loire around Vendôme on 13 December, and Chanzy halted again to reorganize. His pursuers were almost as exhausted. Not so much the inconclusive fighting that began on 15 December, but another break in the weather led to Chanzy's decision to break contact once more and continue the retreat on Le Mans. It was fewer than fifty miles from the river to the city, but the distance was long enough to take most of whatever heart remained out of the survivors of 15th and 16th Corps. They managed to wrestle most of their guns through the mud and slush, but at the price of a level of exhaustion that, according to their commander, would require long to remedy.[60]

The Germans were in no better shape. Fatigue and tension led to repeated clashes of personalities in Mecklenburg's headquarters. One of the grand duke's division commanders interrupted a conference by asking Stosch for orders. When Mecklenburg answered that *he* was in command, the offending general replied, 'No need to be embarrassed; there's nobody here but us girls. Stosch, what should I do?'[61] Frederick Charles's implied answer was 'nothing' – nothing, at least, until the supply trains could come up, with new boots and new uniforms; until his men, replacements and veterans alike, could recover their strength and health; and, not least, until the artillery horses could be brought back into shape to pull the increasingly indispensable guns through slush and mud that would only get worse as spring approached. Too many batteries were operating with short teams. Too many of the well-conditioned horses that left the depots six months earlier had been replaced by animals from anywhere and everywhere: farm horses, captured French cavalry and artillery mounts, and increasing numbers whose original identification marks were German, but from other corps than those whose guns and caissons they now pulled – the products of midnight requisitioning.[62]

III

Moltke's behaviour throughout the Loire campaign reflected his conviction that, with France's real armies removed from the board, Paris was the new *Schwerpunkt* of the campaign, whose capture would finally compel French recognition of reality. If, in hindsight, his decision has a touch of *faute de mieux*, it is reasonable to observe that, since the sixteenth century, he who holds Paris holds France. The city had been worth a mass to Henry of Navarre. To Moltke the Elder it was worth a siege. Enveloping the city, however, was a long way from capturing it. Fortified again and again over the centuries, Paris in 1870 benefited from a defensive system that was near state of the art, a garrison large enough to man its defences, and a size that staggered the imaginations of Moltke's generals and engineers. From a German perspective, the French had another advantage as

---

[60]Chanzy, pp. 158 ff., describes a retreat that virtually shattered his army.
[61]Stosch, p. 216.
[62]*Friedrich Karl, Denkwuerdigkeiten*, vol. II, pp. 423 ff., describes the mid-January state of 2nd Army.
Heeresverpflegung, pp. 188 ff., helps to contextualize German supply problems during the Loire campaign.

well: their undisciplined troops and their unstable government rendered them correspondingly unpredictable, capable of doing anything for any reason, or for no reason at all.[63]

The Germans responded by constructing their own field entrenchments with an eager-
ness and a thoroughness that replicated the American armies of the later Civil War. After
Gravelotte/St Privat and Sedan, there was little talk of redoubts and trenches being unsoldierly. The Germans dug, cut and demolished. Suburban villas became strong points or
vanished for their building material. Trees not needed as breastworks were cut as fire-
wood – after the soldiers finished burning the furniture. 'Sandrart's Landscape Service'
the men of one division called themselves. Verdy summed it up nicely from a conqueror's
position. Running away, he said, is a foolish thing to do. Our soldiers cannot be left on the
road when there are houses beside it. So they break down locked doors and burn furniture because they do not know where to find wood. All this might be avoided, he senten-
tiously declared, if civilians would just remain at home.[64]

Both high commands kept things civilized, with regular parleys and established routes
for movement of selected individuals in or out of the city. Outposts re-established patterns
of 'live and let live' that dated back to the days of mercenaries armed with matchlocks: the
war's outcome was not going to change by shooting each other's hapless sentries. Bread,
sausage, newspapers – the small change of wartime commerce – passed readily across the
lines.[65] Nor was Paris exactly isolated. A submarine cable, on which great hopes had been
placed as a source of communication with the outside world, was discovered by the
Germans, who cut it when they could not decipher the coded messages it carried. More
spectacular were the free-air balloon flights out of the city, sixty-five of them, carrying 164
passengers, 381 carrier pigeons and 2.5 million letters, most of them microfilmed. One balloon was lost, three captured – a remarkable success rate for an untested system. From the
outside, Gambetta sent fifty-one 'pigeon-grams' into the city between 9 October and
27 January, with over forty arriving. Normally the pigeons took a week, sometimes as little
as two days, but winter weather slowed their passage and made them more erratic.[66]

At best, communication between Tours and Paris was sufficiently erratic that Trochu
was responsible for the city's war effort. Partly in response to the fire-eaters in the government and in the streets, he had promised 'a new Saragossa'[67] – this time with the
Germans playing a role still remembered by a French army which had twice suffered
ruinous casualties assaulting that Spanish city in the Napoleonic Wars. The Germans,
however, were not obliging by attacking. Nor was the garrison of Paris an ideal force for
open warfare. It included two regiments of the old army that had escaped the débâcle at

---

[63]Bronsart's comment on French instability of 22 September (p. 84) is typical. Cf. the German officer quoted
in Roth, p. 296.
[64]Verdy, p. 172.
[65]The siege of Paris has its own extensive bibliography. Robert Tombs, 'The Wars against Paris', *Road to Total
War*, pp. 541–64, is the best brief analysis. The best account in English of everyday routines is Alistair Horne,
The Fall of Paris: The Siege and the Commune, 1870–1871 (London, 1962). John Milner, *Art, War and
Revolution in France, 1870–1871. Myth, Reportage, and Reality* (New Haven, CT, 2000) and Hollis Clayson,
Paris in Despair: Art and Everyday Life under Siege (1870–71) (Chicago, 2002), take more apocalyptic tones.
[66]Cf. Ferdinand Lacombe, 'Les transmissions pendant le siège de Paris, 1870–71', *Revue Historique de l'Armée*
22 (1966), no. 4, pp. 113–34; Georges Brunel, *Les Ballons du siège de Paris* (Paris, 1933); and the summary in
Audoin-Rouzeau, p. 365, fn. 4.
[67]Louis Trochu, *Ouevres posthumes* (2 vols., Tours, 1896), vol. I, p. 273.

Sedan, and a number of provisional regiments raised from the depots in Paris. There were some mobile guards and a few irregular volunteer units. The navy provided around 8,500 men, mostly infantry and gunners, the latter arguably the best on either side.[68] The garrison's mass, however, consisted of the National Guard of the Seine, over 300,000 strong, including, in principle, all the able-bodied men not serving somewhere else, most of them green as grass, despite their elevated opinion of themselves as warrior patriots.

Seen in hindsight, Trochu could have done far worse than accept the role of a 'force in being', fixing German troops and attention on Paris, while the rest of the country mobilized its resources and the rest of Europe considered how best to benefit from Bismarck's discomfiture at a protracted war. Instead, he responded to increasing popular pressure by planning a breakout. The exact purposes and objectives of the sortie remain obscure. 'Le plan Trochu', as it was dubbed in the boulevards and cafés of Paris, amounted to little more than a grand rush, not south towards the Loire, the logical direction, but west, across the Seine, where the terrain was more difficult and the defences a bit weaker. Those who survived were expected to push on to Normandy and establish contact by sea with the Army of the Loire![69]

Whatever surprise this extrinsic operation might have achieved was sacrificed in a series of preliminary sorties during late October and early November. Their main achievement was to increase senior officers' confidence in their poorly trained, nearly undisciplined levies, at the price of giving the Germans a solid sense of their opponents' strengths and weaknesses. Political factors, however, made abandoning the operation impossible. For six weeks, Thiers had sought support from the cabinets of Europe. Rejected at every turn, he was convinced that France must make peace on whatever terms it could scrape from Bismarck. Now Bismarck allowed him into Paris to test the temper of the city's defenders. He arrived on 30 October, at the same time as the news of Bazaine's surrender. Instead of discussing options, the radicals demanded war to the knife. Instead of taking drastic action, the government delayed – and Bismarck saw his opportunity. He offered the despondent Thiers an armistice while France convoked a national assembly to decide the question of war or peace. The siege of Paris would remain in effect.

Trochu and his subordinates responded by affirming that Paris would fight to the end and go down in a blaze of glory – a predictable enough reply in context, and one that cannot be dismissed as mere posturing. Trochu understood the internal dynamics of Paris better than Thiers – better as well than many of his subsequent critics. The radicals might not command ongoing, consistent majorities, but they offered a rallying point for a public opinion, civil and military, that had a base-line commitment to resistance to the end, as that concept was generally understood. Would citizens in arms face Prussian bayonets on the final barricades as Paris crumbled in ruins? Perhaps not – even probably not. Would they accept a negotiated settlement while the Prussian siege lines remained in place? Probably not, indeed, almost certainly not. That was where the sortie came in. Its military prospects may have been increasingly limited, but in political terms it offered an answer

---

[68]Noel Kerbourch, 'Les Marins à terre pendant la guerre de 1870–1871', *Revue Historique des Armées* 48 (1992), no. 4, pp. 80–7.
[69]Cf. Trochu, pp. 325 ff. and Auguste A. Ducrot, *La Défense de Paris, 1870–71* (4 vols., Paris, 1875–8), vol. I, pp. 301 ff. Ducrot had escaped from Sedan and been given command of Trochu's two best corps, a sort of army detachment, used as shock troops, and an emergency reserve.

to an otherwise real risk of civil war, initially with the national guard turning against Ducrot's quasi-regulars, and then with the entire city unravelling.[70]

By this time, German morale was beginning to fray a bit. The men besieging Paris had not experienced the full force of the partisan war beginning to sweep the rear areas. On the whole, they still saw themselves as fighting, fairly and in a just cause, for their homeland. At the same time, more or less on general principles, the recalled reservists who made up over half of most battalions, felt they had done their duty and wanted to go home. The stable conditions of the siege also contributed to an unwillingness to take routine risks, especially when the war seemed nearly over.[71] Then the French, once again, resumed the role of an obliging enemy. Reports of Aurelle's advance and the recapture of Orleans led the government to redirect its projected attack south – towards the presumed spearheads of the Army of the Loire, and into the teeth of some of the strongest German defences on the perimeter.

These were manned by the Wuerttemberg Division, whose officers, at least, were anxious to show what their Swabians could do in a stand-up fight. They had almost two weeks to prepare while watching the French clumsily shift men and guns to their chosen breakout sector. After a day's additional delay caused by local flooding, the attack went in on 30 November. The French had planned well. A series of successful secondary attacks pinned down most of the prospective German reinforcements. But the Wuerttembergers, as their descendants were to do in 1916 on the Somme, had dug themselves so thoroughly into two villages, that French artillery – even the heavy fortress guns – had no effect. With plenty of ammunition in hand, they shot down successive waves of French infantry throughout the short winter day, until the badly shaken survivors fell back to their start lines.

Not only the French were shaken. Higher German headquarters, ignoring the Wuerttembergers' matter-of-fact reports that it had all been in a day's work, significantly overestimated the prospects of a second French attack. After a day's truce to bring in the wounded and bury the dead, the Crown Prince of Saxony, commanding the sector, ordered a counter-attack that merely reversed the circumstances of 30 November. This time it was the Germans, including some of the best veteran troops of XII Corps, that made no headway and suffered such heavy losses that Albert broke off the fighting at nightfall.[72]

By mid-December, the handwriting was, nevertheless, on the wall for the republic, as it had been for the empire three months earlier. In conventional military terms the situation was hopeless. Indeed, continuing the struggle brought with it risk of civil war on multiple axes: republicans against conservatives, Paris against the provinces, and soldiers against soldiers in the various provincial armies. Yet the Germans, too, were feeling the pangs of comprehensive overstretch. The campaign on the Loire, originally intended as part of the siege of Paris, had assumed a life of its own. The further Frederick Charles

---

[70]Cf. *inter alia*, Jules Favre, *Gouvernement du défense nationale du juin 30 1870* (3 vols., Paris, 1871–5), vol. I, pp. 312 ff. and Howard, pp. 336 ff. The best general history of the city's political dynamic at this period is Stephane Pick, *De Trochu à Thiers, 1870–1873* (Paris, 1985).

[71]On the subject of German morale generally, see Thomas Rohrkramer, 'Daily Life at the Front and the Concept of Total War', *Road to Total War*, pp. 497–518.

[72]Ducrot, *Défense de Paris*, vol. II, pp. 152 ff. and vol. III, pp. 5 ff., is the best French command-perspective account. For the German side, see Hermann Kunz, *Die grossen Durchbruchsversuch der zweiten Parisier Armee in den Tagen vom 29. November bis 3. Dezember 1870* (Berlin, 1891).

advanced into southern France, the more he risked overstraining already tenuous supply lines and sacrificing any ability to support the siege in an emergency. Paris itself continued to pin down half of Germany's active forces. The south German reserve systems, never comprehensive, were already straining to provide replacements for their units in the field. Over a third of Prussia's population had been exposed to Prussia's military system only since 1867, and had no deep pool of men with even rudimentary active training. That left it up to the provinces of 'old Prussia' to furnish the increasing number of Landwehr battalions required to secure lines of communication and rear areas. When Moltke asked for more men, Roon, grieving a son killed at Sedan, spoke of the growing strain on Prussian society and suggested that military operations must be tailored to available means. Ill feeling between the two men sputtered, then flared.[73]

In the field, 'overstretch' accurately described the situation of the 1st Army: I, VII and VIII Corps were assigned, after the fall of Metz, to clear away the small fortresses that dotted the north and to scatter the French levies forming around Amiens and Arras. Organized and trained by General Charles Bourbaki, former commander of the Imperial Guard and recent fugitive from Metz, these new forces were promising, on the whole. Republican sentiment was strong in the industrial districts, and the men, recruits or recalled reservists, were well armed and well equipped from the region's arsenals and magazines. The regiments were built around strong cadres of officers and men left in the depots, or who had escaped the disasters on the frontier, and stiffened by a few battalions of *Marsouins* formed in the coastal depots. Captain Leonce Patry, one of many evaders from Metz, arrived in Lille on 10 November. By 16 November, he was commanding a company that was a going concern – a sharp contrast to the circumstances to which he had grown accustomed under Bazaine.[74]

On 7 November, Manteuffel took the field with I and VIII Corps and the 3rd Cavalry Division. The North Army was now under General Louis Faidherbe, an old African hand who would prove himself among the best of the republic's field commanders – eminently worthy of the commemorative statues that still dot the municipalities of northern France.[75] Initially, he withdrew slowly, drawing Manteuffel further and further from the German main bodies. At the end of the month, he stood at bay around Amiens. Faidherbe had spread his forces thin in order to hold what seemed key tactical positions, and his levies should have been easy meat for the Prussian veterans. Instead, they fought Manteuffel's army to a near standstill on 27 November, as his subordinates consistently divided their own forces instead of concentrating for one coordinated attack. But as the French retreated north-east on the fortresses of Arras and Lille, Moltke sent Manteuffel west with three of his four divisions, to occupy Rouen and end the potential threat of a Breton redoubt. Rouen fell without a fight and, in mid-December, Moltke explained himself to Manteuffel and Frederick Charles. There were not, and could not be, enough German troops in the field to occupy effectively the whole of France and besiege Paris as well. What was necessary was to keep the republic's field armies off balance without overextending friendly forces, and, at the same time, control the growing plague of irregulars.

---

[73]Bronsart, pp. 240–1.
[74]Patry, pp. 180 ff.
[75]Alain Coursier, *Faidherbe, 1818–1889: du Sénégal a l'Armée du Nord* (Paris, 1989), is an excellent critical biography.

Moltke outlined a barrier system with the 2nd Army holding the line of the Loire in the south, Mecklenburg facing west from bases at Chartres and Dreaux, and the 1st Army securing the north from a rough quadrilateral of Rouen, Amiens, St Quentin and Beauvais. Anything beyond those zones of control was 'Indian country', to be controlled by flying columns and brief offensives.[76]

The chief of staff was not working from abstractions. On 7 December, Gambetta had ordered Faidherbe to mount an offensive towards Paris, with the objective of supporting the city garrison's planned attempt at a breakout. In one of the best-executed republican operations of the war, elements of the 22nd Corps, most of them formed around cadres from regular regiments, captured by surprise the town, fortress and rail junction of Ham on 9 December. Faidherbe followed up the strike by advancing with his main army towards Amiens, brushing aside German occupation forces too thinly spread to be more than tokens. But the commandant of Amiens had taken hostages into the city's citadel (the French, in any case, lacked guns heavy enough to blow it apart) and Manteuffel was coming back from Rouen by forced marches – albeit with just a division and a half, having left three brigades of I Corps to hold down Brittany.

Faidherbe's strategic prospects were not the best. The loss of Rouen had left the North virtually isolated from the rest of France. Operationally, however, he had successfully used Amiens as bait to draw Manteuffel on to his guns; and, tactically, he was able to pick his ground when he decided to make a stand, rather than once more falling back beyond the Germans' reach. His choice would become all too familiar to soldiers of a dozen nations in the next century: about halfway between Amiens and Albert. He deployed his two corps, about 40,000 strong, on the high ground to the east of the Hallue river, where broad, barren slopes offered clear fields of fire, and waited. Manteuffel had only VIII Corps plus some smaller units – 25,000 men and a hundred guns – but was confident enough to send one division forward on 23 December, using the other to probe northward for the French right flank.

The frontal attack was stalled almost immediately. The flanking manoeuvre came up against two fortified villages and, for a while, it was like a reduced-scale version of Gravelotte – without the suicidal charges into massed rifle fire. The junior officers and men of VIII Corps had been there and done that on 16 August, and no one, from division headquarters downwards, was anxious to repeat the experience. A late-afternoon French counter-attack fizzled out under the needle guns at short range. Each side suffered about 1,000 casualties, but French morale received an incalculable boost, especially when Faidherbe kept the ground the next day, thereby securing the victory beyond question.

The 1st Army headquarters knew its expected response was to kick the French off those hills and see them on their way, but had neither the men nor the shells remaining to do more than stay in place. When the French withdrew during the night, Manteuffel did not attempt a pursuit – not least because I Corps, left to hold Rouen, was demanding assistance against an eruption of partisan activity. Faidherbe mounted another offensive in January, this one with the local objective of relieving the fortress of Peronne. On 2 and 3 January, his rapidly seasoning recruits took the measure of the German 15th Division at Bapaume, hammering it so badly that Goeben, still VIII Corps commander, was on the

---

[76]*MMK* 1, vol. III, pp. 462–3.

point of retreating and raising the siege when Faidherbe decided his men had given all they had and broke off operations himself.[77]

Around a strategic semicircle from Orleans to Bapaume, both combatants had fought themselves to stalemate and exhaustion by the end of the year. The myth of 'people's war' so assiduously propagated in the Third Republic, and its German counterpart of a united national effort to create a united fatherland, were both post-war constructions. However extensive their theoretically available resources might be, neither France nor Prussia, to say nothing of the south German states, had the administrative systems or the moral authority necessary to mobilize them effectively and wage an improvised total war.[78] But could the present conflict be settled with the forces on hand? Or did what had begun on both sides as a policy war, short and victorious, face the prospect of spiralling into a broken-backed struggle that would end with third parties picking the combatants' bones? In Tours and in Versailles, men wondered.

---

[77]Louis Leon Faidherbe, *Campagne de l'Armée du Nord en 1870–1871* (Paris, 1871) and the company-level account of Patry, pp. 191 ff., combine for an outstanding reconstruction from the French side. Hermann Graf Wartensleben, *Feldzug 1871. Die Operationen der I. Armee unter General von Manteuffel* (Berlin, 1872), is, correspondingly, among the best of the German army-level histories. Zernin, *Goeben*, vol. II, pp. 87 ff., conveys that general's growing frustration at what he considered a task of making bricks without straw.
[78]Cf. Wilhelm Deist, 'Remarks on the Preconditions to Waging War in Prussia-Germany, 1866–1871' and Gerd Krumeich, 'The Myth of Gambetta and "People's War" in Germany and France, 1871–1914', *Road to Total War*, pp. 311–25 and 641–55.

9

War with France

Napoleon once allegedly dismissed a plan that deployed the French army in a cordon by asking if the unfortunate author was trying to make war or stop smuggling. By 1 December, the disposition of Germany's forces might well have elicited the same sarcastic question. This time, however, the answer might well have been affirmative. With half his effective fighting units pinned down before Paris, Moltke was, in fact, seeking not only to end the war in the field, but to halt at least a counterpart of smuggling: an invisible war that, all of a sudden, seemed to be sapping morale and draining lifeblood from a thousand tiny cuts.

The Unification War of 1870 is conventionally divided into two parts: against the empire and against the republic. Developments within Germany are sometimes interpreted as sufficiently rapid that the war's first half is called the Franco-Prussian War, while the period after Sedan becomes the Franco-German War. That dichotomy, however, assumes an identification of the French people and the French government that is questionable, at best. In truth, almost from the beginning, the war had an extra dimension, a third dimension. That dimension pitted a developing German political/military system against the people of France. That new dimension also exacerbated stresses on a Prussian decision-making apparatus already hard-put to sustain itself in the face of challenges unexpected when the war began. In both areas it foreshadowed future cataclysms.

I

The nineteenth century had witnessed extensive partisan warfare both for and against Napoleon; the Prussian army had significant experience in irregular fighting during the Wars of Liberation.[1] It had also engaged partisans in 1866 in Bohemia, Moravia and Upper Silesia, albeit on a very small scale.[2] In general, however, to the extent that the armies reorganized after 1815 addressed unconventional warfare, it was in a context of suppressing domestic dissent rather than fighting guerrillas.[3] The Prussian General Staff did not

---

[1]Georg Cardinal von Widdern, *Die Streifkorps im deutschen Befreiungskriege 1813 nach kriegsarchivarischen Quellen* (2 vols., Berlin, 1899). *Streifkorps* was a generic name for a task force usually composed of a couple of hundred Russian Cossacks or other Asian cavalry and a hundred-odd Prussian troopers, supplemented by local volunteers and directed against French rear echelons.
[2]W. Etschmann, 'Guerrillas und Franctireurs, 1866 und 1870/71' in *Freund oder Feind? Kombattanten, Nichtkombattantenten und Zivilisten in Krieg und Buergerkrieg seit dem 18. Jahrhundert*, ed. E. A. Schmidl (Frankfurt, 1995), pp. 33–4.
[3]Showalter, 'Europe's Way of War, 1815–64', pp. 28 ff. The best recent anthology on the subject of *The Laws of War*, eds. M. Howard et al. (New Haven, CT, 1994), devotes a single footnote to the Franco-Prussian War.

expect any significant insurgent activity – not least because it expected a quick victory and a negotiated peace.

The French were no better prepared for, or willing to utilize, irregular war. Gambetta, for all his rhetorical insistence on war to the knife, wanted the republic's levies in uniformed and organized formations. Nor were ordinary French civilians, of any class or condition, anxious to try conclusions single-handed with their conquerors. Businessmen solicited German help in maintaining order. Farmers cooperated with requisitions officers. Even relatively small cavalry patrols usually reported 'correct' behaviour by civilians. The choices were admittedly limited. A lieutenant of dragoons who rode into a town at the head of two dozen men and instructed the mayor to produce a good dinner for twenty, ten bottles of champagne and 200 cigars, punctuated his demand by mentioning that 6,000 more Germans would arrive the next day.[4] When the Prussians occupied Reims, a shot was fired from a café window at a passing hussar squadron. Bismarck declared the building must be destroyed and the proprietor court-martialled. Instead, the man's plea of innocence was accepted, and the offence compounded for 200 or 250 bottles of champagne for the hussars. Since that amounted to a bottle and more per trooper, the exchange seemed fair – especially since most of the champagne stocked in the city was owned by German firms, and therefore safe from requisition. Former Union general Philip Sheridan found it all a long way from the Shenandoah Valley, which he had ordered so thoroughly devastated that a crow flying over it would have to carry rations.[5]

Until September, this relatively manageable situation continued. There were exceptions. Along the 3rd Army's line of advance, cutting telegraph wires had been common since the war's first days. Patrols and convoys were sometimes fired upon. Local civilian volunteer forces, sometimes based on shooting clubs, had existed in Alsace and Lorraine since before the Luxembourg crisis of 1868. These initial guerrilla activities, however, were disproportionately the work of stragglers from Wissembourg and Woerth, reinforced, in some cases, by mobilized reservists unable to join their regiments. Civilians in Metz also organized several irregular volunteer units, which did more damage to the Germans during the siege than the whole of Bazaine's moribund army, by striking at supply columns and sniping at outposts.

On the whole, however, German soldiers in the war's first weeks cheerfully asked French civilians for matches, bought drinks in local taverns and played with children whose fathers had been mobilized to fight on the other side. A few Teutonic fire-eaters denounced the French as a folk of degenerate weaklings, ready to bend the knee at the first test; but the evidence is overwhelming that the German conscripts and reservists, many of whom had been in uniform only a few weeks, behaved themselves acceptably. The occasional violent crimes, theft, assault or rape, were dealt with expeditiously in courts martial that usually imposed harsh penalties for guilty verdicts.[6] On the other side, civilians brought before

---

[4]Roth, *Guerre de 1870*, p. 374.

[5]Sheridan's amazement at what he considered the benevolent way Germans treated resistance eventually led him to assert that the French who were continuing the war should be left 'nothing but their eyes to weep with'. Cf. Philip H. Sheridan, *Personal Memoirs of Philip Henry Sheridan* (2 vols., New York, 1888), vol. II, p. 415 and Moritz Busch, *Bismarck in the Franco-German War, 1870–1871* (New York, 1879), vol. I, pp. 126 ff.

[6]Messerschmidt, 'Preussische Armee', pp. 142 ff., discusses the principles behind a Prussian discipline harsh in both principle and reality. Kuehlich, pp. 81 ff., presents the system's application. He makes the point that sentences for military offences like insubordination or sleeping on guard were, in many cases, reduced on review.

military courts on charges of partisan activity were frequently acquitted on grounds of inadequate evidence, or because of poorly presented accusers' testimony. Others were transferred to Germany – 'deported' is the word most often used in post-World War II French accounts – for trial in higher military courts. In practice, that usually meant release, since the war ended before the slow-grinding mills of Prussian army justice dealt with their cases.

What, then, upset the balance?[7] It usually began with requisitioning. The Prussian army and its allied contingents possessed comprehensive and well-organized supply services. From the war's beginning, however, Moltke did not expect to feed his forces from wagon trains alone. Requisitioning did not mean the random levying of goods and services at gunpoint. It was a collective enterprise, supplementing material acquired from public property, such as supply depots, recognized as spoils of war. A community was ordered to produce certain items; German quartermasters made or authorized payment to the local authorities. Such payment seldom approached what the recipients considered fair market value. When it was made in cash, the cash had often been raised by levying contributions of money on towns traversed earlier, thus robbing Pierre to pay Paul. When vouchers were issued, redeeming them took time and effort – in the event, most were settled by the Third Republic as part of the war indemnity. Requisitions were supplemented by 'contributions': cash levies authorized as a substitute for goods unavailable or undelivered; as a penalty for collective offences like aiding partisans; and, at times, to damage the French war effort economically. Opportunities for abuses and corruption flourished as the occupation administration grew more elaborate. Even with goodwill on both sides, language barriers mocked communication. A merchant willing enough to sell stock of foodstuffs, shoes or blankets for cash might baulk at forms in a foreign language or a note in German script. A lieutenant who had studied French in school was, nevertheless, likely to make heavy weather of a village magistrate's patois.

If requisitioning posed problems, quartering exacerbated them. Quartering, assigning soldiers to private and public buildings, was standard Prussian procedure. It contrasted with the French preference for bivouacking, having the men pitch camp at some distance from towns or villages. Each practice was the product of a general military culture. Prussia, with a conscript 'people's army', preferred to cultivate civic ties. France sought to keep its professionals at a distance from civilians and so had them pitch camps in the open. French peasants and townsmen thus had no background for dealing with the presence of their own soldiers, let alone foreigners, in their houses and outbuildings. They had even less when these aliens solicited food and drink.

In theory, soldiers billeted on civilians brought their army rations with them, or received small sums of money to purchase supplies. At times, the Germans did pay, even from their own pockets. But to peasants accustomed to living from harvest to harvest, German coins were a poor replacement for emptied storage bins, barns and chicken coops. More often, especially when the supply wagons had not caught up, soldiers resorted to foraging: individuals and small groups 'liberating' what they needed on their own initiative.

---

[7]The following is based on Kuelich, p. 210 *passim*; Paul B. Hatley, 'Prolonging the Inevitable: The Franc-Tireur and the German Army in the Franco-German War of 1870–1871' (dissertation, Kansas State University, 1999), pp. 103 ff.; van Creveld, *Supplying War*, pp. 96 ff.; Stoneman, pp. 373 ff.; and Roth, *Guerre de 1870*, pp. 372 ff. Sanford Kanter, 'Exposing the Myth of the Franco-Prussian War', *War & Society* 4 (1986), pp. 13–30, also establishes the relatively circumscribed scale of civilian material losses.

Officers first looked the other way as hungry men turned farms and villages upside down searching for food. Later, they began authorizing and organizing informal hunts for the sake of maintaining discipline. At times, the Germans processed them as a game of hide-and-seek: give us what we need or we'll take twice as much. But when the searches turned up nothing, goodwill frequently gave way to threats, and foraging crossed the line into pillage, with women's underwear taken for cleaning rags and lard used as a substitute for rifle oil.

Foraging also encouraged bullying. Apparently to a greater degree than their German counterparts, French peasants in the east let their fowls and piglets forage for themselves as opposed to keeping them penned. Even the most scrupulously honest German – like soldiers of any other nationality and culture – tended to see a difference between taking a chicken from a building and seizing one on the street. For a farm wife to prove ownership of a particular bird was not a promising endeavour. Her efforts, however, easily became a source of amusement for soldiers from a culture whose sense of humour is generally recognized as heavily based on *Schadenfreude*: 'joy at another's hard luck'. Germans enjoyed showing their unwilling hosts how things from housekeeping to barn-cleaning were done in a civilized country. They took pleasure in taking over taverns and pool rooms – especially when their presence generated hostile glares from young men and men not so young. At usual odds of six, eight or a dozen against two or three, arrogance was safe behaviour.

There was little underlying malice involved – just armed immaturity. But being scorned can be worse than being kicked. The friction generated was more pronounced in the countryside than in towns, where it was usually possible for German officers and French officials to sort out the worst of the misunderstandings and miscommunications. On isolated farms and in small villages, too often a blow was the response when civilian importuning grew more annoying than amusing. One village of 686 inhabitants reported its losses: thirteen cows, ninety-five sheep, thirty-eight turkeys, 342 kilograms of bread, 264 litres of milk, 1,026 bottles of wine and brandy, and over a hundred days' worth of labour from commandeered horses.[8] A reckoning kept with such exactness was a poor prospect for post-war reconciliation.

German misbehaviour of all kinds lost nothing in its retelling through the 'little press', the provincial journals whose initial differentiation was between a militaristic Prussia and a more humane and liberal German south. However, distinctions between north and south, good and bad, increasingly blurred into a single image of conquering oppressors.[9] Small wonder that as the German armies approached Paris, they found increasing numbers of villages abandoned: barns burned and animals driven off, streets torn up and wells blocked. Initially, this was more of a nuisance than a problem. On 30 September, for example, Verdy noted with amusement finding a barricade of artichokes.[10]

However, with the railroads increasingly drawn upon to transport siege material, and with organic horse transportation suffering from a steady erosion of animals and vehicles, the Germans besieging Paris became increasingly self-supporting, using troops to gather local crops left unharvested and process them with local machines left undamaged, or repaired by German craftsmen in the pioneer and train formations. It was, in many ways,

[8] Roth, *Guerre de 1870*, p. 391.
[9] Bodo Rollka, 'Das Preussenbild in der "kleinen Presse" Frankreichs 1870/71', *Jahrbuch fuer die Geschichte Mittel-und Ostdeutschlands* 31 (1982), pp. 129–54.
[10] Verdy, pp. 172–3.

easier to guard that kind of work than it was to protect railway lines. Van Creveld's suggestion that these activities diverted the Germans from their main mission of making war on Paris does not withstand close examination. While the French had a good number of successes against pickets and outposts, carelessness rather than numerical weakness was the usual problem. The number of men required for food producing was, moreover, small compared with the numbers available in the rear echelons of the siege: teamsters, cavalry-men and all the rear echelons of a modern army. Markets were also established, to which local farmers brought goods for sale under German military protection – a pattern prefiguring the 'oil-spot' technique of pacification subsequently used widely in French colonies, which might have involved some flattery by imitation.

The second step to partisan war was the republic's call for national mobilization. Conscription had always been unpopular, and 'republic' was by no means the rallying cry in the countryside that it was for Paris. Some young men were correspondingly unwilling to report, but were ready enough to fight on their own terms among their friends and neighbours. Other new soldiers simply walked away from camps that offered neither food nor instruction.[11] When the war ministry established pay for partisans comparable to that for men in organized formations, the choice became even easier. While exact numbers are impossible to determine, the best estimates are around 350 units incorporating approximately 60,000 men.[12]

Those numbers do not, however, include the 'classic' *franc-tireur*: peaceful townsman or peasant by day, scourge of the invader by night, as an individual or in small groups of friends and neighbours – a model dominant enough and sufficiently positive to be the subject of one of G. A. Henty's novels of derring-do written for proper British boys.[13] One prefect summarized the ideal nicely: 'Your fatherland ... only expects that each morning three or four resolute men will leave their village and go where nature has prepared a suitable place for hiding and for firing on the Prussians without danger'.[14]

Such activities were usually poorly coordinated, or uncoordinated, with any wider efforts. In what might be called traditional guerrilla actions against outposts, patrols and supply columns, the 'pure' partisan was usually no more than a nuisance.[15] The material damage he did was easily repaired – particularly when inflicted in the immediate rear of the main German armies, which had large numbers of men available for short-term work details. Railroads were another story. Small partisan groups operating on their own, however, usually did not have the equipment, the know-how or the time to do more than temporarily interrupt service. Loosening or removing a few lengths of rail, even when a train was derailed, amounted to harassment and little more. What really counted were viaducts, bridges, tunnels – permanent works whose destruction took not only skill, but large amounts of explosives.

---

[11]Cf. G. de Bonin, *Les levées dans le département de l'Yonne pendant la guerre de 1870–71 et la défense locale* (Auxerre, 1915).

[12]Audoin-Rouzeau, pp. 198 and 369 (both figures exclude Paris).

[13]G. A. Henty, *The Young Franc-Tireurs and Their Adventures in the Franco-Prussian War* (London, 1872). It is correspondingly difficult to see him adding either *The Young Communards* or *The Young Uhlans* to his long list of publications.

[14]Quoted in Geoffrey Best, *Humanity in Warfare* (London, 1980), p. 198.

[15]Verdy, p. 164.

Two days after the largest and most successful raid of the war, Verdy commented that 'we have wondered for a long time why they have not done more damage to the railways'.[16] Railway demolition in the American Civil War had proven a task sufficiently complex that it took armies years to learn it.[17] In September, an 'Alsace-Lorraine Legion' was formed in Bordeaux, purportedly trained for operations against railroads. Effective demolitions, however, were usually the work of retreating regulars – as at Nanteuil, on a main route to Paris, where half a dozen mines blocked a long tunnel with loose sand, and later sand-slides made repair impossible. Instead, it was necessary to build a bypass, which was not completed until 22 November – a major contribution to the delay in bringing up material for the bombardment of Paris. Ironically, German cavalry raiding ahead of their advancing armies did more damage to railroads in some sectors than did partisans behind the lines. In the course of the war the Germans repaired sixty-eight bridges and viaducts, of which they themselves accounted for exactly half. The French railroads' total loss in damages calculated after the war amounted to 33 million francs – not negligible, but hardly a budget-wrecker.[18]

It also took the Germans a while to learn how to protect vulnerable installations. Too often, their bivouacs and strong points were too far away, with only outposts stationed at the actual bridge or tunnel. It was well enough to order troops to construct shelters and defences with fields of fire covering what they were supposed to protect, but the infantry had no training in that kind of work, and the lines of communications had no spare pioneers to supervise such construction. Nor, as a rule, did the garrisons have enough cavalry to patrol their areas of responsibility systematically.[19]

It was not about casualties. By best reckoning, only around 1,000 German soldiers were killed by partisans in the whole course of the war. What the guerrillas did was add to risk and discomfort in the German rear echelons without altering the conflict's course. That was one reason why unit-level reactions escalated so rapidly to various forms of summary justice, ending with a rope or a firing squad. Another was the sense of isolation, brought about by a new form of irregular warfare, engendered by technology. Cutting telegraph lines was as low-skill, low-risk a form of resistance as was possible in 1870. Yet interrupted communications could be disproportionately disconcerting to outposts and small garrisons, particularly in the broken, sparsely settled country in the east and south of France. What did the suddenly silent telegraph mean? A teenager with a pocket knife, a tenfold superior raiding force or a major French offensive? Repairing the breaks also involved risk, given the small size of the usual working parties. Taking a few shots at a couple of linemen and their escort of half a dozen troopers was not the same as tackling a wagon train and fifty riflemen. And even when nothing happened, the stress remained – particularly since the soldiers involved were overwhelmingly Landwehr, men settled in life. To borrow from Rudyard Kipling, they wanted to finish their little

---

[16]Ibid., p. 247.

[17]An excellent case study in the limits of anti-rail operations at this period, even when undertaken by large forces, is David Evans, *Sherman's Horsemen. Union Cavalry Operations in the Atlanta Campaign* (Bloomington, IN, 1996).

[18]Hermann Budde, *Die franzoesischen Eisenbahnen im Deutschen Kriegsbetriebe* (Berlin, 1904), pp. 64 ff. and Jacqumin, pp. 316 ff., who also lists the sites of destruction and damage.

[19]Georg Cardinal von Widdern, *Der Krieg an den Rueckwaertigen Verbindungen der deutschen Heere 1870–71*, (5 vols., Berlin, 1893–9), vol. III, no. 2, pp. 177 ff.

bit and then go home to their tea. And they could be savage when that scenario was threatened.[20]

Since the sixteenth century, a consensus had developed in Europe that civil populations were required to remain conspicuously aloof from any kind of hostilities. In return, the combatants were responsible for civilian safety. A Prussian decree of 1867, applying in wartime to all the German armies under Prussian command, established armed civilians as subject to the death penalty. Other authorized responses to civilian resistance included destroying buildings from which shots were fired, taking hostages for the good behaviour of a community and levying punitive contributions on an offending place or region. All three were applied almost from the war's beginning.[21] All were intended, in principle, as measured deterrents, not only suppressing misguided individuals by limited applications of force, but encouraging communities to suppress their own hotheads with no subsequent questions being asked. In the circumstances of 1870, however, none seemed sufficiently effective to secure order in the German rear – in particular, to protect the railroads that seemed increasingly vulnerable as they grew more necessary to German operations in the heart of France.[22]

Belief and fact, however, are not always the same. Railway service, particularly on the main lines connecting Germany with Paris, was affected far less by the kinds of minor damage inflicted by local partisans than by traffic jams. As had been the case in 1866, depots in Germany tended to push trains forward with little concern for when or whether they could be unloaded. A front-loaded army organization provided no labour formations for such mundane tasks. As corps penetrated deeper into France, their train battalions found increasing difficulty maintaining connections with the railheads. The heavy concentrations of troops around Metz, then Sedan, further exacerbated crowding. Few French railway stations were large enough to handle heavy military traffic on a regular basis, lacking, in particular, the ramps and sidetracks necessary for quick loading and unloading. Smaller double-track lines, at times, had single-track stretches interspersed, or one track down for maintenance or to repair demolitions. Small wonder that lines were blocked as far back as Frankfurt and Cologne. As early as 5 September, over 2,300 freight cars of supplies for the 2nd Army alone were in place on five different rail lines. Between 1 and 26 October, twenty-nine of 292 trains sent from Wissembourg to Nancy – a routine regional run – never arrived.

No officer was likely to step forward and claim responsibility for that degree of rear echelon chaos. It was far easier to file reports blaming the partisans – whose activities were, in fact, often a final straw for overworked and overstressed train crews and administrative personnel. A rifle slug ricocheting off a locomotive, or a loosened rail spotted in time to

---

[20]Kuehlich, pp. 317 ff., describes the offhand execution of partisans, the burning of houses – even, in some cases, the use of artillery against villages.

[21]Frederick III, *War Diary*, p. 95.

[22]Cardinal von Widdern, *Rueckwaertigen Verbindungen* (all five volumes) and *Der kleine Krieg und der Etappendienst* (2nd ed., rev., Berlin, 1899), incorporate a wealth of narrative data. Bernhard Winterhalter, 'Die Behandlung der franzoesische Zivilbevoelkerung durch die deutschen Truppen im Kriege 1870/71' (dissertation, Freiburg, 1952), provides the framework of laws and regulations that shaped much, though not all, of the army's behaviour. Cf. also, Mark Stoneman, 'The Bavarian Army and French Civilians in the War of 1870–71' (MA thesis, Augsburg, 1994) (the source of the article cited above) and Fernand Thiebault Schneider, 'Der Krieg in franzoesischer Sicht' in *Entscheidung 1870*, pp. 191 ff.

avoid derailment, could be enough to produce demands for action from the civilians who made the railroads run. Increasing numbers of these were German – around 3,500 by the end of the war – and they were not shy about asserting that being shot at was not part of their job description. The train crews, moreover, were responsible to the ministry of commerce, not the ministry of war. The resulting jurisdictional squabbles only exacerbated friction on the spot.[23]

As early as 21 August, Moltke officially recognized captured mobile guards as soldiers, despite their improvised uniforms. The same day he denied that right to *francs-tireurs*, although they too officially wore clothing distinguishable as a uniform. The difference was the latter's mission to ambush and shoot German stragglers.[24] The high command also authorized harsh reprisals against any community near which 'incidents' occurred – reprisals ranging, eventually, to the destruction of entire villages. This policy was sustained and enhanced by the growing conviction, common to Moltke, Bismarck and William, that France was the home of revolution, and the partisans were merely an extreme manifestation of the 'People's War' that threatened the future stability of Europe itself.[25] It became enough of an official line that one correspondent was expelled from France in December 1870 for advocating moderation and conciliation in his despatches.[26]

On 15 December, VII Corps, which, after the surrender of Metz saw as much irregular fighting as any large formation, issued an eighteen-point memorandum to all officers and officer candidates. Its principal injunctions were:

1. Most surprise attacks are the fault of the unit, and reflect more concern for securing comfortable billets than for security. Troops should never occupy quarters in places they cannot hold. Even for overnight stays, strong points (alarm houses) must be designated, on which the men can fall back in emergencies and whose locations are known to all. If secure quarters cannot be prepared, the troops must bivouac in the open.

2. On the march, never forget you are in enemy country. Never move without guides who are also to be regarded as hostages. Never return to a place by the same route you left. In establishing march lengths, allow time for searching villages you pass through. Should weapons be found, take them along or destroy them on the spot.

3. Detachments remaining in one place for a longer period of time must make their strong points into fortified points, with food and water for several days.

4. Detachments on the march are to keep in touch by strong patrols. No patrol sent more than a short distance from the main body must be smaller than six men. Orders and despatches must also be strongly escorted – one or two men accompanying an officer are insufficient.

5. Hostages are to be taken in places that seem suspicious. It is to be made known everywhere than any location from which civilians fire on soldiers will be burned

---

[23]Cf. Sukstorf, pp. 184 ff. and 403 ff.; Budde, pp. 138 ff. and 280 ff.; and van Creveld, *Supplying War*, pp. 94–5.

[24]*Moltkes Militaerische Werke* 1, vol. III, pp. 239 and 241–2.

[25]See Foerster, 'Prussian Triangle', for a developed presentation of this subject.

[26]Erich Schneider, 'Gegen Chauvinismus und Voelkerhass. Die Berichte des Kriegskorrespondent Hermann Vogt aus dem deutsch-franzoesischen Krieg von 1870/71', *Francia* 14 (1986), pp. 389–434.

down. Civilians *caught in the act* [italics in the original] of taking 'treacherous measures' against our troops may be dealt with on the spot 'according to the uses of war'.[27]

Most literature on the subject of irregular war in 1870–71 shows a pronounced tendency to assert the brutality of German anti-partisan measures, without offering much in the way of supporting examples.[28] Officers of all the German contingents believed it necessary to be 'steel-hard' with partisans, and so depicted themselves in hindsight. Practice, however, more usually involved an outburst of colourful threats, sometimes accompanied by intimidating behaviour such as isolating the men of a village, but eventually winding down to a few exemplary drumhead executions – or none at all, with the alleged *francs-tireurs* instead taken into custody and removed to prison. The overwhelming weight of reprisals was directed against property, not people. By comparison with previous insurgencies – the Vendée, Spain or southern Italy in the Napoleonic Era; Algeria or Mexico in the emerging Age of Imperialism; the border states and the up-country South in the American Civil War – German behaviour in 1870–1 can legitimately be described as restricted, if not exactly restrained.

That relative moderation reflected the rapid progress of the war. The Prussian/German army of 1870 had only time enough to develop an approach towards partisans. In 1914, it had a doctrine. In 1939, it had an ideology. In the early stages of World War I, reports of civilian guerrilla activity quickly reached senior command levels and led to direct orders for reprisals.[29] Most German officers confronting partisans in 1870–1 were on their own. And individuals left to their own moral devices tended, in the last analysis, to draw back from guerrilla war's 'nihilist edge'.[30] Whatever the institutionalized toughness of the Prussian army in particular, that mentality did not extend to ordering large-scale executions as a matter of routine.

At the same time, the German army failed – or refused – to develop a distinction between civilian resistance and organized raiding: 'little war'. The relative ineffectiveness of small local forces meant that an increasing amount of partisan activity was assumed by larger formations, usually town-based and generally town-recruited. A reasonably typical force was such as that made up of the four companies of the 56th Provisional Regiment, plus forty artillerymen trained in demolition, despatched from the fortress of Langres on 8 December against the rail bridge at Château-Vilain.[31] While they could usually count on passive goodwill in the sense of their presence not being reported to the Germans, these raiders were far from fish in the water along Maoist lines. They tended to use local guides and informers without much regard for later consequences, and were highly unlikely to stay in the neighbourhood once their mission was accomplished. The farmers and villagers were left unsupported to face reprisals that, especially for communities near railroads, steadily escalated.

---

[27]In *Entscheidung 1870*, eds. W. von Groote, U. von Gersdorff (Stuttgart, 1970), pp. 368 ff. See also, for the corps's anti-irregular operations, Hans Fabricius, *Auxerre-Châtillon: Die Kriegsereignisse und Operationen in der Luecke zwischen der II. Deutschen Armee und dem XIV Armee-Korps zum 20. Januar 1871* (Berlin, 1900).
[28]Kuehlich, p. 319.
[29]John Horne and Alan Kramer, *German Atrocities 1914: A History of Denial* (New Haven, CT, 2001), pp. 98 ff.
[30]Michael Fellman, 'At the Nihilist Edge: Reflections on Guerrilla Warfare during the Civil War' in *Road to Total War*, pp. 519–40. Cf. Manfred Messerschmitt, 'Voelkerrecht und Kriegsnotwendigkeit in der deutschen militaerischen Tradition seit den Einigungskriegen', *German Studies Review* 6 (1985), pp. 237–70.
[31]Cardinal von Widdern, *Rueckwaertige Verbindungen*, vol. III, no. 2, pp. 18 ff.

On 18 January 1871, another strike force started from a base camp near Langres: around 300 men from the grandiloquently named 'Vanguard of the *Chasseurs des Vosges*', a *franc-tireur* unit organized in December and including a large number of old soldiers. Despite freezing weather that reduced their numbers by a third, the raiders moved sixty miles unobserved, mostly at night, through a region patrolled by the Germans, and hit Fontenoy-sur-Moselle around 5 a.m. on 22 January. They took the small garrison by surprise and drove it out, destroyed a key viaduct on the rail line to Paris and withdrew in a matter of hours.

Operationally, the success came too late. The Germans had just been able to put into service some of the smaller northern lines recently secured by Manteuffel, and were able to re-route traffic for the seventeen days it took to repair the damage. Fontenoy was, nevertheless, one of the best planned and executed raids of the entire war, and a partisan operation in a classic sense: a bolt from the blue in an area generally considered quiet, producing concrete results and demonstrating that there was no safety anywhere. It was not a partisan activity in the popular sense, though, since it did not depend on local guerrillas in civilian clothes. The force was an organized formation, and its men wore military caps and brown blouses identifiable as uniforms.

That made no difference to the battalion sent to reoccupy Fontenoy. The Prussians subjected the town to a three-day sack that left it in ruins. According to French sources, they executed civilians almost at random on grounds of assisting the raiders, throwing corpses, and perhaps wounded, into burning buildings. Moltke also ordered harsh reprisals: forced labour to repair the damage and a fine of 10 million francs imposed on German-occupied Lorraine. When a demand for 500 French workers went unheeded, the occupation authorities shut down the entire *département*'s factories and workshops, then forbade paying unemployed workmen. The Germans, one might say, had learned their lesson as well. Fontenoy was at once a signpost and an open door to a way of war that would come to grim fruition in the next century.[32]

Other *franc-tireur* units operated more along lines established by the Austrian Croats and French 'Legions' in the eighteenth century, or the Russian and Prussian *Streifkorps* during the Wars of Liberation, in close cooperation with larger field forces. *Francs-tireurs* collected intelligence by mixing with the vendors and merchants who traded with German garrisons. *Francs-tireurs* performed tactical reconnaissance, compensating significantly for the republic's shortage of cavalry able to do more than kill its own horses. *Francs-tireurs* harassed careless bivouacs and shot up unwary outposts. Some of the best of them served with the Army of the Loire, cooperating with the 17th Corps to contribute to Mecklenburg's frequent discomfitures in the autumn of 1870. During the Orléans campaign, *francs-tireurs* developed increasingly sophisticated means of disrupting telegraphic communications between Moltke and Frederick Charles. Instead of merely cutting lines, the French transposed them. That caused messages to arrive randomly and at wrong locations, and required repair teams to search pole to pole for the source of the

---

[32]The most detailed accounts of the raid and its aftermath are 'Der Ueberfall bei Fontenoy-sur-Moselle am 22. Januaer, 1871', *Kriegsgeschichtliche Einzelschriften* 2, ed. Grosser Generalstab (Berlin, 1883) and Herman Kunz, *Der Ueberfall bei Fontenoy sur Moselle am 22. Januaer 1871* (Berlin).The French versions include Amédée Brenet, *La France et l'Allemagne devant le droit international pendant les opérations militaires de la guerre de 1870–71* (Paris, 1902), pp. 12 ff. and H. Genevois, *Les Coups de main pendant la guerre* (Paris, 1896), pp. 111 ff. Cf. *Moltkes Militaerische Werke* 1, vol. III, pp. 531–2.

problem. From a German perspective, the irregulars' handiwork was difficult to distinguish from that of unorganized insurgents. Reprisals continued and escalated. The irregulars themselves, however, could also hope for treatment as prisoners of war – particularly if they wore the dark-blue blouse associated with the Army of the Loire as an improvised uniform – and if they were captured in large numbers.[33]

The greatest challenges and the greatest successes of the Third Republic's irregular warfare took place in eastern France, where partisans and organized forces cooperated more closely than anywhere else. After the fall of Strasbourg, its conquerors, now organized as XIV Corps, were transferred to Dijon and made responsible for protecting the army's southern lines of communications against a mixed bag of national guards and partisans. These included the legendary guerrilla leader, Giuseppe Garibaldi. He had arrived in Tours in October to offer his services to a government that would have preferred to dispense with them, but eventually sent him into the Vosges to organize the region's irregulars.

The old revolutionary may have been past his prime in calendar years, but beginning in mid-November, he and his more enterprising subordinates took full advantage of the broken terrain to give their German opposite numbers lessons in large-scale irregular warfare. Garishly uniformed men, occasionally supported by a few guns, shot up supply columns, overran outposts and otherwise thoroughly disrupted the southern sector. Partisans blew up railroad bridges and sabotaged tracks, on one occasion sending three scarce locomotives into the Meuse. The Germans took hostages. Prominent citizens were required to ride the locomotive or the forward cars. Flight cost 1,200 francs for a first offence. A second was worth 5,000 francs and a prison term to be served in Prussia. If a train was derailed near a town, the inhabitants were fined 25,000 francs. The Germans despatched 'flying columns' in pursuit of partisans and irregulars. But since the bulk of the available forces were Landwehr, the tendency was to make the task forces strong enough numerically to compensate for presumed lower quality. There was nothing 'flying' about the mixed bags of horse, foot and guns that stumbled through eastern France in pursuit of enemies that, far from disappearing into the civilian population, simply outmarched and outwitted their ostensible pursuers.[34]

The Vosges were a formidable obstacle to the movement of both large bodies of troops and smaller detachments ignorant of the terrain. Werder learned of one engagement only when a messenger slipped through the French, disguised as a *franc-tireur*. Initial reactions in royal headquarters were, nevertheless, along the lines that Werder was more ready to seek winter quarters than to seek out the enemy, and that the best response to successful ambushes was the court-martialling of officers taken by surprise.[35] It was not so much, however, that the Germans were losing the 'little war', as that the French were winning it.

---

[33]At Châteaudun, for example, forty-four irregulars received POW status: Thiebault Schneider, p. 195. Hatley, pp. 151 ff., is the best survey of the war in the south from the irregulars' perspective. The blue blouse, common outer garb of the French working man, proved as big a stumbling block for Germans as black pyjamas did for US soldiers in Vietnam.

[34]Hatley, pp. 220 ff. and Robert Molis's excellent *Les Francs-Tireurs et les Garibaldi. Soldats de la République, 1870–71 en Bourgogne* (Paris, 1995), emphasize the campaign's irregular aspects. Cf. the contemporary narratives of Joseph P. Bordone, *Garibaldi et L'Armée des Vosges* (Paris, 1871) and Ludwig Loehlein, *The Operations of the Corps of General von Werder*, tr. F. T. Maxwell (Chatham, 1872).

[35]Bronsart, pp. 186 and 214.

More than in any other theatre – thanks primarily to Garibaldi – the French coordinated raids and more conventional operations. Garibaldi's organized force amounted to around 18,000. Another 20,000 were scattered throughout the Côte d'Or, responsible only to local committees of public safety. Coordinating their activities proved impossible, as various officers and officials exchanged charges of treason and sabotage. One local official called Garibaldi's troops 'hyenas in search of carrion', sustaining themselves by exploiting increasingly scarce civilian resources. But the irregulars fought so fiercely to hold the city of Dijon that the German general commanding the assault was pleased to grant terms of amnesty to all combatants, eschew reprisals and require no more than a 'damage deposit' of 500,000 francs, to be returned if the municipality behaved itself.

It was a far cry from Châteaudun, but consistent with Werder's overall policy of respecting, and encouraging, individual and collective decisions to remain outside the fighting. That, of course, was exactly what Gambetta and Garibaldi sought to prevent. After Dijon, the irregulars continued to embarrass and discomfit their conventionally minded adversaries. On 19 November, a detachment led by one of Garibaldi's sons surprised and overran a battalion of Landwehr occupying the town of Châtillon-sur-Seine, taking over 200 prisoners and scattering the rest. A week later, 300 more drove the German garrison out of Auxonne, with the support and participation of the townspeople. By the end of the month, Garibaldi mounted an attack to retake Dijon itself.

The strongly held city proved too tough a mouthful for the irregulars, who, by this time, were increasingly shedding their character as partisans, donning uniforms and acculturating to the norms of the reorganized line army. Garibaldi, moreover, saw to it that his men observed the laws of war towards wounded and prisoners. German officers in the theatre, many of whom respected him as a man of honour and principle, reciprocated sufficiently to avoid the mutual escalation of reprisals so often characteristic of irregular warfare under any conditions. Nevertheless, royal headquarters perceived the situation to be sufficiently out of control that, at the end of November, VII Corps was sent south to aid Werder's mixed bag of Prussian reservists and Badenese active regiments.

The corps had been left after the surrender of Metz to secure Lorraine and cover the main rail line to Paris. Its place in the rear echelon would be taken by eighteen newly organized Landwehr battalions that Moltke convinced Roon were vitally needed in the theatre of operations.[36] But a larger threat was coalescing in the south, a threat potentially far more serious than a few thousand armed amateurs.

Bourbaki's half of the Army of the Loire initially consisted of three corps, the 15th, 18th and 20th – 50,000 men, more or less. Freycinet proposed to use them as a nucleus, concentrating another 60,000 men, currently dispersed throughout eastern France, under Bourbaki's command in the Saône valley, then sending the entire mass north to recapture Dijon, cut German communications with Paris and, perhaps, eventually cooperate with the Army of the North in a massive strategic envelopment that would trap the entire German army deep in France, sandwiched between the defences of Paris and the newly emerged provincial armies, savaged by partisans and cut off from supplies and reinforcements.[37]

---

[36]Bronsart, p. 218.
[37]Cf. the presentation in *Guerre 1870–71. Campagne du Général Bourbaki en l'Est*, vol. I, pp. 47 ff., with Freycinet, *Guerre en Province*, pp. 222 ff. and Howard, pp. 411 ff.

Gambetta approved at once. Bourbaki, initially dazzled, grew less sanguine by the day. He was just enough a soldier of the mid-nineteenth century to recognize that the plan depended essentially on the capacity of the French railroad network first to concentrate his amorphous army, then to move it into the heart of the designated theatre of operations and, finally, to keep it supplied during the hard marching and hard fighting he expected. Instead, shortages of rolling stock and ineffective administration combined with the poor discipline of the troops involved virtually to gridlock the railroads for two weeks. Not until 30 December was Bourbaki in a position to advance, with four corps of largely inexperienced troops, led by uninspired commanders, and feeling thoroughly discomfited from their recent respective encounters with the railway system. It was August 1870 all over again, with the stage set for another illustration of the axiom that when history repeats itself, the second performance is usually a farce.[38]

The French confusion had succeeded in baffling the Germans as well. Not until the Prussian legation in Berne, Switzerland, confirmed that Bourbaki was moving east towards Belfort did Moltke see his way clear to act.[39] That decision reflected more sentiment than strategy, from Gambetta and Freycinet downwards. The frontier fortress had been under siege since October. Its defences, significantly improved shortly before the war, were the strongest of any secondary post in France, and its garrison had successfully withstood the limited pressures of an investment pursued half-heartedly by relatively weak forces. That was enough, given the series of disasters paralleling it, to make Belfort's survival an ongoing front-page item in the republic's newspapers. At the same time, Belfort was in no immediate danger of capitulating. Nor could its relief provide anything but cosmetic support for the republic's war effort.[40] Yet, in the context of previous decisions, it seemed almost predictable when Bourbaki, instead of marching north by north-east towards Paris, was assigned the *beau geste* of relieving Belfort, and only then turning on even the main German forces in his sector, to say nothing of doing something to relieve Paris.

Moltke responded by creating a new Army of the South – Werder's corps and VII Corps, reinforced by II Corps from outside Paris. The commander was Manteuffel, who had done well enough against the Army of the North, and his chief of staff was the redoubtable Wartensleben. Moltke's initial orders, stressing the need for haste, but giving his subordinates a good deal of leeway in moving their troops, suggest that, in the previous five months, he had relearned much about the risks of over-controlling distant theatres of operations.[41] And, in fact, by the time the Army of the South was concentrated, Werder's improvised XIV Corps had done all the fighting necessary.

For all the barbs levelled at him *in absentia* by junior staff officers at royal headquarters, Werder was deliberate, but not timid, and, in his biographer's words, 'anything but soft'.[42] He understood better than many of his post-war critics, the qualities and limitations of

---

[38]Howard, pp. 411 ff., is the best overview of the offensive's initial stages.
[39]Bronsart, p. 274.
[40]Eric Grosjean, *Belfort, la sentinelle de la liberté, 1870–1871* (Colmar, 1970), is a good general-audience modern narrative of the siege and its auras. Frobenius, vol. II, pp. 178 ff. and Mueller, vol. IV, pp. 47 ff., give the technical details of the German side.
[41]*Moltkes Militaerische Werke* 1, vol. III, pp. 508 ff.
[42]Ernst Schmidt, *General der Infanterie Graf von Werder. Ein Lebens und Charakterbild* (Oldenbourg, 1913), pp. 68 ff.

the mixed-bag formation he commanded. To a good extent, Werder also had the measure of the improvised armies he confronted. The French had numbers, and sometimes *élan*, on their side. The Badenese and reservists of XIV Corps had coherence, administration and discipline – just not as much of any of them as first-line Prussian troops. Taking advantage of these qualities by 'making haste slowly' was a better policy than seeking an immediate grapple with an adversary that, given sufficient time, was likely to establish the basis for his own defeat.

Bourbaki played the obliging enemy to perfection. He moved slowly; he failed to galvanize his troops to exploit initial local successes; and he gave Werder over a week in which to concentrate. On 15 January, Bourbaki finally sent his men forward along the Lisaine River. Werder, by then, had 40,000 men against Bourbaki's 110,000. But he was occupying some of the best field entrenchments the Germans constructed during the entire war, and he had the advantage of weather. The cold was brutal – eighteen degrees of frost on one night, and the unseasoned Landwehr men, the older ones, in particular, suffered accordingly. Werder had ordered the roads behind his lines kept cleared and shovelled. He was able to rotate his front-line units, bringing them back to the villages where shelter, fires and hot coffee waited. The French, on the offensive, did not feel able to pull back from their forward positions. Few of their senior officers seemed to have considered the possibility, perhaps because they feared the consequences for morale. Even fires were forbidden, and though the order was universally ignored, its issuing did nothing to enhance the soldiers' confidence in their leadership. After three days of on-and-off fighting, Bourbaki fell back, leaving 6,000 casualties behind him.[43]

Werder followed cautiously as Manteuffel's other two corps swung in from the west against Bourbaki's flank and rear. Initially, Manteuffel hoped for a second Koeniggraetz, catching Bourbaki between his column and Werder's. In the event, bad roads and marching fatigue held back the Germans long enough for Bourbaki to bring his army safely to the Swiss border. Seeking to wipe away his disgrace, Bourbaki shot himself in the head. It was somehow fitting that he only grazed his skull, leaving his successor to arrange the details of withdrawal across the frontier and internment.

By some accounts, the German high command was not entirely disappointed by that outcome. Feeding and caring for the 80,000 men who still remained in Bourbaki's ranks was no trifling matter under winter conditions and a long way from German supply bases. The Prussian/German army had already compelled the submission of two French field armies, including most of the country's best troops. Little further glory was to be gained in the capitulation of Bourbaki's disintegrating rabble. Negotiations for a general ceasefire, moreover, were progressing satisfactorily, and another ignominious surrender might well impel the French to continue the war for the sake of honour.[44]

---

[43]Herman Kunze, *Die Entscheidungskaempfe des General von Werder im Januaer 1871* (2 vols., Berlin, 1895), is the most detailed account from the German side. Cf. also Loehlein, pp. 109 ff. and *La Guerre de 1870–71. Campagne en l'Est*, pp. 208 ff., for a French perspective on the Lisane.

[44]Cf. Hermann Graf Wartensleben-Carow, *Operations of the South Army in January and February, 1871* (London, 1972); Lt. Col. Dutriez, 'L'Agonie de "L'Armée Bourbaki" (Haut-Doubs, 28 Janvier au 1er Février 1971)', *Revue Historique des Armées* 34 (1978), no. 5, pp. 189–206; and Dietmar Bellinger, 'Die Bourbakis in der Schweiz: Ein Neutralitaetsfall vor 120 Jahren', *Oesterreichische Militaerische Zeitschrift* 29 (1991), pp. 331–6.

II

Those tentative negotiations were part of a larger, more complex and more familiar story. From the initial stages of the siege of Paris, Moltke had prepared to bombard the city's fortifications. Siege guns and ammunition were ordered up from Germany; work began on assembling locally available trench stores like timber; and royal authorization was secured for preliminary fire plans. Moltke and his 'demigods', however, regarded these as no more than prudential measures. Great cities, Moltke argued, were not captured; they fell of their own accord. Paris was believed to have enough supplies for only six weeks. Most of the senior officers and policy-makers on the German side were convinced that the Parisians had neither the stomach nor the civic discipline to go hungry for any length of time. Moltke said he expected the city to capitulate once its milk supply gave out. Once that proved a vain hope, he still believed strangling Paris was preferable to shelling it, even as guns and ammunition slowly accumulated in the depots established outside the city. Strasbourg had cost a million talers' worth of ammunition. What would be the price of Paris?[45]

Merely enveloping Paris successfully was the greatest challenge posed to date in the history of modern fortress warfare. The city's huge circumference demanded amounts of men and material dwarfing any previous effort. Maintaining lateral and rear communications among the besiegers required an elaborate telegraph system to supplement more conventional means, like runners and orderly officers. There was no question that the defences of Paris would absorb shells like a sponge, arguably straining an already overworked logistical system to breaking point. Even bombarding the outlying forts offered, at best, limited results. Those so-called 'lesser' works were, in fact, usually constructed to take heavy pounding relative to their size, using up an attacker's ammunition and material, wearing out his guns. Such an operation was only promising in the context of a direct assault on the city's defences, a replication of Dueppel on a corps- and army-sized scale. No one, from King William down, was anxious even to consider the losses such an operation was certain to entail.[46]

As for seeking to impel surrender by shelling the city itself, recent and remote Prussian experience – from that gained by Frederick the Great in front of Prague in 1757, to that of besieging French-occupied strong points left behind in Germany during the Wars of Liberation – indicated that area bombardment of even relatively small urban centres did nothing to hasten their surrender. In the present war, Strasbourg had been shelled for five days, but capitulated only when a 'practicable breach' was made in the fortress itself. The more usual effect of random shelling was to make the attackers look like barbarians, and, at this stage of the war, Moltke was still concerned both with minimizing civilian suffering and maintaining the moral high ground for Prussia. In early October, the general staff urged Bismarck to prepare the civilized world for the consequences should Paris decide to immolate itself in a last-ditch defence, then capitulate. The army could not feed the city's 2 million inhabitants from its own resources for a single day. The work of

---

[45]Kessel, *Moltke*, p. 576; Bronsart, p. 109; and Roon, vol. III, p. 218.

[46]Verdy, pp. 159 ff. Cf. W. von Blume, *Die Beschiessung von Paris 1870/1 und die Ursachen der Verzoegerung* (Berlin, 1899) and the review essay by Werner Dunkel, 'Die Verzoegerung der Beschiessung von Paris 1870–71 und ihre Literatur', *Zeitschrift fuer Heereskunde* 40 (1978), pp. 113–19.

the *francs-tireurs* was making it impossible to make up the difference by forwarding supplies by rail. Hundreds of thousands of civilians might starve while under Prussian authority.[47]

By November, that position was coming under systematic fire. The press, which came late to support the war, and was initially spoiled by great battles, now lacked similarly newsworthy material, and sought, on its own initiative, to sustain reader interest by promoting the bombardment of Paris as justified retribution for every wrong plausibly inflicted on Germany from west of the Rhine since the Middle Ages.[48] Bismarck used his considerable influence in German journalistic circles to encourage that viewpoint. In his mind, diplomatic considerations alone were enough to seek the quickest possible conclusion to the war. His choleric temperament had focused on the politicians, the propagandists and the people of Paris as the principal obstacles to that end. Lurking on the fringes of his perspective was also a belief that a certain reputation for ferocity might prove a useful weapon in the diplomatic arsenal of the new Germany he was constructing outside of Paris. And finally, Bismarck was anxious to reassert a primacy over the soldiers that he considered increasingly challenged every day the war dragged on. The chancellor understood Moltke's by now familiar argument for military supremacy in decision-making while a war was being fought. He understood also the risks to his position of accepting it on anything like a long-term basis. Increasingly, for Bismarck, the bombardment of Paris was less important for its own sake than as a touchstone: whose influence would prevail with the public, the army and, above all, with William, supreme warlord and constitutionally authorized commander-in-chief?[49]

Bismarck worked assiduously at making converts to his position in the royal headquarters. He drew support from the assertion of General Gustav von Hindersin, inspector-general of the artillery and the grand old man of the Long Arm, that a formal siege in the traditional style was possible.[50] Roon came into line, increasingly angered by the general staff's criticisms at what it called his failure to meet the field army's manpower and logistical needs.[51] While Blumenthal and the crown prince continued to support Moltke, other senior officers, like Albert of Saxony, disheartened by the apparent lack of progress on both military and political fronts, began expressing sympathy for the chancellor's position.[52]

Bismarck had a positive taste for dramatic situations, and a temper so fierce that, in later years, he kicked to death one of his own pet dogs – a large mastiff. Moltke, a private person, who set store by an orderly work day and disliked theatrics, was being driven to distraction by what later generations would describe as the 'media circus' that had grown up around the siege. Increasingly as well, the chief of staff was playing politics, seeking to assert control of what he regarded as essentially a military decision in the face of civilian

---

[47]Bronsart, pp. 109–10.
[48]Cf. Martin Winckler, 'Die Rolle der Presse bei der Vorbereitung des deutschen-franzoesischen Krieges 1870/71' in *Presse und Geschichte. Beitraege zur historischen Kommunikationsforschung* (Munich, 1977), pp. 171–94 and Ursula E. Koch, *Berliner Presse und europaeisches Geschehen 1871* (Berlin, 1978).
[49]Craig, *Politics of the Prussian Army*, pp. 204 ff. and Ritter, *Sword and Scepter*, vol. I, pp. 220 ff., are the most detailed analyses in English.
[50]Bronsart, p. 108.
[51]Roon, vol. III, p. 221 *passim*.
[52]Hassel, *Albert von Sachsen*, vol. II, p. 432.

ignorance, apart from the actual wisdom of the policy in question.[53] He might not have directly sabotaged the forwarding of guns and shells, but he did nothing to light fires under reluctant subordinates.

Many of the key participants, moreover, were elderly men. Moltke celebrated his seventieth birthday on 26 October. Hindersin, Roon and King William himself were also into their seventies. (Roon and Hindersin would retire immediately after the war.) While they were not exactly sleeping in tents, their improvised living quarters scarcely afforded the routines of home. Small wonder that the tone of discourse frequently reminds this author of watching as a boy his septuagenarian grandfather and his friends arguing the sequence of play in a *Schafskopf* game – an event sometimes ending with the swinging of fists and canes.

'Fog and friction', in any case, were imposing delays without any help from above. Prussia's siege artillery had no organic transport capacity. The sheer weight of the guns and ammunition was too much for many of the purchased and requisitioned local vehicles expected to move them from the railheads to the parks and battery positions. The development of the siege works around the city's periphery had absorbed for entrenchments construction material originally intended for gun sites. The increasingly hard winter meant the further diversion of labour and material to shelters for men, horses and even equipment – the alternative being unacceptably high sick lists, especially among unseasoned replacements in their thirties and their equine counterparts. What was built required maintenance. Wastage and pilfering soared beyond peacetime rates. Much against their respective wills, on 25 November, Hindersin and the army's chief engineer reported that it would be impossible to begin any bombardment until early 1871.[54]

During the interval, Moltke's perspective began to change. Events on the Loire showed the French were still very much in the war. Despatches from Berlin suggested trouble in parliament if the bombardment did not begin soon. On 12 December, Moltke told Roon he did not consider a bombardment impossible. Blumenthal believed the chief of staff was willing to consider a 'political' bombardment – that is, one that would not be followed by an attack, or, more brutally expressed, a terror attack. On 17 December, a council of war, with William present and Bismarck absent, agreed that a full-scale bombardment of the southern sector of the defences would begin once a reserve of 500 shells per gun was in position.[55]

Bismarck's often-noted absence from that conference was part of a pattern of, at best, sporadic attendance, the consequence of his habit of working late at night, then sleeping into the morning, past the 10 a.m. hour when such meetings usually took place. It had not been a problem until 5 December, when Moltke sent Trochu a letter announcing the surrender of Orleans. In the chief of staff's mind this was a military matter: both a blow at Parisian morale and a traditional soldiers' courtesy requiring no more than a routine 'for your information' routing to Bismarck. Bismarck signed off, but informed William that he

[53]A central theme of Wilhelm Busch, *Das deutsche Grosse Hauptquartier und die Bekaempfung von Paris, 1870–71* (Stuttgart, 1905).

[54]The details are presented in *Die Thaetigkeit der Belagerungsartillerie vor Paris im Kriege 1870/71, Kriegsgeschichtliche Einzelschriften*, ed. Grosser Generalstab (Berlin, 1884), vol. 4 and Mueller, vol. IV, pp. 67 ff.

[55]Cf. *Moltkes Militaerische Werke 1*, vol. III, p. 445; Blumenthal, p. 219; and Bronsart, p. 220.

wished, in future, to be present at any military conferences discussing similar situations, in case they might include a political dimension.[56]

The request was not by itself unreasonable – in a working environment informed by normal mutual goodwill. But Bismarck, never an easy colleague, was beginning to get on Moltke's nerves. By December, few officers at headquarters would go out of their way to oblige Bismarck in anything, and made certain the irascible minister-president knew it.[57] *'Zehn Minuten vor der Zeit / Ist Soldatenhoeflichkeit'* ('Ten minutes early is a soldier's good manners') was a rule of thumb in the Prussian/German army long after 1870. Much like their US successors, moreover, German officers prided themselves on getting an early start to the day. Might staff officers have entertained a sense that if a certain 'civil official in a cuirassier's tunic'[58] insisted on participating in military conferences where his presence was marginal, then it was his business to get himself there on time?

Moltke's fraying imperturbability was tested further on 21 December, when the belea-guered French launched another sortie, this one on the fortified village of Le Bourget, held by five companies of the Prussian Guard. The course of events was a microcosmic model for the Great War. The first wave of attackers fought their way into the position and maintained a foothold for most of the day by sheer courage. But the guardsmen's support-ing artillery broke up all attempts to reinforce the initial success. At twilight the attack was called off – to be succeeded in the next few days by an attempt to approach Le Bourget by sapping. In hard-frozen ground the effort proved futile, and had a significant negative effect on military and civilian morale. But from the German side, the assault on Le Bourget suggested that Paris remained far from losing its military vitality.[59]

William responded promptly. On 23 December, he put Hohenloe in command of the bombardment. By any reckoning the army's best gunner, the prince had his orders from the king in person. Since a siege had not convinced 'the sovereign rabble of Paris' to make peace, William declared, bombardment must bring them to capitulate. It was Hohenloe's job to 'finally light a fire under the attack'. And in case he missed the point, Moltke's staff officers made it plain that he was to consider the problem from a 'strategic' and not a nar-row technical perspective.[60] Hohenloe, who had cut his teeth on army politics, did not miss the point. The bombardment of Paris began on 5 January.

Prussian siege batteries did a textbook job of silencing the defences of Mont Avron, then turned their attentions to the city proper. As a rule, the bombardment was conducted by night, beginning around 10 p.m., lasting four or five hours, and delivering between 200 and 500 rounds on target. Certain points stood out: the unexpected effective range of the Prussian guns, especially the new rifles from the firm of Krupp, and the limited amount of damage they inflicted. The long ranges – popular at battery level because the French could

---

[56]Bronsart, pp. 208–9 and accompanying footnotes; Kessel, *Moltke*, pp. 578–9; and Ritter, *Sword and Scepter*, vol. I, p. 397.
[57]Waldersee, flattered by dinner invitations and what he interpreted as an offer to make him governor of Paris, was an exception. Waldersee, vol. I, pp. 96–7 and 117. One is reminded of the widely attributed dinner-party put-down: 'We know what you are, madam, we are just establishing the price.'
[58]Bronsart had an acid tongue and a pen to match (p. 249).
[59]Cf. Hohenloe, *Aus meinem Leben*, vol. IV, pp. 359 ff.; Kunze, *Le Bourget*; and Ducrot, *Défense de Paris*, vol. III, pp. 106 ff.
[60]Hohenloe, *Aus meinem Leben*, vol. IV, p. 367 and Bronsart, pp. 248 and 251.

not reply effectively – in turn, made observation a somewhat random process: the Invalides and the Pantheon became favourite targets, not from Hunnish delight in wanton destruction, but because their domes were visible from a large number of gun positions. Damage, however, even in heavily shelled neighbourhoods, was minimal, with boys collecting and selling shell fragments as souvenirs, and initial anxiety giving way, first to indignation, then indifference, as Paris continued to go about its business.

If experience indicated anything about a bombardment, it was the necessity for sustained effort. Interruptions for any reason gave the defenders a chance to repair damages, and usually had the same effect on morale as the cessation of a dentist's drill, however temporary, on the person in the chair. The Germans kept it up for three weeks. The sheer amount of effort that involved seemed to promise success, and, at first, the fires breaking out across the city heightened German optimism. Then the guns began wearing out. The craft of metal casting had not progressed far enough to withstand round after round, one full charge after another. Suspect pieces were taken off line. Others exploded, often without warning, and with corresponding effect on crew morale. The foot artillerymen were nevertheless successful in suppressing the outlying French batteries and pushing their own closer and closer to the city's centre. Even then, it was noticed that guns were notoriously difficult to knock out, and gun positions hard to destroy. Crews might suffer heavy casualties or be driven into bombproof shelters when German fire was at its heaviest, but time after time, they came back to man their pieces once more, especially the sailors, whose training and heritage demanded keeping the guns in action as long as the ship was afloat. The defences of Paris continued to hold the Germans at a distance that grew increasingly respectful.

Nor was Paris itself exactly devastated by its three weeks of shelling. While statistics vary, no more than around a hundred people were killed and fewer than 300 injured. As many as 1,500 buildings suffered some damage. In material terms, this was no harbinger of disaster, but the shelling was enough to push public opinion over the edge. Food was scarce enough that zoo animals were being slaughtered and marketed as delicacies. Enough army horses had been slaughtered and eaten to create a public taste for horsemeat that survives into the twenty-first century. Dogs, cats and birds disappeared into cooking pots. The bitterest winter in many years cost the city most of its trees. Hunger and cold were followed by disease – typhoid, smallpox, pneumonia. In the first week of the siege, deaths from all causes totalled 1,266. In the eighteenth week, 14–21 January, the total was over 4,400 – again, hardly remarkable by later standards, but enough to increase demands that the garrison do something except endure.[61]

From the beginning of the siege, activists had spoken of a 'torrential sortie', with everyone able to bear arms storming out of every exit simultaneously. It had been dismissed as persiflage – the suggestion that the onslaught be led by choirs of virgins particularly bemused Ducrot.[62] Then, on 9 December, news of Bourbaki's advance reached the city. It was almost three weeks old, but the hard-pressed government responded by ordering not quite an ultimate attack, but an offensive by every unit the garrison could put into the field. Trochu, tired and pessimistic, was reluctant to cooperate. Some of his subordinates,

---

[61]Horne remains the best account of the bombardment. Mueller, vol. IV, pp. 193 ff. and *Thaetigkeit der Belagerungsartillerie*, pp. 74 ff., present details of service in the Prussian batteries.
[62]Ducrot, *Défense de Paris*, vol. III, pp. 310 ff.

however, thought the attack worth a try. Some moderates, generals and cabinet ministers alike, regarded the operation as a necessary final gesture, to clear the grounds for a negotiated peace by submerging the radicals in the corpses of their followers. It was no accident that the national guard, military focus of hostility to the government, was given a leading role in the plan. To date, the guard had not been significantly engaged, because of its poor armament and its lack of training as much as from doubts about its political reliability. Now the guard would have its chance, providing half of the 100,000 men expected to descend on the German positions like a thunderbolt from St Valerien on the morning of 19 January.[63]

The sortie's focal point was admirably chosen – from a defender's perspective. Since the beginning of the siege, the ground around Saint-Cloud had been the sector of the 9th Division of V Corps. Its commander, Brigadier General von Sandrart, was another Prussian general who had learned from experience the advantages of defence. Nor were Germans exactly averse to changing the landscape around Versailles by digging, dismantling and demolishing, making sure everything possible within the laws and customs of war was done to help the locals recognize there was a war on and they were losing.[64] Sandrart's regiments had put their backs into constructing a system of defences in depth, prefiguring those of the Great War. Its front lines were held by outposts, supported by a network of fortified farms and houses interspersed with battery positions. Everywhere ranges were marked, ammunition was plentiful and the men were well fed and as warmly clad as possible. The French attack – predictably – was several hours late. Even so, it achieved some initial success before sticking fast in front of the main Prussian positions. Dynamite, invented in 1866 and making its first tactical appearance as a 'secret weapon' to demolish obstacles, instead froze solid in the cold. Too many guns remained too far in the rear. The national guards tried hard in the early going, but began to unravel as the attack stalled. At nightfall, Trochu ordered a retreat that became a rout as the tired, demoralized men drew nearer to Paris. Casualties were not high – around 4,000 – but this day marked the end of the Paris garrison as an active fighting force, and the end of Paris as a centre of military resistance.[65]

The government's initial reaction was to seek a scapegoat. The obvious choice was Trochu, who by now made no secret of his conviction that surrender was inevitable. Refusing to resign, he was dismissed as military commander by a government still insisting that more could be done. That attitude permeated the streets as well. A mini-revolt on 22 January, combined with a report that only two days' worth of flour remained in the official stores, began changing minds at high levels. News of Faidherbe's defeat and withdrawal in the north had reached the capital a few days earlier. Even if Bourbaki somehow pulled off a miracle in the south, his army was too far from Paris for its consequences to be felt before civil war or famine broke out. On 23 January, the government authorized Favre to negotiate a ceasefire.[66]

---

[63]Trochu, *Ouevres posthumes*, pp. 520 ff.; Ducrot, *Défense de Paris*, vol. III, pp. 294 ff.; and the overviews of Roth, *Guerre de 1870*, pp. 300 ff. and Howard, pp. 363 ff.

[64]Bronsart, pp. 275–6; Noelle Sauvee-Dauphin, 'L'Occupation prussienne à Versailles' in *La Guerre de 1870/71*, pp. 231–48.

[65]Cf. Trochu, *Ouevres posthumes*, vol. I, pp. 528 ff. and Ducrot, *Défense de Paris*, vol. IV, pp. 72 ff., for details. Hermann Kunz, *Die Schlacht vor dem Mont Valerien am 19 Januar 1871* (Berlin, 1891), in a conclusion reading as though it had been written thirty years later, describes the fighting as reflecting the importance in defensive operations of firepower, fire discipline and well-developed field fortifications.

[66]Favre, vol. II, pp. 334 ff. and Ducrot, *Défense de Paris*, vol. IV, pp. 192 ff.

III

The foreign minister met with Bismarck that same evening, after a disconcerting voyage across the Seine in a boat sieved by bullet holes. The two men had met before, in September, and when Bismarck mentioned that Favre's hair had grown whiter since last they met, it was a not-so-subtle reminder that France's situation had worsened as well.[67] But while Bismarck might have hoped to keep France diplomatically isolated, he saw no real possibility of excluding it from Europe's power structure. Why, then, provoke its ill will by pursuing the annexation of Alsace-Lorraine? Since the two diplomats' last meeting, the issue had been thrashed out in every possible forum. Neither public opinion nor interest groups east of the Rhine spoke with one voice on the subject.[68] Industrialists feared the possible economic consequences of dealing with a region so thoroughly integrated into the French economic system, especially the competition from Alsatian textile factories. The *Zollverein* even preferred to have the proposed new provinces retain their economic orientation towards France.[69] Social Democrats, and an increasing number of progressives generally, questioned both the morality and the wisdom of an annexation policy.[70]

Another special interest group, the general staff, weighed in by emphasizing the advantages accruing to France by possessing a salient that thrust deep into Germany, with the railway hub of Strasbourg enabling rapid introduction of troops and supplies on the eve of the next war. The speed and efficiency of Prussian mobilization had made the difference in 1870, but it was both impossible and unwise to rely on sustaining that exponential advantage indefinitely. France, moreover, had made a spectacular number of other military errors in 1870 – errors whose correction lay beyond German capacities to prevent. Annexing the border provinces, and transforming Metz into a German bone in the throat of France, was an obvious insurance policy against the future, drawn-out 'industrialized people's war' Moltke, in particular, increasingly feared.[71] Finally, annexation was a way of bringing home defeat to a France thus far unwilling to acknowledge it, and satisfying the belief – certainly not restricted to Moltke alone – that the lives of German soldiers could not be compensated by a cash indemnity alone. Land and people were the only fitting payment for lost lives.[72]

Special pleaders of all sorts, however, were increasingly submerged beneath a nationalist chorus that demanded Alsace-Lorraine as a symbol of victory. Newspapers and politicians encouraged each other in a patriotic and flag-waving counterpoint that owed only something to Bismarck's later encouragement. As the war progressed, irredentism supplemented nationalism. French possession of Alsace-Lorraine was described, especially in

---

[67]Favre, vol. II, pp. 377 ff.

[68]Fritz Bronner, *1870/71: Elsass-Lothringen: Zeitgenoessische Stimmen fuer und wider die Eingliederung in das Deutsche Reich* (2 vols., Frankfurt, 1970), is an exhaustive and exhausting compendium.

[69]Cf. Raymond Poidevin, 'Les industriels allemands devant l'annexion de l'Alsace-Lorraine', *Guerre de 1870/71*, pp. 355–65 and, for background, Michael Hau, 'Industrialization and Culture: The Case of Alsace', *Journal of European Economic History* 29 (2000), pp. 295–306.

[70]Andrew Bonnell, 'Between Internationalism, Nationalism, and Particularism: German Social Democrats and the War of 1870–71', *Australian Journal of Politics and History* 38 (1992), pp. 375–85.

[71]Bronsart, p. 269 and Kessel, *Moltke*, p. 573.

[72]He considered the fortress worth an army of 120,000 men. Stadelmann, p. 230. Cf. Pflanze, vol. I, pp. 484–5 and Stig Foerster, 'Helmuth von Moltke und das Problem des industrialiserten Volkskrieges im 19. Jahrhundert' in *Generalfeldmarschall von Moltke*, pp. 103–15.

academic and intellectual circles, as a great historical injustice, to be righted by restoring the lost brethren to a new Germany. Instead of muting the annexation rhetoric, Bismarck escalated it. From the early days of the war, he argued that Napoleon and his advisors were acting for the people of France, and in the name of a national will to power that threatened the stability of Europe as a whole. On 25 August, he instructed all German papers to support annexations in the interest of security.[73] He continued ordering and encouraging journalistic coverage favouring that policy.

Alsace-Lorraine also increasingly emerged as a *sine qua non* of imperial unification. It was a low common denominator, a demand giving concrete form to a war whose aims seemed otherwise to be part of Heine's Reich of dreams. Even Moltke, thirty years earlier, had published an article calling for the provinces' 'return' on the bases of national origin and historical right. The south German papers and the south German parliaments presented the Alsace-Lorraine question in terms of a moral justification for their armies' participation as equals in a German national mission, with an intensity that increased as the marginal military role of the lesser states grew more apparent.[74]

To some degree, Bismarck was responding to circumstances. In the summer of 1870, he had carefully prepared to localize the conflict by reinforcing the specific reasons of the other great powers for remaining neutral. As the war continued with no signs of winding down, even after Napoleon's surrender, Bismarck emphasized domestic pressure for annexation as a warning against outside intervention, presenting himself simultaneously as its victim and its mouthpiece.[75] It was a focal point of his British policy, in particular. Initial widespread sympathy for Prussia's position – much of it reflecting long-standing suspicion of France – gave way to intense criticism of Prussia for prolonging the war and its suffering. Bismarck, in turn, insisted that Germany would fight to the last for right, justice and defensible frontiers. A British government, all too well aware of its inability to call the hand with military force, folded its cards.[76]

Localizing the fighting, however, did not mean localizing the peacemaking. Individual self-interest, combined with the lingering heritage of the Concert of Europe, meant that a

---

[73]Stern, *Gold and Iron*, p. 139, makes the point that Bismarck's intransigence spiked at a time when he would have been legitimately worried about his sons. Both were serving with combat units: one was erroneously reported killed at Vionville; the other was three times wounded in the same battle.

[74]Walter Lipgens, 'Bismarck, die oeffentliche Meinung und die Annexion von Elsass und Lothringen', *Historische Zeitschrift* 199 (1964), pp. 31–112 and 'Bismarck und die Frage der Annexion 1870: Eine Erwiderung', ibid. 206 (1968), pp. 586–617, makes a detailed case for Bismarck as the generator of the annexation movement. Lothar Gall, 'Zur Frage der Annexion von Elsass und Lothringen 1870', ibid., pp. 263–326; Eberhard Kolb, 'Bismarck und das Aufkommen der Annexionsforderungen 1870', ibid. 209 (1969), pp. 318–56; and Josef Becker, 'Baden, Bismarck und die Annexion von Elsass und Lothringen', *Zeitschrift fuer die Geshchichte des Oberrheins* 115 (1967), pp. 167–204, describe the independent development of public support for the policy. In an example of German academic controversy at its best and most professional, the trio carry the intellectual day – but not by much.

[75]Pflanze, vol. I, p. 488.

[76]Cf. Klaus Hildebrand, 'Grossbritannien und die deutsche Reichsgruendung' in *Europa und die Reichsgruendung*, ed. E. Kolb, *Historische Zeitschrift*, Beiheft 6 (Munich, 1980), pp. 9–62; Peter Peel, *British Public Opinion and the Wars of German Unification, 1864–1871* (College Park, MD, 1981); Thomas Schaarschmidt, *Aussenpolitik und oeffentliche Meinung in Grossbritannien waehrend des Deutsch-Franzoesischen Krieges von 1870/71* (New York, 1993); and Michael Pratt, 'A Fallen Idol: The Impact of the Franco-Prussian War on the Perception of Germany by British Intellectuals', *International History Review* 7 (1985), pp. 543–75.

protracted conflict was likely to invite unwelcome 'good offices' from Europe's foreign ministries – offers difficult to refuse without putting Germany in France's recent position as chief disturber of the diplomatic peace. Much of Bismarck's growing antagonism towards Moltke reflected the splenetic frustration of a man who recognized that, however well his opposite number had done in the military sphere, the army's achievements were falling increasingly short of meeting the requirements of diplomacy. As early as October, Britain proposed to Russia that the neutral powers cooperate in arranging an acceptable peace. Russia's refusal was explained when it repudiated the clauses of the Crimean settlement that provided for neutralizing the Black Sea. Bismarck felt he had no choice but to support St Petersburg's initiative. In Britain, there was talk of war with Russia in the newspapers, the parliament and the cabinet. Austria, too, voiced objections to this flagrant violation of international law. Bismarck's brokering of a conference on the subject, beginning in mid-January, toned down the rhetoric – but also created a possible forum for intervention in the German–French matter. In that context, at least, the overtures from Paris had not come a day too soon.[77]

Nor were international relations the only problem area. Bismarck recognized, more comprehensively than is generally understood, the complex internal tensions that produced what Michael Stuermer calls the 'restless Reich'. Since September, the south German governments had been discussing among themselves, and with Bismarck, the terms of a permanently unified Germany. With the Prussian government, for all practical purposes, transferred to its field headquarters at Versailles, negotiations were correspondingly influenced by both the military atmosphere and the progress of military affairs. In a direct reversal of their positions on the bombardment of Berlin, Crown Prince Frederick called for arm-twisting. Bismarck insisted a slow hand was a sure hand; any concessions made to win the adherence of the southern states, in particular, would be obscured by time. Predictably, Bismarck's position prevailed in two months of complex negotiation, persuasion and occasional bribery that involved parliaments as well as princes, and succeeded as much by balancing discontents as by developing any positive consensus. When William of Prussia was proclaimed 'German Emperor' as William I on 18 January, he showed his displeasure by brushing past Bismarck with neither word nor greeting.[78]

Helmuth von Moltke was as eager as Bismarck to see the surrender of Paris – but by January, he was by no means certain that the city's fall would mean the end of the war. Instead, he increasingly described it as the next step to a fight to the finish and an imposed peace. He discussed putting a surrendered Paris under martial law and sending the entire organized garrison across the Rhine as prisoners. The besieging Germans, then, would be free to fan out into the provinces and crush any remaining organized resistance.

[77]Eberhard Kolb, *Der Weg aus dem Krieg. Bismarcks Politik im Krieg und die Friedensanbahnung 1870/71* (Munich, 1989), is the definitive analysis of Bismarck's diplomacy and its matrix. Russia's successful challenge to the Crimean system is discussed in Beyrau, pp. 184 ff.; Mosse, pp. 291 ff.; and, more generally, his *The Rise and Fall of the Crimean System, 1855–1871. The Story of a Peace Settlement* (London, 1963). Austria's response is covered in Lutz, pp. 342 ff.
[78]Pflanze, vol. I, pp. 490 ff. and Gall, *White Revolutionary*, p. 369, remain the best general accounts. Dieter Albert, 'Koenig Ludwig II. von Bayern und Bismarck', *Historische Zeitschrift* 270 (2000), pp. 39–64, stresses the Bavarian monarch's role in William's coronation.

A massive war indemnity would complete the task of rendering France prostrate for generations.[79]

This strategy has been so vehemently criticized ever since that there is some merit in asking whether it should be taken as a serious statement of Moltke's desires, as opposed to a pessimistic scenario he considered more possible than did a certain highly placed amateur in military affairs. Moltke's principal biographer suggests that, by this time, his conflict with Bismarck was personal rather than professional.[80] In a conversation with the crown prince on 8 January, Moltke became – for him – almost confidential in expressing his sense of offence at what he considered Bismarck's arbitrary and ill-considered desire to decide both military and political matters himself, taking no counsel with the responsible experts.[81] Bronsart, with an intelligent and ambitious subordinate's eye for personalities, observed that it might be best for Prussia if Bismarck and Moltke always attended every meeting where the king was present. Their temperaments, however, were too different to make that feasible under high-stress conditions.[82] In any public exchange of words with the chancellor, the normally taciturn Moltke usually drew a short straw – not least because he was used to being deferred to by his associates. Bismarck deferred to no one. On 13 January, Crown Prince Frederick invited the two men to his quarters for a long talk followed by dinner – a command performance intended to clear the air. Instead, the general and the minister locked horns to a point where Frederick was repeatedly constrained to interfere. Bismarck finally took the evening over the top by arguing that advancing on Paris after Sedan had been a mistake! 'Agreement', in Frederick's words, 'was clearly out of the question'.[83]

Frederick also came away convinced that Bismarck wanted peace while Moltke was determined on a war of annihilation. Bismarck reinforced the dichotomy by insisting that accepting Moltke's position would make any long-term peaceful reordering of Europe an impossibility. Even if France could be crushed without sparking direct intervention by the other powers, such a policy would render Germany's position permanently dependent on the kind of force a brand new empire was in no position to develop.[84] Then Moltke answered another letter from Paris on his own responsibility, this one a complaint about damages to hospitals.[85] Bismarck saw this as a challenge and, on 18 January, took the issue before William. It is an indication of how seriously he regarded the subject that he did not give the new emperor a chance to recover from the tension surrounding his coronation. And it is an indication of William's deep fund of common sense that he scarcely hesitated in supporting his chancellor. Allowing a week for tempers to cool, on 25 January, the king issued two cabinet orders that made Bismarck clearly responsible for any negotiations

---

[79]Cf. Moltke's memorandum of 14 January to William, discussed in A. O. Meyer, 'Moltke und Bismarck' in *Stufen und Wandlungen der deutschen Einheit*, eds. K. v. Raumer and T. Scheider (Stuttgart, 1943), pp. 338 ff.; Hermann Oncken, *Grossherzog Friedrich I von Baden und die deutsche Politik von 1854–1871* (2 vols., Stuttgart, 1927), vol. II, pp. 300–1; and the general presentations in Ritter, vol. I, pp. 223 ff. and Stadelmann, pp. 246 ff.
[80]Kessel, *Moltke*, pp. 581–2.
[81]Frederick III, *War Diary*, p. 253.
[82]Bronsart, pp. 279–80.
[83]Frederick III, *War Diary*, pp. 257–8.
[84]Bismarck to William, 14 January 1871, *Die gesammelten Werke*, vol. VI b, pp. 665 ff.
[85]*Moltkes Militaerische Werke* 1, vol. III, p. 517.

with the French and required Moltke to keep Bismarck fully informed of future military operations.[86]

Moltke initially drafted a sizzling response along the lines of 'is that all I deserve?', suggesting that perhaps he should resign and leave the future conduct of the war entirely to Bismarck. The one he sent was considerably milder – perhaps, in part, because Moltke was able to recall his own long-standing postulate that it was the army's task to win wars, but that meant bringing about conditions for peace. More than many of his counterparts and some of his successors, Moltke recognized that literally destroying an enemy's capacity for resistance was inherently impossible. Even in defeat, states and societies retained a significant capacity to fight back. It had been true of Prussia in 1762, Spain in 1809 and Russia in 1812. Now, the point was being made again in France. Moltke never acknowledged it, except perhaps to himself, but Favre's request for a ceasefire may have been as welcome to the chief of staff as it was to Bismarck.

That did not make him reluctant to push for a clear settlement of what he considered the crucial point at issue. Exactly what material should be passed to the chancellor, in what circumstances, could be negotiated. But in Moltke's opinion, the chief of staff and the chancellor were mutually independent agencies under the direct authority of the king.

Those were strong ideas for a man who, until a few years earlier, had not been officially authorized to report directly even to the war minister. They opened as well a new spectrum of possibilities for William. Few rulers have been offered an opportunity to drive such blood horses in tandem, unchecked by any other institution of government. But William might also have understood that the Wars of Unification and the military reforms preceding them had already increased the army's power and pretensions. To move even further in that direction risked weakening the state's political and diplomatic elements, with obvious consequences for domestic and foreign policy. On a more pragmatic level, what was the guarantee that the estrangement between chief and chancellor would be permanent? What was to stop them cooperating at some time in the future to box in the crown? William was no Machiavelli, to rejoice in the prospect of permanent intrigue to keep apart subjects grown over-mighty. If anything, he was heartily sick of the recent weeks of backstabbing, and sought to restore something resembling collegiality to his high council.

He addressed the issue by not addressing it. He made no reply to Moltke's memo – even the unsent draft avoided addressing the chief of staff's position. At the same time, William did not officially increase Bismarck's authority over the military, though Moltke made certain the chancellor was invited to discussions of projected operations.[87] It seems reasonable to suggest that both Bismarck and Moltke still defined themselves as the king's servants, and that each believed he had pushed his position to the limit. If no direct answer was forthcoming, that itself was an answer for anyone who knew William. He was telling them to get on with their jobs – with an 'or else' possibly implied.

Bismarck also had Favre to deal with. The Frenchman bore instructions so vague they amounted to no instructions at all. Tasked to find out what terms were available, he hoped to secure time for the election of a national assembly, whose first order of business should

---

[86]Cf. Craig, *Politics of the Prussian Army*, pp. 210 ff.; Kessel, *Moltke*, pp. 584 ff.; and Ritter, vol. I, p. 224.

[87]Bronsart, pp. 309 ff. and Kessel, *Moltke*, pp. 586 ff., reconstruct the events. Stadelmann, pp. 434 ff. and 503 ff., contain the drafts of the memos and the author's perceptive commentary. Boerner, p. 208, suggests the king's reasoning.

be deciding whether to make peace. If Paris were compelled to surrender, Favre hoped to keep the Germans out of the city once resistance ceased. And, as a last resort, he was ready to offer complete capitulation, making the Germans, under the laws of war, responsible for everyone in the city, soldier or civilian. Favre was sufficiently aware of the German logistics and administrative problems to be reasonably confident that the latter option would intimidate even Moltke.

Bismarck, after a bit of posturing, leaped. He offered to abandon the more or less desultory negotiations still under way with Empress Eugénie and a rapidly disintegrating Bonapartist exile movement. That meant recognizing the legitimacy of the government of national defence. Favre, in return, agreed to sign an armistice binding the whole of France.[88]

As Bismarck left the first conference on the evening of 23 January, he whistled a hunting call signalling the end of the chase.[89] He was at some pains not to inform Moltke of the French minister's arrival – a 'so there, too!' response to perceived slights that led Moltke, who had little sense of irony, to describe the minister's behaviour as inappropriate and say that perhaps he could now hope to be relieved of his burdens.[90] Considering himself firmly in the saddle, Bismarck lost few opportunities to apply a curb bit to Moltke as the details of what the chancellor insisted on calling a convention rather than a surrender were settled. On 28 January, the document was signed. It gave France three weeks to elect a national assembly to discuss future measures leading to permanent peace. Paris was to pay an immediate indemnity of 200 million francs. Most of the garrison would be disarmed, but German troops would occupy the city's outer fortifications. For the rest of the country, a demarcation line was established, with each army withdrawing ten kilometres behind it to avert unfortunate incidents – the Germans provided the deciding information in most of the doubtful cases.

Though Moltke grumbled at some details, he had no problem accepting his own argument that, with the guns silent, diplomats spoke instead of soldiers. Initially, on the French side at least, the tone was of uncompromising resistance, with Gambetta, in particular, insisting that the war continue, whatever the cost. His resignation on 6 February, cleared the path for more moderate positions. Some French generals believed another round of fighting would produce better terms. Moltke and his demigods obliged them by making plans for operations intended to destroy any French forces still in the field.

The hammer came down when a sorely tried French electorate voted overwhelmingly against the war hawks. In an election that returned a high proportion of local leaders and notables, from both right and left, as opposed to national figures, around 200 republicans faced a 400-strong bloc of Orleanists, legitimists who supported the House of Bourbon, and assorted other conservatives. Thiers, the new government's new premier, made the long trip to Paris to seek what terms he could. The price of defeat came high: Alsace; Eastern Lorraine, including Metz; an indemnity of 5 billion francs, with military occupation to be maintained until payment in full; and, finally, perhaps the bitterest pill of all, a victory march through Paris. These were consensus demands, reflecting a reasonable agreement of Germany's people and Germany's rulers, for all that Bismarck periodically

---

[88]Favre, vol. II, pp. 377 ff.
[89]Frederick III, *War Diary*, p. 282.
[90]Bronsart, p. 306.

blamed the soldiers for some of them, like the annexation of Metz. They were meant, on the one hand, to cement the German Empire, the creation of which had arguably been Bismarck's real primary war aim. They were meant as well to convince France that the war was over, and attempts to revise the outcome would bring only the same result.

On 26 February, the preliminary terms of peace were signed by the negotiators. On 1 March they were ratified by the French National Assembly — an unexpectedly quick decision that reduced the German spectacular in Paris to a smaller dimension, which, perhaps, avoided unpleasant incidents. Instead, participants and observers alike were surprised by the mutual goodwill and good humour shown by both sides. Perhaps indeed, to invert Nietzsche, a good party hallows any cause.

Epilogue

The solution of the German Question turned out to be a 'little Germany' that was also the primary power in Europe. It was one possible outcome among several. What Hegelians called the stream of time was not a flood. Its course was shaped at every turn by synergies of contingencies. While not exactly accidents, neither were they predetermined, and all were flexible. As the body of this work demonstrates, different dynamics among Bismarck, Moltke and William; different foreign policies in Paris, Vienna or St Petersburg; different military policies in the German states, France or Austria; a different outcome in one or two among half a dozen military operations; and history's cue taps its balls into different pockets with no less aplomb.

I

Contingency continued to shape the German experience after the guns of 1870 fell silent. The peace treaty's final negotiations began in Brussels, then came close to gridlock when Bismarck attempted to squeeze marginal advantages from French domestic problems. Relocated to Frankfurt, the negotiations concluded with the treaty's signature on 10 May 1871, and its formal ratification three weeks later.[1] Both events were anticlimactic. William had returned to Berlin in March; most of the German troops boarded trains for home in the same period. They returned to victory parades, triumphal arches and commemorative statuary in varying degrees of bad taste.[2] They had the satisfaction of seeing their most one-sided victory become the new Reich's defining holiday. Sedan Day, celebrated on 1 September, combined top-down efforts to facilitate national consolidation with local initiatives, linking the celebration with both traditional patriotic festivals and contemporary celebratory patriotism. Not until the Wilhelmine era did it become top-heavy with a ponderous chauvinism that alienated even many of the veterans it purported to honour.[3]

---

[1] Cf. Robert Giesberg, *The Treaty of Frankfurt: a Study in Diplomatic History* (Philadelphia, 1966) and Hans Herzfeld, *Deutschland und das geschlagene Frankreich, 1871–1873* (Berlin, 1924).

[2] Cf. Thomas Nipperdey, 'Nationalidee und Nationaldenkmal im deutschland im 19. Jahrhundert', *Historische Zeitschrift* 206 (1968), pp. 259–85; Rudy Koshar, *From Monuments to Traces: Artifacts of German Memory, 1870–1990* (Berkeley, CA, 2000), pp. 29 ff.; and Reinhold Lurz, *Kriegerdenkmaeler in Deutschland*, vol. II, *Einigungskriege* (Heidelberg, 1985).

[3] For Sedan Day's protean nature, cf. *inter alia*, Alon Confino, 'Localities of a Nation: Celebrating Sedan Day in the German Empire', *Tel Aviver Jahrbuch fuer Deutsche Geschichte* 26 (1997), pp. 61–74; Nils Freytag, 'Sedantage in Muenchen: Gemeindefeiern, Komitefeste und Vereinsgedenken', *Zeitschrift fuer Bayerische*

There were reasons enough to celebrate. Unification's price in lives and suffering had been cheap: under 30,000 deaths, even in 1870–1. Most of those deaths were recorded; by comparison to the American Civil War, few separate graves were marked 'unknown'. While public monuments were not usually 'democratic', in the sense of listing each individual commemorated, there were many exceptions, especially at local levels.[4] The wars' relative brevity worked against the emergence of individuals as public heroic figures, at the expense of the ordinary soldier.[5] Nothing like a 'lost generation' mentality developed among the young men who marched into Bohemia and France. If anything, the war deaths from specific cohorts, gymnasium classes or university fraternities, for example, had a reverse effect, providing foci for a nostalgia that increased with the passage of time, and had as much to do with fading youth as constructed memory. Nor had the conflicts borne heavily on the victors' economies. While the south German states had significant problems, Prussia had been able to finance 1864 and 1866 by regular means: the state treasury and the international capital market. Loans and public subscriptions carried the burden of 1870–1, and there was the French indemnity to balance the books. War, in short, still seemed like good business, at least at the great-power level.[6]

And yet the Wars of Unification, in some ways, resembled the dragon gold of the medieval minnesingers in bringing no luck. Four consequences, at least, were to leave the Second Reich with a bitter aftertaste. The first began when republican France mobilized its political and economic resources for one of the most remarkable – and unexpected – financial achievements of the nineteenth century. By September 1873, the indemnity was paid in full – a year and a half ahead of schedule, and an early riddance to the burdens of military occupation and Bismarck's periodic heavy-handed pressure.

France also had the last laugh. Much of the indemnity eventually went into public circulation, through war-loan repayment, railway and military building programmes, and pensions to veterans and families. It contributed significantly to an overheated economy and a speculative boom that attracted a disproportionate number of small investors, who were the first ones caught when the bubble burst in 1873. The *Gruenderzeit*, for all its short duration, put an unfortunate stamp of ostentation and excess on the new Germany, in everything from architecture to fashion. The epoch also nurtured widespread distrust of the liberals who had encouraged the initial surge of investment. It deepened and extended antagonism towards 'the Jews', who were scapegoated as profiting disproportionately from stock-market manipulations and swindles.

Arguably even more significant than the *Gruenderzeit*'s nurturing of anti-liberalism and anti-Semitism were its contributions to anti-modernism. The decade of unification had fundamentally altered the historic geographic and political parameters of Germany. The succeeding period of speculation and depression encouraged shame and guilt among those ordinary people caught in the various undertows. The long-standing values of

---

Landesgeschichte 61 (1998), pp. 383–406; and Claudia Lepp, 'Protestanten Feiern ihre Nation: Die Kulturprotestantischen Urspruenge des Sedantages', *Historisches Jahrbuch* 118 (1998), pp. 210–22.

[4]George L. Mosse, *Fallen Soldiers: Reshaping the Memory of the World Wars* (New York, 1990), pp. 48 ff.

[5]Cf. Rene Schillling, *'Kriegshelden'. Deutungsmuster heroischer Maennlichkeit in Deutschland 1813–1945* (Paderborn, 2002).

[6]See the overview by Wilhelm Treue, 'Die Finanzierung der Kriege 1864–1871 durch die deutschen Laender', *Vierteljahrschrift fuer Sozial- und Wirtschaftsgeschichte* 75 (1988), pp. 1–14.

Lutheranism, Prussianism and the 'home town', though frequently more praised than practised, had in common an emphasis on moderation. The nail that stood up could expect to be hammered down. To overreach was to invite catastrophe. Those small investors who had been tempted by the economic prospects of the post-unification years, frequently came away with more that just a sense of having made a mistake, or even of having been cheated. What remained after the now useless stock shares had been burned or put away in trunks was a sense of having done something wrong, of having been complicit in one's own fate.[7] That sense may have contributed to the image of a twenty-year depression, long discredited by economic historians.[8] Yet the Second Reich never quite managed to escape the cynicism that followed so closely on its creation. It did not bode well for a new nation that its popular cultures grew increasingly escapist, whether the dreams were of Socialist revolution, rural nostalgia or generational transcendence.

Nor did it bode well that the events of 1864–71 left the new Germany in the hands of an unreconstructed revolutionary – or, perhaps better said, an unreconstructed croupier. Bismarck's achievements, against all odds and expectations, between 1862 and 1871, only intensified his determination to keep control of the levers of power. Grown accustomed to a dynamic system, he now found himself responsible for creating a stable one. His spectacular successes deconstructing the Confederation and Prussian systems gave him a corresponding taste for living on the edge after 1871. Certainly, no state built on a combination of what Otto Pflanze calls 'Hohenzollern authoritarianism, Prussian militarism, and German nationalism' would have been easy to govern.[9] Its constitutional structure was unlikely to be anything but complex, clumsy and ambiguous. But Bismarck intended to structure the state's power so as to keep as much of it as possible in his own hands. The same pattern ruled in domestic politics. It took time everywhere for parliamentary systems of any kind developed for the participants to evoke functioning ground rules, to establish distinctions between cooperation and collusion. Bismarck consciously worked against that process in Germany, seeking to rule by dividing: exploiting fault lines, keeping not only parties but individuals isolated or antagonistic, turning differences of opinion into factions kept apart by principle.[10]

For Bismarck, manipulating the complex system he had created so as to keep tensions and antagonisms at a maximum was easier, surer and, not least, more personally gratifying than the alternatives.[11] For Germany, this approach nevertheless raised the question of what happened when, as was inevitable, the table changed dealers. Was Bismarck's system a legacy only Bismarck could operate? Would his successors face the problem of gluing toothpicks together as a precondition of decisive activity in any sphere?

That question spread into international affairs as well. The third dragon's gift of the Wars of Unification was Bismarck's assumption of an insurmountable Franco-German antagonism

---

[7]This line of argument is more fully developed in Fritz Stern, 'Money, Morals, and the Pillars of Society' in *The Failure of Illiberalism. Essays on the Political Culture of Modern Germany* (New York, 1972).

[8]S. B. Saul, *The Myth of the Great Depression, 1873–1893* (London, 1969).

[9]Pflanze, vol. I, p. 505.

[10]Wolfgang J. Mommsen, 'A Delaying Compromise: the Division of Authority in the German Constitution of 1871' in *Imperial Germany 1867–1918*, tr. R. Deveson (London, 1995), pp. 20–40.

[11]See, particularly, Michael Stuermer, 'Staatsstreichgedanken im Bismarckreich', *Historische Zeitschrift* 209 (1969), pp. 566–615.

as their consequence. When Bismarck declared, shortly after Sedan, that 'France will not forgive us our victories', he was not merely referring to the series of battles that had doomed the Second Empire.[12] Bismarck saw France's basic, objective interests, independent of its form of government, as demanding a weak central Europe. That situation, after 1871, was best achieved by playing the emerging German Empire against the equally new state of Austria-Hungary. By itself, a policy of appeasement and conciliation directed from Berlin to Vienna was no guarantee of averting the result. France must be directly and permanently weakened as well, to a point where any reasonable calculation would be against seeking to revise the results of 1870–1. Yet to accept France as an eternal enemy was to give a permanent hostage to fortune, to accept an enmity Germany might eventually be unable to afford.[13]

That risk seemed easier to assume in the context of the fourth direct legacy of the Wars of Unification: an army considered 'competent by definition', in a Second Reich lacking symbols of integration. Militarism, the systematic exaltation of alleged soldierly ways and virtues, had never been a Prussian characteristic. There had never been the fusion of the military and the civilian that defines a militaristic state. The leadership had been decidedly civilian; the army's role was decidedly instrumental.[14]

After 1871, that began to change, as association with the military experience became central to German self-identification,[15] and not only for males. The bipolar pattern of male warriors and female helpmates historically central to the western way of war was reinforced by the events of 1864–71. The blunders were sufficiently limited to avert any significant call to 'take the toys from the boys'. A case can even be made that German males were unusually competent, seldom making the same diplomatic or military mistakes more than twice. The wars were fought on enemy territory, providing correspondingly fewer opportunities for women to assume victim roles. The levels of loss and sacrifice did not create significant opportunity for women to establish independent status as nurturers. One might say that, by 1870, doctors were too competent, filling that role for the first time in history in so far as it emerged in a short and limited war. As it developed from its mid-century matrix, women's function relative to war was primarily to serve as symbols of its opposite: the peace whose preservation was not even seen as a beautiful dream by the practical men of affairs who ran the new Reich. To the extent that women participated in those affairs, it was in male contexts and on male terms: as volunteers and auxiliaries in civic functions rather than as autonomous actors. Even among the Social Democrats, the integration of women into the party structure was seen as a pragmatic decision rather than a principled one.[16]

---

[12]Bismarck to Keudell, 6 September 1870 in *Fuerst und Fuerstin Bismarck. Erinnerungen von 1846 bis 1871*, ed. R. Keudell (Berlin, 1901), p. 457.

[13]Allan Mitchell, *Bismarck and the French Nation, 1848–1890* (New York, 1971) and *The Germans in France after 1870: The Formation of the French Republic* (Chapel Hills, NC, 1979). Cf. also Markus Voekel, 'Geschichte als Vergeltung. Zur Grundlegung des Revanchegedankens in der deutsch-franzoesschen Historikerdiskussion von 1870–71', *Historische Zeitschrift* 257 (1993), pp. 63–107.

[14]Michel Salewski, 'Preussischer Militarismus – Realitaet oder Mythos? Gedanken zu einem Phantom', *Zeitschrift fuer Religions-und Geistesgeschichte* 53 (2001), pp. 19–34, brilliantly challenges conventional wisdom on the subject.

[15]Ute Frevert, 'Das Militaer als "Schule der Maennlichkeit". Erwartungen, Angebote, Erfahrungen im 19. Jahrhundert' in *Militaer und Gesellschaft im 19. und 20. Jahrhundert* (Stuttgart, 1997), pp. 134–63.

[16]Cf. Jean H. Quataert, *Reluctant Feminists in German Social Democracy, 1885–1917* (Princeton, 1979); 'German Patriotic Women's Work in War and Peacetime' in *Road to Total War*, pp. 449–77; Roger Chickering, ' "Casting

The public memory of the Wars of Unification was, to a significant degree, defined by its organized veterans, who emerged from Germany's multilateral *Vereinsleben* to become the nation's first mass movement. After 1871, ex-servicemen's associations, incorporating both war veterans and discharged reservists, flourished. Though always public, they were initially more social than political. Their purposes were to sustain the comradeship and camaraderie associated with active military service, to foster nationalist, monarchic and patriotic values and, not least in the years before Bismarck's social welfare programmes, to provide for their members in times of need. These organizations affirmed a common myth rather than introduced a particular one. Nor were they exclusive. Ordinary meetings were primarily devoted to eating, drinking and card-playing. If the more elaborate ceremonies included periodic marches with flags, bands and speeches, the speeches were conventionally low-common-denominator national/patriotic. The concluding festivities included anyone wishing to participate.

Like their Civil War counterparts across the Atlantic, the veterans of the Wars of Unification were not anxious to repeat their experiences – or see them replicated by a new generation and thereby sacrifice their own uniqueness.[17] They stressed both military qualities and peacefulness as German national characteristics. The true German was a citizen in arms, prepared to defend his fatherland but never seeking trouble. That mindset blended well with the notion of Germany as a sated power that Bismarck marketed enthusiastically and sincerely, both domestically and internationally after 1871. Not until the 1890s would government efforts to mobilize veterans' organizations in the causes of anti-socialism and military preparedness attract younger generations of peacetime veterans, who saw themselves as restricted to a permanent second-rate status compared to their seniors who had actually been 'out there' in Denmark, Bohemia or France.[18]

II

The Wars of Unification left more to the new empire than authoritarianism and division. First, they made the new Germany legitimate. While its emergence may not have been inevitable, none of the credible alternatives had any widespread appeal after 1871. In pragmatic terms, the events of 1866 and 1870–1 had demonstrated to the lesser states, beyond reasonable challenge, the advantages of participation in a large-scale military system.[19] The end of the old imperial/Confederation order generated a certain nostalgia, but nothing in Austria's – or rather Austria-Hungary's – post-Koeniggraetz history generated much sense north of the Inn of dazzling Greater German opportunities under Habsburg

---

Their Gaze More Broadly": Women's Patriotic Activism in Imperial Germany', *Past and Present* 118 (1988), pp. 156–85; and Ann Taylor Allen, *Feminism and Motherhood in Germany, 1800–1914* (New Brunswick, NJ, 1991).

[17]Cf. Stuart McConnell, *Glorious Contentment: The Grand Army of the Republic, 1865–1900* (Chapel Hill, NC, 1992).

[18]Cf. Thomas Rohrkraemer, *Der Militarismus der 'kleinen Leute': Die Kriegervereine im Deutschen Kaiserreich* (Munich, 1990); 'Heroes and Would-Be Heroes: Veterans and Reservists' Associations in Imperial Germany' in *Anticipating Total War: The German and American Experiences, 1871–1914*, eds. M. Boemke et al. (New York, 1999), pp. 189–215; and Alfred Kelly, 'Whose War? Whose Nation? Tensions in the Memory of the Franco-German War of 1870–1871' in ibid., pp. 281–306.

[19]Othmar Hackl, *Die Bayerischen Kriegsakademie (1867–1914)* (Munich, 1989), is a case study illustrating the point. The academy never sacrificed its Bavarian identity, but never questioned Bavaria's position in the Reich.

auspices forfeited by the new order.[20] The Second Reich's federal organization meant that local mores – and local power structures – were widely respected. In that context, tensions arising from 'Prussianization' also reflected generational conflict over modernization, values and behaviours imported from 'outside' by the new central government. Conscription, for example, posed significant challenges to paternal and religious authority by providing an alternative rite of passage into manhood.[21]

If regionalism did not pose a challenge to legitimacy, neither did factionalism. Of the Reich's ethnic minorities, the Poles had nowhere else to go, since no prospects for re-establishing Polish independence existed outside the context of cataclysmic war. The integration of Alsatians into the new state was more successful for a longer period than French nationalism has been willing to concede.[22] Jews embraced the Reich with an enthusiasm that denied an anti-Semitism whose influence up to 1914 was, in any case, limited enough to seem trivial in retrospect.[23] Catholics made up a one-third of the religious minority in a state whose dominant ethos was moving towards Protestantized secularism. But even the bitter *Kulturkampf* of the 1870s was not enough to alienate them permanently from the empire for which their sons, too, had fought.[24] An embryonic working class almost had to be driven out of the imperial consensus by the anti-socialist legislation of the 1880s.[25] Liberal and progressive elements felt themselves so well satisfied with the new imperial system that, by most accounts, they offered too little resistance to Bismarck's political manipulations during the 1870s.[26]

The common denominator in each of these cases was that no particular element of German society, whether defined in economic, political or ethnic terms, felt itself sufficiently excluded or sufficiently victimized to reject its chances in the system. Bismarck's demonstrated virtuosity at manipulating interest groups and creating new ones, usually described in negative terms, offered hope as well.

Characteristic at this stage of the pluralistic systems generated by democracy, nationalism and industrialization since the 1780s, was that no one was really sure how to run them effectively.[27] The French revolutionaries had sought to deal with political opposition by criminalizing it. Tsarist Russia introduced 'orthodoxy, autocracy and nationality' as benchmarks. Napoleon III sought to put himself above classes and interests, manipulating domestic and foreign policies to balance discontents. The United States had nearly self-destructed over an

---

[20]For the analysis of what happened instead, the growing association of Greater German attitudes with Little German chauvinism in Pan-Germanism, see, particularly, Roger Chickering, *We Men Who Feel Most German: A Cultural Study of the Pan-German League, 1886–1914* (Boston, 1984).

[21]David Blackbourn describes the tension between the lesser and the greater worlds eloquently in *Class, Religion, and Local Politics: The Centre Party in Wuerttemberg before 1914* (London, 1980).

[22]François Roth, *La Lorraine annexé, 1870–1918* (Nancy, 1976), is a massive argument that the transfer was doomed from the start by mutual intransigence. Dan P. Silverman, *Reluctant Union: Alsace-Lorraine and Imperial Germany, 1871–1918* (University Park, PA, 1972), takes a more pragmatic perspective.

[23]R. S. Levy, *The Downfall of Antisemitic Political Parties in Imperial Germany* (New Haven, 1975).

[24]Ronald J. Ross, *The Beleaguered Tower. The Dilemma of Political Catholicism in Wilhelmine Germany* (Notre Dame, IN, 1976).

[25]Vernon L. Lidtke, *The Outlawed Party* (Princeton, 1996).

[26]Langewiesche, *Liberalism in Germany*, pp. 128 ff.

[27]See Mommsen, 'Society and State in Europe in the Age of Liberalism, 1870–1890' in *Imperial Germany*, pp. 57–74.

issue, slavery, that proved ultimately unsusceptible of compromise in the context of a federal system. For decades afterwards, reunification was a manifestation of *force majeure* as well as mutual consent. The British two-party system was of short duration, and even then more myth than fact. That Bismarck's domestic political structure threw oil did not make it worth trading in for a new one. To shift metaphors, the advantages of staying in the game for another round outweighed the prospects of kicking over the table.[28]

As for the Reich's international relations, Bismarck was convinced, at least as firmly as Moltke, that Germany had fought, in 1870, under near optimal military and diplomatic conditions – conditions unlikely to arise, or become possible to create, in the predictable future. He remained unsusceptible to the 'victory disease' that generated a significant overrating of the new German Empire's capacity to shape events in Europe by direct intervention. He did not share the pseudo-social Darwinist conviction that the next victory over a 'degenerate' France would be a matter of weeks. Frontier revisions had seemed a correspondingly necessary immediate risk. Then the Third Republic, having negotiated a reasonable peace relative to its circumstances, promptly eviscerated itself in a civil war.

The Paris Commune highlighted the minority status of 'Gambetta Republicans', already well aware of their vulnerability. The conservatives wanted to be rid of them. They were outflanked on the radical left,[29] and all factions of political France still feared any initiative that might unleash the countryside's 'dark masses'.[30] The result was France's withdrawal from the European position that the rapid payment of reparations might have enabled the country to claim. For at least a decade, as it sought to define itself and re-knit its social fabric, the republic would inherit Prussia's historic role as the least of Europe's great powers.[31]

Bismarck, nevertheless, ultimately felt more comfortable with his ability simultaneously to reassure Britain of Germany's benevolent attentions, and to keep a balance in the east between Russia and Austria, than he did with the possibility of confronting France again under the same geographic and diplomatic conditions as in 1870. Germany's position relative to its eastern neighbours was enhanced by the independent decisions of Russia and Austria-Hungary to turn their diplomatic ambitions south and east, towards a decaying Asia and an Ottoman Empire that seemed ripe for the plucking. Even before the Treaty of Frankfurt, Bismarck had become involved in a sequence of attempts at brokering that eventually turned him into the circus-rider of Europe: standing on the backs of two spirited horses, working to keep them galloping in the same direction. Eventually, that would strain even his talents. During most of the 1870s, however, Germany's chancellor was able to sustain his diplomatic trick-riding act.[32]

As for Britain, neither of the two emerging dominant parties, nor their leaders, saw any reason to challenge Bismarck's insistence that the new Germany was a satiated power whose leaders wanted only peace and stability in Europe. Successive foreign secretaries

---

[28]A point demonstrated in Margaret Lavina Anderson, *Practicing Democracy. Elections and Political Culture in Imperial Germany* (Princeton, 2000).

[29]William Serman, *La Commune de Paris (1871)* (Paris, 1986).

[30]Alain Corbin, *Le village des cannibales* (Paris, 1990).

[31]Moltke and the general staff, nevertheless, did not regard it as an easy target. See James Stone, 'The War Scare of 1875 Revisited', *Militaergeschichtliche Mitteilungen* 53 (1994), pp. 304–26.

[32]See Hermann Lutz, 'Von Koeniggraetz zum Zweibund: Aspekte europaeischer Entscheidungen', *Historische Zeitschrift* 217 (1973), pp. 347–80 and Reinhard Wittram, 'Bismarcks Russlandpolitik nach der Reichsgruendung', ibid. 186 (1958), pp. 261–84.

might have had reasons to question that paradigm. The successes of the German army, however, acted as a deterrent to expressing doubt by challenge. The 1871 proto-techno-thriller, *The Battle of Dorking*, with its depiction of a near-future Britain prostrate before a German invasion, drew loud protests from critics who described the scenario as impossible as long as the Royal Navy kept the seas, and some complaint as well from land-warfare specialists who declared that large-scale invasion under modern conditions was by no means as easy as *Dorking* implied.[33] What was obvious was the impossibility of reversing the scenario: of projecting British land power on to the continent in the face of a hostile Germany, even on the scale of the Napoleonic Wars, without making precisely the kind of diplomatic commitments successive British governments were determined to avoid − or without developing an army beyond any feasible political possibilities. In short, however deep might run underlying Anglo-German antagonisms, common sense dictated under-playing, indeed submerging them, for the foreseeable future.[34]

In fact, a Franco-Russian alliance did not emerge for over twenty years. Britain took over a decade longer to sign on and form the Triple Entente. And the relationship had nothing significant to do with France's loss of its eastern provinces. Diplomacy, in short, was at least as much a product of contingency and opportunity after 1871, as were domestic political developments.

What about the army? That Germany had been united by the sword was a postulate unchallenged in the new Reich. To the public mind at least, the intellectuals, the businessmen, the politicians, the diplomats, even Bismarck himself, had ultimately stood aside for the soldiers. In 1898, the *Berliner Illustrierte Zeitung*, a leading popular magazine, polled its readers on significant people and events of the past hundred years. The public's choice as the nineteenth century's greatest thinker was Helmuth von Moltke.[35]

Yet the army of the Second Reich did not use its status as a means of expanding its spectrum of domestic influence directly. Instead, after 1871, it sought to enhance its position by concentrating even more closely on keeping abreast or ahead of the rapidly changing techniques of making war. Military modernization facilitated the army's role as an instrument of social integration, and increased its power relative to other institutions, but was not undertaken primarily for either purpose.[36]

The Imperial German Army's 'way of war', after 1871 developed around four specific points, each a legacy of 1864−71. The first was the need for decision. The Wars of Unification had confirmed the long-standing Prussian tradition of applying maximum force in the pursuit of limited objectives. As a satisfied power, Germany was also the fulcrum of Europe. Protracted conflict, with its accompanying risk of becoming general, could only threaten both of its positions. The war with the French Republic was a foreshadowing of a worst-case scenario. A combination of improvised organized forces with irregulars and partisans

---

[33]I. F. Clarke, *Voices Prophesying War* (rev. ed., Oxford, 1992), pp. 27 ff.

[34]Paul Kennedy, *The Rise of the Anglo-German Antagonism, 1860–1914* (London, 1980).

[35]*Facsimile Querschnitt durch die Berliner Illustrierte*, ed. F. Luft (Munich, 1965), pp. 46 ff.

[36]Cf. Dennis E. Showalter, 'Army and Society in Imperial Germany: the Pains of Modernization', *Journal of Contemporary History* 18 (1983), pp. 583–618 and Eric Dorn Brose, *The Kaiser's Army: The Politics of Military Technology during the Machine Age* (New York, 2001). For an opposing position, handicapped by its limited time frame, see Bernd F. Schulte, *Die deutsche Armee 1900–1914. Zwischen Beharren und Veraendern* (Duesseldorf, 1977).

had not changed the conflict's outcome. It had, however, dragged out an end game that left both combatants materially debilitated to a point where third-party involvement was a rational option. Such a conflict could not be lightly risked again.[37]

Averting that risk depended on speed. Rapid mobilization and concentration had given Prussia an initiative that had proven decisive in both of its major wars. The Danish experience had offered a counterpoint: a set of unappealing signposts to the consequences of initiating war in stages. Any doubts on that point could be dispelled by studying the behaviour of the Austrian and French Empires. To fight the kind of war that made 'victory' a meaningful concept, the Second Reich needed, above all, to keep inside the decision loops of its potential adversaries.

That, in turn, required preparation. And preparation depended on autonomy. The Bismarck–Moltke friction during the Wars of Unification is best understood in the context of a cabinet system. Both men saw themselves in an essentially collegial relationship, with any institutional superiority of one office over the other as being adjustable – or better said, subject to modification. Certainly, Moltke did not regard Bismarck in the same way a French general of the Third Republic regarded the premier. A more appropriate parallel would be the tensions between the Departments of State and Defense in the US cabinets during the Vietnam Wars, or after 9/11. Bismarck, moreover, worked consistently and successfully to nurture and exacerbate conflicts within the military, separating the war ministry, the military cabinet and the general staff, and setting them against each other as a means of limiting the soldiers' direct, effective involvement in politics. The result was a German army sufficiently divided internally to be resistible enough in domestic political contexts – when civilian authority made the effort necessary to resist it.[38]

The soldiers' readiness to emphasize direct preparation for war was fostered as well by the continued pattern of limited mobilization for which Roon spoke even in the Franco-Prussian War's darker days. Between 1871 and 1914, the Second Reich moved closer and closer to a *de facto* selective service system, in which only around half the men eligible in a given year were inducted into the active army. The rest were assigned to what is best understood as an inactive reserve, a pool to be drawn on for replacements and garrison troops should that prove necessary. Incomplete mobilization, in turn, generated an increasing imbalance between Germany's diplomatic pretensions – or, depending on perspective, the requirements of Germany's diplomatic position – and its ability to sustain that position in arms.[39]

That represented a 180-degree turn from the situation of the 1860s, when the Prussian army's military effectiveness was at least equal to Bismarck's diplomatic virtuosity. The soldiers' response was increasing emphasis on decisive battle: the battle of annihilation, or *Vernichtungsschlacht*. Despite its apocalyptic ring, the term did not mean literal

---

[37]Showalter, 'German Grand Strategy: A Contradiction in Terms?' and, from a different perspective, Stig Foerster, 'Facing "People's War": Moltke the Elder and Germany's Military Options after 1871', *Journal of Strategic Studies* 10 (1987), pp. 209–30.

[38]Cf. the distinguished works by Michael Schmid, *Der Eiserne Kanzler und die Generaele. Deutsche Ruestungspolitik in der Aera Bismarck (1871–1890)* (Paderborn, 2002) and Stig Foerster, *Der doppelte Militarismus. Die deutsche Heeresruestungspolitik zwischen Status-Quo-Sicherung und Aggression 1890–1913* (Stuttgart, 1985).

[39]Jack Dukes, 'Militarism and Arms Policy Revisited: The Origins of the German Army Law of 1913' in *Another Germany: A Reconsideration of the Imperial Era*, eds. J. Dukes and J. Remak (Boulder, CO, 1988), pp. 19–40.

extermination. *Vernichtungsschlacht* involved the comprehensive defeat, physical and psychological, of the enemy at all levels, from rank and file to the highest command. It meant the breaking of both will and the capacity for continued resistance. It was intended as the single hammer blow, delivered by an army superior at its cutting edge to any in Europe, that would guarantee the Reich's future existence in an environment that, increasingly, did not wish Germany well.[40]

Ironically, the army's very emphasis on operational-level preparation for the next war generated increasing doubt whether a battle of annihilation could be accomplished in a single engagement, as at Koeniggraetz, or even a sequence like the two-week run of victories from Vionville to Sedan. Schlieffen's turn-of-the-century thinking, usually considered the apogee of general staff wisdom, aimed at gaining a decisive edge, less by a single sweeping campaign than a series of interlocking counter-attacks against expected French offensives, followed by a second campaign intended to bring France to the negotiating table. The parallels between this concept and what would have happened in a best-case scenario against a competent enemy in 1870 are too striking to overlook. The improbability of its execution in the diplomatic and military contexts of 1914 is no less obvious.[41]

In blood, in money, even in principle, the new Germany had been cheaply bought – perhaps too cheaply, creating unrealizable expectations of future equivalent successes. Bismarck had not promised the German people blood, toil, tears or sweat. There was no Valley Forge in the military mix, no legacy of public sacrifice. The Wars of Unification had been 'policy wars' in a way even the wars of Frederick the Great had not achieved. They were triumphs of the state rather than the body politic. That fundamental dissonance would gnaw away at the Second Reich until its final collapse in 1914. But that is a story for another time – and perhaps another book.

---

[40]Cf. Jehuda Wallach, *The Dogma of the Battle of Annihilation: The Theories of Clausewitz and Schlieffen and Their Impact on the German Conduct of Two World Wars* (Westport, CT, 1986) and Antullio Echevarria, *After Clausewitz. German Military Thinkers before the Great War* (Lawrence, KS, 2000).

[41]Cf. Terence Zuber, *Inventing the Schlieffen Plan. German War Planning 1871–1914* (New York, 2002) and Robert T. Foley, 'Attrition: Its Theory and Application in German Strategy, 1880–1916' (dissertation, King's College, University of London, 1999).

Further Reading

The exhaustive – and exhausting – literature on German unification is best traced through this volume's footnotes. What is offered here is not a bibliography in the standard sense, but rather the book's subtext: a summary and overview of the works that, over a span of forty years, have shaped my ideas and informed my writing on a subject that remains as compelling as it is complex. Recognizing that the work's audience will be overwhelmingly English-speaking, and hoping that it will include general readers as well as academic specialists, I concentrate on works in English.

Three massive general histories, each synthesizing the best scholarship of the later twentieth century, provide the backdrop. Thomas Nipperdey, *German History from Napoleon to Bismarck, 1800–1866*, tr. Daniel Nolan (Dublin, 1996), stresses the continuities between the Reich of the eighteenth century and the post-Napoleonic order of the nineteenth. Heinrich Lutz, *Zwischen Habsburg und Preussen. Deutschland 1815–1866* (Berlin, 1985), stresses the three-way tensions between Prussia, Austria and the lesser states. James J. Sheehan, *German History, 1770–1866* (Oxford, 1989), has a cultural/intellectual emphasis. The anthology edited by Stig Foerster and Joerg Nagler, *On the Road to Total War. The American Civil War and the German Wars of Unification, 1861–1871* (New York, 1997), does not develop the comparative dimension promised by its title, but is neverthe-less invaluable for its essays. William Carr, *The Origins of the Wars of German Unification* (London, 1991), is one of the best volumes in the excellent Longman series on the origins of modern war, and its diplomatic focus balances the present work.

The above list is complemented by two evergreens: Gordon Craig, *The Politics of the Prussian Army* (rev. ed., New York, 1964) and Gerhard Ritter, *The Sword and The Scepter: The Problem of Militarism in Germany*, tr. Heinz Nordau (Coral Gables, FL, 1969), vol. I. The insights and conclusions of Craig and Ritter on the subject of unification may be crit-icized, but can never be dismissed.

For personalities, Otto Pflanze, *Bismarck and the Development of Germany* (3 vols., Princeton, NJ, 1990), vol. I, remains a mother lode of insight and analysis. Complementing it is Lothar Gall, *Bismarck. Der Weisse Revolutionaer* (Frankfurt, 1980) and its English transla-tion, *Bismarck. The White Revolutionary* (2 vols., Boston, 1986). Ernst Engelberg, *Bismarck: Urpreusse und Reichgruender* (2nd ed., rev., Frankfurt, 1985), reflects a German Democratic Republic scholarly legacy that, at its best, was more than propaganda.

There is still, surprisingly, no good biography in English of Helmuth von Moltke the Elder. Eberhard Kessel, *Moltke* (Stuttgart, 1857), remains the best in any language. Rudolf Stadelmann, *Moltke und der Staat* (Krefeld, 1950), is a dated but still useful analysis of Moltke's political ideas. Arden Bucholz, *Moltke and the German Wars, 1864–1871* (New York, 2001), discusses Moltke in the context of the German army's organizational culture.

Neither imperial France nor Habsburg Austria have generated an equivalent body of biography. There are stimulating, amusing and critical biographies of Napoleon III; none, however, is definitive – perhaps because historians find him difficult to take seriously. Roger Price, *The French Second Empire: An Anatomy of Political Power* (New York, 2001), takes a long step in the right direction by its analysis of imperial patterns of governance.

For the respective military systems, Dierk Walter, *Preussische Heeresreformen 1807–1870* (Paderborn, 2003), is a masterful overview of the Prussian army's institutional development. Arden Bucholz, *Moltke, Schlieffen, and Prussian War Planning* (Providence, RI, 1991), concentrates on the general staff. Frank Kuehlich, *Die deutsche Soldaten im Krieg von 1870/71* (Frankfurt, 1995), is a neglected mine of information about life in the ranks – much of it applicable to earlier periods as well. Dennis Showalter, *Railroads and Rifles: Soldiers, Technology, and the Unification of Germany* (Hamden, CT, 1975) remains useful for the technological aspects. Hermann Rahne, *Mobilmachung* (East Berlin, 1983), has a good treatment of the Wars of Unification.

Juergen Angelow, *Von Wien nach Koeniggraetz. Die Sicherheitspolitik des Deutschen Bundes im Europaeischen Gleichgewicht* (Munich, 1966), offers the Confederation perspective from a policy level. Heinz Helmert, *Militaersystem und Streitkraefte im Deutschen Bunde am Vorabend des preussischen-oesterreichischen Krieges von 1866* (Berlin, 1964) is institutionally and tactically focused. Of the lesser states, Bavaria is by far the best served, with Wolf D. Gruener, *Das Bayerische Heer von 1825–1864* (Boppard, 1972) and Detlef Vogel, *Der Stellenwert des Militaers in Bayern (1849 bis 1875)* (Boppard, 1981). Paul Sauer, *Das wuerttembergischen Heer in der Zeit des Deutschen und norddeutschen Bundes* (Stuttgart, 1958), is a good institutional history.

The most up-to-date treatment of the Habsburg army is in Geoffrey Wawro's acid-etched *The Austro-Prussian War. Austria's War with Prussia and Italy in 1866* (New York, 1996). Antonio Schmidt-Brentano, *Die Armee in Oesterreich: Militaer, Staat und Gesellschaft 1848–67* (Boppard, 1975), is more positive about the army's roles and its effectiveness. For the French, combine Richard Holmes, *The Road to Sedan: The French Army, 1866–70* (London, 1984), Thomas Adriance, *The Last Gaiter Button. A Study of the Mobilization and Concentration of the French Army in the War of 1870* (Westport, CT, 1987) and Jean Casevitz, *Une loi manqué: la loi Niel, 1867–68; L'armée française a la vielle de la Guerre de 1870* (Paris, 1960).

Ian Beckett, *The American Civil War and the Wars of the Industrial Revolution* (London, 1999), is an excellent introduction for beginners in the military aspects of this subject. Philip Howes, *The Catalytic Wars. A Study of the Development of Warfare 1860–1870* (London, 1998), incorporates strong comparative and transatlantic dimensions. Among works on specific conflicts, Sabrina Mueller, *Soldaten in der deutschen Revolution von 1848/49* (Paderborn, 1999), has a social history emphasis. There is no good military study of the Danish War of 1864; the best treatment is in Bucholz, *Moltke and the German Wars*. For 1866, Wawro is the best modern analysis, though Gordon Craig, *The Battle of Koeniggraetz* (Philadelphia, 1964), is still a solid summary. For 1870–1, Michael Howard, *The Franco-Prussian War* (London, 1960), continues to set the standard. It is complemented in English by Geoffrey Wawro, *The Franco-Prussian War* (Cambridge, 2003), noteworthy for its operational presentations.

In a flourishing French literature on the war and its consequences, Stephane Audoin-Rouzeau, *1870. La France dans la Guerre* (Paris, 1918) and François Roth, *La Guerre de 1870*

(Paris 1990), stand out. The war itself has attracted less attention among German scholars. Matthias Steinbach, *Abgrund Metz* (Munich, 2002), merits citation for its ingenious use of the city and fortress of Metz as a focal point for an analysis of the war's nature and consequences.

Among the many specialized works on the war, David Wetzel, *A Duel of Giants* (Madison, WI, 2001), analyses its diplomatic origins with flair and insight. David Ascoli, *A Day of Battle. Mars-la-Tour, 16 August 1870* (London, 1987), presents the war's tactical aspects. Alistair Horne, *The Fall of Paris* (London, 1965), covers the great siege. Mark Stoneman, 'The Bavarian Army and French Civilians in the War of 1870–1871: A Cultural Interpretation', *War in History* 8 (2000), pp. 271–93, discusses the complex relations of soldiers and civilians, and their long-term consequences.

Index

Brendan Behan
The Complete Plays

The Quare Fellow, The Hostage,
Richard's Cork Leg,
Moving Out, A Garden Party, The Big House

'It seems to be Ireland's function, every twenty years or so, to provide a playwright who will kick English drama from the past into the present. Brendan Behan may well fill the place vacated by Sean O'Casey.' Kenneth Tynan, *Observer*

This volume contains everything Behan wrote in dramatic form in English. First come the three famous full-length plays: *The Quare Fellow*, set in an Irish prison, is 'something very like a masterpiece' (John Russell Taylor); *The Hostage*, set in a Dublin lodging-house of doubtful repute, 'crowds in tragedy and comedy, bitterness and love, caricature and portrayal, ribaldry and eloquence, patriotism and cynicism, symbolism and music-hall songs, all on top of one another, apparently higgledy-piggledy, and yet wonderfully combining into a spiritual unity' (*The Times*); and *Richard's Cork Leg*, set largely in a graveyard, which is nevertheless 'a joyous celebration of life' (*Guardian*). There follow three little-known one-act plays originally written for radio and all intensely autobiographical, *Moving Out, A Garden Party* and *The Big House*.

The introduction, by Alan Simpson, who knew Behan well and first directed his work on stage, provides the essential biographical details as well as candid insights into Behan's working methods and his political allegiances. Also included in the volume is a wide-ranging bibliography.

Brendan Behan was born in Dublin in 1923, while his father, a housepainter and Republican activist, was in jail. Behan left school at fourteen but spent two years in Borstal and a further four (1942–46) in prison for political activities. Out of these experiences came his autobiography, *Borstal Boy* (1958), and his first stage play, *The Quare Fellow* (1954). His first radio plays were broadcast in Ireland in 1952 and he was writing a column for the *Irish Press* in 1954; but it was with the enormous success of Joan Littlewood's London productions of *The Quare Fellow* (in 1956) and *The Hostage* (in 1958), combined with Behan's much publicised drinking bouts, that he achieved international fame. A third play, *Richard's Cork Leg*, was left almost complete at his death in 1964 and was edited and directed by Alan Simpson for the 1972 Dublin Theatre Festival.

CPSIA information can be obtained at www.ICGtesting.com
Printed in the USA
LVOW092157030812

292910LV00003B/5/P